Oh My Goddess!

ああっ女神さまっ

HAND IN HAND

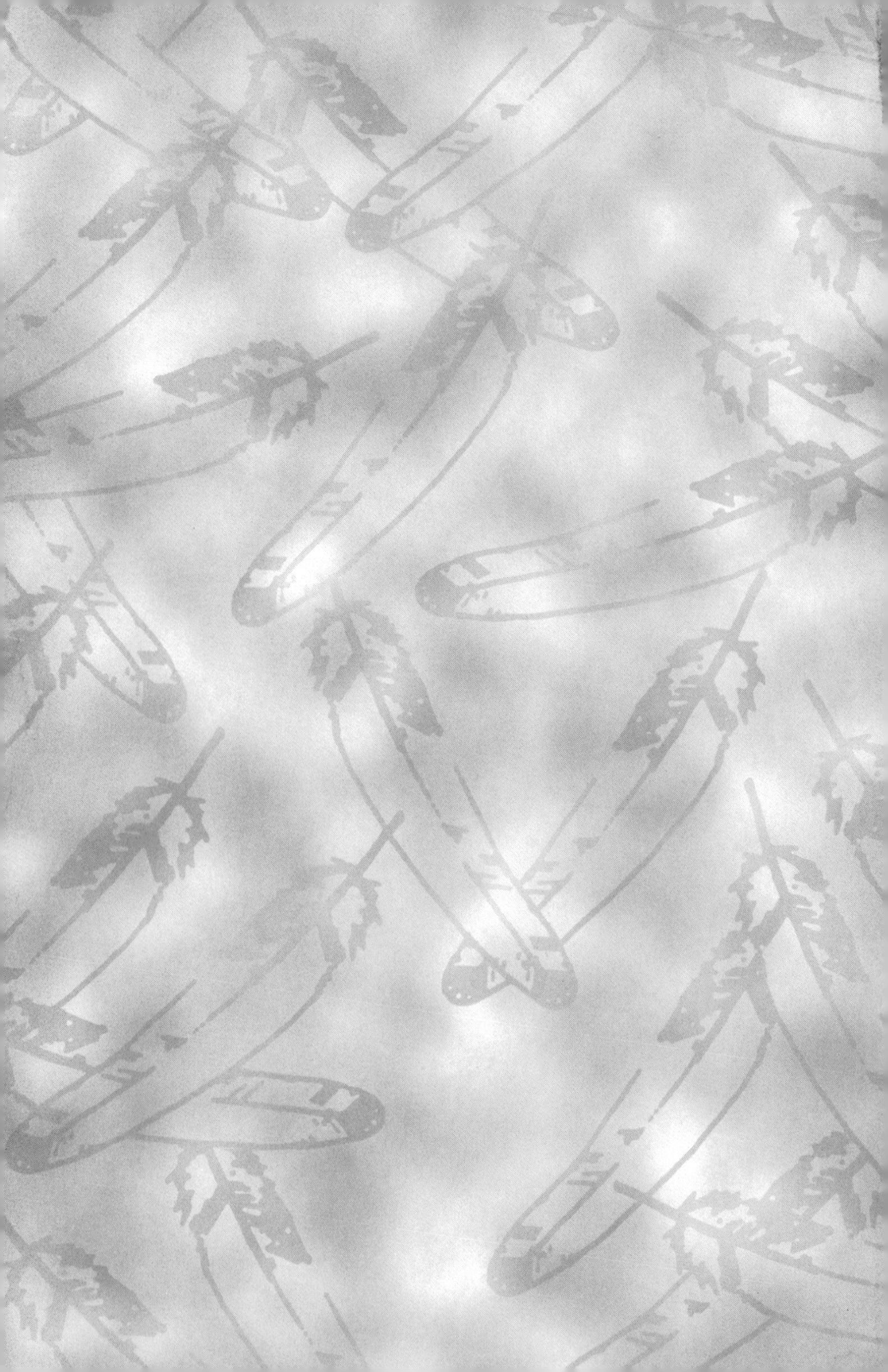

Oh My Goddess!

ああ女神さま

HAND IN HAND

STORY AND ART BY

Kosuke Fujishima

TRANSLATION BY

Dana Lewis & Toren Smith

LETTERING AND TOUCH-UP BY

Susie Lee & PC Orz

DARK HORSE COMICS®

PUBLISHER
Mike Richardson

SERIES EDITORS
Mike Hansen & Tim Ervin-Gore

COLLECTION EDITOR
Chris Warner

COLLECTION DESIGNER
Amy Arendts

ART DIRECTOR
Mark Cox

English-language version produced by Studio Proteus
for Dark Horse Comics, Inc.

OH MY GODDESS Vol. XV: Hand in Hand

This volume collects issues one through five of the Dark Horse comic book series *Oh My Goddess! Part X* and issues one and two of the Dark Horse comic book series *Oh My Goddess! Part XI*.

Published by
Dark Horse Comics, Inc.
10956 SE Main Street
Milwaukie, OR 97222

www.darkhorse.com

To find a comics shop in your area, call the Comic Shop
Locator Service toll-free at 1-888-266-4226

First edition: February 2003
ISBN: 1-56971-921-7

1 3 5 7 9 10 8 6 4 2
Printed in Canada

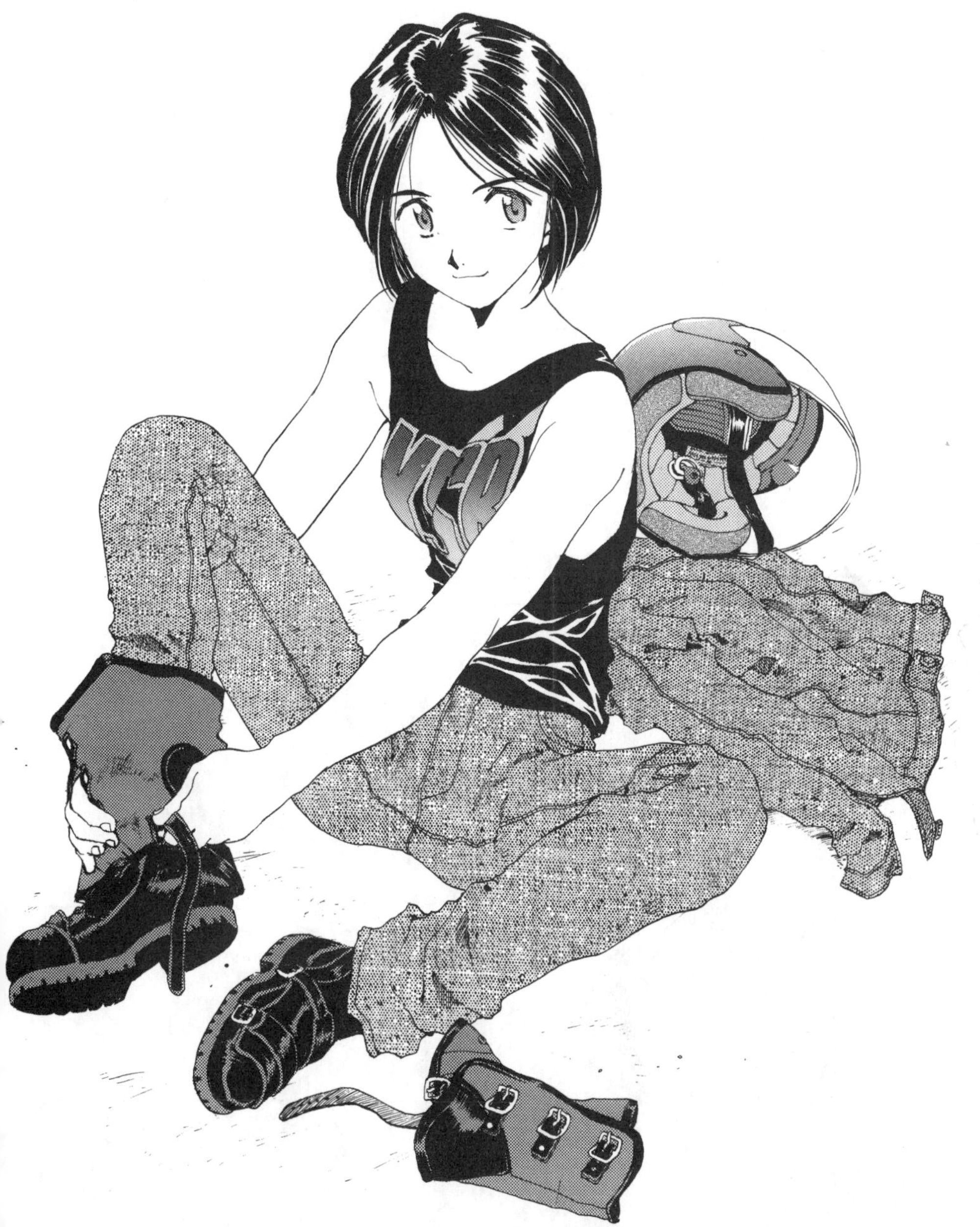

MEGUMI VERSUS THE QUEEN

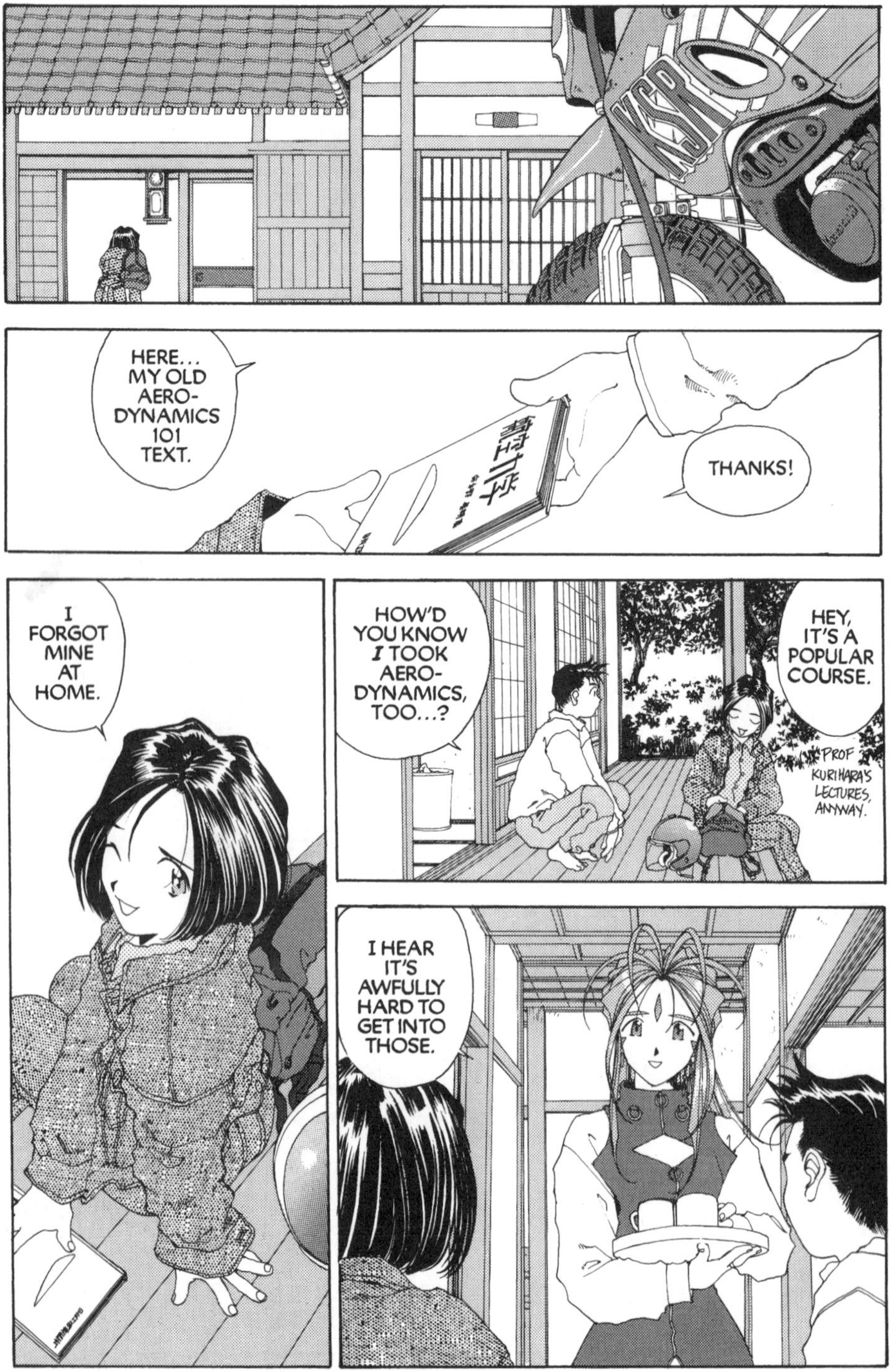
HERE... MY OLD AERO-DYNAMICS 101 TEXT.
THANKS!
I FORGOT MINE AT HOME.
HOW'D YOU KNOW *I* TOOK AERO-DYNAMICS, TOO...?
HEY, IT'S A POPULAR COURSE.
PROF KURIHARA'S LECTURES, ANYWAY.
I HEAR IT'S AWFULLY HARD TO GET INTO THOSE.

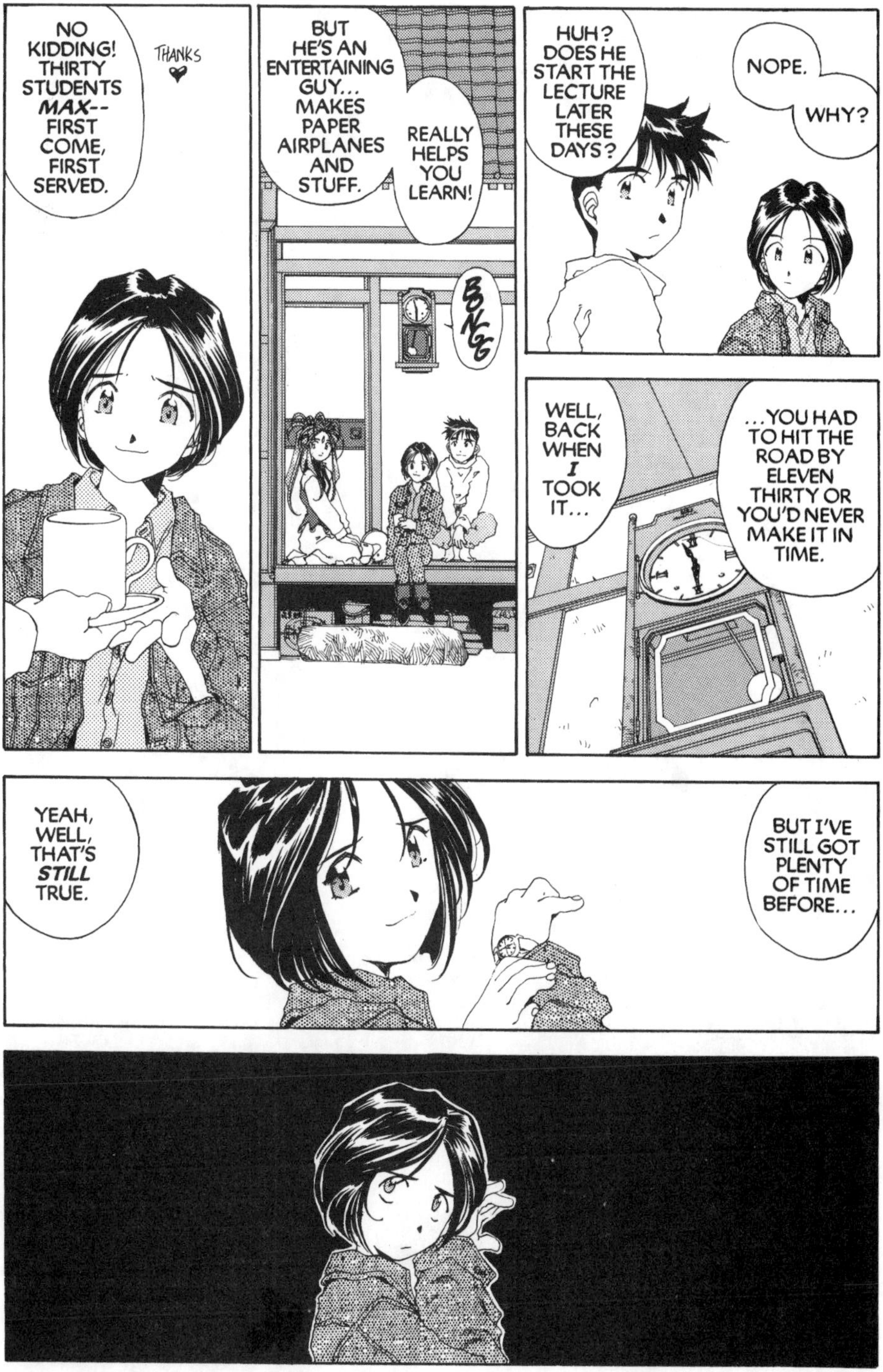
NO KIDDING! THIRTY STUDENTS MAX-- FIRST COME, FIRST SERVED.
THANKS
BUT HE'S AN ENTERTAINING GUY... MAKES PAPER AIRPLANES AND STUFF.
REALLY HELPS YOU LEARN!
BONGG
HUH? DOES HE START THE LECTURE LATER THESE DAYS?
NOPE.
WHY?
WELL, BACK WHEN I TOOK IT...
...YOU HAD TO HIT THE ROAD BY ELEVEN THIRTY OR YOU'D NEVER MAKE IT IN TIME.
YEAH, WELL, THAT'S STILL TRUE.
BUT I'VE STILL GOT PLENTY OF TIME BEFORE...

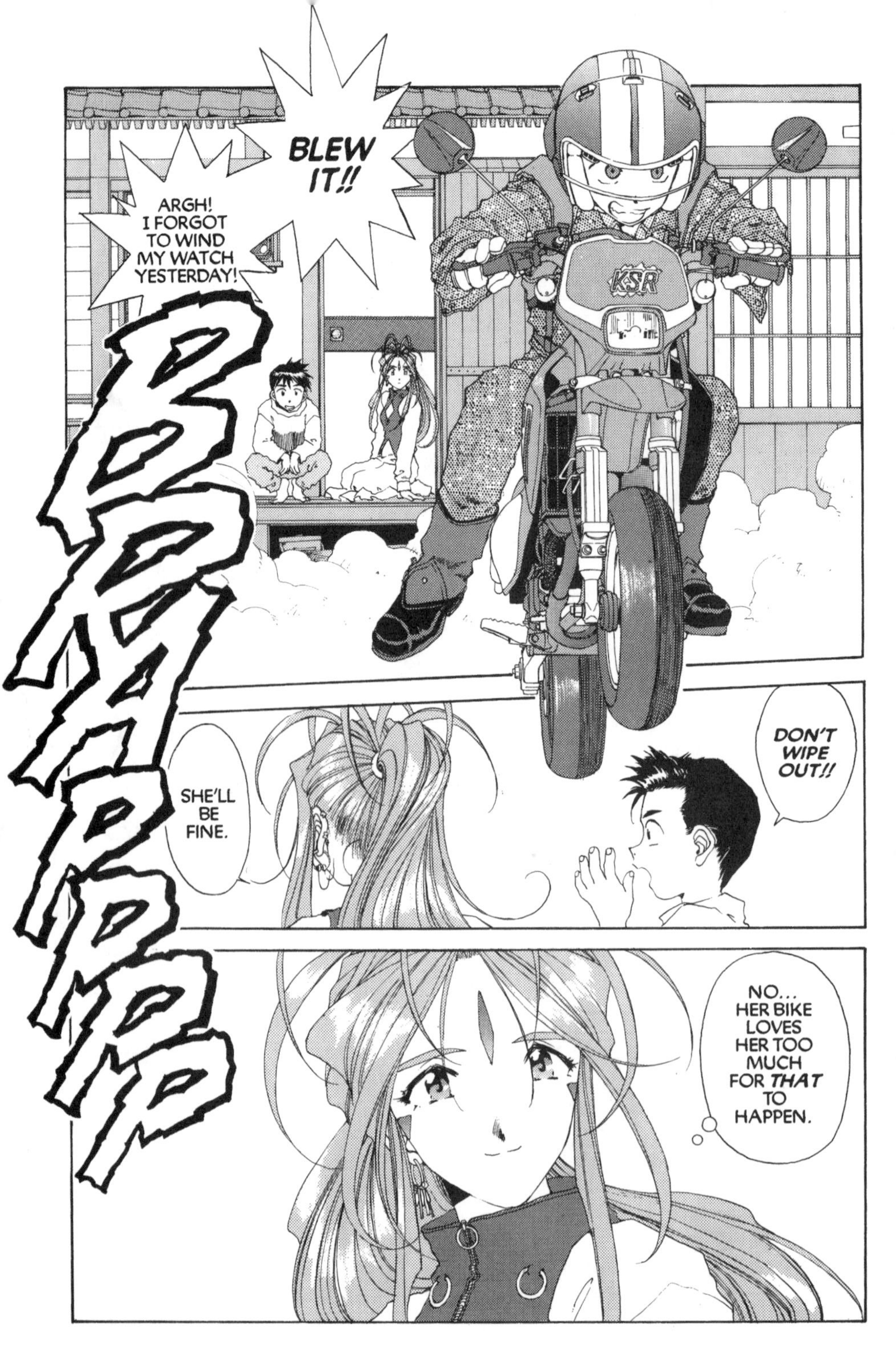
ARGH! I FORGOT TO WIND MY WATCH YESTERDAY!
BLEW IT!!
SHE'LL BE FINE.
DON'T WIPE OUT!!
NO... HER BIKE LOVES HER TOO MUCH FOR *THAT* TO HAPPEN.

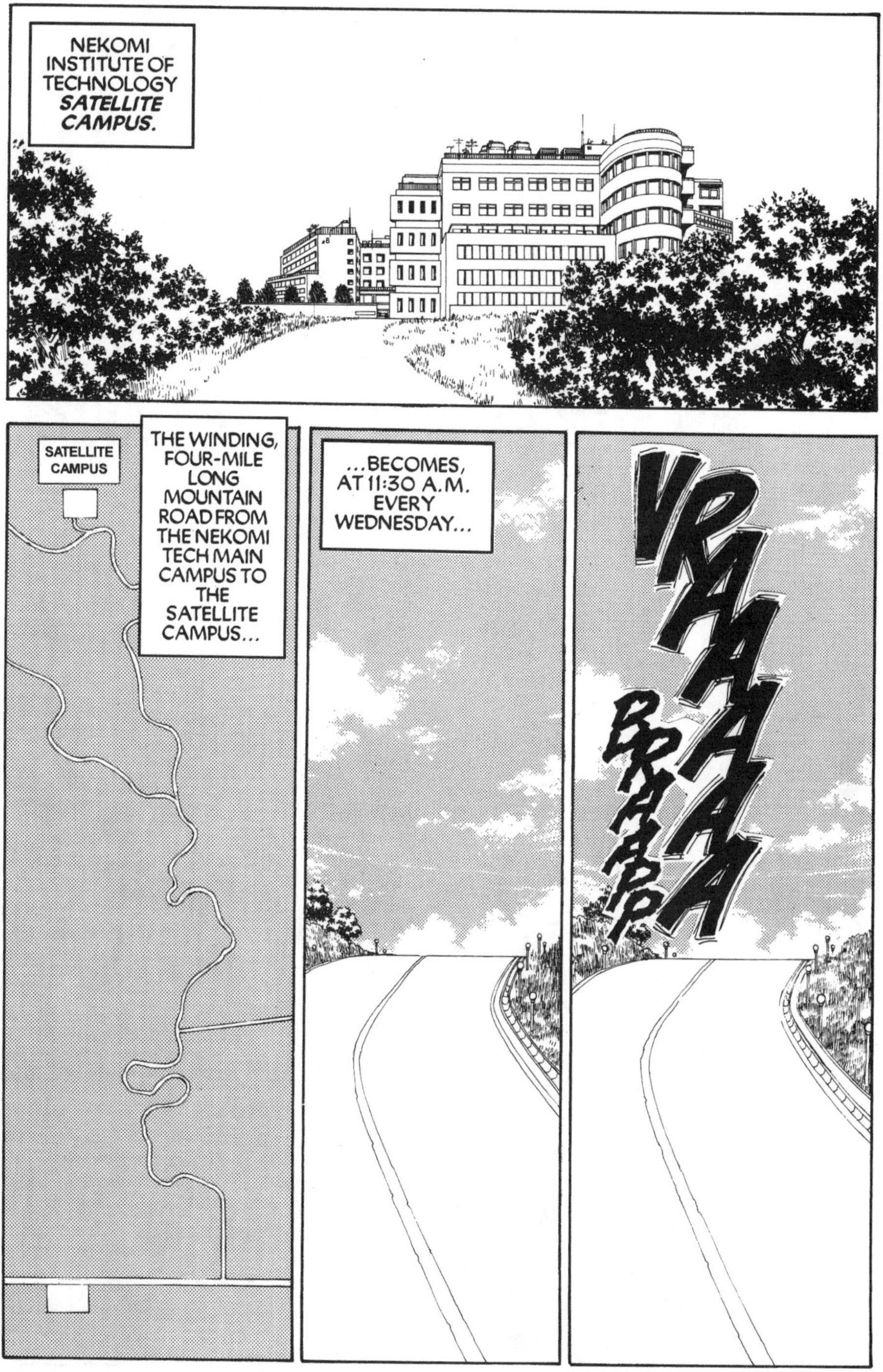
NEKOMI INSTITUTE OF TECHNOLOGY *SATELLITE CAMPUS.*
SATELLITE CAMPUS
THE WINDING, FOUR-MILE LONG MOUNTAIN ROAD FROM THE NEKOMI TECH MAIN CAMPUS TO THE SATELLITE CAMPUS...
...BECOMES, AT 11:30 A.M. EVERY WEDNESDAY...
VRAAAAA
BRAAPP

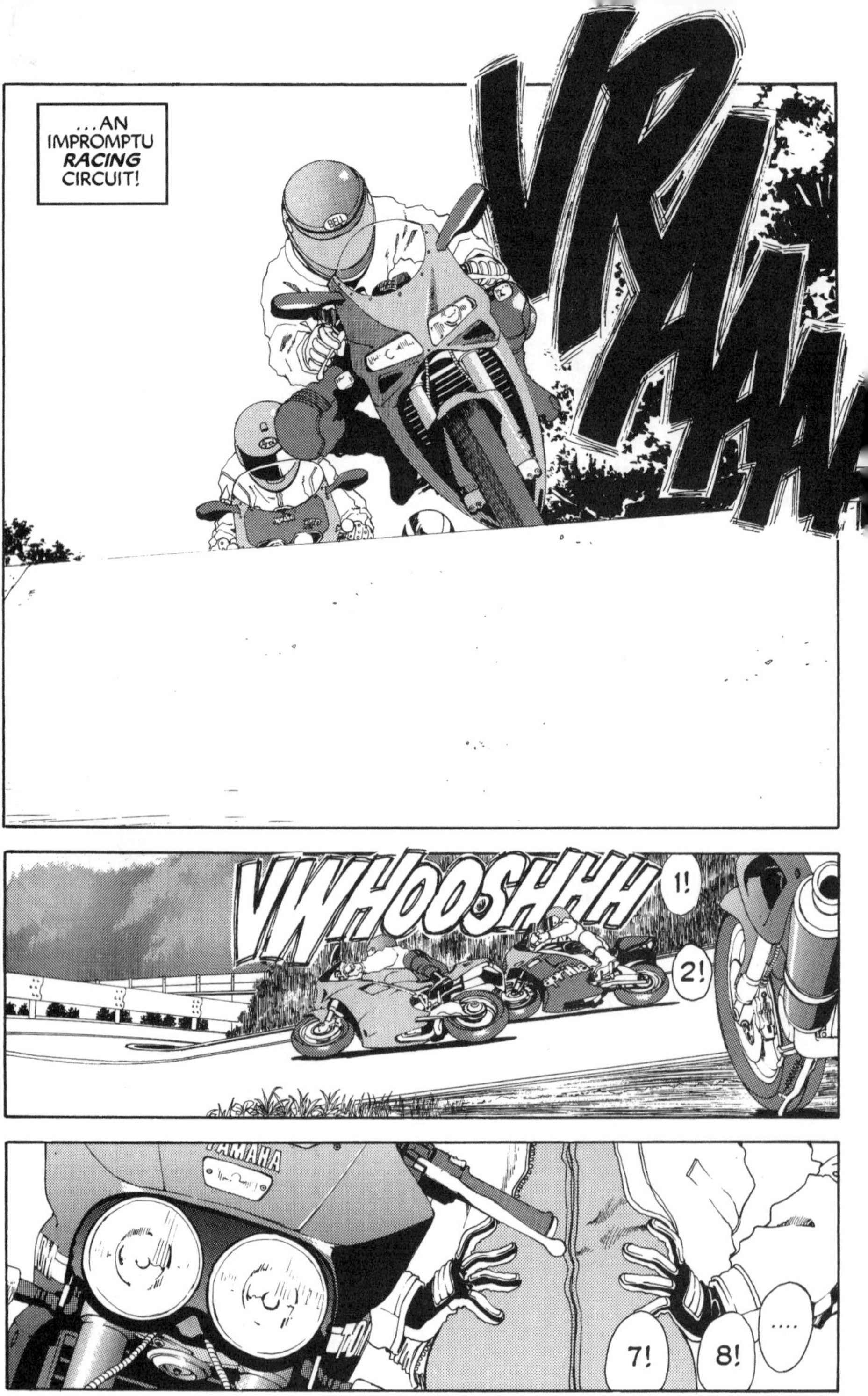
...AN IMPROMPTU *RACING* CIRCUIT!
VWHOOSHHH
1!
2!
7!
8!
....

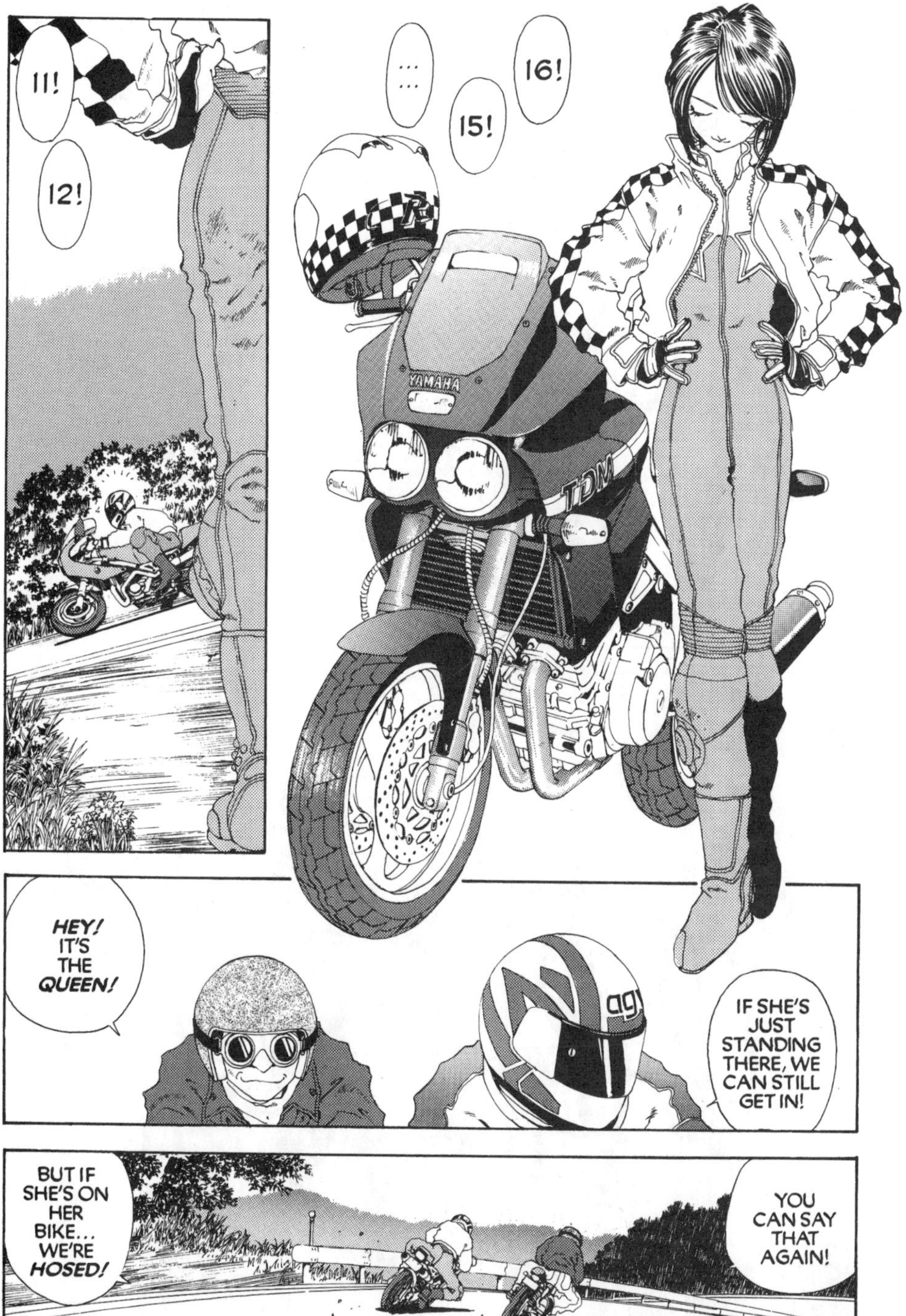
11!
12!
......
15!
16!
HEY! IT'S THE QUEEN!
IF SHE'S JUST STANDING THERE, WE CAN STILL GET IN!
BUT IF SHE'S ON HER BIKE... WE'RE HOSED!
YOU CAN SAY THAT AGAIN!

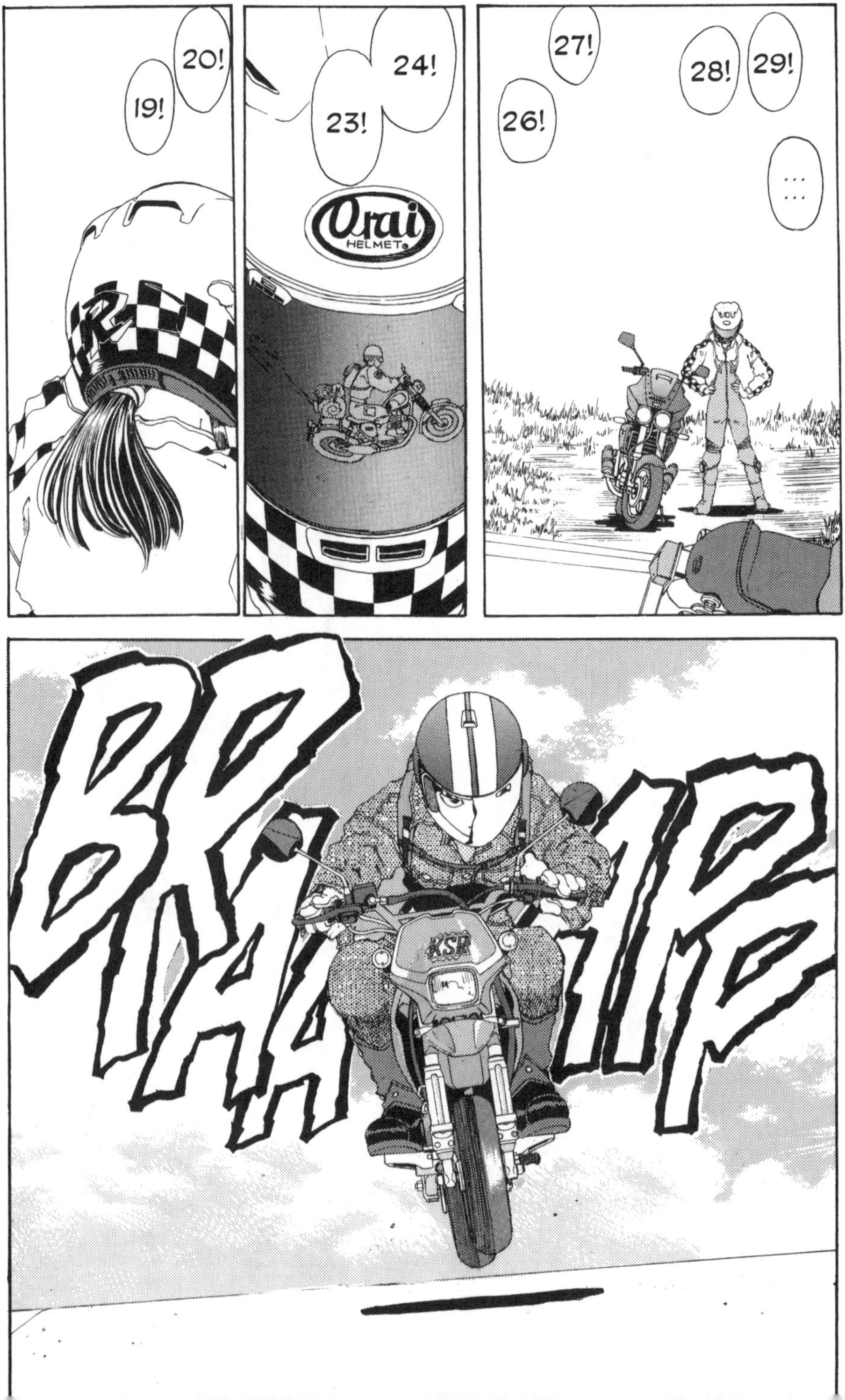
19!
20!
Orai
HELMET
23!
24!
26!
27!
28!
29!
......
KSR

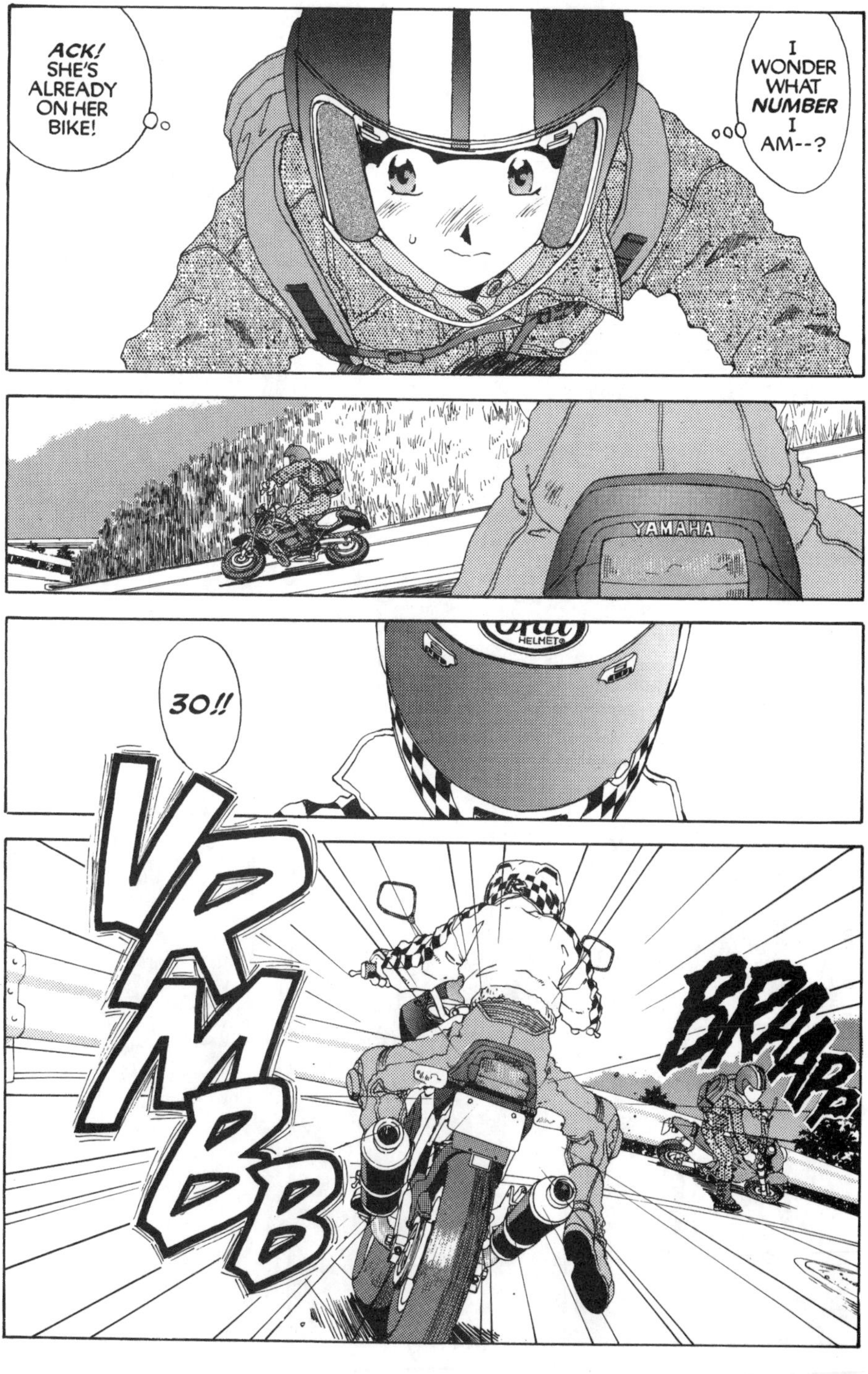
ACK! SHE'S ALREADY ON HER BIKE!
I WONDER WHAT ***NUMBER*** I AM--?
YAMAHA
30!!
VRMBB
BRRAPP

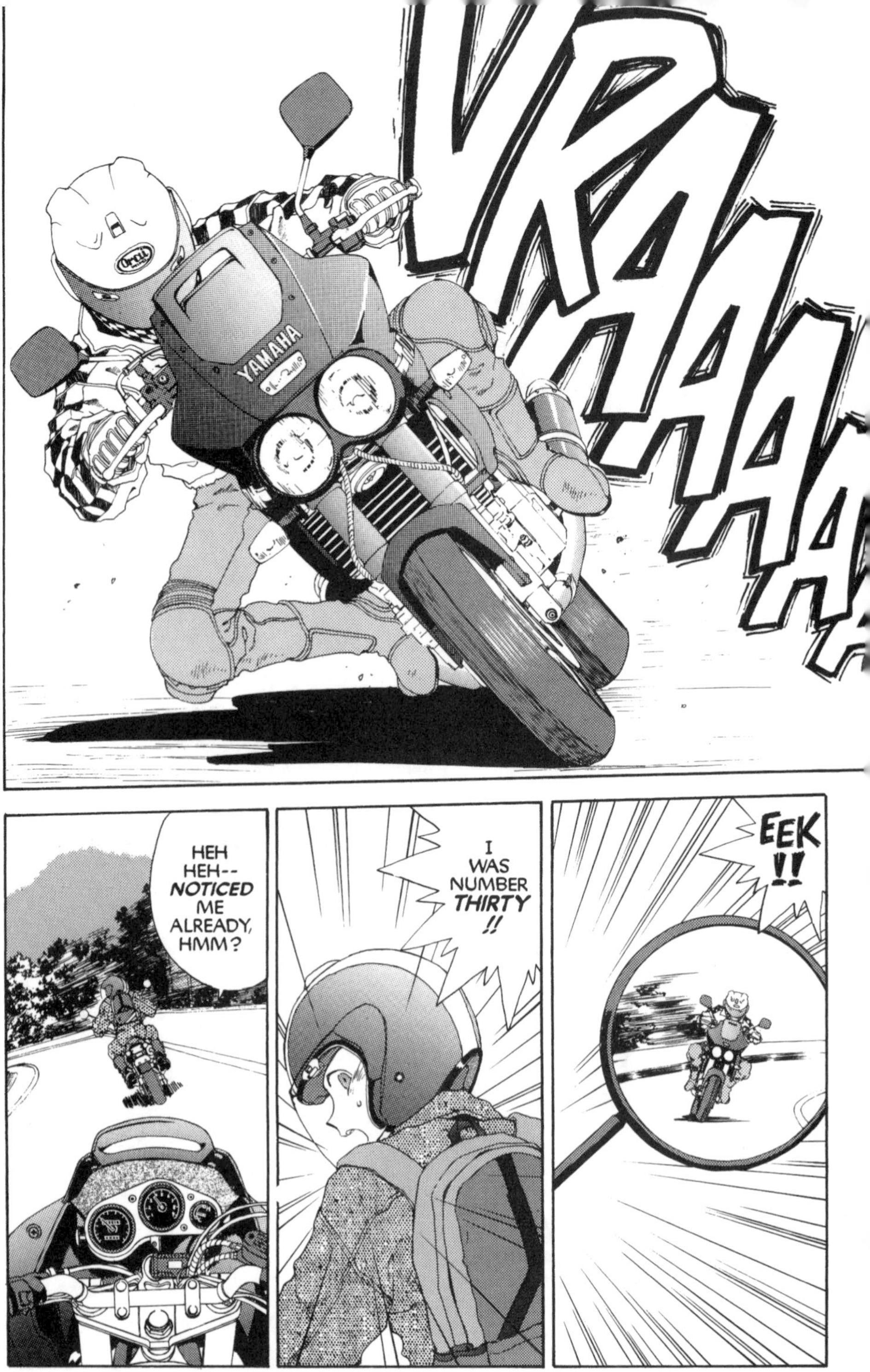
VRAAAA
YAMAHA
HEH HEH-- *NOTICED* ME ALREADY, HMM?
I WAS NUMBER *THIRTY* !!
EEK !!

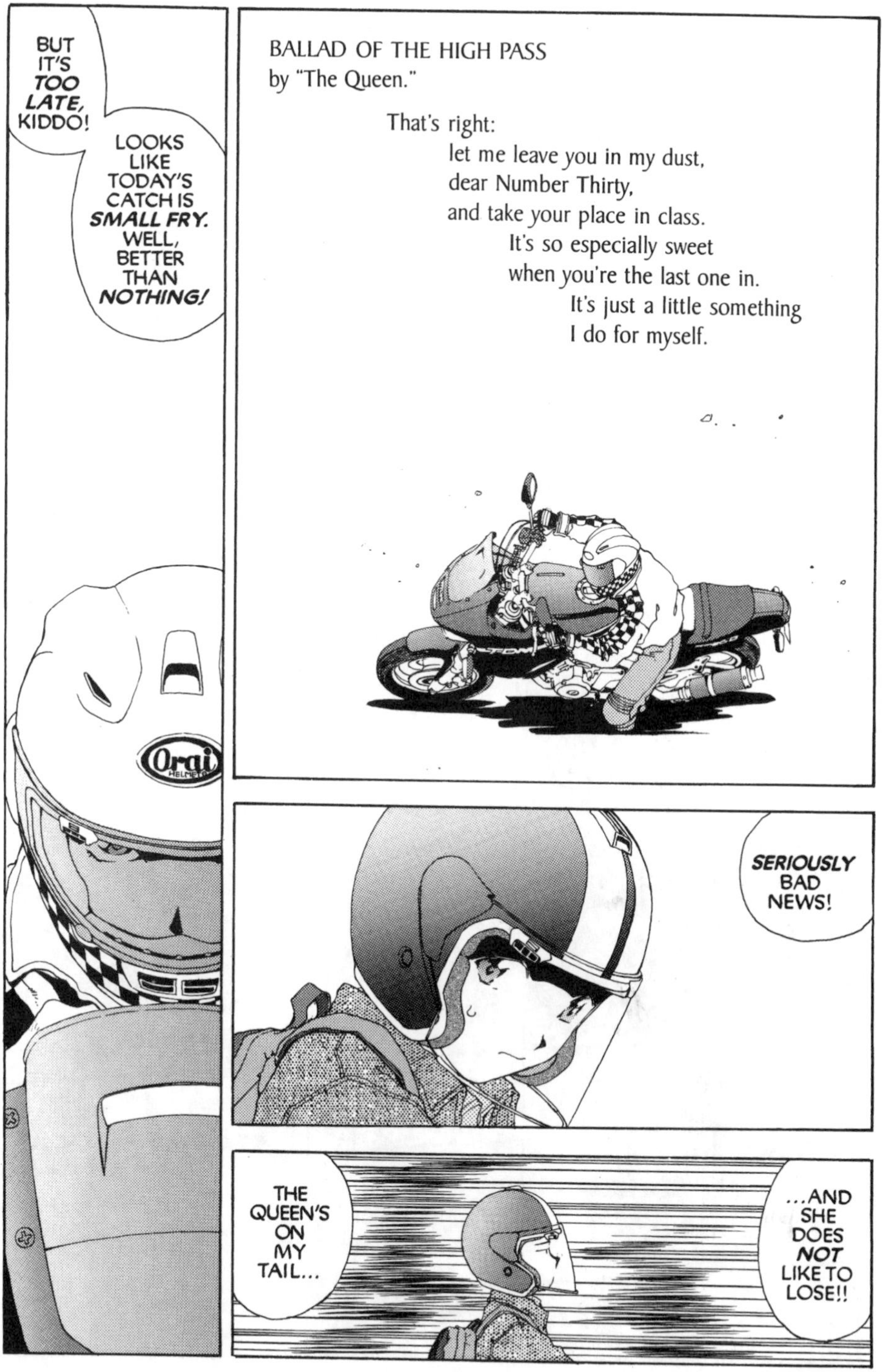
BUT IT'S TOO LATE, KIDDO!
LOOKS LIKE TODAY'S CATCH IS SMALL FRY. WELL, BETTER THAN NOTHING!
Orai
BALLAD OF THE HIGH PASS
by "The Queen."
That's right:
let me leave you in my dust,
dear Number Thirty,
and take your place in class.
It's so especially sweet
when you're the last one in.
It's just a little something
I do for myself.
SERIOUSLY BAD NEWS!
THE QUEEN'S ON MY TAIL...
...AND SHE DOES NOT LIKE TO LOSE!!

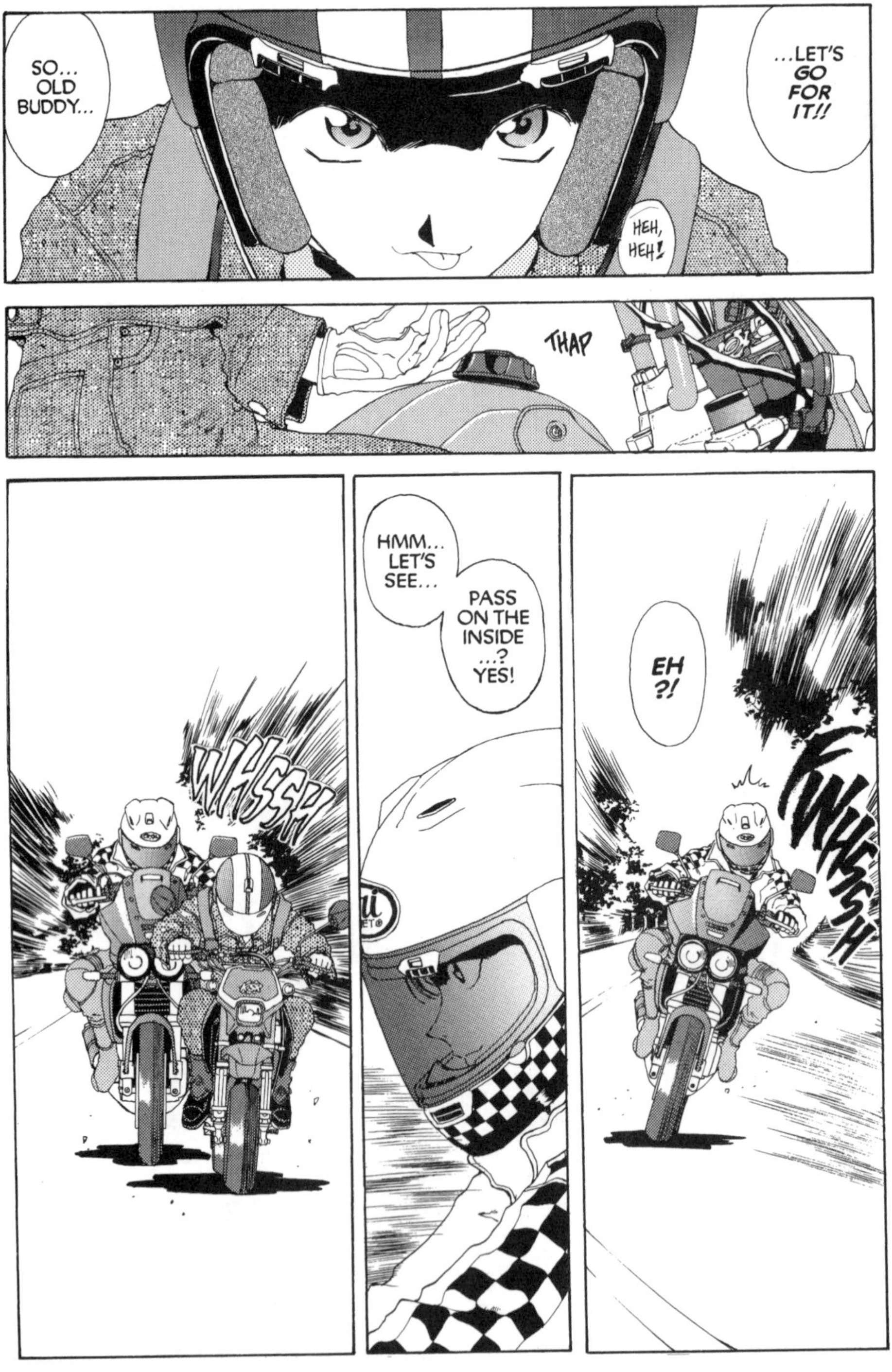
SO... OLD BUDDY...
...LET'S GO FOR IT!!
HEH, HEH!
THAP
WHSSH
HMM... LET'S SEE...
PASS ON THE INSIDE ...? YES!
EH?!

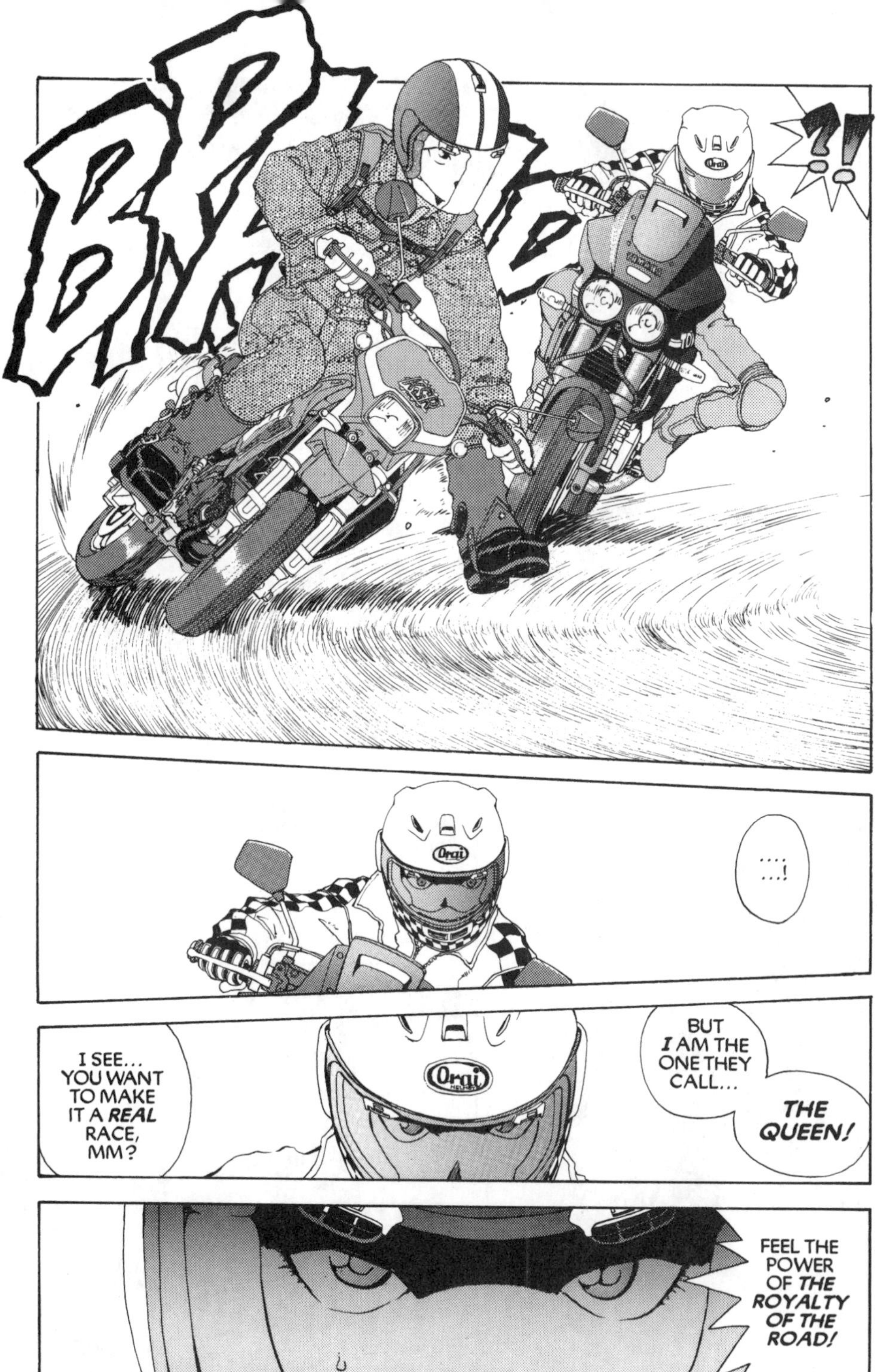
?!
……!
I SEE… YOU WANT TO MAKE IT A *REAL* RACE, MM?
BUT *I* AM THE ONE THEY CALL…
THE QUEEN!
FEEL THE POWER OF ***THE ROYALTY OF THE ROAD!***

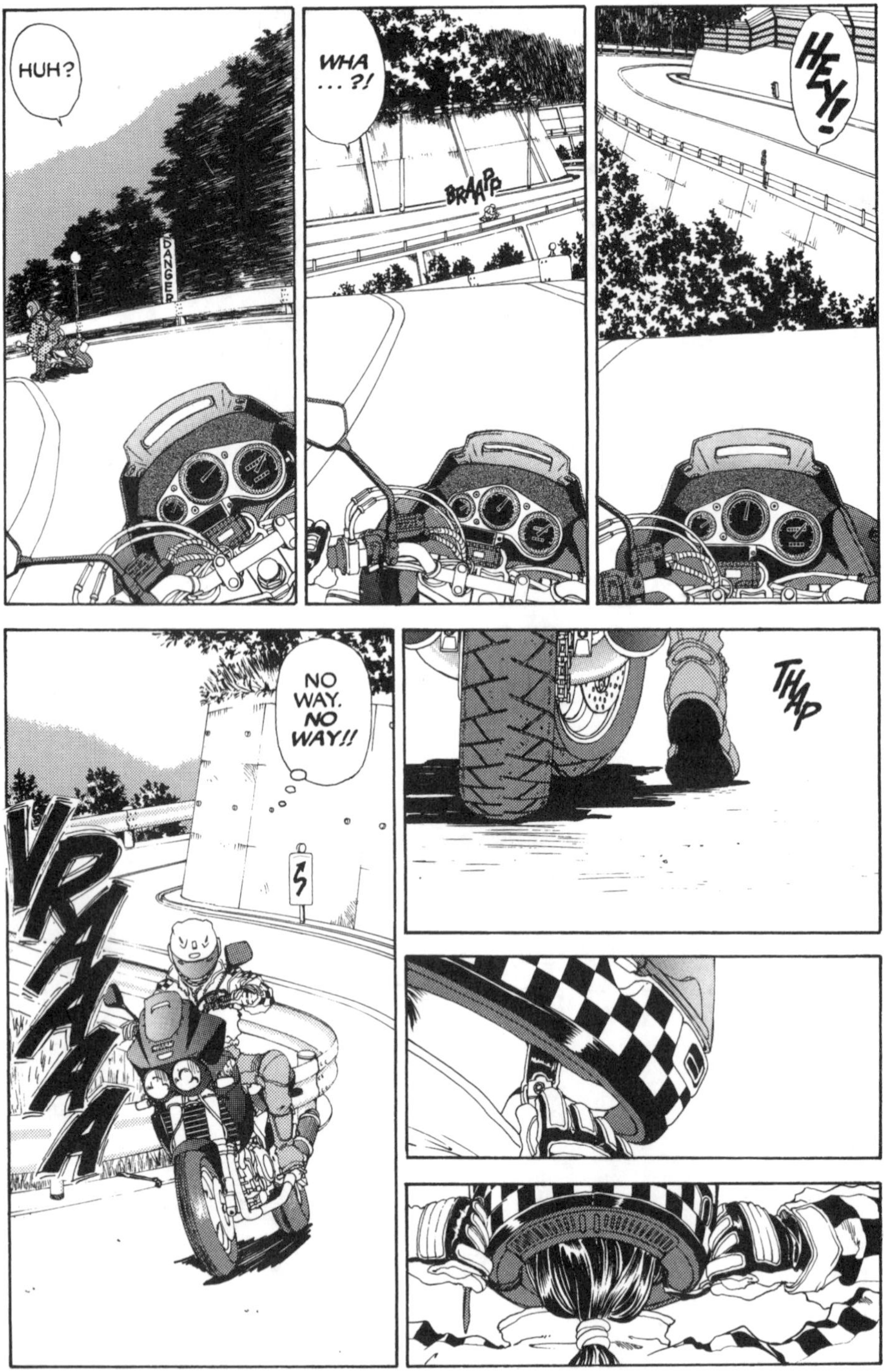
HUH?
DANGER
WHA . . . ?!
BRAAPP
HEY!!
NO WAY. NO WAY!!
VRAAAAAA
THAP

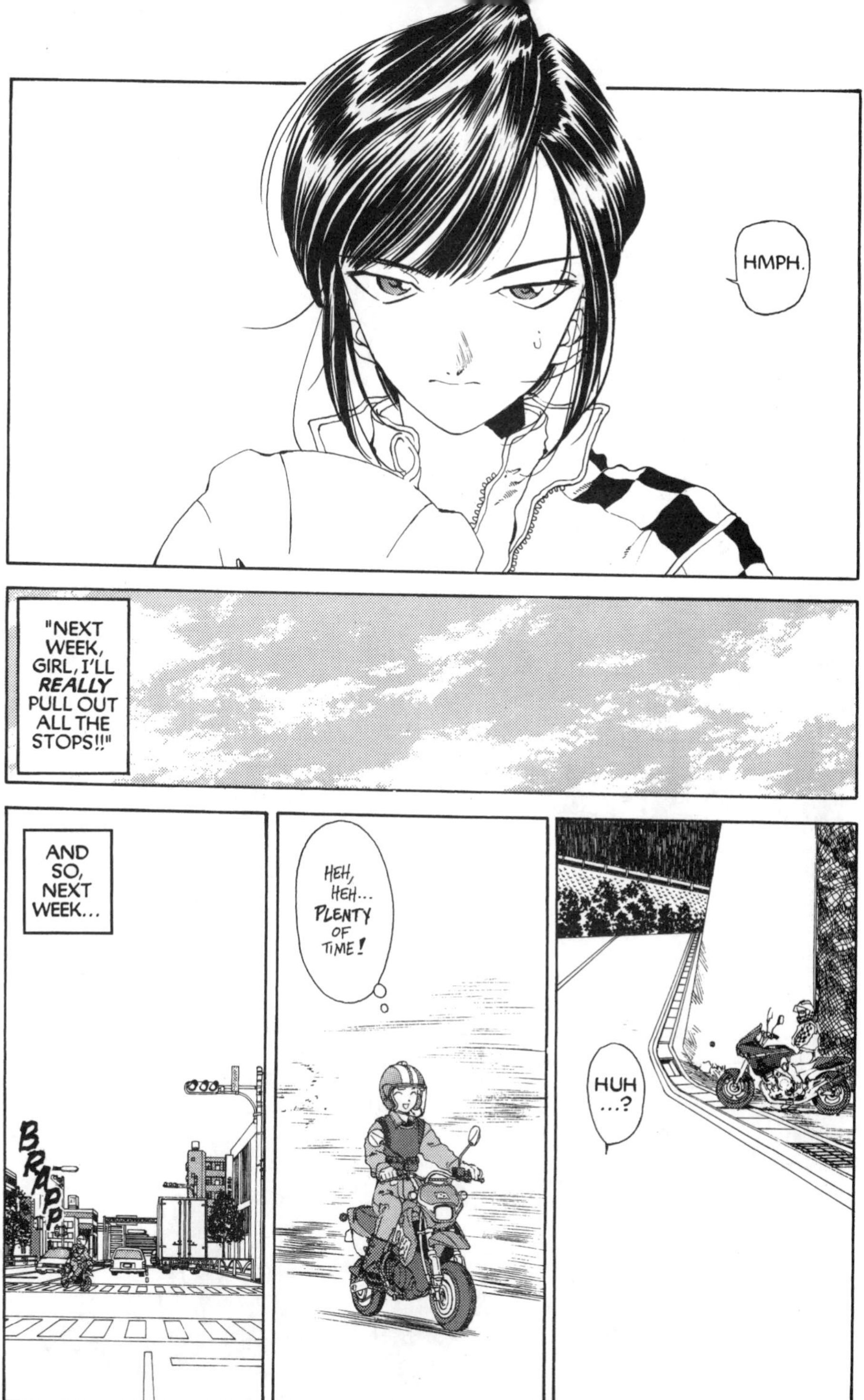
HMPH.
"NEXT WEEK, GIRL, I'LL *REALLY* PULL OUT ALL THE STOPS!!"
AND SO, NEXT WEEK...
BRAPP
HEH, HEH... PLENTY OF TIME!
HUH ...?

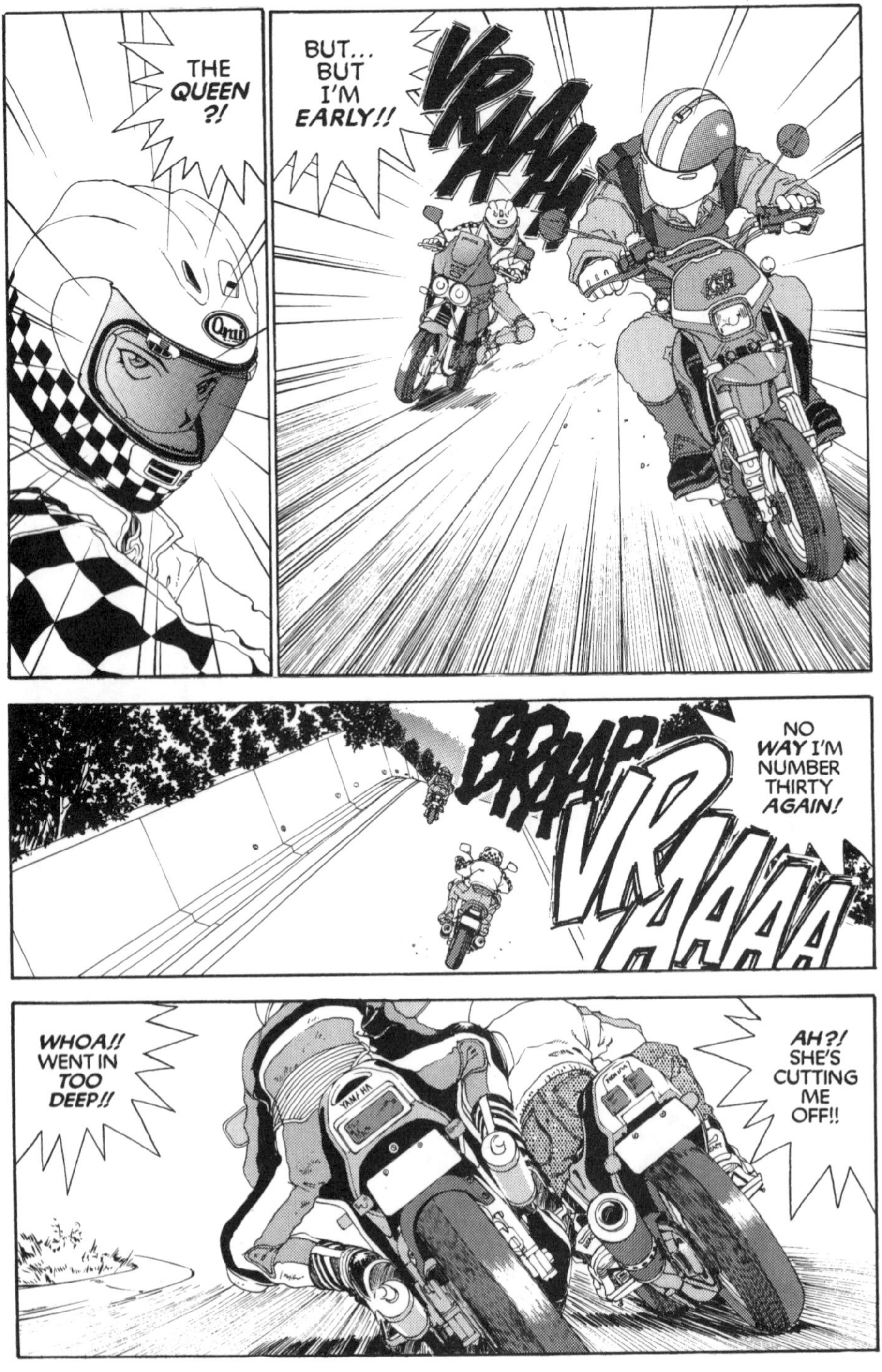

THE *QUEEN* ?!
BUT... BUT I'M *EARLY!!*
NO *WAY* I'M NUMBER THIRTY *AGAIN!*
VRAAAAA
WHOA!! WENT IN *TOO DEEP!!*
AH?! SHE'S CUTTING ME OFF!!

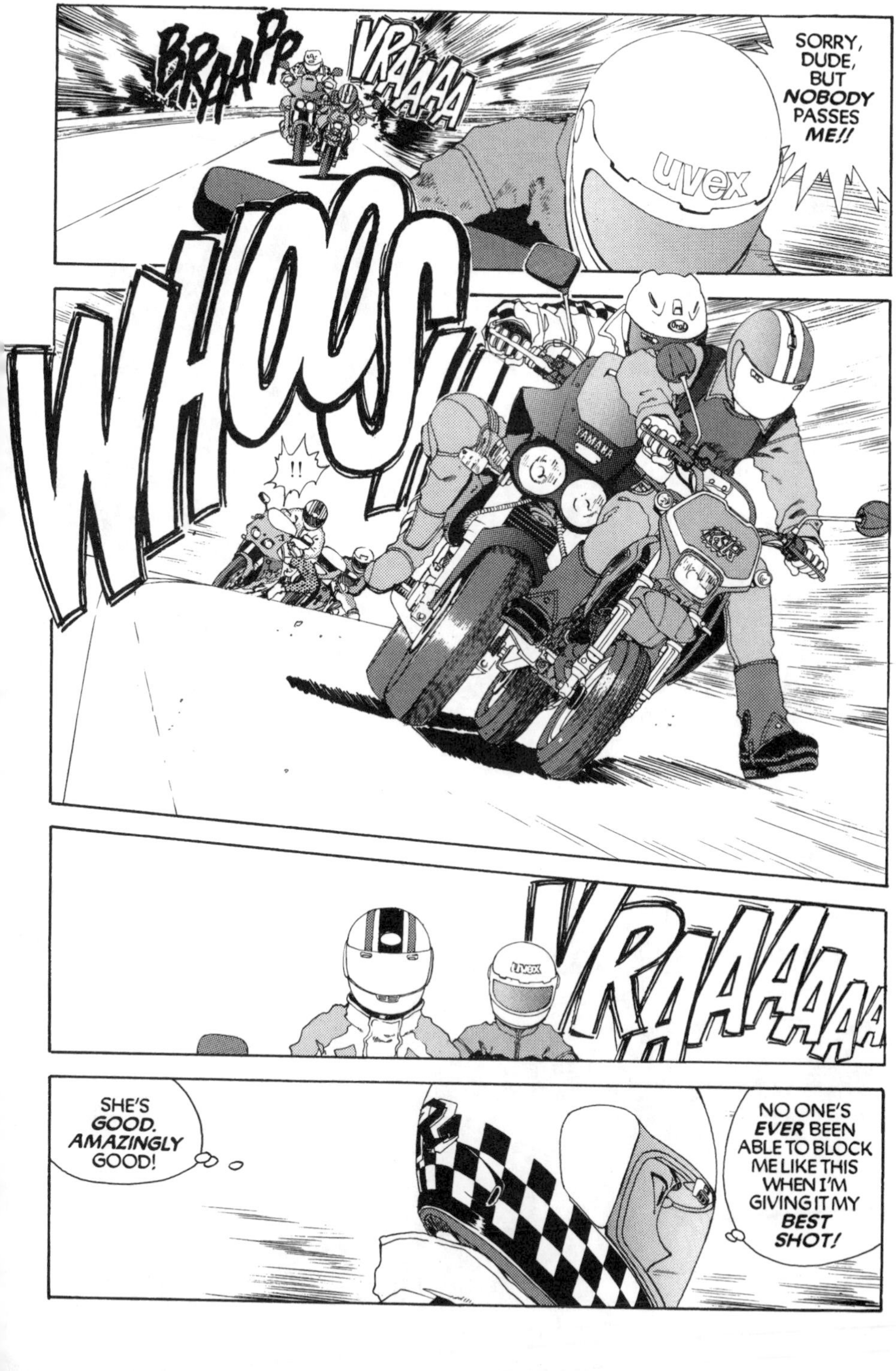
BRAAPP
VRAAAA
SORRY, DUDE, BUT NOBODY PASSES ME!!
uvex
WHOOS
!!
VRAAAAAA
SHE'S GOOD. AMAZINGLY GOOD!
NO ONE'S EVER BEEN ABLE TO BLOCK ME LIKE THIS WHEN I'M GIVING IT MY BEST SHOT!

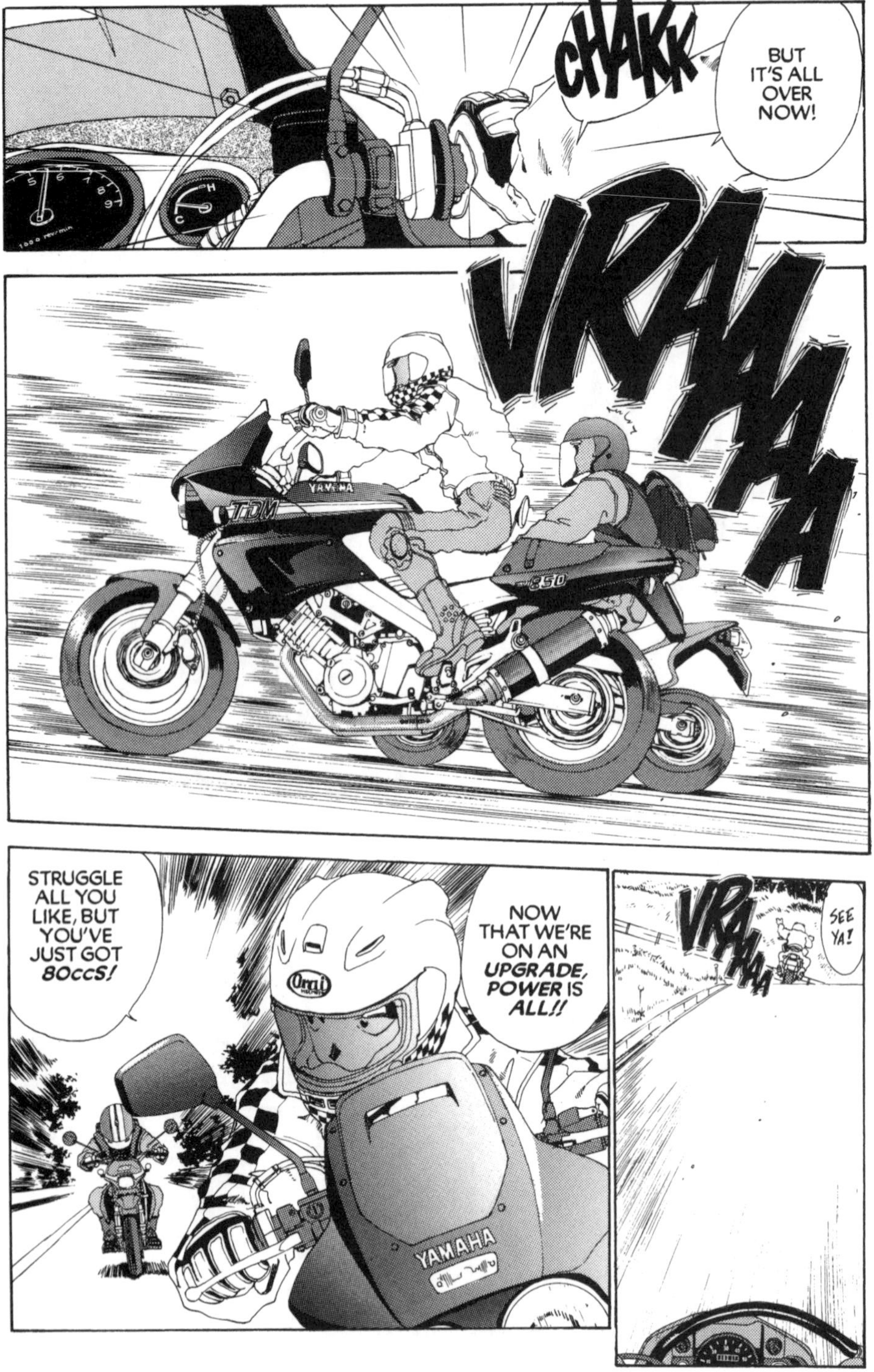
CHAKK
BUT IT'S ALL OVER NOW!
VRAAAAA
STRUGGLE ALL YOU LIKE, BUT YOU'VE JUST GOT *80ccS!*
NOW THAT WE'RE ON AN *UPGRADE, POWER* IS *ALL!!*
VRAAAAA
SEE YA!

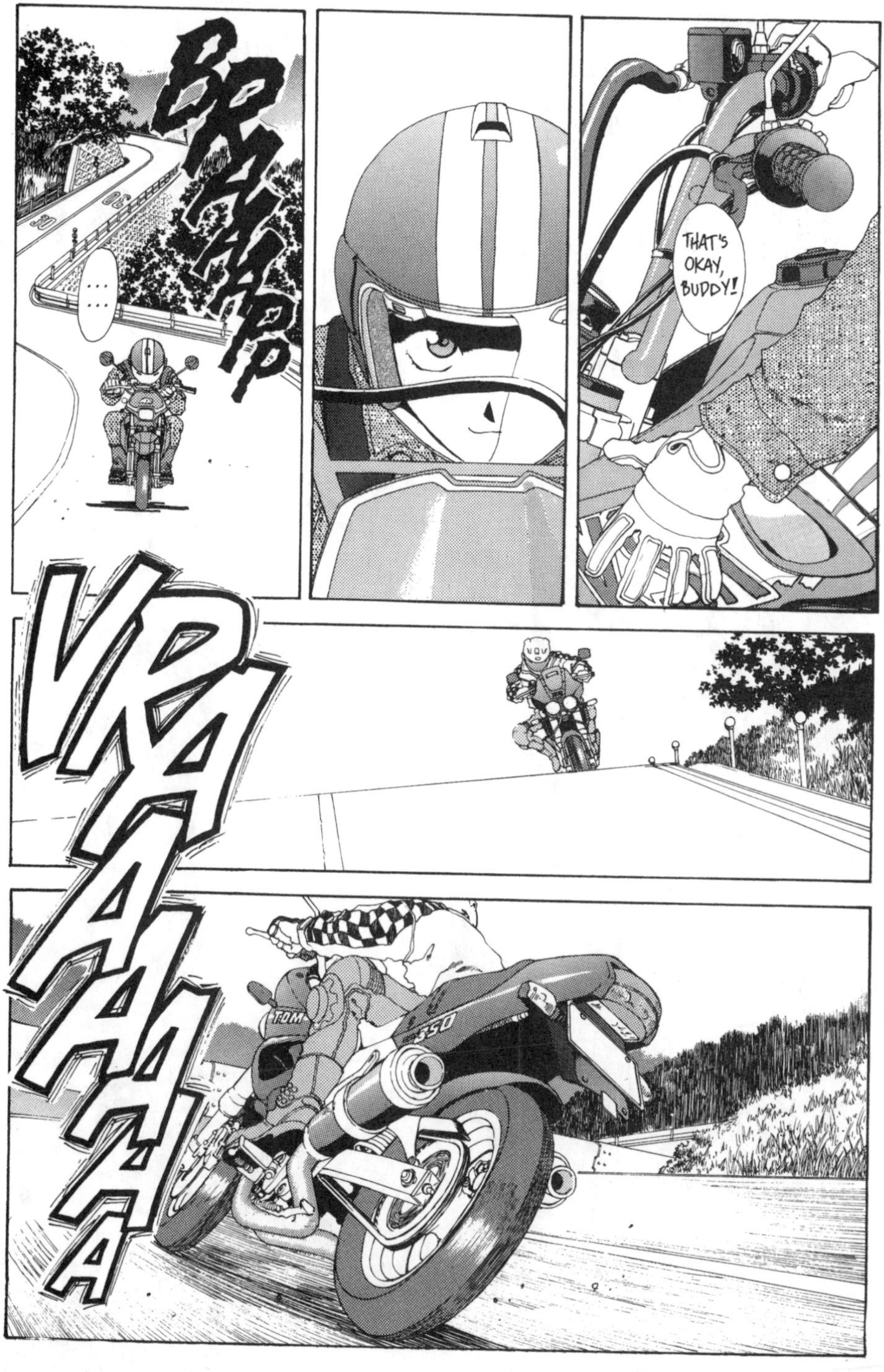
BRRMMPP
...
THAT'S OKAY, BUDDY!
VRAAAAAA

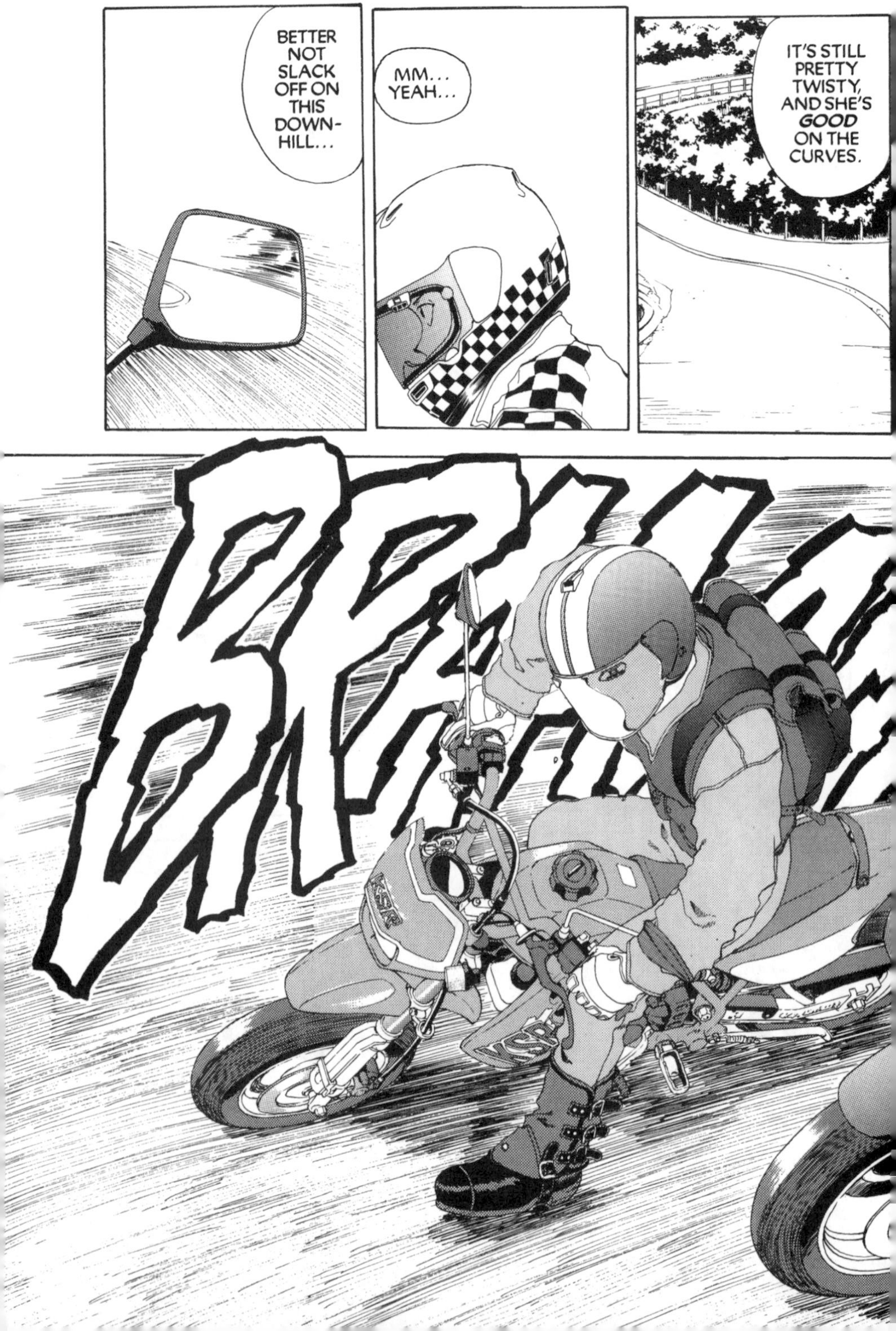
BETTER NOT SLACK OFF ON THIS DOWN-HILL...
MM... YEAH...
IT'S STILL PRETTY TWISTY, AND SHE'S *GOOD* ON THE CURVES.

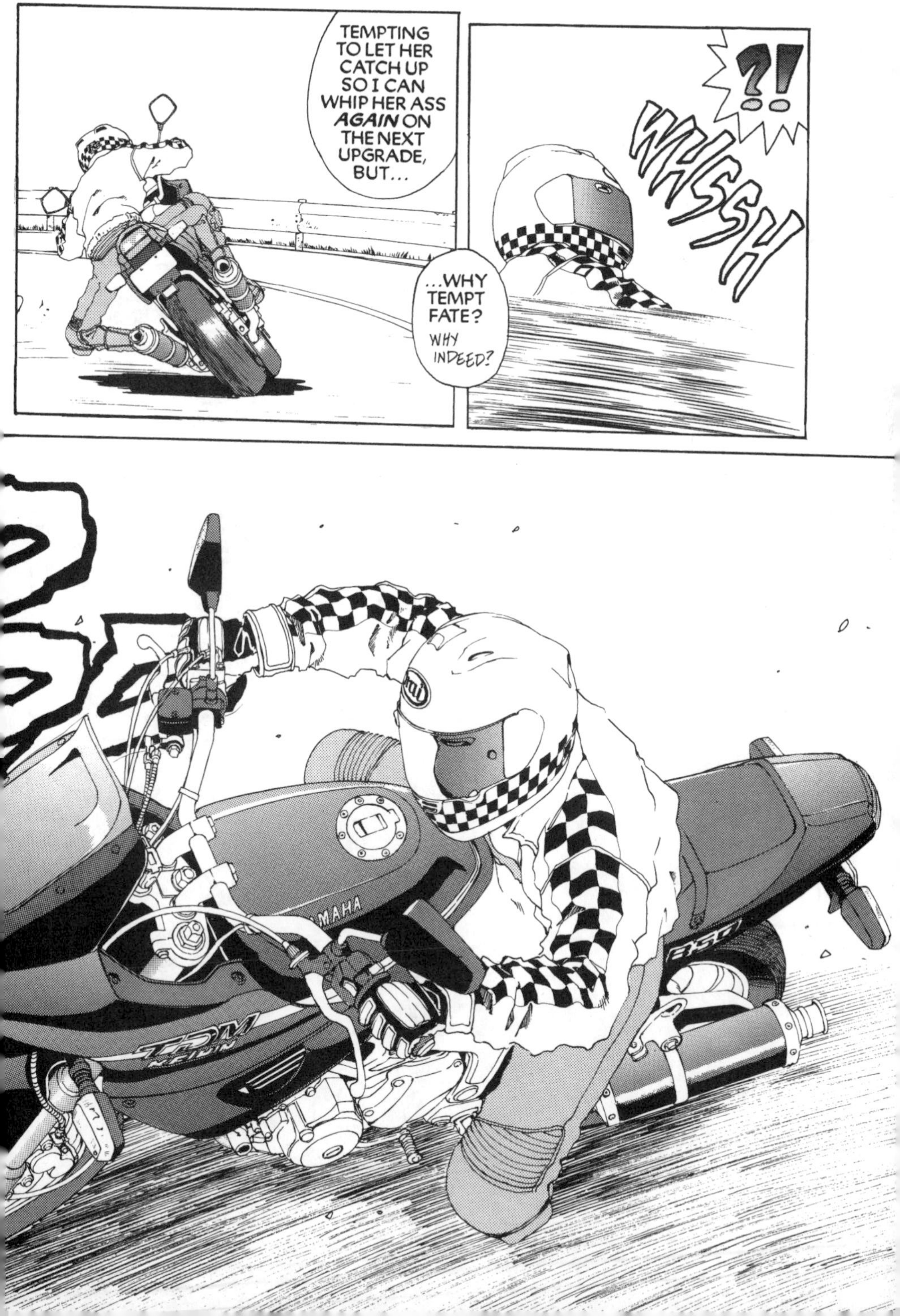
TEMPTING TO LET HER CATCH UP SO I CAN WHIP HER ASS *AGAIN* ON THE NEXT UPGRADE, BUT...
...WHY TEMPT FATE?
WHY INDEED?
?!
WHSSH

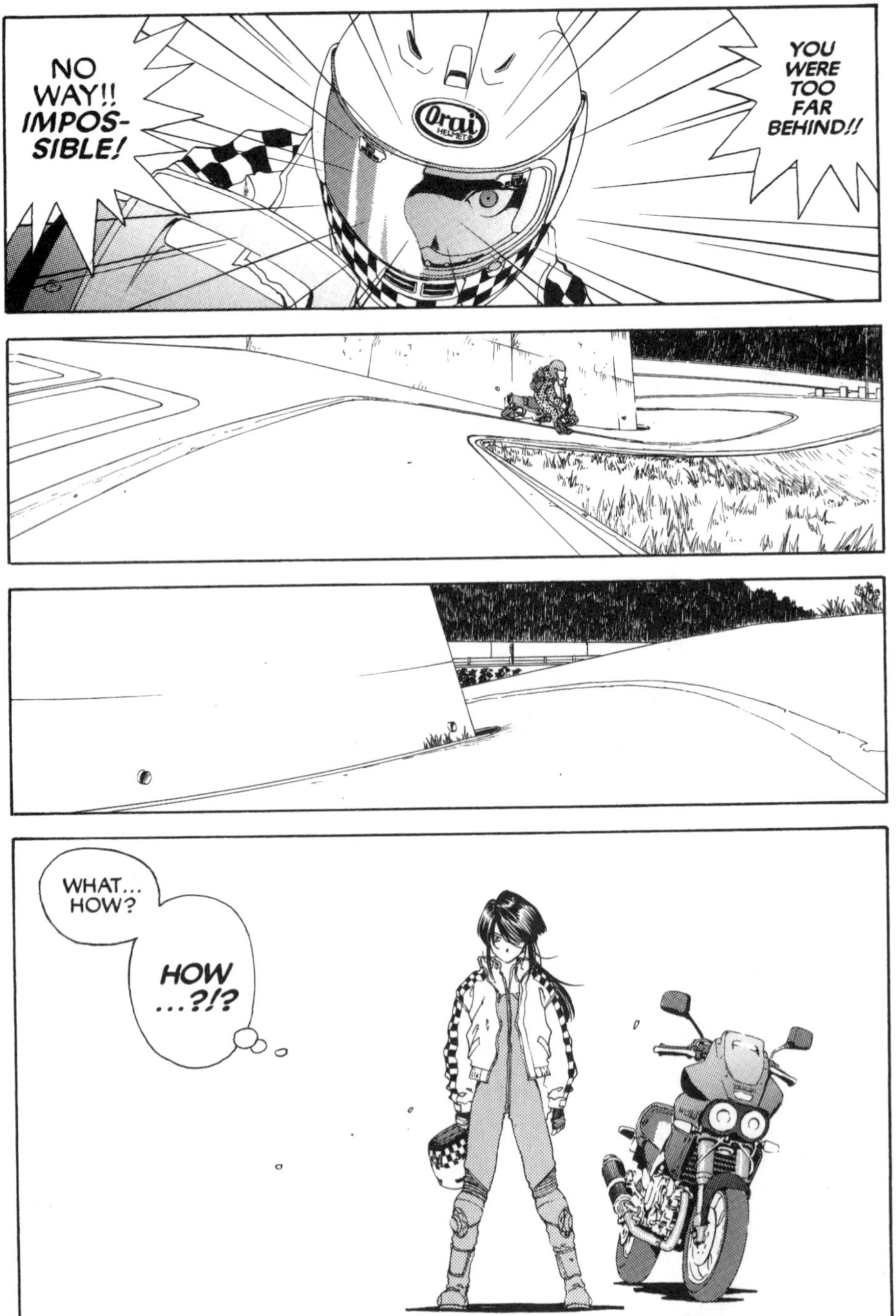
NO WAY!! IMPOS-SIBLE!
YOU WERE TOO FAR BEHIND!!
WHAT... HOW?
HOW ...?!?

THE SECRET OF SPEED

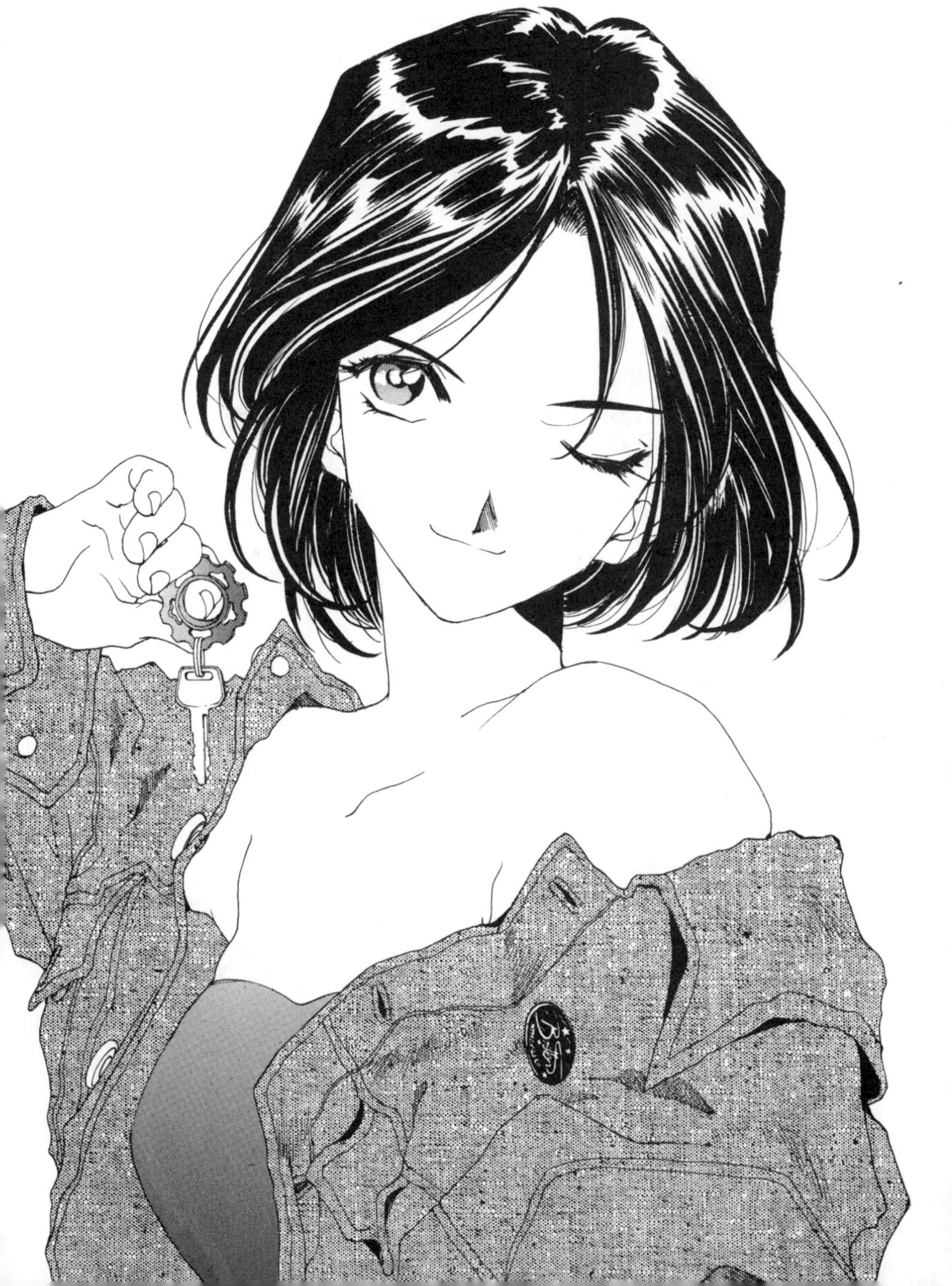

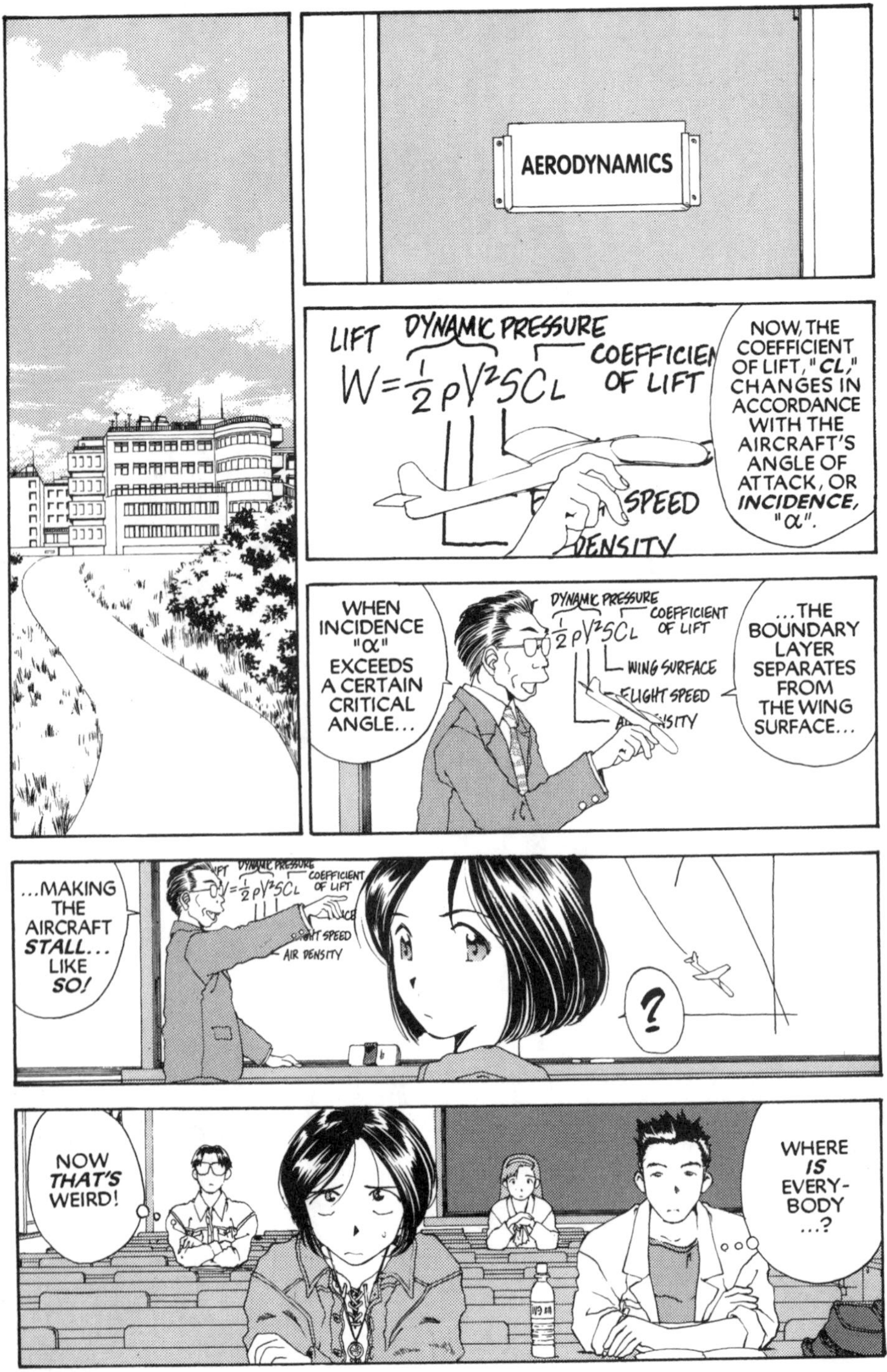
AERODYNAMICS
LIFT
DYNAMIC PRESSURE
W=1/2ρV²SCL
COEFFICIEN
OF LIFT
SPEED
DENSITY
NOW, THE COEFFICIENT OF LIFT, "CL," CHANGES IN ACCORDANCE WITH THE AIRCRAFT'S ANGLE OF ATTACK, OR INCIDENCE, "α".
WHEN INCIDENCE "α" EXCEEDS A CERTAIN CRITICAL ANGLE...
DYNAMIC PRESSURE
COEFFICIENT OF LIFT
WING SURFACE
FLIGHT SPEED
...THE BOUNDARY LAYER SEPARATES FROM THE WING SURFACE...
...MAKING THE AIRCRAFT STALL... LIKE SO!
COEFFICIENT OF LIFT
AIR DENSITY
?
NOW THAT'S WEIRD!
WHERE IS EVERYBODY...?

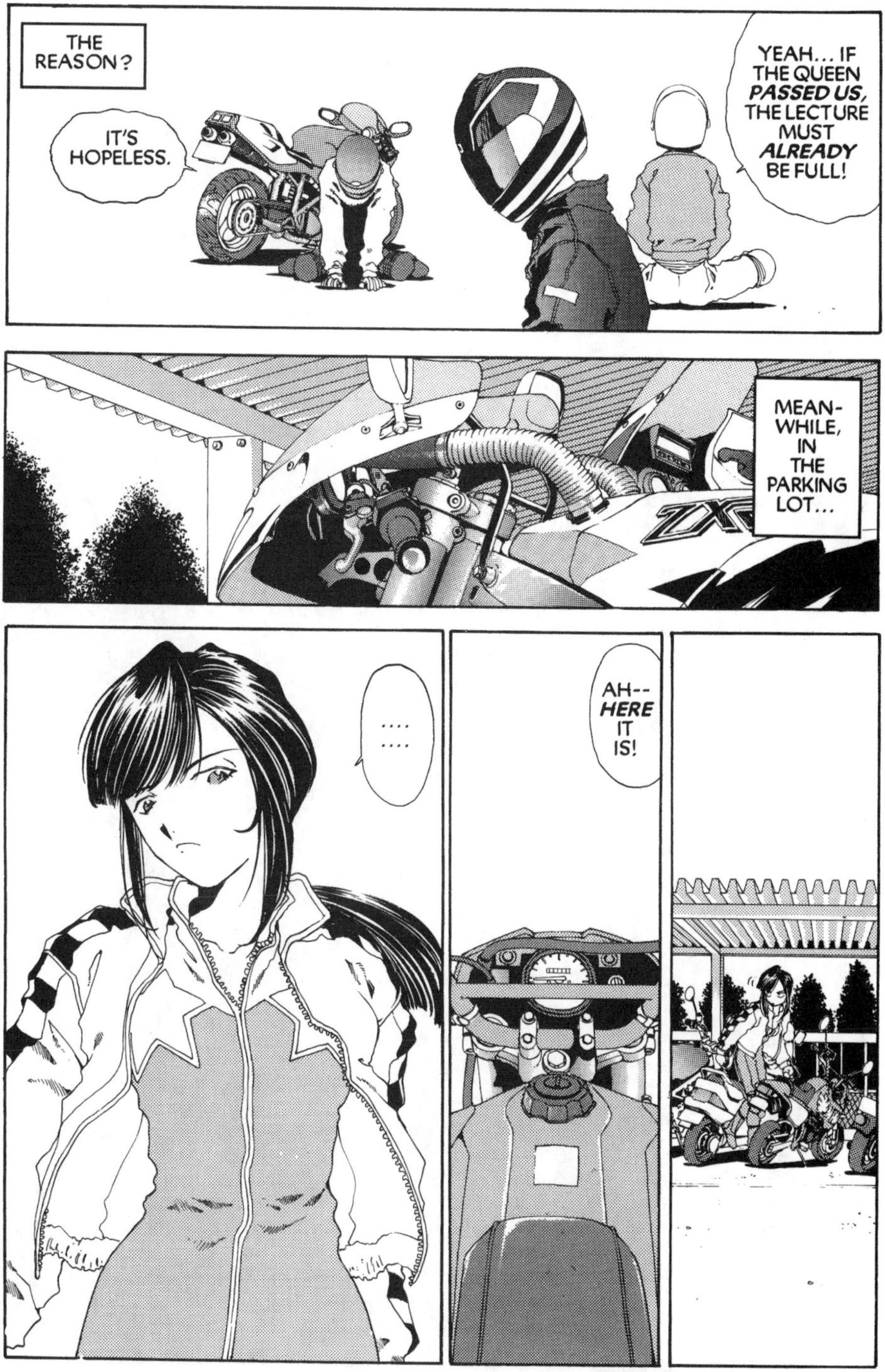
THE REASON?
IT'S HOPELESS.
YEAH... IF THE QUEEN PASSED US, THE LECTURE MUST ALREADY BE FULL!
MEAN-WHILE, IN THE PARKING LOT...
ZX
....
AH-- HERE IT IS!

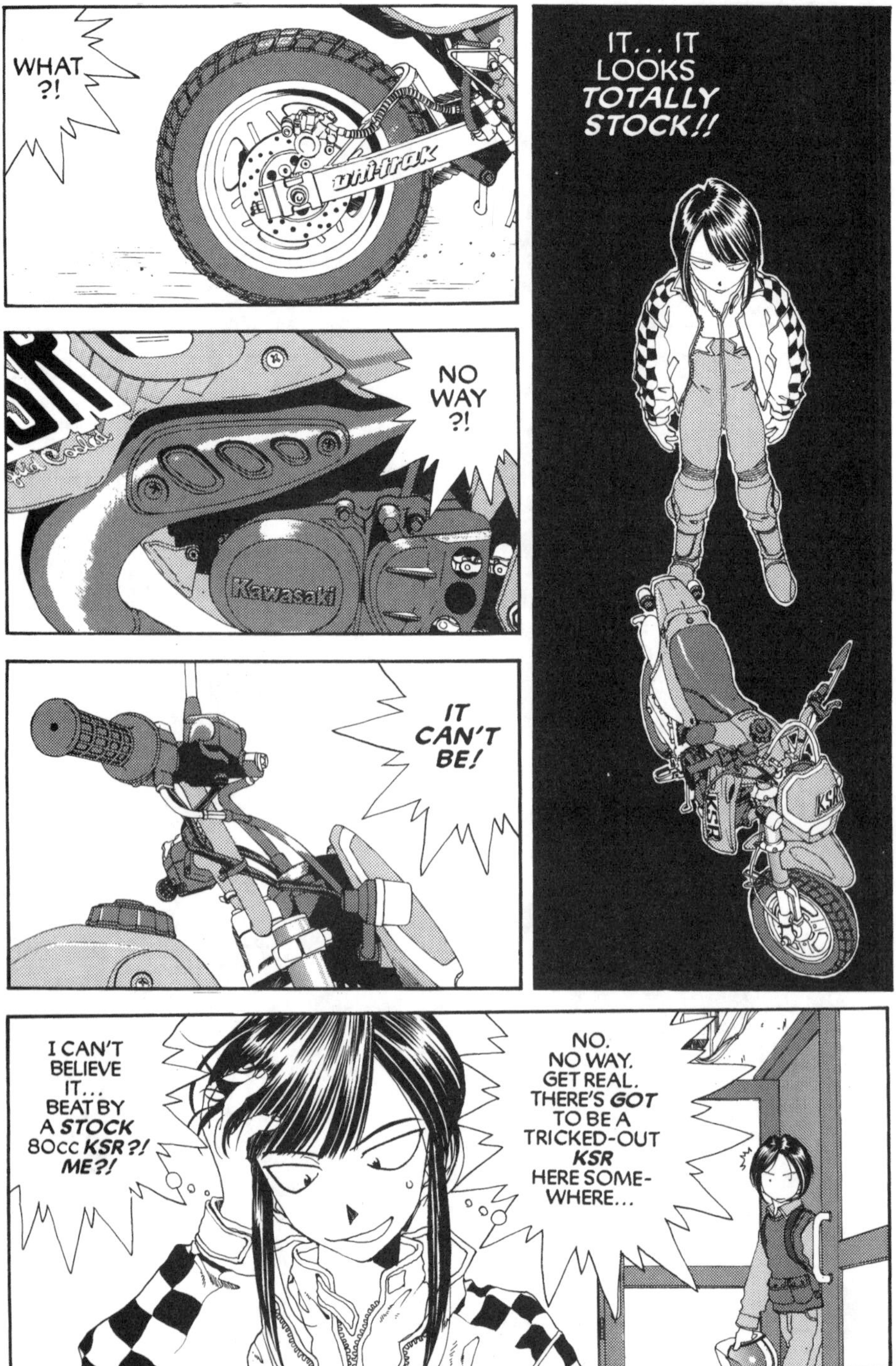
WHAT ?!
uni-trak
NO WAY ?!
Kawasaki
IT CAN'T BE!
IT... IT LOOKS TOTALLY STOCK!!
KSR
I CAN'T BELIEVE IT... BEAT BY A STOCK 80cc KSR?! ME?!
NO. NO WAY. GET REAL. THERE'S GOT TO BE A TRICKED-OUT KSR HERE SOME-WHERE...

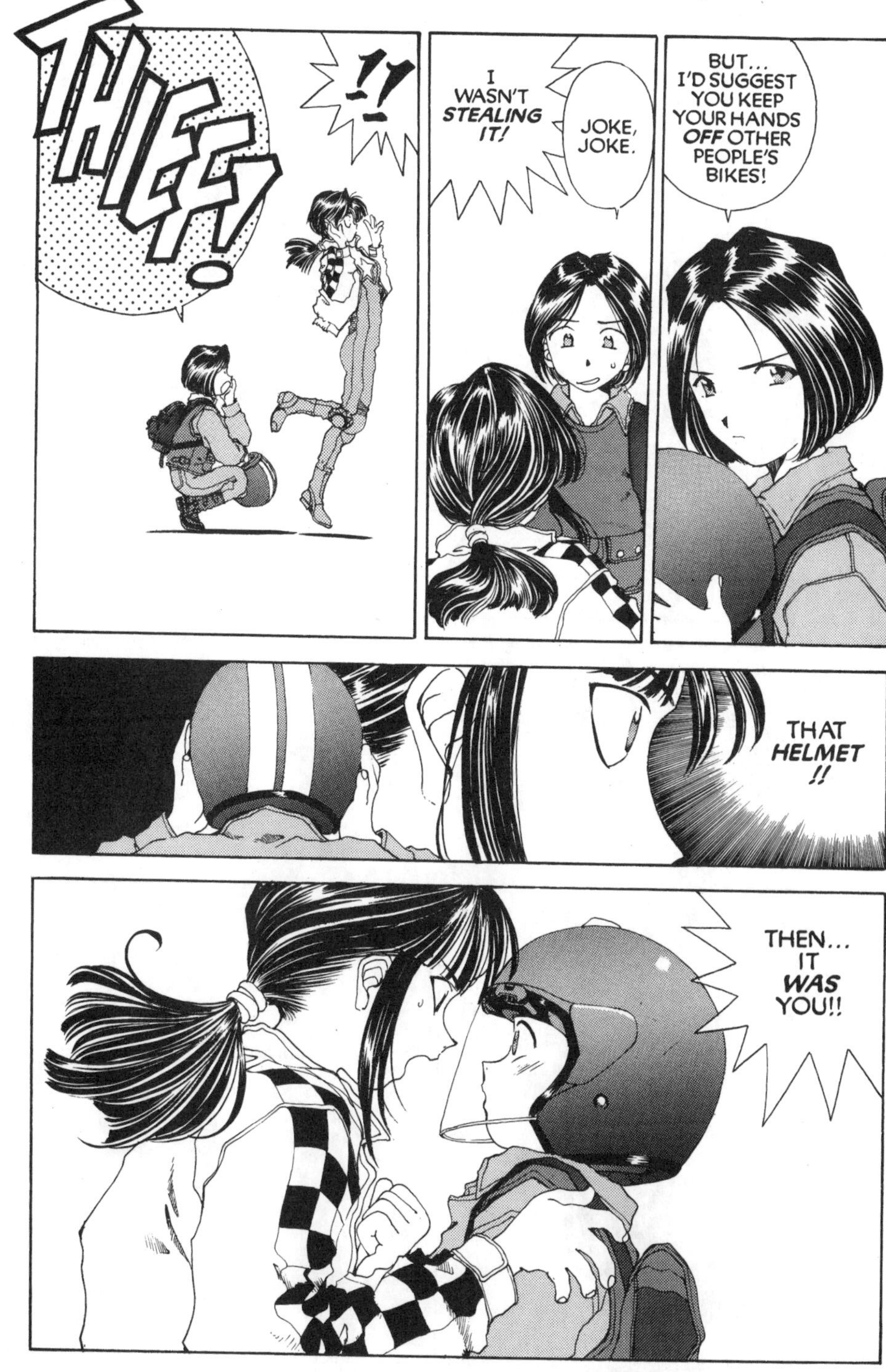
THIEF!
!!
I WASN'T STEALING IT!
JOKE, JOKE.
BUT... I'D SUGGEST YOU KEEP YOUR HANDS OFF OTHER PEOPLE'S BIKES!
THAT HELMET!!
THEN... IT WAS YOU!!

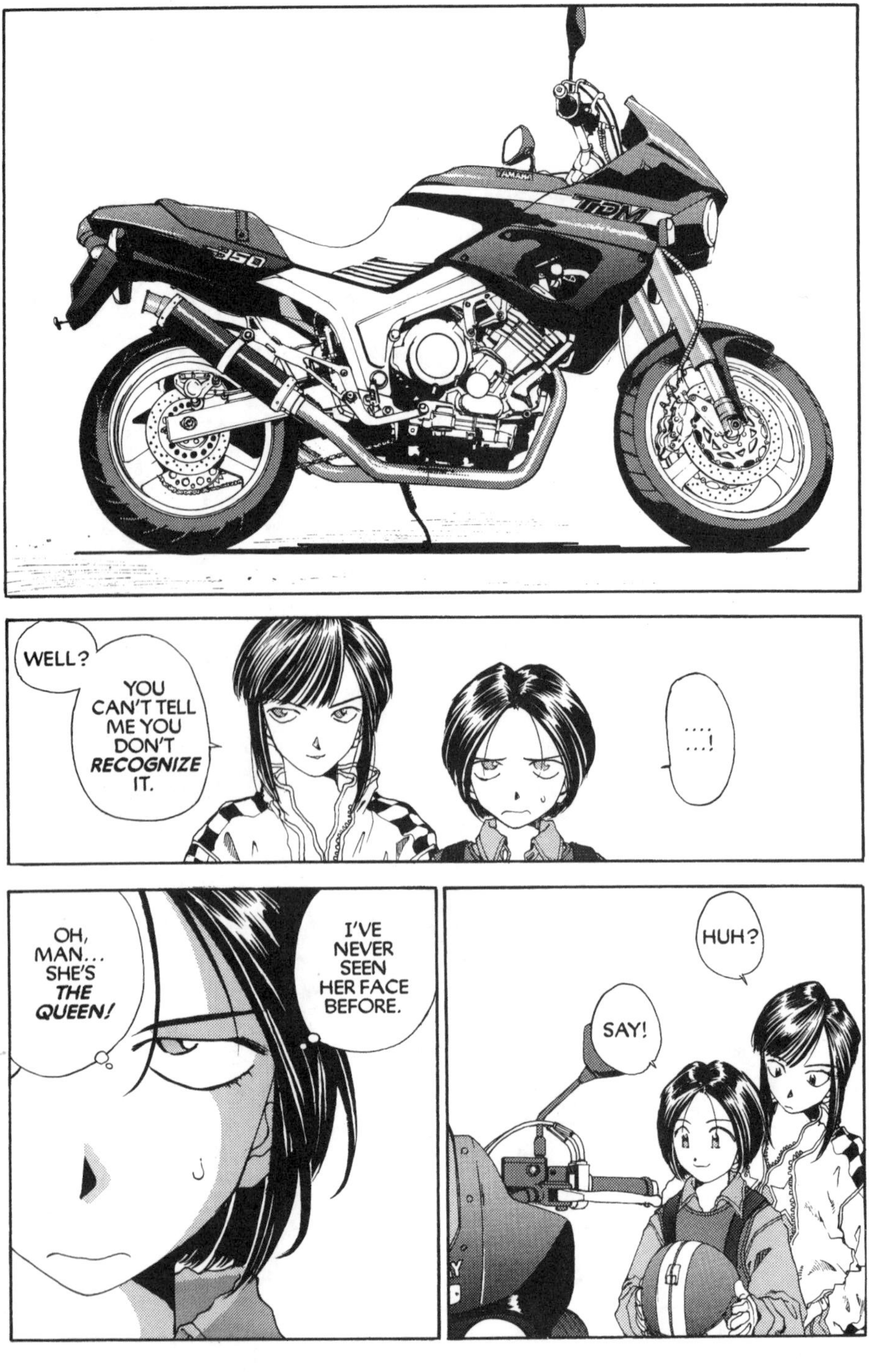
TDM
850
WELL?
YOU CAN'T TELL ME YOU DON'T *RECOGNIZE* IT.
……!
OH, MAN… SHE'S ***THE QUEEN!***
I'VE NEVER SEEN HER FACE BEFORE.
HUH?
SAY!

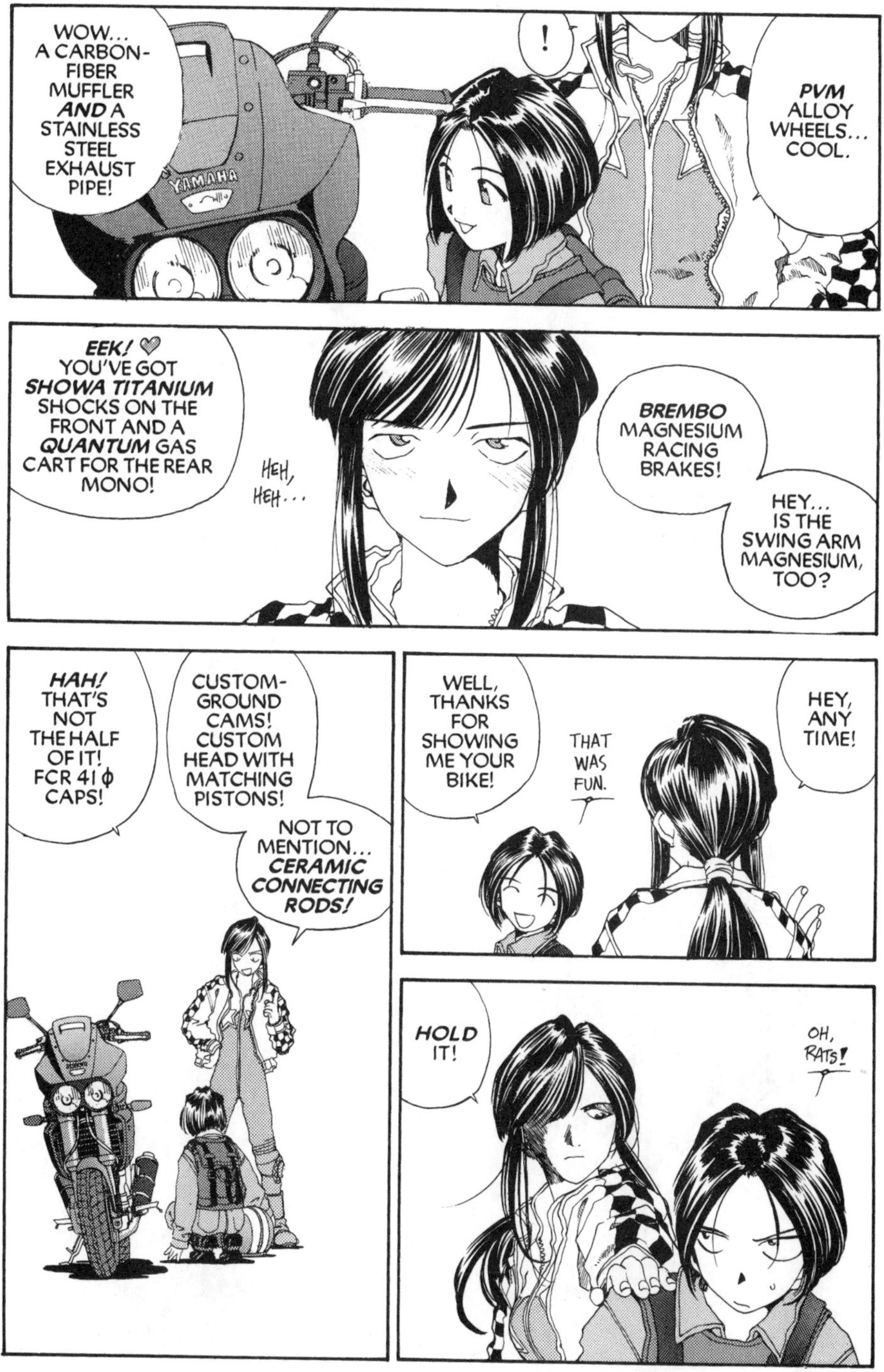
WOW... A CARBON-FIBER MUFFLER AND A STAINLESS STEEL EXHAUST PIPE!
YAMAHA
!
PVM ALLOY WHEELS... COOL.
EEK! ♡ YOU'VE GOT SHOWA TITANIUM SHOCKS ON THE FRONT AND A QUANTUM GAS CART FOR THE REAR MONO!
HEH, HEH...
BREMBO MAGNESIUM RACING BRAKES!
HEY... IS THE SWING ARM MAGNESIUM, TOO?
HAH! THAT'S NOT THE HALF OF IT! FCR 41 ϕ CAPS!
CUSTOM-GROUND CAMS! CUSTOM HEAD WITH MATCHING PISTONS!
NOT TO MENTION... CERAMIC CONNECTING RODS!
WELL, THANKS FOR SHOWING ME YOUR BIKE!
THAT WAS FUN.
HEY, ANY TIME!
HOLD IT!
OH, RATS!

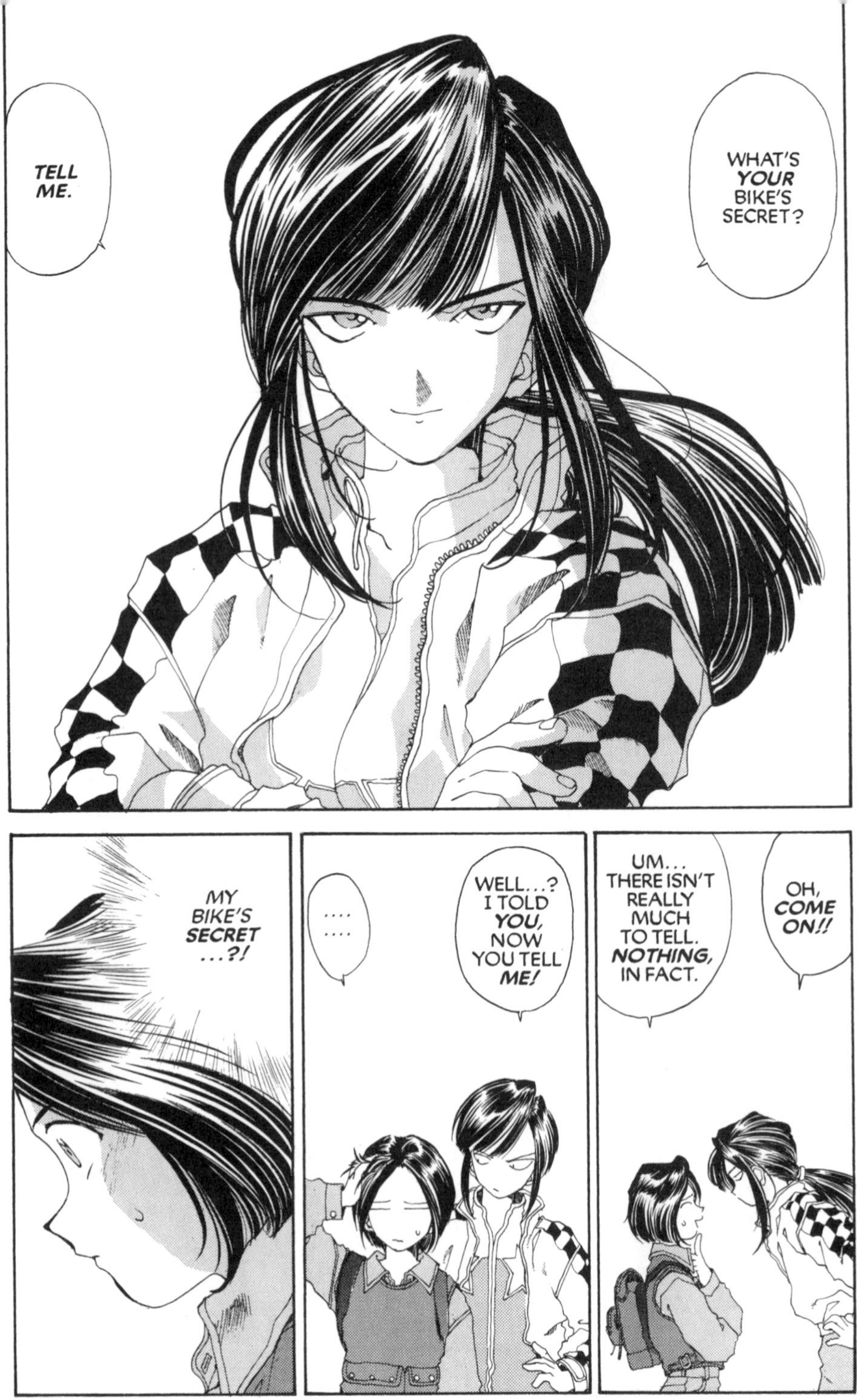
TELL ME.
WHAT'S YOUR BIKE'S SECRET?
MY BIKE'S SECRET ...?!
....
WELL...? I TOLD YOU, NOW YOU TELL ME!
UM... THERE ISN'T REALLY MUCH TO TELL. NOTHING, IN FACT.
OH, COME ON!!

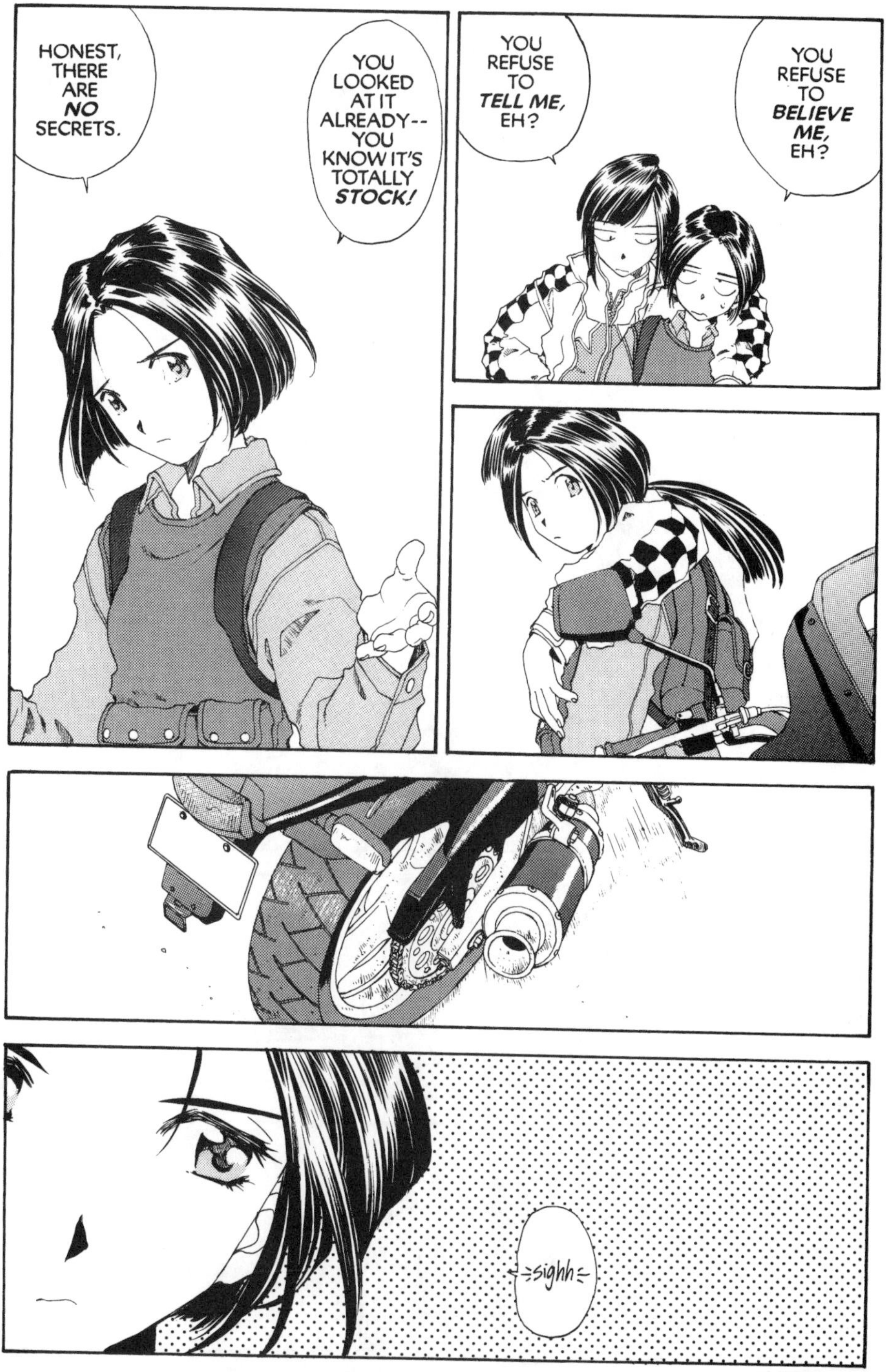
HONEST, THERE ARE NO SECRETS.
YOU LOOKED AT IT ALREADY-- YOU KNOW IT'S TOTALLY STOCK!
YOU REFUSE TO TELL ME, EH?
YOU REFUSE TO BELIEVE ME, EH?
sighh

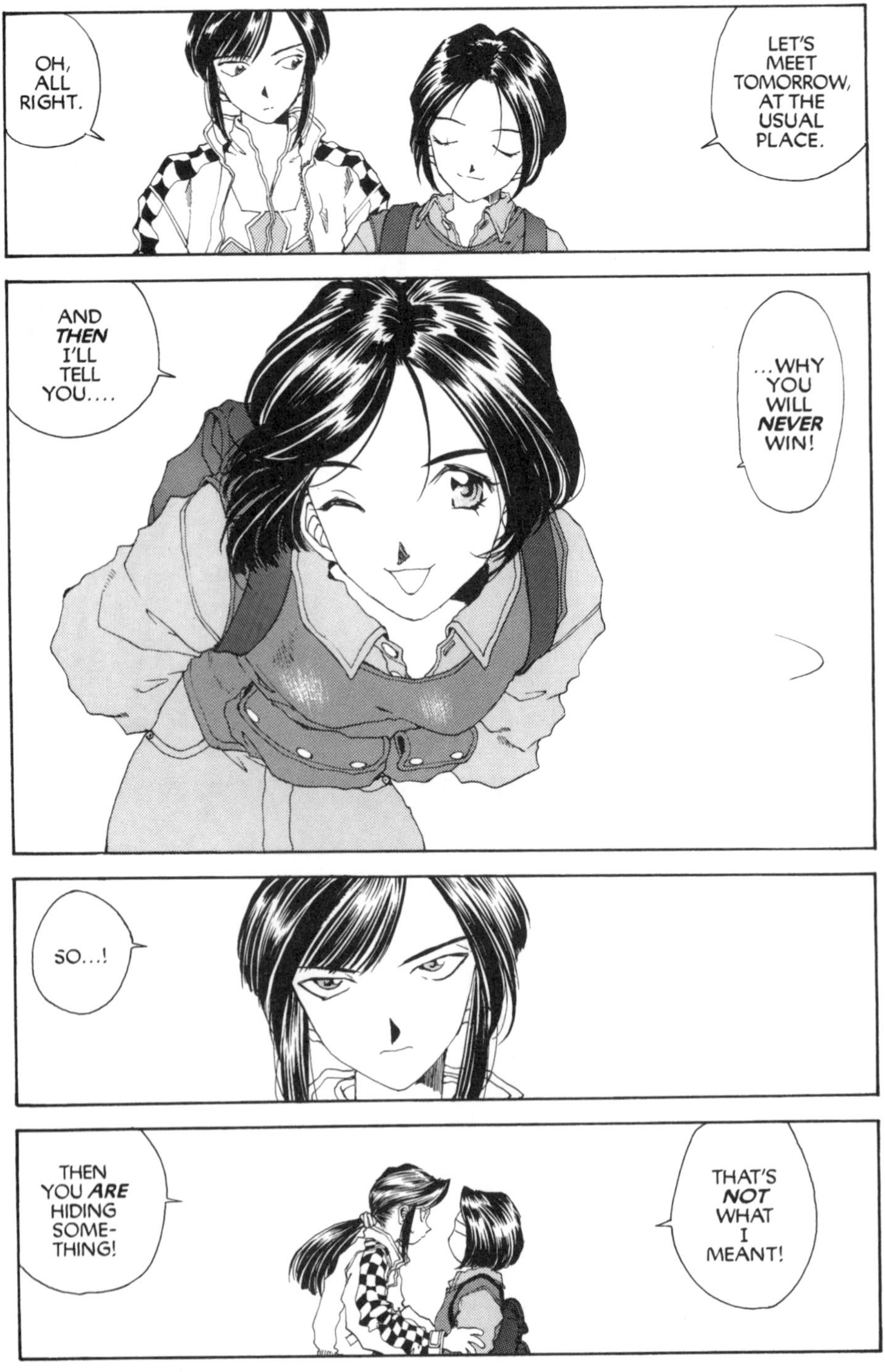

OH, ALL RIGHT.
LET'S MEET TOMORROW, AT THE USUAL PLACE.
AND *THEN* I'LL TELL YOU....
...WHY YOU WILL *NEVER* WIN!
SO...!
THEN YOU *ARE* HIDING SOME-THING!
THAT'S *NOT* WHAT I MEANT!

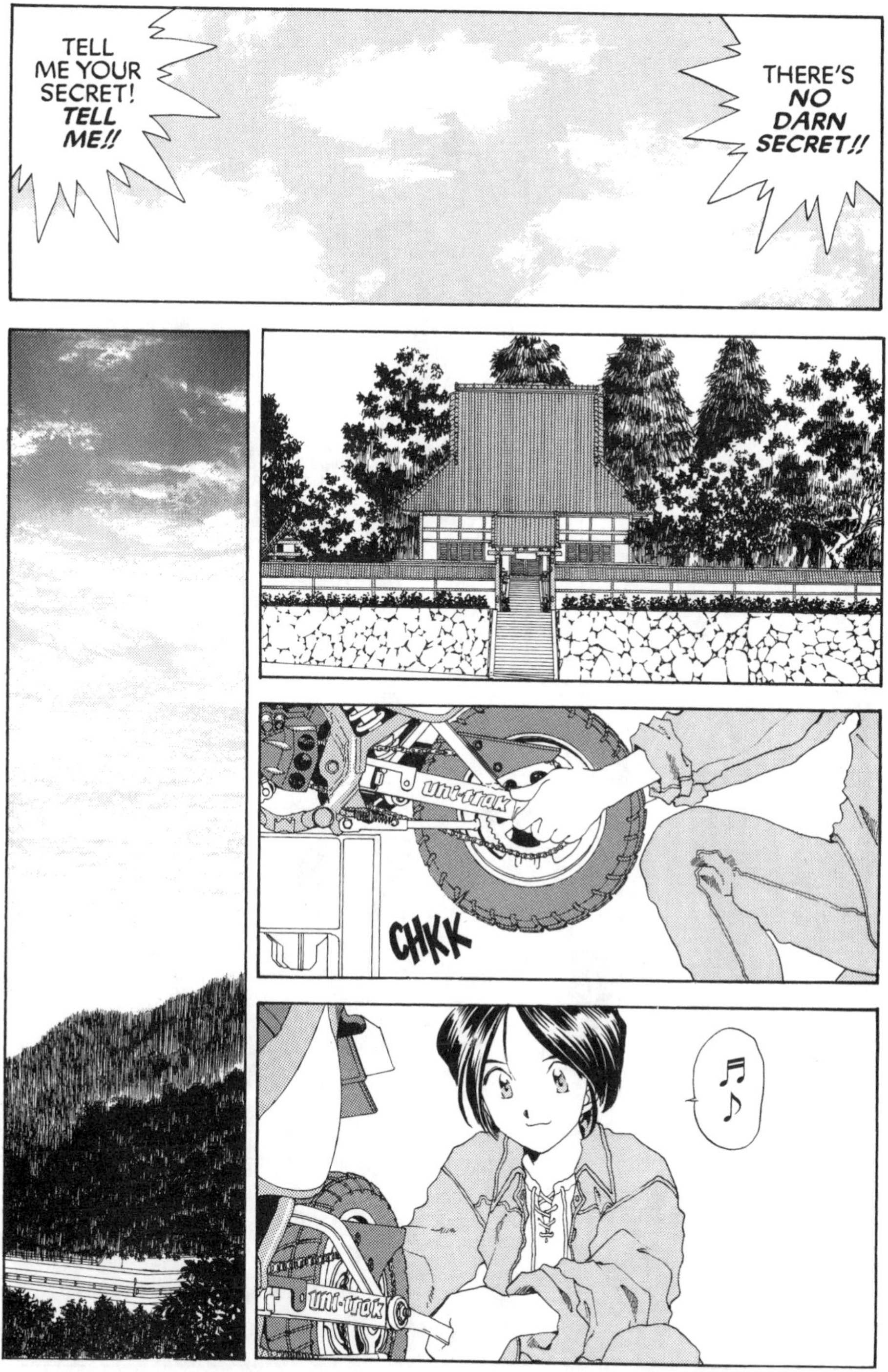
TELL ME YOUR SECRET! **TELL ME!!**
THERE'S **NO DARN SECRET!!**
uni-trak
CHKK
♬ ♪
uni-trak

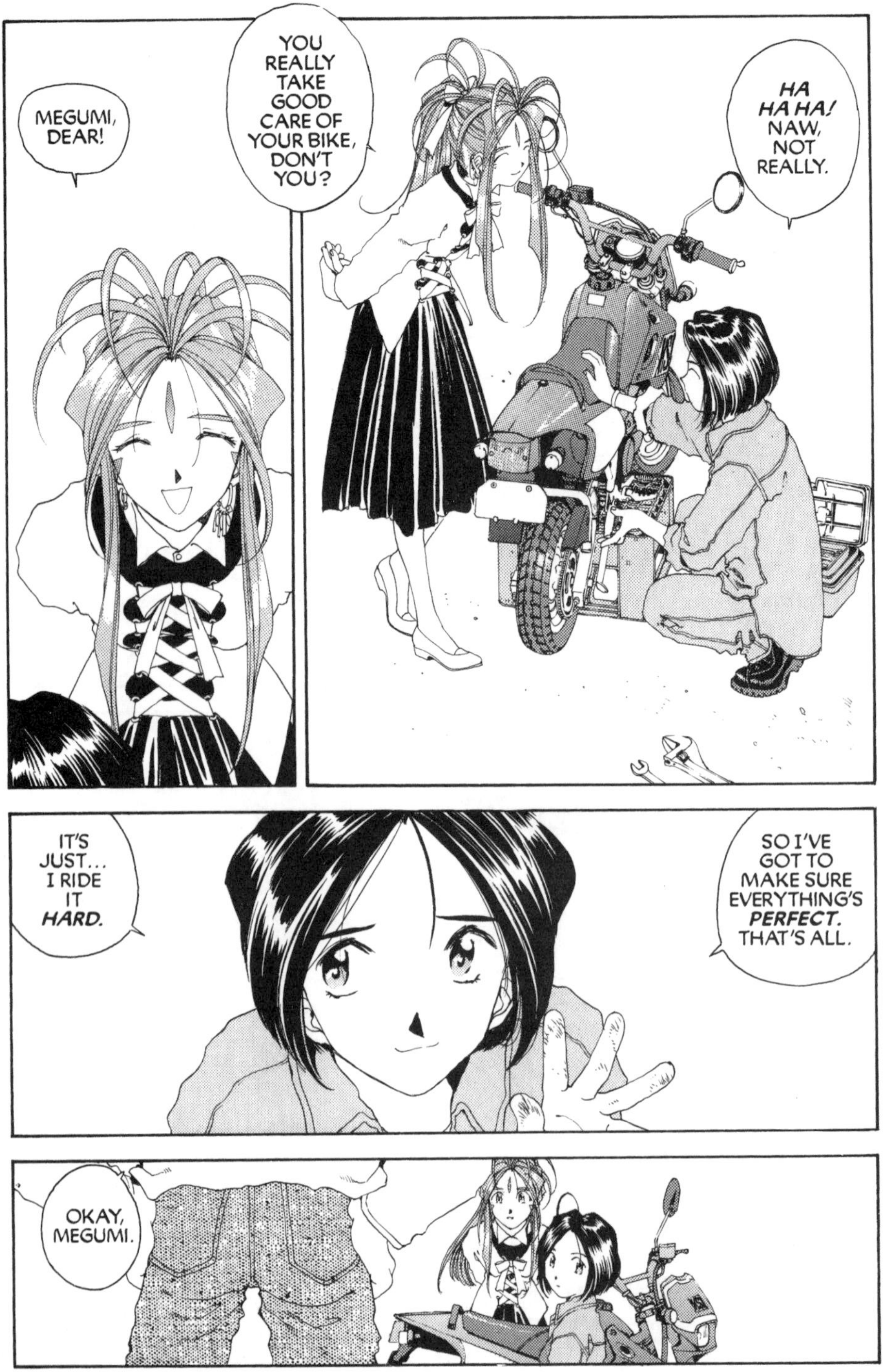
MEGUMI, DEAR!
YOU REALLY TAKE GOOD CARE OF YOUR BIKE, DON'T YOU?
HA HA HA! NAW, NOT REALLY.
IT'S JUST... I RIDE IT HARD.
SO I'VE GOT TO MAKE SURE EVERYTHING'S PERFECT. THAT'S ALL.
OKAY, MEGUMI.

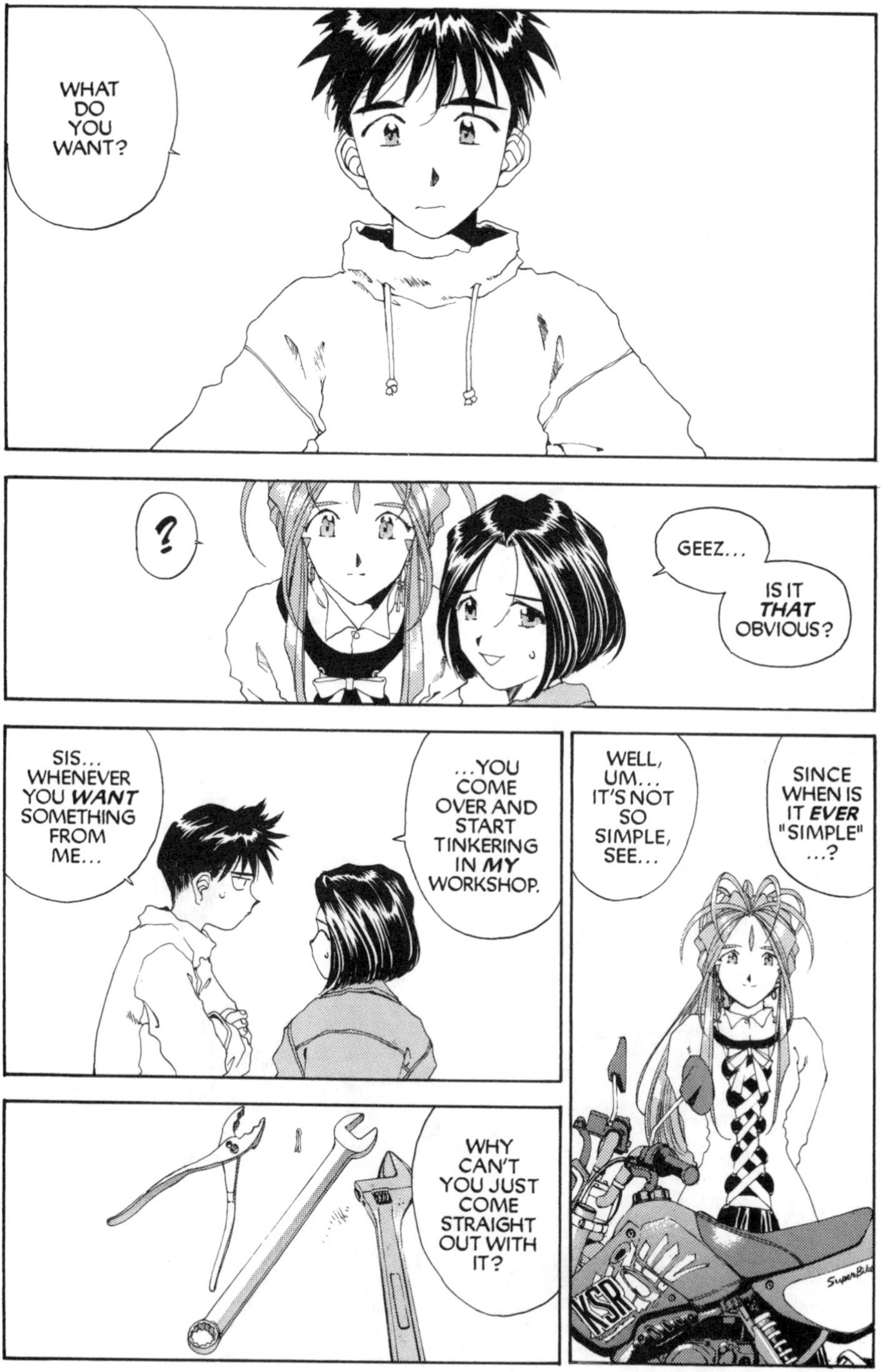

WHAT DO YOU WANT?
?
GEEZ...
IS IT *THAT* OBVIOUS?
SIS... WHENEVER YOU *WANT* SOMETHING FROM ME...
...YOU COME OVER AND START TINKERING IN *MY* WORKSHOP.
WHY CAN'T YOU JUST COME STRAIGHT OUT WITH IT?
WELL, UM... IT'S NOT SO SIMPLE, SEE...
SINCE WHEN IS IT *EVER* "SIMPLE" ...?
KSR

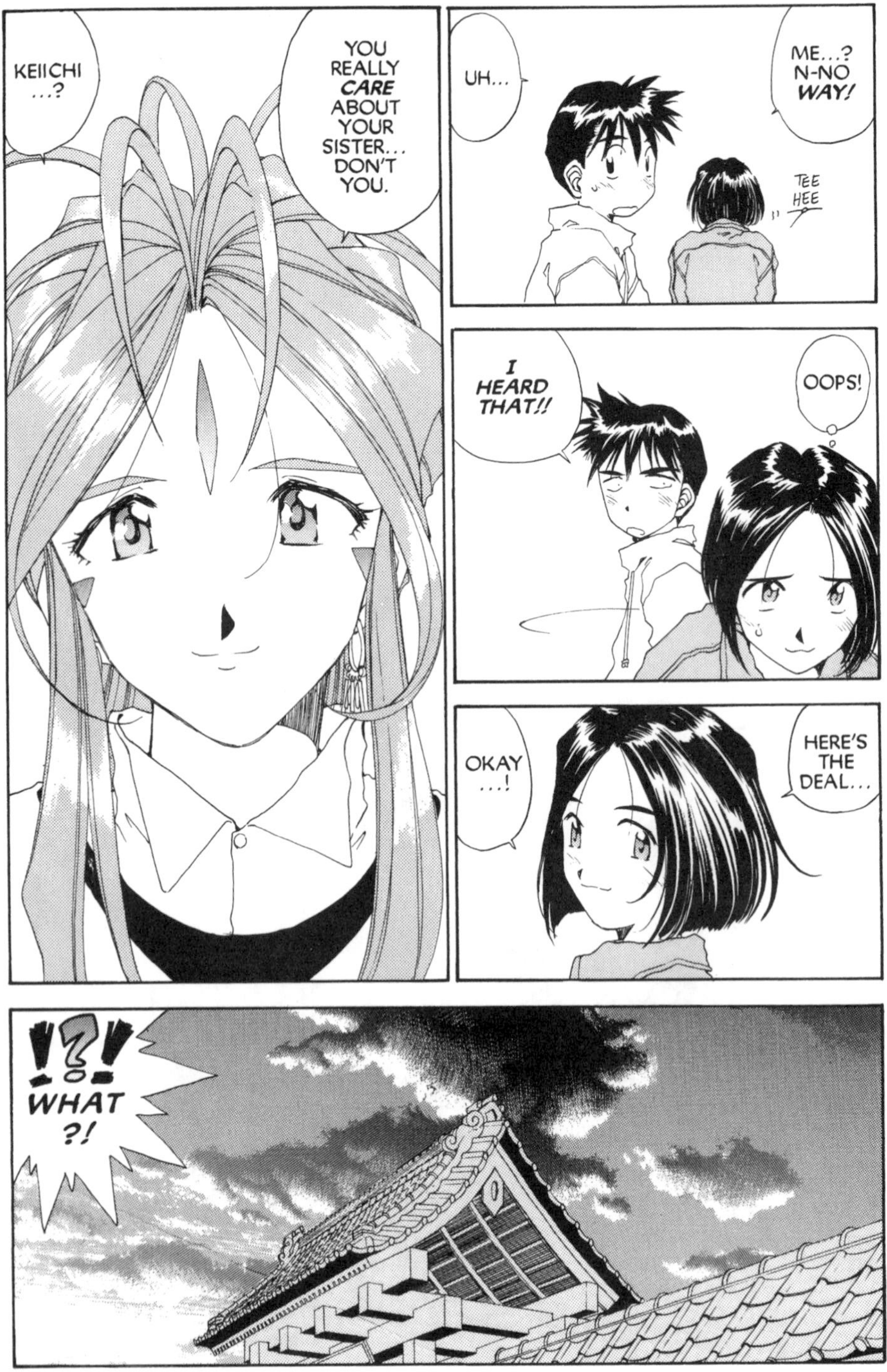
KEIICHI ...?
YOU REALLY *CARE* ABOUT YOUR SISTER... DON'T YOU.
UH...
ME...? N-NO *WAY!*
TEE HEE
I HEARD THAT!!
OOPS!
OKAY ...!
HERE'S THE DEAL...
!?! WHAT ?!

TWO HEARTS BEAT AS ONE

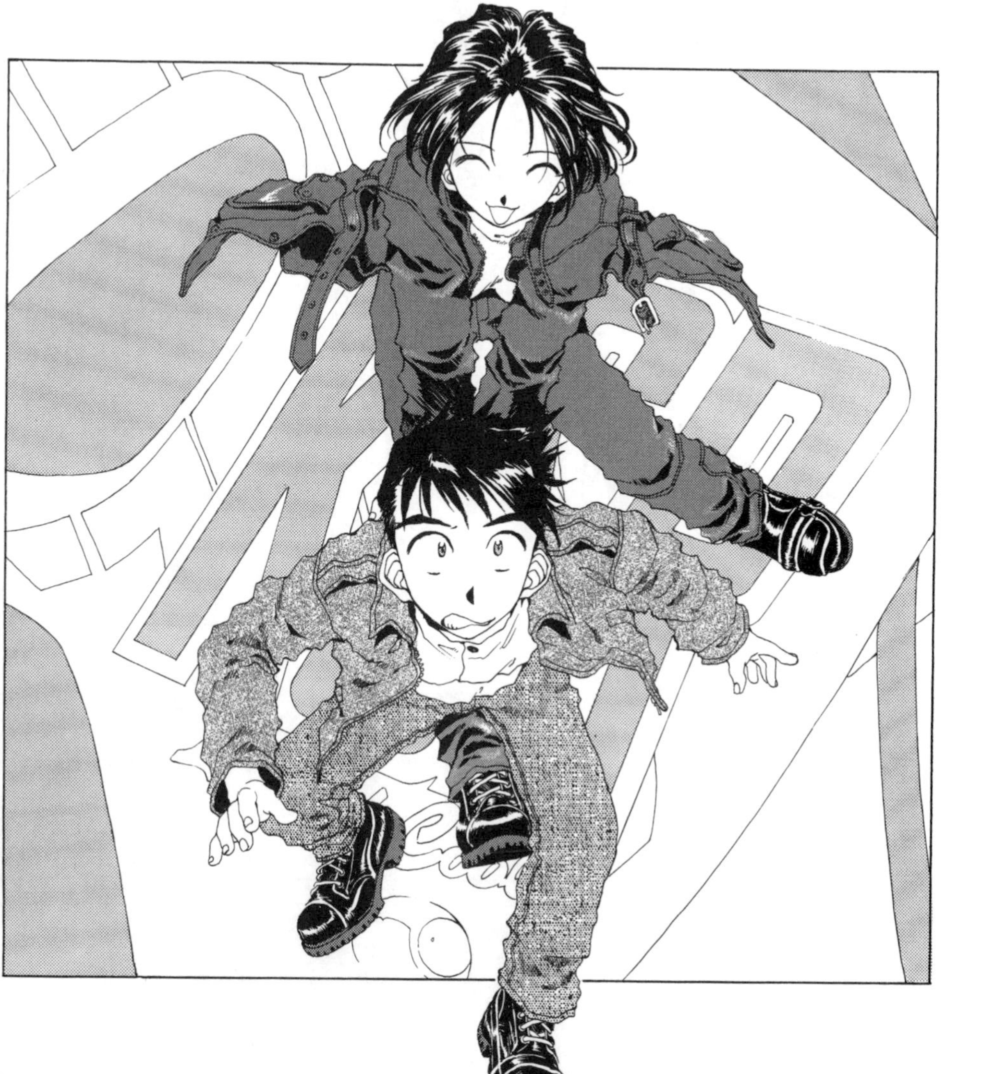

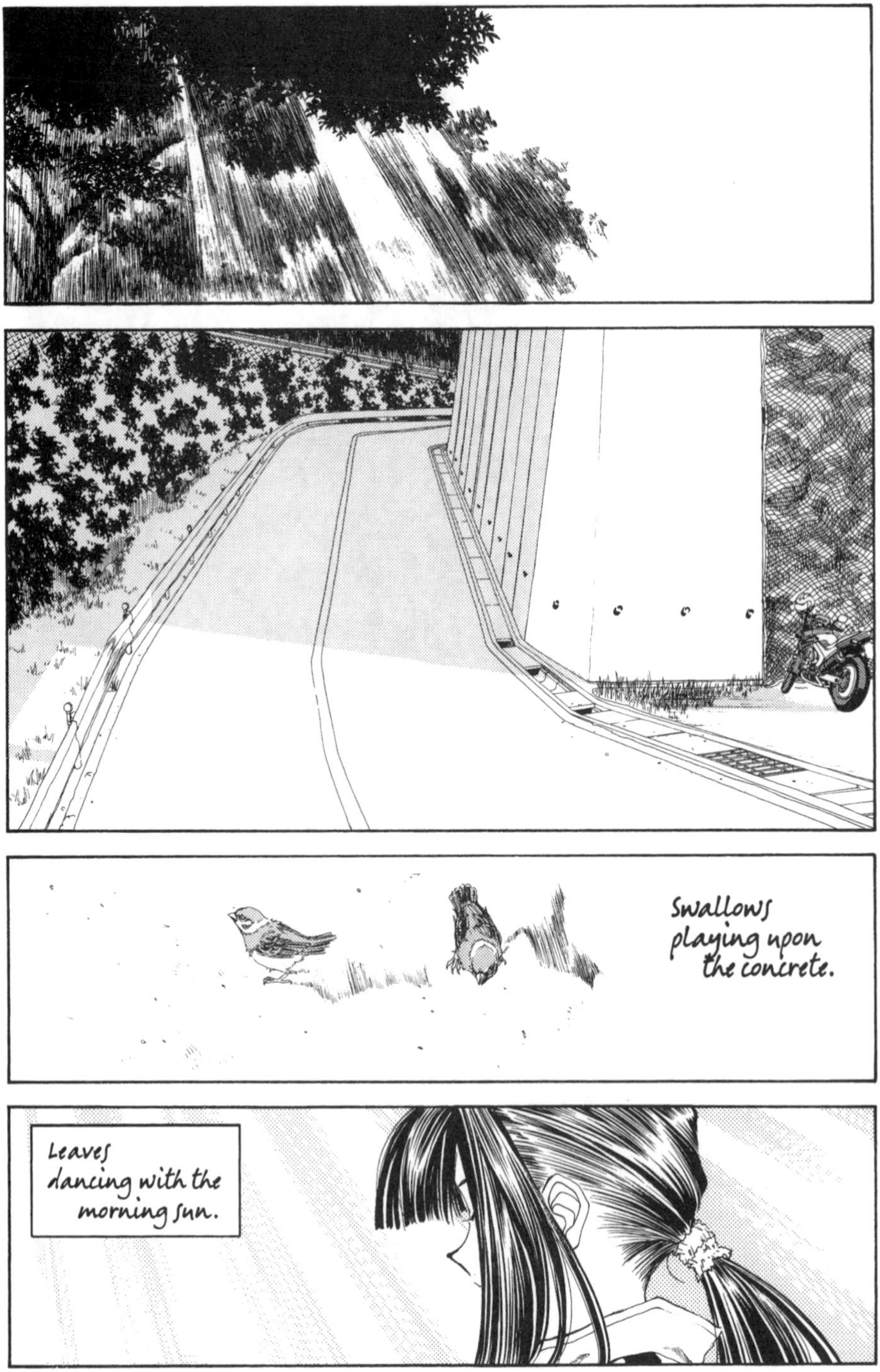
Swallows playing upon the concrete.
Leaves dancing with the morning sun.

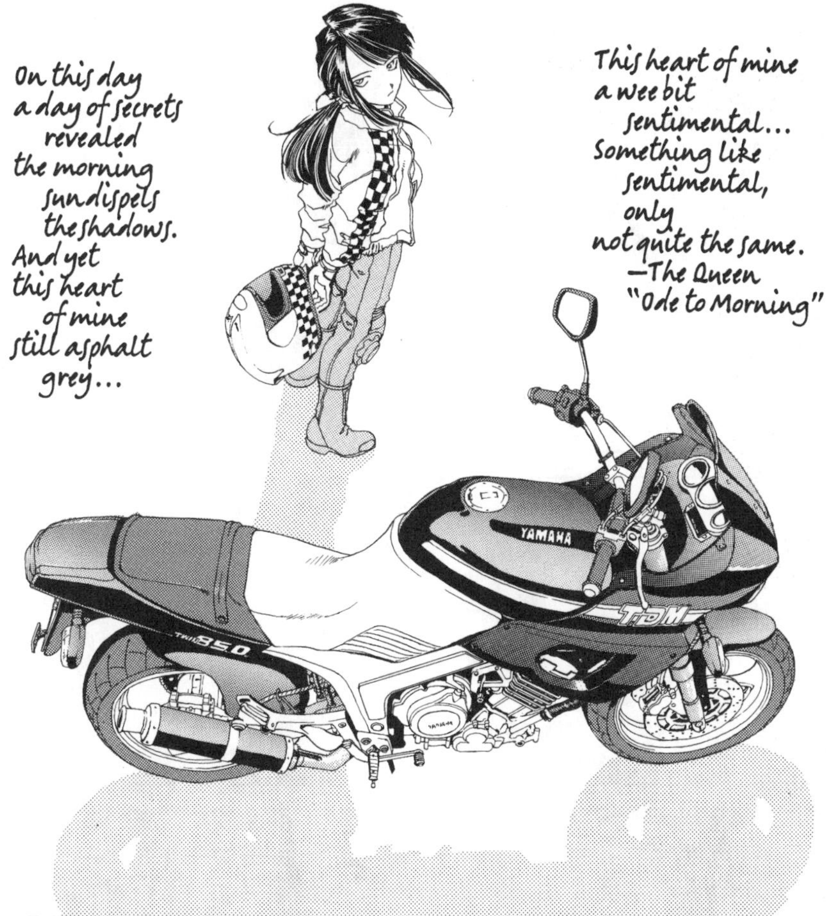
On this day
a day of secrets
revealed
the morning
sun dispels
the shadows.
And yet
this heart
of mine
still asphalt
grey...
This heart of mine
a wee bit
sentimental...
Something like
sentimental,
only
not quite the same.
—The Queen
"Ode to Morning"
YAMAHA
TDM
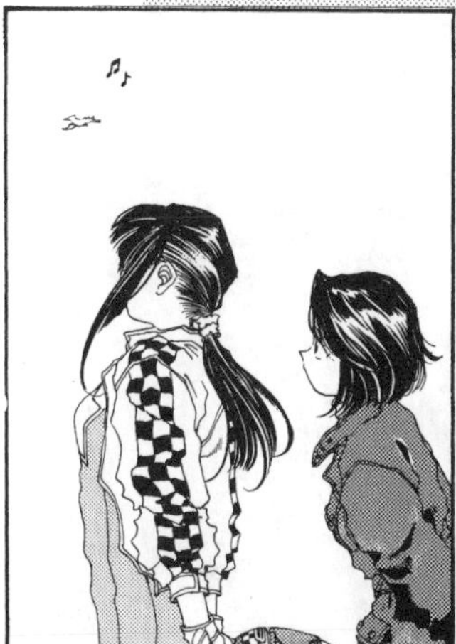
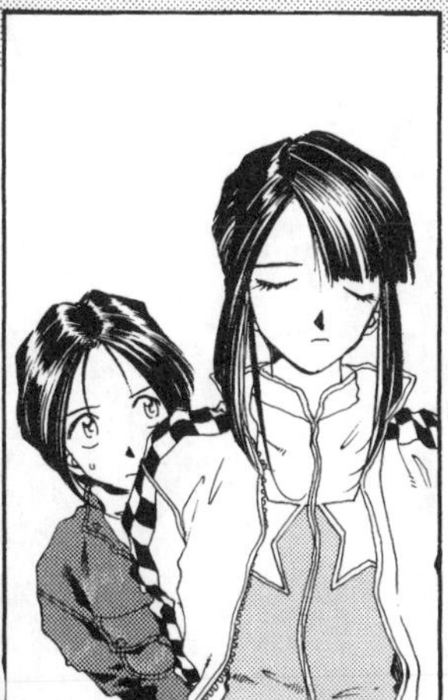
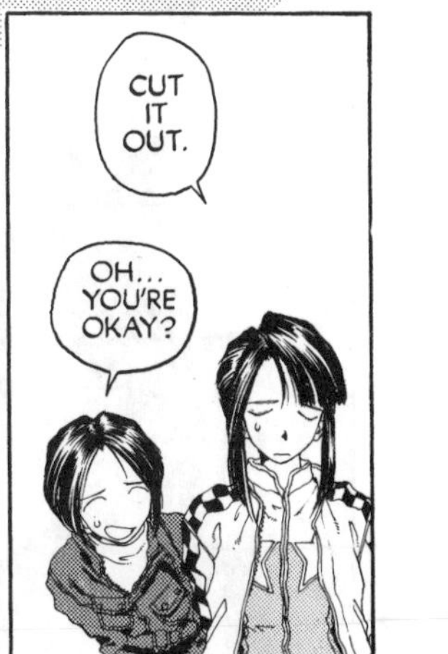
CUT IT OUT.
OH... YOU'RE OKAY?

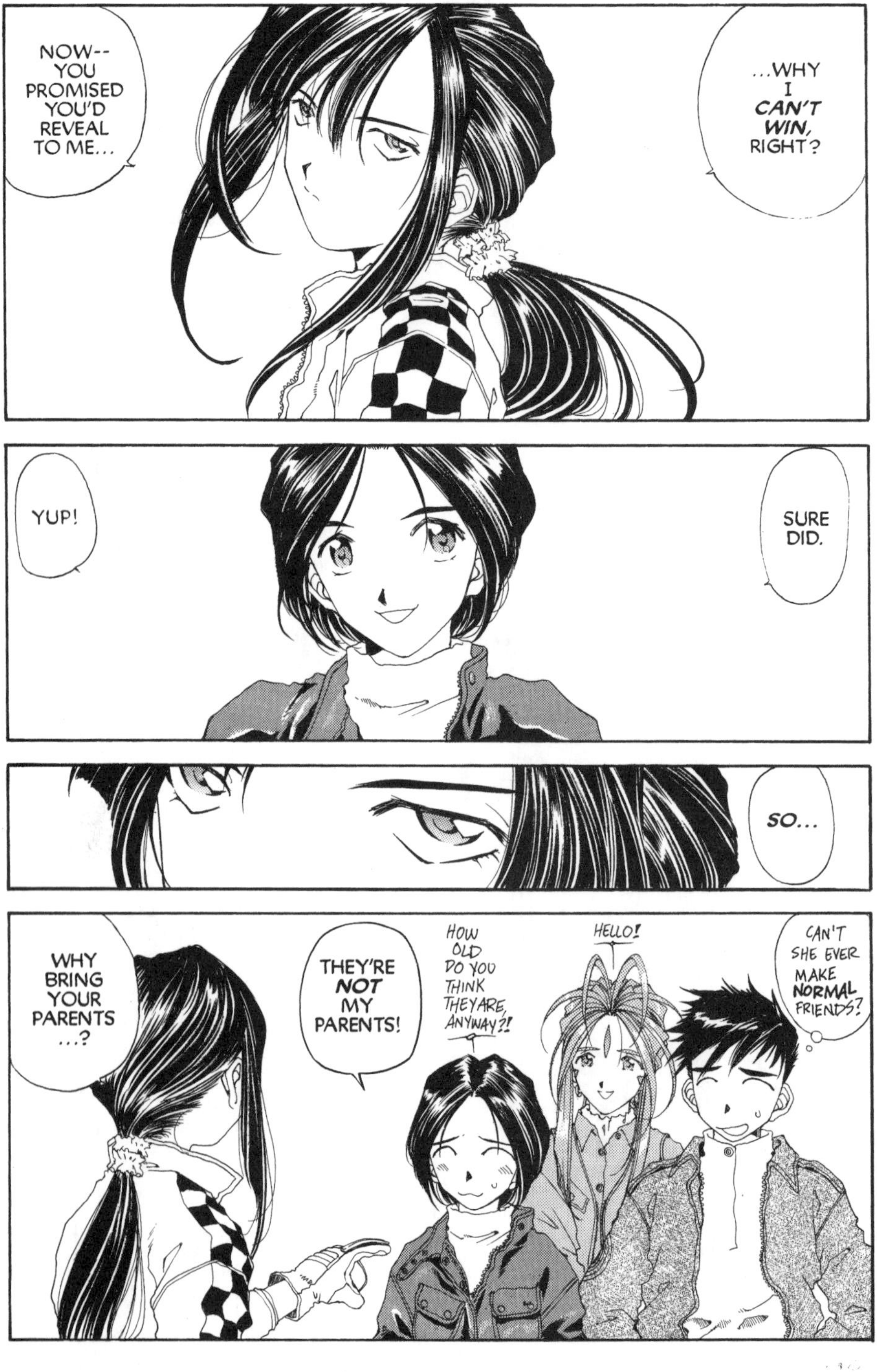
NOW-- YOU PROMISED YOU'D REVEAL TO ME...
...WHY I ***CAN'T WIN,*** RIGHT?
YUP!
SURE DID.
SO...
WHY BRING YOUR PARENTS ...?
THEY'RE ***NOT*** MY PARENTS!
HOW OLD DO YOU THINK THEY ARE, ANYWAY?!
HELLO!
CAN'T SHE EVER MAKE **NORMAL** FRIENDS?

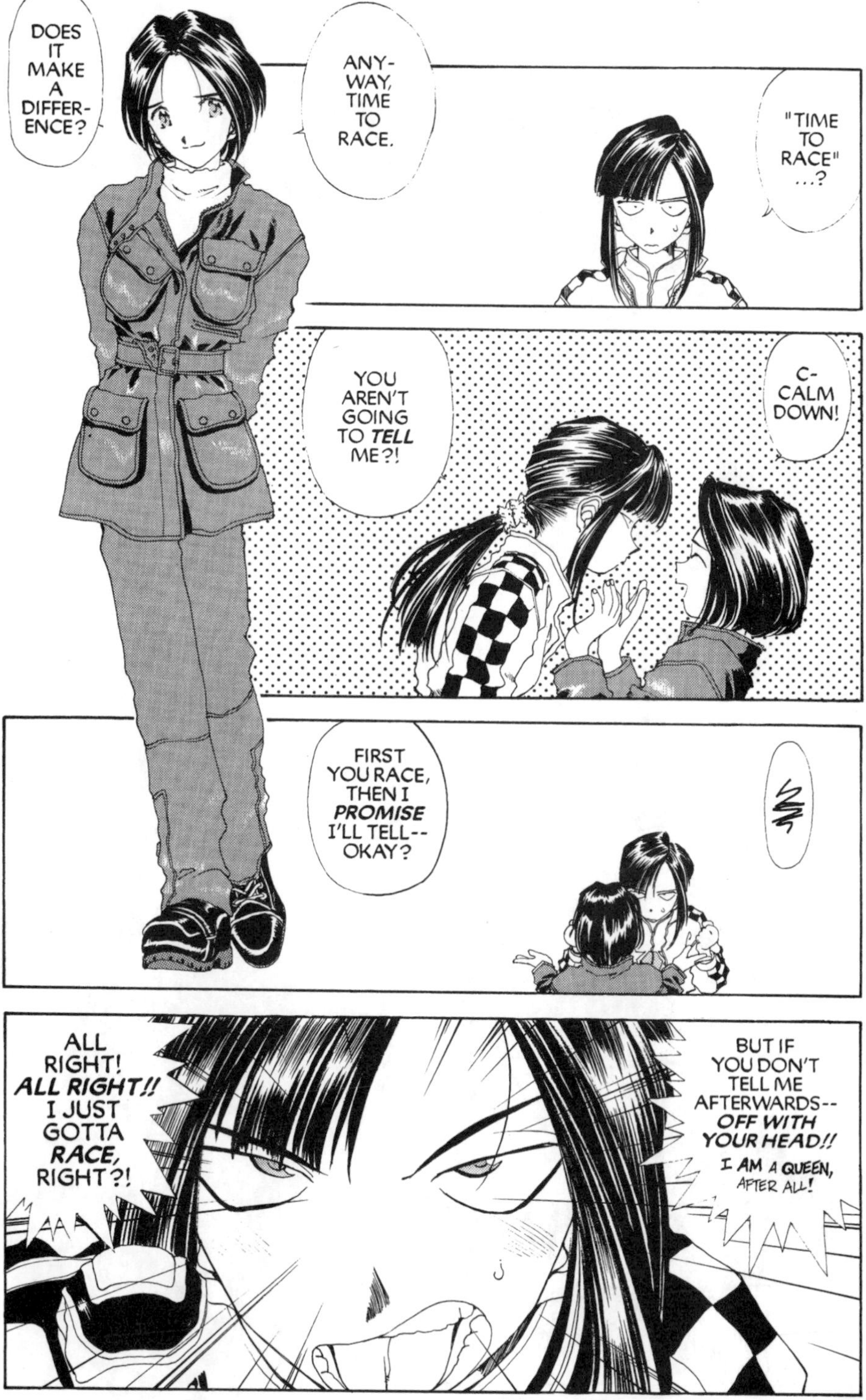
DOES IT MAKE A DIFFERENCE?
ANY-WAY, TIME TO RACE.
"TIME TO RACE" ...?
YOU AREN'T GOING TO *TELL* ME?!
C-CALM DOWN!
FIRST YOU RACE, THEN I *PROMISE* I'LL TELL--OKAY?
ALL RIGHT! *ALL RIGHT!!* I JUST GOTTA *RACE*, RIGHT?!
BUT IF YOU DON'T TELL ME AFTERWARDS-- *OFF WITH YOUR HEAD!!*
I AM A QUEEN, AFTER ALL!

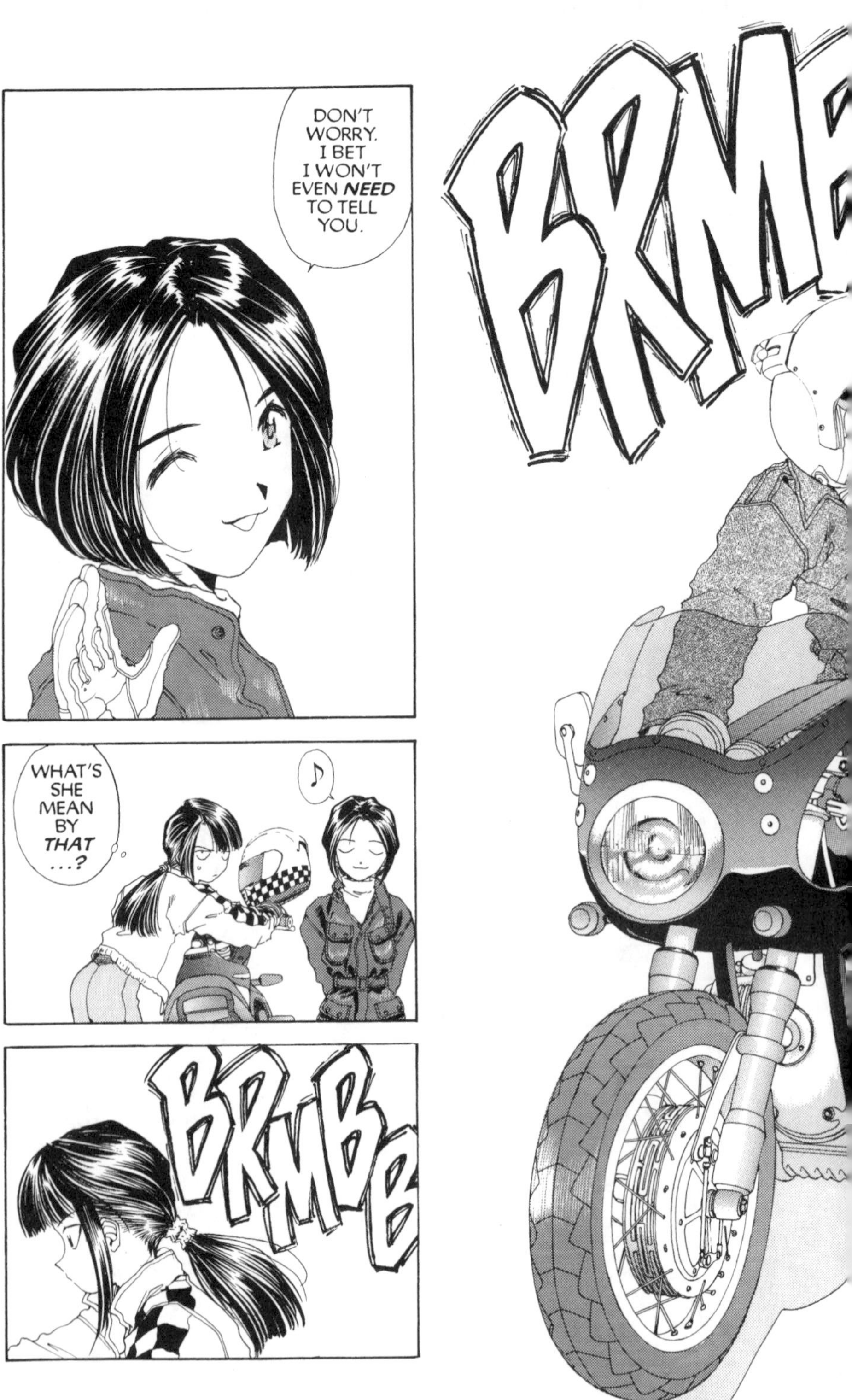
DON'T WORRY. I BET I WON'T EVEN ***NEED*** TO TELL YOU.
WHAT'S SHE MEAN BY ***THAT*** . . .?
♪
BRMB
B
BRM

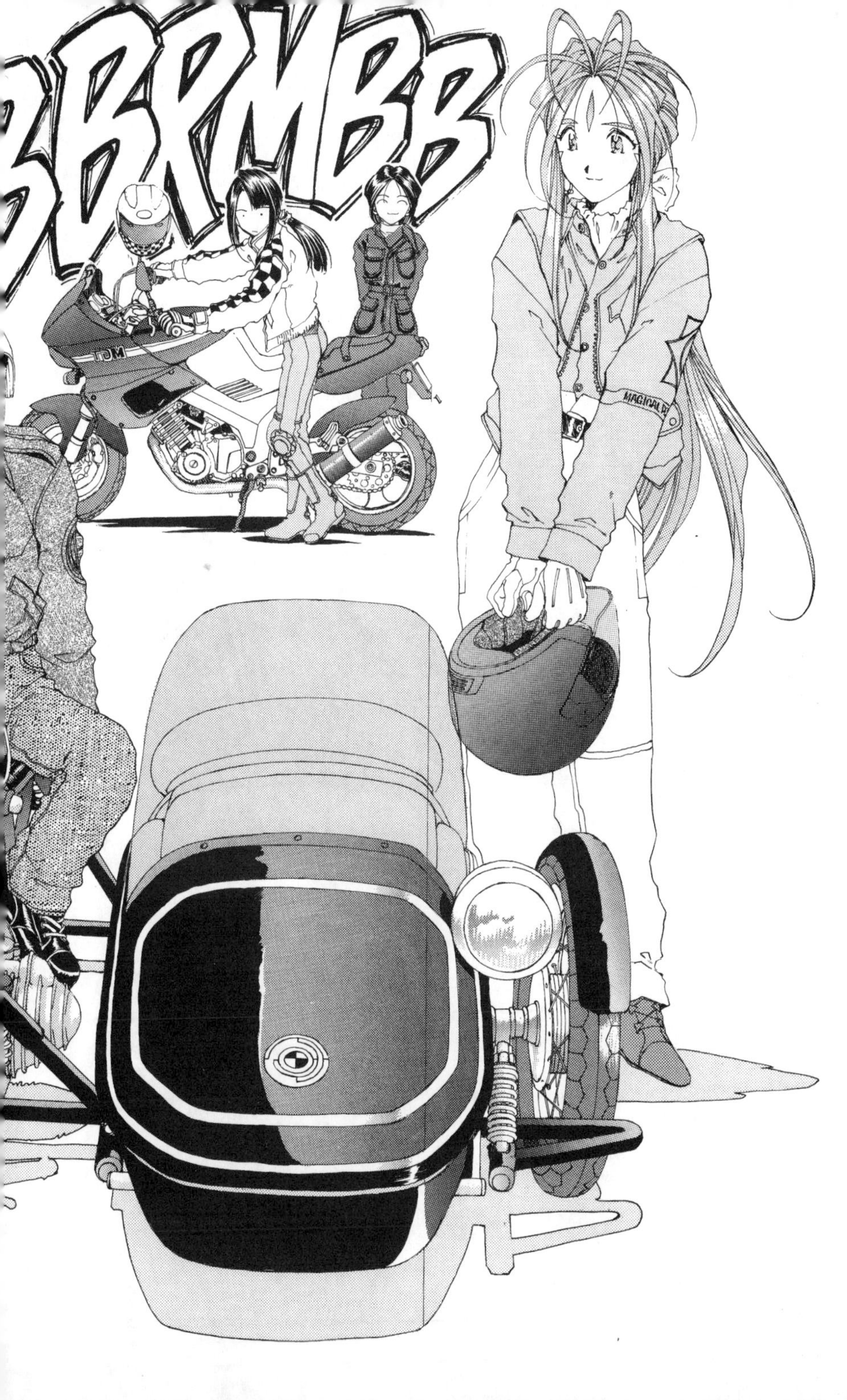
BBRMBB

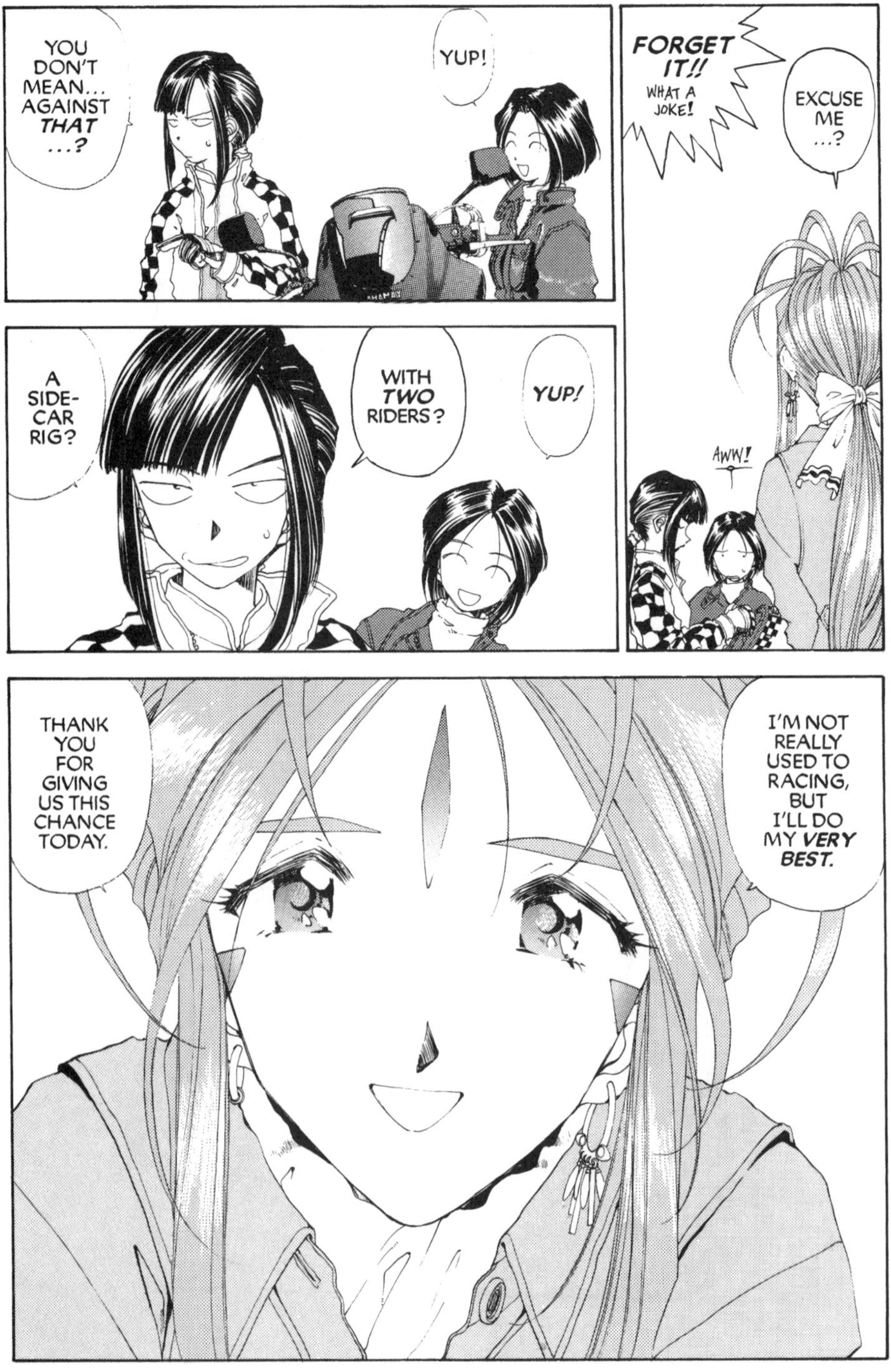
YOU DON'T MEAN... AGAINST *THAT* ...?
YUP!
A SIDE-CAR RIG?
WITH *TWO* RIDERS?
YUP!
FORGET IT!!
WHAT A JOKE!
EXCUSE ME ...?
AWW!
THANK YOU FOR GIVING US THIS CHANCE TODAY.
I'M NOT REALLY USED TO RACING, BUT I'LL DO MY *VERY BEST.*

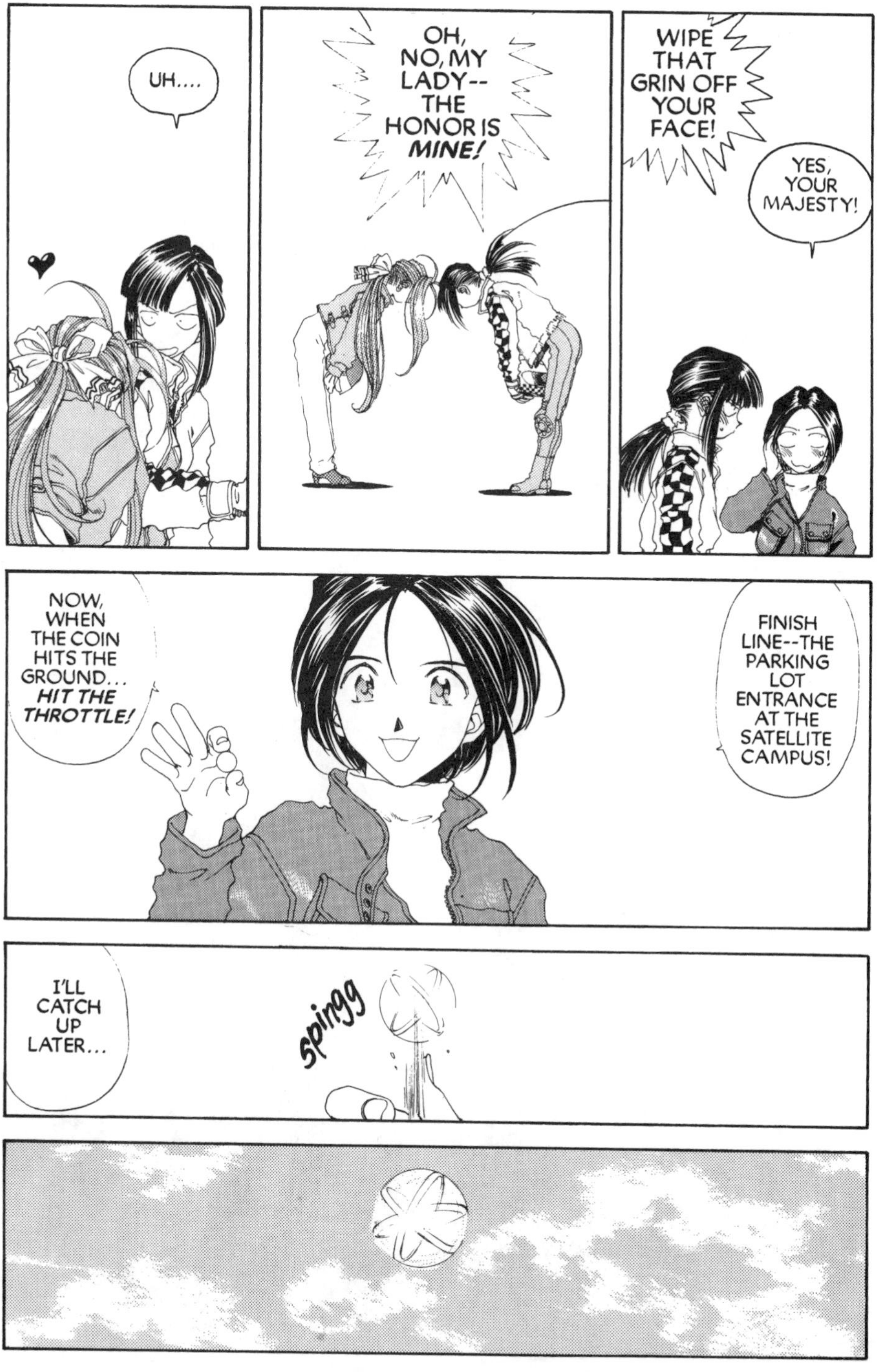
UH....
OH, NO, MY LADY-- THE HONOR IS *MINE!*
WIPE THAT GRIN OFF YOUR FACE!
YES, YOUR MAJESTY!
NOW, WHEN THE COIN HITS THE GROUND... *HIT THE THROTTLE!*
FINISH LINE--THE PARKING LOT ENTRANCE AT THE SATELLITE CAMPUS!
I'LL CATCH UP LATER...
spingg

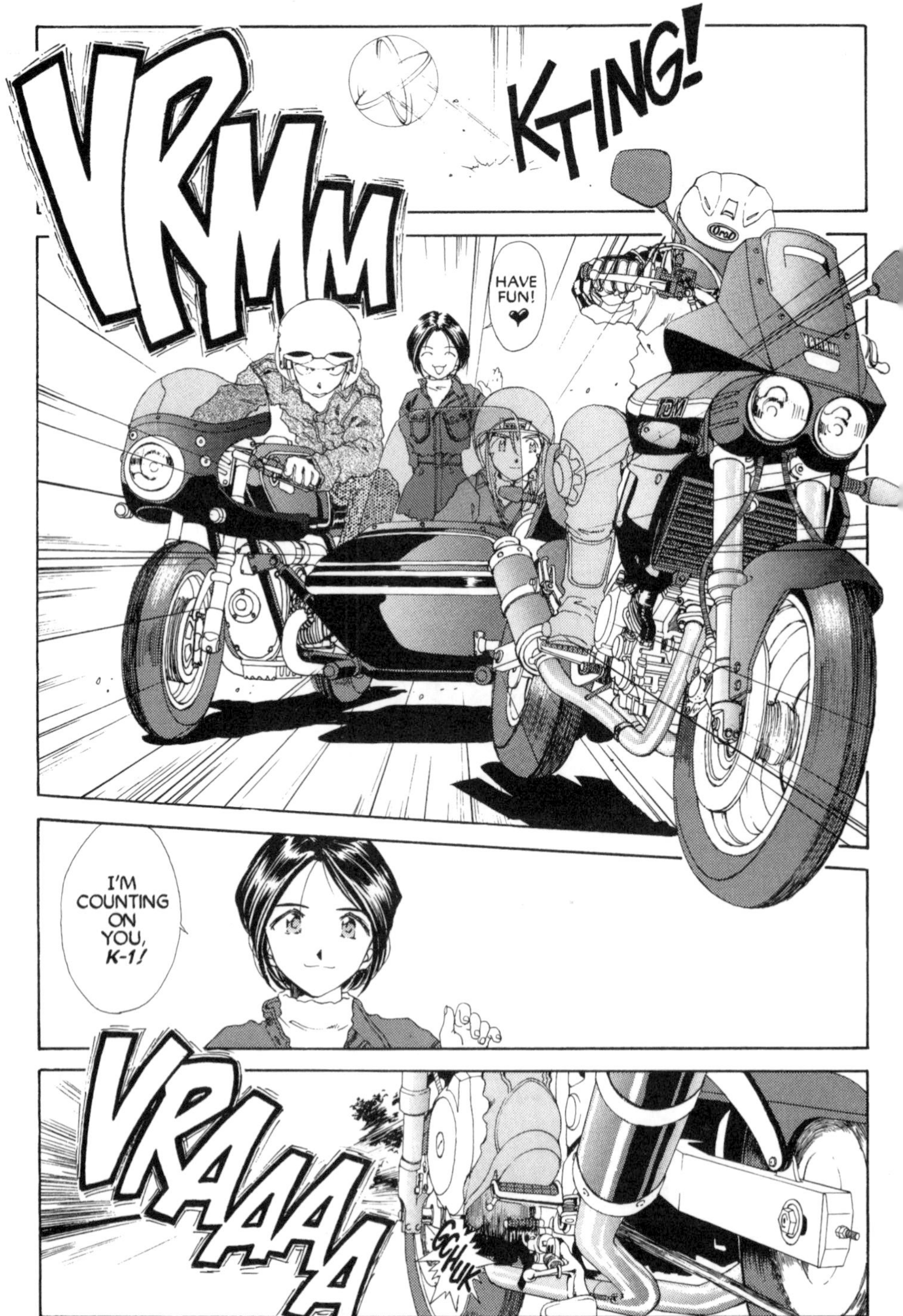
VRMMM
KTING!
HAVE FUN! ♥
I'M COUNTING ON YOU, K-1!
VRAAAA
GCHUK

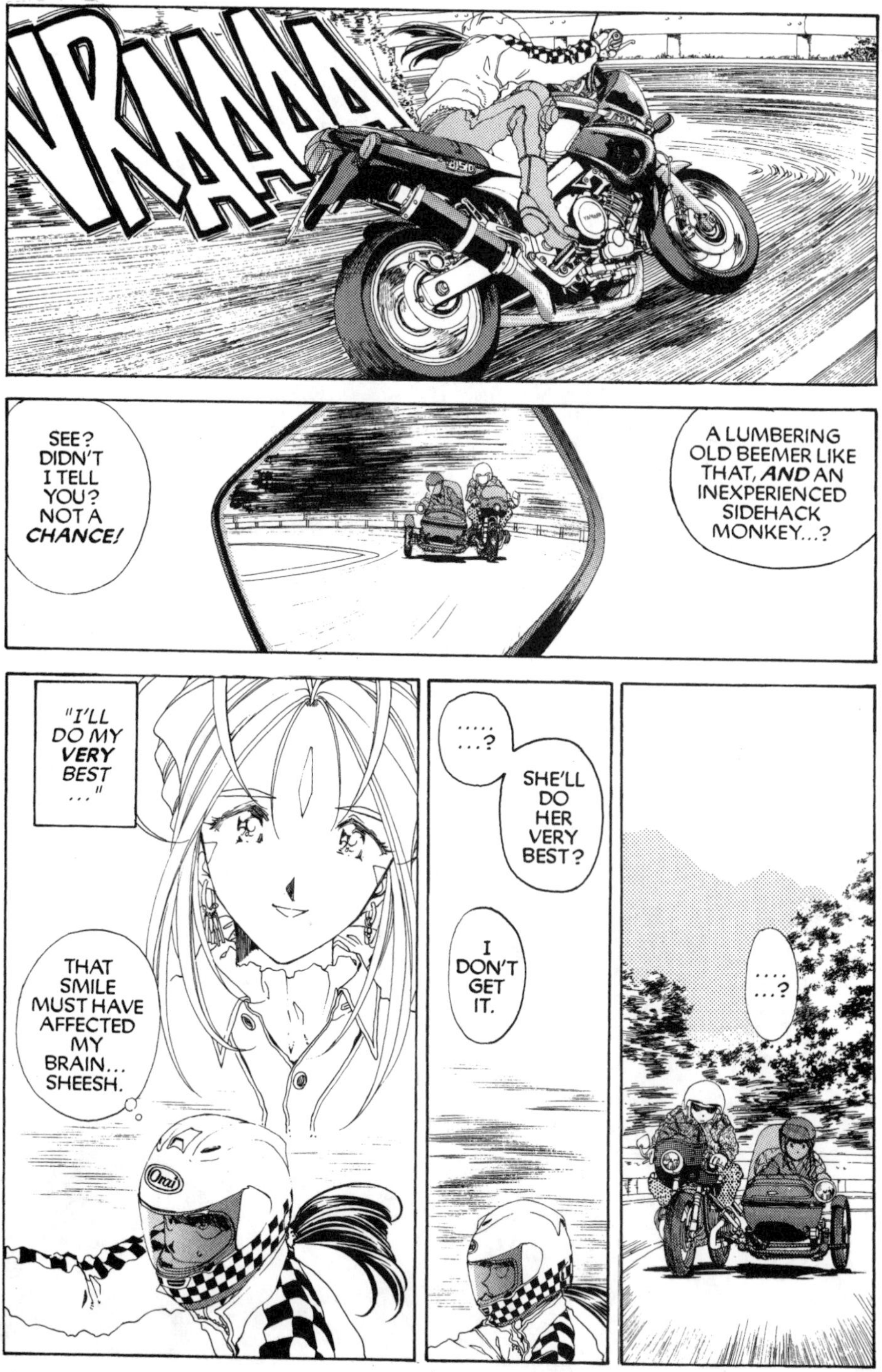
VRAAAAA
SEE? DIDN'T I TELL YOU? NOT A *CHANCE!*
A LUMBERING OLD BEEMER LIKE THAT, ***AND*** AN INEXPERIENCED SIDEHACK MONKEY...?
"*I'LL DO MY* ***VERY*** *BEST ...*"
THAT SMILE MUST HAVE AFFECTED MY BRAIN... SHEESH.
...., ...?
SHE'LL DO HER VERY BEST?
I DON'T GET IT.
...., ...?

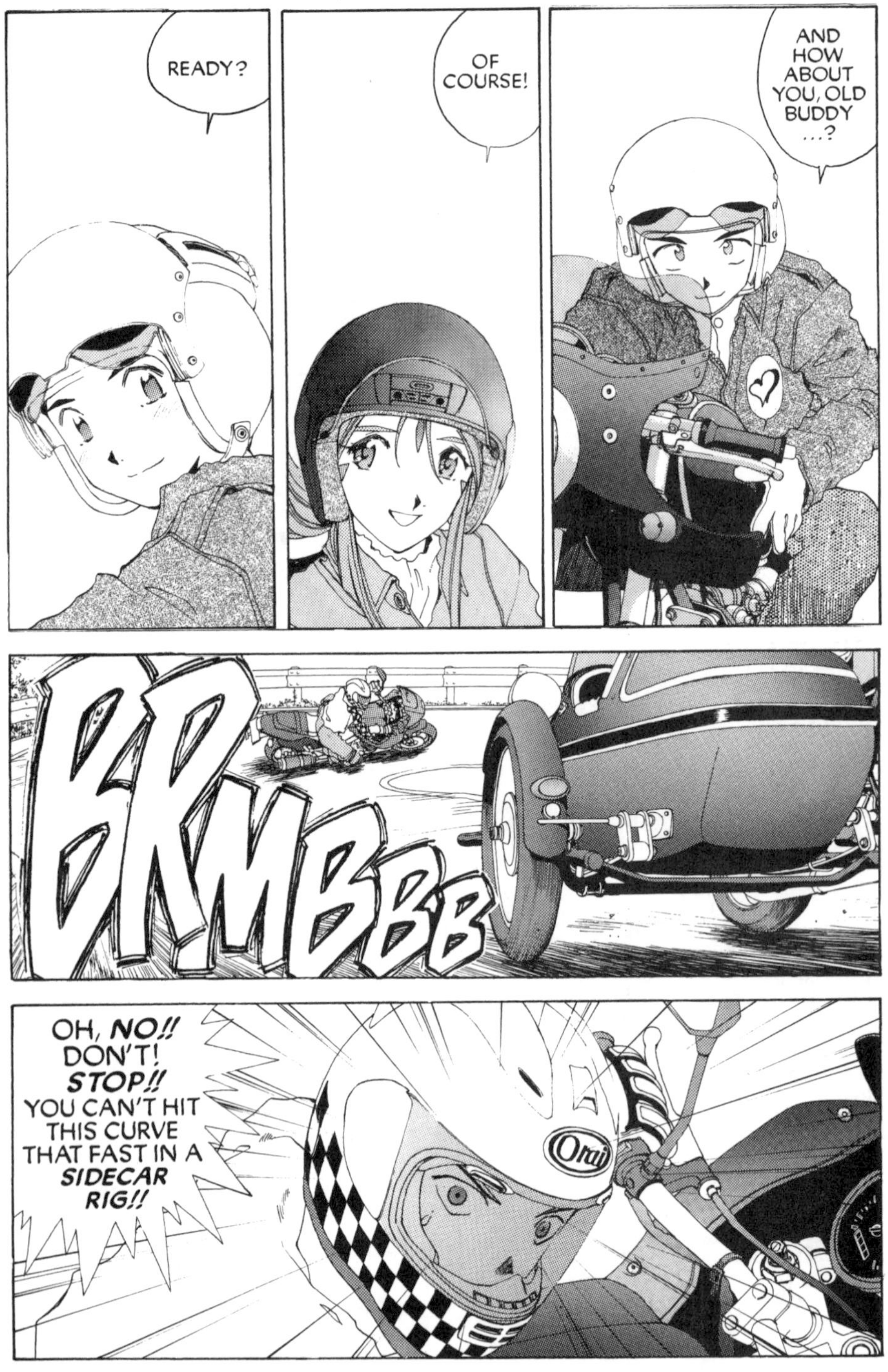
READY?
OF COURSE!
AND HOW ABOUT YOU, OLD BUDDY ...?
BRMBBB
OH, NO!! DON'T! STOP!! YOU CAN'T HIT THIS CURVE THAT FAST IN A SIDECAR RIG!!

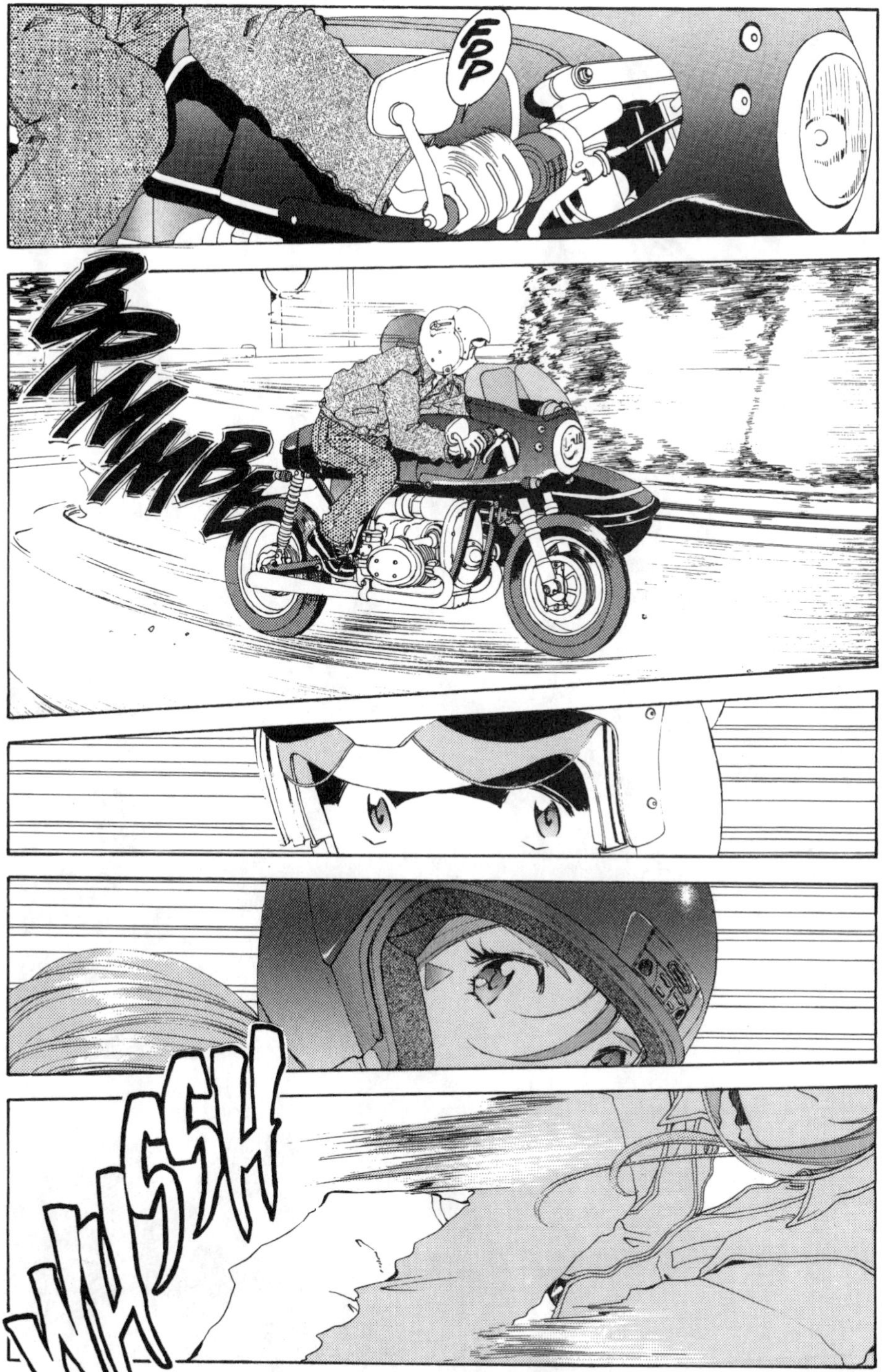
EPP
BRMMBB
WHSSH

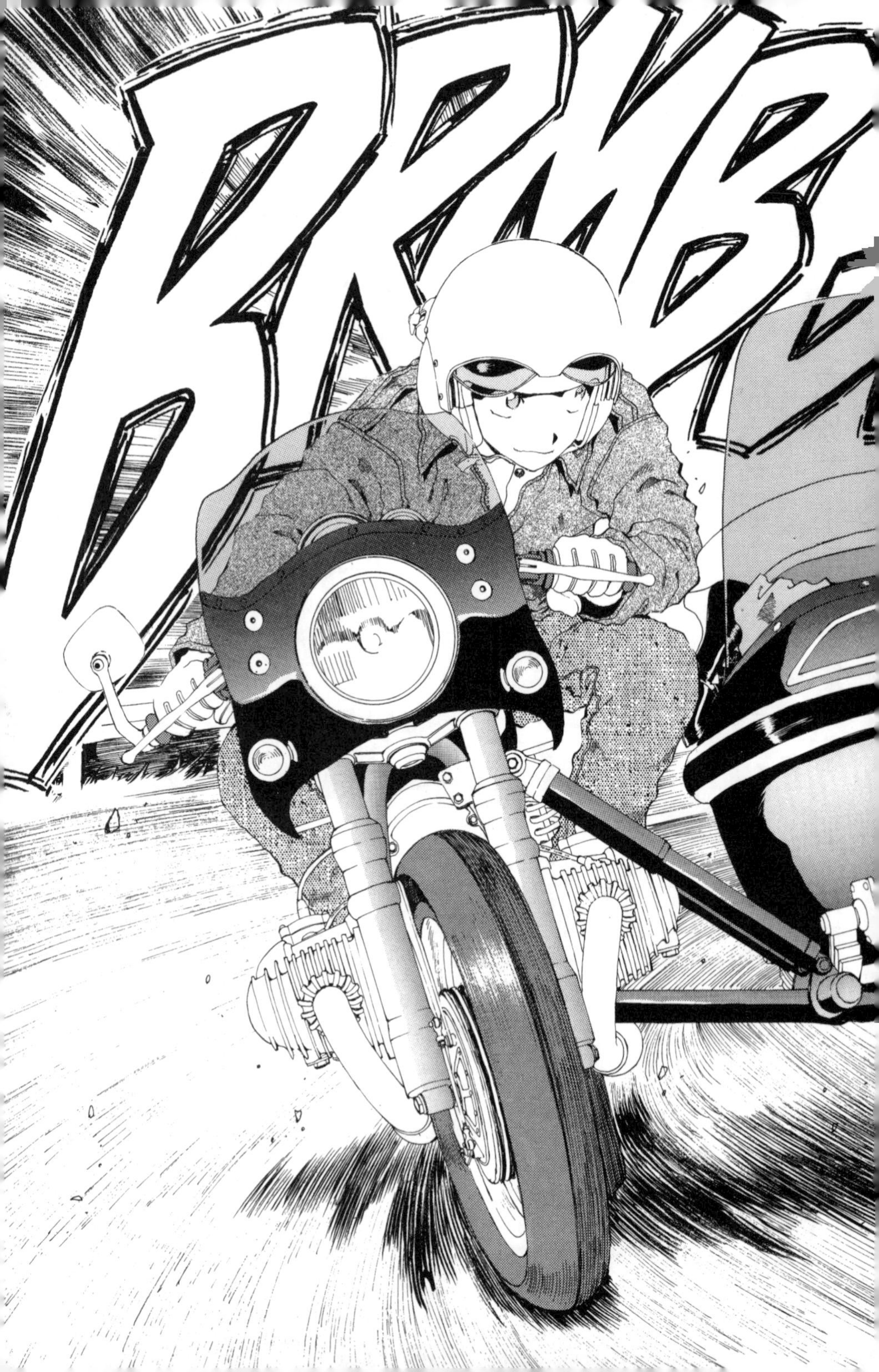
BRMB

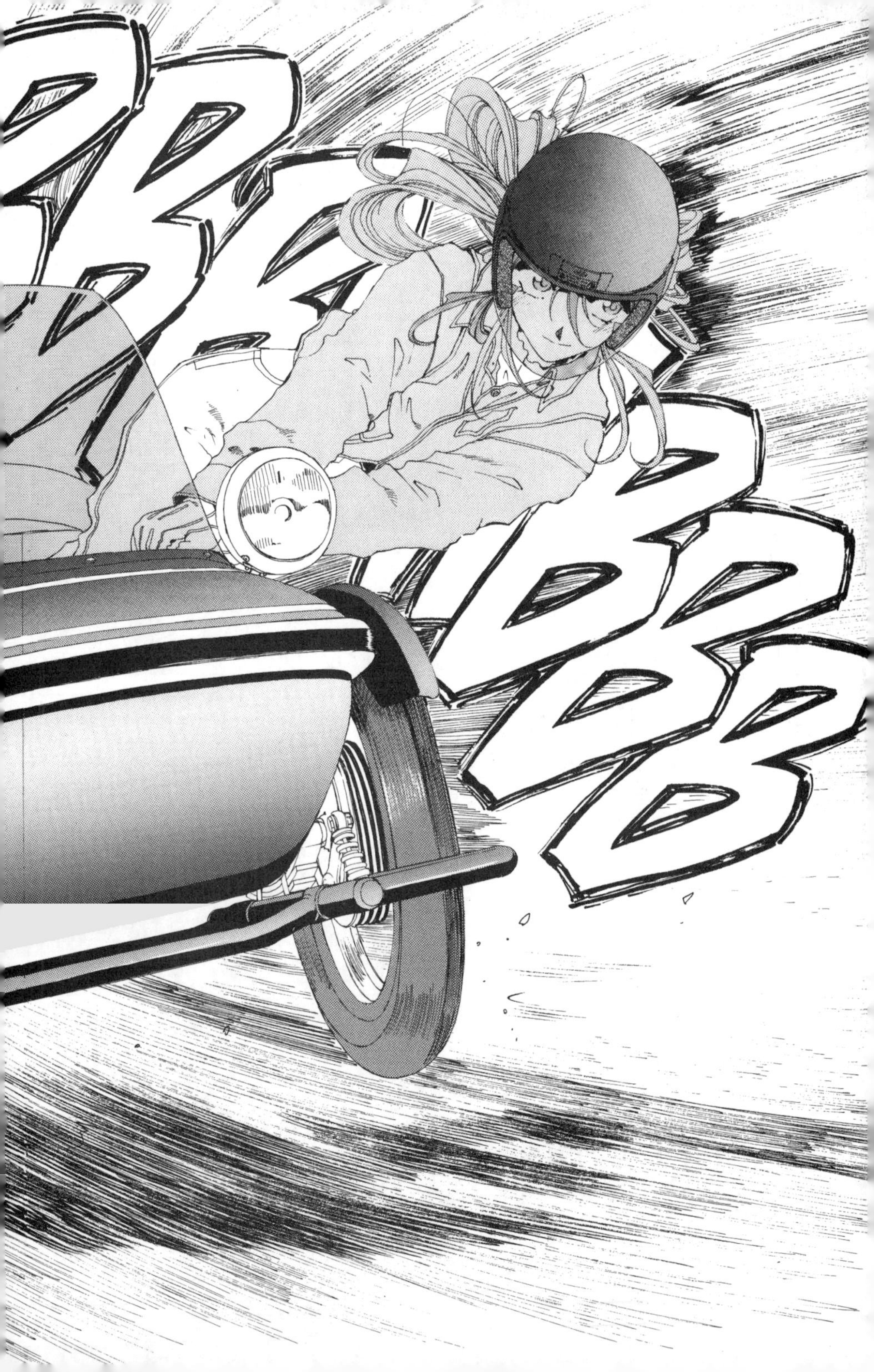

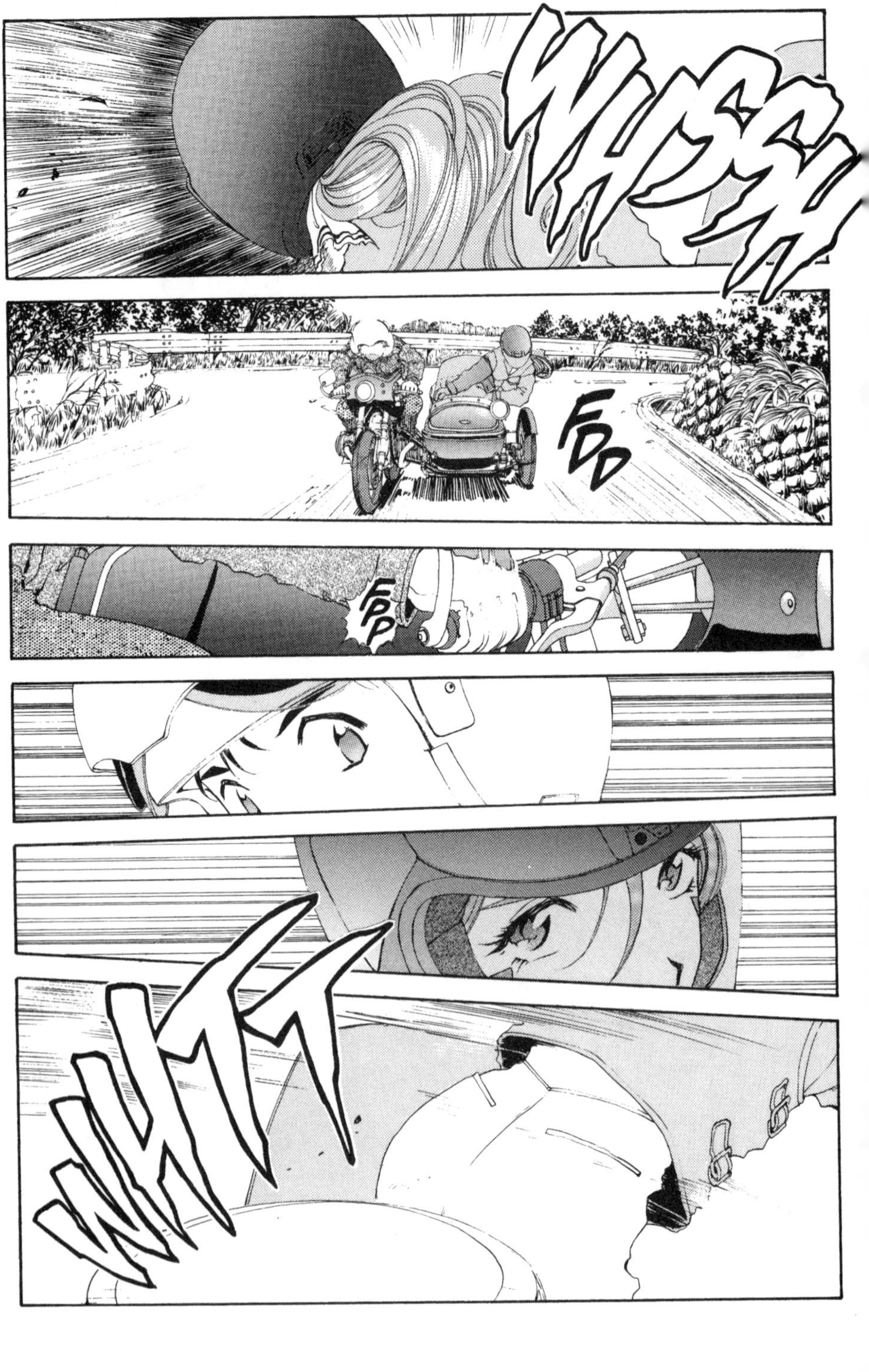
WHSSH
FDD
FDP
WHTT

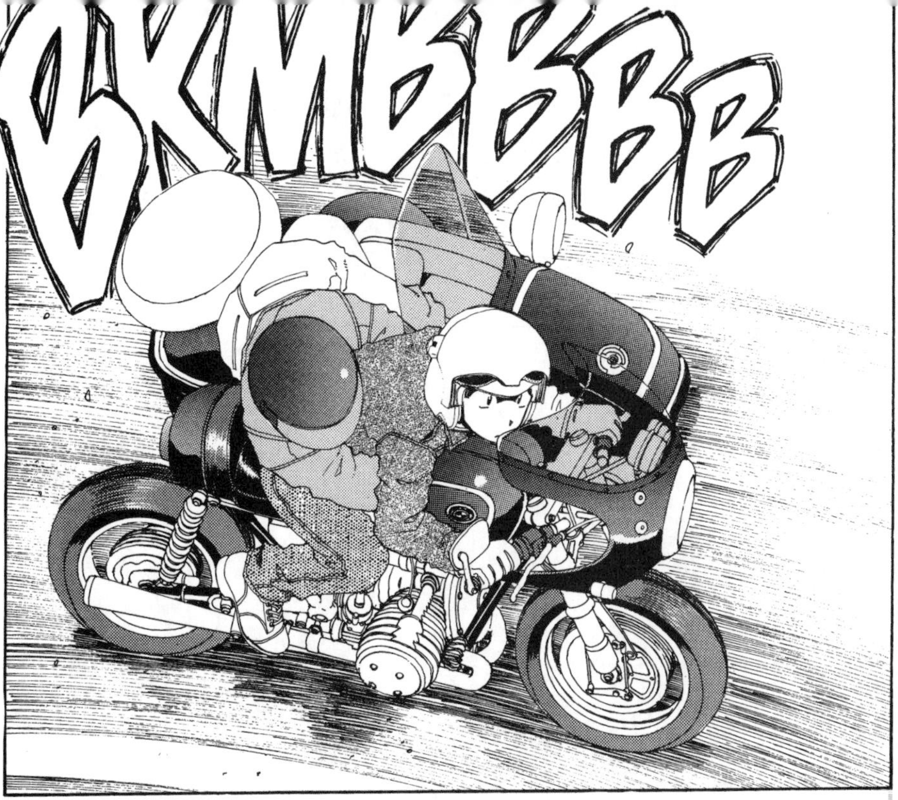
BKMBBBB

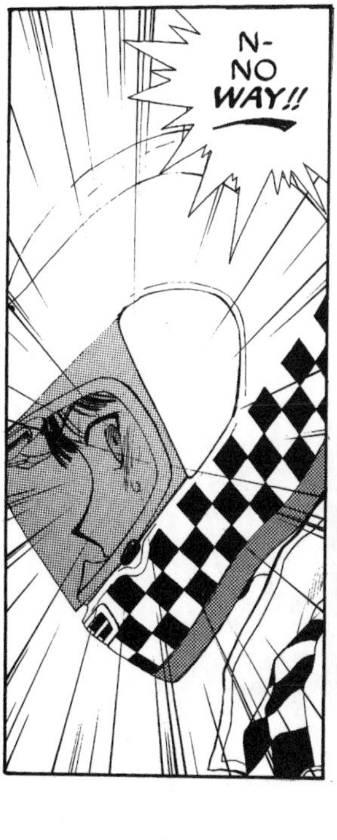
N-
NO
WAY!!

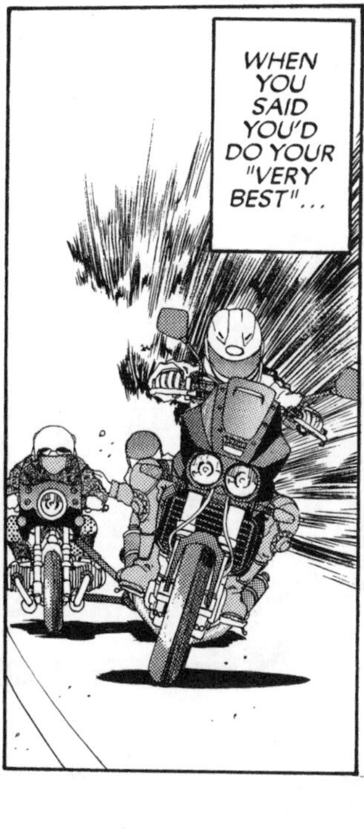
WHEN YOU SAID YOU'D DO YOUR "VERY BEST"...

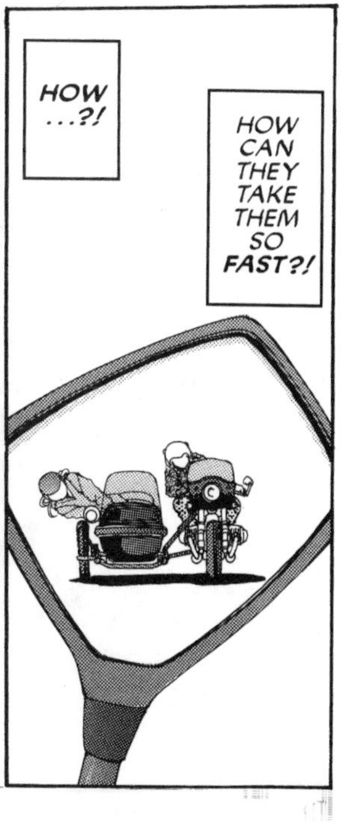
HOW ...?!
HOW CAN THEY TAKE THEM SO FAST?!

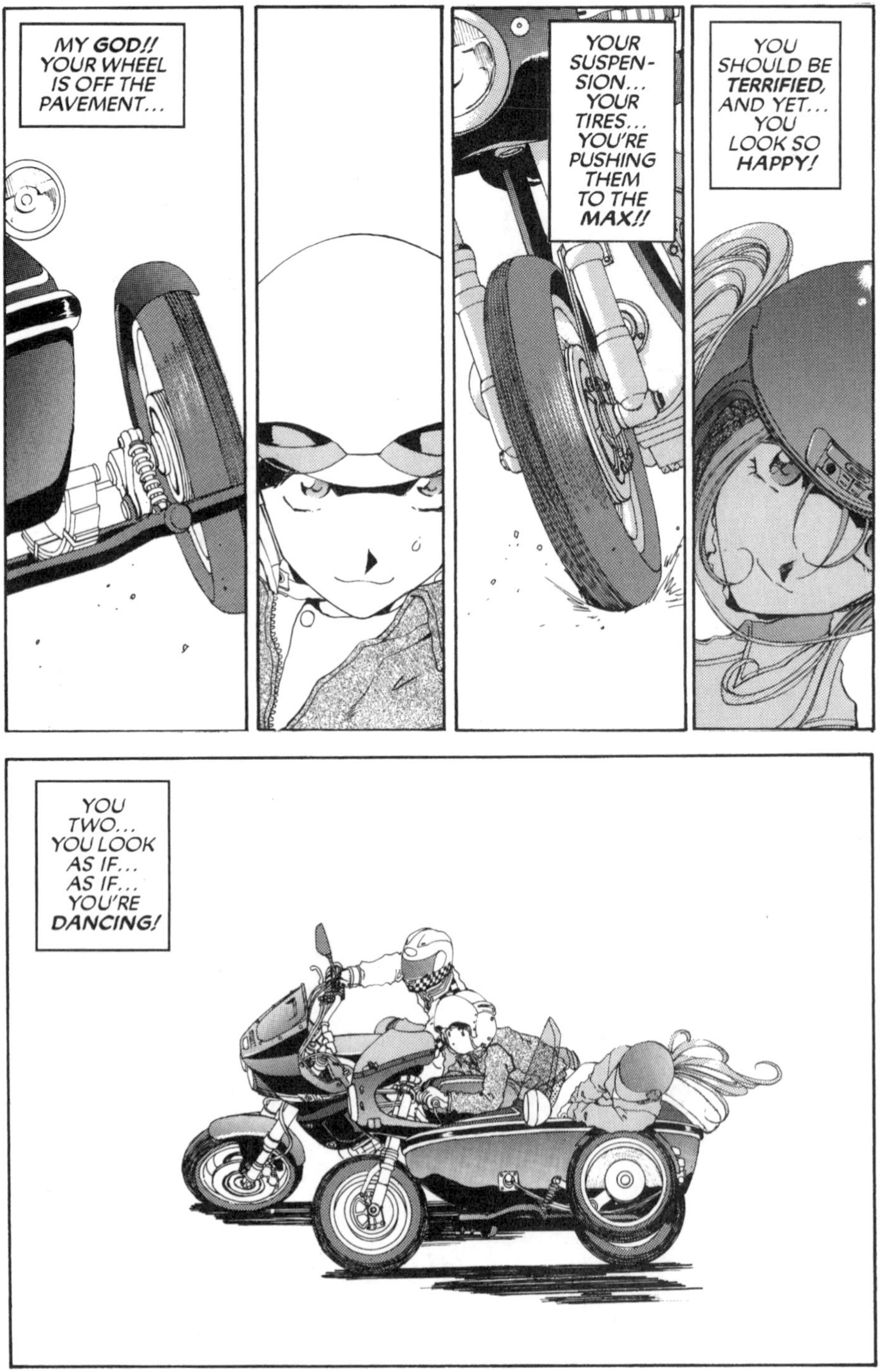
MY **GOD!!** YOUR WHEEL IS OFF THE PAVEMENT...
YOUR SUSPEN-SION... YOUR TIRES... YOU'RE PUSHING THEM TO THE **MAX!!**
YOU SHOULD BE **TERRIFIED,** AND YET... YOU LOOK SO **HAPPY!**
YOU TWO... YOU LOOK AS IF... AS IF... YOU'RE **DANCING!**

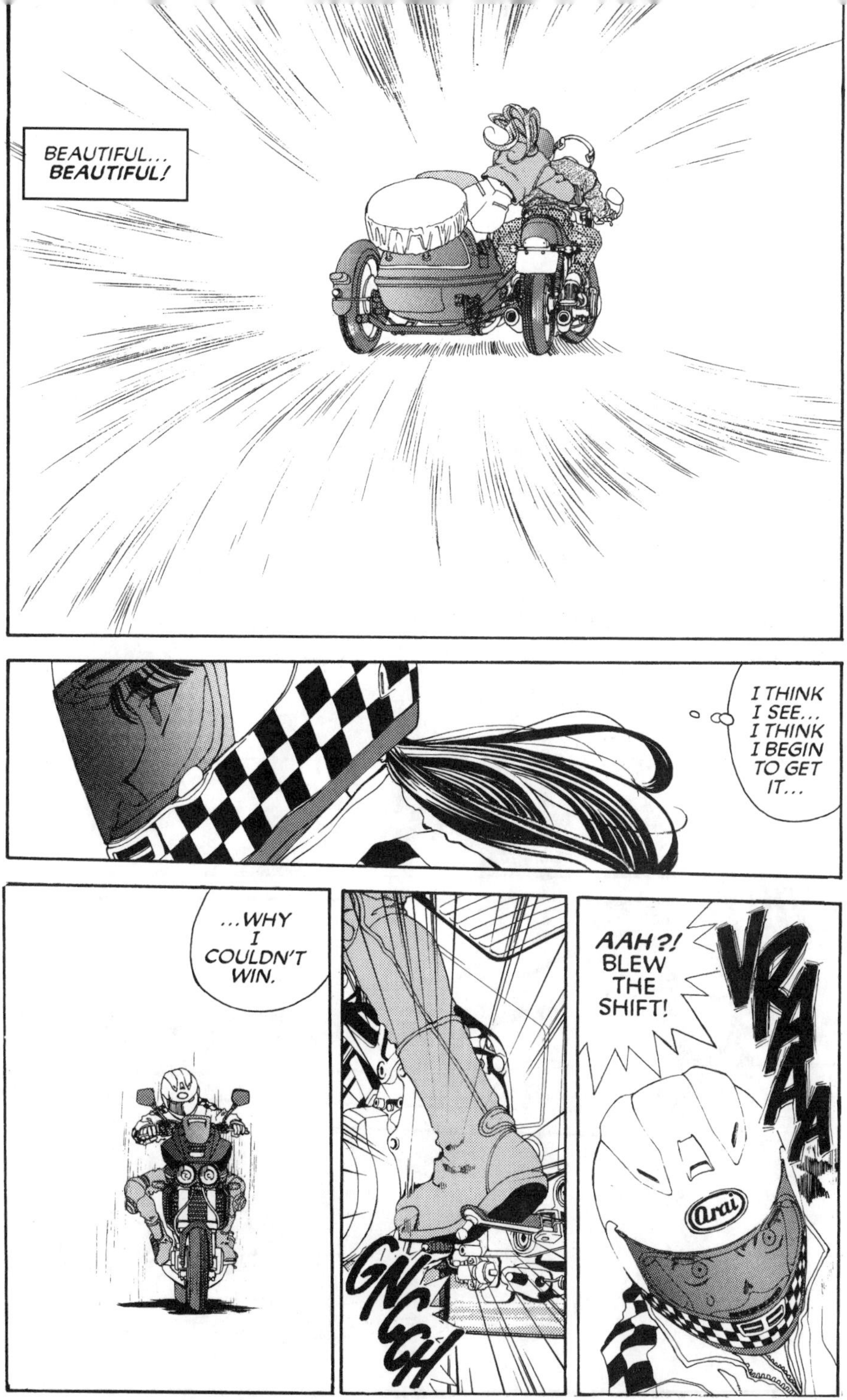
BEAUTIFUL... BEAUTIFUL!
I THINK I SEE... I THINK I BEGIN TO GET IT...
...WHY I COULDN'T WIN.
GNCCH
AAH?! BLEW THE SHIFT!
VRAAA

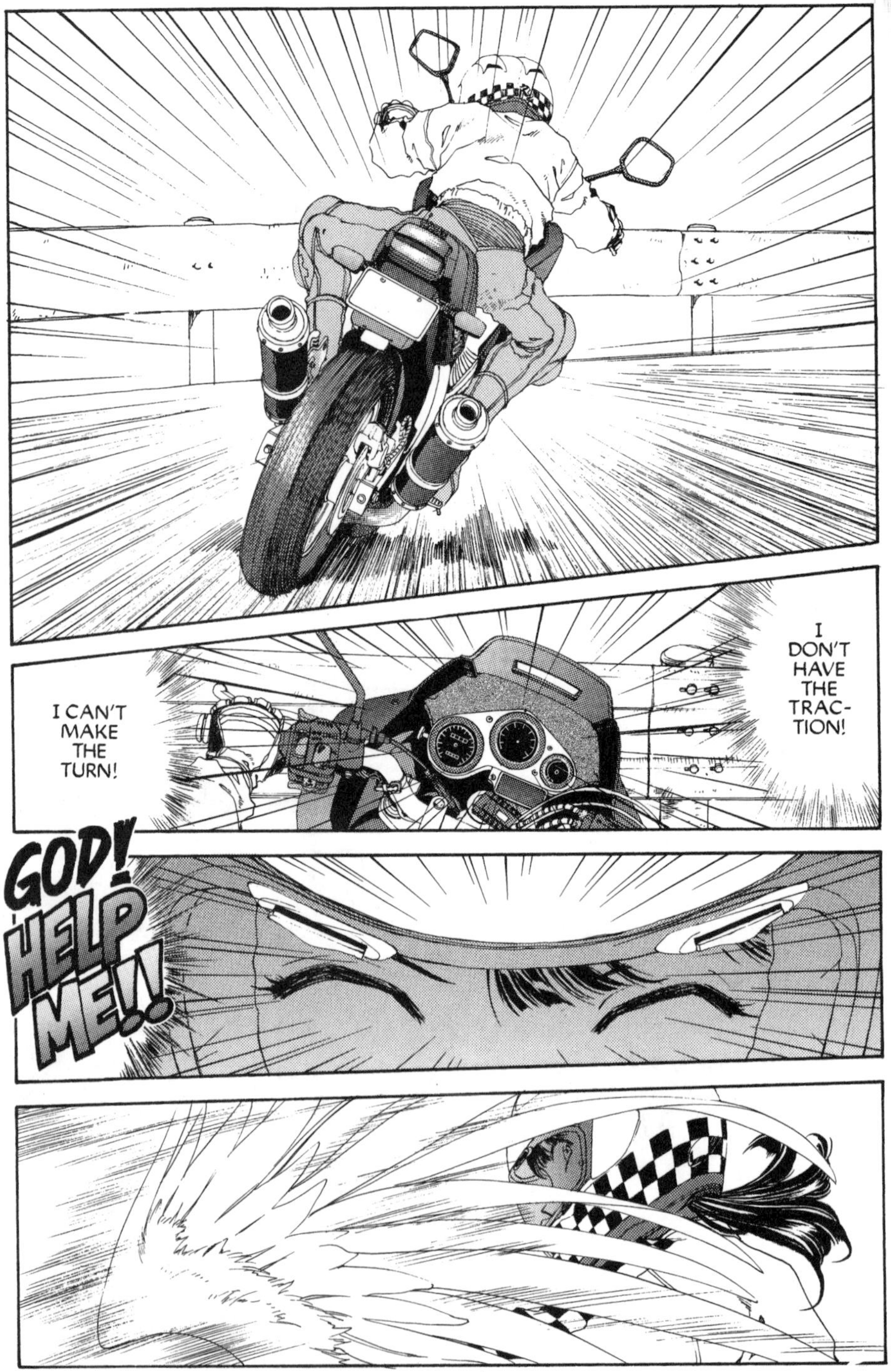
I CAN'T MAKE THE TURN!
I DON'T HAVE THE TRAC-TION!
GOD! HELP ME!!

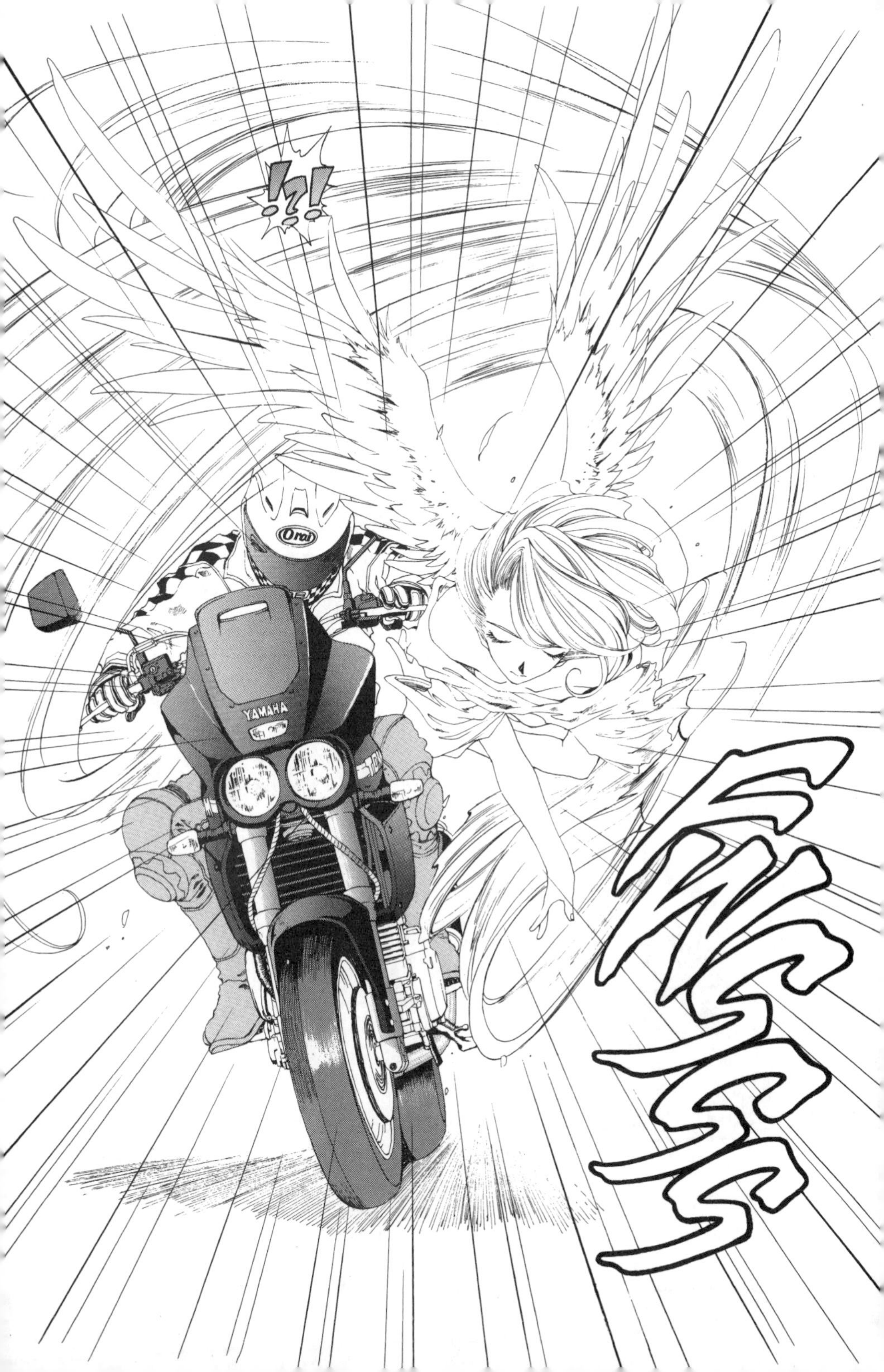
!?!
FWSSSS

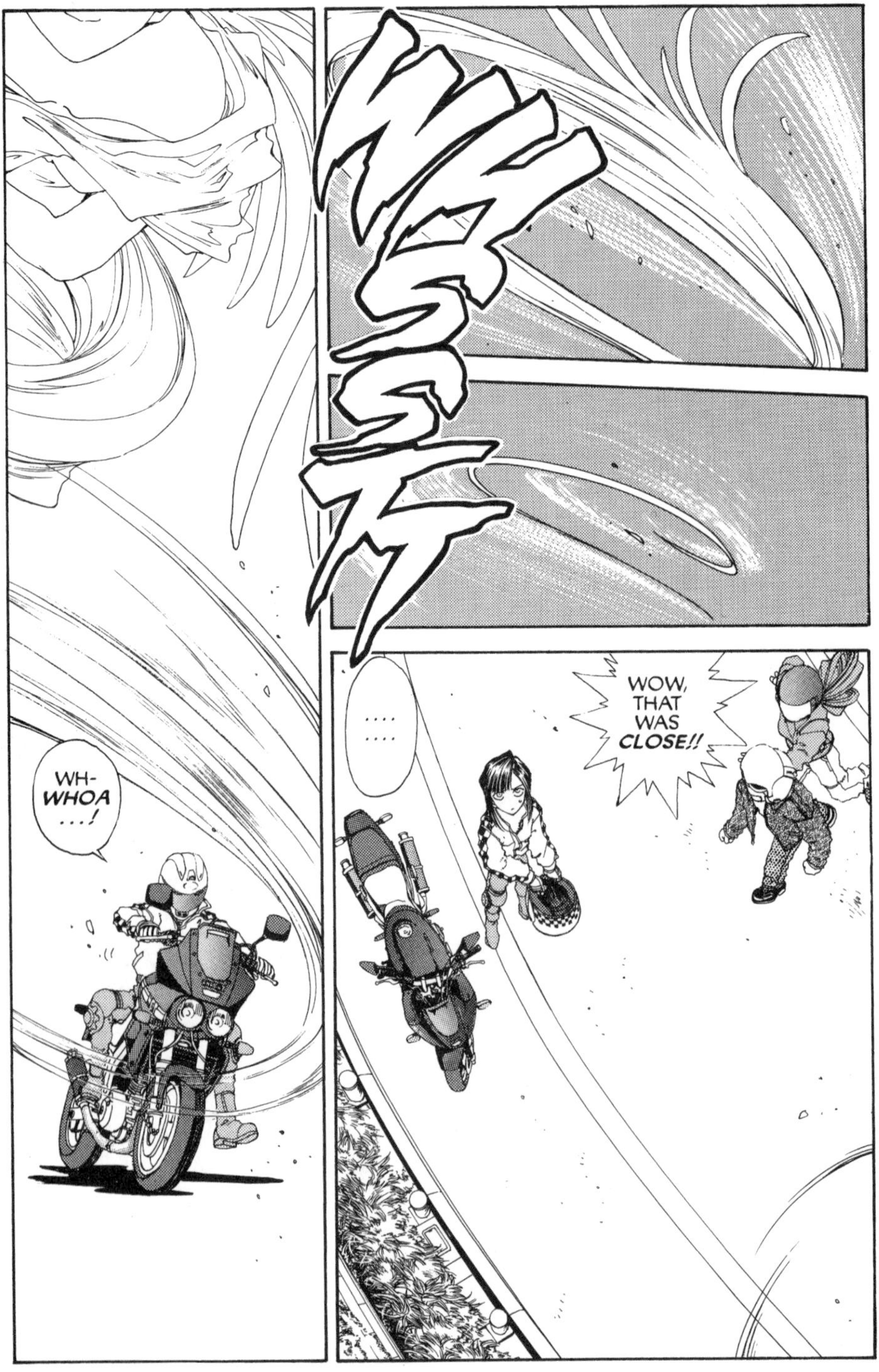
WH- WHOA ...!
....
....
WOW, THAT WAS CLOSE!!

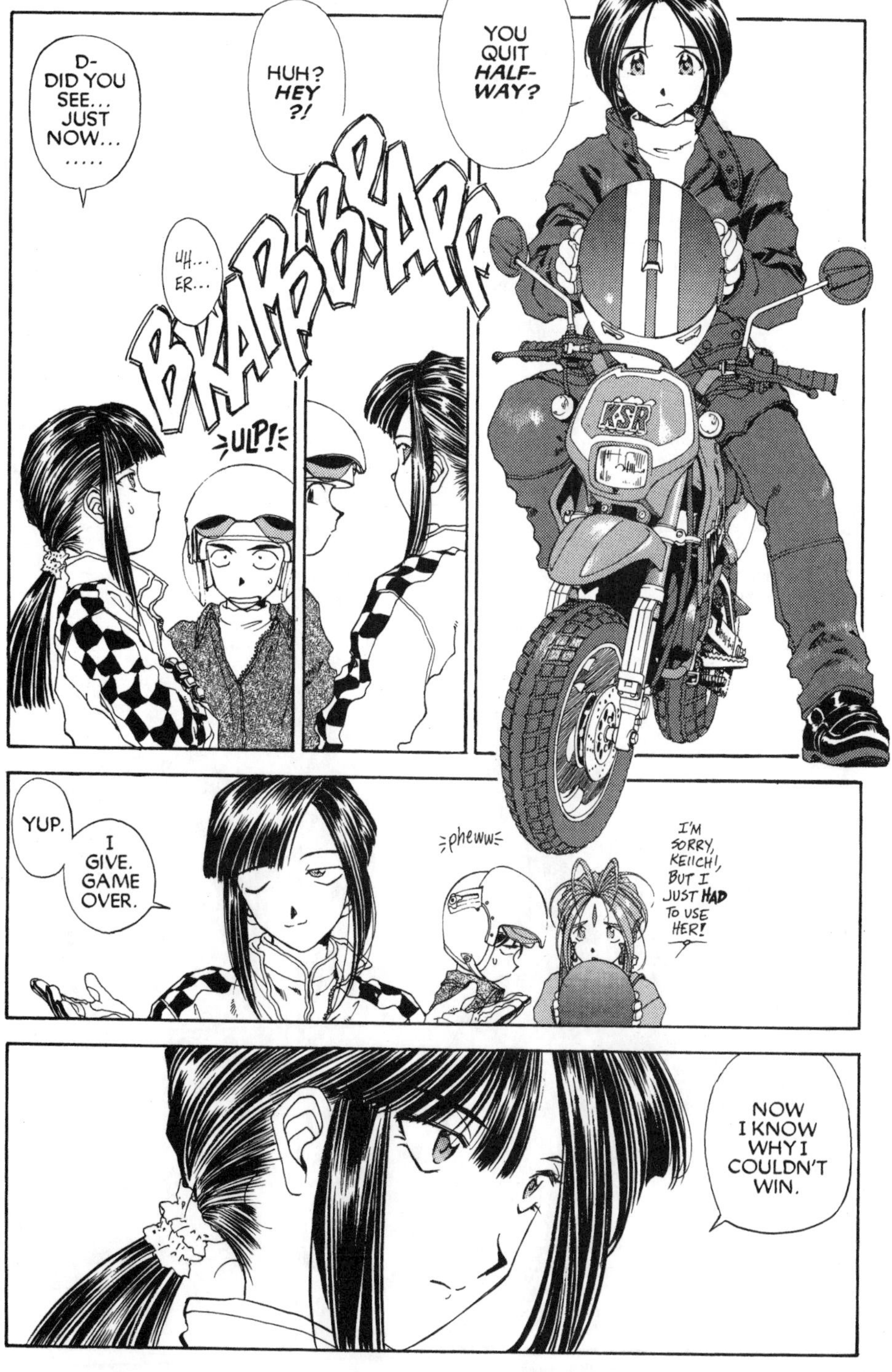
D- DID YOU SEE... JUST NOW... .....
UH... ER...
BRAPPBRAPP
ULP!
HUH? HEY ?!
YOU QUIT HALF-WAY?
YUP. I GIVE. GAME OVER.
pheww
I'M SORRY, KEIICHI, BUT I JUST HAD TO USE HER!
NOW I KNOW WHY I COULDN'T WIN.

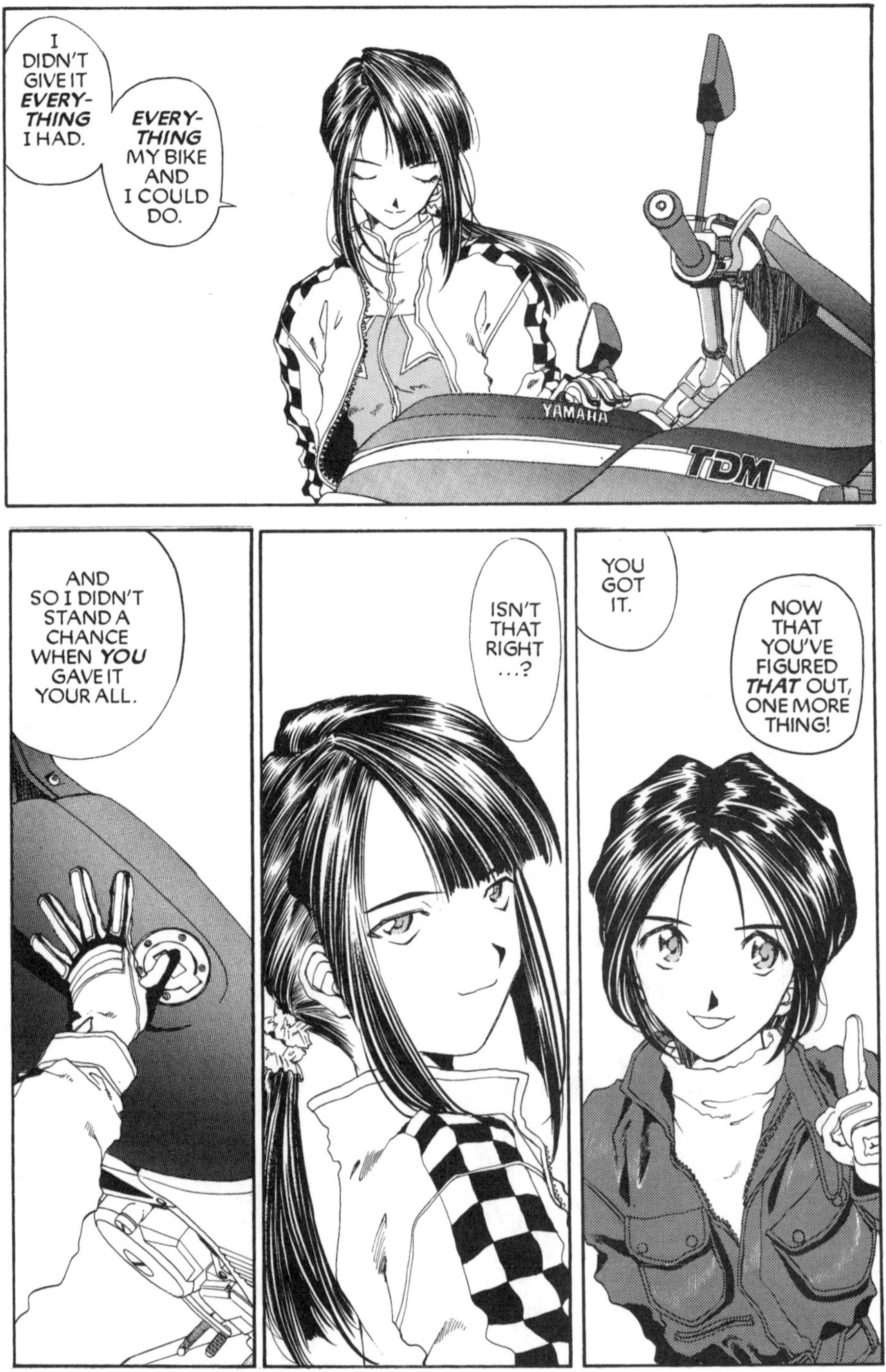
I DIDN'T GIVE IT *EVERYTHING* I HAD.
EVERYTHING MY BIKE AND I COULD DO.
YAMAHA
TDM
AND SO I DIDN'T STAND A CHANCE WHEN *YOU* GAVE IT YOUR ALL.
ISN'T THAT RIGHT ...?
YOU GOT IT.
NOW THAT YOU'VE FIGURED *THAT* OUT, ONE MORE THING!

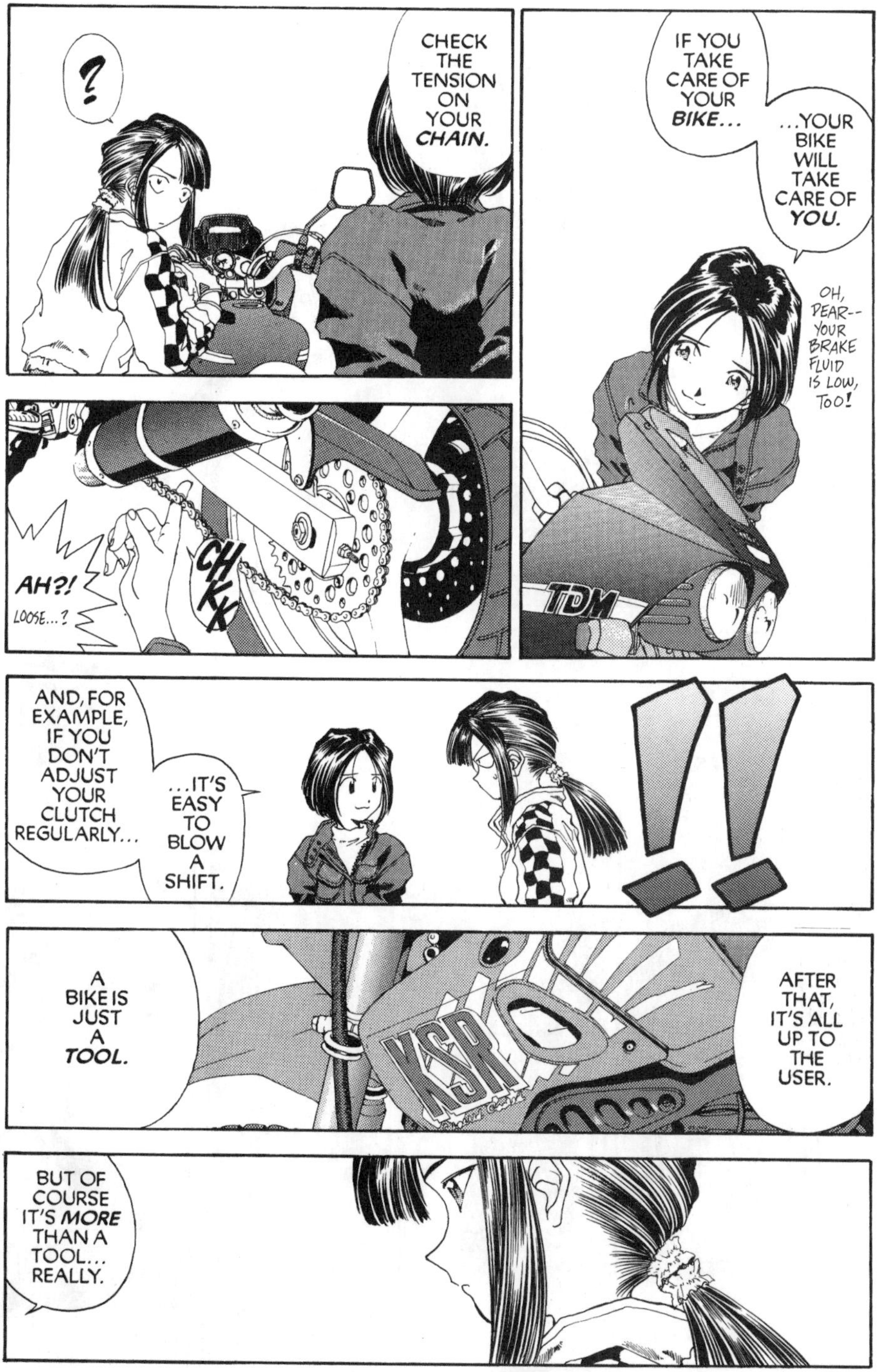
?
CHECK THE TENSION ON YOUR *CHAIN*.
AH?!
LOOSE...?
CHKK
IF YOU TAKE CARE OF YOUR *BIKE*...
...YOUR BIKE WILL TAKE CARE OF *YOU*.
OH, DEAR--YOUR BRAKE FLUID IS LOW, TOO!
AND, FOR EXAMPLE, IF YOU DON'T ADJUST YOUR CLUTCH REGULARLY...
...IT'S EASY TO BLOW A SHIFT.
!!
A BIKE IS JUST A *TOOL*.
KSR
TDM
AFTER THAT, IT'S ALL UP TO THE USER.
BUT OF COURSE IT'S *MORE* THAN A TOOL... REALLY.

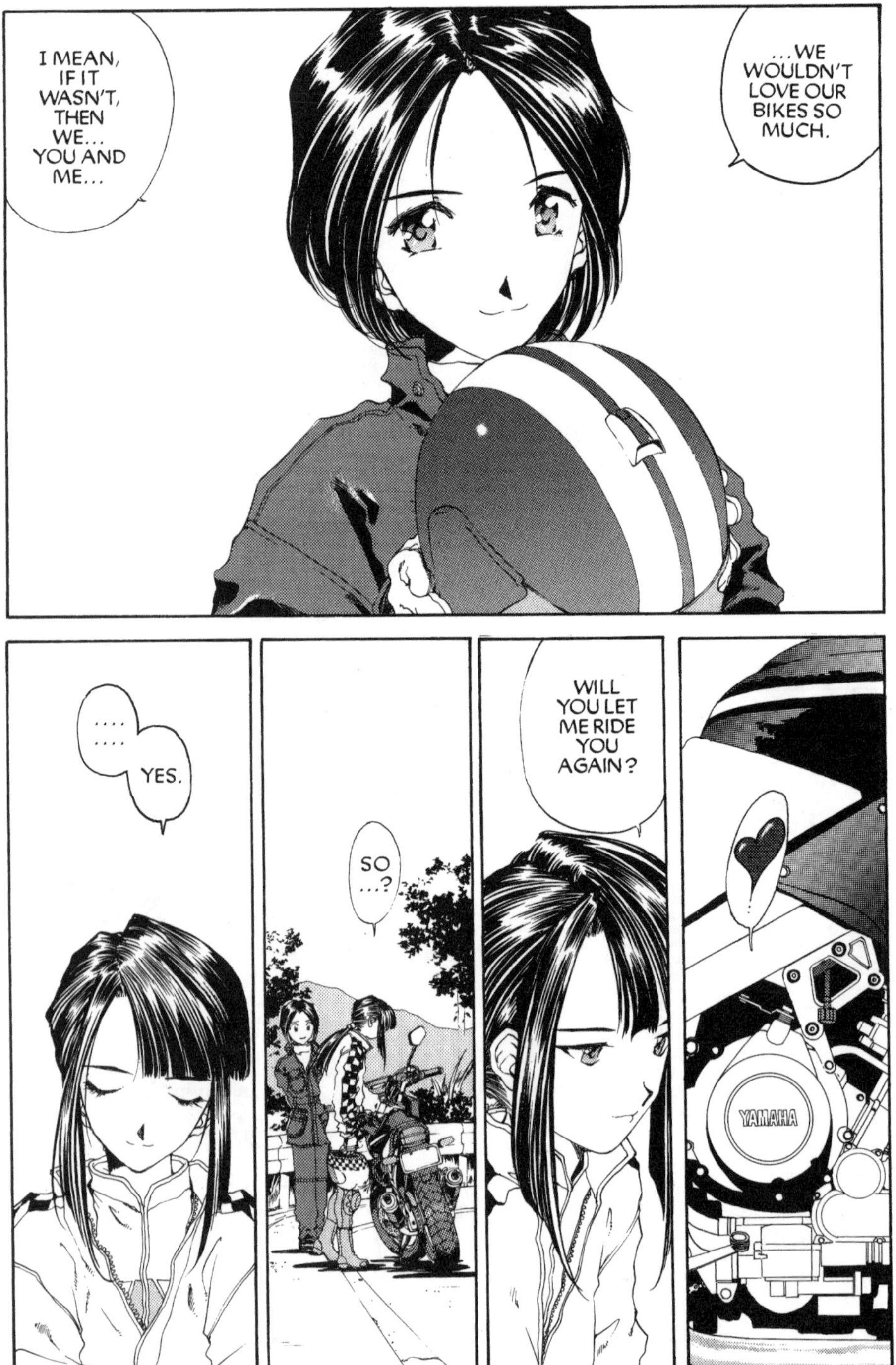
I MEAN, IF IT WASN'T, THEN WE... YOU AND ME...
...WE WOULDN'T LOVE OUR BIKES SO MUCH.
....
....
YES.
SO ...?
WILL YOU LET ME RIDE YOU AGAIN?
YAMAHA

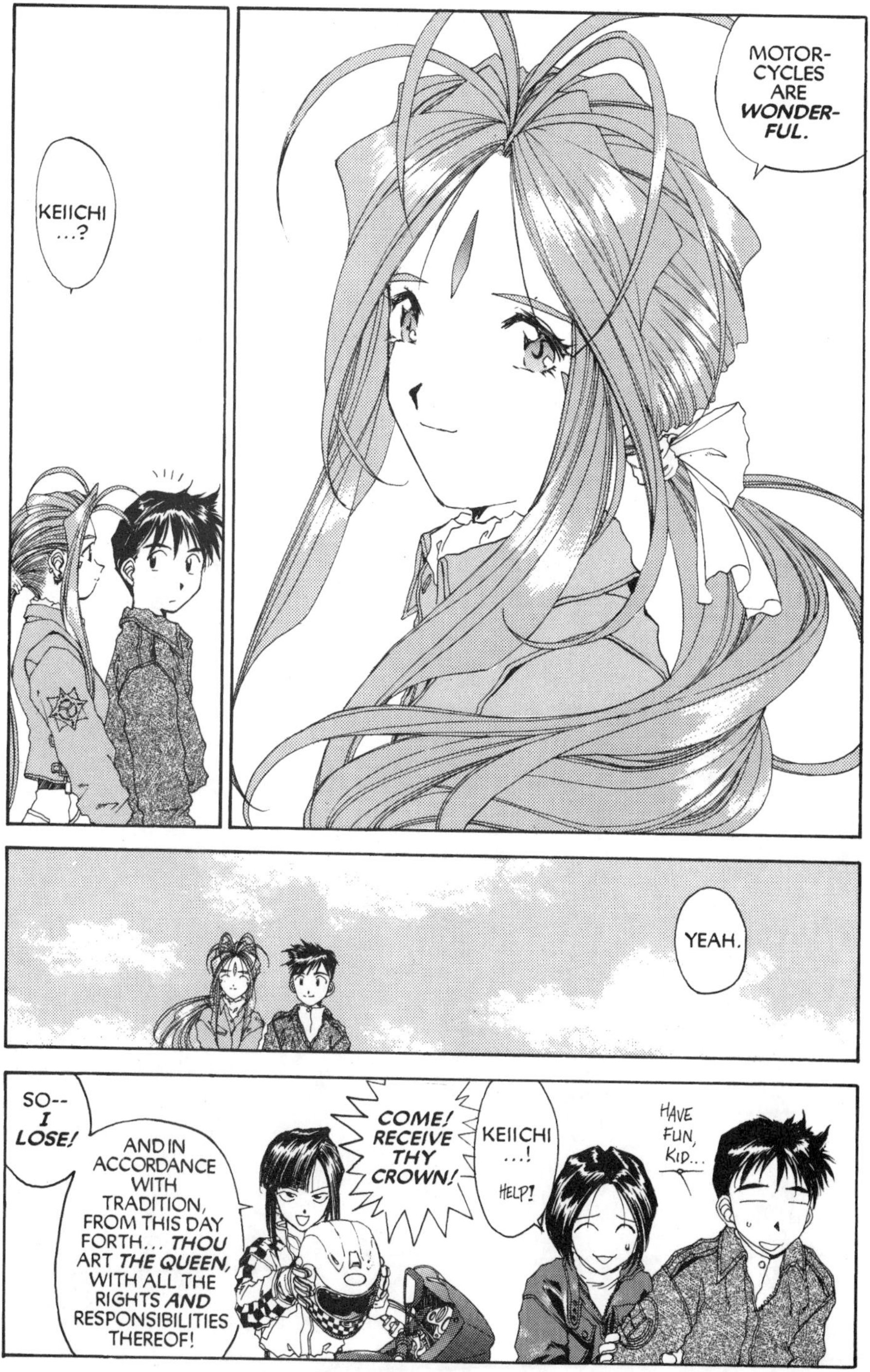
KEIICHI ...?
MOTOR-CYCLES ARE WONDER-FUL.
YEAH.
SO-- I LOSE!
AND IN ACCORDANCE WITH TRADITION, FROM THIS DAY FORTH... THOU ART THE QUEEN, WITH ALL THE RIGHTS AND RESPONSIBILITIES THEREOF!
COME! RECEIVE THY CROWN!
KEIICHI ...!
HELP!
HAVE FUN, KID...

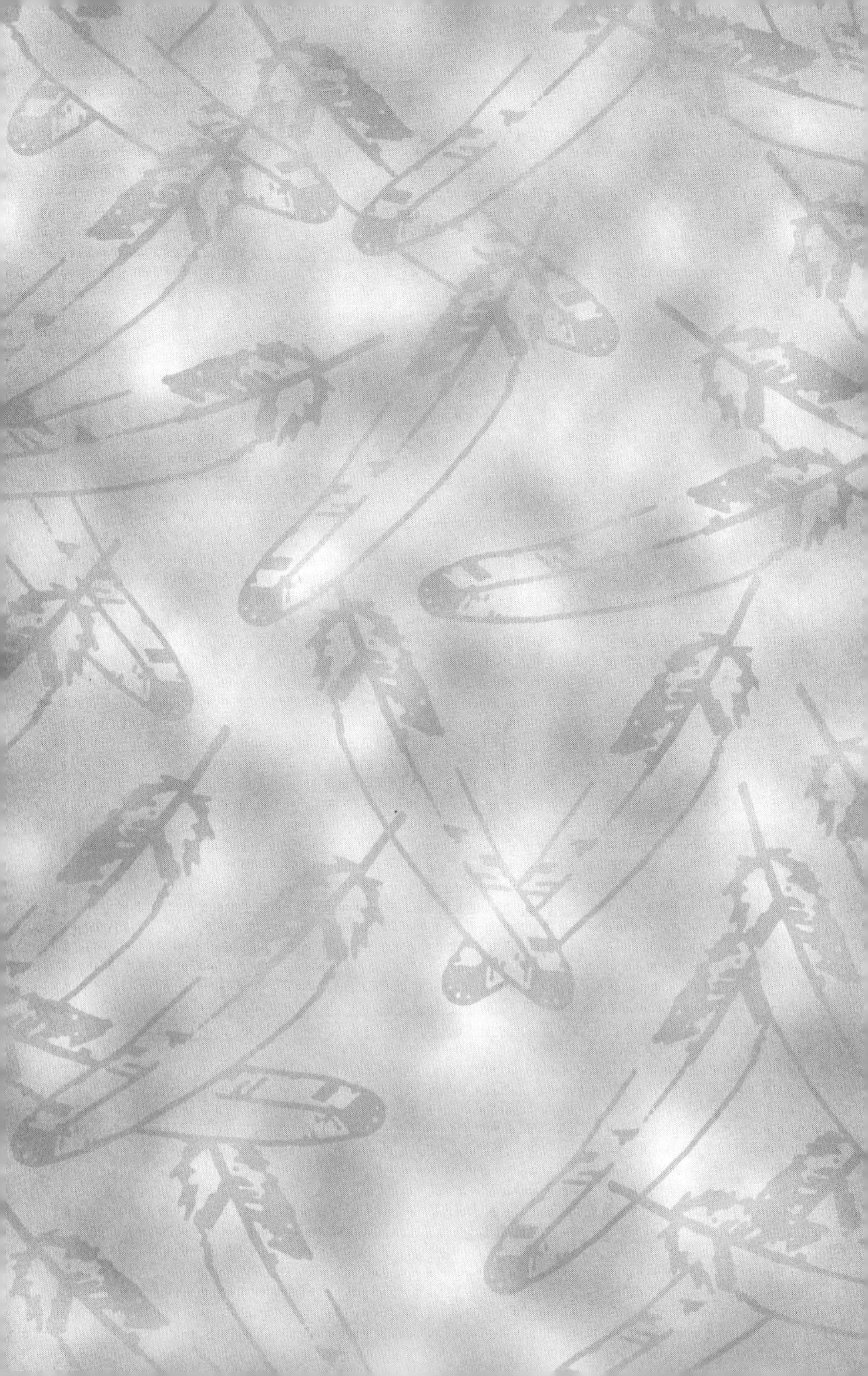

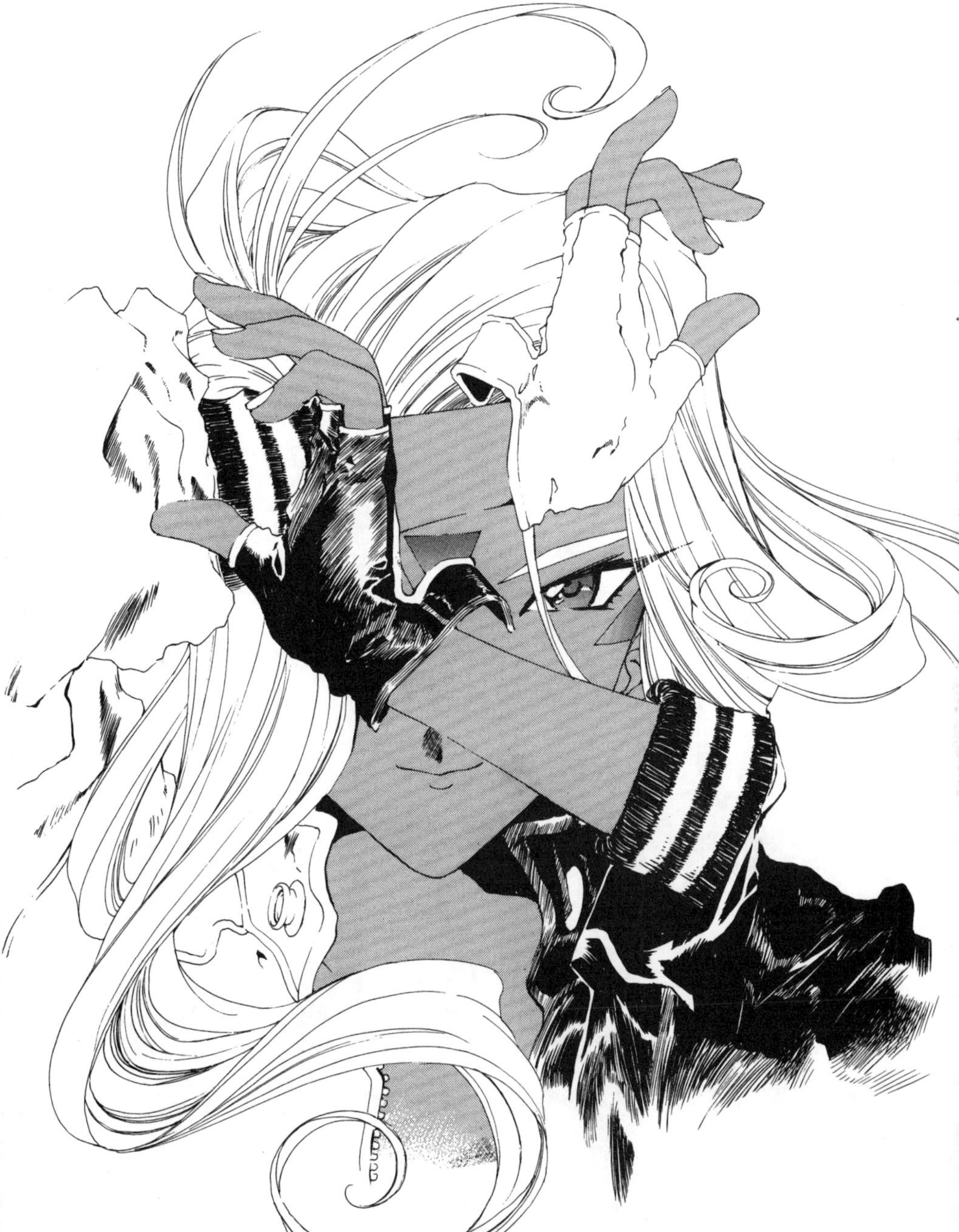

ANOTHER ME

ANGELS ARE HOT!

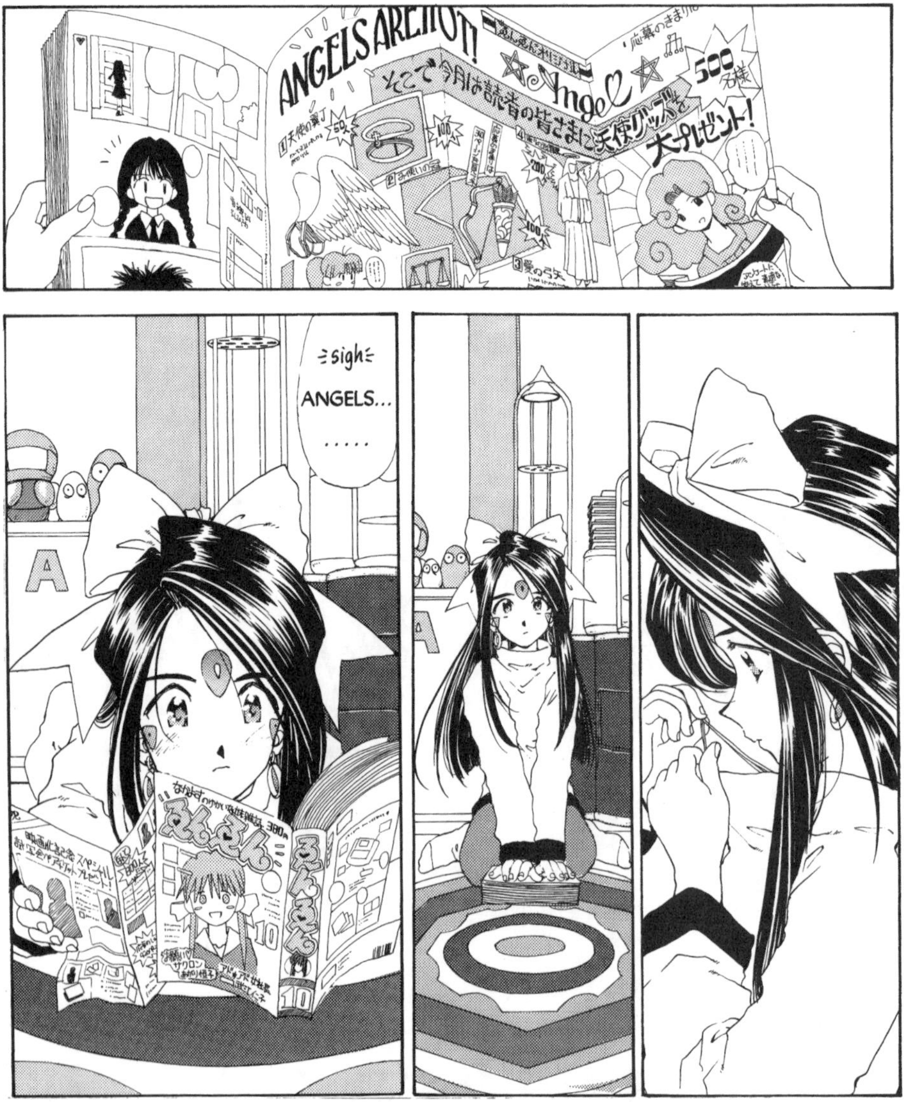
ANGELS ARE HOT!
そこで今月は読者の皆さまに天使グッズを大プレゼント!
500名様
天使の翼
愛の弓矢
sigh
ANGELS...
.....

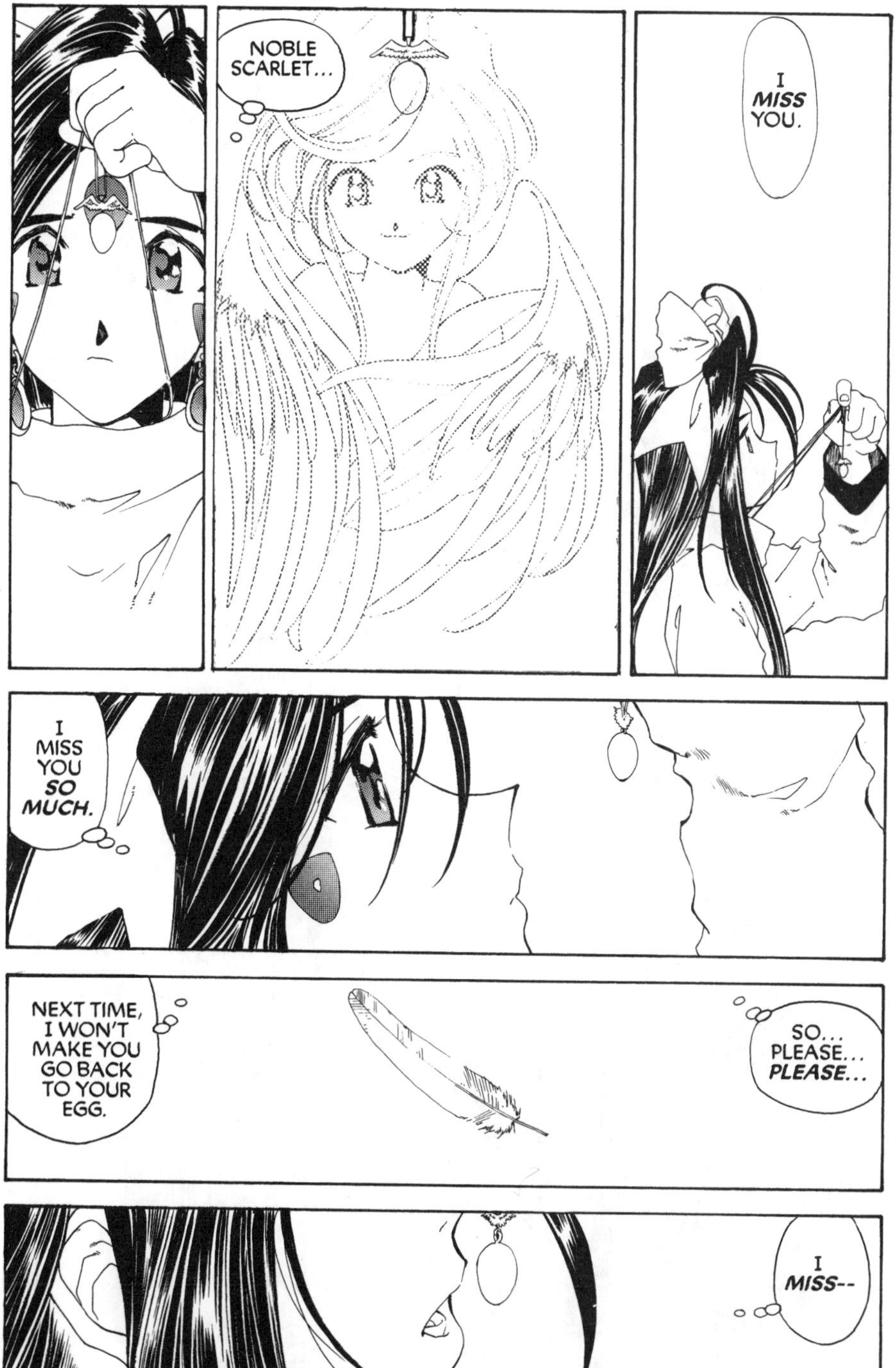
NOBLE SCARLET...
I *MISS* YOU.
I MISS YOU *SO MUCH.*
NEXT TIME, I WON'T MAKE YOU GO BACK TO YOUR EGG.
SO... PLEASE... *PLEASE...*
I *MISS--*

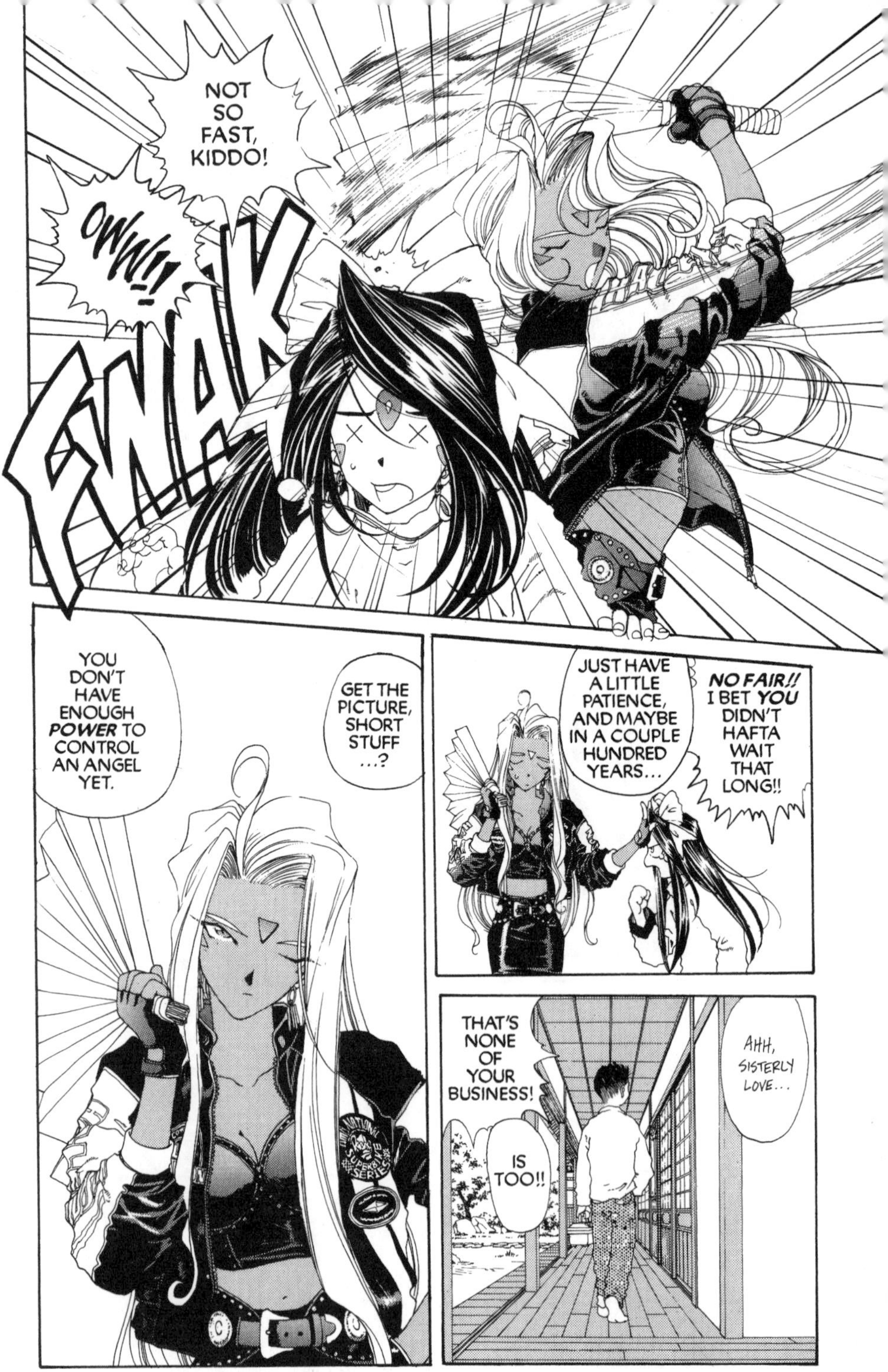
NOT SO FAST, KIDDO!
OWW!!
FWAK
YOU DON'T HAVE ENOUGH **POWER** TO CONTROL AN ANGEL YET.
GET THE PICTURE, SHORT STUFF ...?
JUST HAVE A LITTLE PATIENCE, AND MAYBE IN A COUPLE HUNDRED YEARS...
NO FAIR!! I BET ***YOU*** DIDN'T HAFTA WAIT THAT LONG!!
THAT'S NONE OF YOUR BUSINESS!
IS TOO!!
AHH, SISTERLY LOVE...

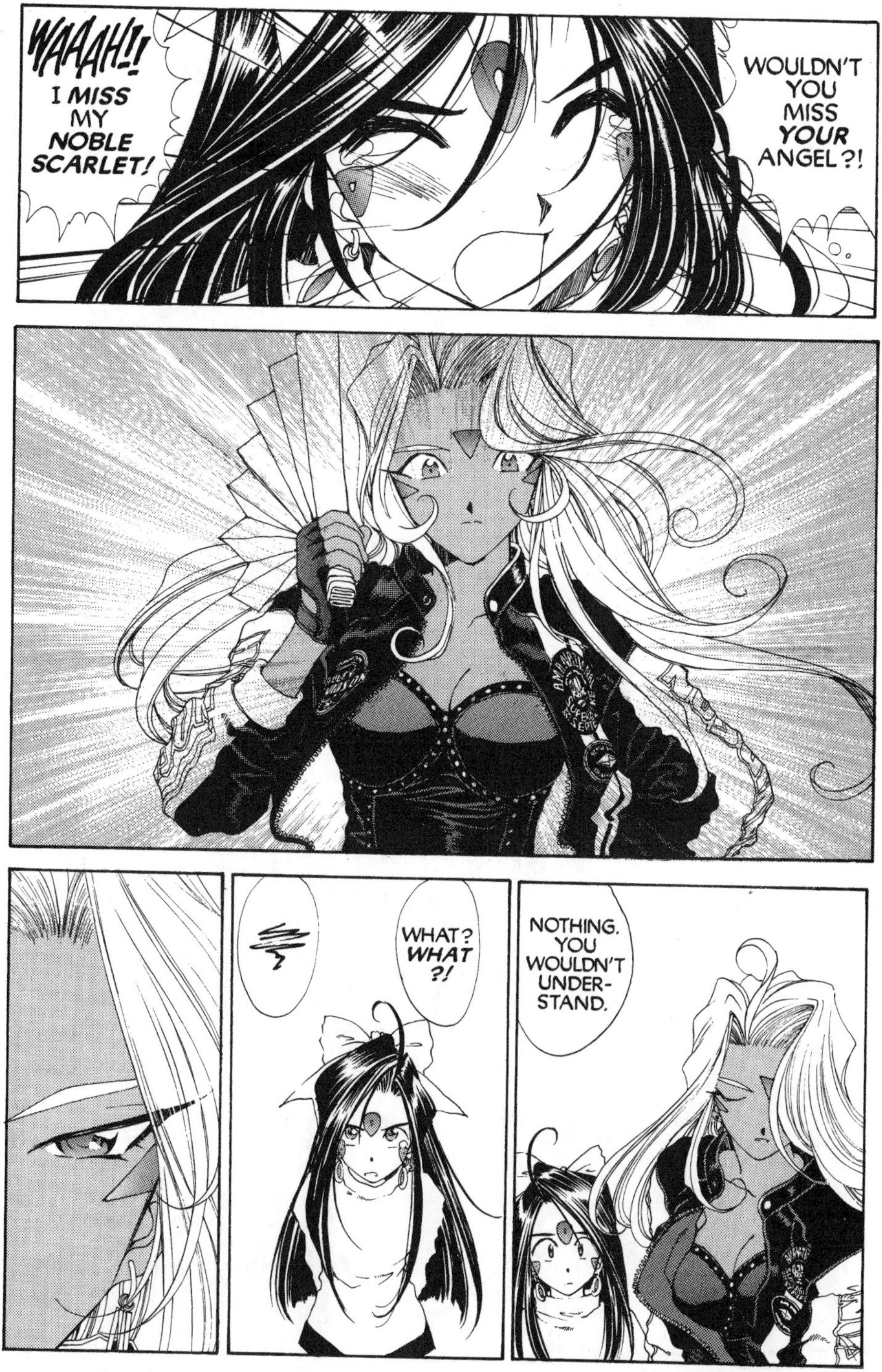
WAAAH!!
I MISS MY NOBLE SCARLET!
WOULDN'T YOU MISS YOUR ANGEL?!
WHAT? WHAT?!
NOTHING. YOU WOULDN'T UNDER-STAND.

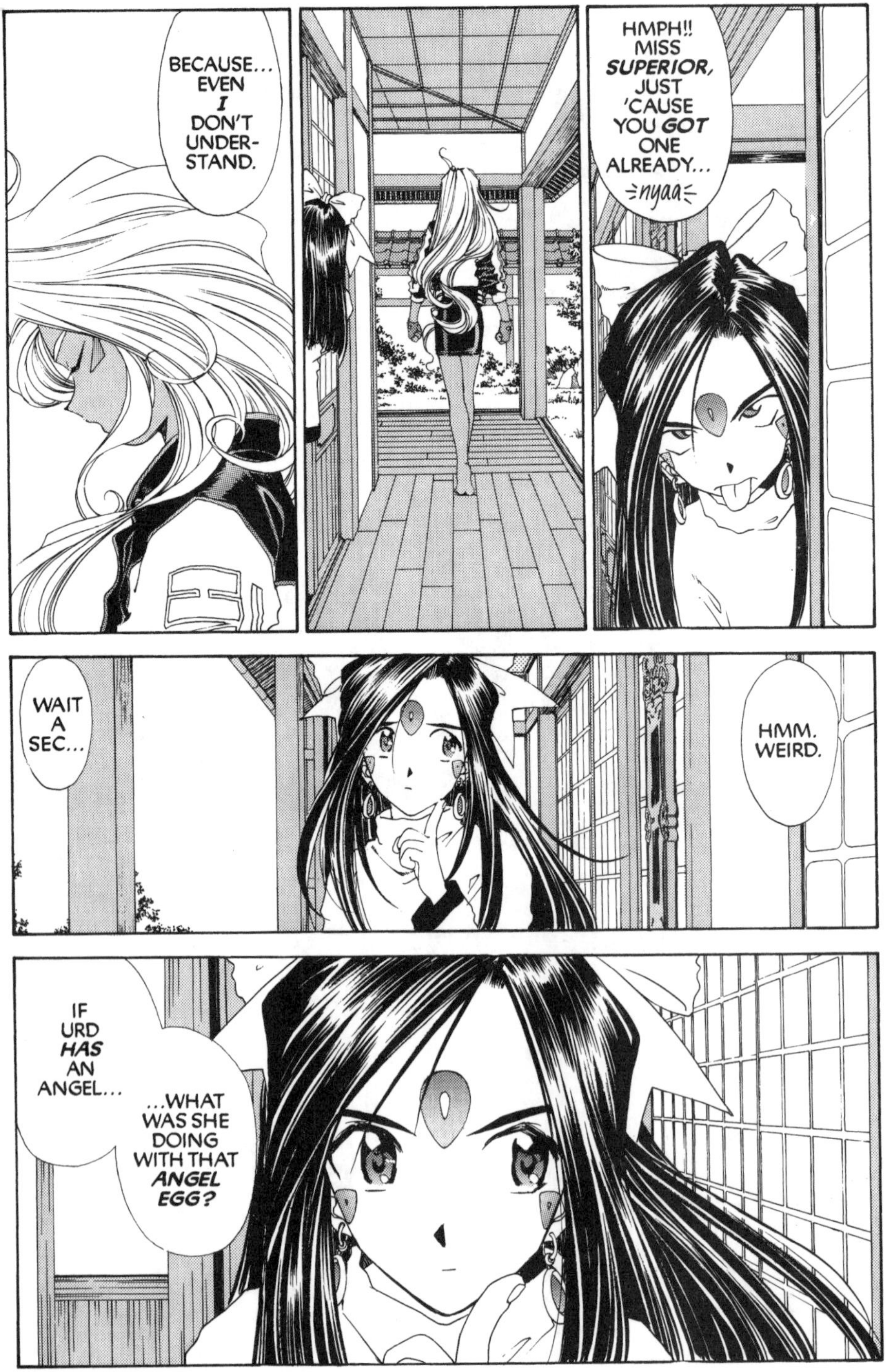
BECAUSE... EVEN I DON'T UNDER-STAND.
HMPH!! MISS SUPERIOR, JUST 'CAUSE YOU GOT ONE ALREADY...
nyaa
WAIT A SEC...
HMM. WEIRD.
IF URD HAS AN ANGEL...
...WHAT WAS SHE DOING WITH THAT ANGEL EGG?

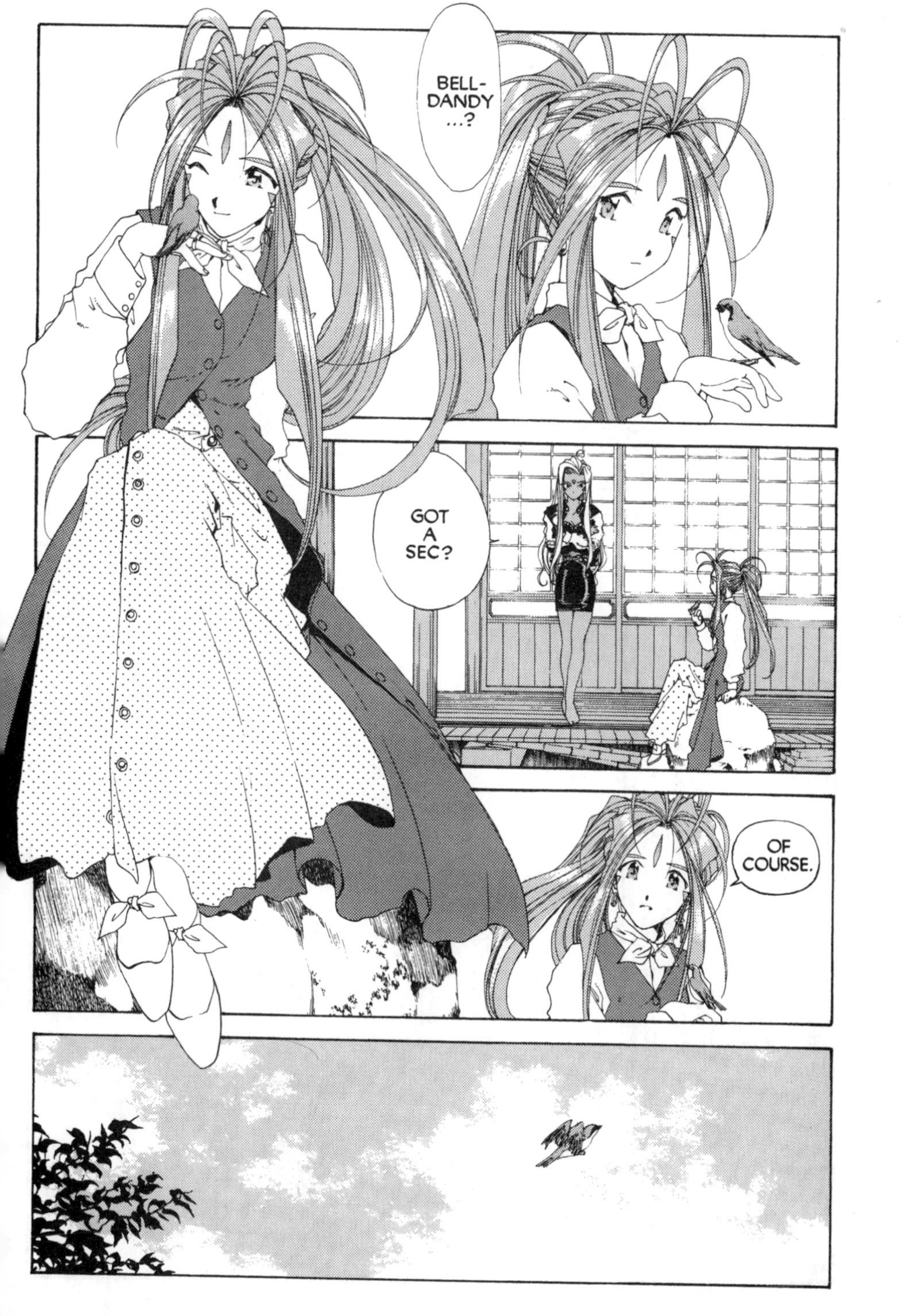
BELL-DANDY ...?
GOT A SEC?
OF COURSE.

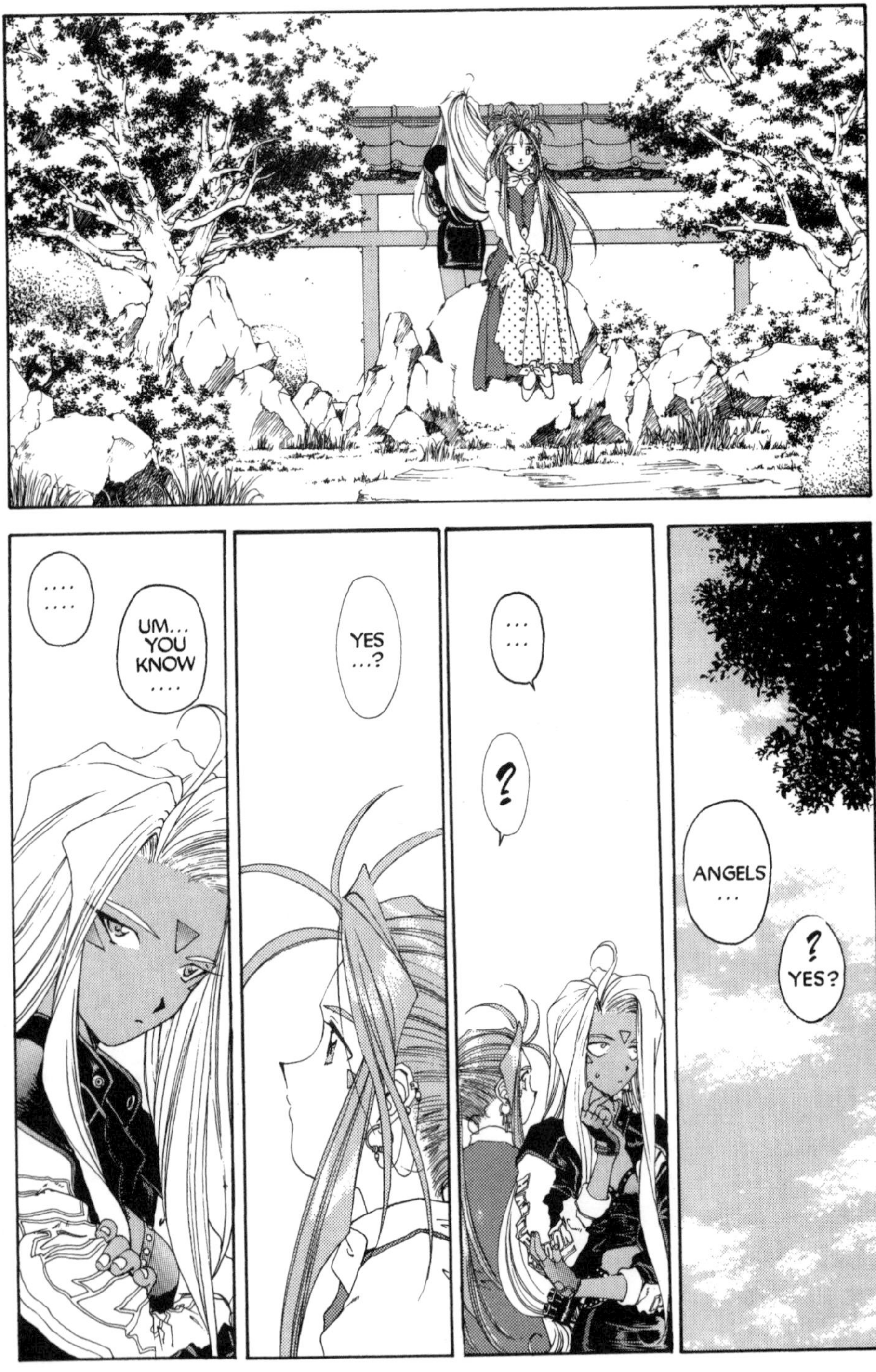
....
....
UM... YOU KNOW ....
YES ...?
...
...
?
ANGELS ...
? YES?

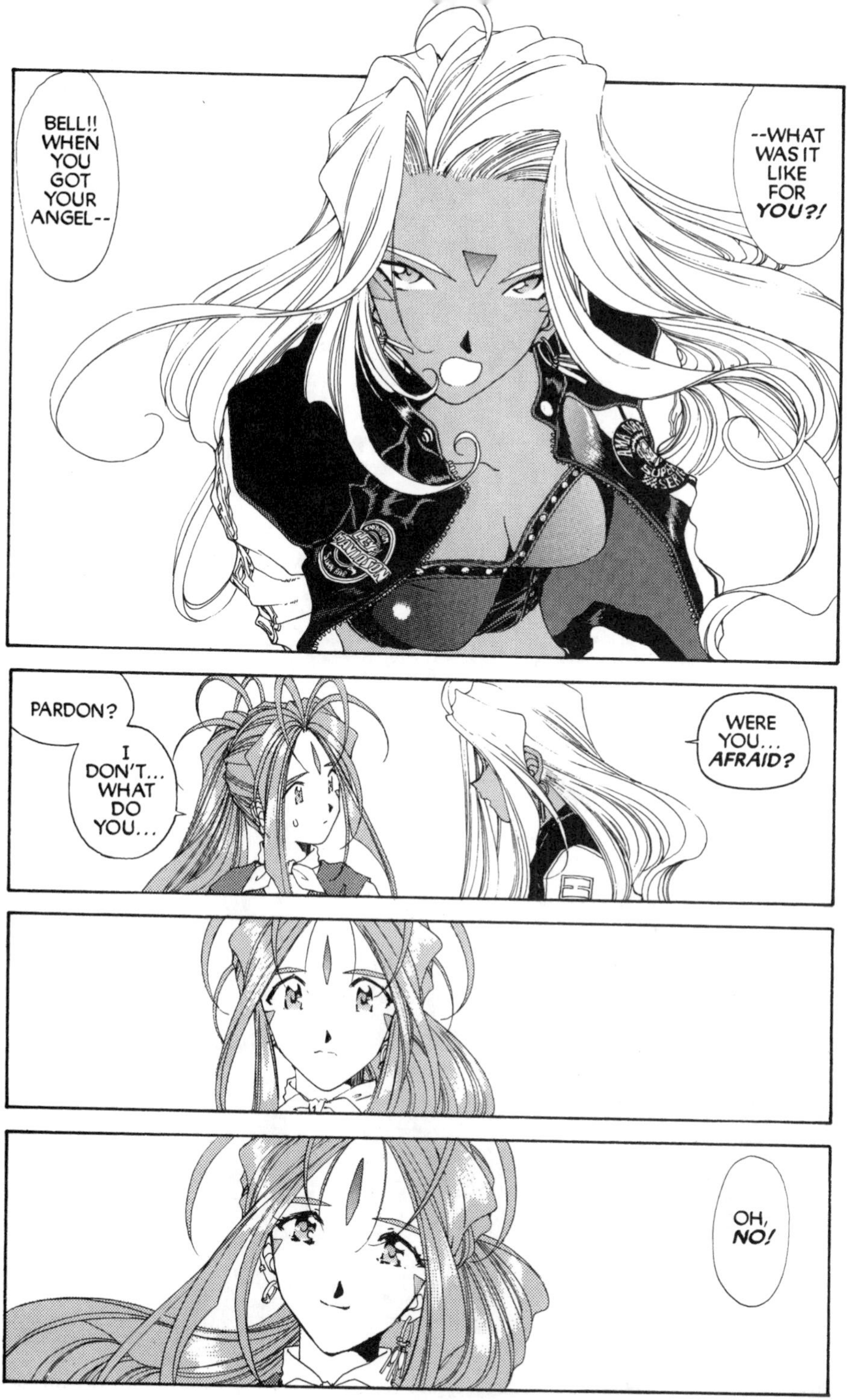
BELL!! WHEN YOU GOT YOUR ANGEL--
--WHAT WAS IT LIKE FOR *YOU?!*
PARDON?
I DON'T... WHAT DO YOU...
WERE YOU... *AFRAID?*
OH, *NO!*

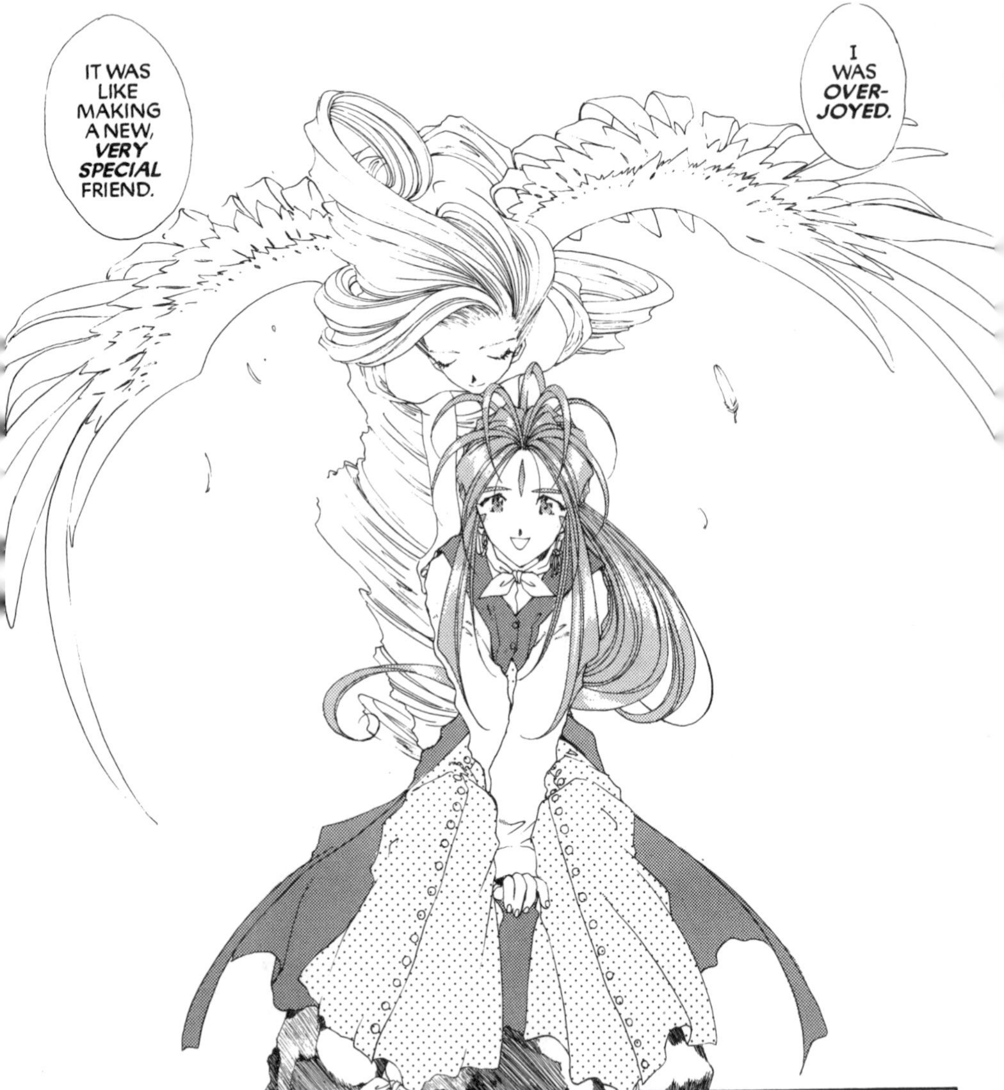
IT WAS LIKE MAKING A NEW, **VERY SPECIAL** FRIEND.
I WAS **OVER-JOYED.**

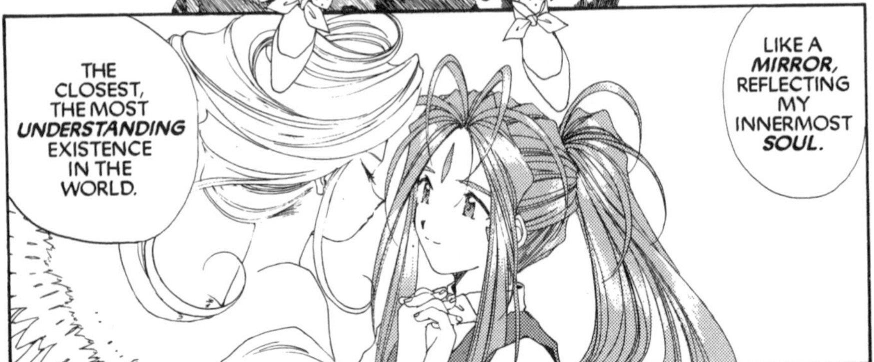
THE CLOSEST, THE MOST **UNDERSTANDING** EXISTENCE IN THE WORLD.
LIKE A **MIRROR,** REFLECTING MY INNERMOST **SOUL.**

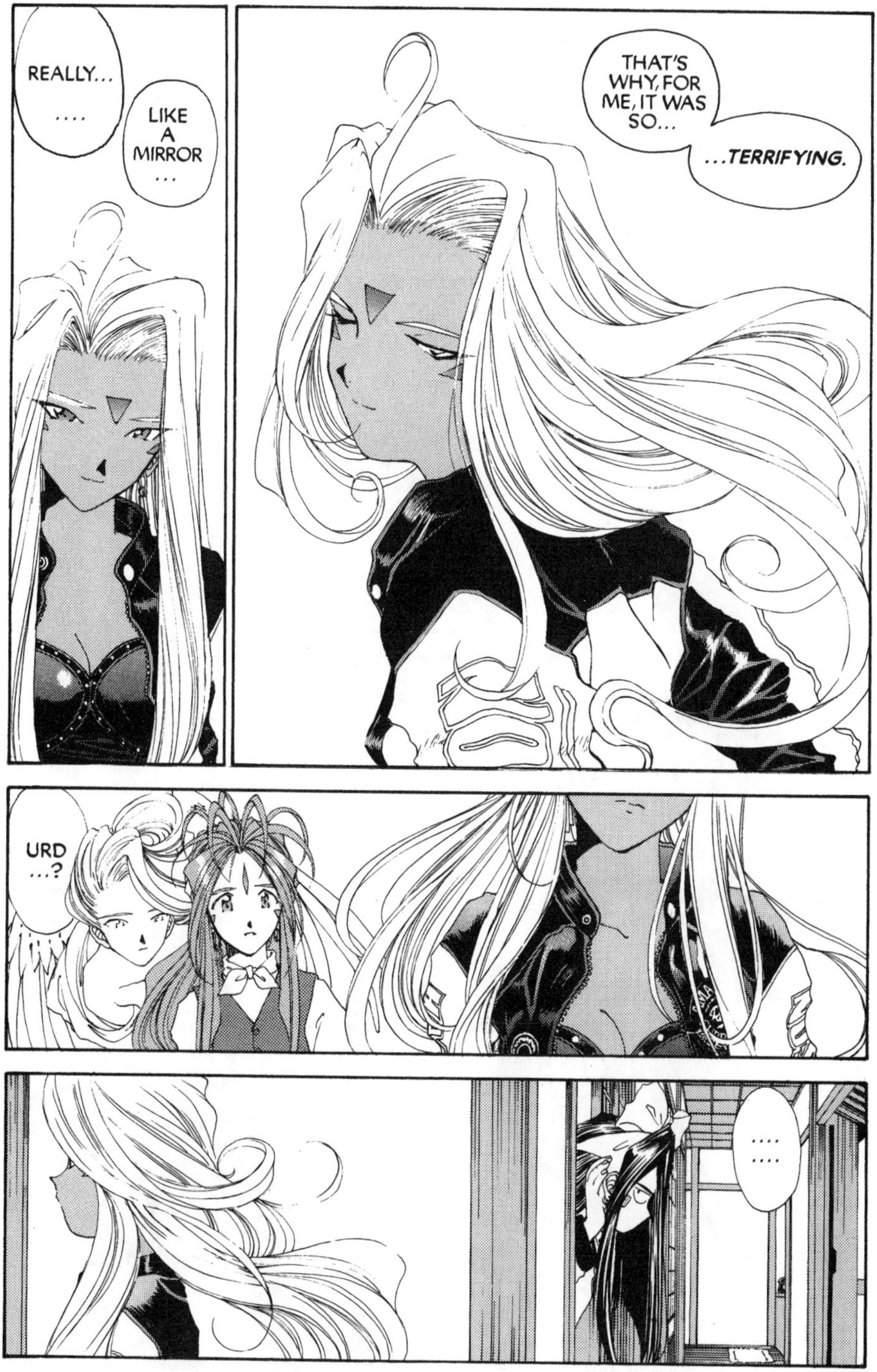

THAT'S WHY, FOR ME, IT WAS SO...
...TERRIFYING.
REALLY...
....
LIKE A MIRROR ...
URD ...?
....
....

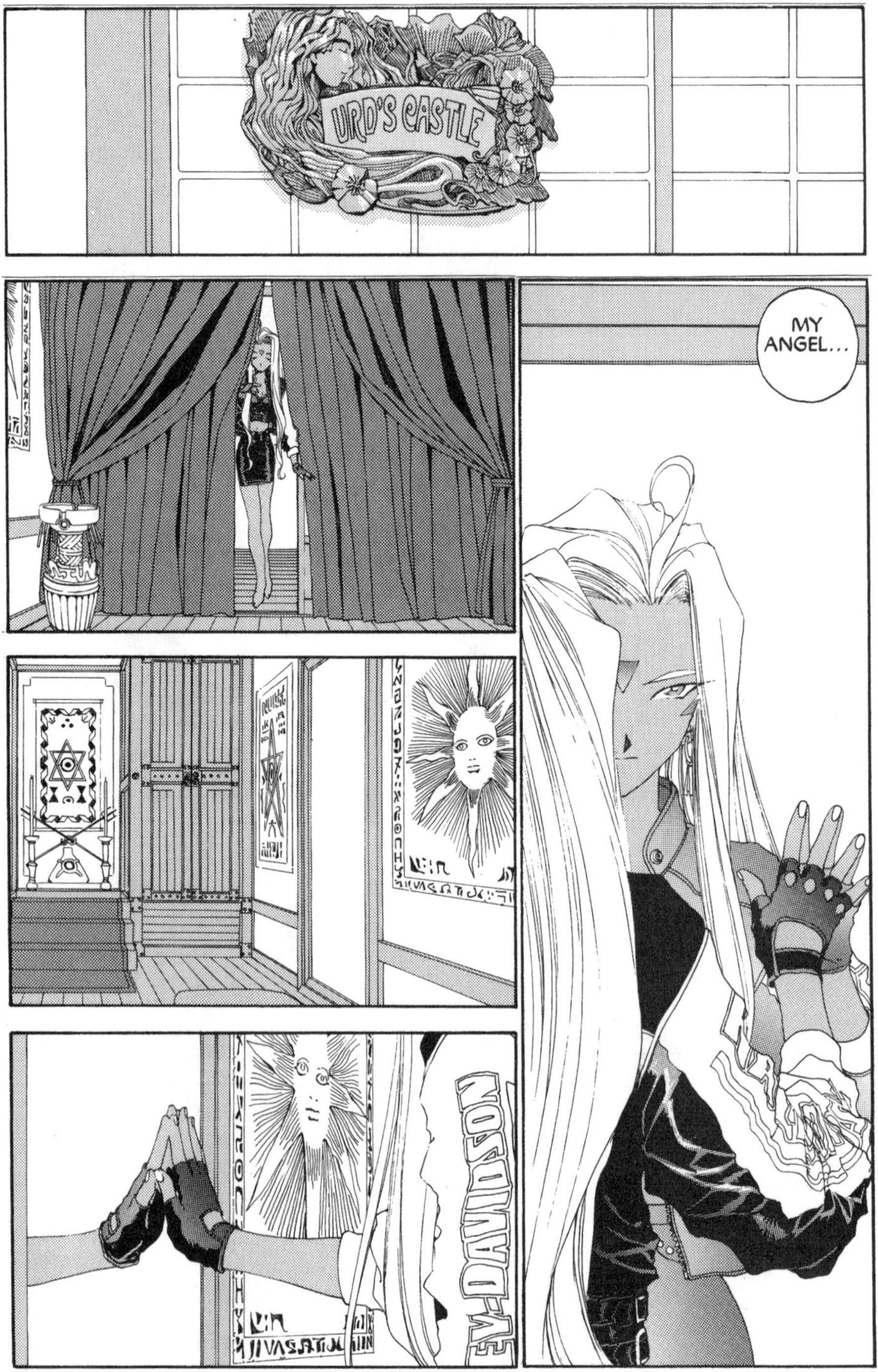
URD'S CASTLE
EY-DAVIDSON
MY ANGEL...

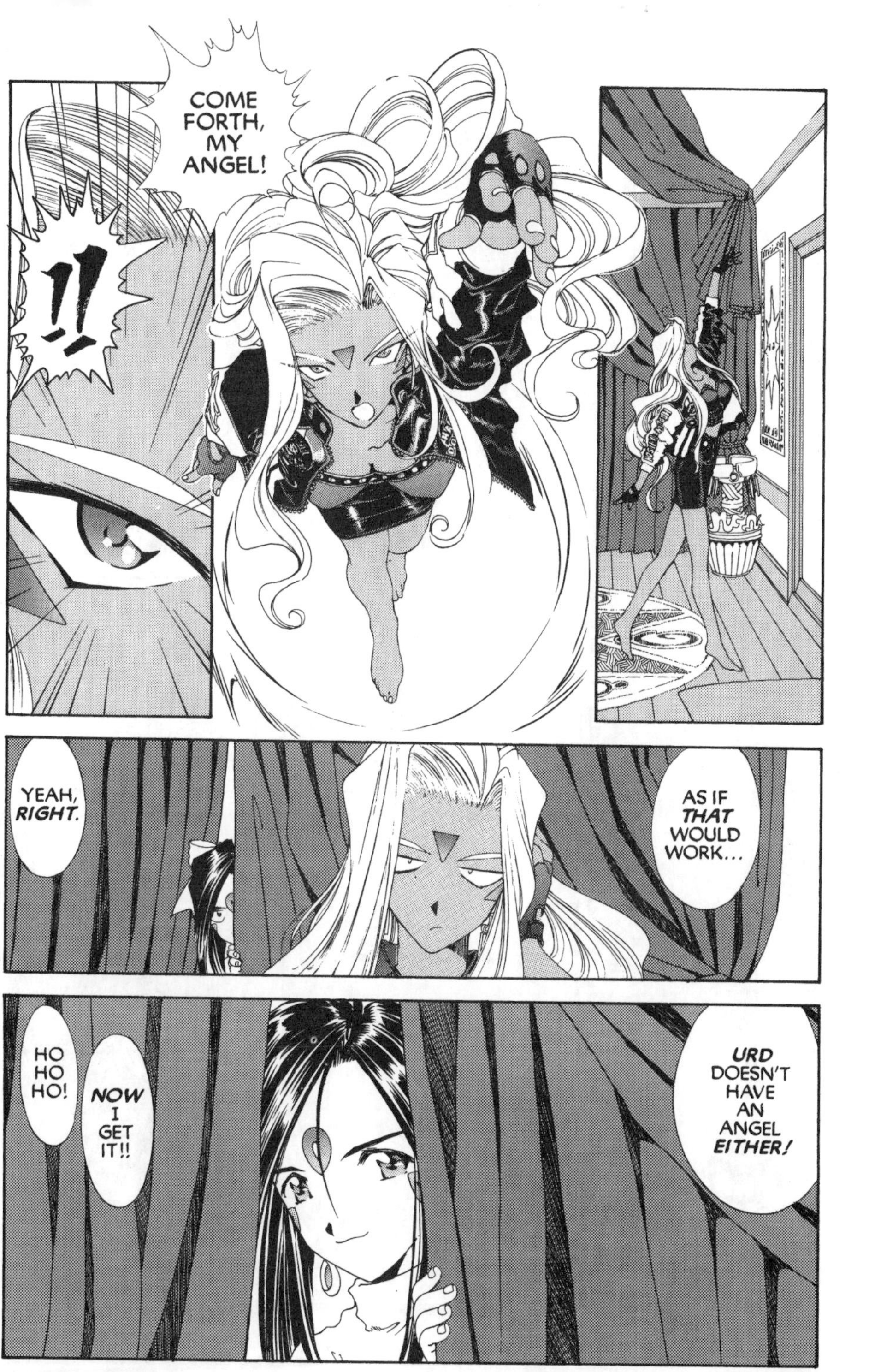
!!
COME FORTH, MY ANGEL!
YEAH, *RIGHT.*
AS IF *THAT* WOULD WORK...
HO HO HO!
NOW I GET IT!!
URD DOESN'T HAVE AN ANGEL *EITHER!*

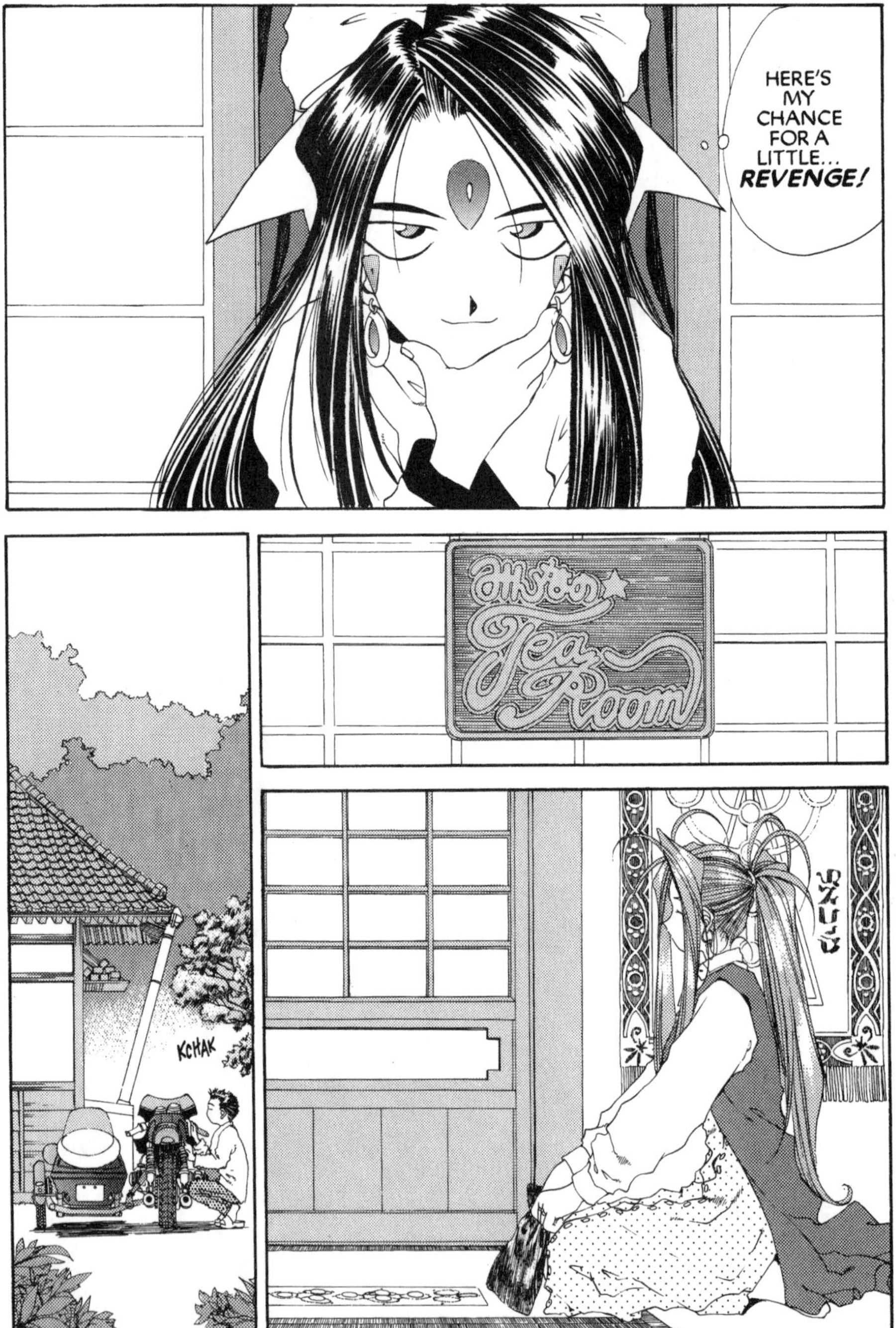
HERE'S MY CHANCE FOR A LITTLE... **REVENGE!**
KCHAK
Tea Room

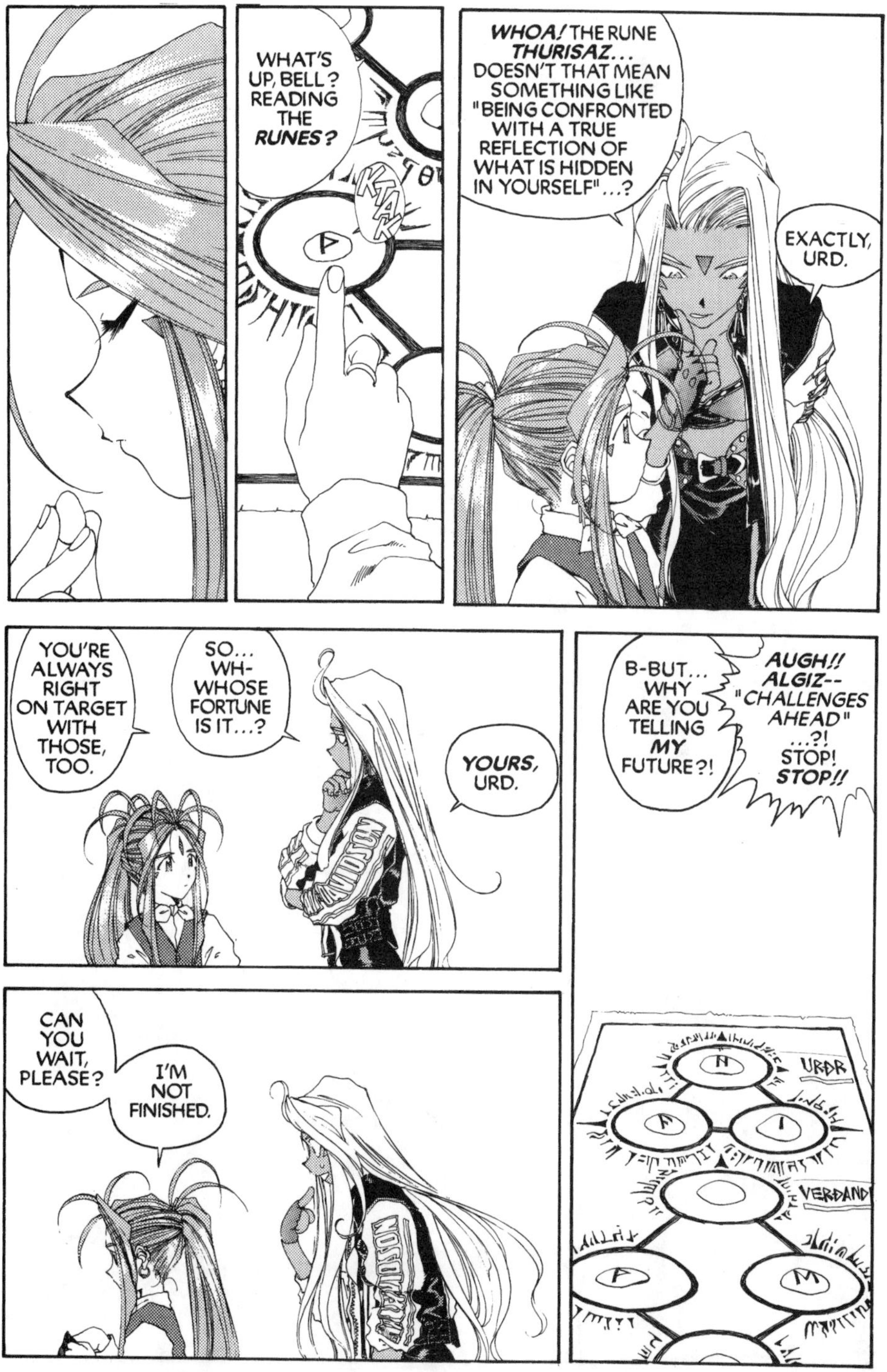
WHAT'S UP, BELL? READING THE *RUNES?*
KTAK
WHOA! THE RUNE *THURISAZ*... DOESN'T THAT MEAN SOMETHING LIKE "BEING CONFRONTED WITH A TRUE REFLECTION OF WHAT IS HIDDEN IN YOURSELF"...?
EXACTLY, URD.
YOU'RE ALWAYS RIGHT ON TARGET WITH THOSE, TOO.
SO... WH-WHOSE FORTUNE IS IT...?
YOURS, URD.
CAN YOU WAIT, PLEASE?
I'M NOT FINISHED.
B-BUT... WHY ARE YOU TELLING *MY* FUTURE?!
AUGH!! ALGIZ-- "*CHALLENGES AHEAD*"...?! STOP! *STOP!!*
URÐR
VERDAND

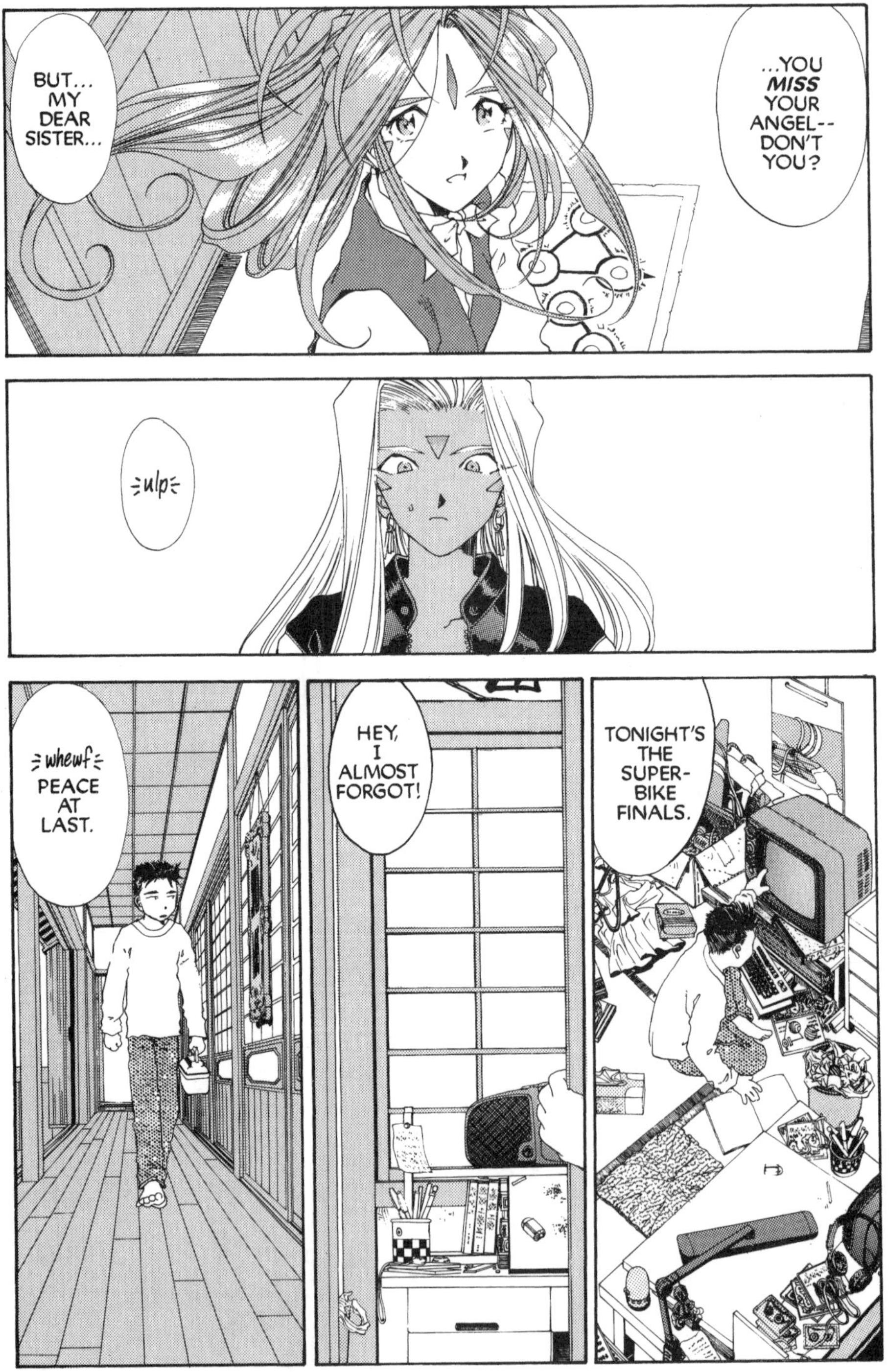
BUT... MY DEAR SISTER...
...YOU MISS YOUR ANGEL-- DON'T YOU?
ulp
whewf PEACE AT LAST.
HEY, I ALMOST FORGOT!
TONIGHT'S THE SUPER-BIKE FINALS.

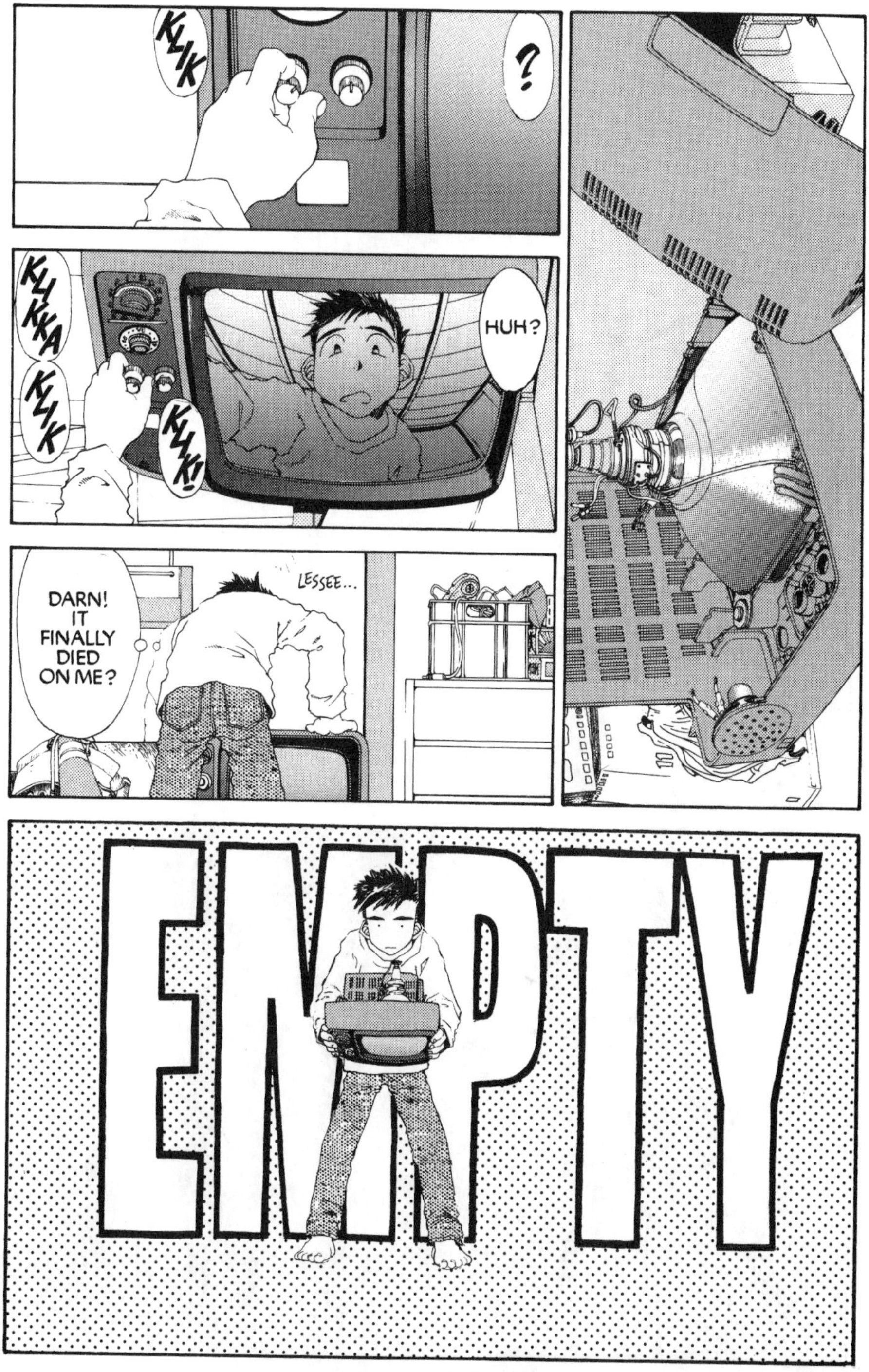
KLIK
?
KLIKKA
KLIK
KLIK!
HUH?
DARN! IT FINALLY DIED ON ME?
LESSEE...
EMPTY

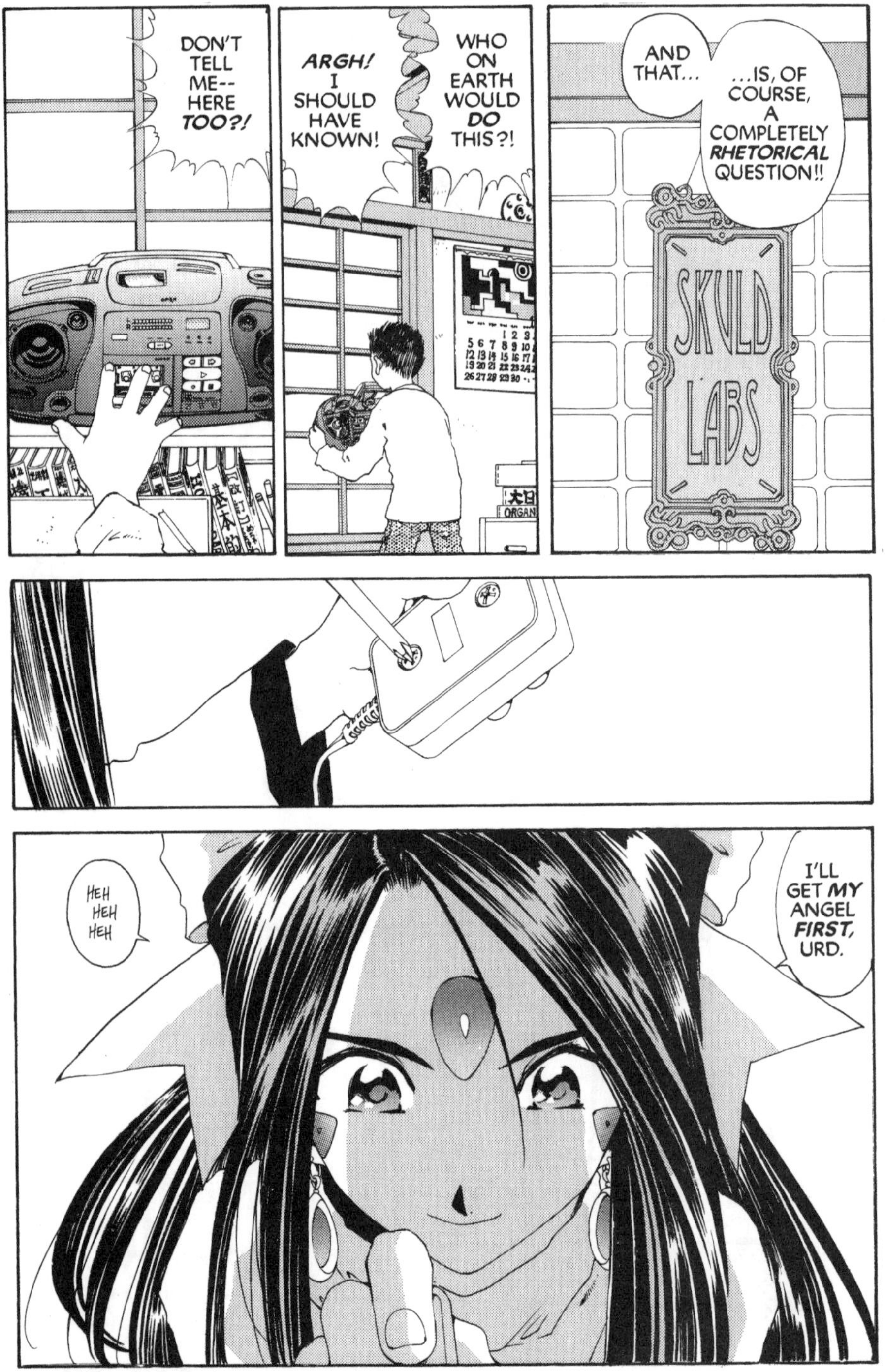
DON'T TELL ME-- HERE *TOO?!*
WHO ON EARTH WOULD *DO* THIS?!
ARGH! I SHOULD HAVE KNOWN!
AND THAT...
...IS, OF COURSE, A COMPLETELY *RHETORICAL* QUESTION!!
SKULD LABS
HEH HEH HEH
I'LL GET *MY* ANGEL *FIRST,* URD.

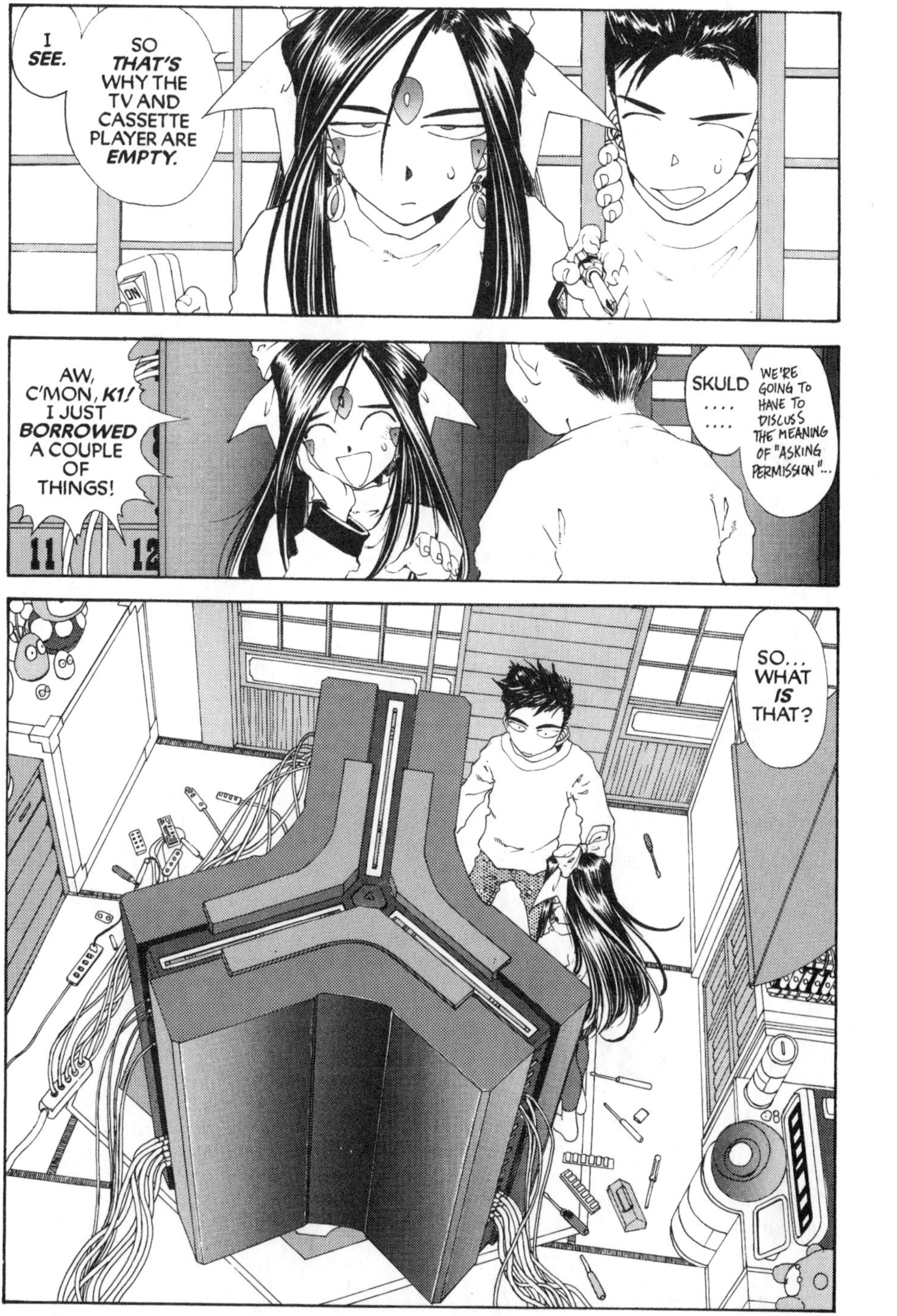
I SEE.
SO THAT'S WHY THE TV AND CASSETTE PLAYER ARE EMPTY.
AW, C'MON, K1! I JUST BORROWED A COUPLE OF THINGS!
SKULD ....
WE'RE GOING TO HAVE TO DISCUSS THE MEANING OF "ASKING PERMISSION"...
SO... WHAT IS THAT?

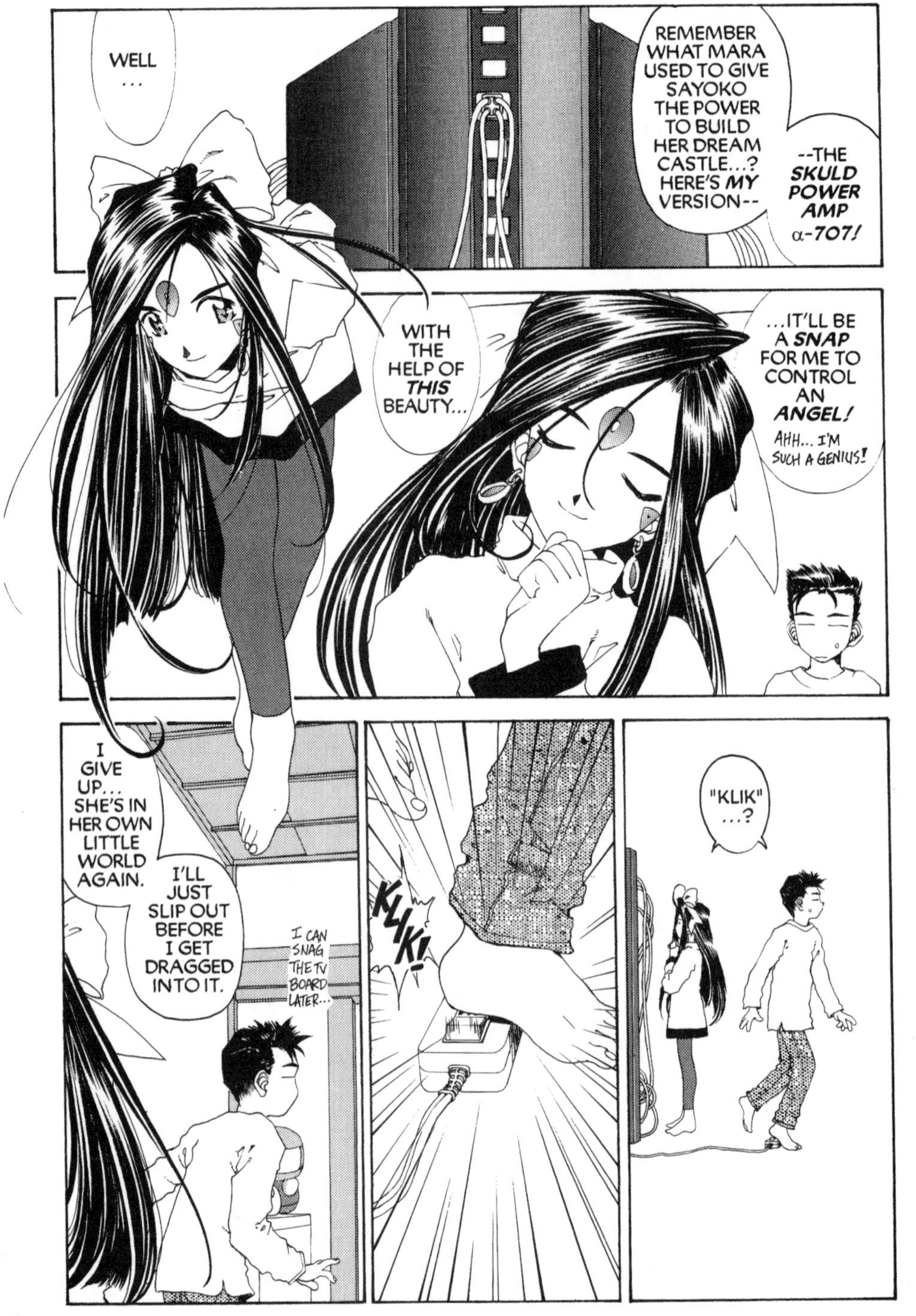
WELL ...
REMEMBER WHAT MARA USED TO GIVE SAYOKO THE POWER TO BUILD HER DREAM CASTLE...? HERE'S MY VERSION--
--THE SKULD POWER AMP α-707!
WITH THE HELP OF THIS BEAUTY...
...IT'LL BE A SNAP FOR ME TO CONTROL AN ANGEL!
AHH... I'M SUCH A GENIUS!
I GIVE UP... SHE'S IN HER OWN LITTLE WORLD AGAIN.
I'LL JUST SLIP OUT BEFORE I GET DRAGGED INTO IT.
I CAN SNAG THE TV BOARD LATER...
KLIK!
"KLIK" ...?

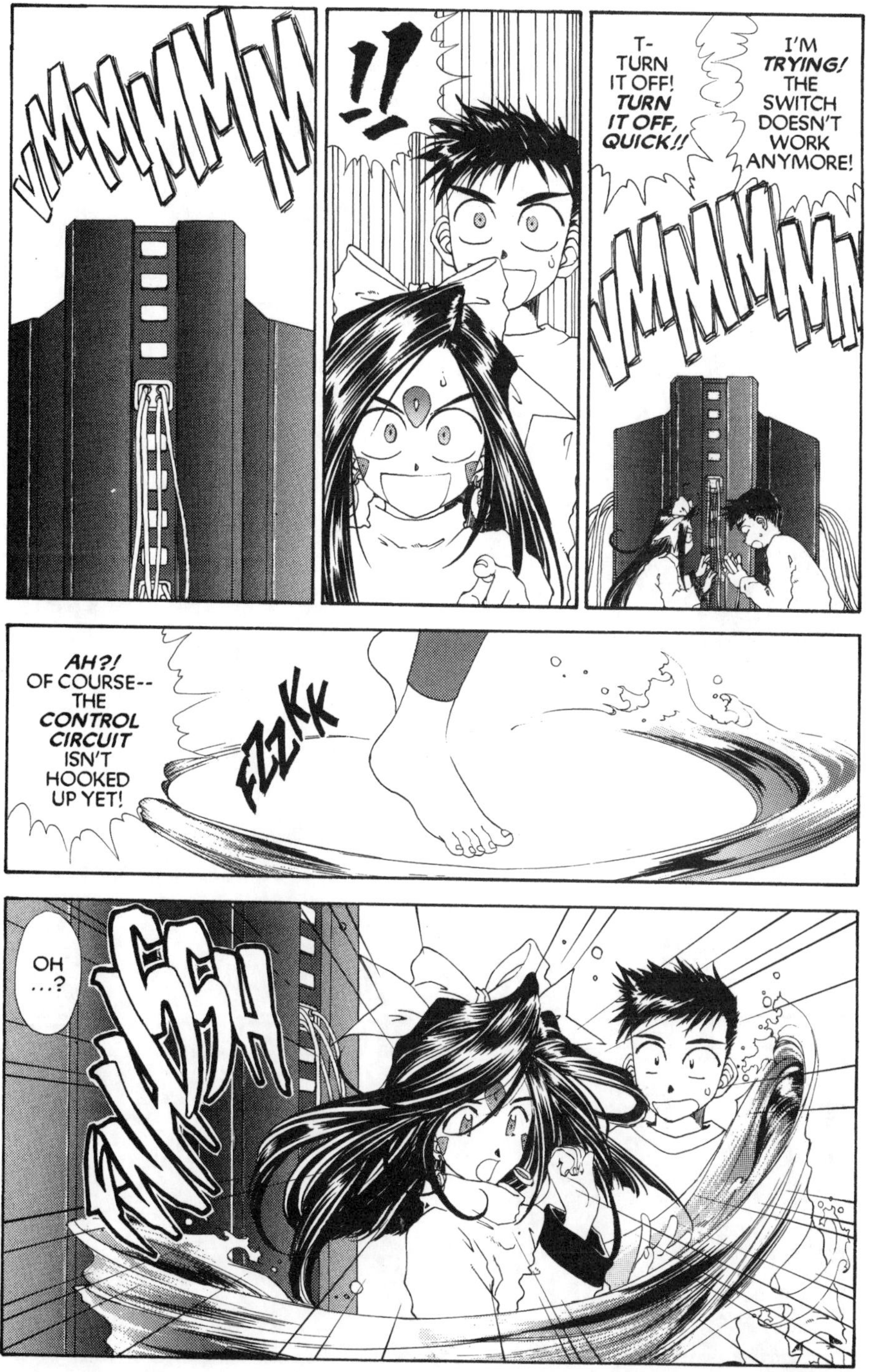
VMMMMMM
!!
T- TURN IT OFF! TURN IT OFF, QUICK!!
I'M TRYING! THE SWITCH DOESN'T WORK ANYMORE!
VMMMMMM
AH?! OF COURSE-- THE CONTROL CIRCUIT ISN'T HOOKED UP YET!
FZZKK
OH ...?
FWSSH

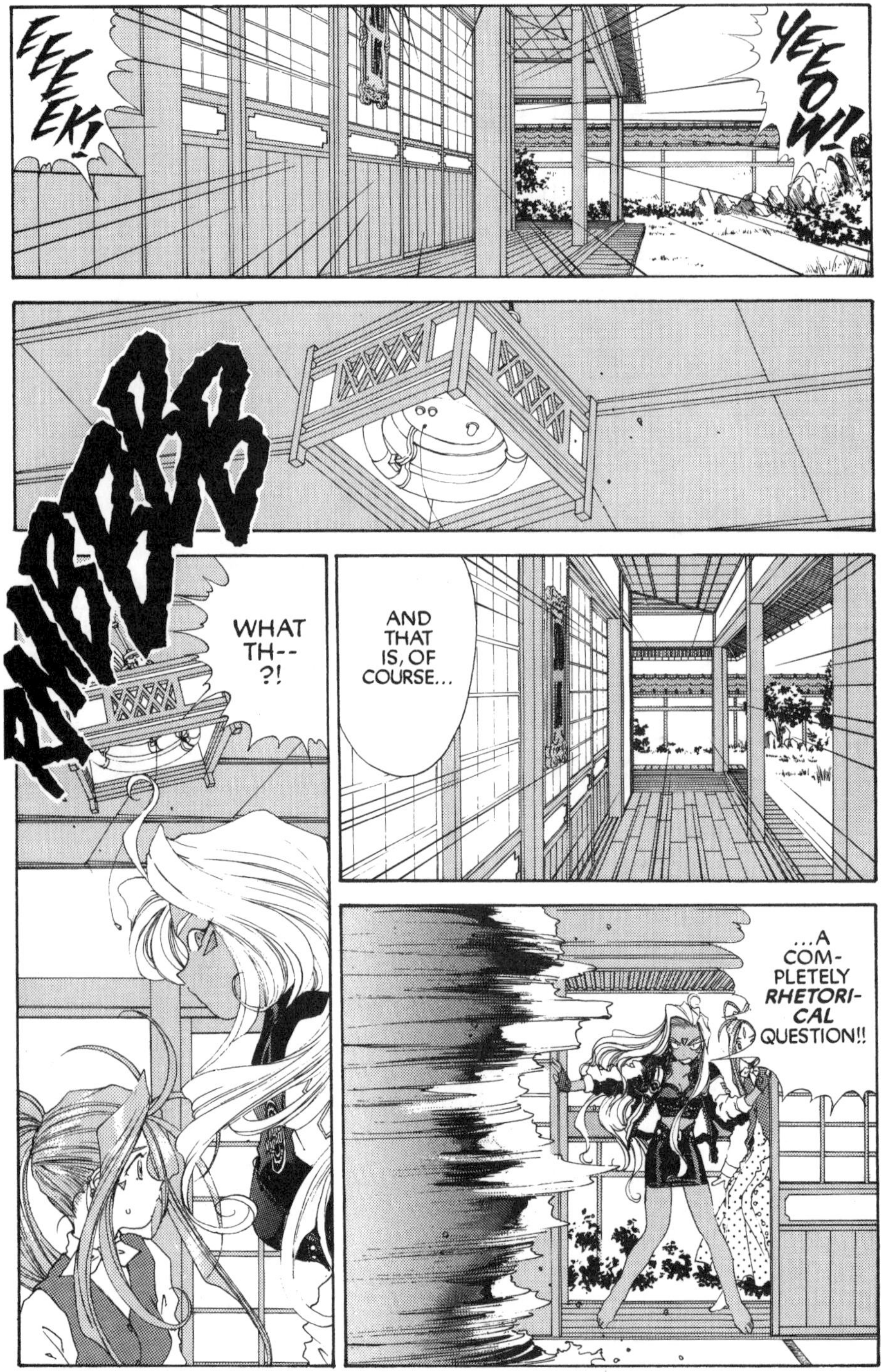
EEEEEK!
YEEOW!
RMBBBB
WHAT TH-- ?!
AND THAT IS, OF COURSE...
...A COMPLETELY *RHETORICAL* QUESTION!!

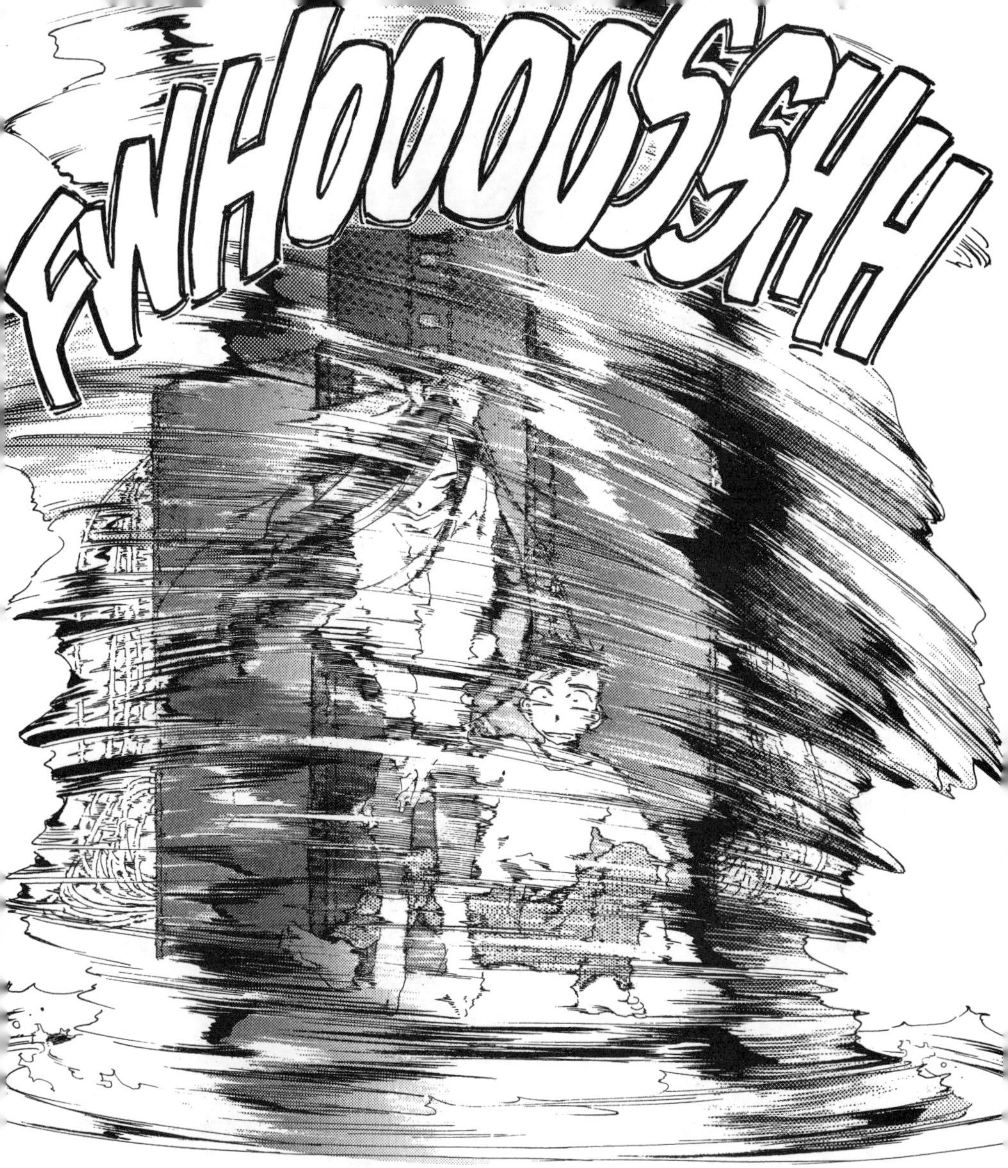
FWHOOOOSSH

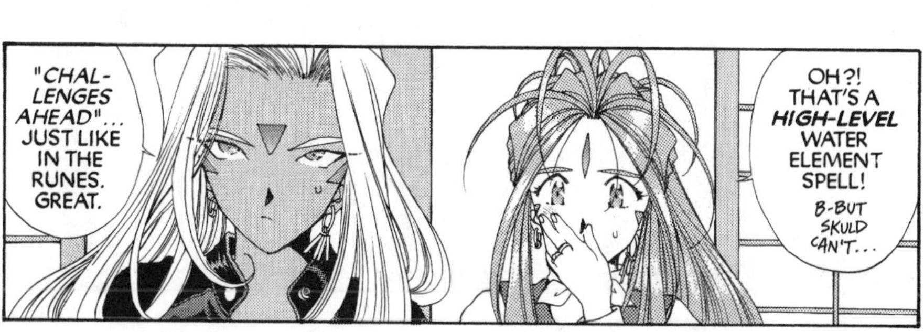
"CHALLENGES AHEAD"... JUST LIKE IN THE RUNES. GREAT.
OH?! THAT'S A HIGH-LEVEL WATER ELEMENT SPELL!
B-BUT SKULD CAN'T...

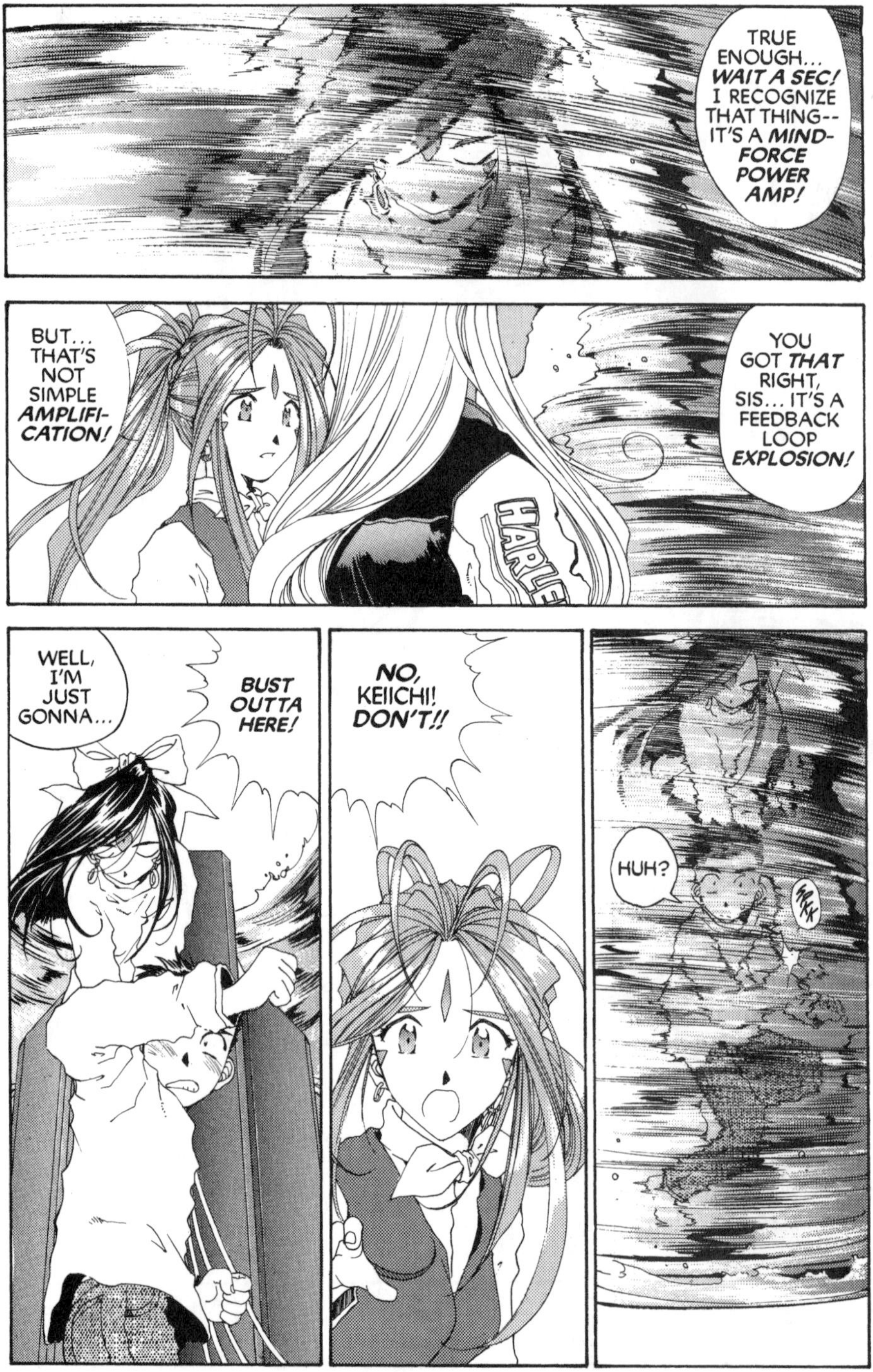
TRUE ENOUGH... *WAIT A SEC!* I RECOGNIZE THAT THING-- IT'S A *MIND-FORCE POWER AMP!*
BUT... THAT'S NOT SIMPLE *AMPLIFICATION!*
YOU GOT *THAT* RIGHT, SIS... IT'S A FEEDBACK LOOP *EXPLOSION!*
WELL, I'M JUST GONNA...
BUST OUTTA HERE!
NO, KEIICHI! *DON'T!!*
HUH?

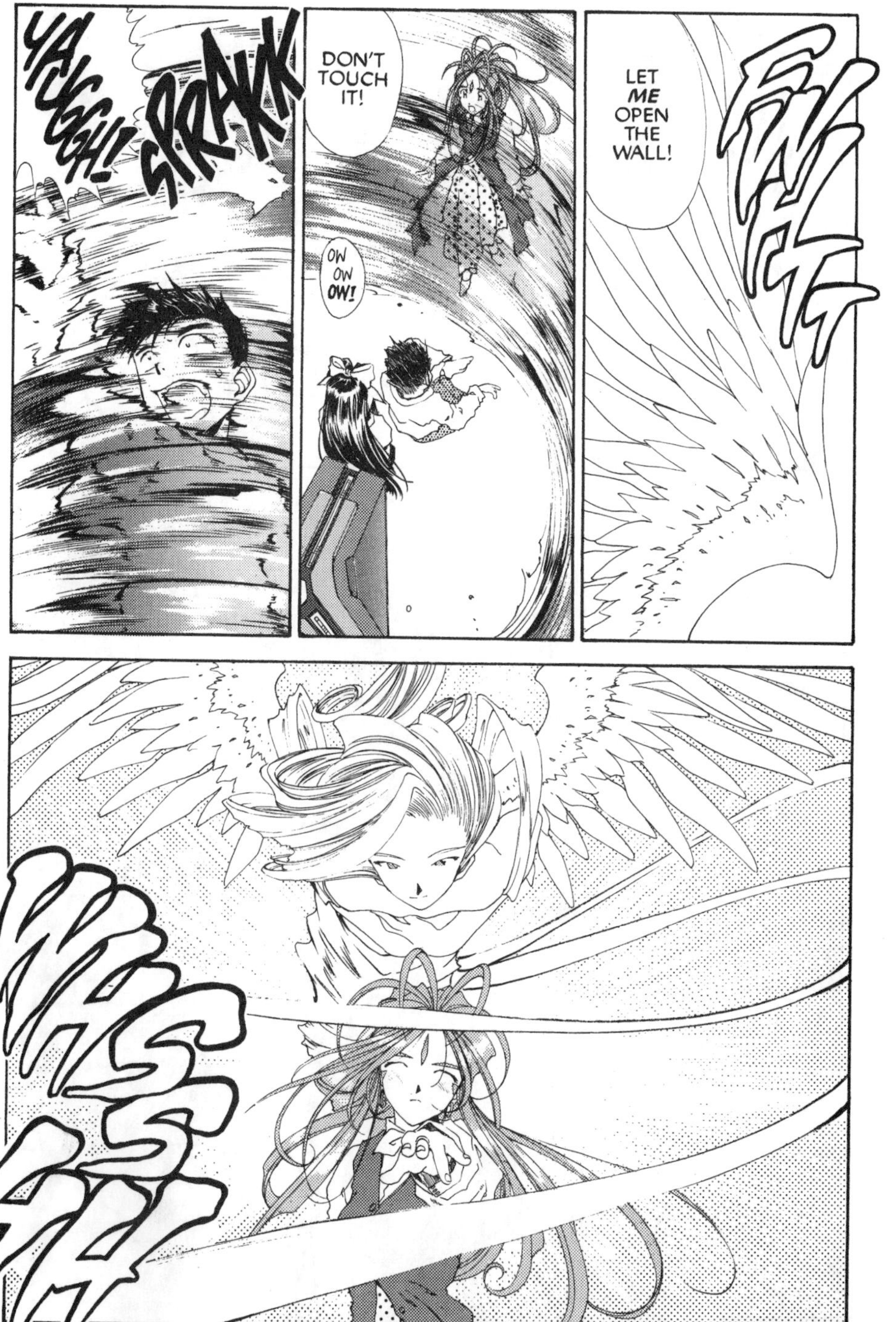
YAUGGH!
SPRAKK
DON'T TOUCH IT!
OW OW OW!
LET ME OPEN THE WALL!

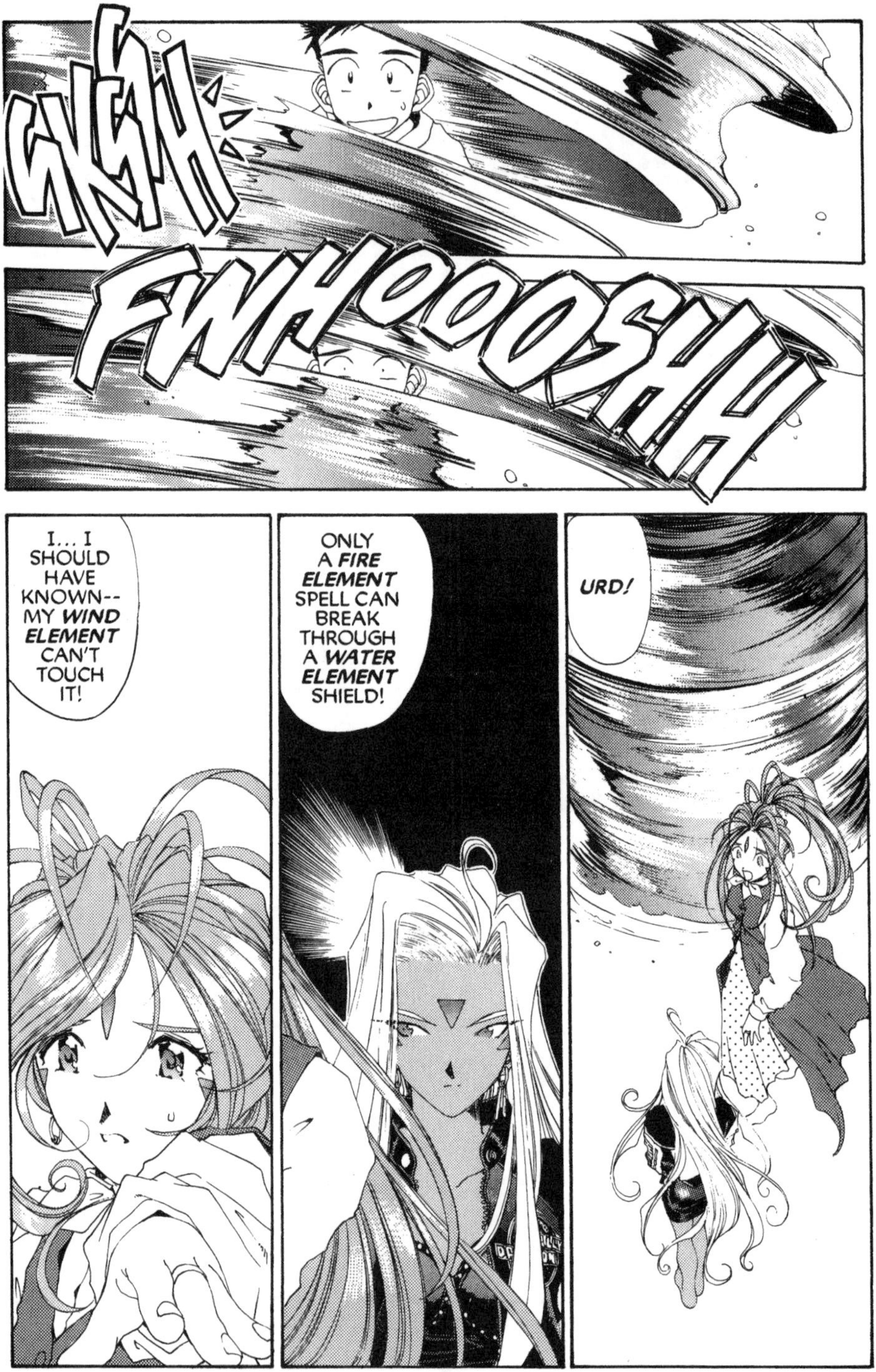
GKSH!
FWHOOOSHH
I... I SHOULD HAVE KNOWN-- MY WIND ELEMENT CAN'T TOUCH IT!
ONLY A FIRE ELEMENT SPELL CAN BREAK THROUGH A WATER ELEMENT SHIELD!
URD!

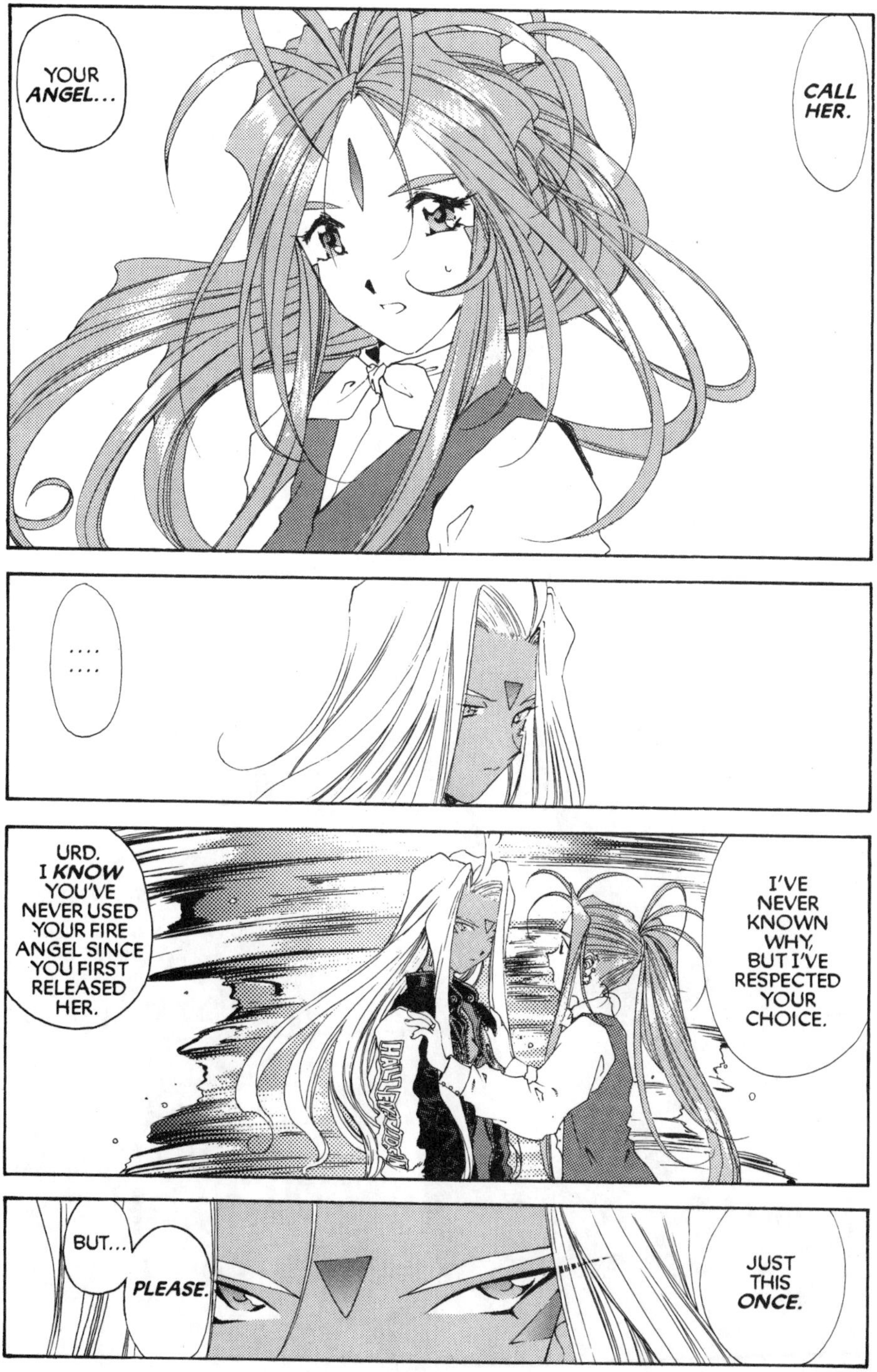
YOUR ANGEL...
CALL HER.
....
URD. I KNOW YOU'VE NEVER USED YOUR FIRE ANGEL SINCE YOU FIRST RELEASED HER.
I'VE NEVER KNOWN WHY, BUT I'VE RESPECTED YOUR CHOICE.
BUT...
PLEASE.
JUST THIS ONCE.

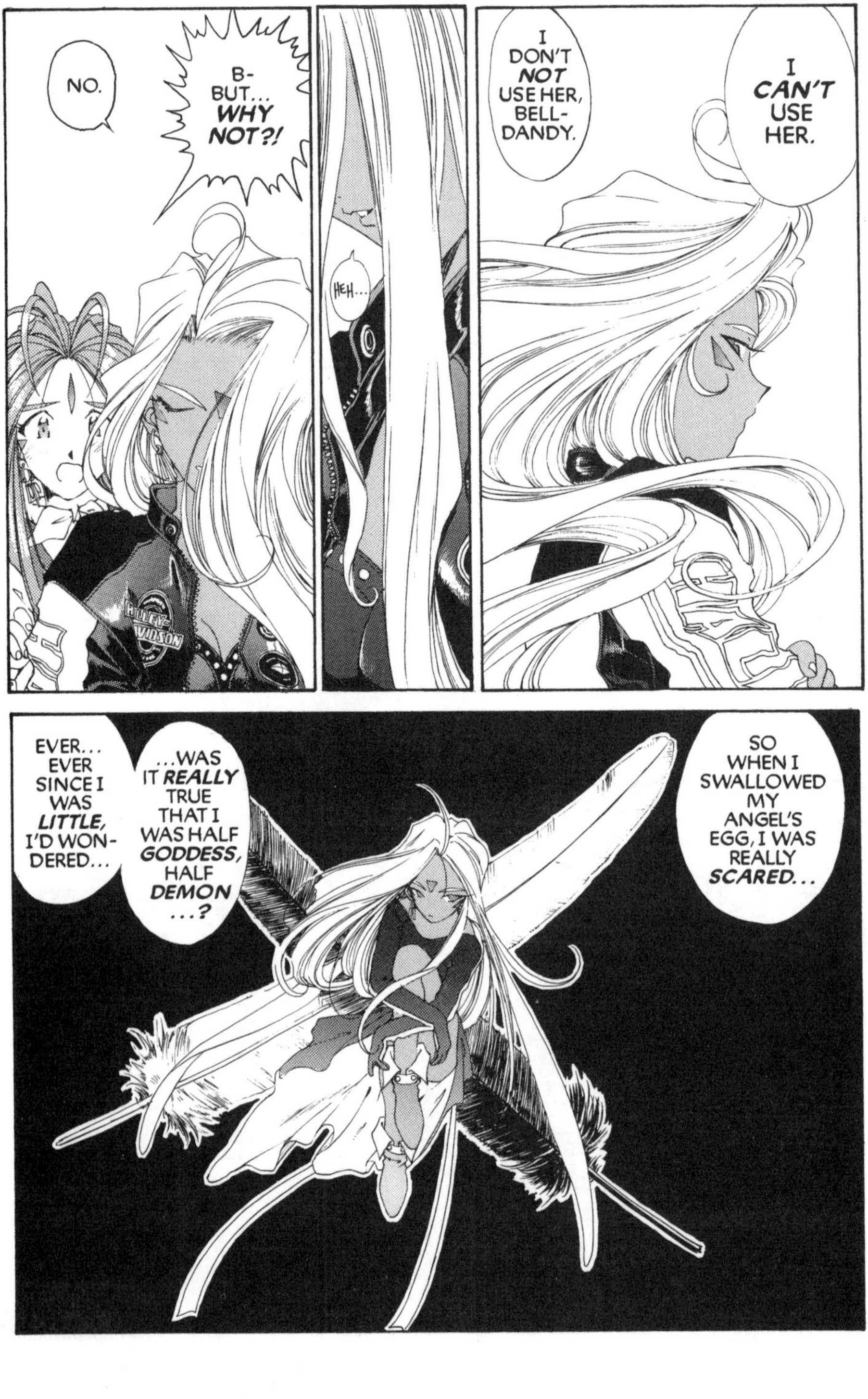
NO.
B-BUT... *WHY NOT?!*
HEH...
I DON'T *NOT* USE HER, BELL-DANDY.
I *CAN'T* USE HER.
EVER... EVER SINCE I WAS *LITTLE,* I'D WONDERED...
...WAS IT *REALLY* TRUE THAT I WAS HALF *GODDESS,* HALF *DEMON* ...?
SO WHEN I SWALLOWED MY ANGEL'S EGG, I WAS REALLY *SCARED...*

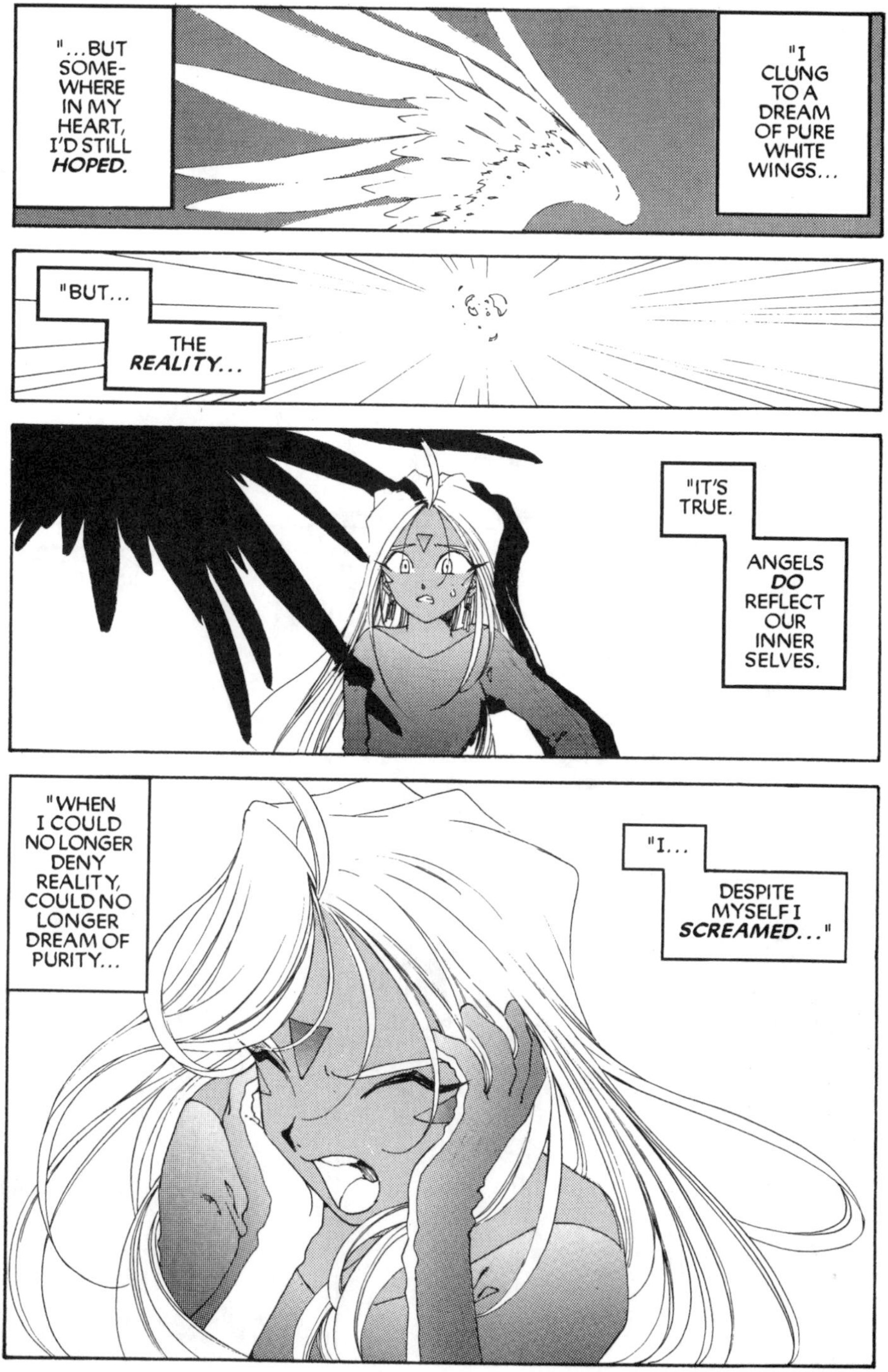
"...BUT SOME-WHERE IN MY HEART, I'D STILL ***HOPED.***
"I CLUNG TO A DREAM OF PURE WHITE WINGS...
"BUT...
THE ***REALITY...***
"IT'S TRUE.
ANGELS ***DO*** REFLECT OUR INNER SELVES.
"WHEN I COULD NO LONGER DENY REALITY, COULD NO LONGER DREAM OF PURITY...
"I...
DESPITE MYSELF I ***SCREAMED...***"

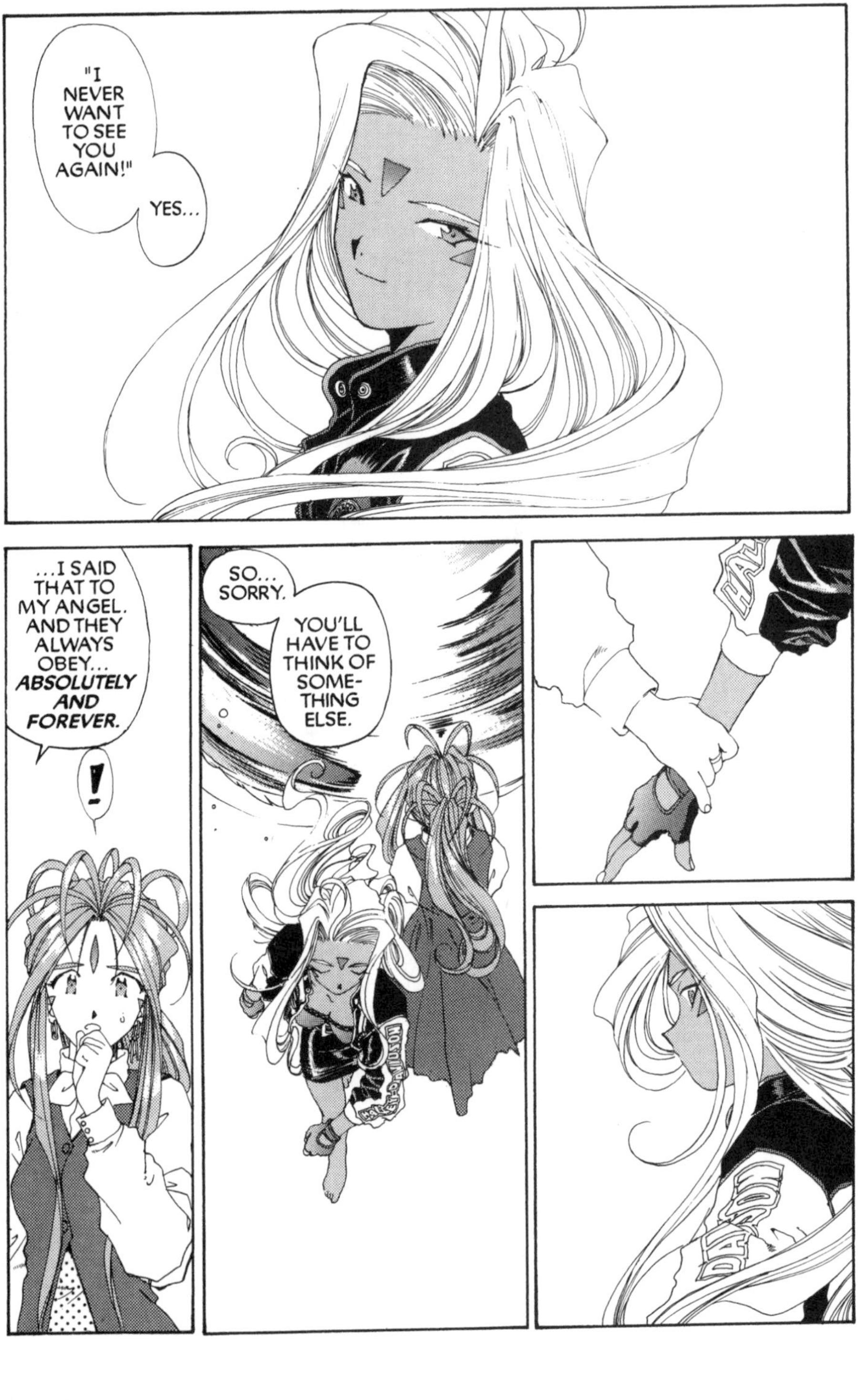
"I NEVER WANT TO SEE YOU AGAIN!"
YES...
...I SAID THAT TO MY ANGEL. AND THEY ALWAYS OBEY... *ABSOLUTELY AND FOREVER.*
!
SO... SORRY.
YOU'LL HAVE TO THINK OF SOMETHING ELSE.

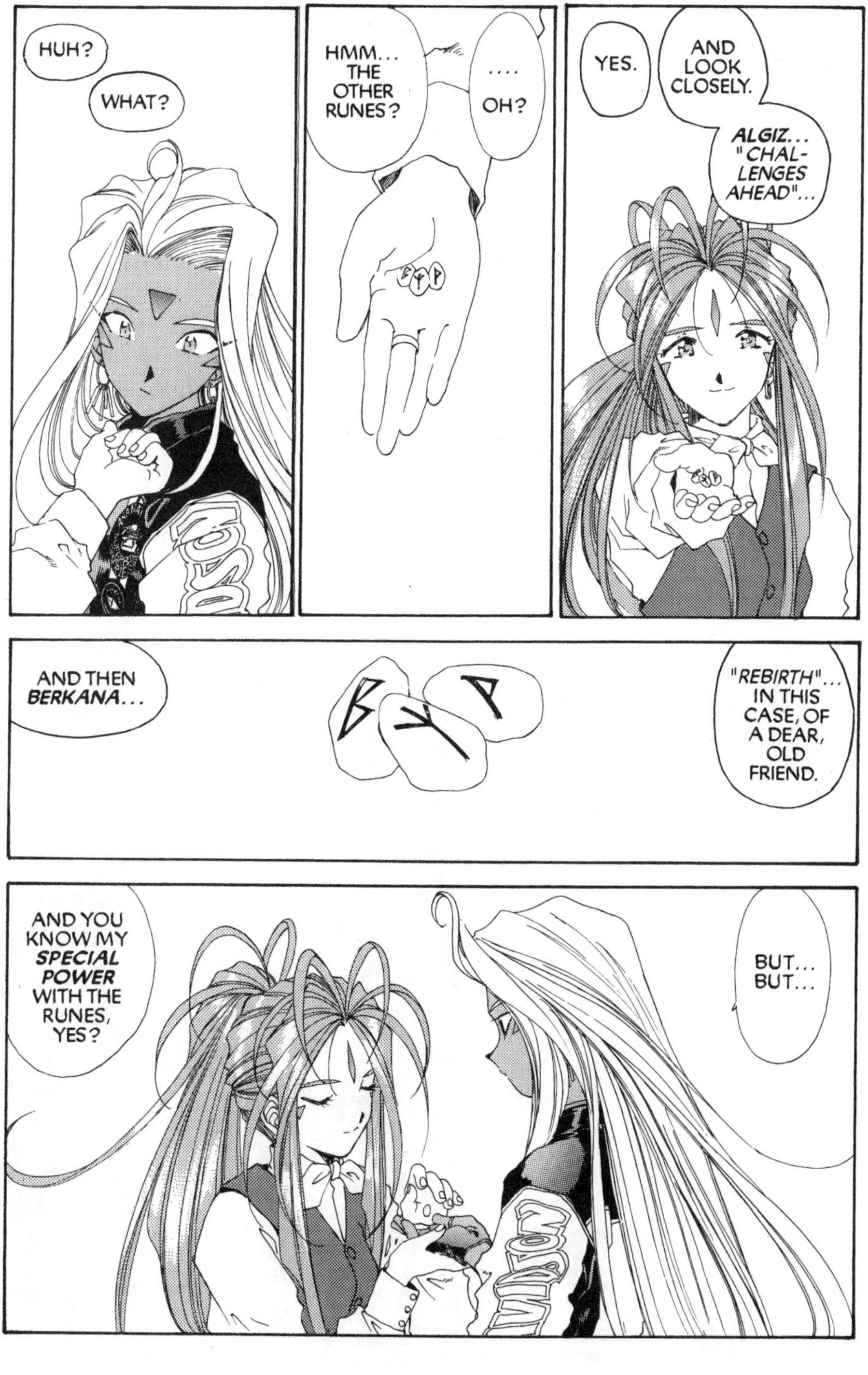
HUH?
WHAT?
HMM... THE OTHER RUNES?
.... OH?
YES.
AND LOOK CLOSELY.
ALGIZ... "CHALLENGES AHEAD"...
AND THEN *BERKANA*...
"*REBIRTH*"... IN THIS CASE, OF A DEAR, OLD FRIEND.
AND YOU KNOW MY *SPECIAL POWER* WITH THE RUNES, YES?
BUT... BUT...

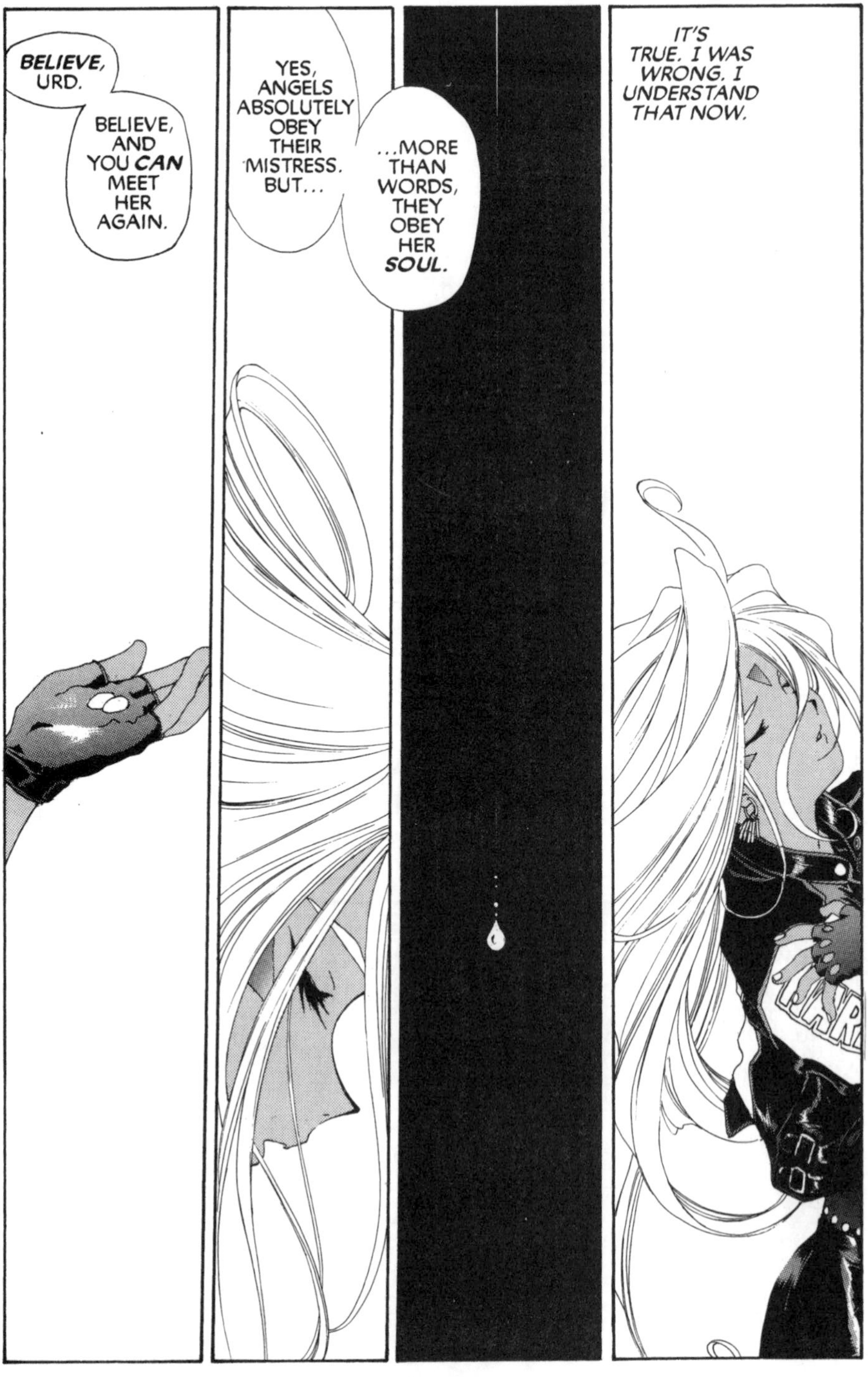
BELIEVE, URD.
BELIEVE, AND YOU CAN MEET HER AGAIN.
YES, ANGELS ABSOLUTELY OBEY THEIR MISTRESS. BUT...
...MORE THAN WORDS, THEY OBEY HER SOUL.
IT'S TRUE. I WAS WRONG. I UNDERSTAND THAT NOW.

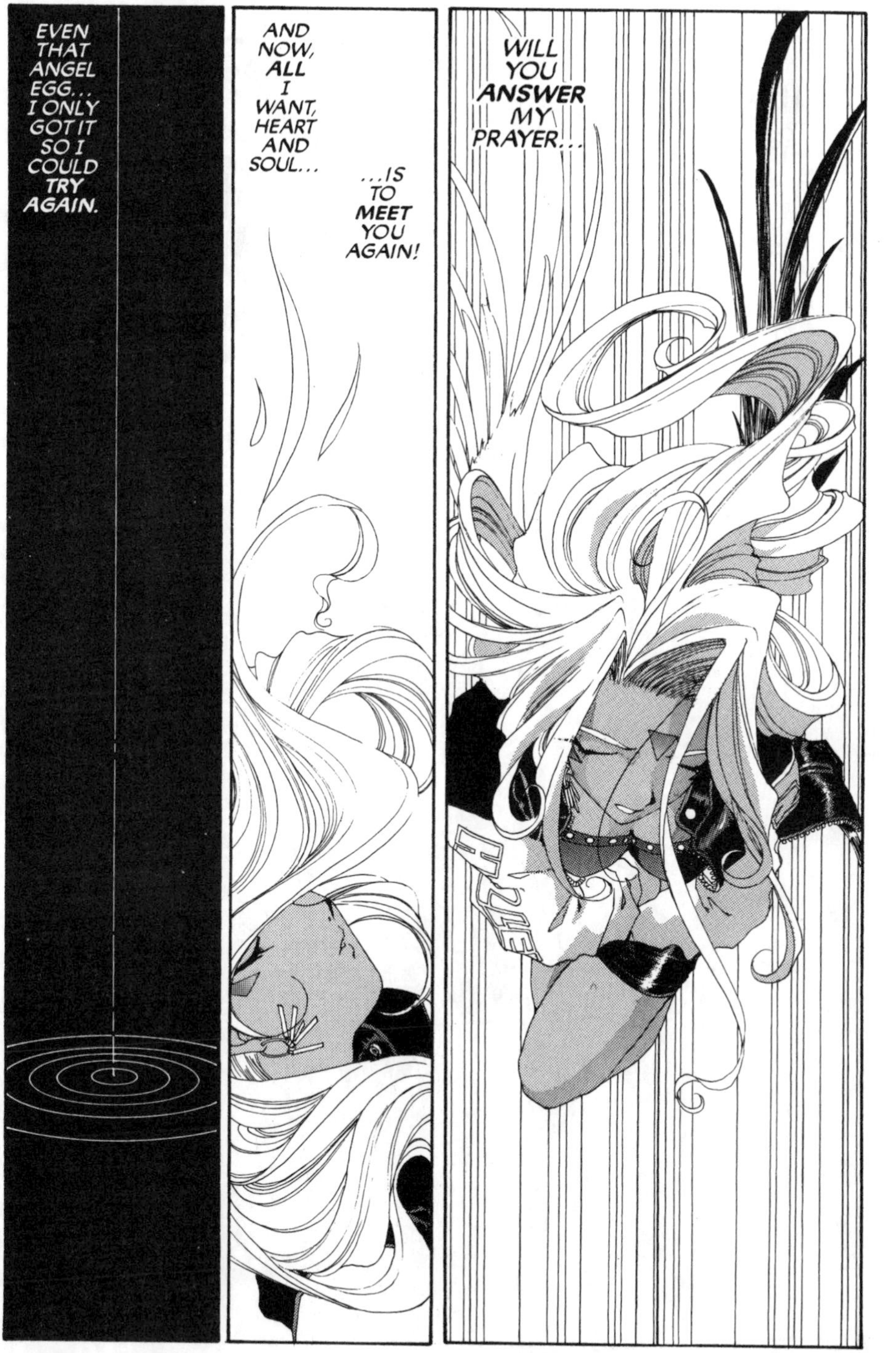
EVEN THAT ANGEL EGG... I ONLY GOT IT SO I COULD **TRY AGAIN.**
AND NOW, **ALL** I WANT, HEART AND SOUL...
...IS TO **MEET** YOU AGAIN!
WILL YOU **ANSWER** MY PRAYER...

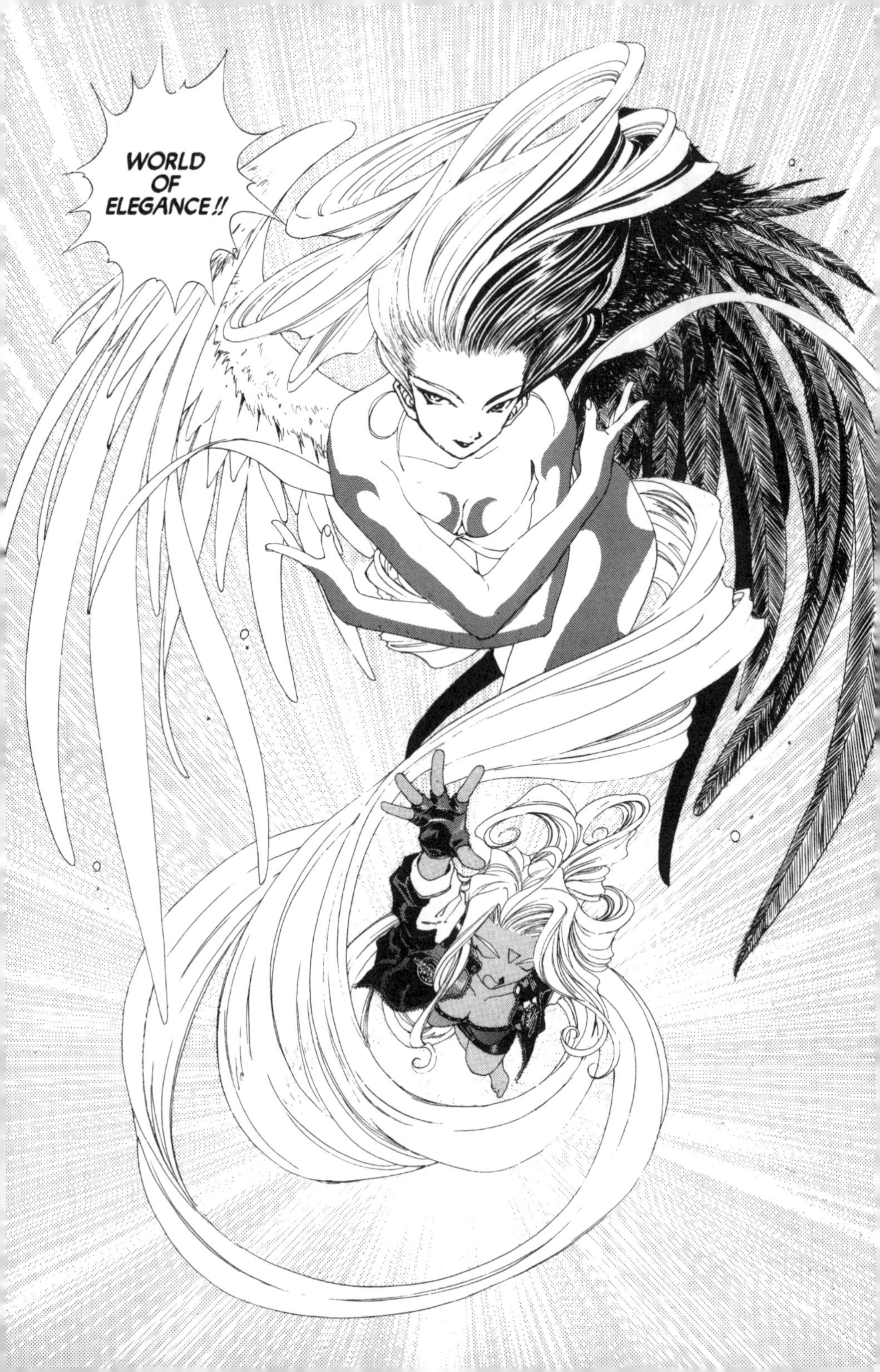
WORLD OF ELEGANCE!!

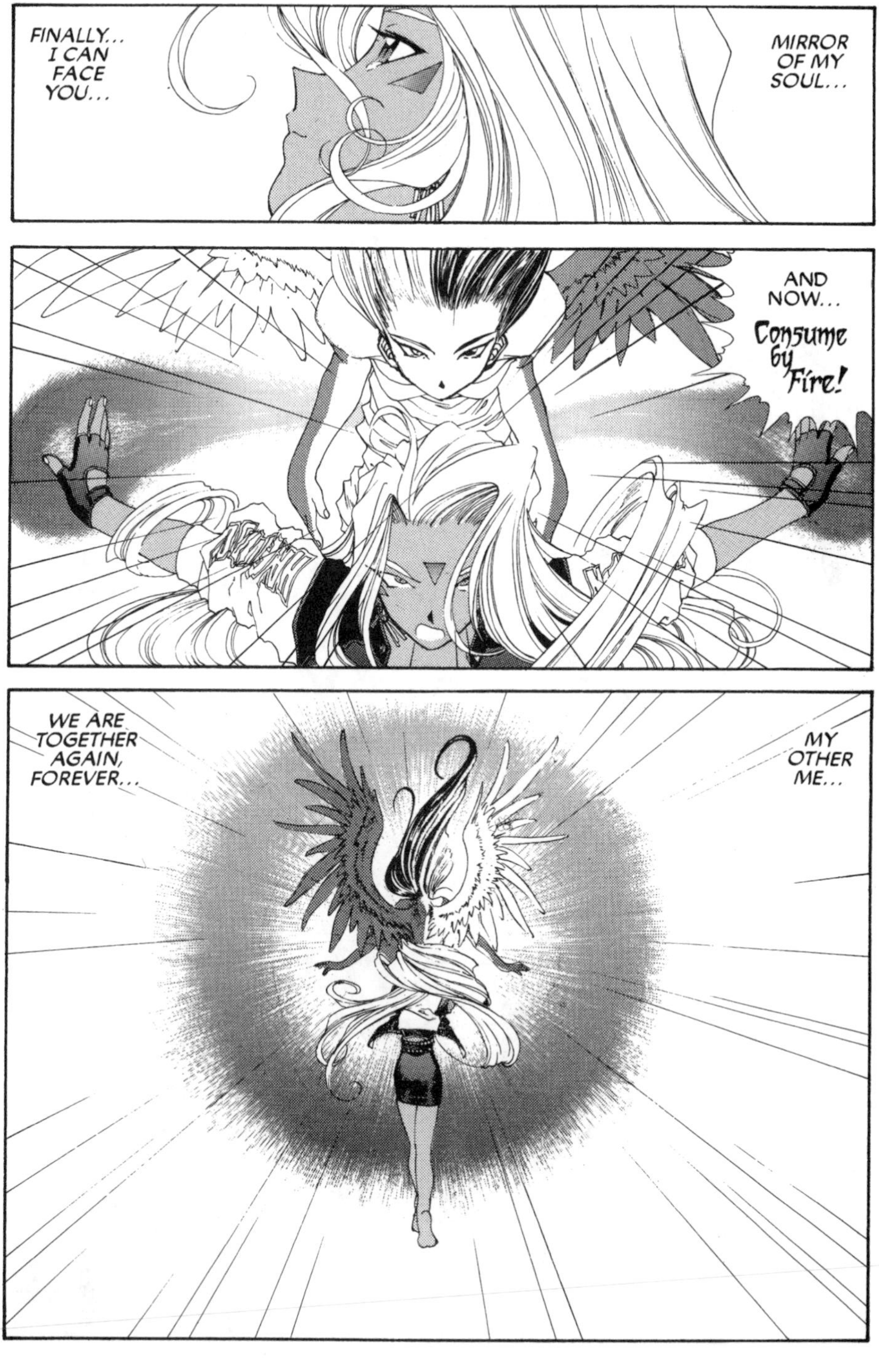
FINALLY... I CAN FACE YOU...
MIRROR OF MY SOUL...
AND NOW...
Consume by Fire!
WE ARE TOGETHER AGAIN, FOREVER...
MY OTHER ME...

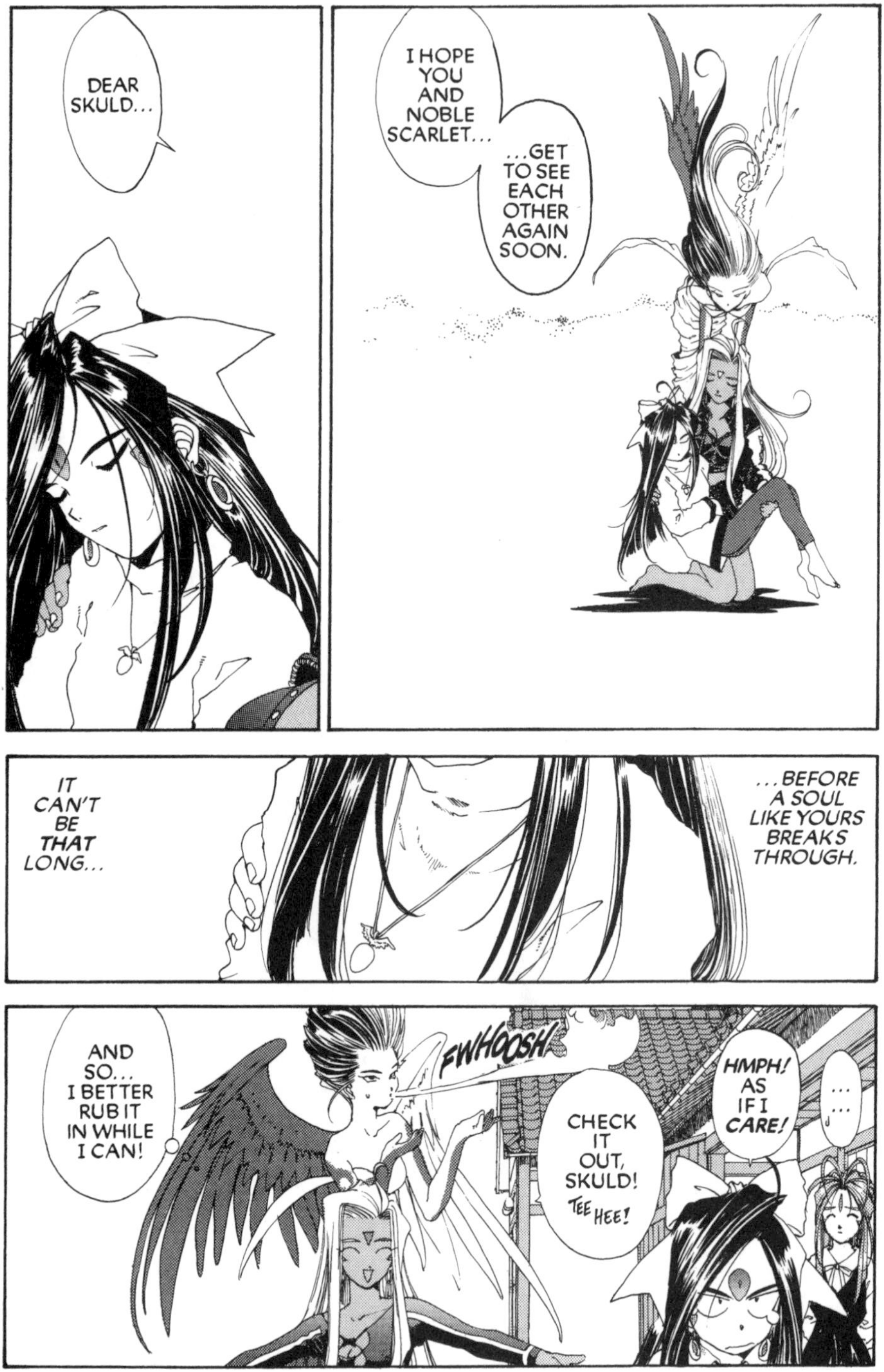
DEAR SKULD...
I HOPE YOU AND NOBLE SCARLET...
...GET TO SEE EACH OTHER AGAIN SOON.
IT CAN'T BE THAT LONG...
...BEFORE A SOUL LIKE YOURS BREAKS THROUGH.
AND SO... I BETTER RUB IT IN WHILE I CAN!
FWHOOSH
CHECK IT OUT, SKULD!
TEE HEE!
HMPH! AS IF I CARE!
......

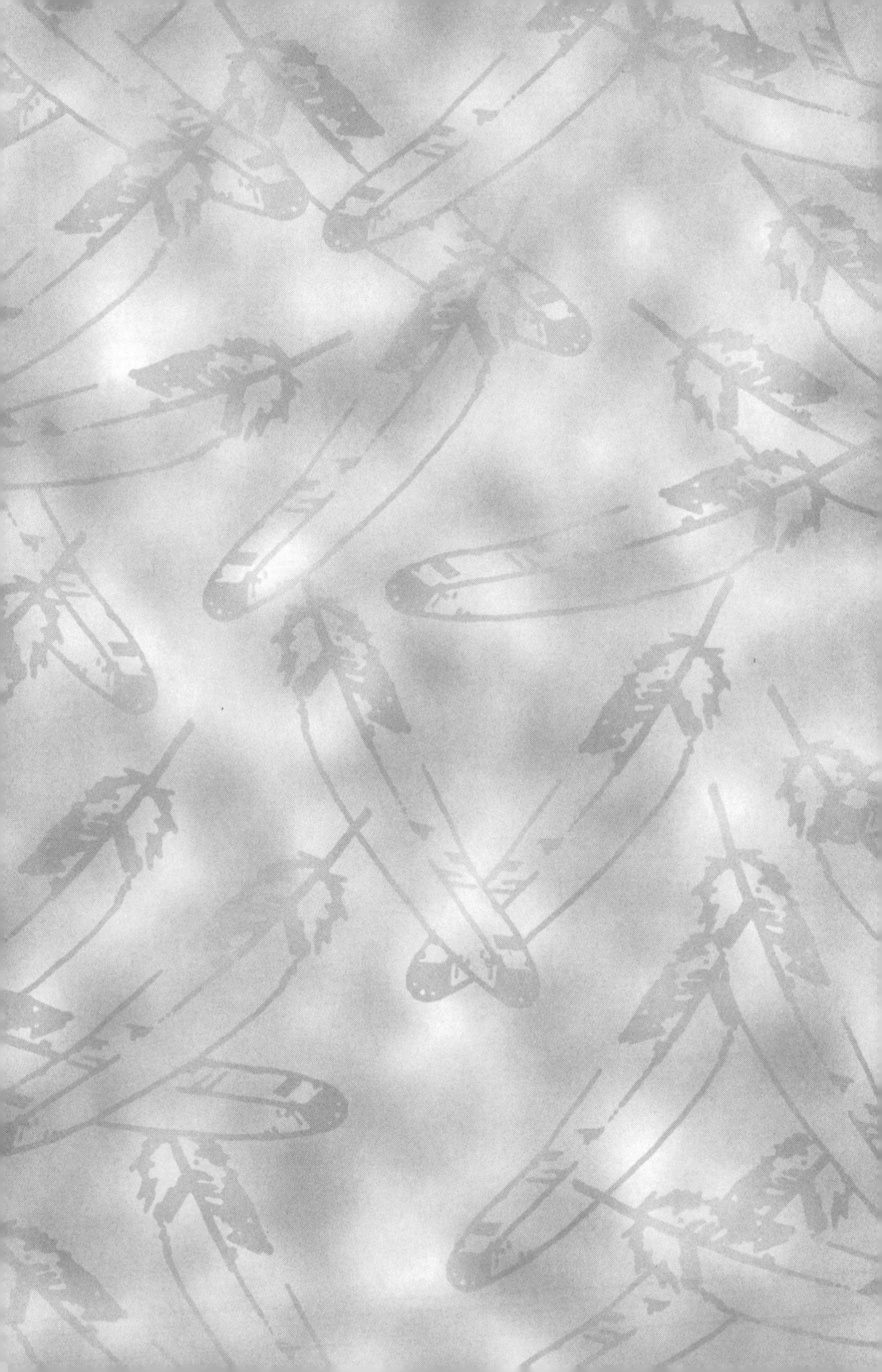

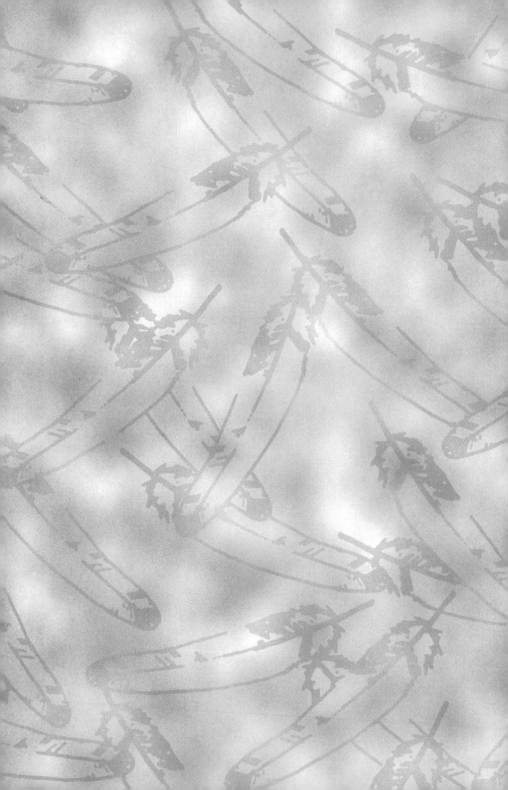

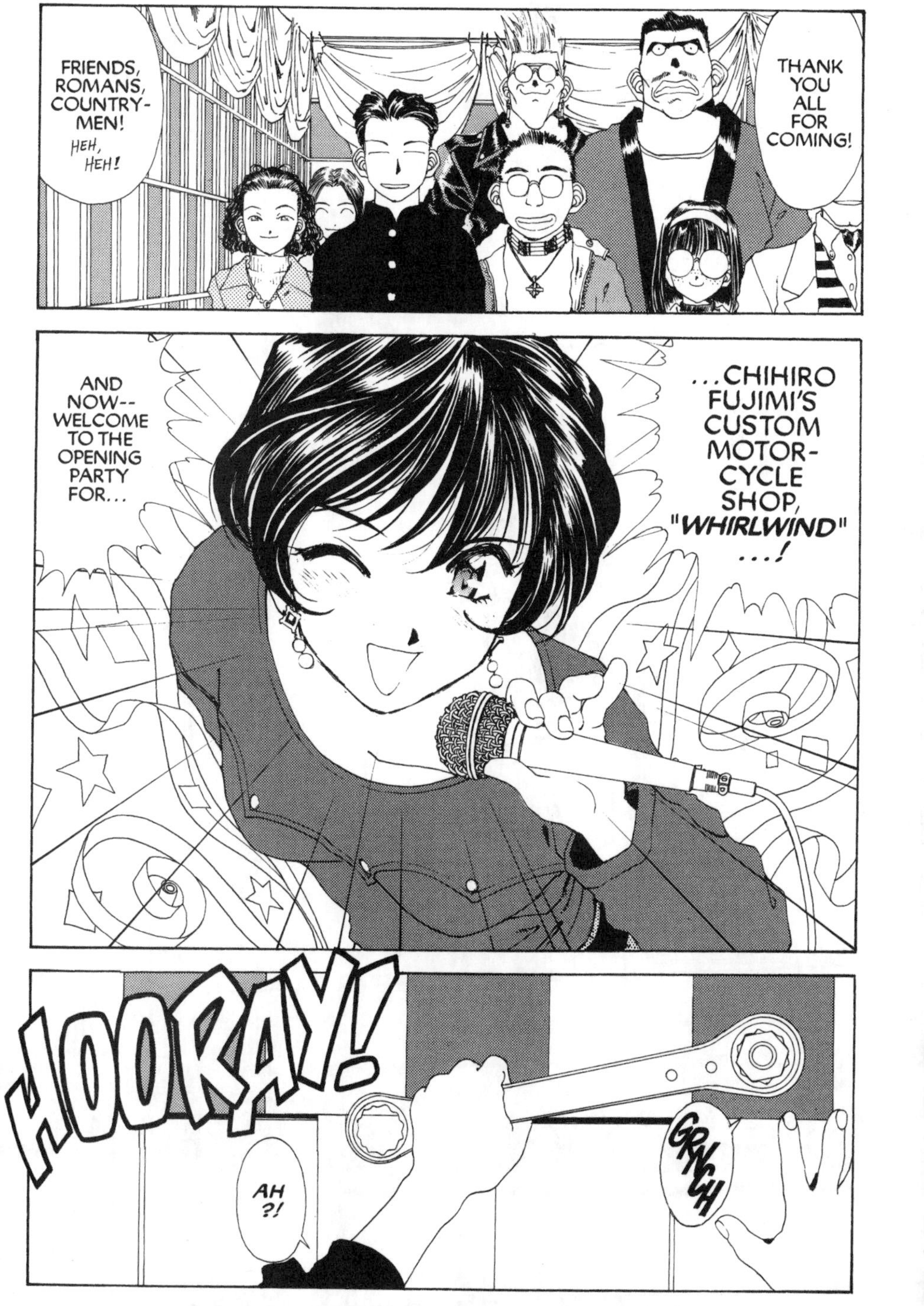
FRIENDS, ROMANS, COUNTRY-MEN!
HEH, HEH!
THANK YOU ALL FOR COMING!
AND NOW-- WELCOME TO THE OPENING PARTY FOR...
...CHIHIRO FUJIMI'S CUSTOM MOTOR-CYCLE SHOP, "WHIRLWIND" ...!
HOORAY!
AH ?!
GRNCH

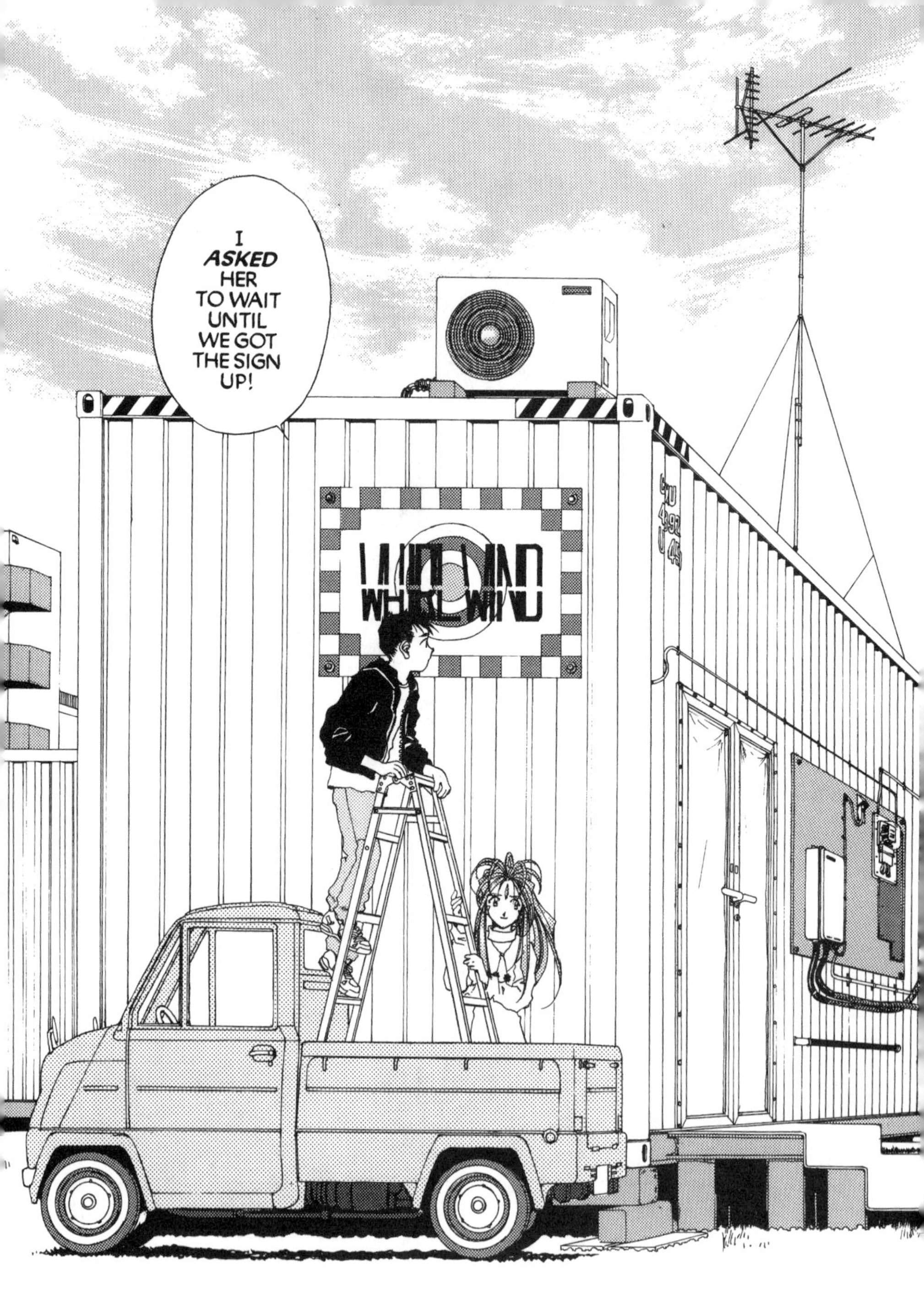
I *ASKED* HER TO WAIT UNTIL WE GOT THE SIGN UP!
WHIRLWIND

NEVER LET GO

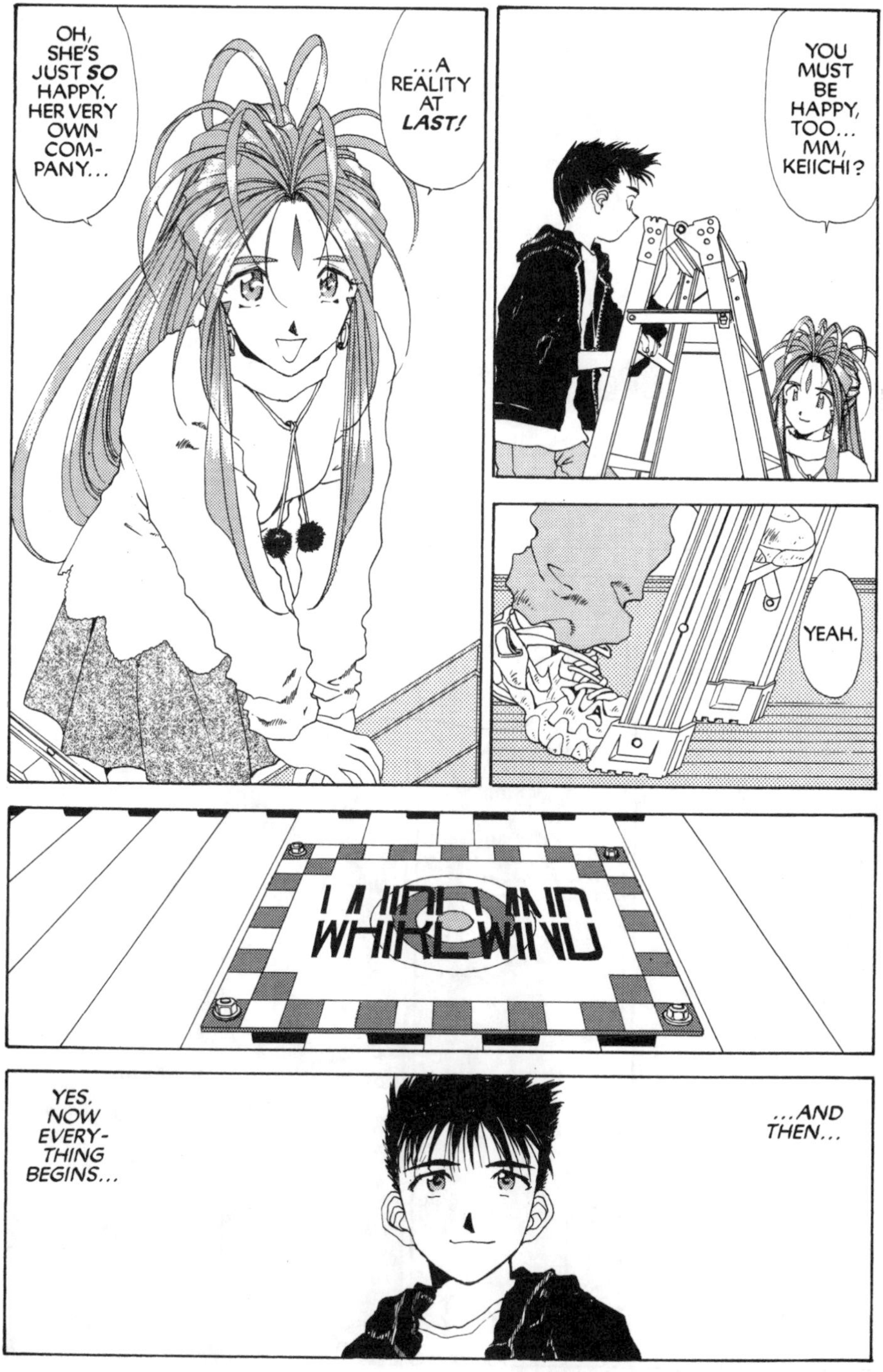

OH, SHE'S JUST **SO** HAPPY. HER VERY OWN COM-PANY...
...A REALITY AT ***LAST!***
YOU MUST BE HAPPY, TOO... MM, KEIICHI?
YEAH.
WHIRLWIND
YES. NOW EVERY-THING BEGINS...
...AND THEN...

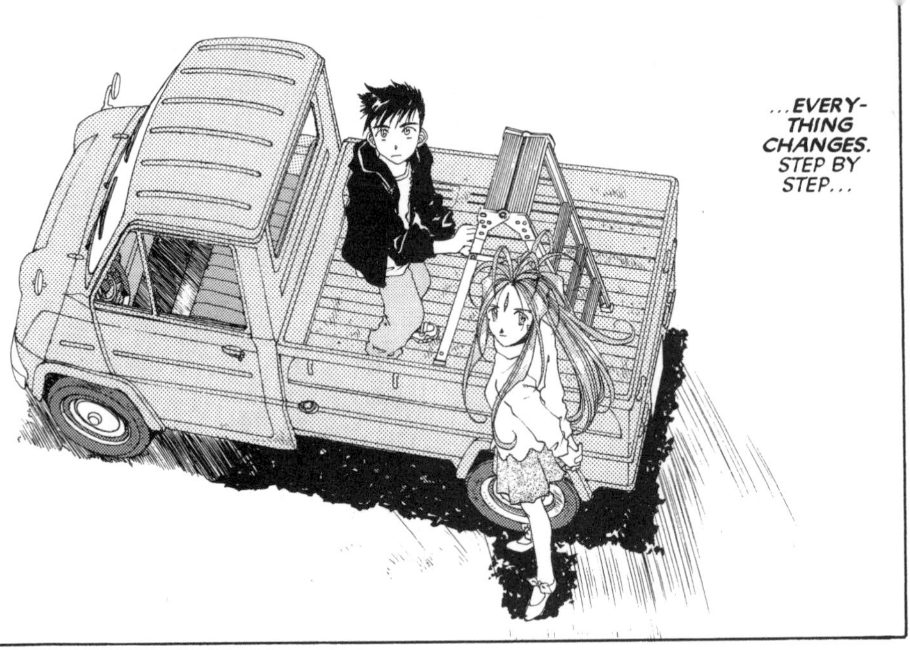
...EVERY-THING CHANGES. STEP BY STEP...

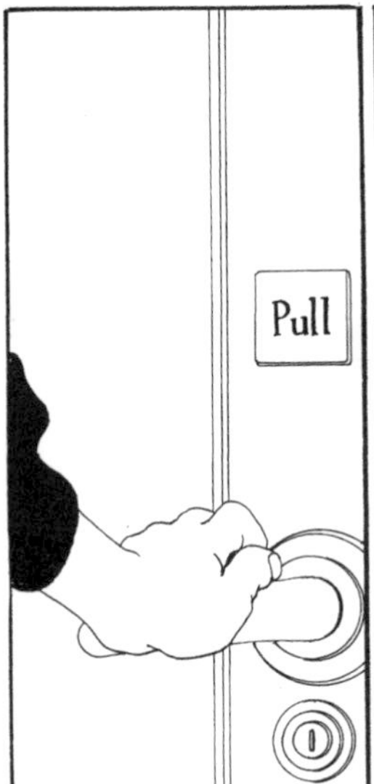
Pull

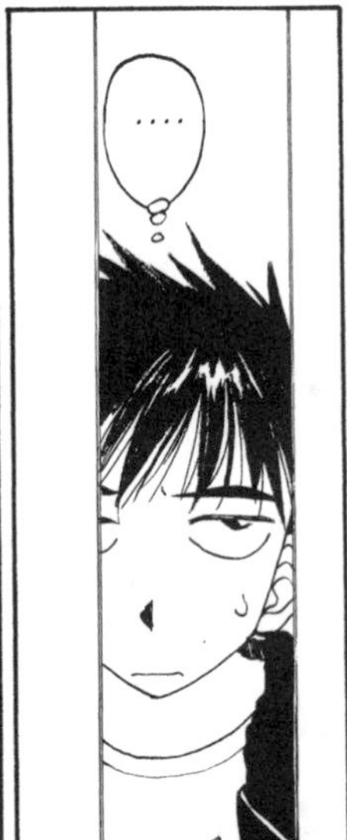
....
Push

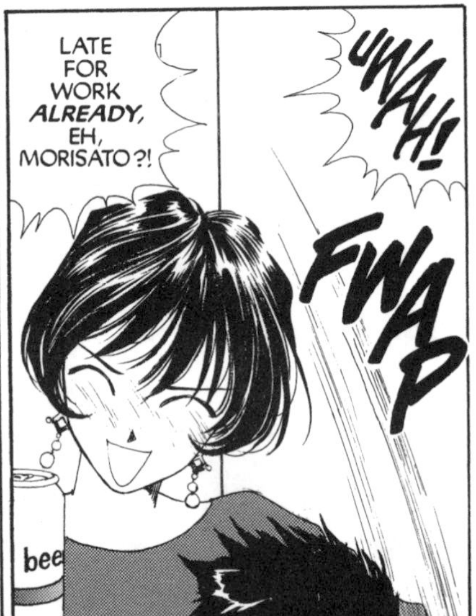
LATE FOR WORK *ALREADY,* EH, MORISATO?!
UWAH!
FWAP

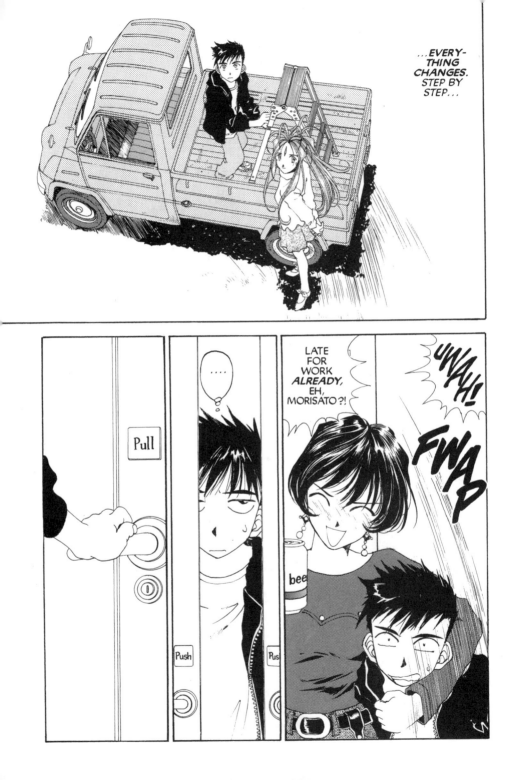

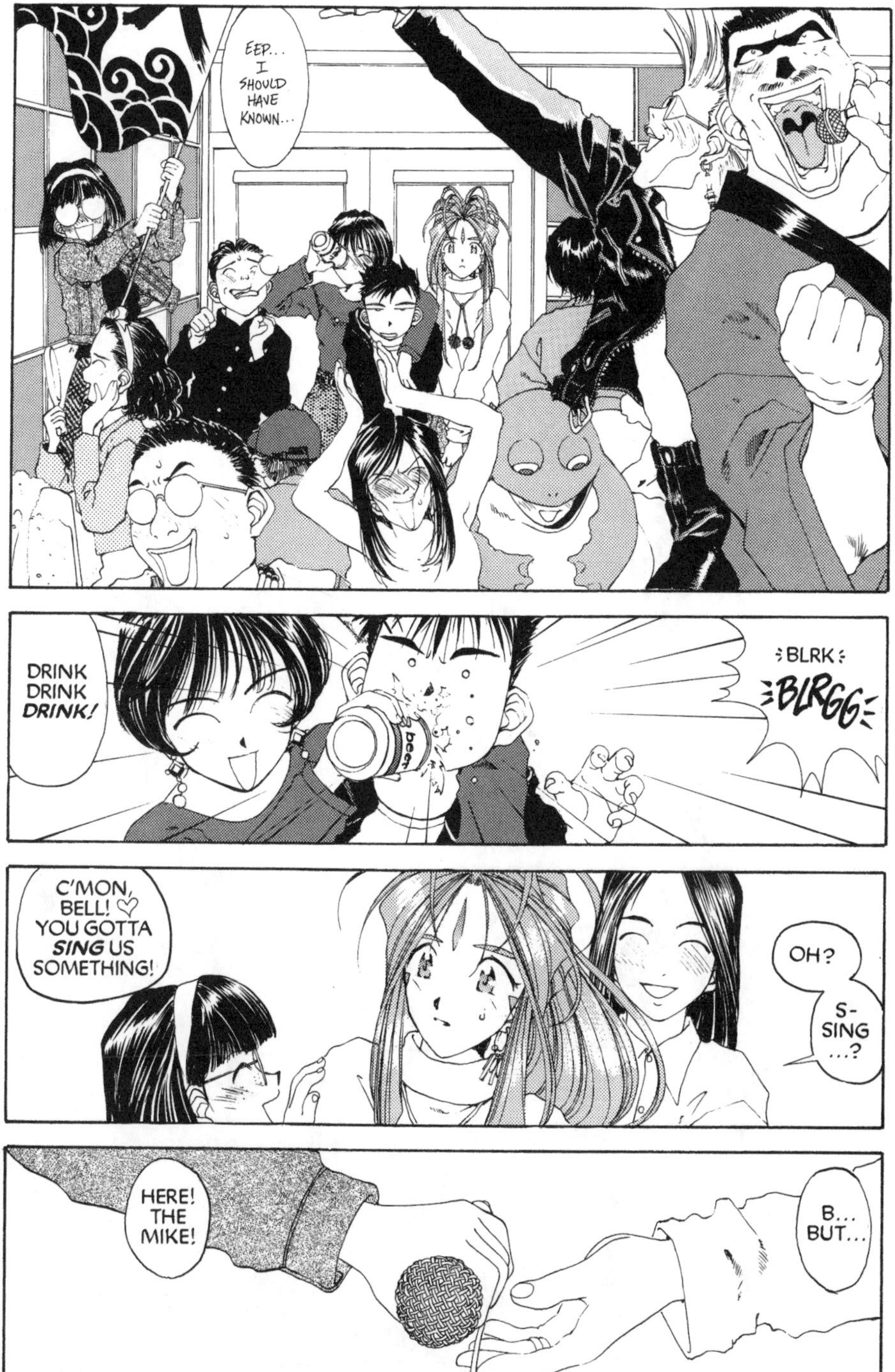
EEP... I SHOULD HAVE KNOWN...
DRINK DRINK DRINK!
BLRK
BLRGG
C'MON, BELL! ♡ YOU GOTTA SING US SOMETHING!
OH?
S-SING ...?
HERE! THE MIKE!
B... BUT...

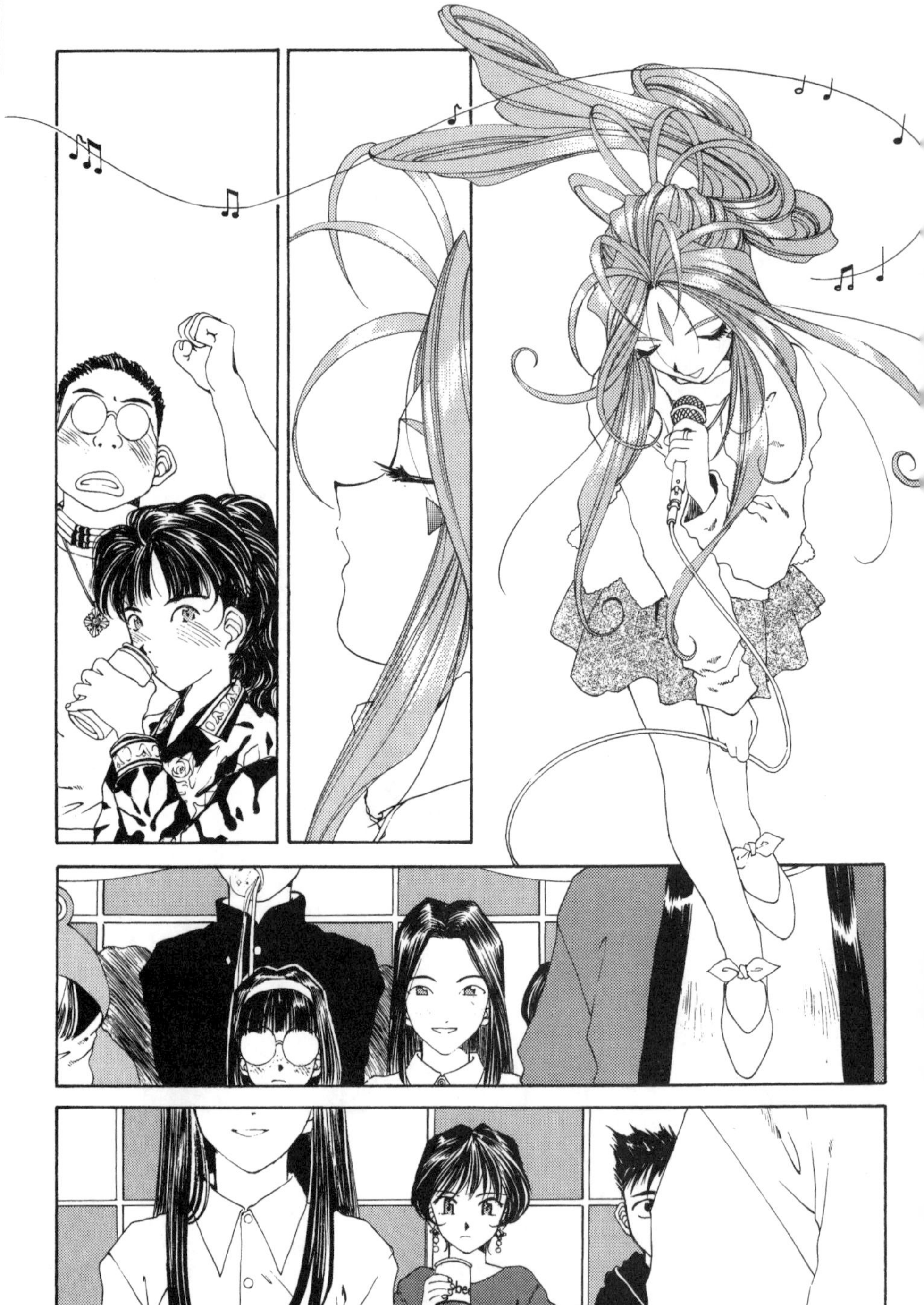

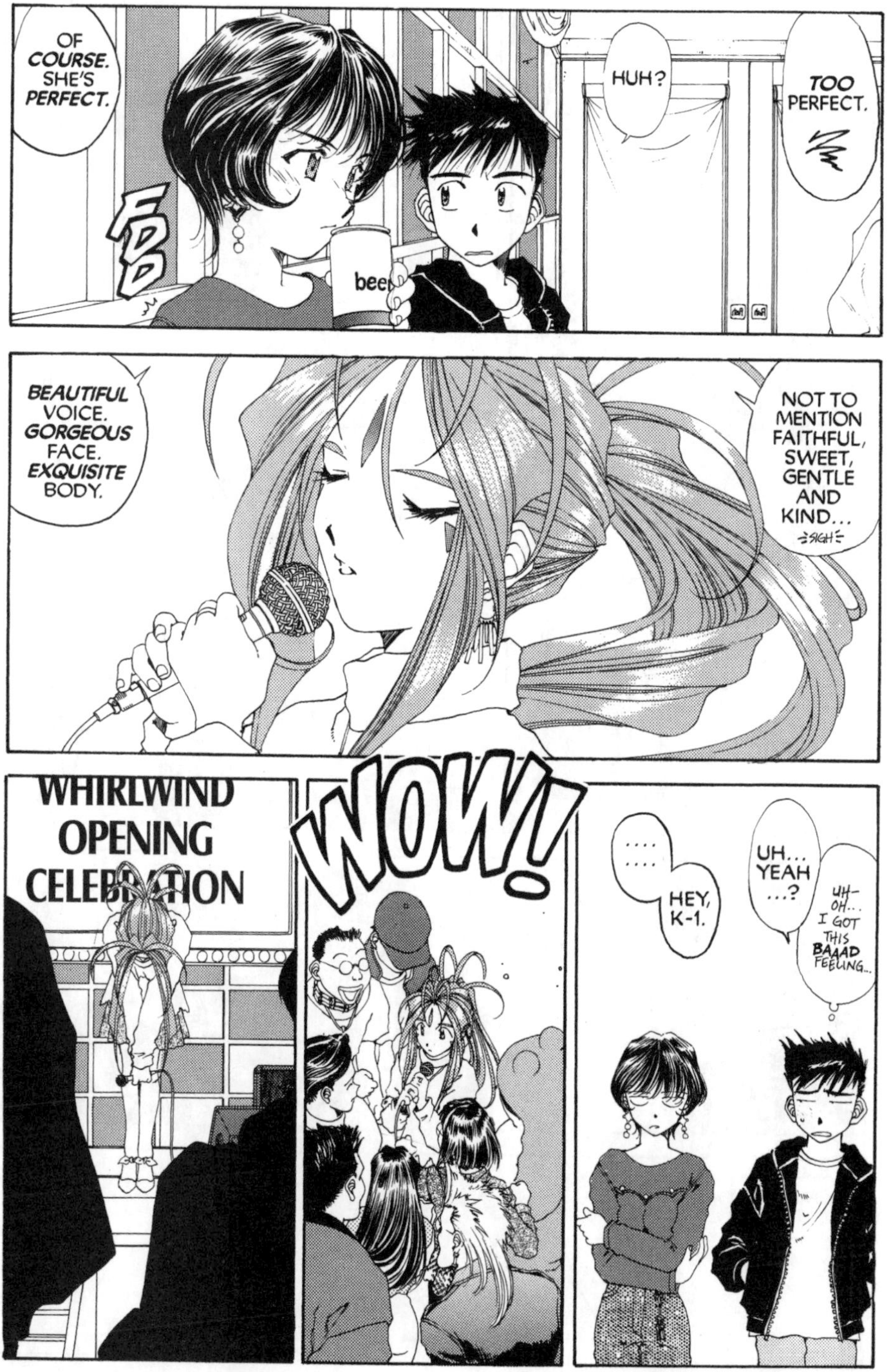
OF COURSE. SHE'S PERFECT.
FDD
beer
HUH?
TOO PERFECT.
BEAUTIFUL VOICE. GORGEOUS FACE. EXQUISITE BODY.
NOT TO MENTION FAITHFUL, SWEET, GENTLE AND KIND...
SIGH
WHIRLWIND OPENING CELEBRATION
WOW!
....
....
HEY, K-1.
UH... YEAH ...?
UH-OH... I GOT THIS BAAAD FEELING...

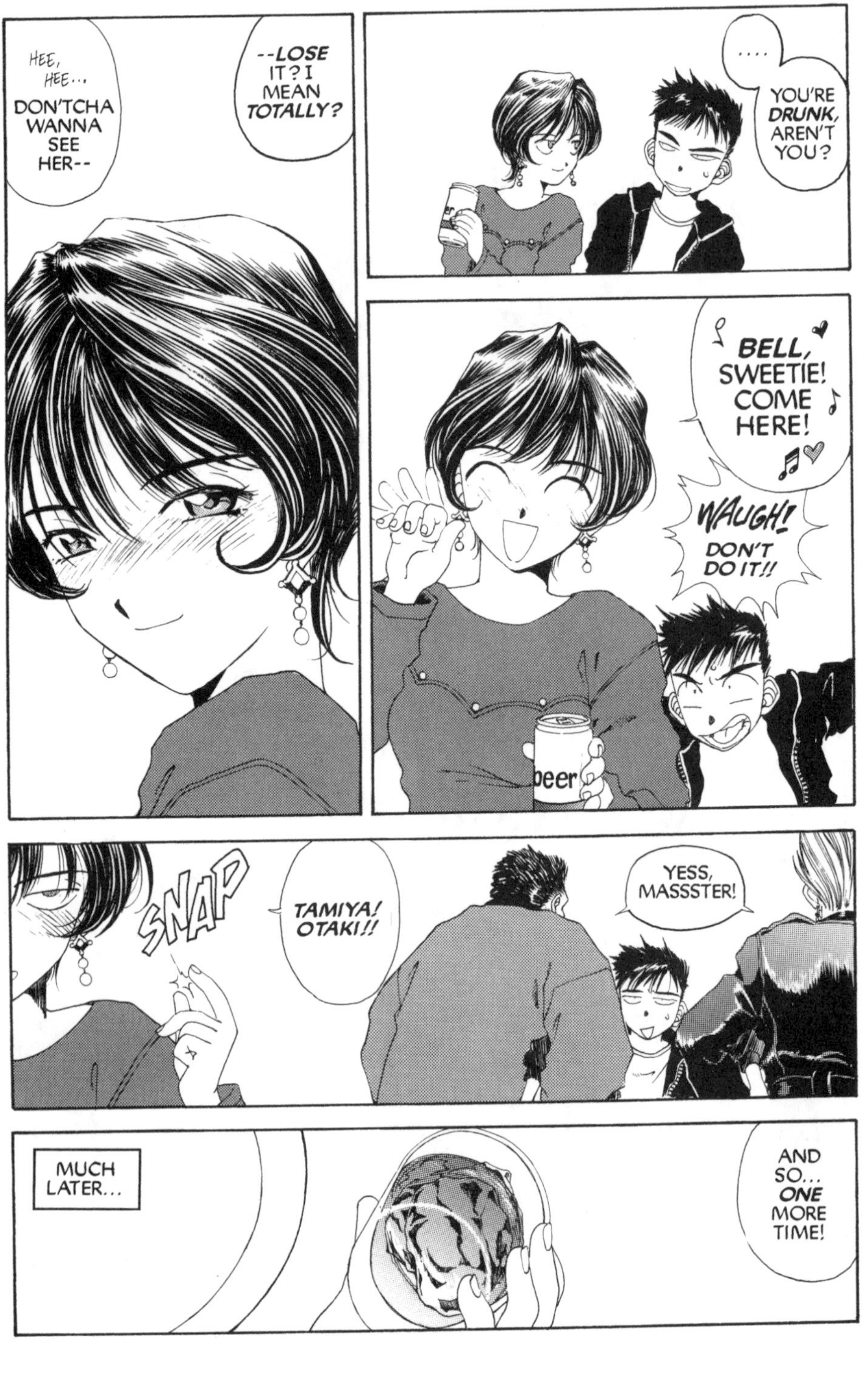
HEE, HEE... DON'TCHA WANNA SEE HER--
--LOSE IT? I MEAN TOTALLY?
....
YOU'RE DRUNK, AREN'T YOU?
BELL, SWEETIE! COME HERE!
WAUGH! DON'T DO IT!!
beer
SNAP
TAMIYA! OTAKI!!
YESS, MASSSTER!
MUCH LATER...
AND SO... ONE MORE TIME!

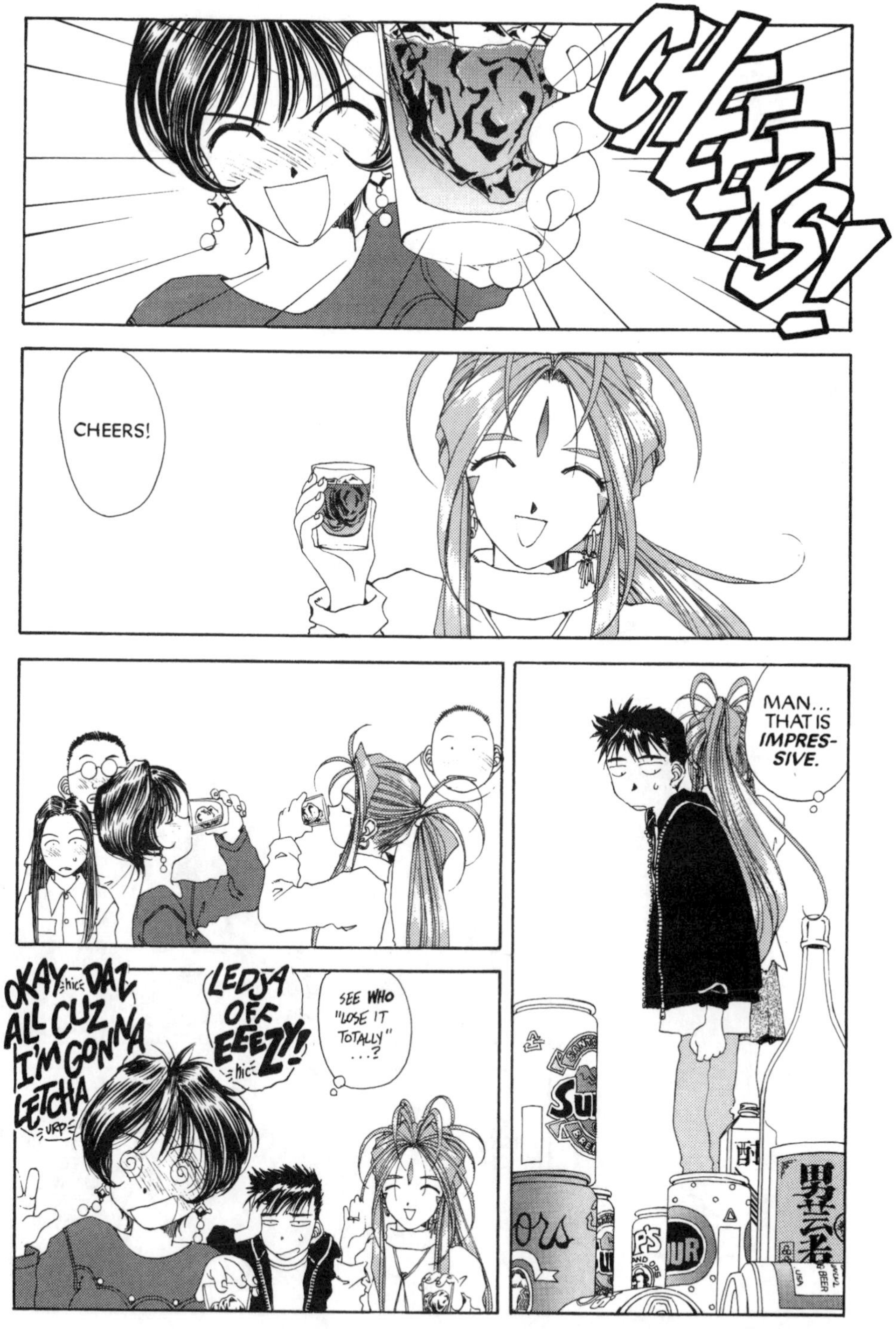
CHEERS!
CHEERS!
OKAY—hic—DAZ ALL CUZ I'M GONNA LETCHA
URP
LEDJA OFF EEEZY!
hic
SEE WHO "LOSE IT TOTALLY" ...?
MAN... THAT IS IMPRESSIVE.

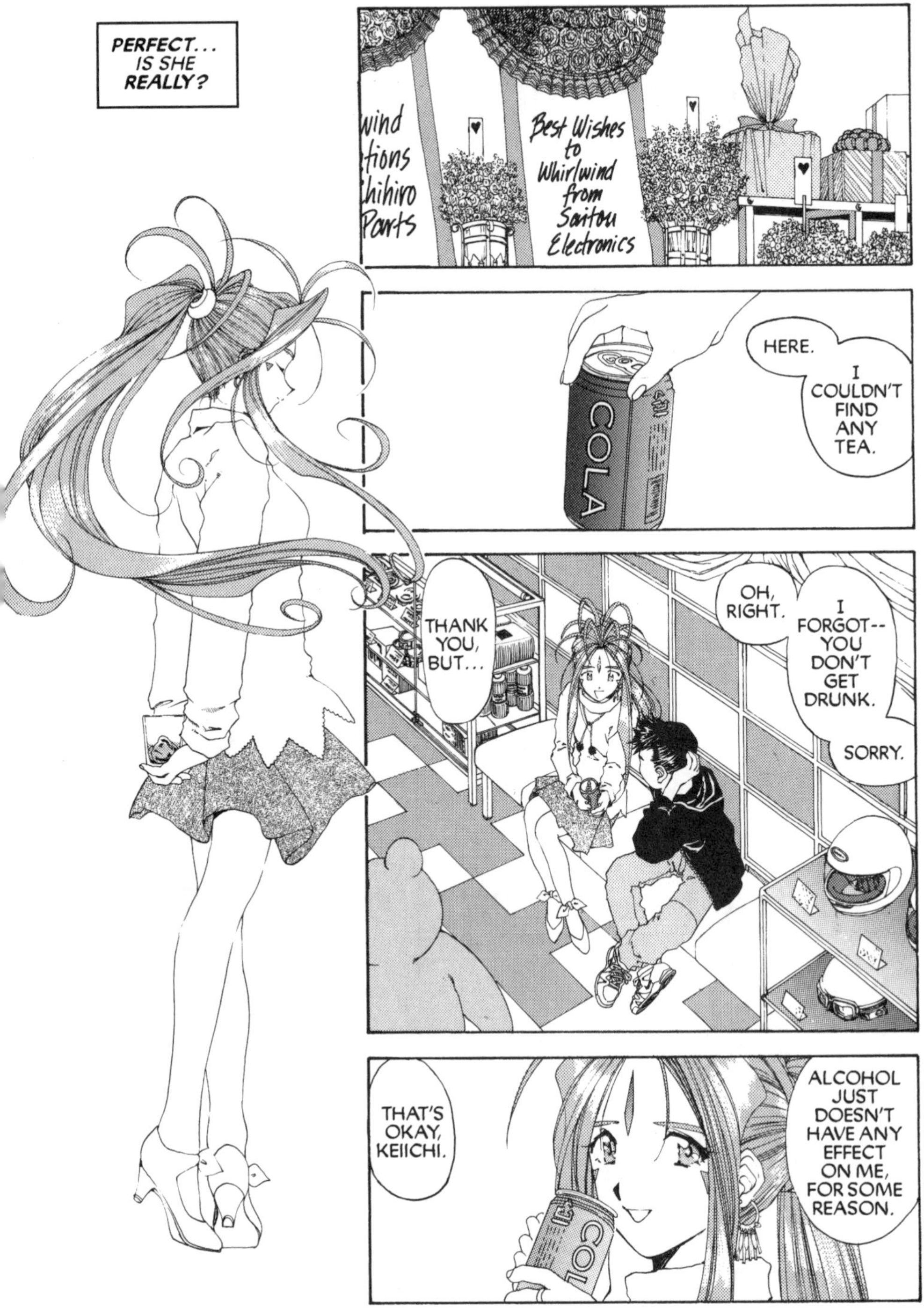
PERFECT... IS SHE REALLY?
Best Wishes to Whirlwind from Saitou Electronics
HERE.
I COULDN'T FIND ANY TEA.
COLA
THANK YOU, BUT...
OH, RIGHT.
I FORGOT--YOU DON'T GET DRUNK.
SORRY.
THAT'S OKAY, KEIICHI.
ALCOHOL JUST DOESN'T HAVE ANY EFFECT ON ME, FOR SOME REASON.

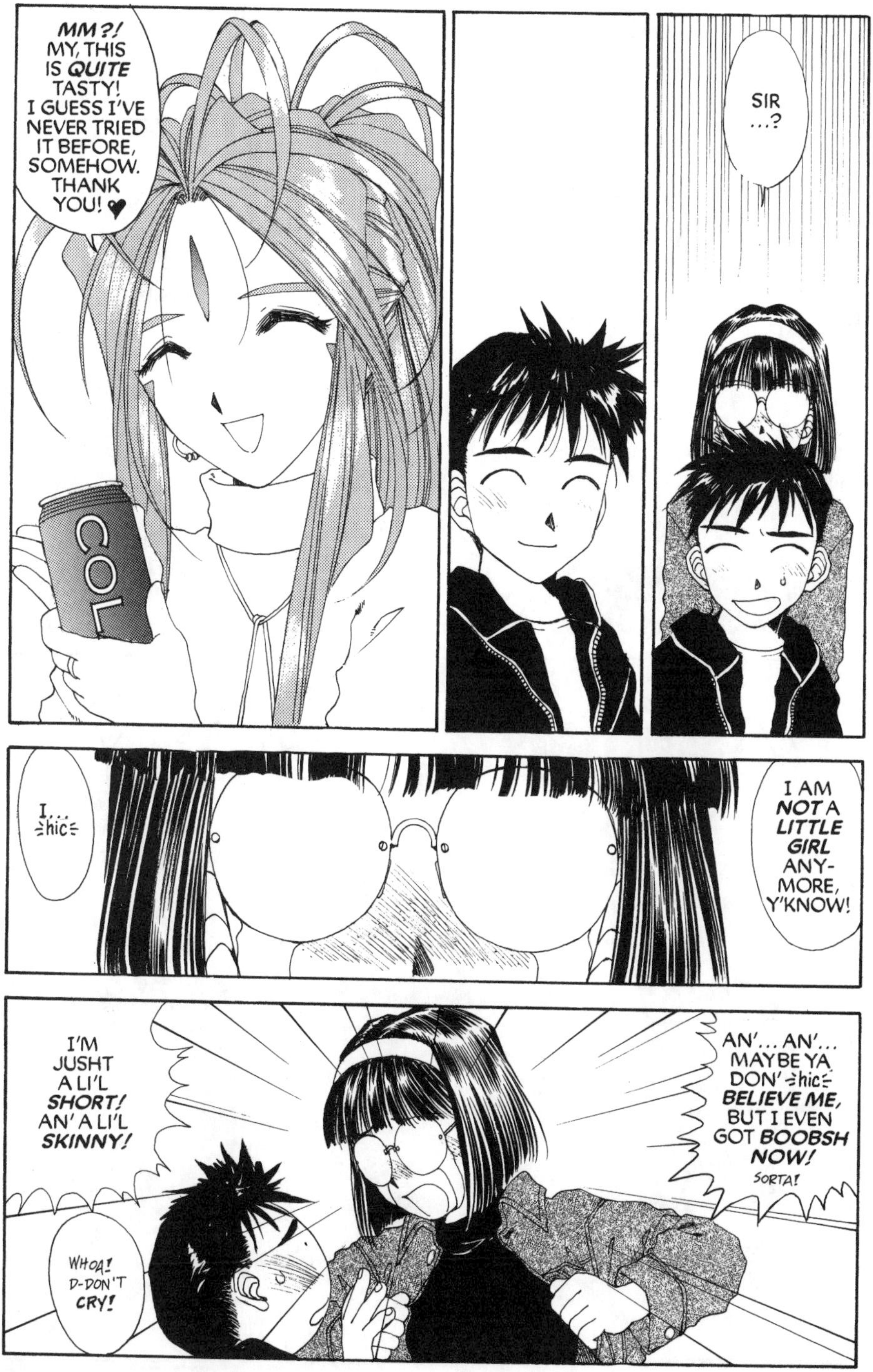
MM?! MY, THIS IS QUITE TASTY! I GUESS I'VE NEVER TRIED IT BEFORE, SOMEHOW. THANK YOU! ♥
COL
SIR ...?
I... hic
I AM NOT A LITTLE GIRL ANY-MORE, Y'KNOW!
I'M JUSHT A LI'L SHORT! AN' A LI'L SKINNY!
AN'... AN'... MAYBE YA DON' hic BELIEVE ME, BUT I EVEN GOT BOOBSH NOW!
SORTA!
WHOA! D-DON'T CRY!

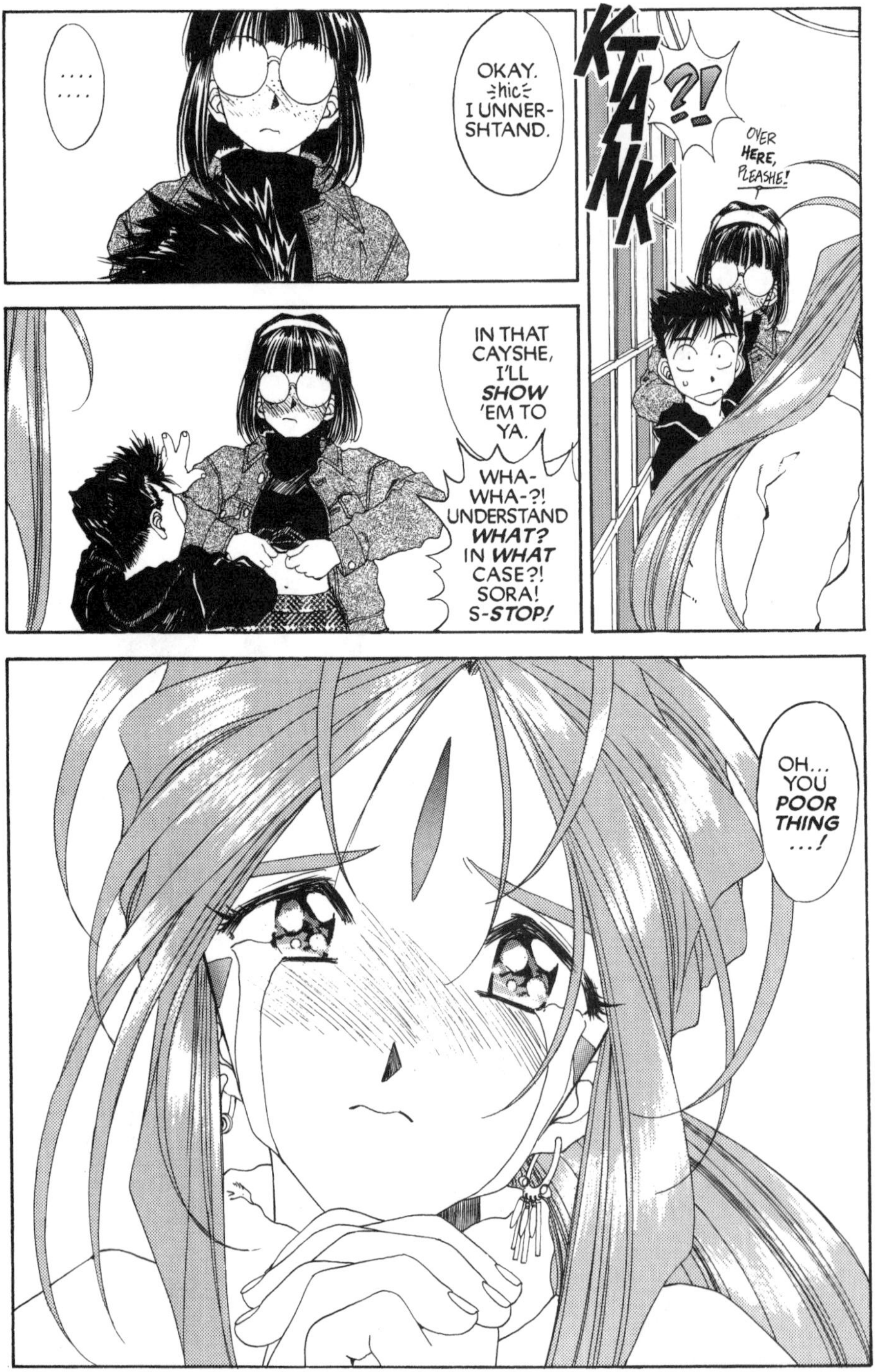
....
....
OKAY. hic I UNNER-SHTAND.
KTANK
?!
OVER HERE, PLEASHE!
IN THAT CAYSHE, I'LL SHOW 'EM TO YA.
WHA-WHA-?! UNDERSTAND WHAT? IN WHAT CASE?! SORA! S-STOP!
OH... YOU POOR THING ...!

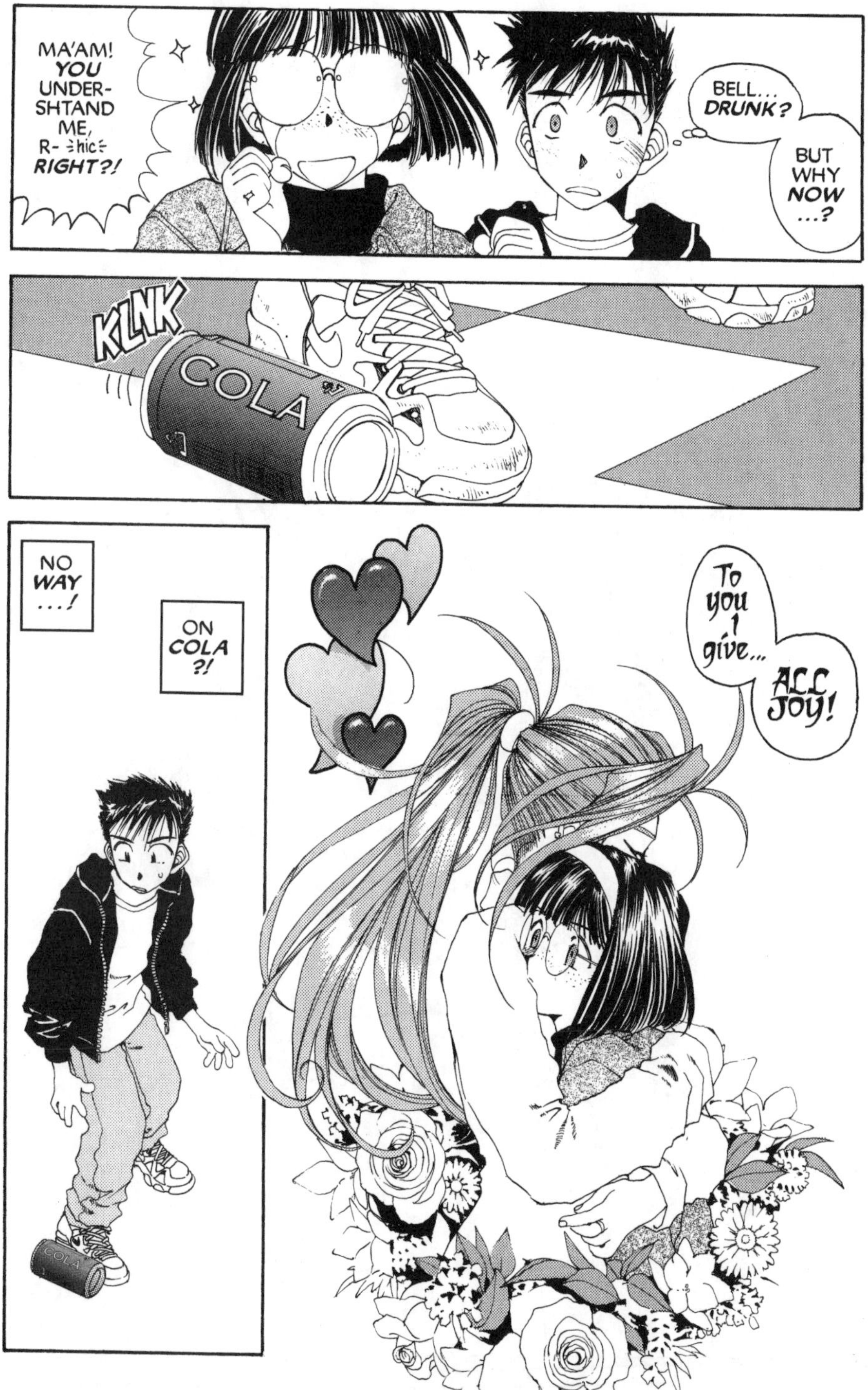
MA'AM! YOU UNDER-SHTAND ME, R- hic RIGHT?!
BELL... DRUNK?
BUT WHY NOW ...?
KLNK
COLA
NO WAY ...!
ON COLA ?!
To you I give... ALL JOY!

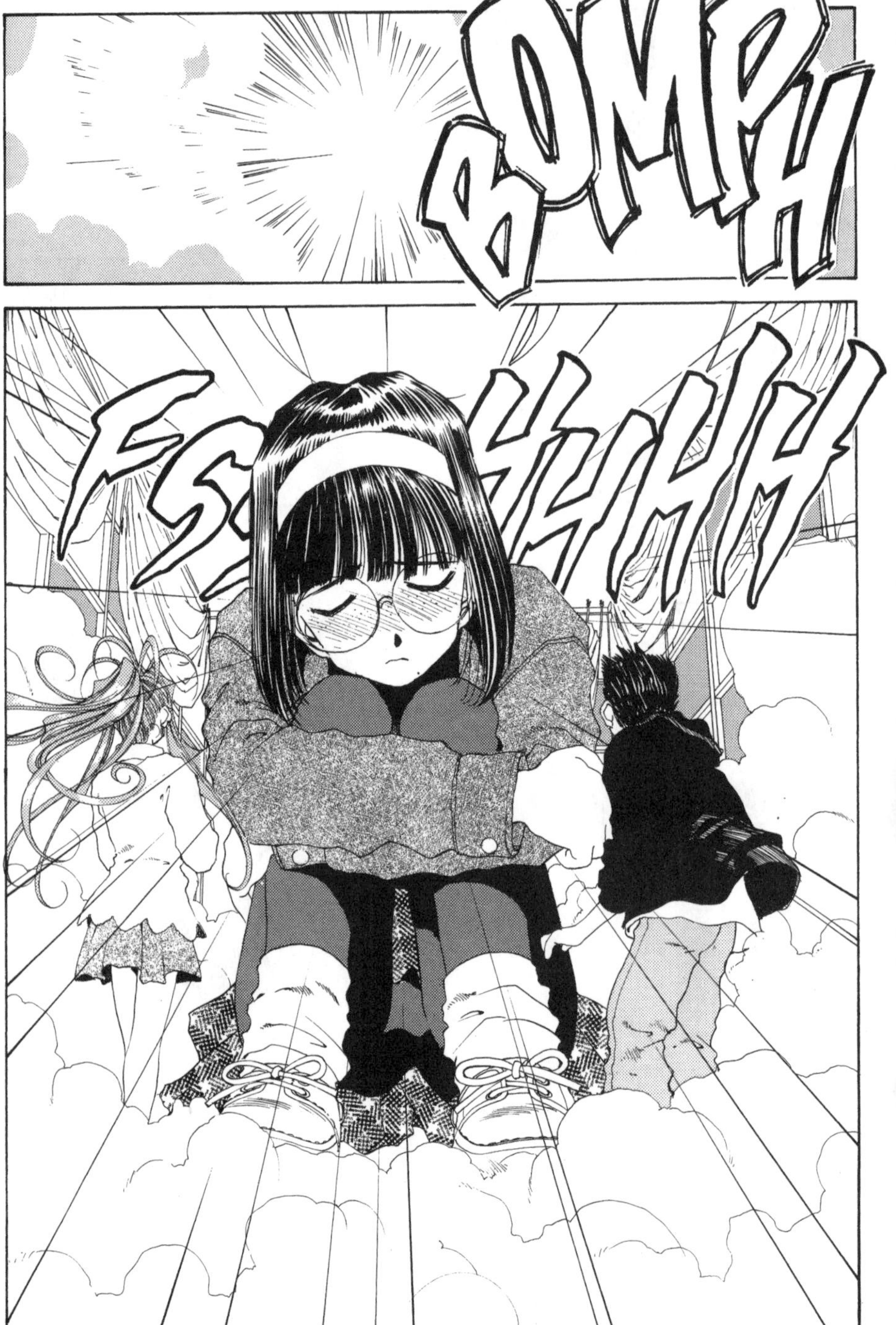
BOMPH
FSSHHHH

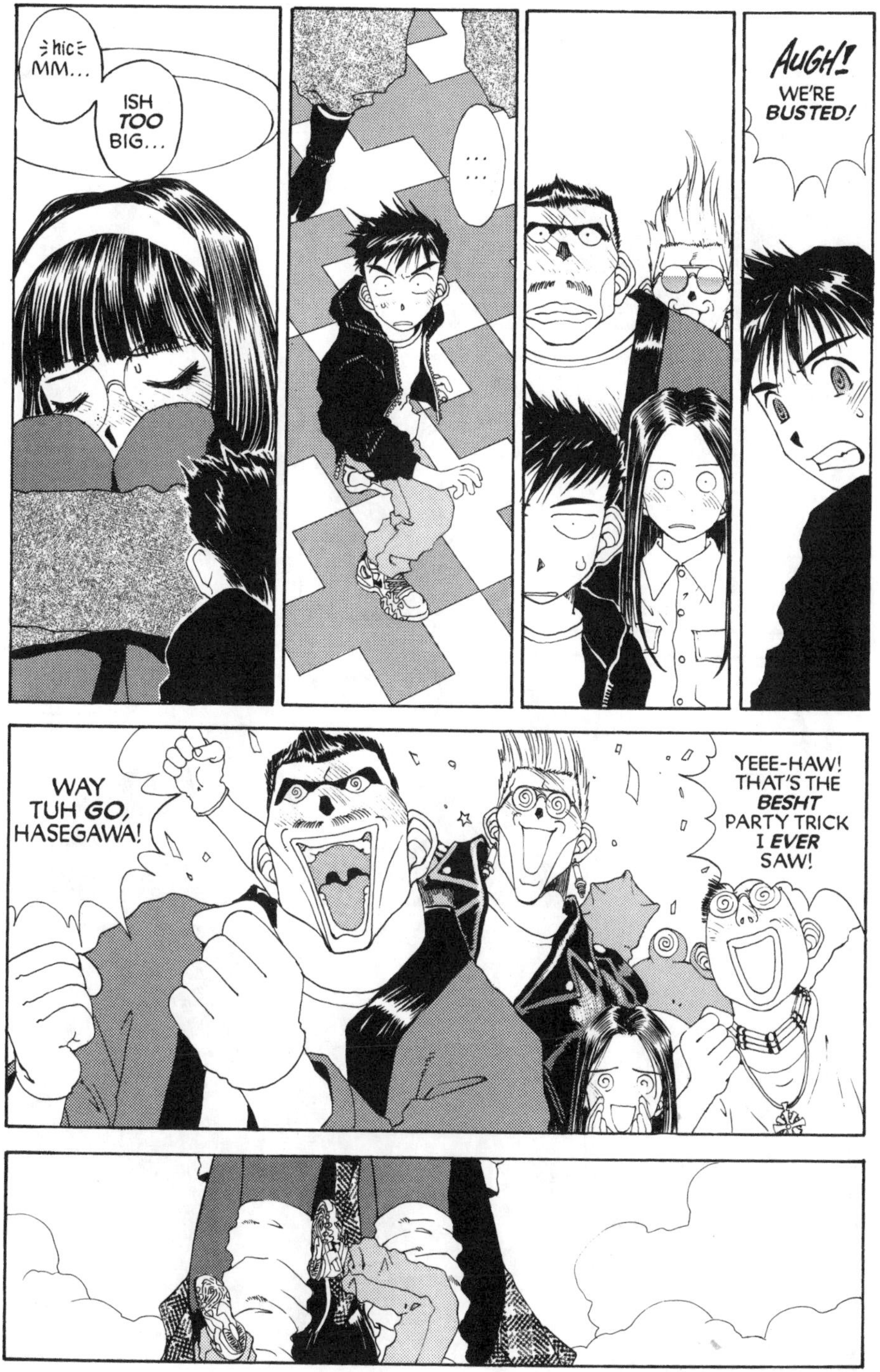

≡hic≡ MM...
ISH *TOO* BIG...
...
...
AUGH! WE'RE *BUSTED!*
WAY TUH *GO,* HASEGAWA!
YEEE-HAW! THAT'S THE *BESHT* PARTY TRICK I *EVER* SAW!

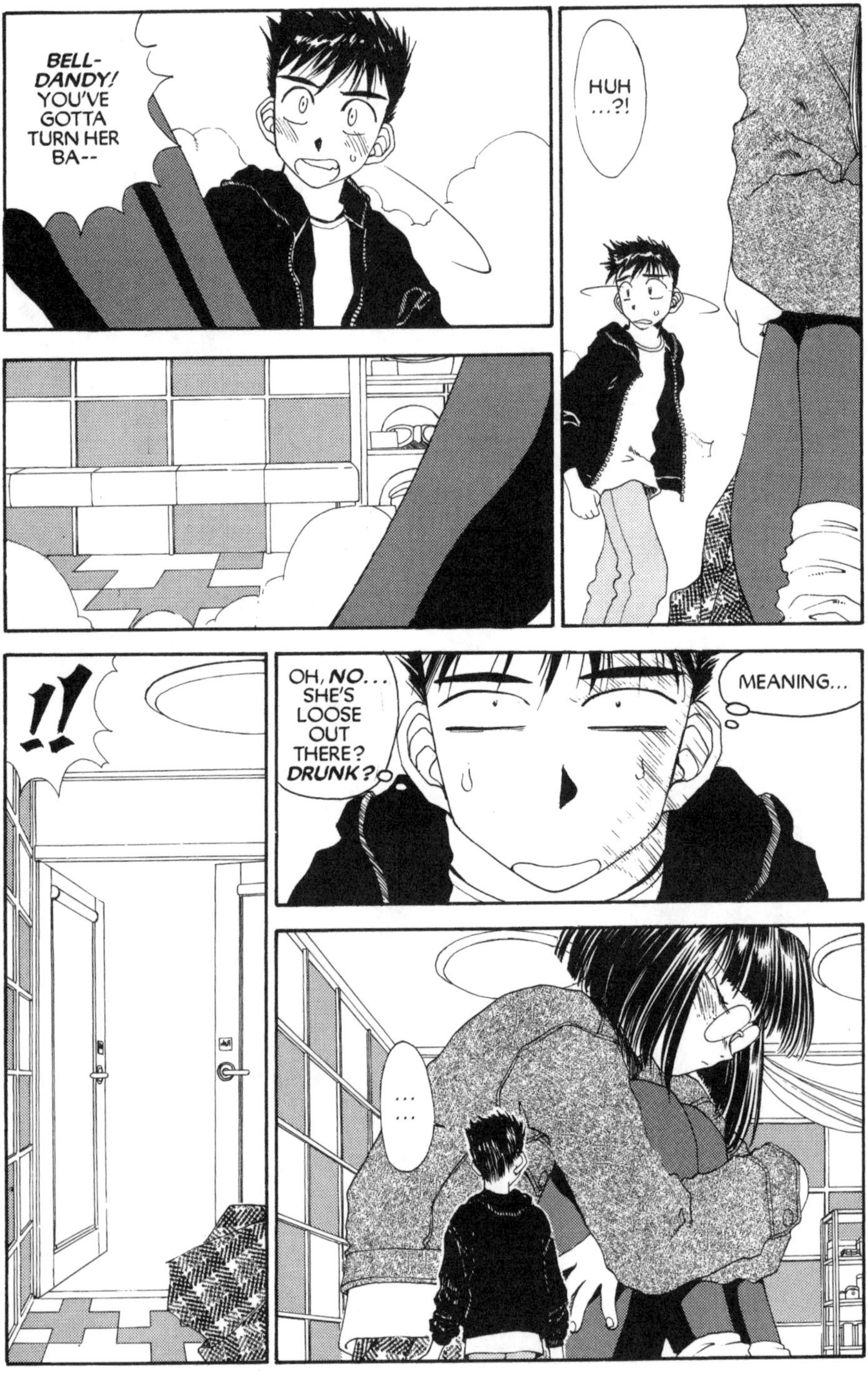
BELL-DANDY! YOU'VE GOTTA TURN HER BA--
HUH ...?!
!!
OH, NO... SHE'S LOOSE OUT THERE? DRUNK?
MEANING...
... ...

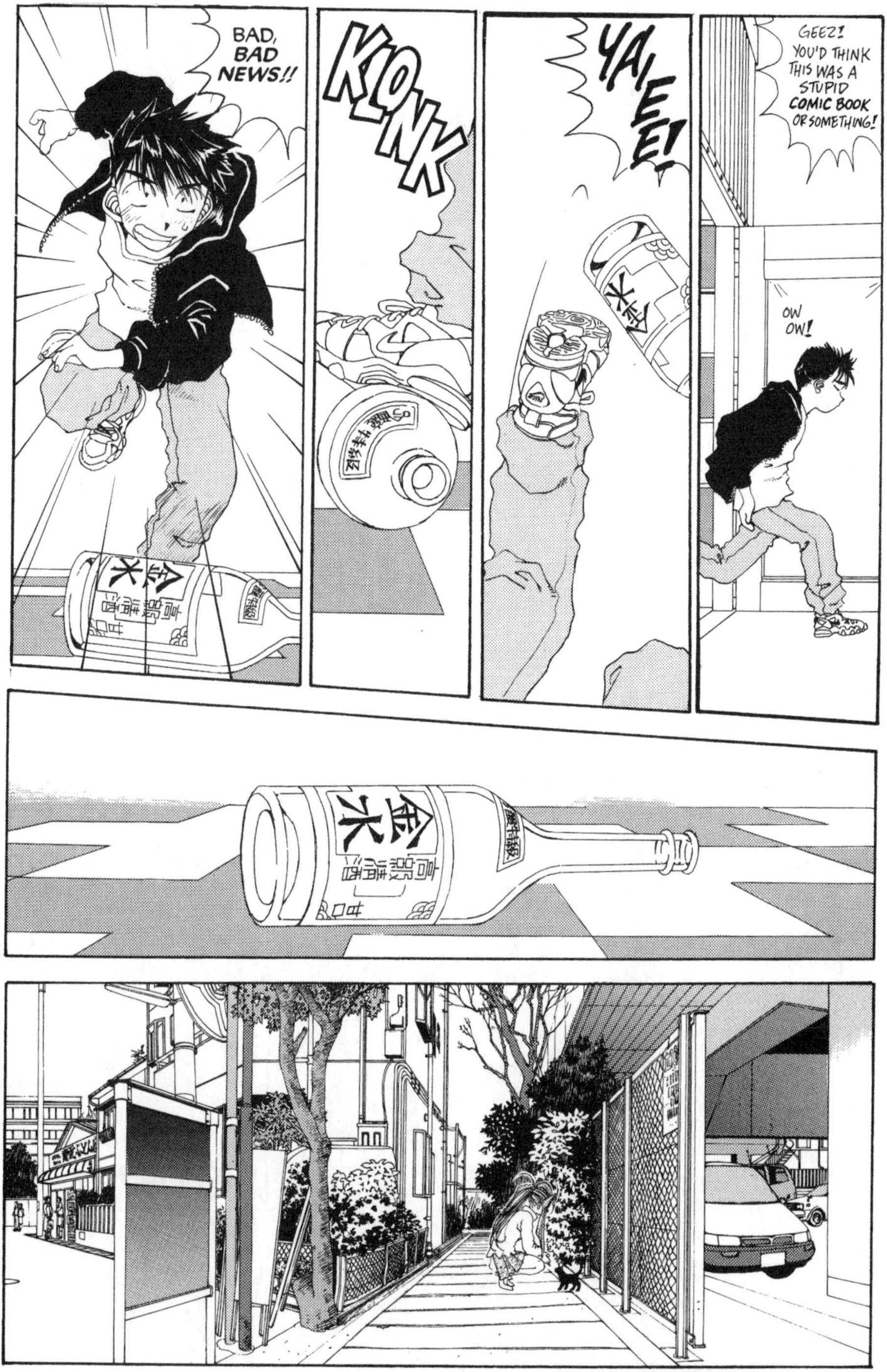
BAD, BAD NEWS!!
KLONK
YAIEEE!
GEEZ! YOU'D THINK THIS WAS A STUPID COMIC BOOK OR SOMETHING!
OW OW!

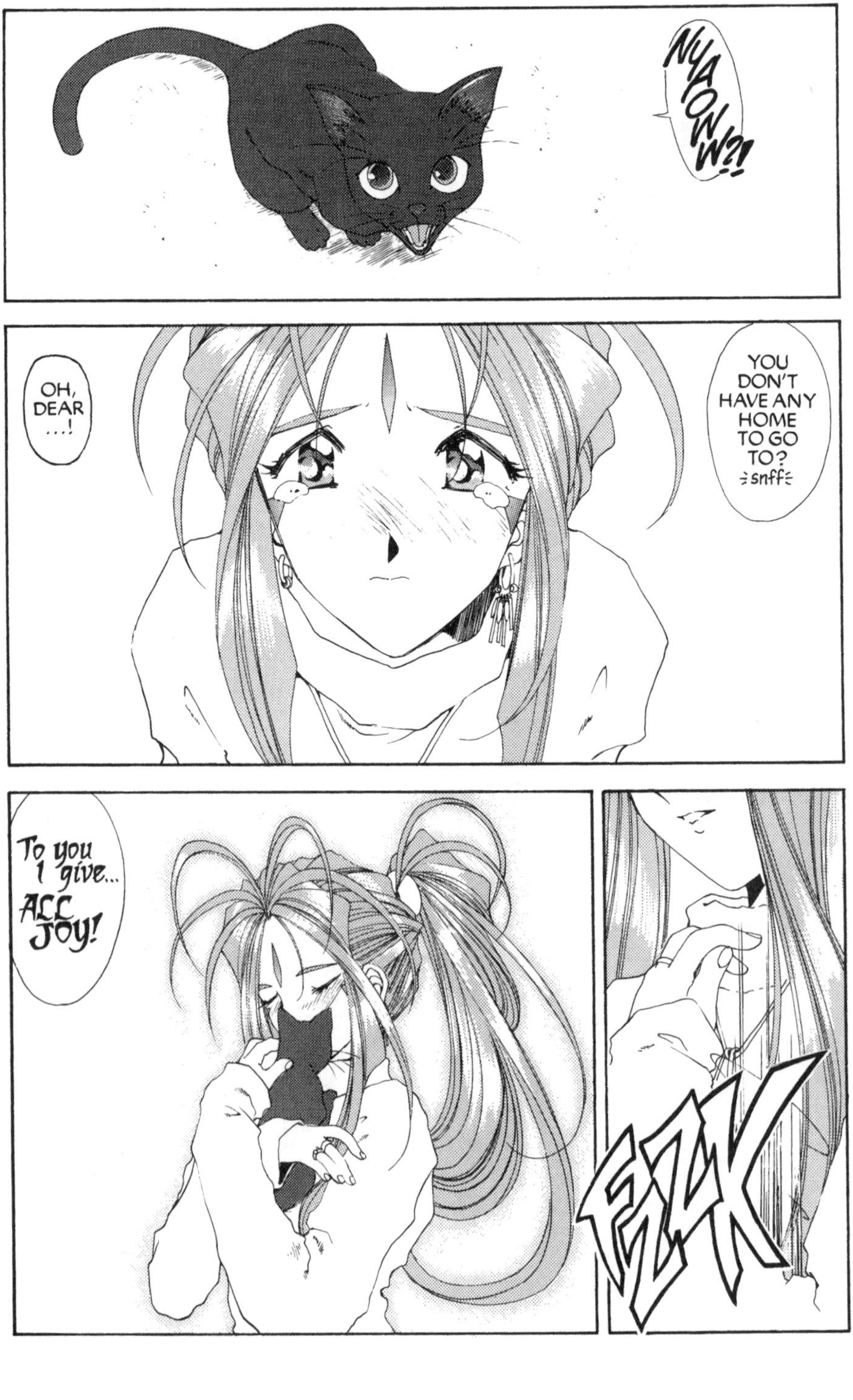
NYAOWW?!
OH, DEAR ...!
YOU DON'T HAVE ANY HOME TO GO TO? snff
To you I give... ALL JOY!
FZZK

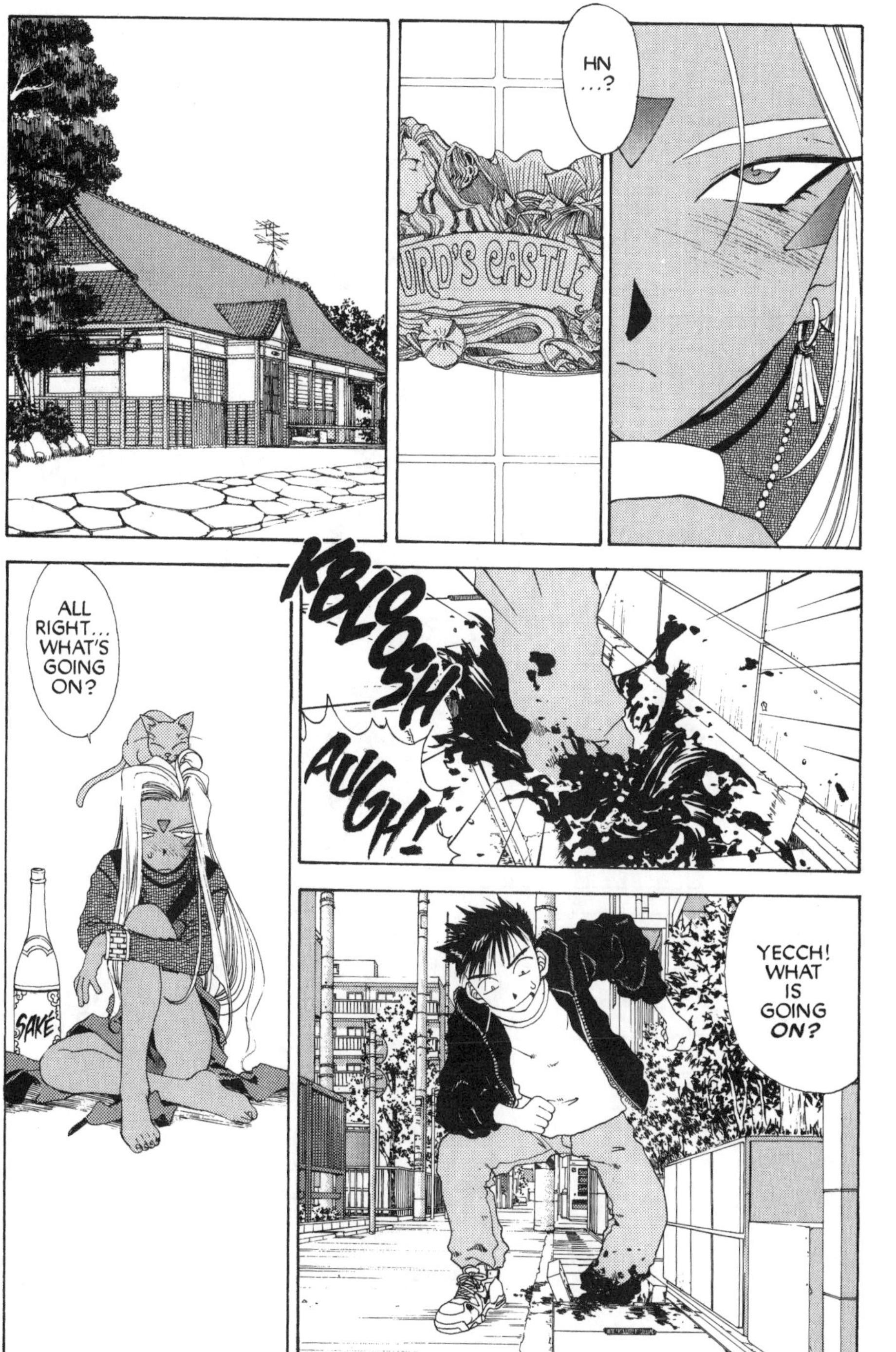
HN ...?
URD'S CASTLE
ALL RIGHT... WHAT'S GOING ON?
SAKÉ
KBLOOSH
AUGH!
YECCH! WHAT IS GOING ON?

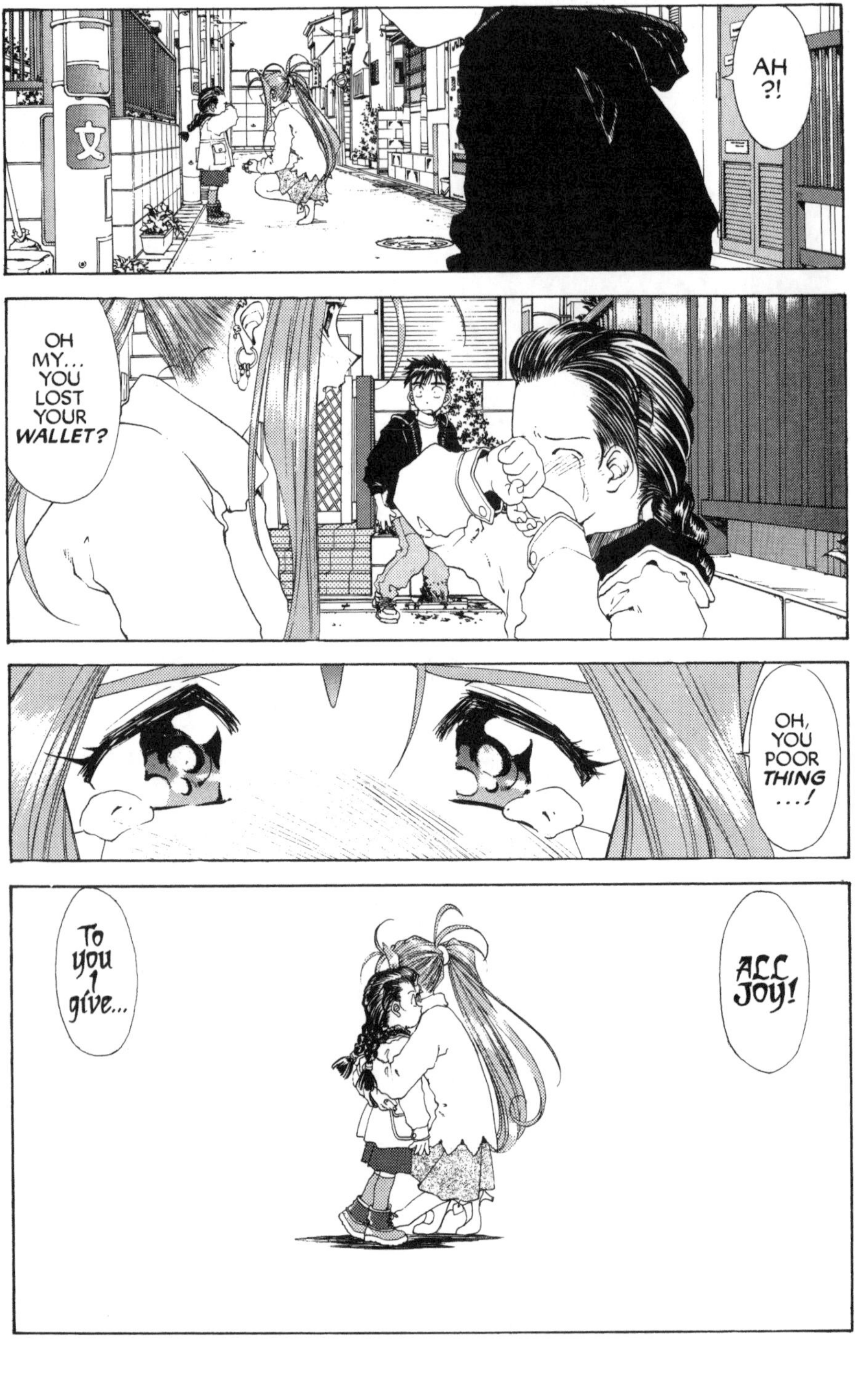

文
AH ?!
OH MY... YOU LOST YOUR *WALLET?*
OH, YOU POOR *THING* ...!
To you I give...
ALL JOY!

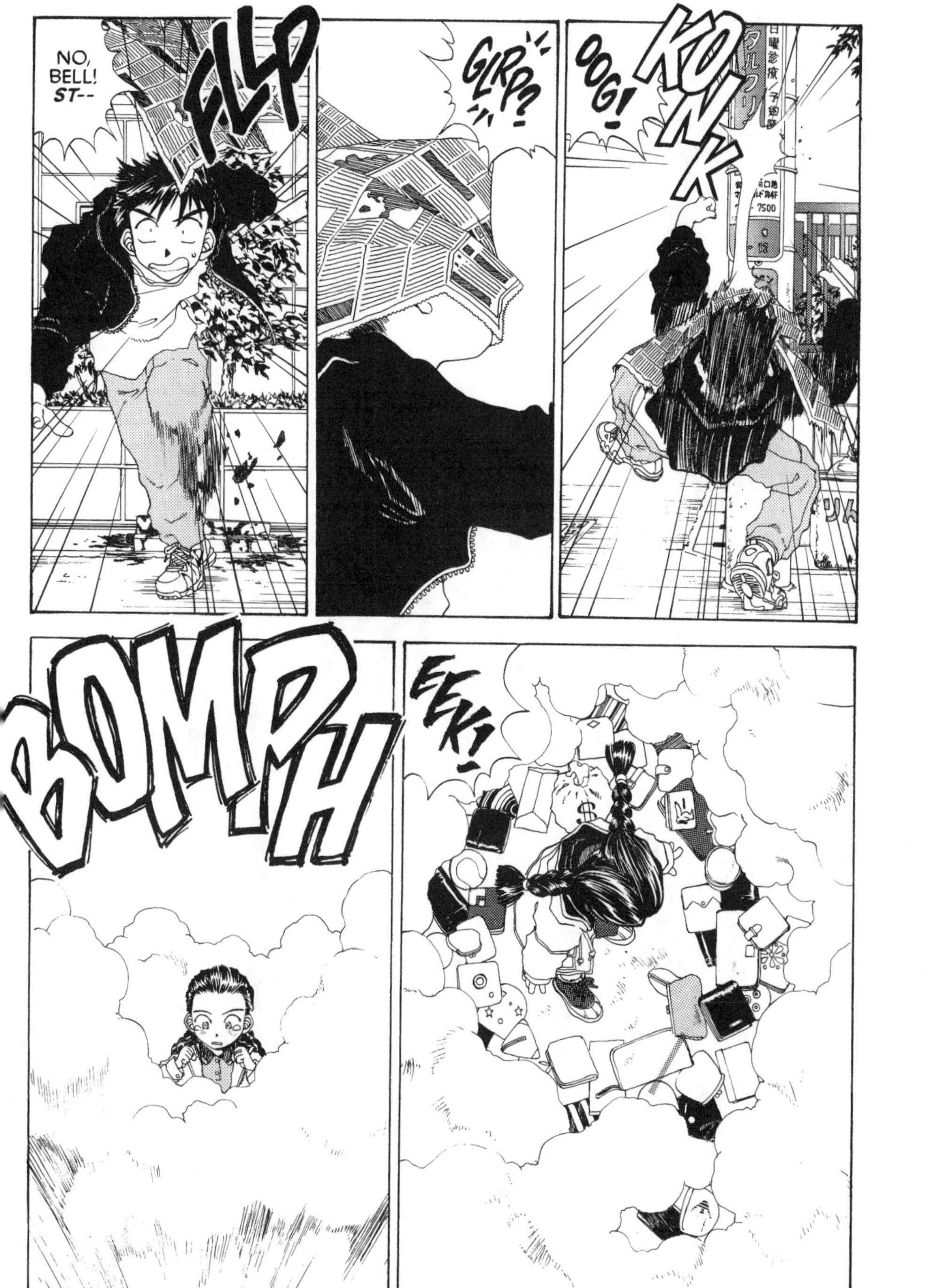
NO, BELL! ST--
FLLP
GLRP?!
OOG!
KONK
BOMPH
EEK!

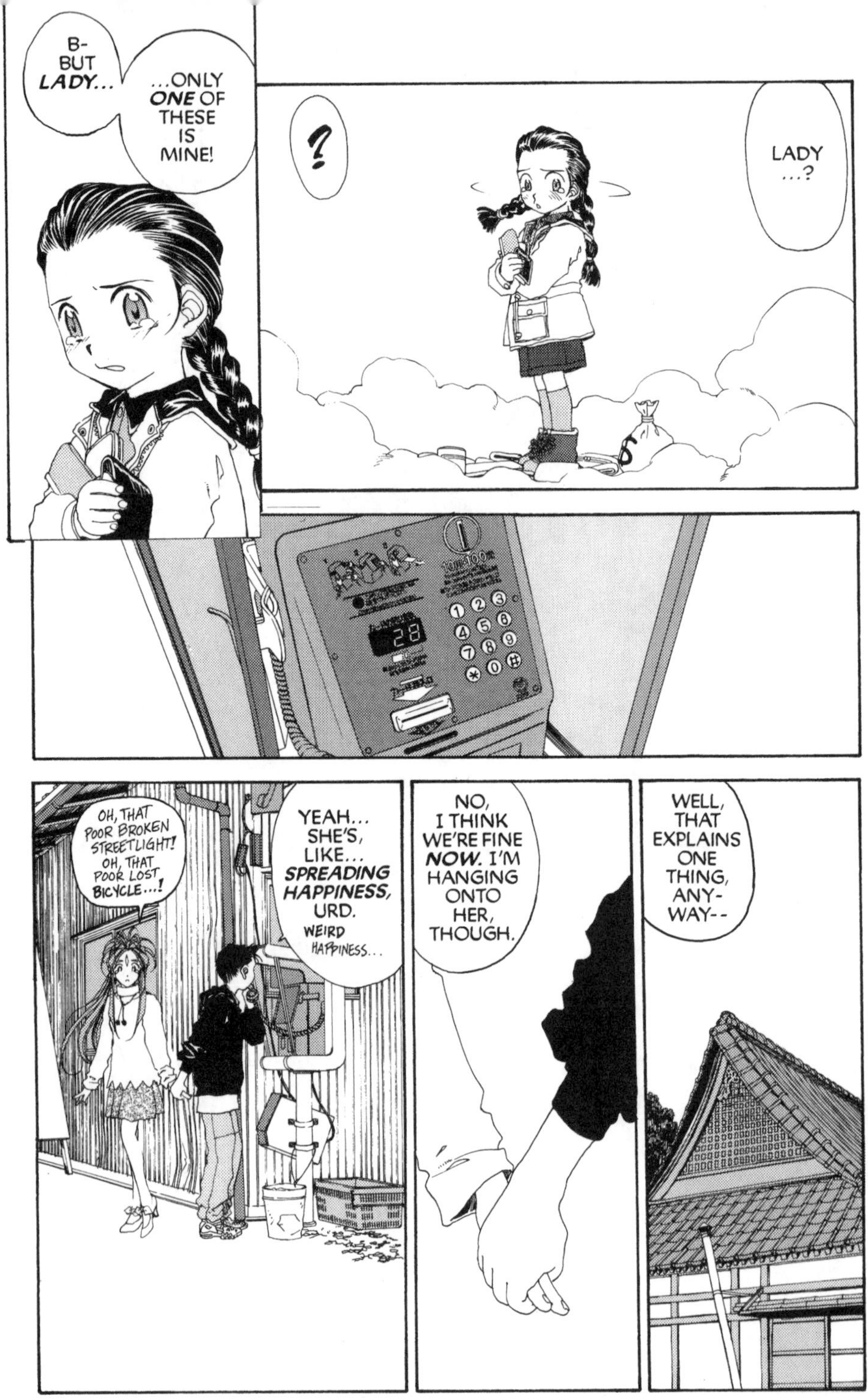
B-BUT LADY...
...ONLY ONE OF THESE IS MINE!
?
LADY ...?
OH, THAT POOR BROKEN STREETLIGHT! OH, THAT POOR LOST BICYCLE...!
YEAH... SHE'S, LIKE... SPREADING HAPPINESS, URD.
WEIRD HAPPINESS...
NO, I THINK WE'RE FINE NOW. I'M HANGING ONTO HER, THOUGH.
WELL, THAT EXPLAINS ONE THING, ANY-WAY--

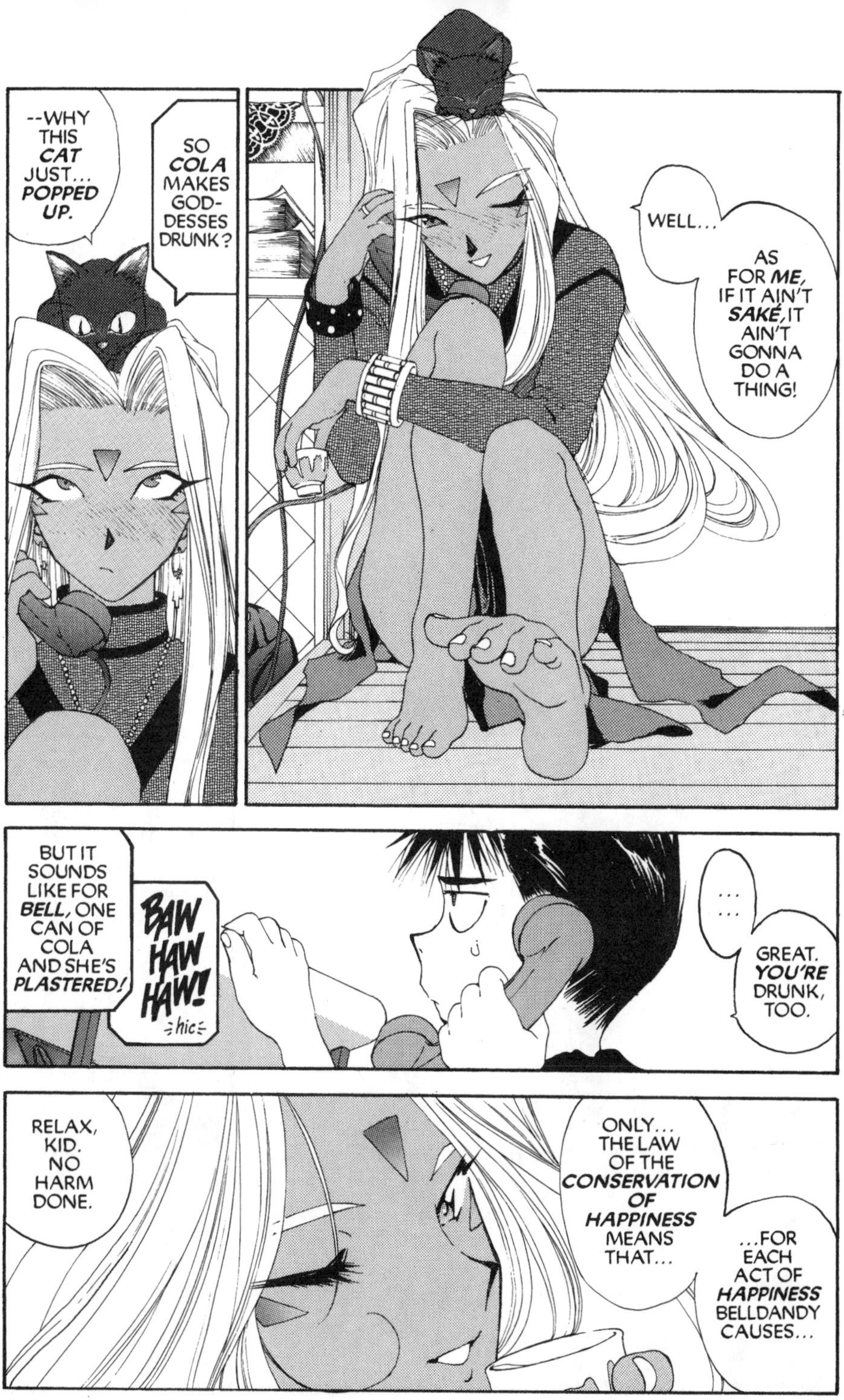
--WHY THIS CAT JUST... POPPED UP.
SO COLA MAKES GOD-DESSES DRUNK?
WELL...
AS FOR ME, IF IT AIN'T SAKÉ, IT AIN'T GONNA DO A THING!
BUT IT SOUNDS LIKE FOR BELL, ONE CAN OF COLA AND SHE'S PLASTERED!
BAW HAW HAW!
hic
......
GREAT. YOU'RE DRUNK, TOO.
RELAX, KID. NO HARM DONE.
ONLY... THE LAW OF THE CONSERVATION OF HAPPINESS MEANS THAT...
...FOR EACH ACT OF HAPPINESS BELLDANDY CAUSES...

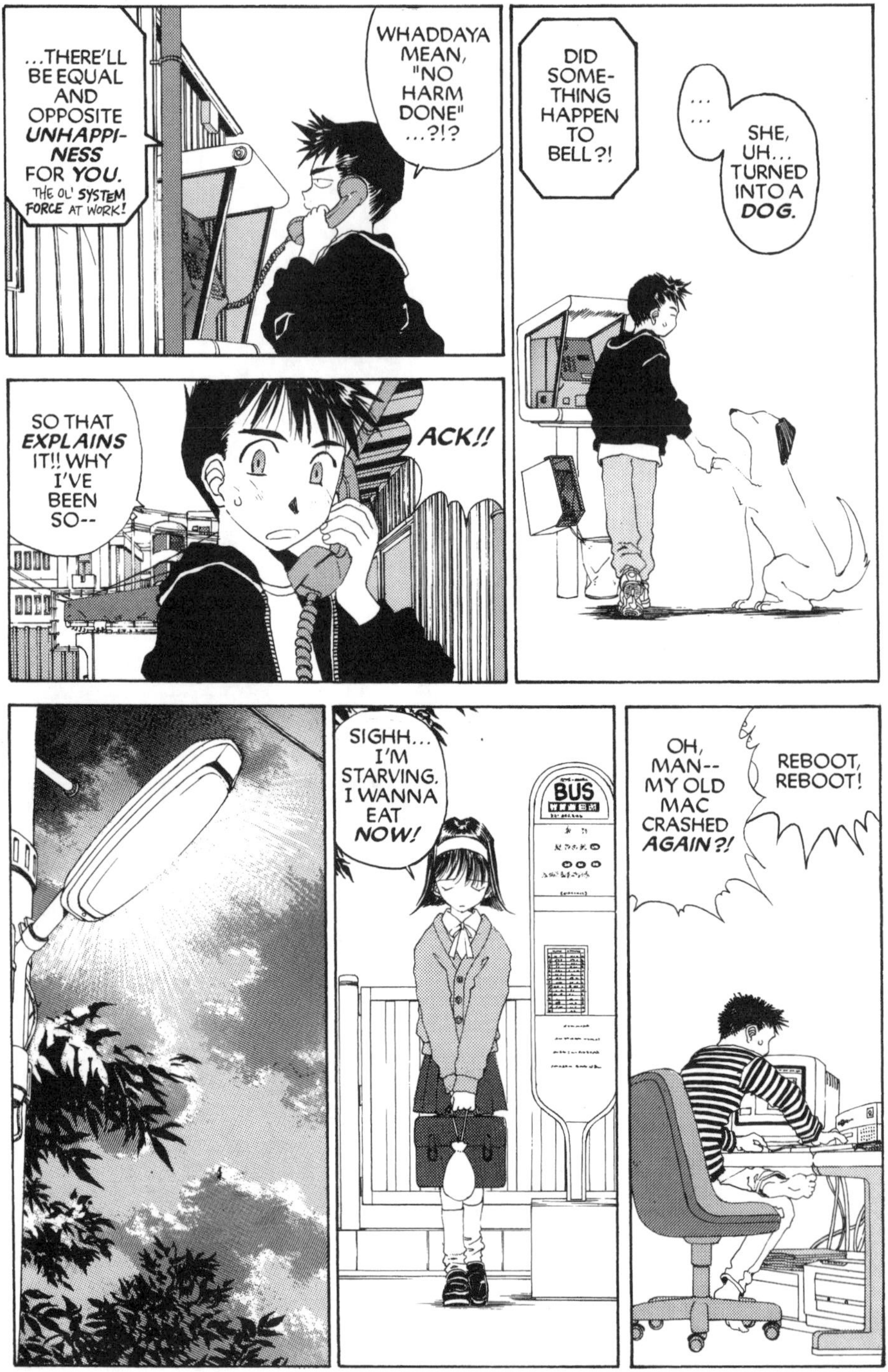
...THERE'LL BE EQUAL AND OPPOSITE UNHAPPINESS FOR YOU. THE OL' SYSTEM FORCE AT WORK!
WHADDAYA MEAN, "NO HARM DONE" ...?!?
SO THAT EXPLAINS IT!! WHY I'VE BEEN SO--
ACK!!
DID SOMETHING HAPPEN TO BELL?!
... ...
SHE, UH... TURNED INTO A DOG.
SIGHH... I'M STARVING. I WANNA EAT NOW!
BUS
OH, MAN-- MY OLD MAC CRASHED AGAIN?!
REBOOT, REBOOT!

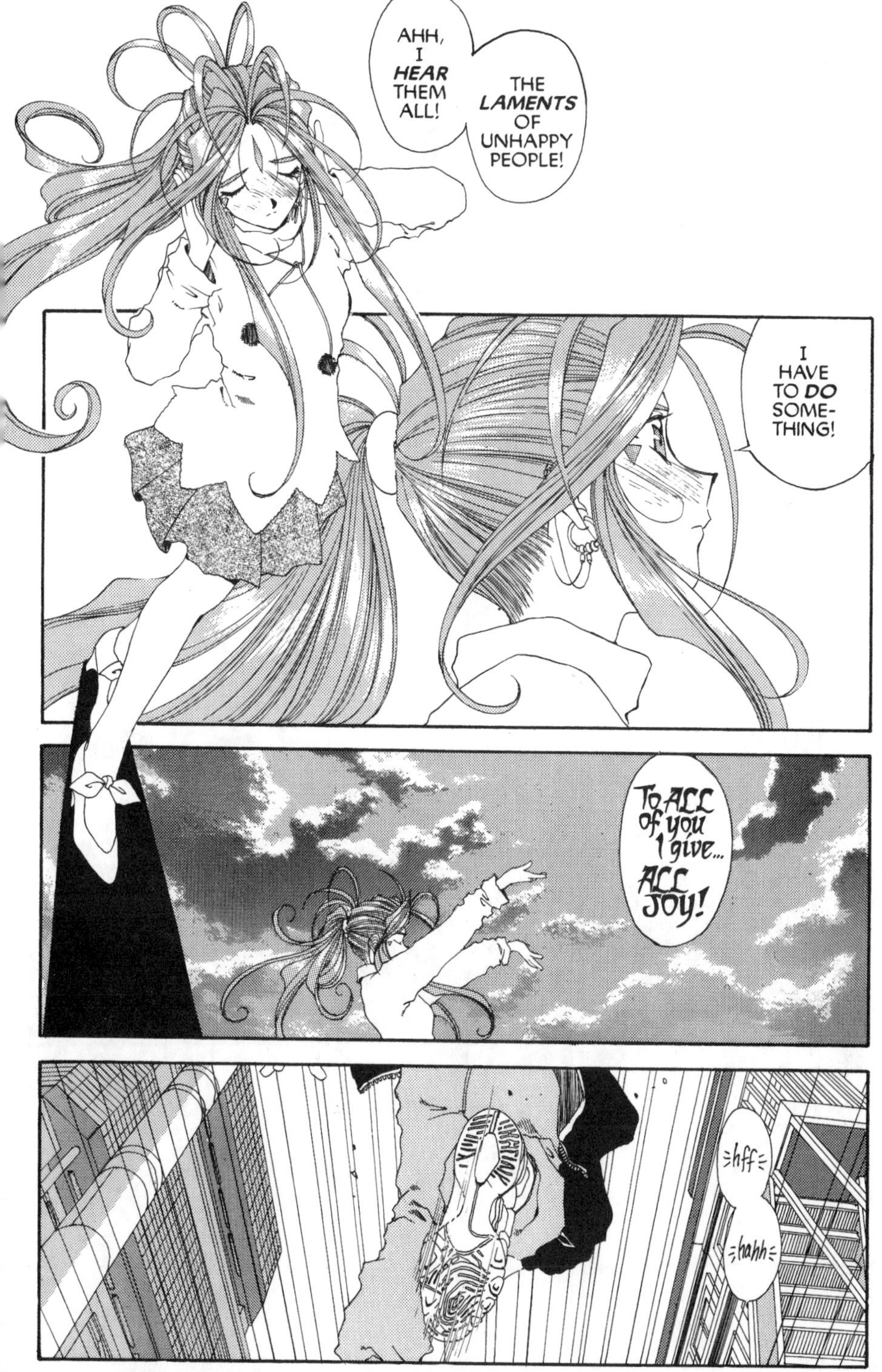
AHH, I HEAR THEM ALL!
THE LAMENTS OF UNHAPPY PEOPLE!
I HAVE TO DO SOME-THING!
To ALL of you I give... ALL JOY!
hff
hahh

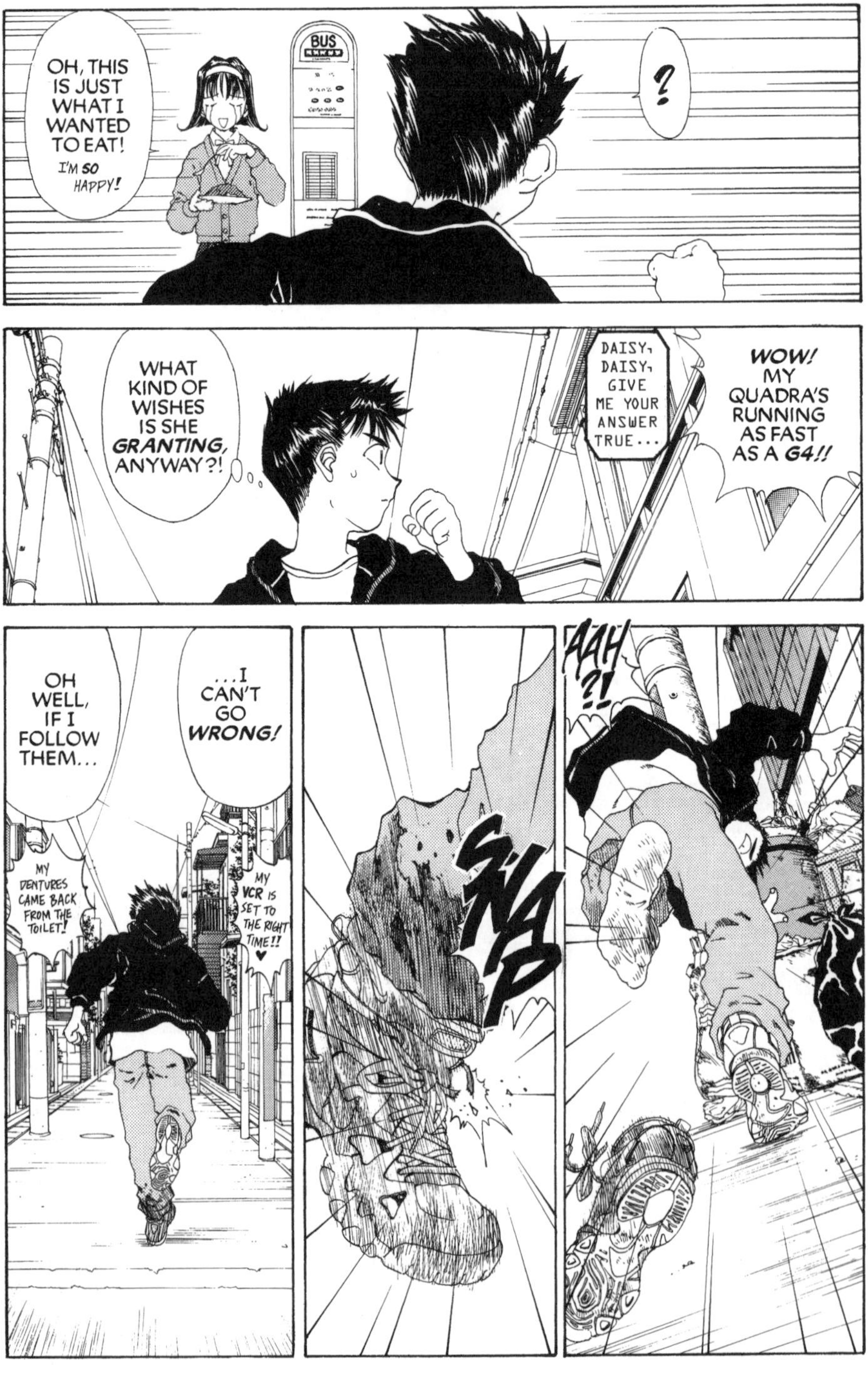
OH, THIS IS JUST WHAT I WANTED TO EAT!
I'M SO HAPPY!
?
WHAT KIND OF WISHES IS SHE GRANTING, ANYWAY?!
DAISY, DAISY, GIVE ME YOUR ANSWER TRUE...
WOW! MY QUADRA'S RUNNING AS FAST AS A G4!!
OH WELL, IF I FOLLOW THEM...
...I CAN'T GO WRONG!
MY DENTURES CAME BACK FROM THE TOILET!
MY VCR IS SET TO THE RIGHT TIME!! ♥
SNAP
AAH?!

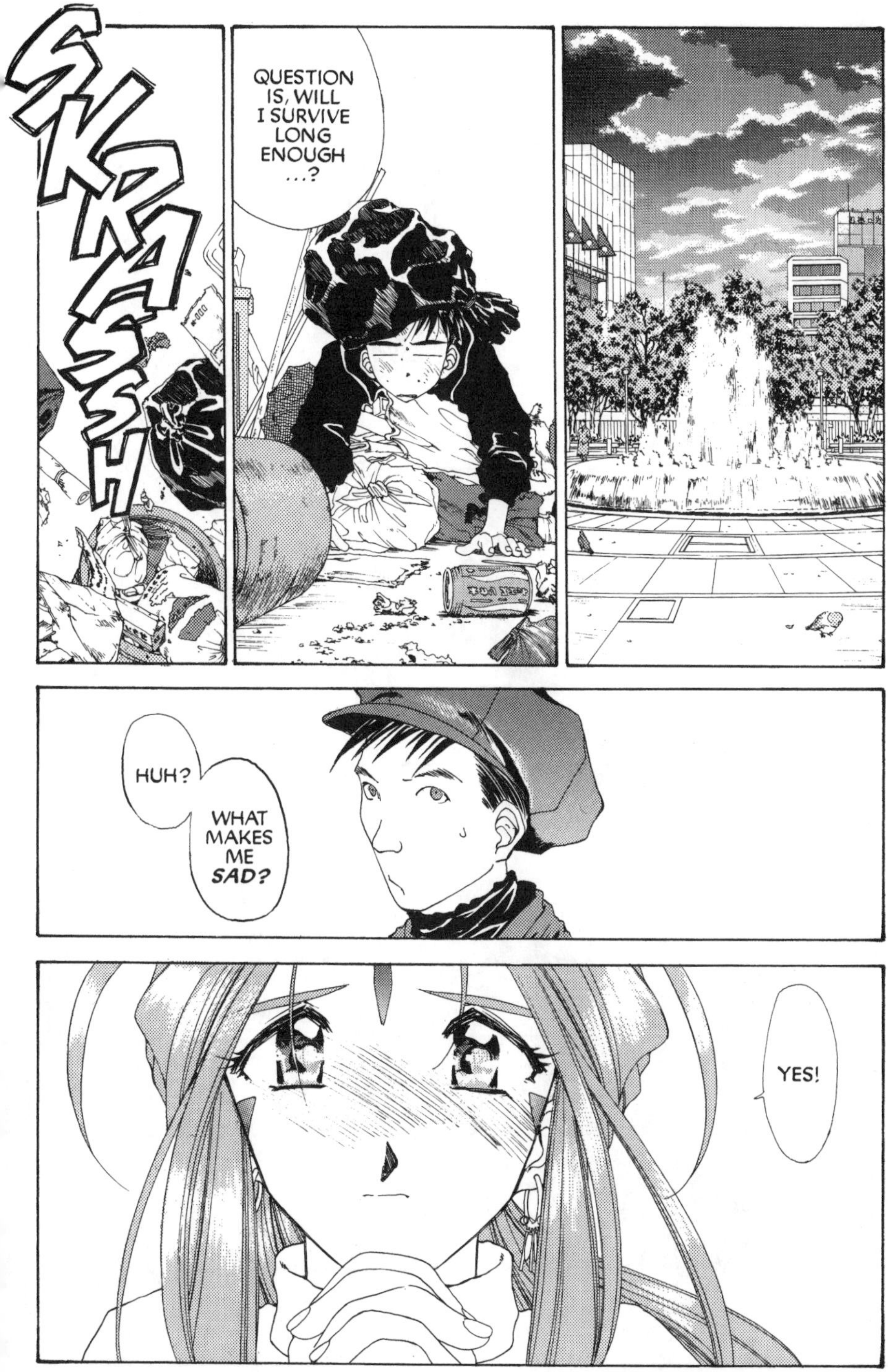
SKRASSH
QUESTION IS, WILL I SURVIVE LONG ENOUGH ...?
HUH?
WHAT MAKES ME SAD?
YES!

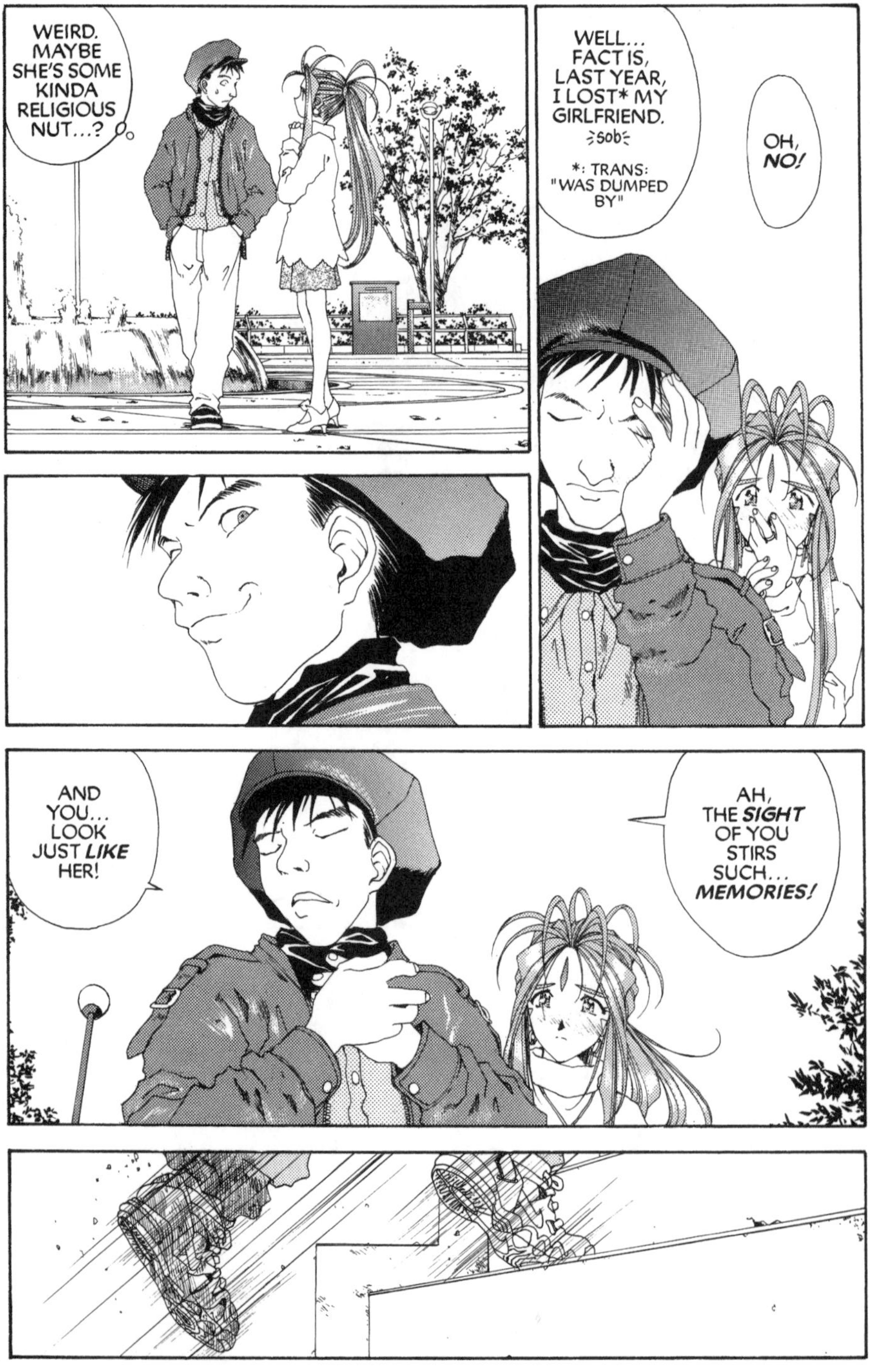
WEIRD. MAYBE SHE'S SOME KINDA RELIGIOUS NUT...?
WELL... FACT IS, LAST YEAR, I LOST* MY GIRLFRIEND.
sob
*: TRANS: "WAS DUMPED BY"
OH, NO!
AND YOU... LOOK JUST LIKE HER!
AH, THE SIGHT OF YOU STIRS SUCH... MEMORIES!

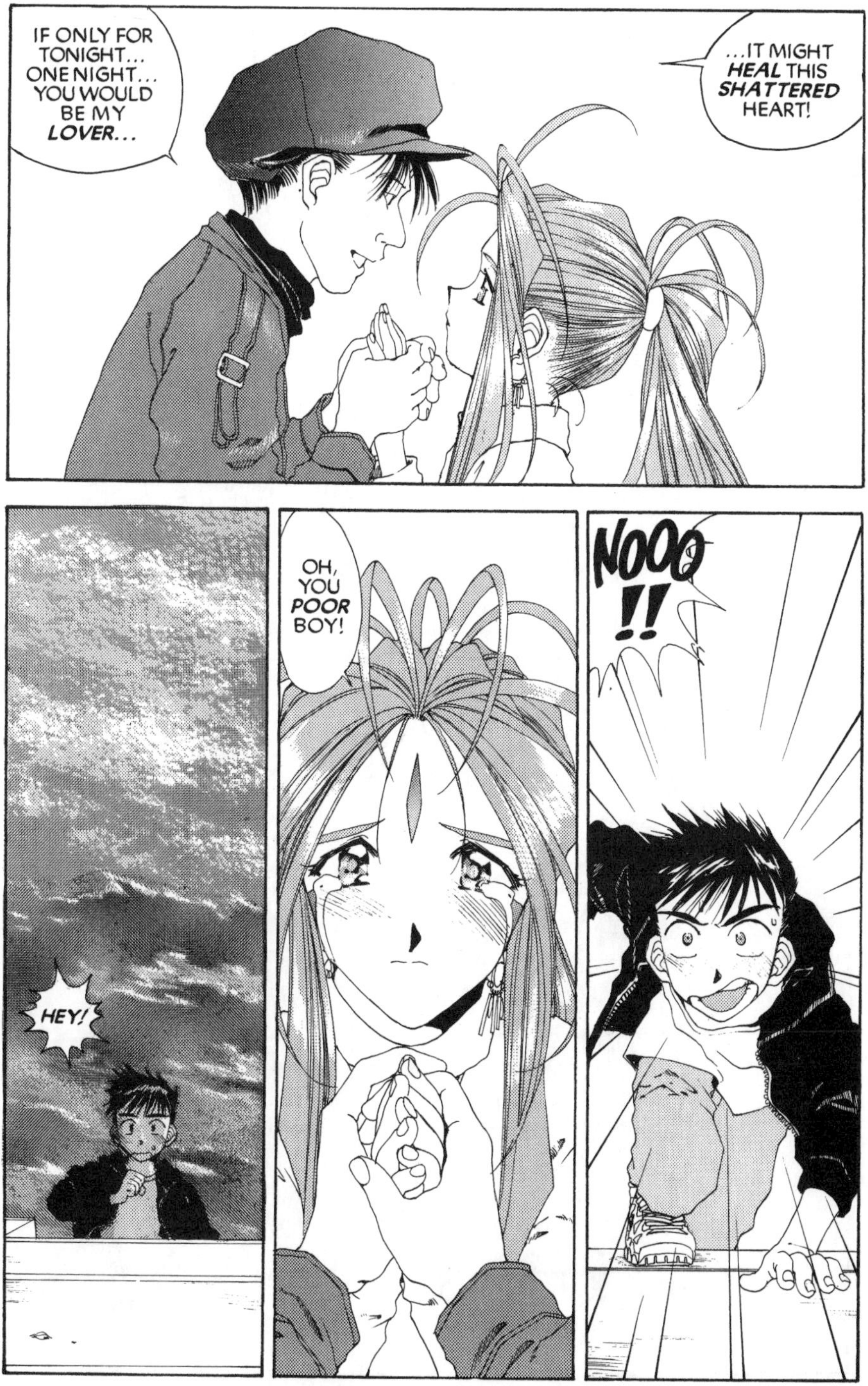
IF ONLY FOR TONIGHT... ONE NIGHT... YOU WOULD BE MY *LOVER...*
...IT MIGHT *HEAL* THIS *SHATTERED* HEART!
HEY!
OH, YOU *POOR* BOY!
NOOO !!

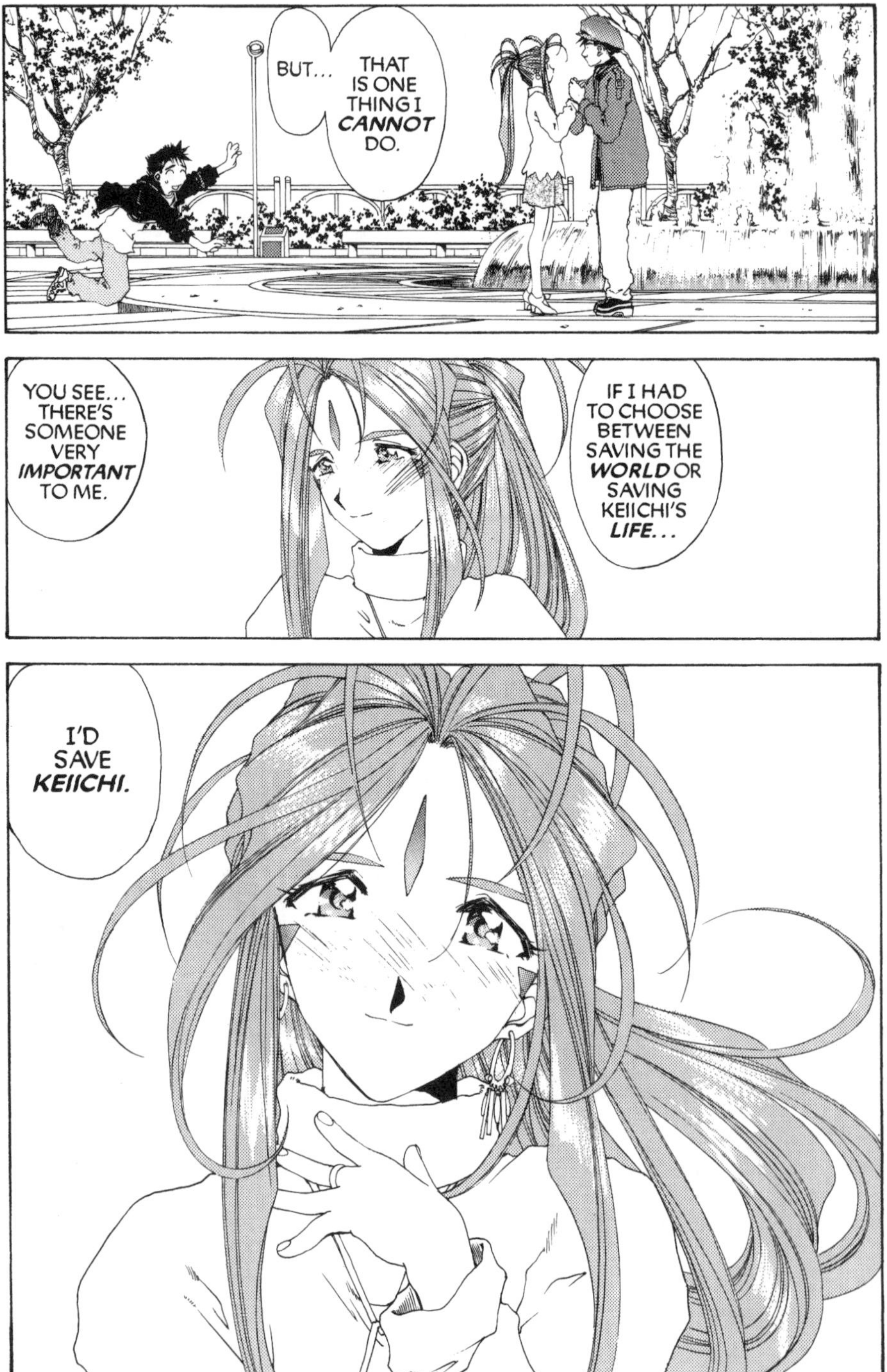

BUT... THAT IS ONE THING I CANNOT DO.
YOU SEE... THERE'S SOMEONE VERY IMPORTANT TO ME.
IF I HAD TO CHOOSE BETWEEN SAVING THE WORLD OR SAVING KEIICHI'S LIFE...
I'D SAVE KEIICHI.

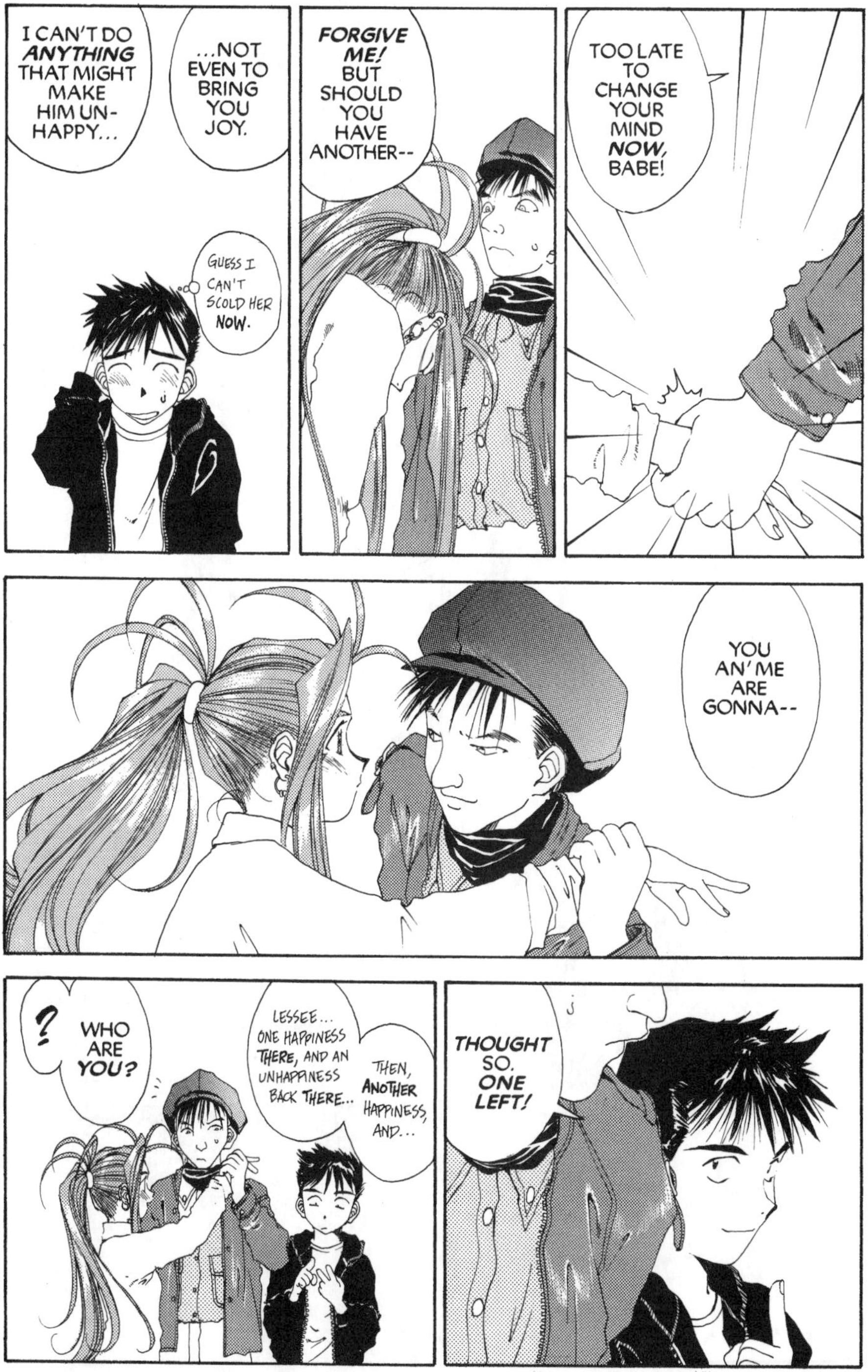
I CAN'T DO ANYTHING THAT MIGHT MAKE HIM UN-HAPPY...
...NOT EVEN TO BRING YOU JOY.
GUESS I CAN'T SCOLD HER NOW.
FORGIVE ME! BUT SHOULD YOU HAVE ANOTHER--
TOO LATE TO CHANGE YOUR MIND NOW, BABE!
YOU AN' ME ARE GONNA--
?
WHO ARE YOU?
LESSEE... ONE HAPPINESS THERE, AND AN UNHAPPINESS BACK THERE...
THEN, ANOTHER HAPPINESS, AND...
THOUGHT SO. ONE LEFT!

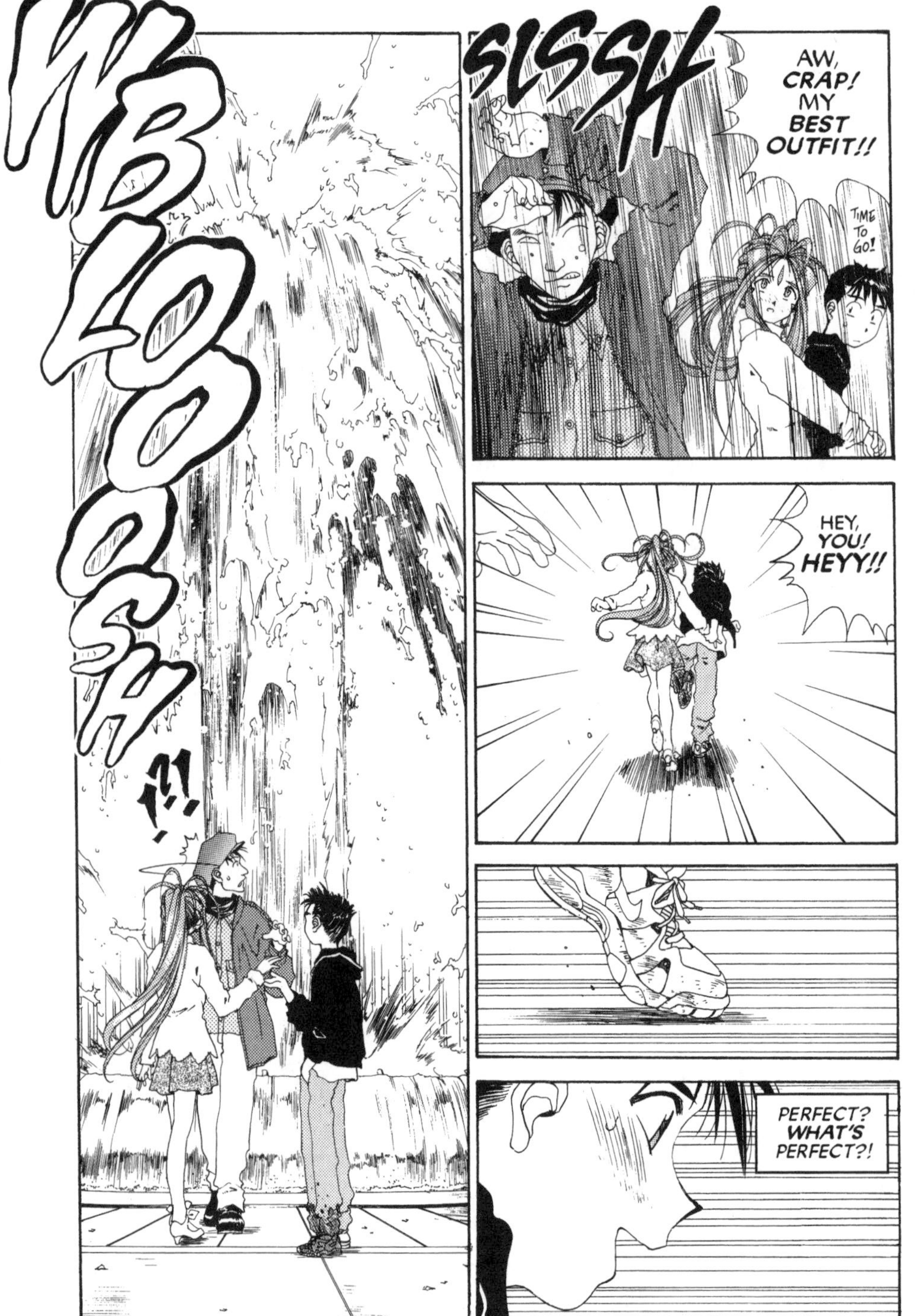
WBLOOOSH
!?!
SISSH
AW, CRAP! MY BEST OUTFIT!!
TIME TO GO!
HEY, YOU! HEYY!!
PERFECT? WHAT'S PERFECT?!

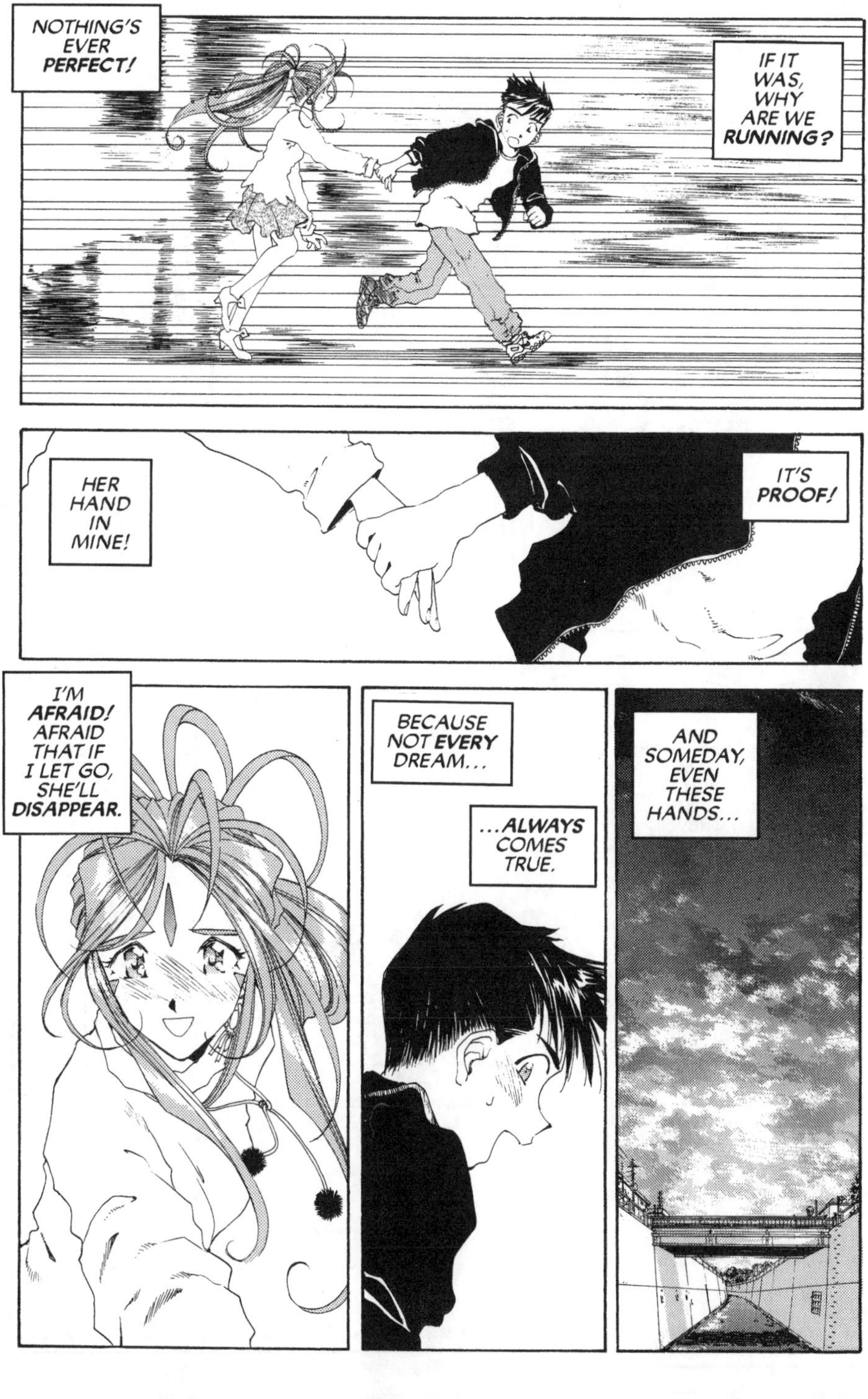
NOTHING'S EVER **PERFECT!**
IF IT WAS, WHY ARE WE **RUNNING?**
HER HAND IN MINE!
IT'S **PROOF!**
I'M **AFRAID!** AFRAID THAT IF I LET GO, SHE'LL **DISAPPEAR.**
BECAUSE NOT **EVERY** DREAM...
...**ALWAYS** COMES TRUE.
AND SOMEDAY, EVEN THESE HANDS...

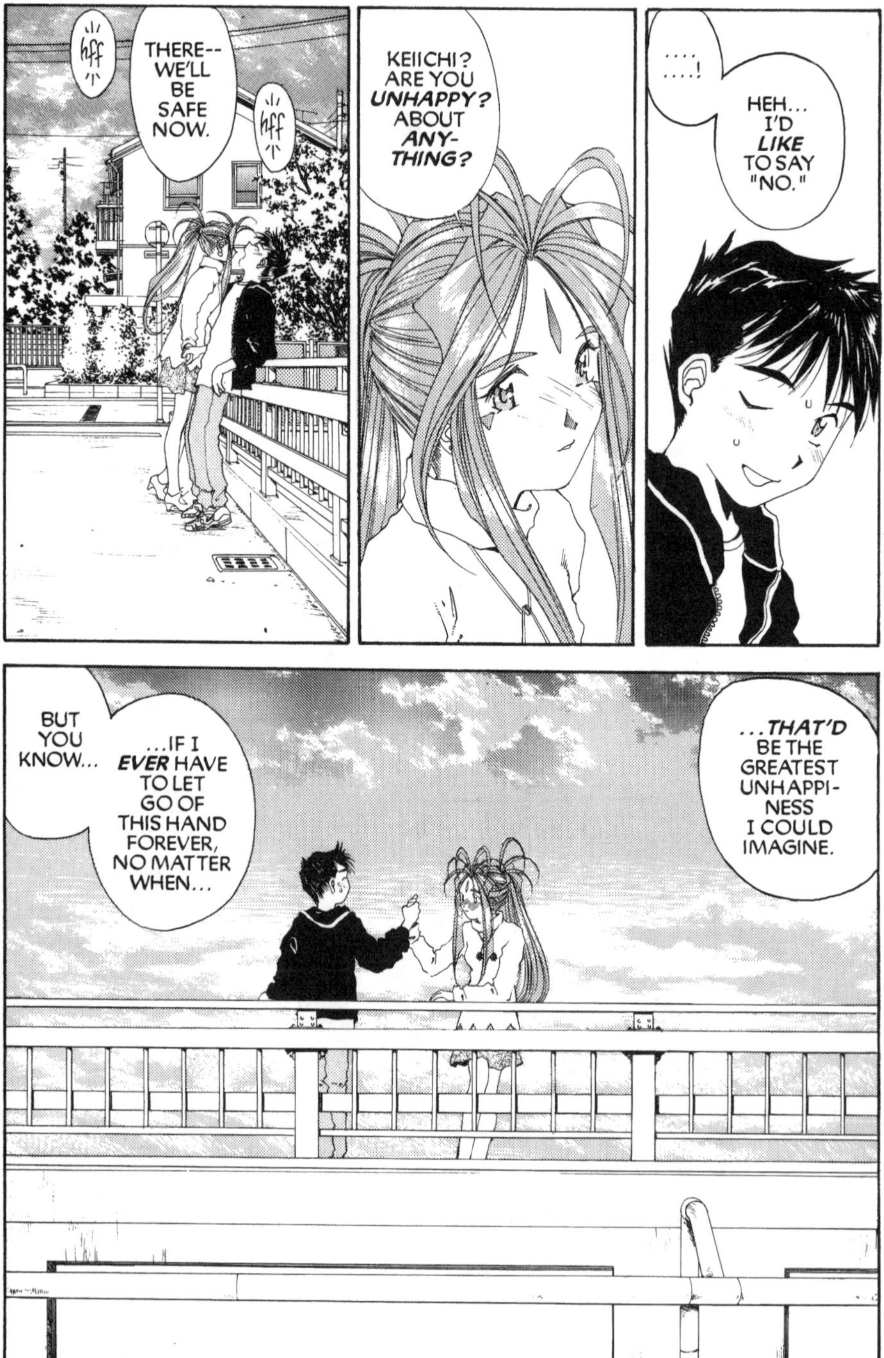
hff
THERE-- WE'LL BE SAFE NOW.
hff
KEIICHI? ARE YOU *UNHAPPY?* ABOUT *ANY-THING?*
....
....!
HEH... I'D *LIKE* TO SAY "NO."
BUT YOU KNOW...
...IF I *EVER* HAVE TO LET GO OF THIS HAND FOREVER, NO MATTER WHEN...
...*THAT'D* BE THE GREATEST UNHAPPI-NESS I COULD IMAGINE.

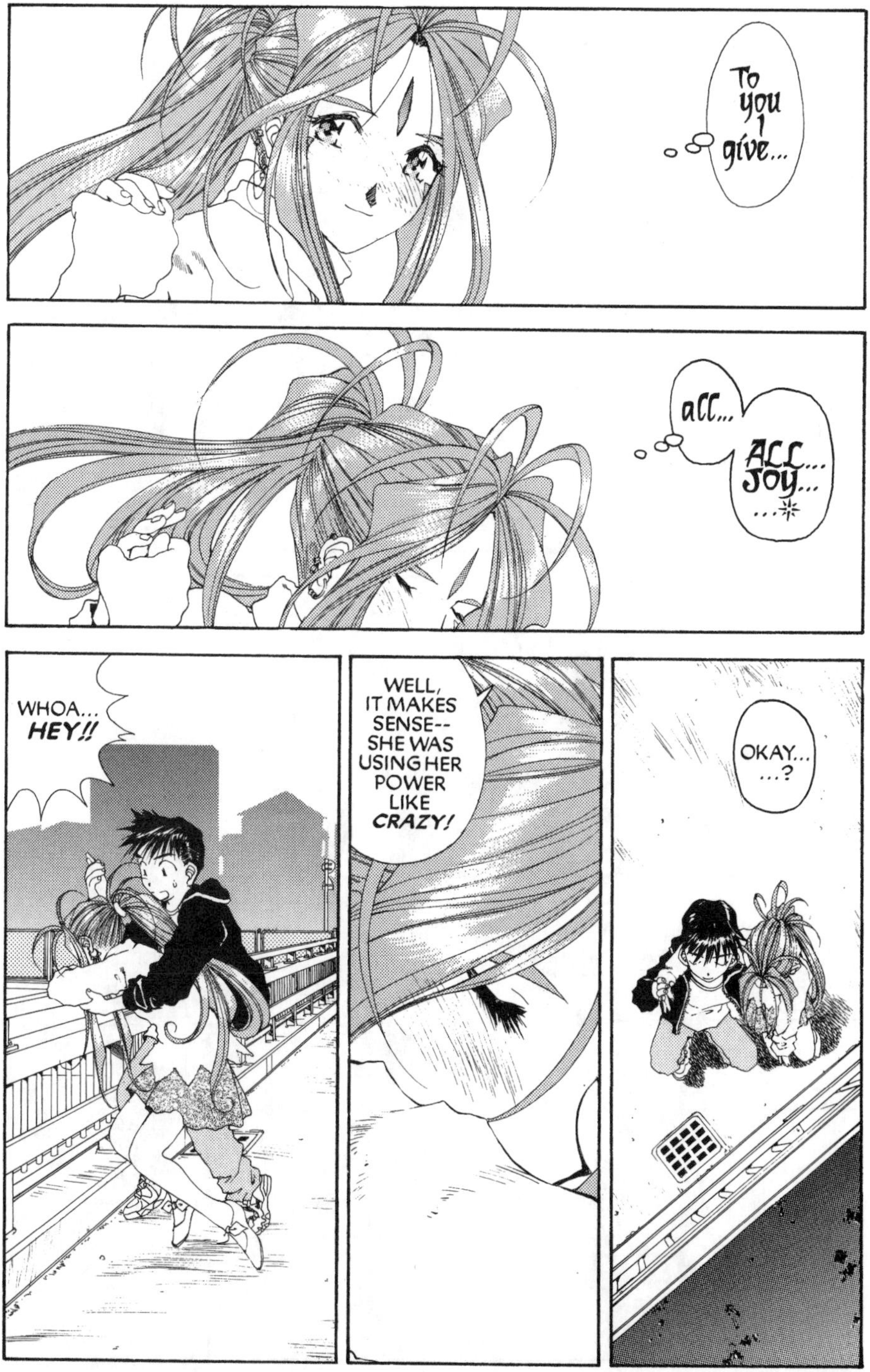
To you I give...
all... ALL... JOY... ...
WHOA... HEY!!
WELL, IT MAKES SENSE-- SHE WAS USING HER POWER LIKE CRAZY!
OKAY... ...?

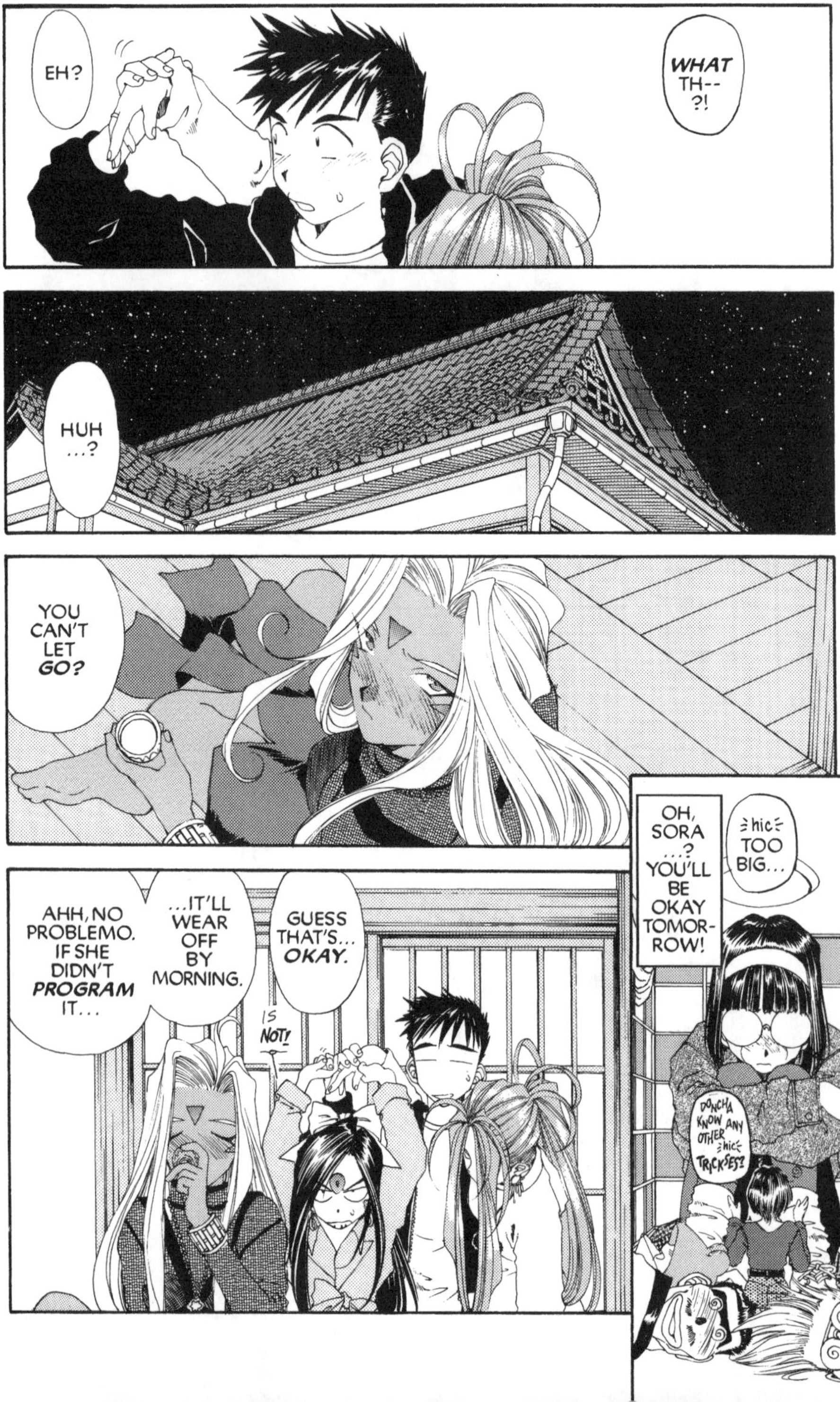

EH?
WHAT TH-- ?!
HUH ...?
YOU CAN'T LET GO?
AHH, NO PROBLEMO. IF SHE DIDN'T PROGRAM IT...
...IT'LL WEAR OFF BY MORNING.
GUESS THAT'S... OKAY.
IS NOT!
OH, SORA ...? YOU'LL BE OKAY TOMORROW!
hic TOO BIG...
DONCHA KNOW ANY OTHER hic TRICKSES?

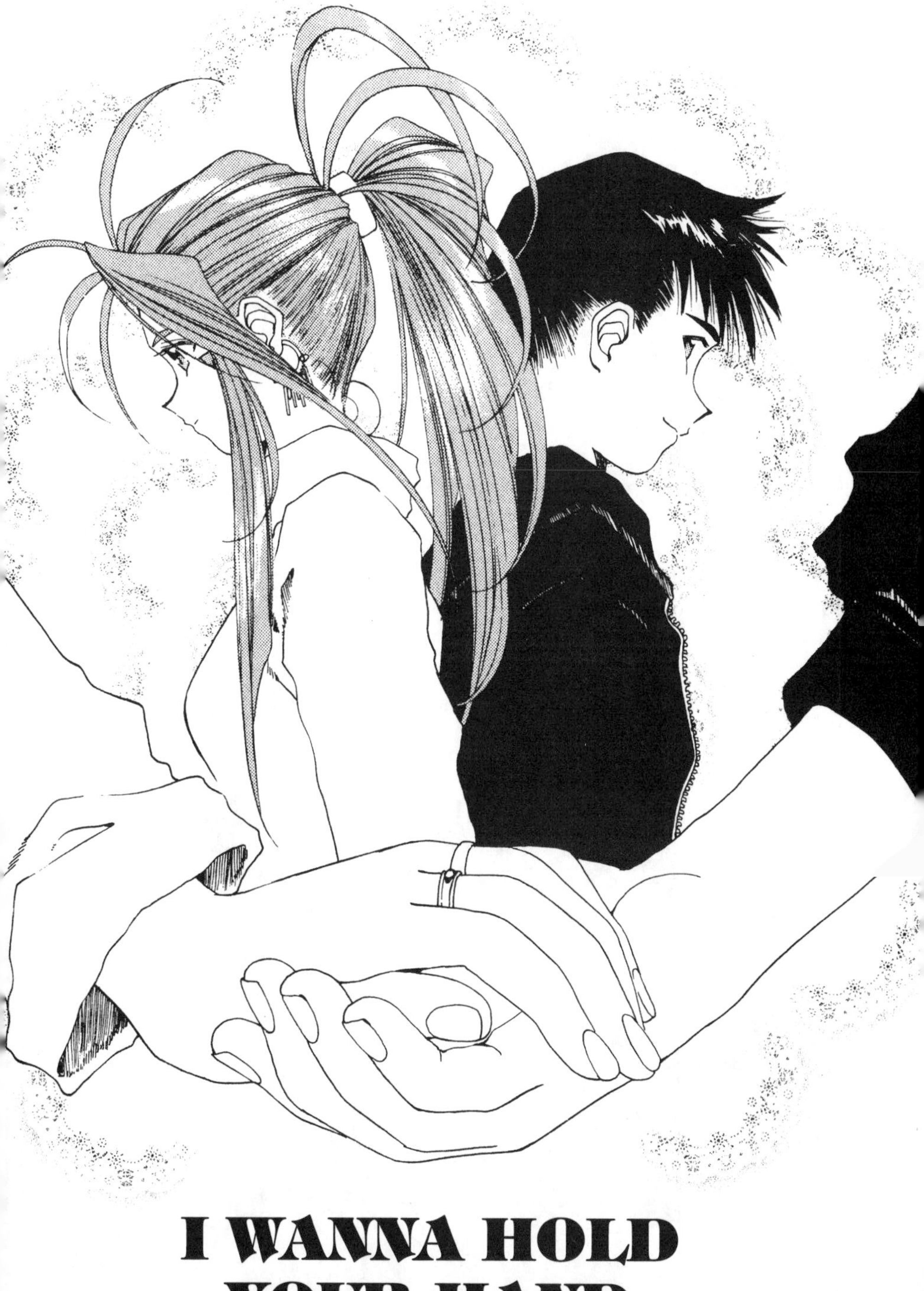

I WANNA HOLD YOUR HAND

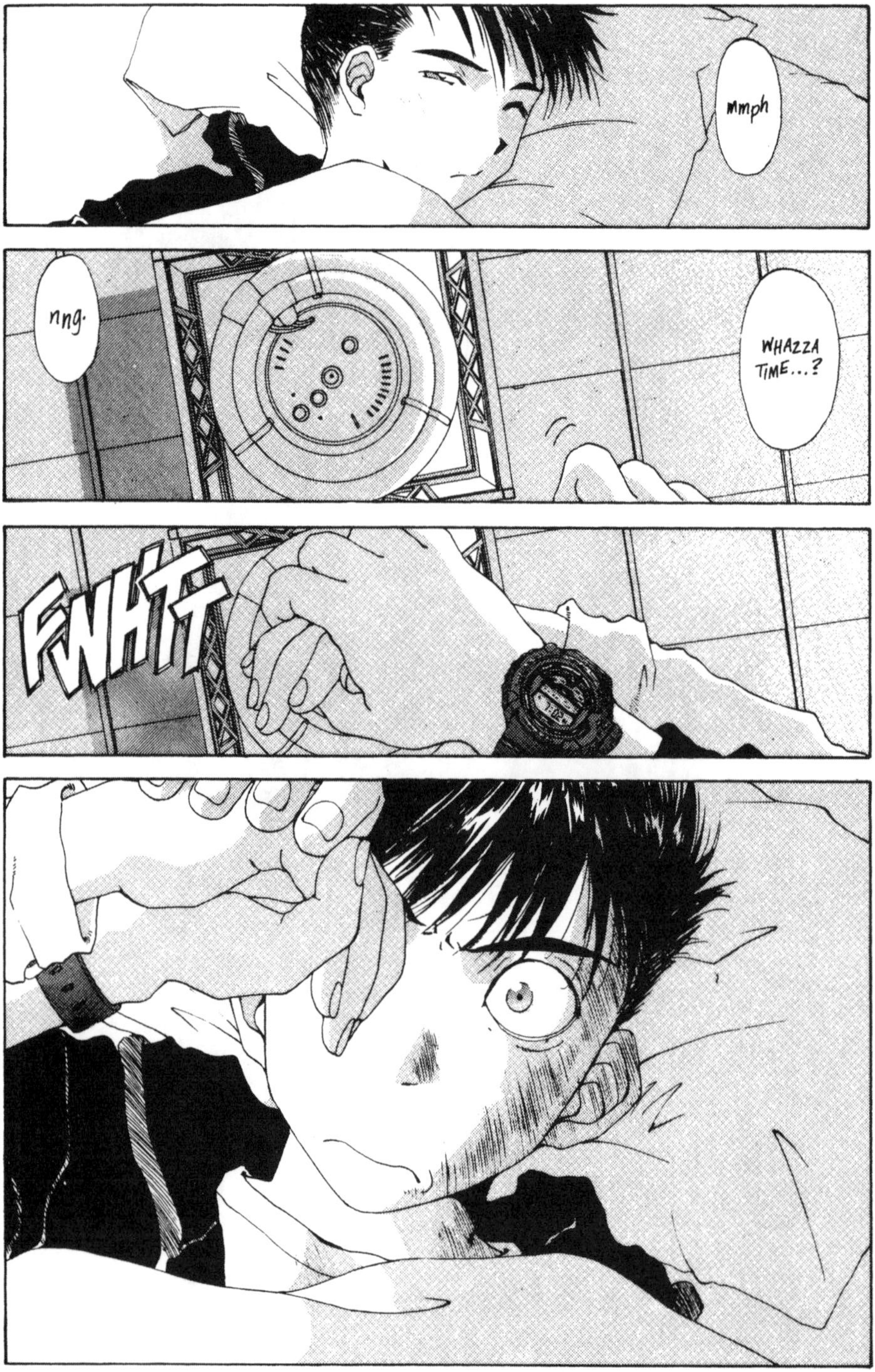
mmph
nng.
WHAZZA TIME...?
FWHTT

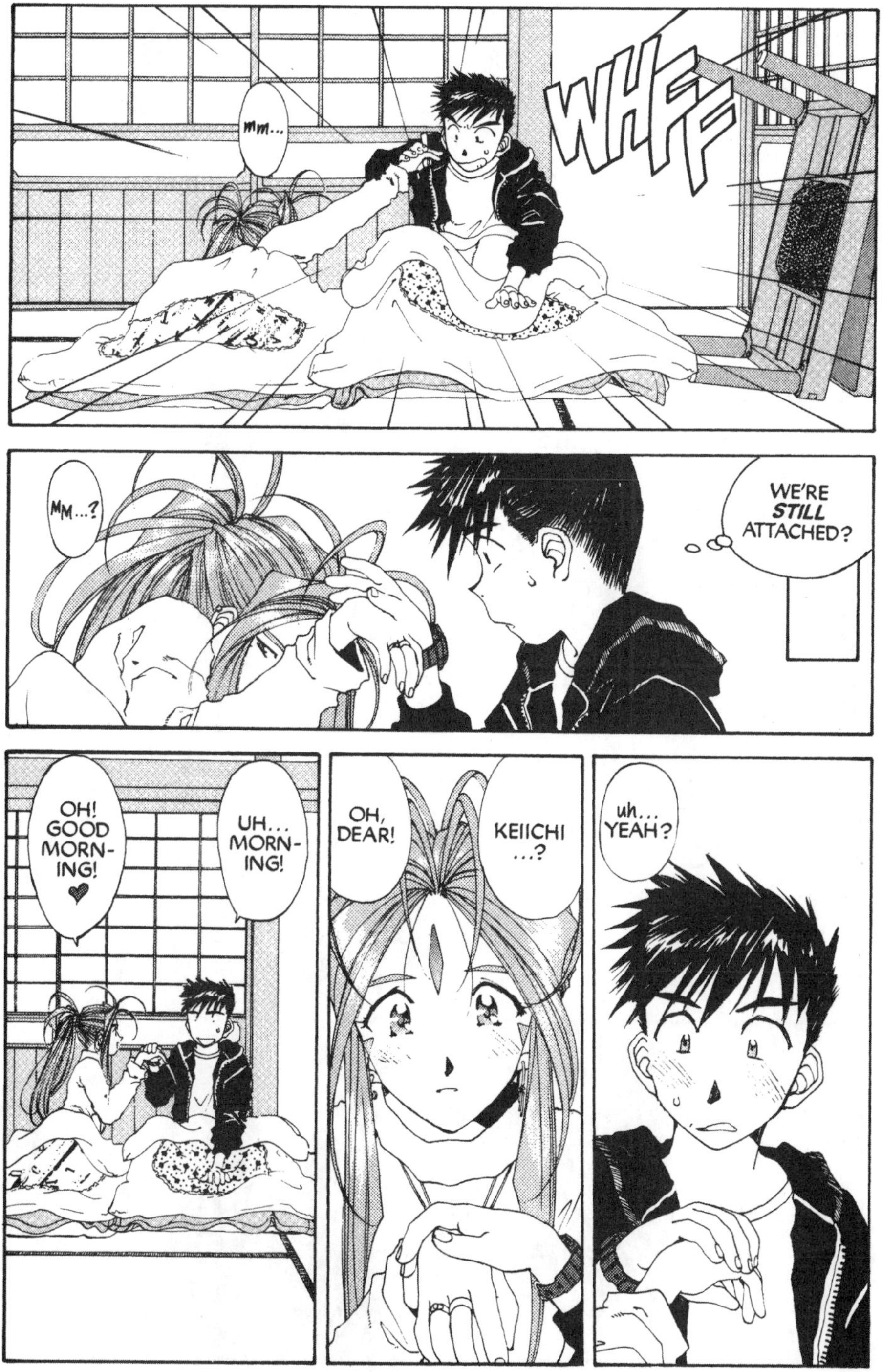
MM...
WHFF
MM...?
WE'RE STILL ATTACHED?
OH! GOOD MORNING! ♥
UH... MORNING!
OH, DEAR!
KEIICHI ...?
uh... YEAH?

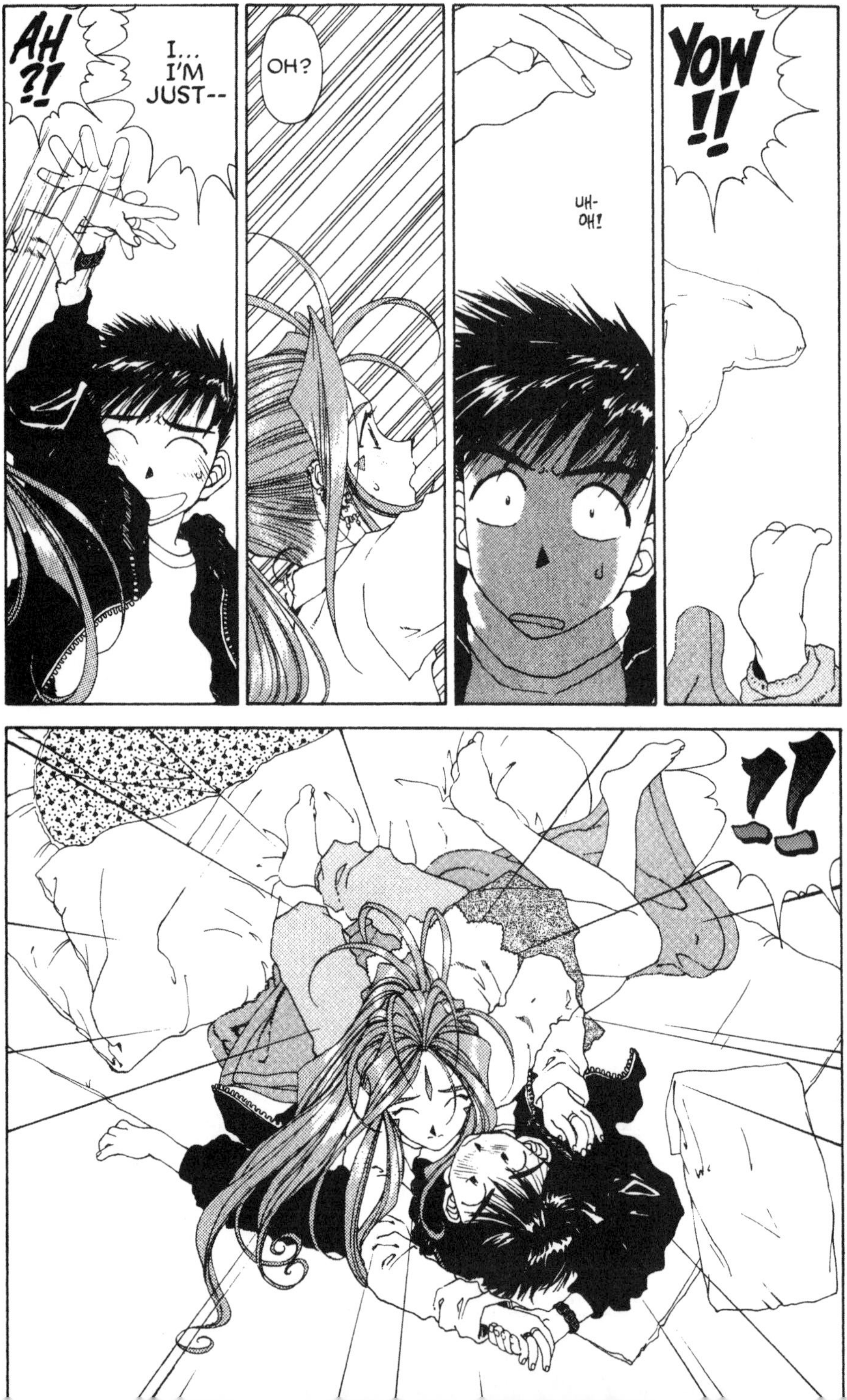
YOW!!
UH-OH!
OH?
AH?!
I... I'M JUST--
!!

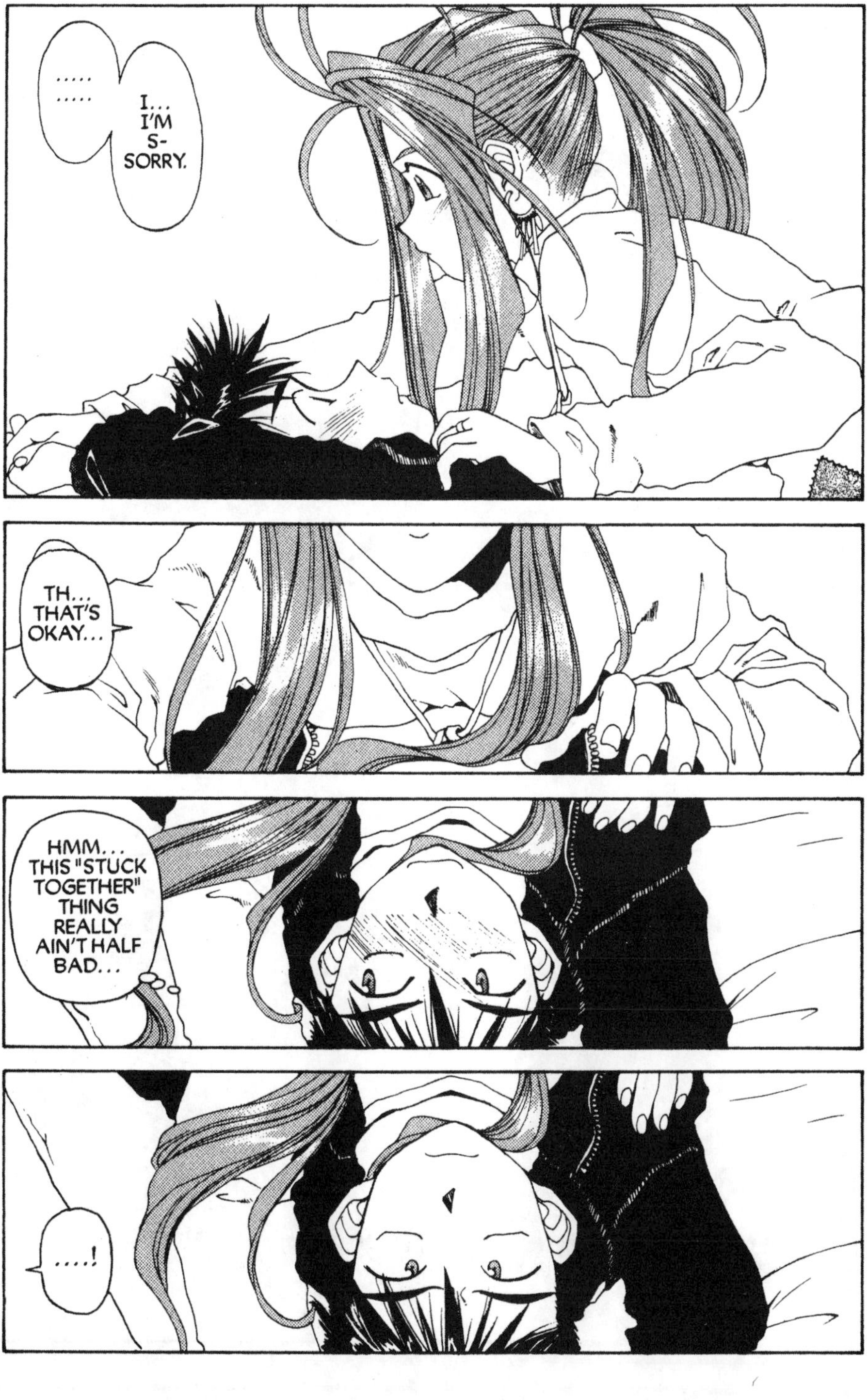

.....
.....
I... I'M S-SORRY.
TH... THAT'S OKAY...
HMM... THIS "STUCK TOGETHER" THING REALLY AIN'T HALF BAD...
.....!

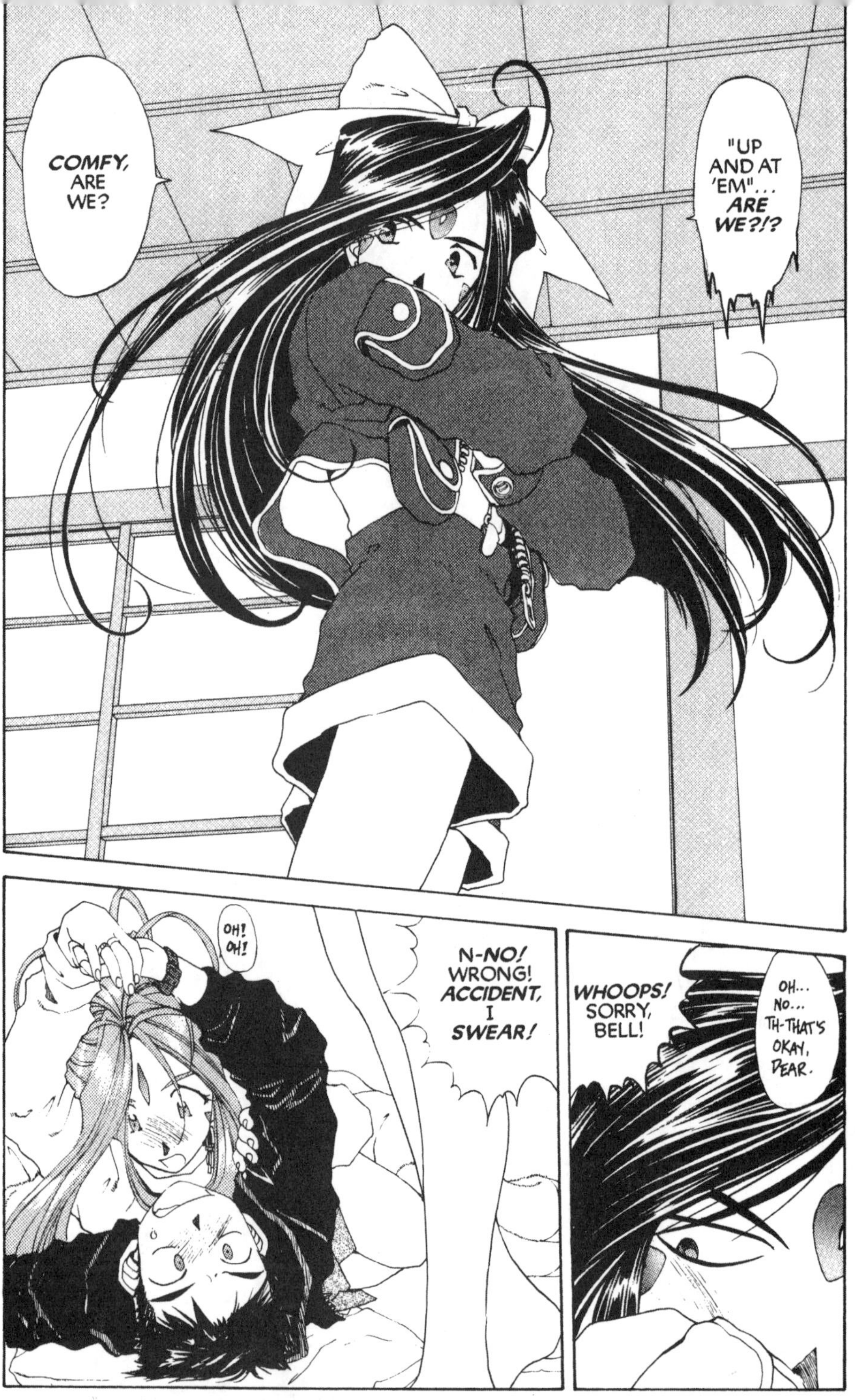
COMFY, ARE WE?
"UP AND AT 'EM"... ARE WE?!?
OH! OH!
N-NO! WRONG! ACCIDENT, I SWEAR!
WHOOPS! SORRY, BELL!
OH... NO... TH-THAT'S OKAY, DEAR.

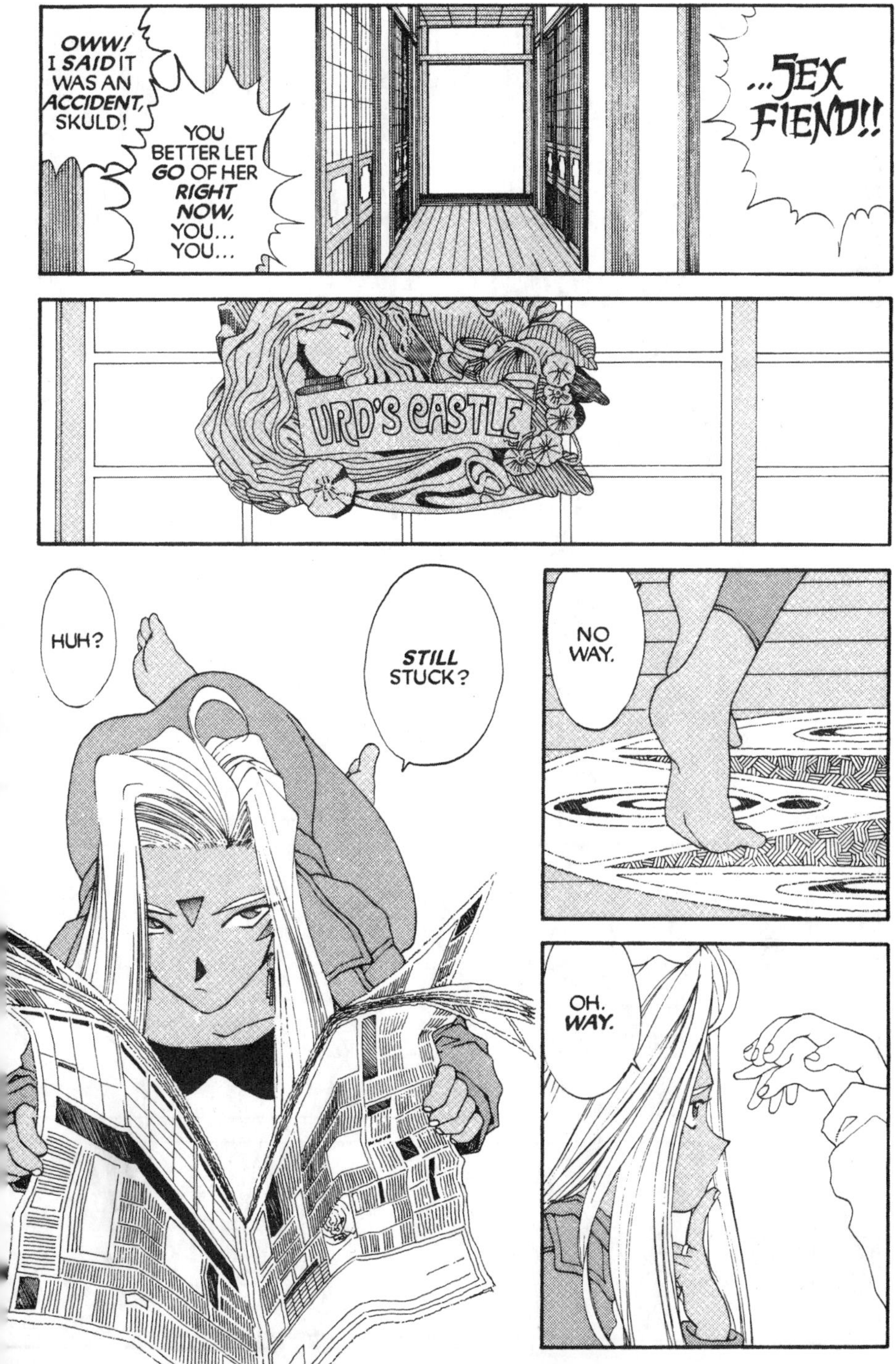
OWW! I SAID IT WAS AN ACCIDENT, SKULD!
YOU BETTER LET GO OF HER RIGHT NOW, YOU... YOU...
...SEX FIEND!!
URD'S CASTLE
HUH?
STILL STUCK?
NO WAY.
OH. WAY.

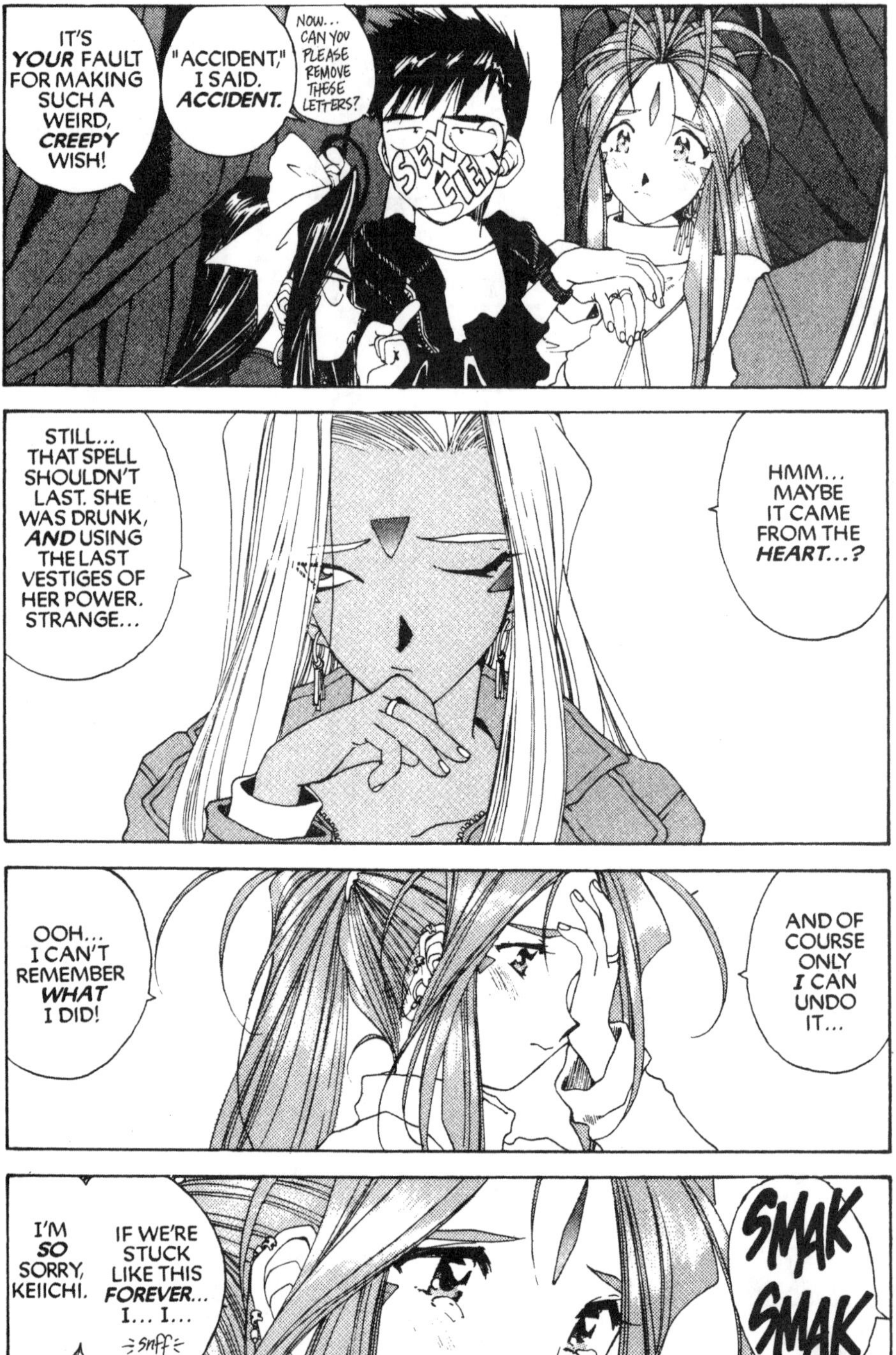
IT'S YOUR FAULT FOR MAKING SUCH A WEIRD, CREEPY WISH!
"ACCIDENT," I SAID. ACCIDENT.
NOW... CAN YOU PLEASE REMOVE THESE LETTERS?
SEX SIEN
STILL... THAT SPELL SHOULDN'T LAST. SHE WAS DRUNK, AND USING THE LAST VESTIGES OF HER POWER. STRANGE...
HMM... MAYBE IT CAME FROM THE HEART...?
OOH... I CAN'T REMEMBER WHAT I DID!
AND OF COURSE ONLY I CAN UNDO IT...
I'M SO SORRY, KEIICHI.
IF WE'RE STUCK LIKE THIS FOREVER... I... I...
snff
SMAK SMAK

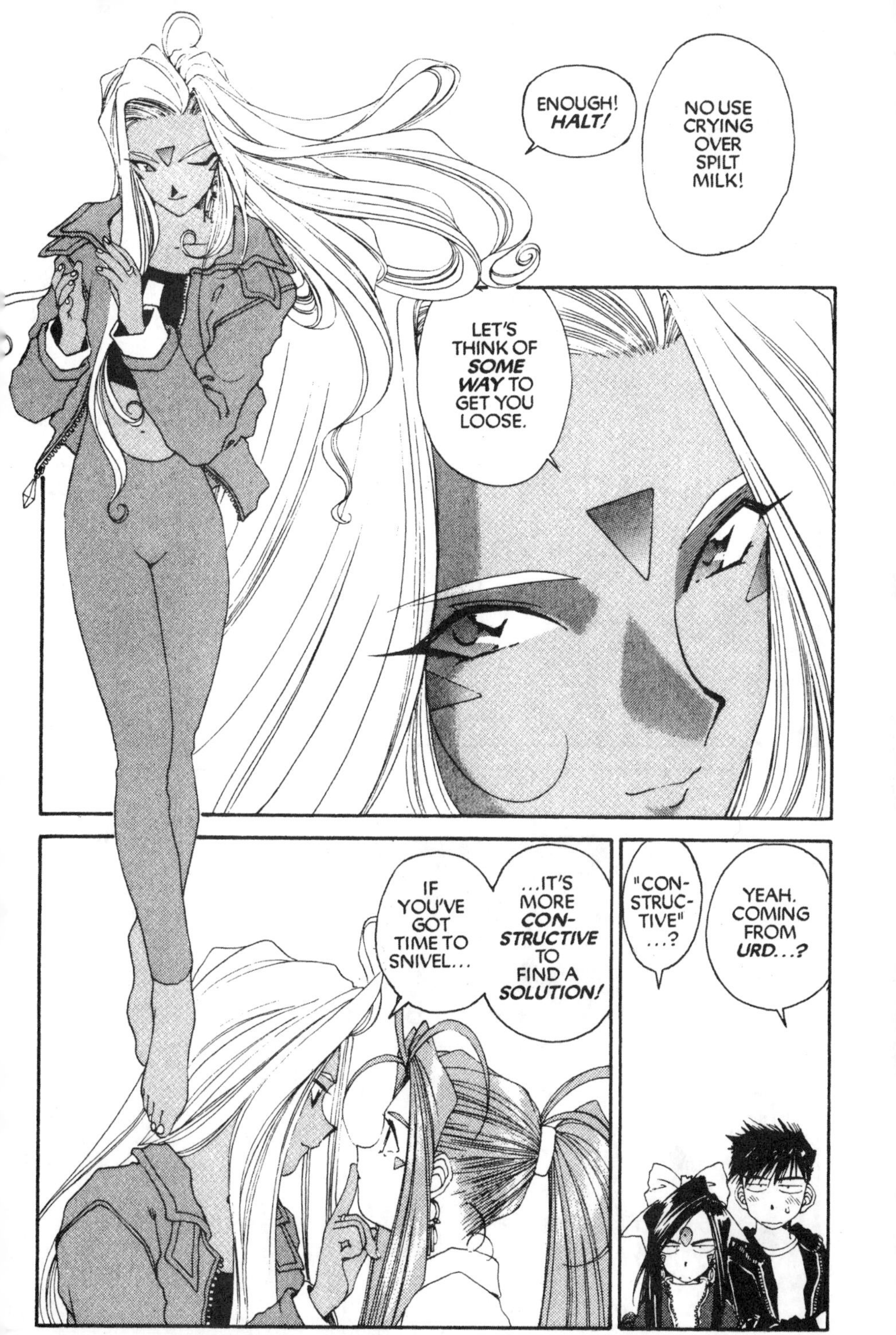
ENOUGH! *HALT!*
NO USE CRYING OVER SPILT MILK!
LET'S THINK OF ***SOME WAY*** TO GET YOU LOOSE.
IF YOU'VE GOT TIME TO SNIVEL...
...IT'S MORE ***CON-STRUCTIVE*** TO FIND A ***SOLUTION!***
"CON-STRUC-TIVE" ...?
YEAH. COMING FROM ***URD...?***

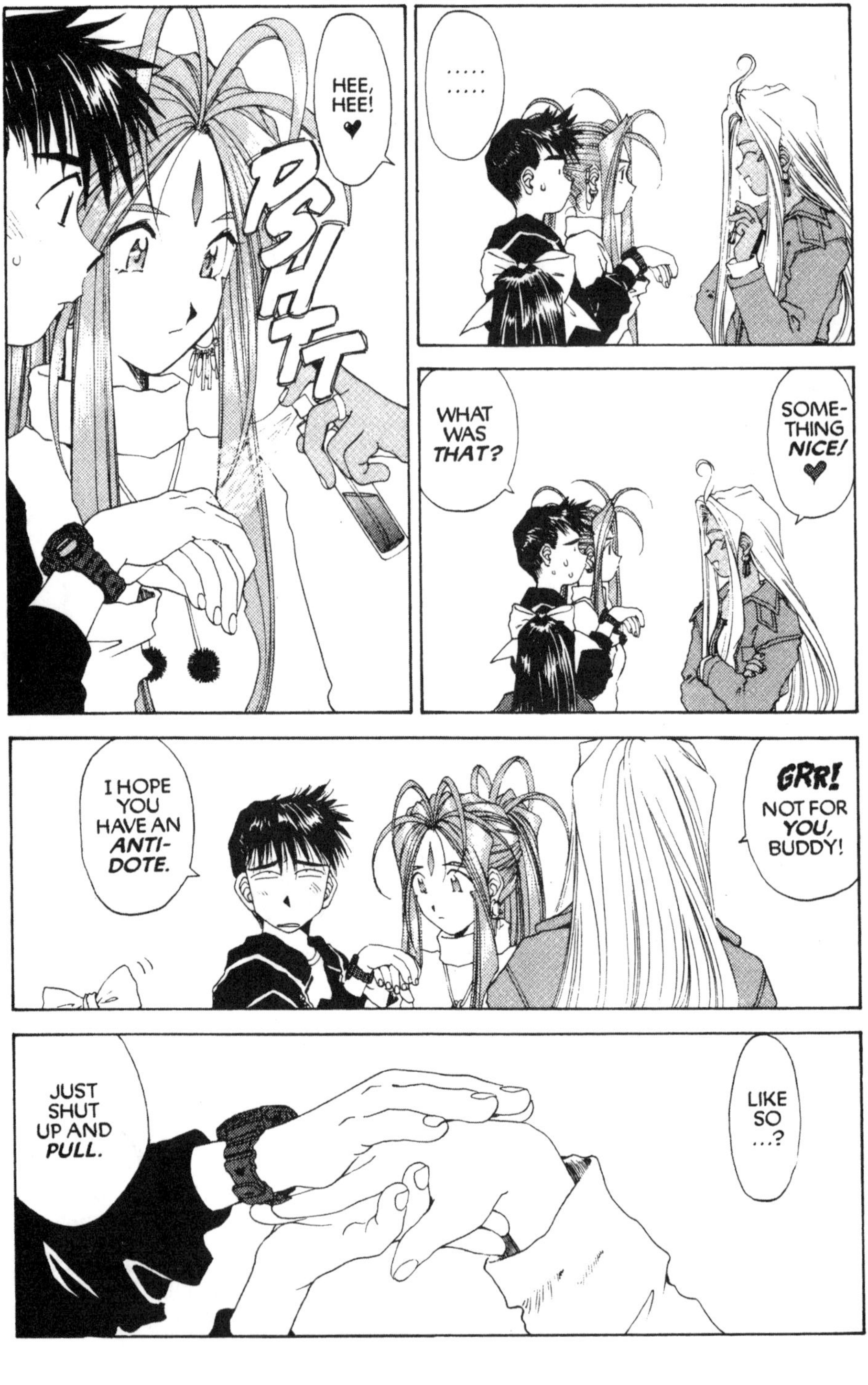
HEE, HEE! ♥
PSHTT
......
......
WHAT WAS *THAT?*
SOME-THING *NICE!* ♥
I HOPE YOU HAVE AN *ANTI-DOTE.*
GRR! NOT FOR *YOU,* BUDDY!
JUST SHUT UP AND *PULL.*
LIKE SO ...?

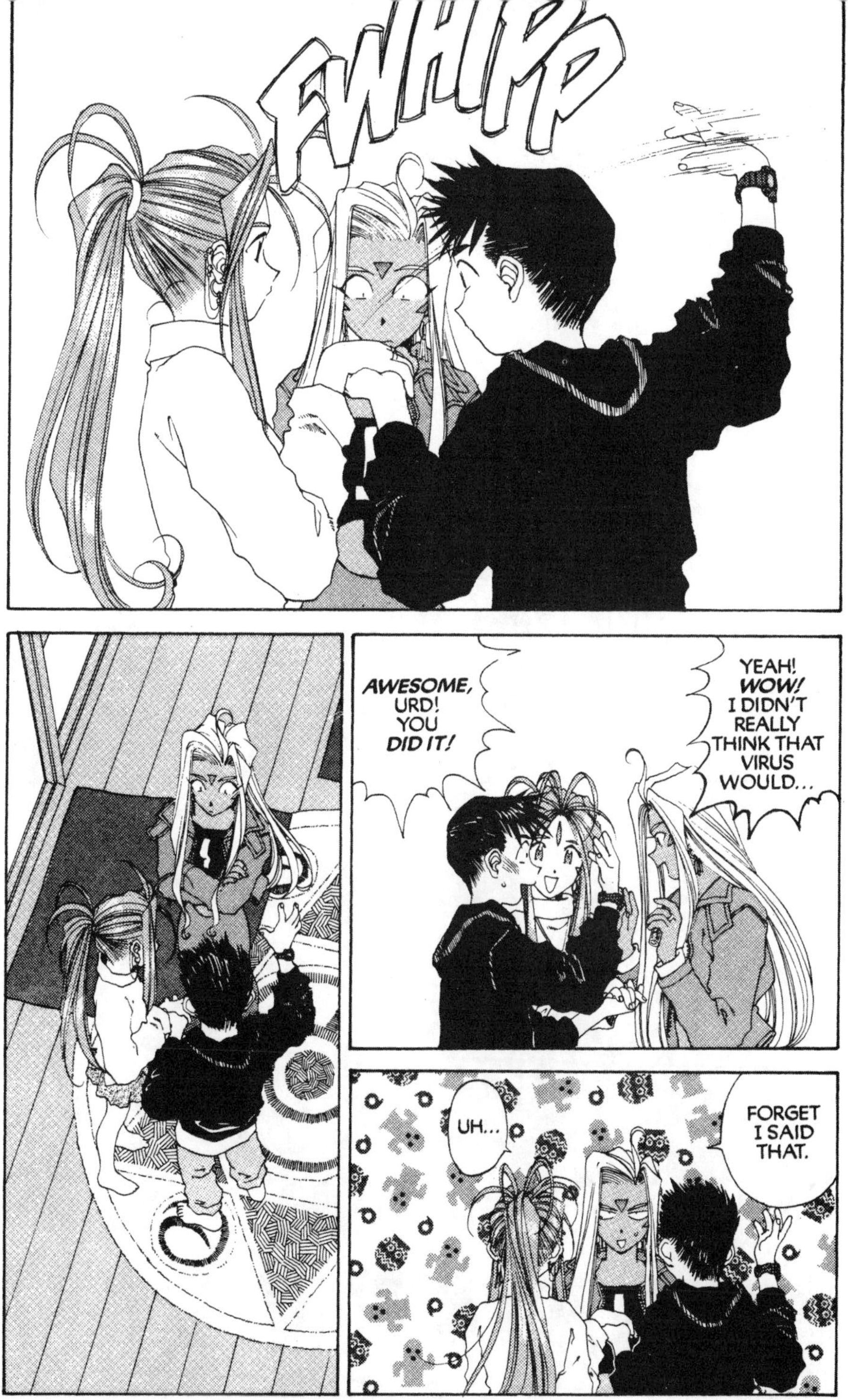
FWHIPP
AWESOME, URD! YOU DID IT!
YEAH! WOW! I DIDN'T REALLY THINK THAT VIRUS WOULD...
UH...
FORGET I SAID THAT.

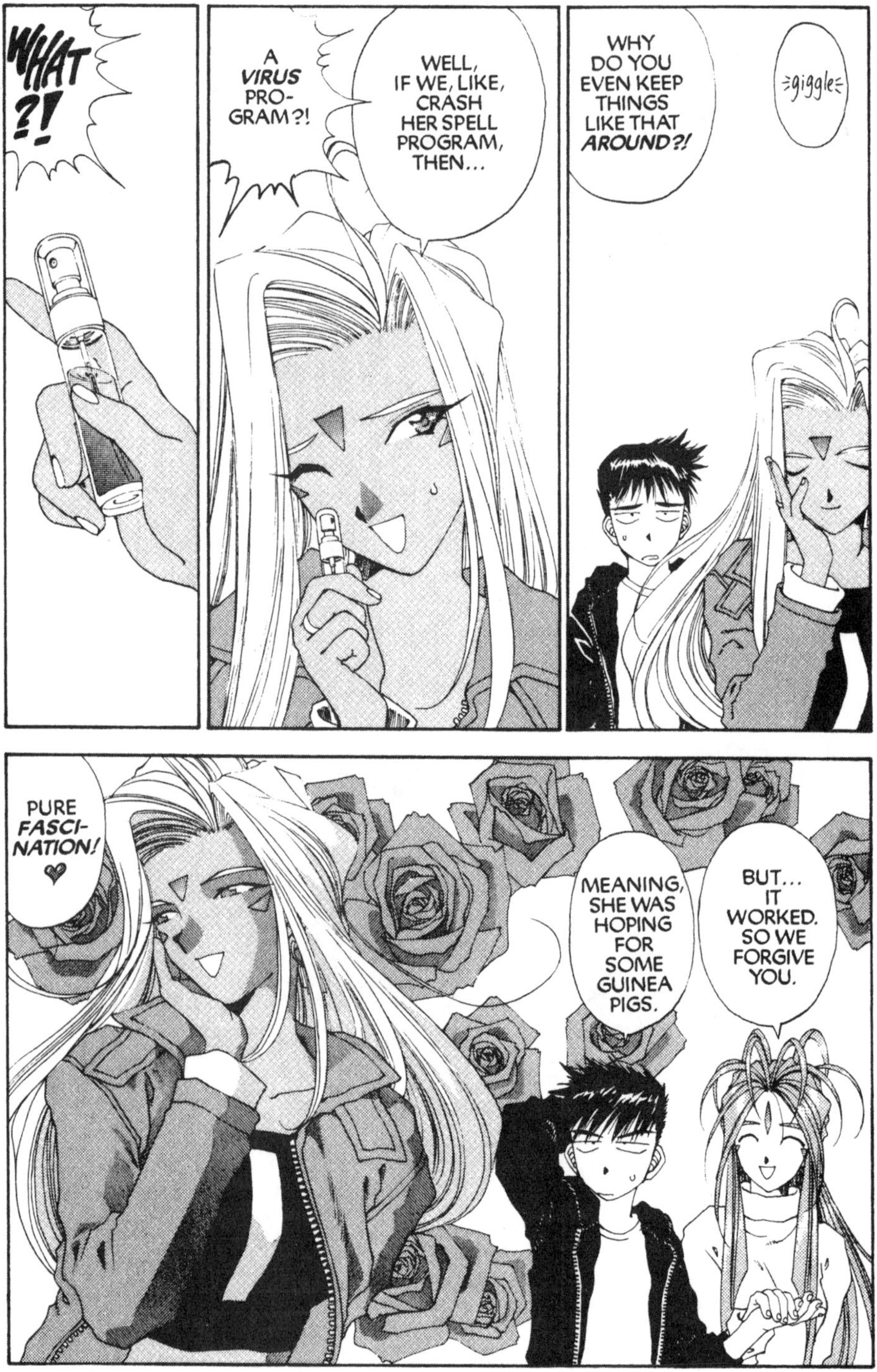
WHAT?!
A VIRUS PROGRAM?!
WELL, IF WE, LIKE, CRASH HER SPELL PROGRAM, THEN...
WHY DO YOU EVEN KEEP THINGS LIKE THAT AROUND?!
giggle
PURE FASCINATION! ♥
MEANING, SHE WAS HOPING FOR SOME GUINEA PIGS.
BUT... IT WORKED. SO WE FORGIVE YOU.

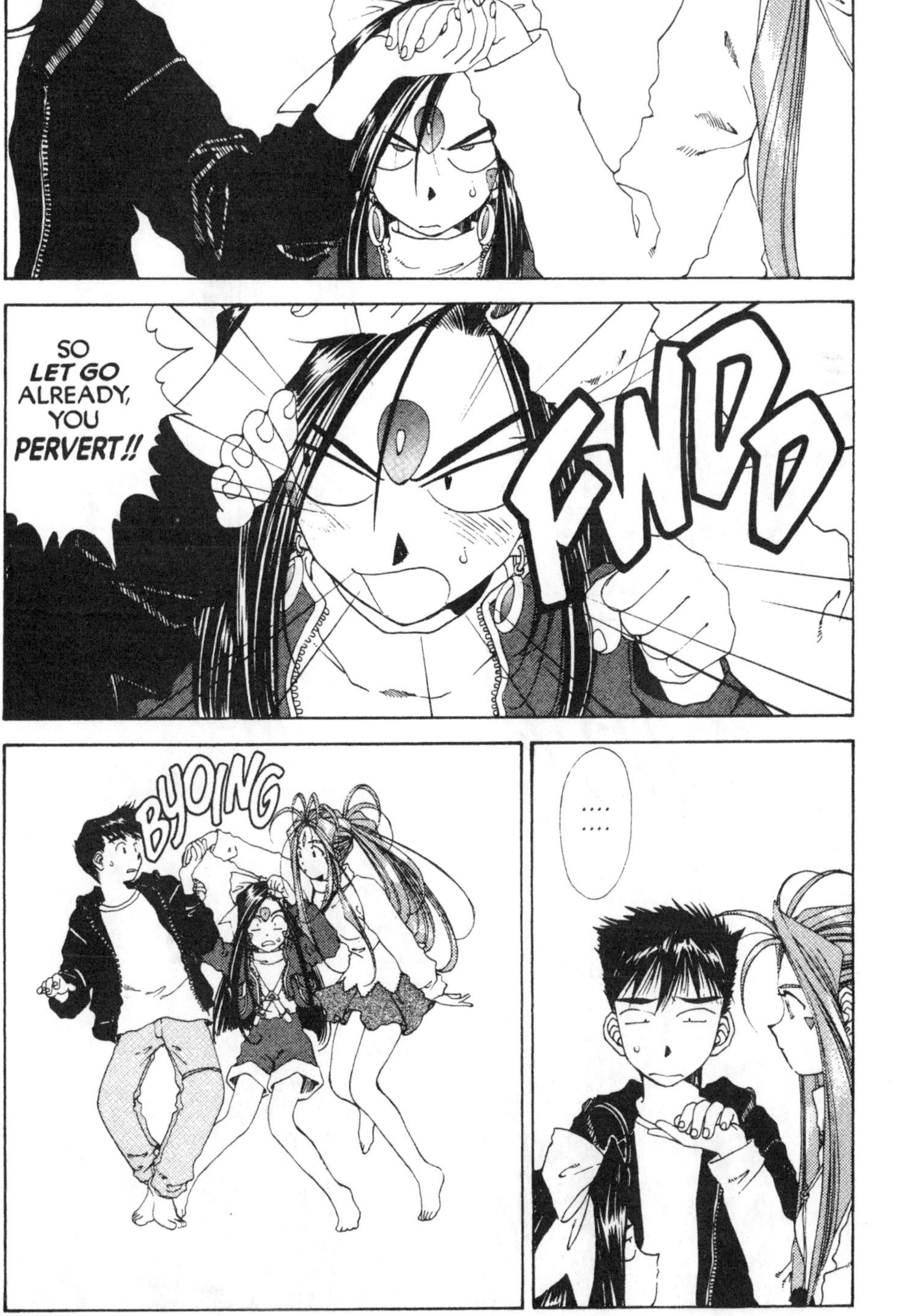
SO *LET GO* ALREADY, YOU **PERVERT!!**
FWOD
BYOING
....
....

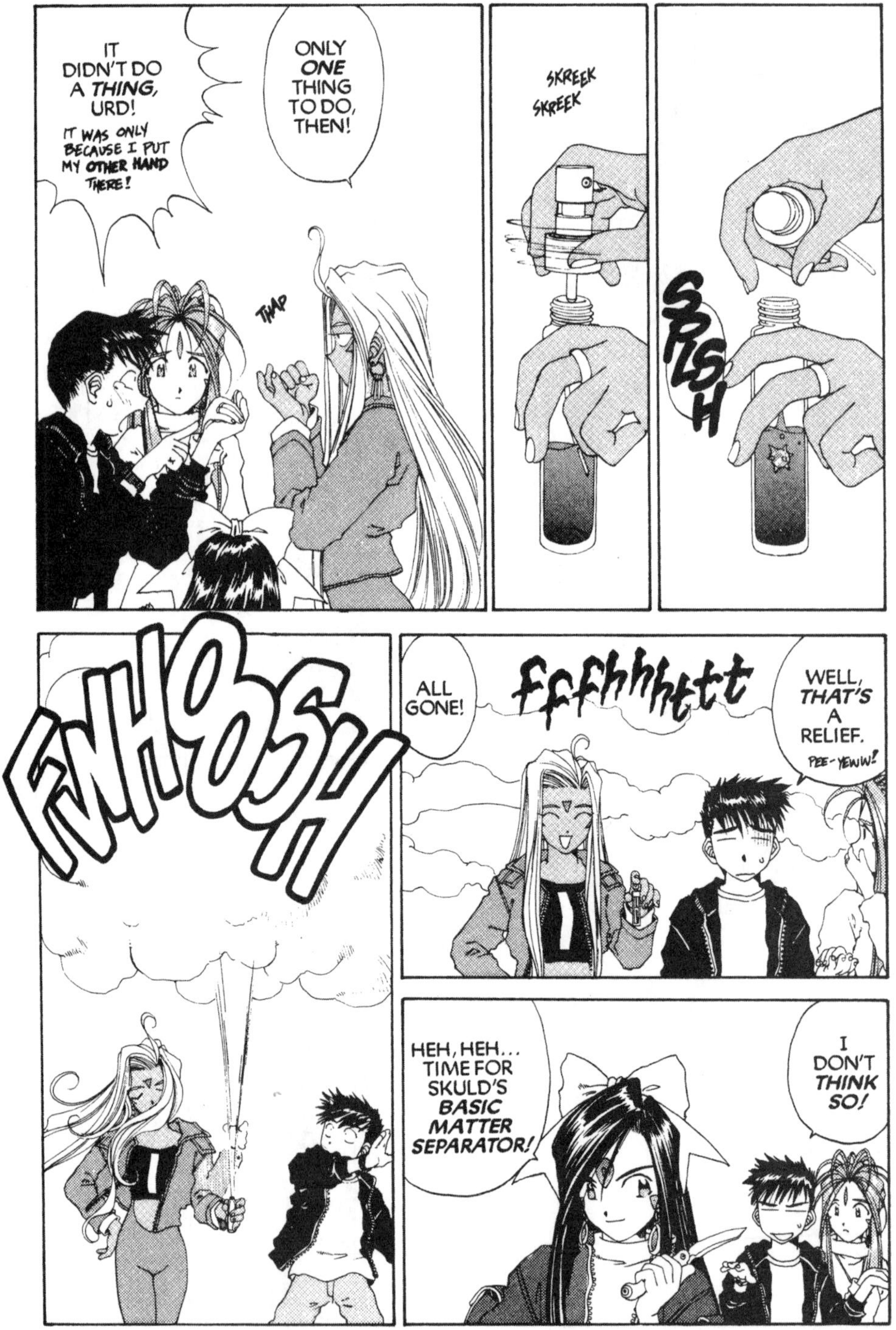
IT DIDN'T DO A THING, URD!
IT WAS ONLY BECAUSE I PUT MY OTHER HAND THERE!
ONLY ONE THING TO DO, THEN!
THAP
SKREEK
SKREEK
SPLSH
FWHOOSH
ALL GONE!
FFFHHHTTT
WELL, THAT'S A RELIEF.
PEE-YEWW!
HEH, HEH... TIME FOR SKULD'S BASIC MATTER SEPARATOR!
I DON'T THINK SO!

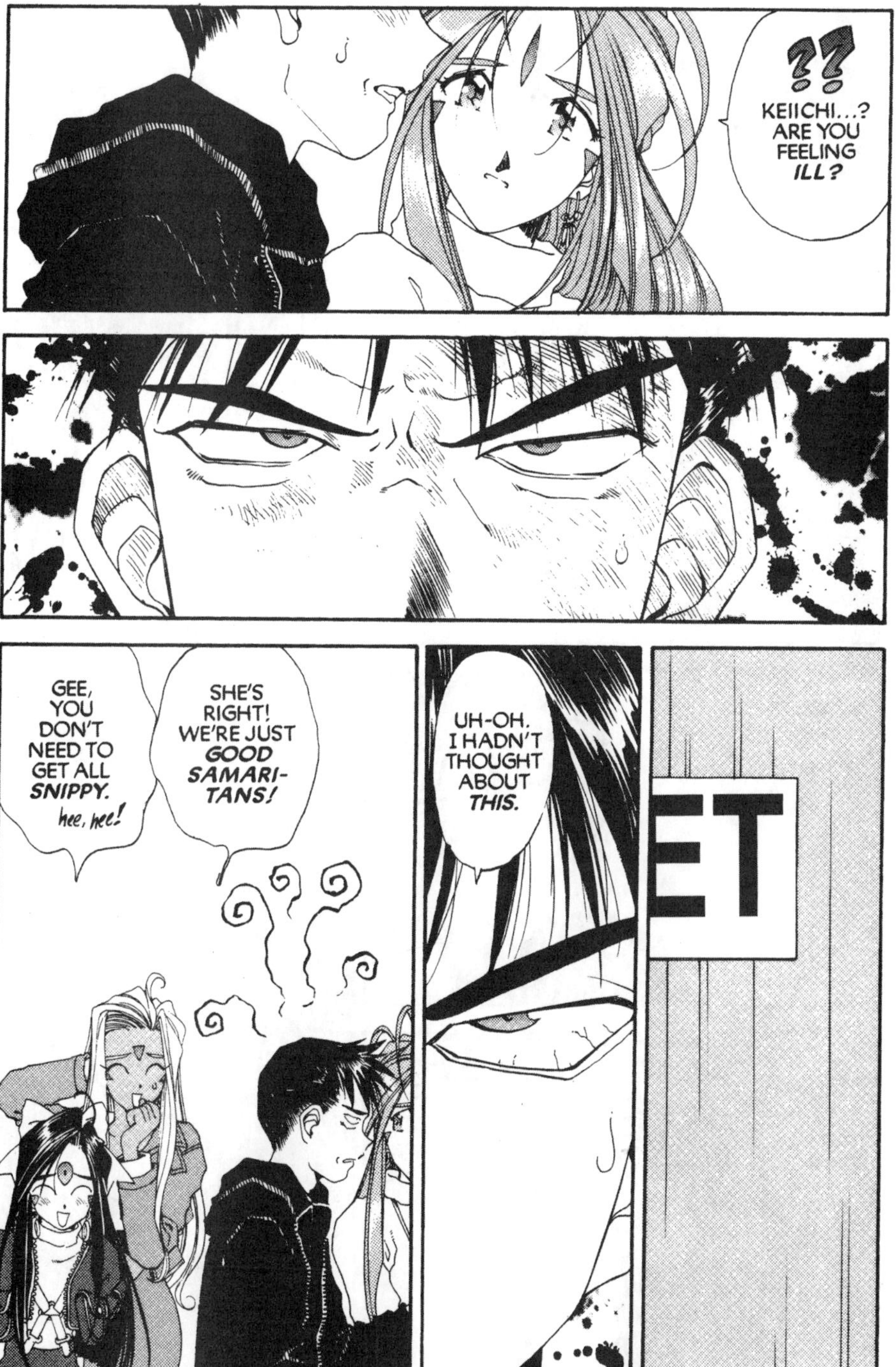
??
KEIICHI...? ARE YOU FEELING ILL?
GEE, YOU DON'T NEED TO GET ALL SNIPPY.
hee, hee!
SHE'S RIGHT! WE'RE JUST GOOD SAMARITANS!
UH-OH. I HADN'T THOUGHT ABOUT THIS.
ET

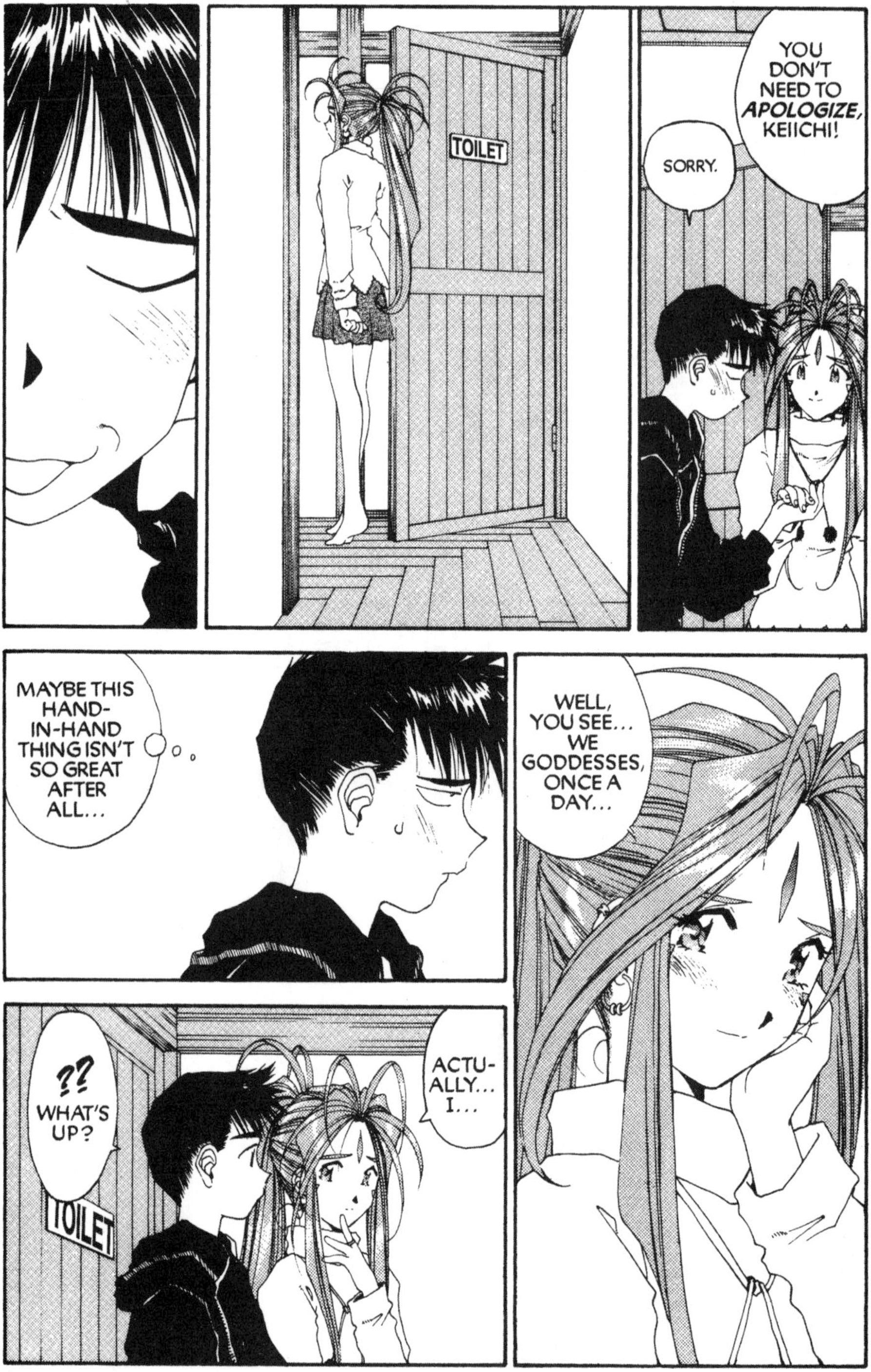
TOILET
SORRY.
YOU DON'T NEED TO *APOLOGIZE*, KEIICHI!
MAYBE THIS HAND-IN-HAND THING ISN'T SO GREAT AFTER ALL...
?? WHAT'S UP?
TOILET
ACTU-ALLY... I...
WELL, YOU SEE... WE GODDESSES, ONCE A DAY...

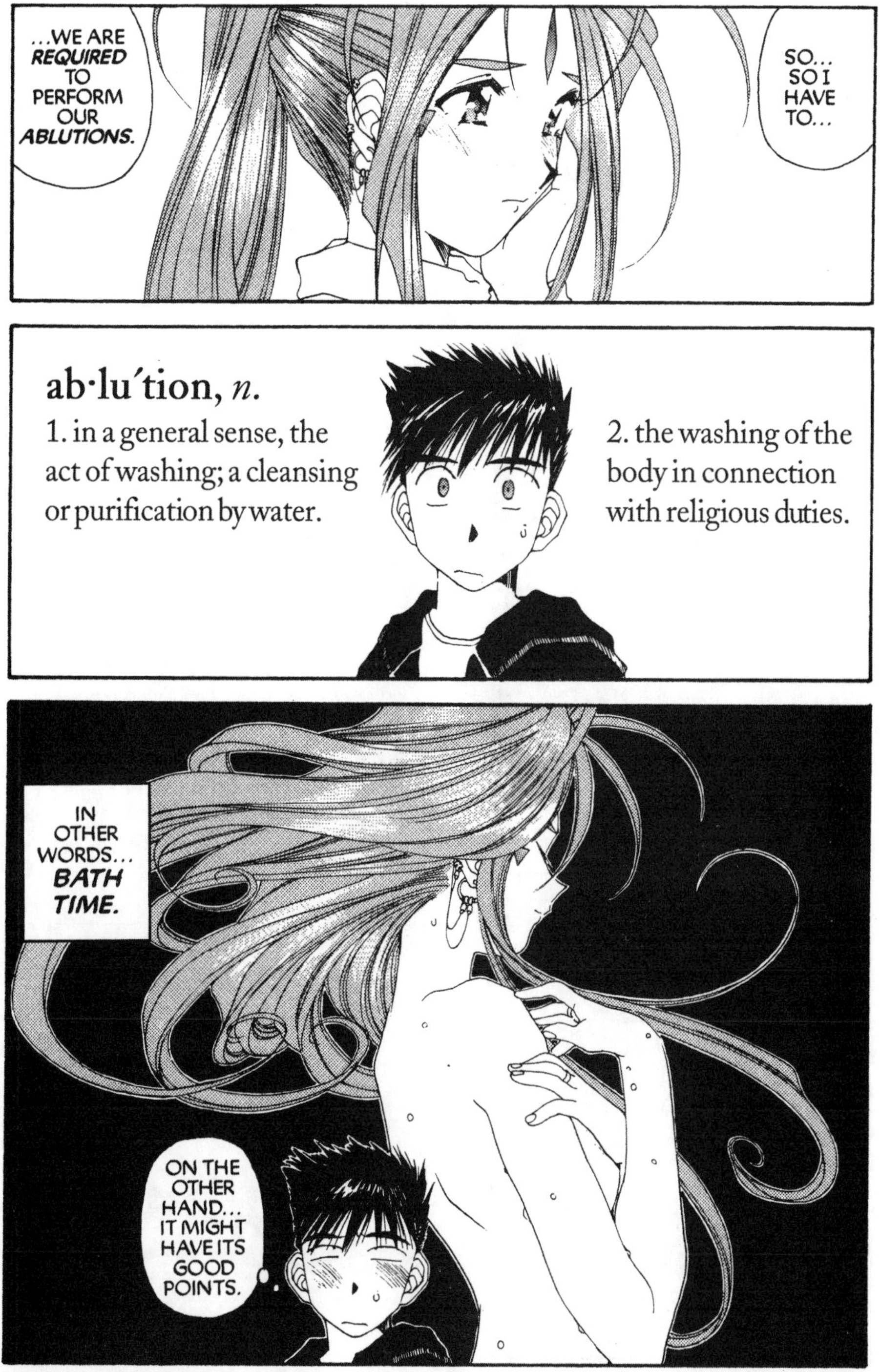
...WE ARE *REQUIRED* TO PERFORM OUR *ABLUTIONS.*
SO... SO I HAVE TO...
ab·lu′tion, *n.*
1. in a general sense, the act of washing; a cleansing or purification by water.
2. the washing of the body in connection with religious duties.
IN OTHER WORDS... *BATH TIME.*
ON THE OTHER HAND... IT MIGHT HAVE ITS GOOD POINTS.

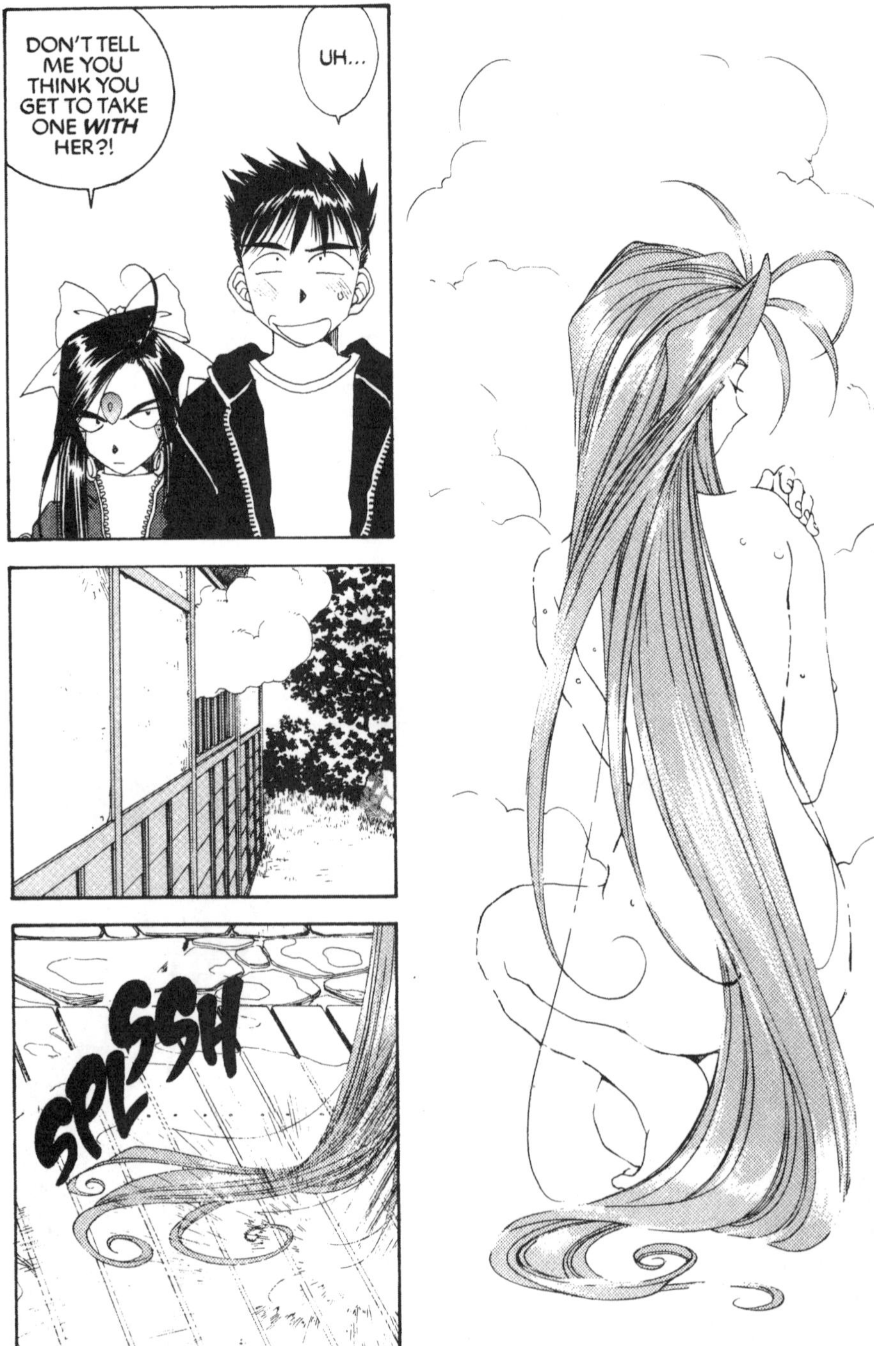
DON'T TELL ME YOU THINK YOU GET TO TAKE ONE *WITH* HER?!
UH...
SPLSSH

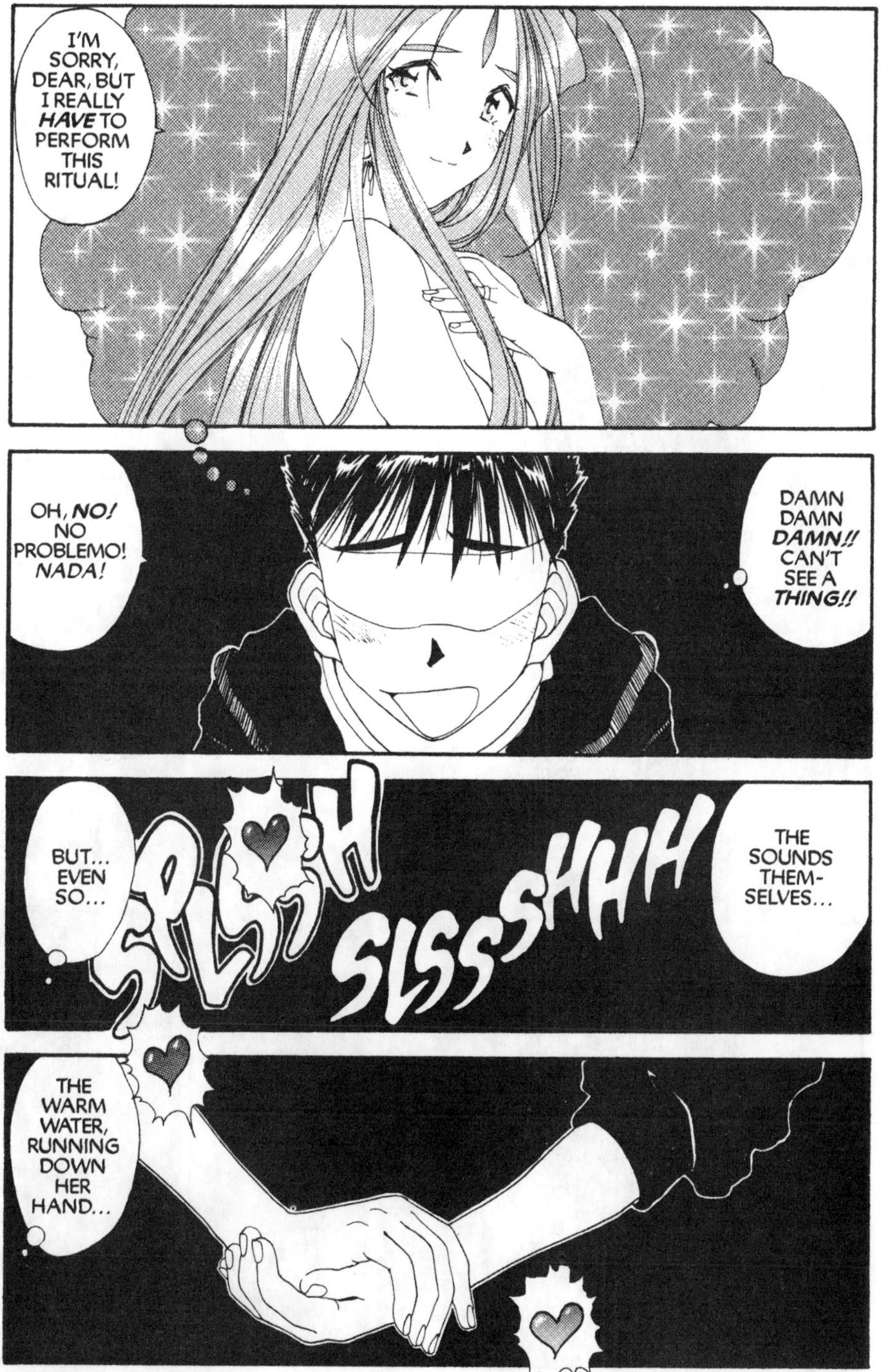
I'M SORRY, DEAR, BUT I REALLY *HAVE* TO PERFORM THIS RITUAL!
OH, *NO!* NO PROBLEMO! *NADA!*
DAMN DAMN *DAMN!!* CAN'T SEE A *THING!!*
BUT... EVEN SO...
SPLASH
SLSS-SHHH
THE SOUNDS THEM-SELVES...
THE WARM WATER, RUNNING DOWN HER HAND...

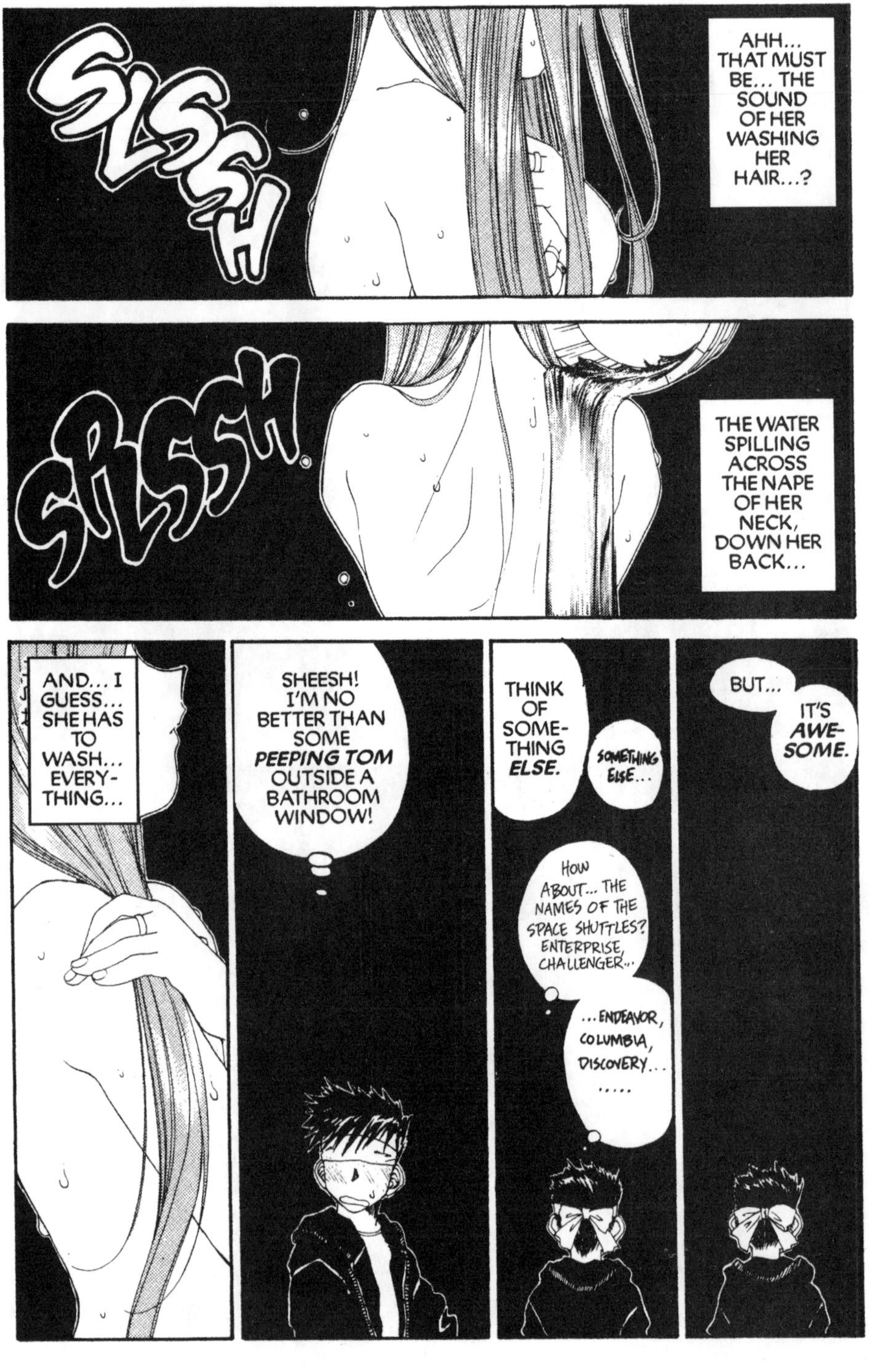
SLSSH
AHH... THAT MUST BE... THE SOUND OF HER WASHING HER HAIR...?
SRSSH
THE WATER SPILLING ACROSS THE NAPE OF HER NECK, DOWN HER BACK...
AND... I GUESS... SHE HAS TO WASH... EVERY-THING...
SHEESH! I'M NO BETTER THAN SOME PEEPING TOM OUTSIDE A BATHROOM WINDOW!
THINK OF SOME-THING ELSE.
SOMETHING ELSE...
HOW ABOUT... THE NAMES OF THE SPACE SHUTTLES? ENTERPRISE, CHALLENGER...
...ENDEAVOR, COLUMBIA, DISCOVERY... .....
BUT...
IT'S AWE-SOME.

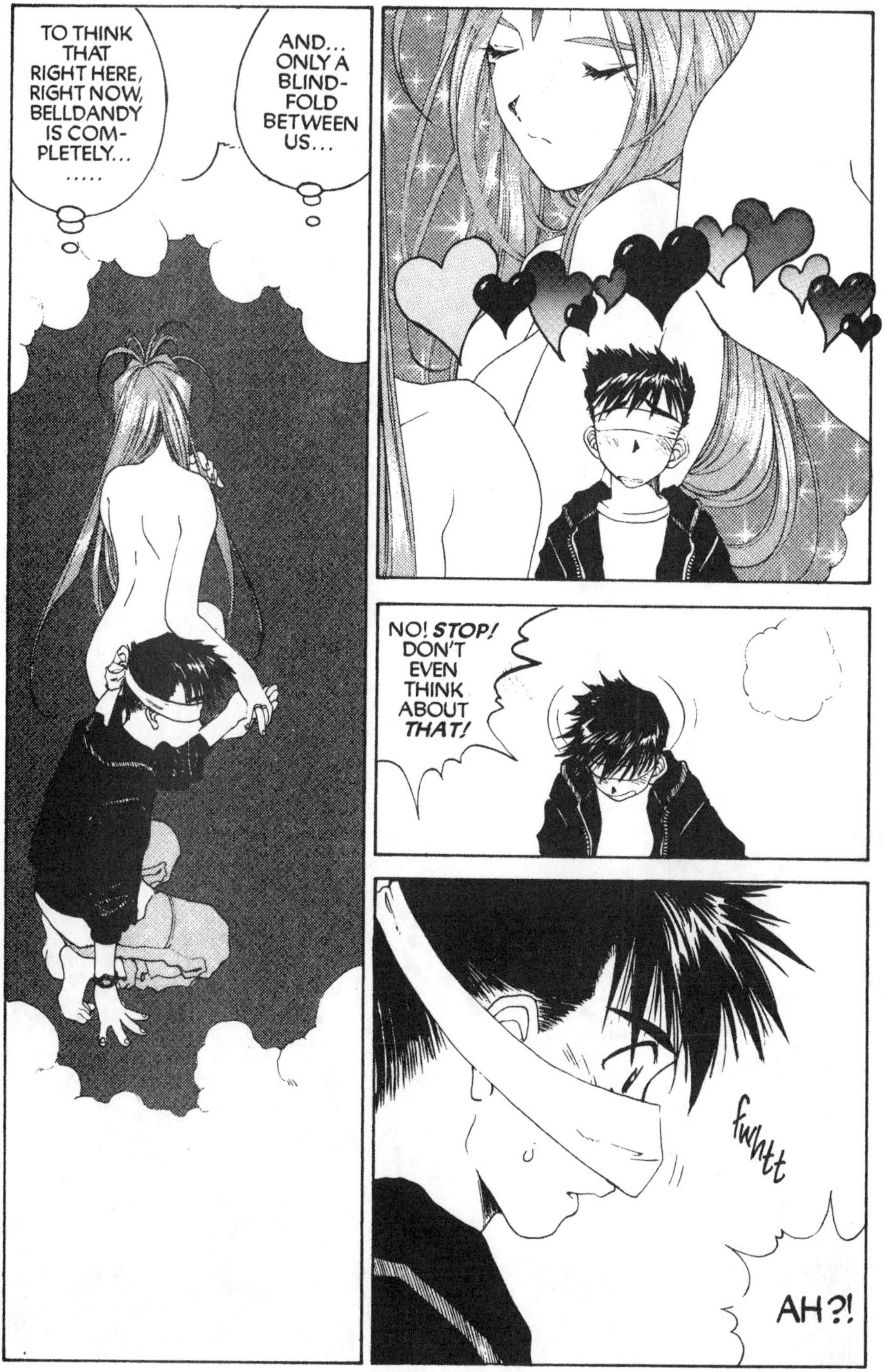
TO THINK THAT RIGHT HERE, RIGHT NOW, BELLDANDY IS COMPLETELY... .....
AND... ONLY A BLINDFOLD BETWEEN US...
NO! *STOP!* DON'T EVEN THINK ABOUT *THAT!*
fwhtt
AH?!

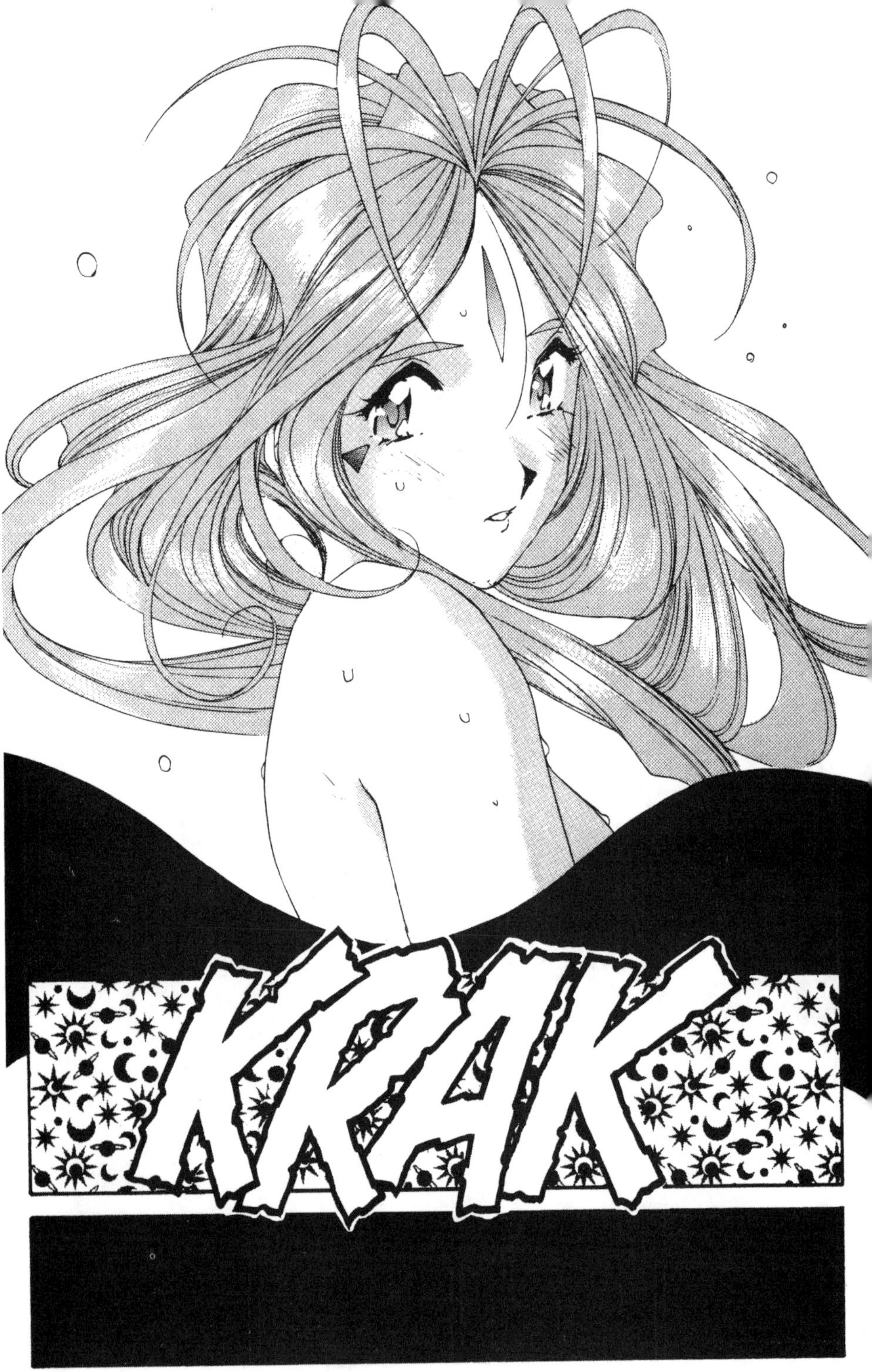
KRAK

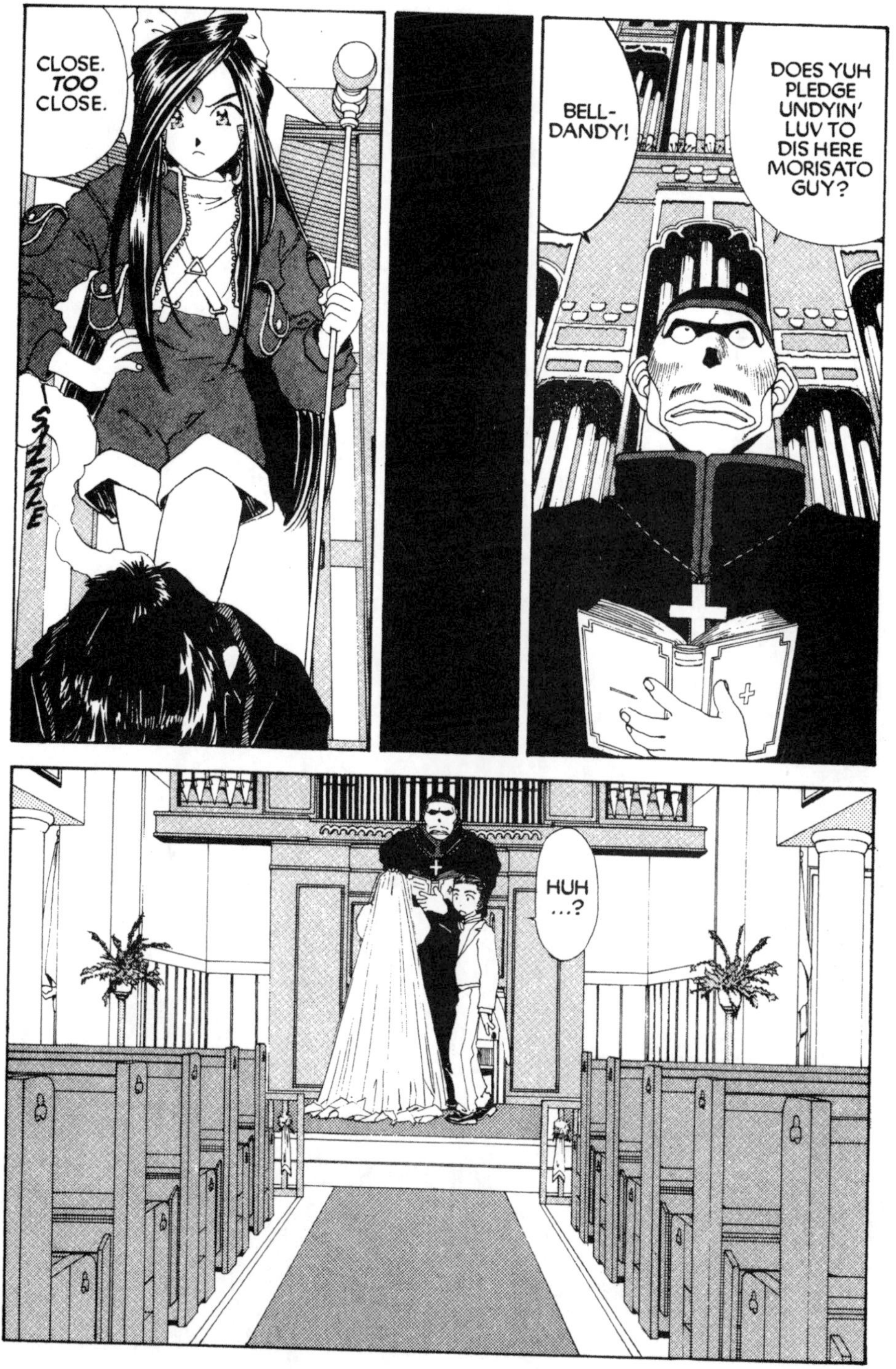
CLOSE. TOO CLOSE.
SIZZLE
BELL-DANDY!
DOES YUH PLEDGE UNDYIN' LUV TO DIS HERE MORISATO GUY?
HUH ...?

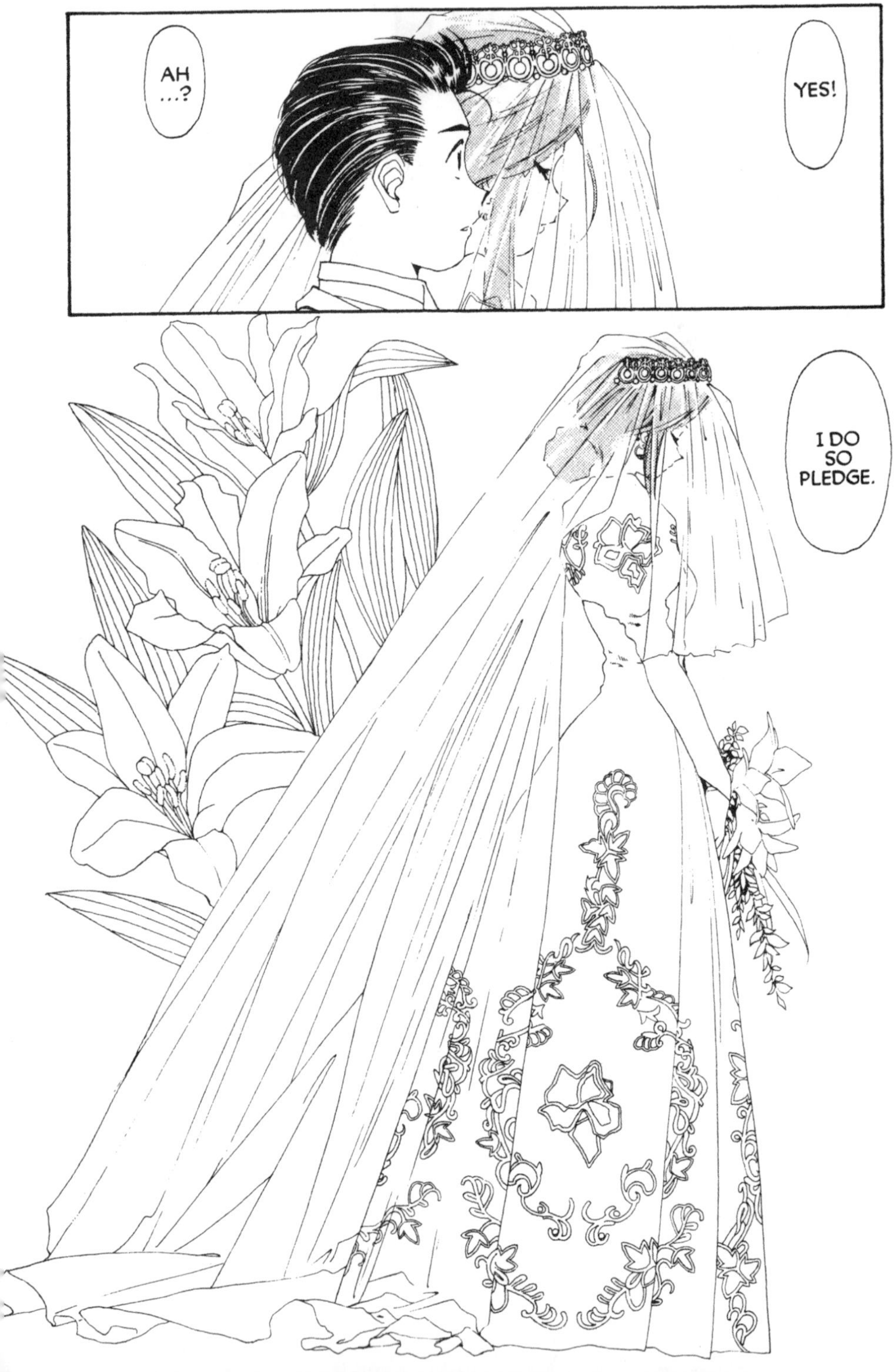
YES!
AH ...?
I DO SO PLEDGE.

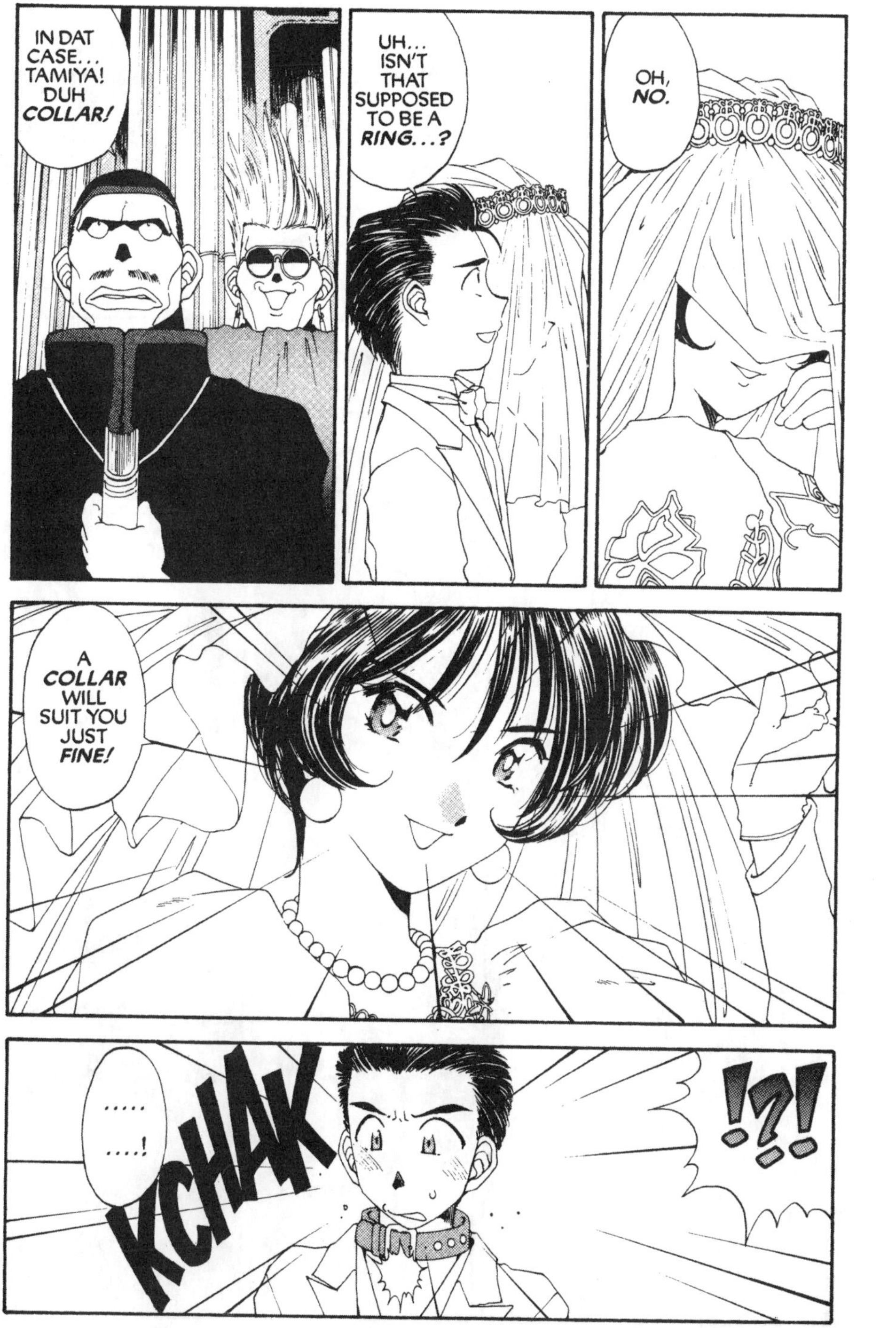
IN DAT CASE... TAMIYA! DUH COLLAR!
UH... ISN'T THAT SUPPOSED TO BE A RING...?
OH, NO.
A COLLAR WILL SUIT YOU JUST FINE!
....!
KCHAK
!?!

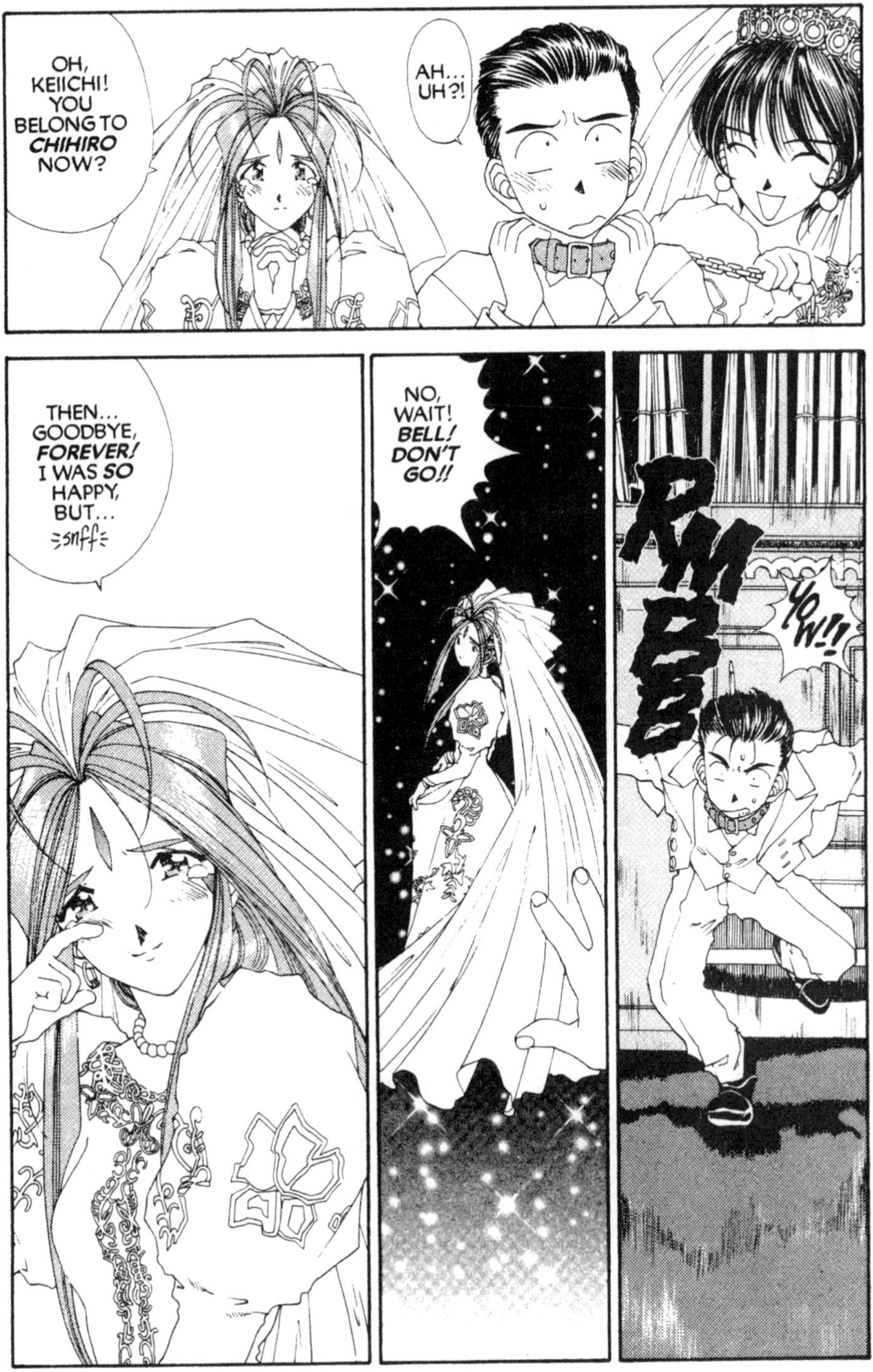
OH, KEIICHI! YOU BELONG TO CHIHIRO NOW?
AH... UH?!
THEN... GOODBYE, FOREVER! I WAS SO HAPPY, BUT... =snff=
NO, WAIT! BELL! DON'T GO!!
RMBBB
YOW!!

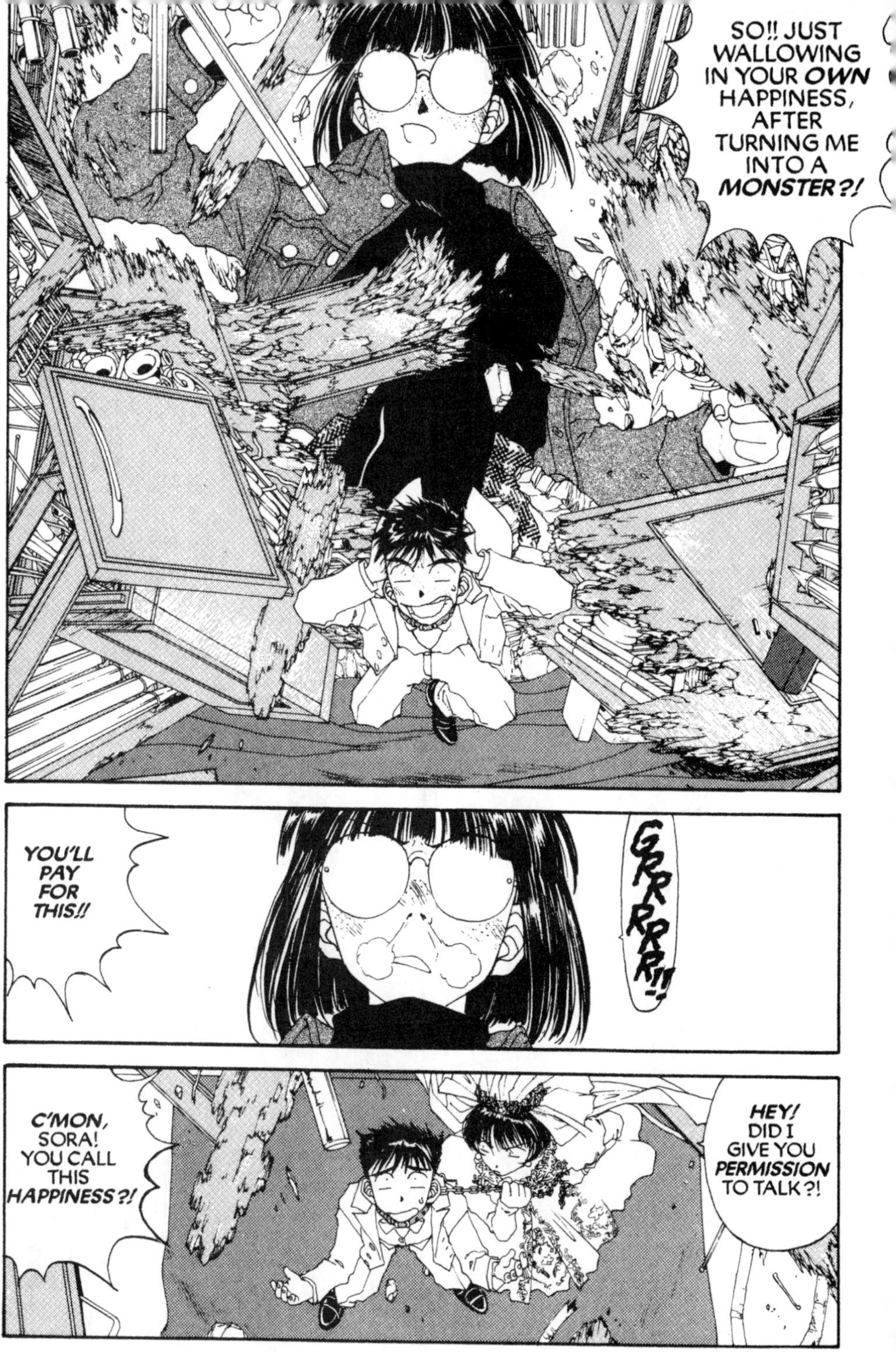
SO!! JUST WALLOWING IN YOUR *OWN* HAPPINESS, AFTER TURNING ME INTO A ***MONSTER?!***
YOU'LL PAY FOR THIS!!
GRRRRRR!!
*C'MON, SORA! YOU CALL THIS **HAPPINESS?!***
HEY! DID I GIVE YOU ***PERMISSION*** TO TALK?!

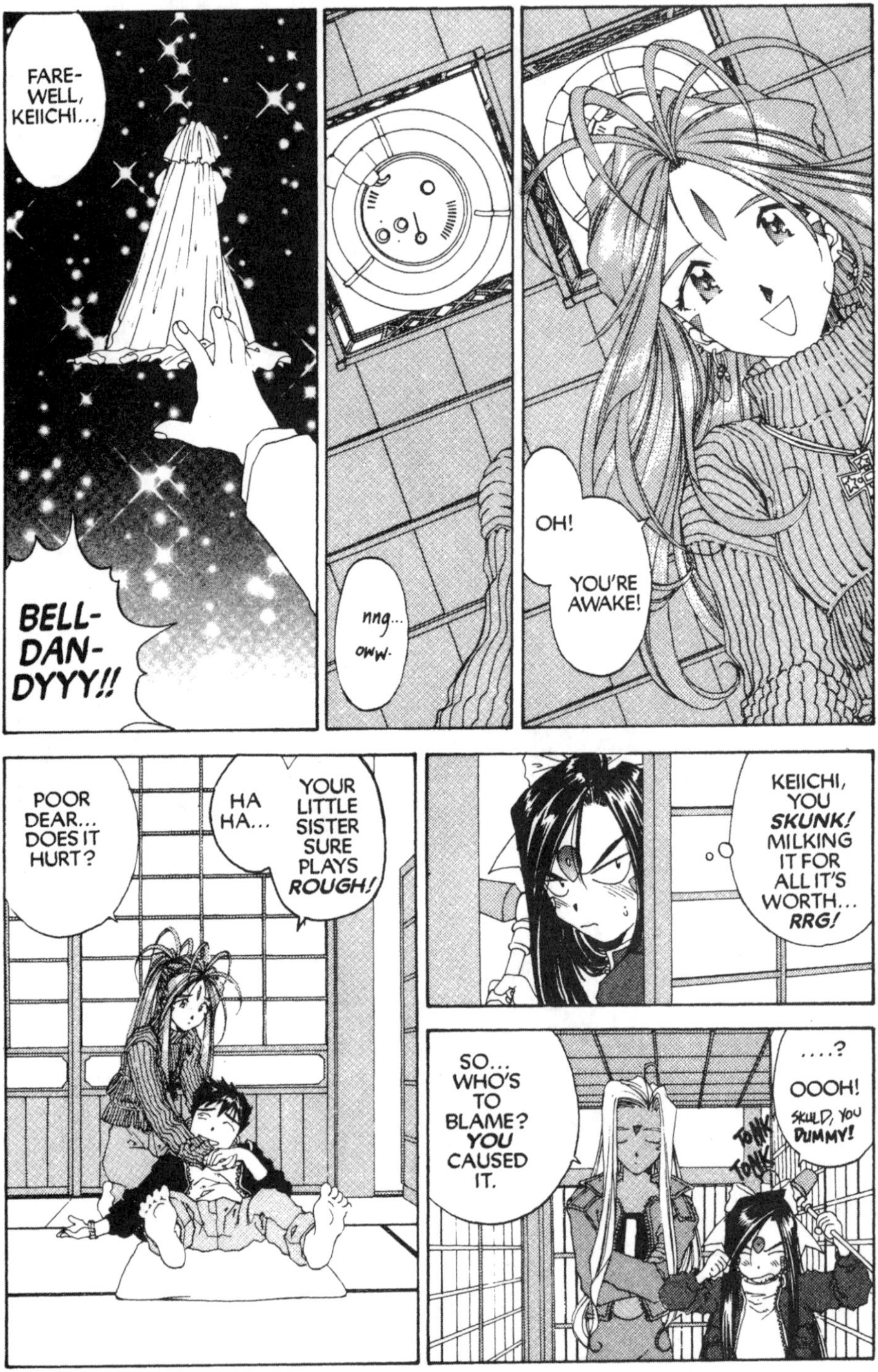
FARE-WELL, KEIICHI...
BELL-DAN-DYYY!!
nng... oww.
OH!
YOU'RE AWAKE!
POOR DEAR... DOES IT HURT?
HA HA...
YOUR LITTLE SISTER SURE PLAYS ROUGH!
KEIICHI, YOU SKUNK! MILKING IT FOR ALL IT'S WORTH... RRG!
SO... WHO'S TO BLAME? YOU CAUSED IT.
TONK TONK
....?
OOOH!
SKULD, YOU DUMMY!

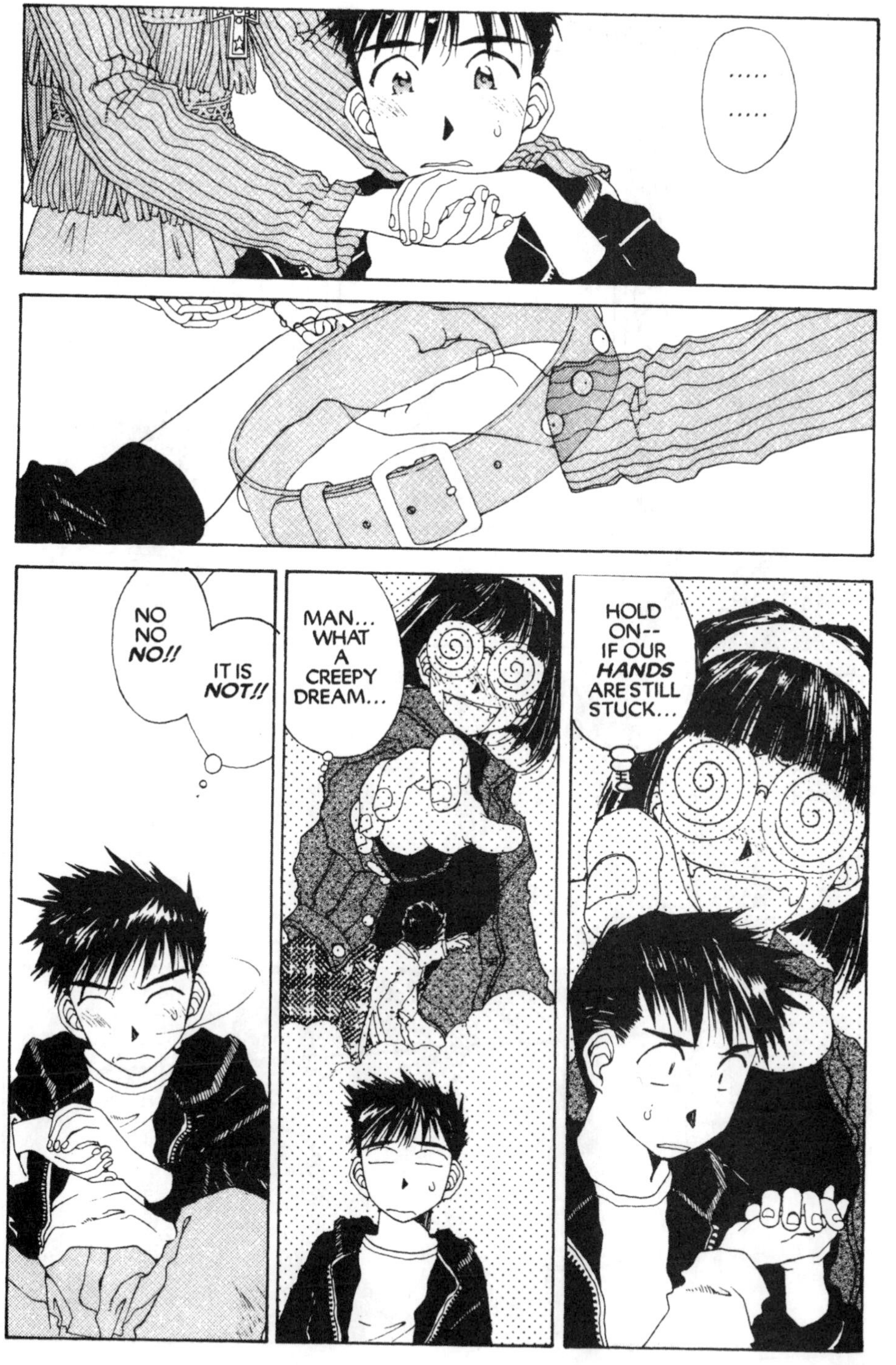
......
......
NO NO NO!!
IT IS NOT!!
MAN... WHAT A CREEPY DREAM...
HOLD ON-- IF OUR HANDS ARE STILL STUCK...

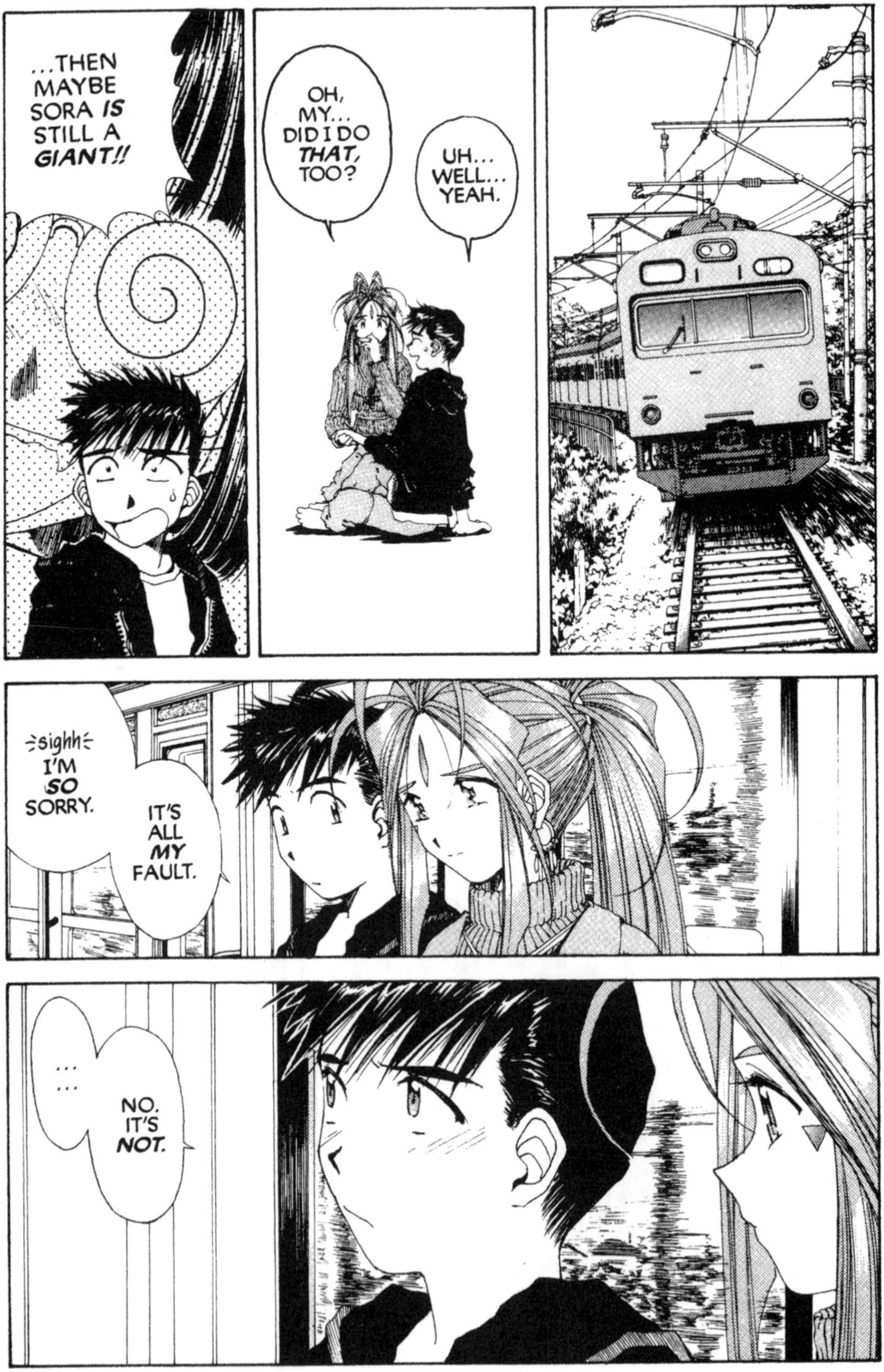
...THEN MAYBE SORA *IS* STILL A *GIANT!!*
OH, MY... DID I DO *THAT*, TOO?
UH... WELL... YEAH.
≑sighh≑ I'M *SO* SORRY.
IT'S ALL *MY* FAULT.
... ...
NO. IT'S *NOT*.

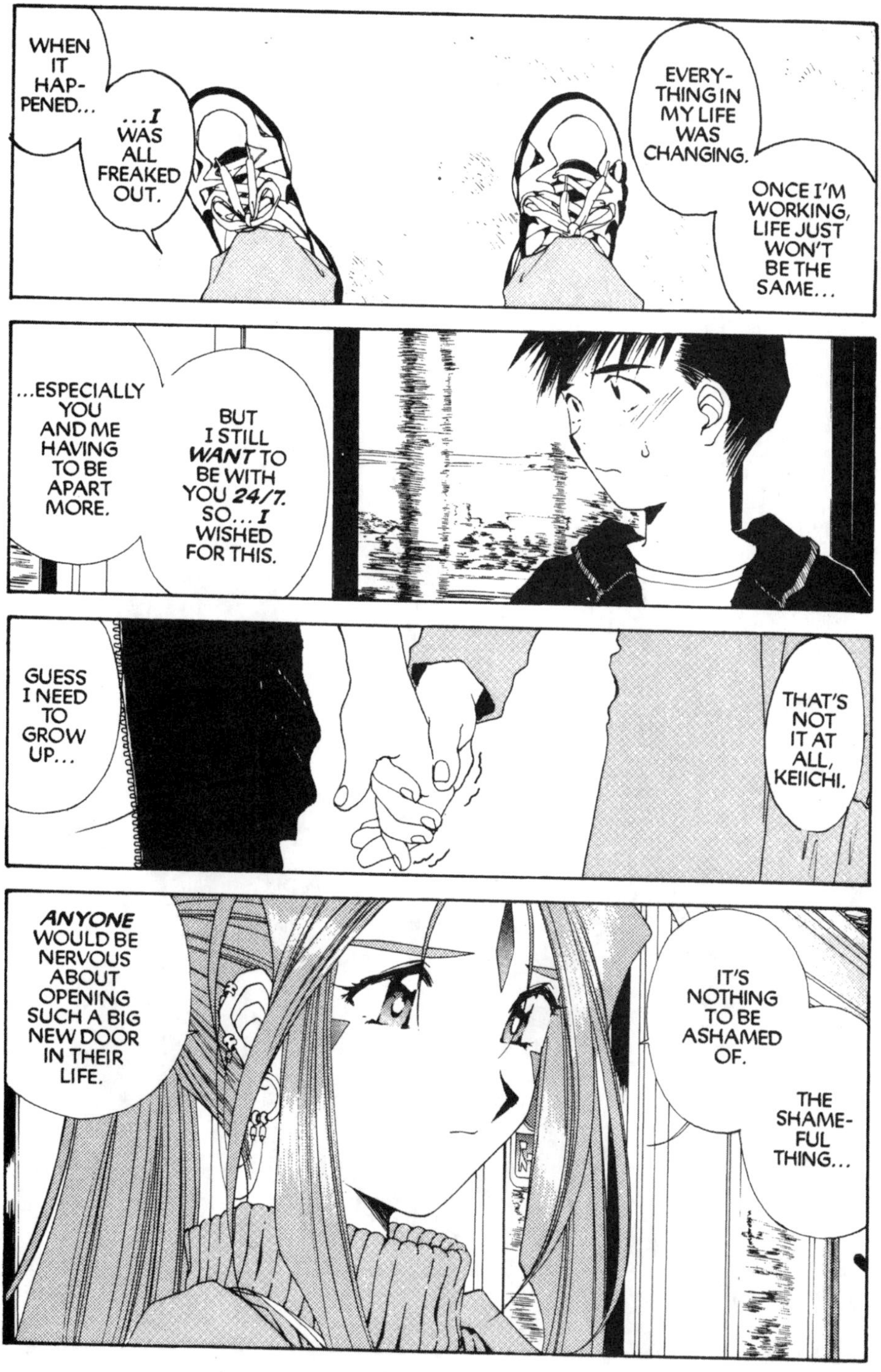
WHEN IT HAPPENED...
...*I* WAS ALL FREAKED OUT.
EVERYTHING IN MY LIFE WAS CHANGING.
ONCE I'M WORKING, LIFE JUST WON'T BE THE SAME...
...ESPECIALLY YOU AND ME HAVING TO BE APART MORE.
BUT I STILL ***WANT*** TO BE WITH YOU *24/7.* SO... *I* WISHED FOR THIS.
GUESS I NEED TO GROW UP...
THAT'S NOT IT AT ALL, KEIICHI.
ANYONE WOULD BE NERVOUS ABOUT OPENING SUCH A BIG NEW DOOR IN THEIR LIFE.
IT'S NOTHING TO BE ASHAMED OF.
THE SHAMEFUL THING...

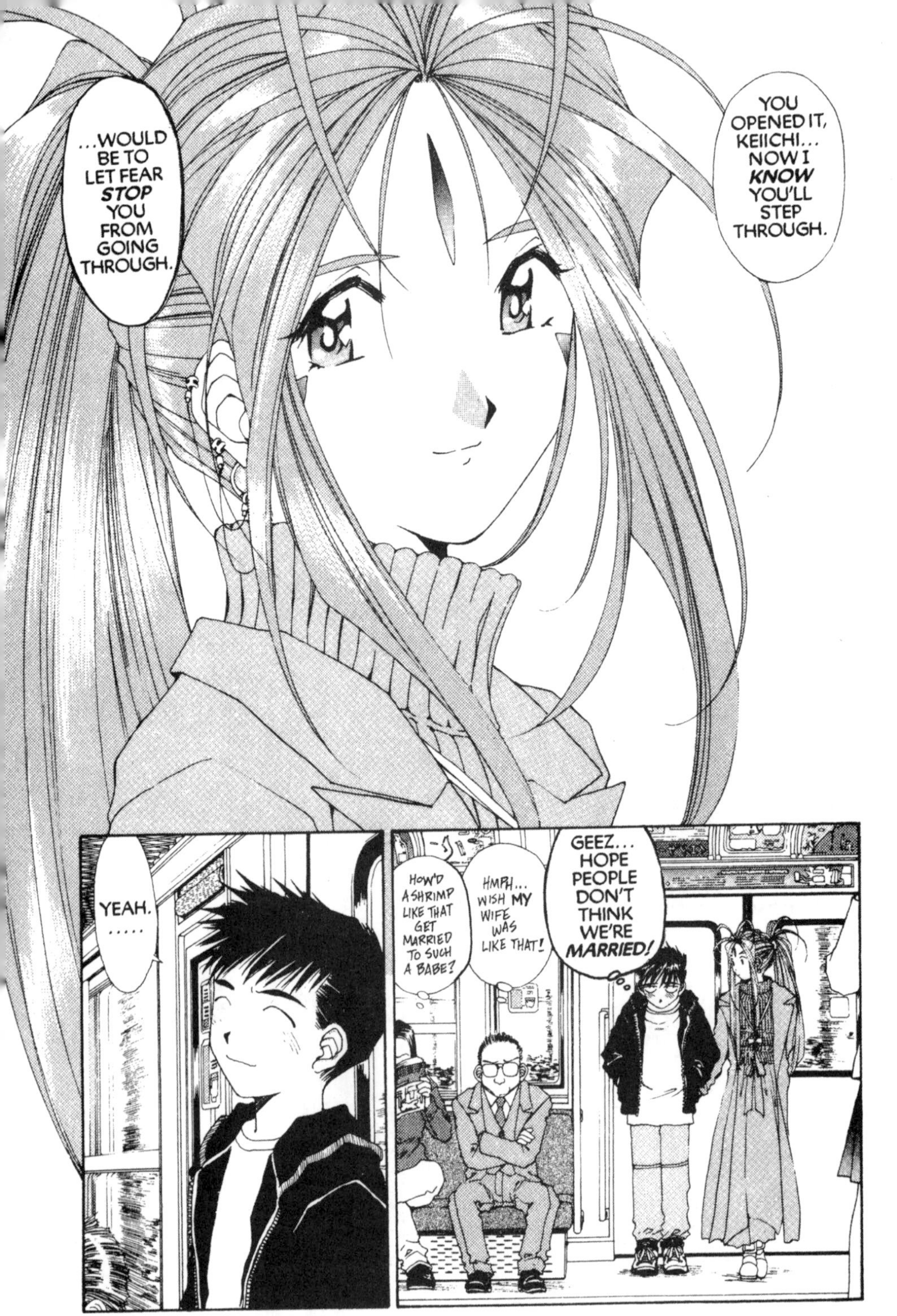
...WOULD BE TO LET FEAR **STOP** YOU FROM GOING THROUGH.
YOU OPENED IT, KEIICHI... NOW I **KNOW** YOU'LL STEP THROUGH.
YEAH. .....
HOW'D A SHRIMP LIKE THAT GET MARRIED TO SUCH A BABE?
HMPH... WISH **MY** WIFE WAS LIKE THAT!
GEEZ... HOPE PEOPLE DON'T THINK WE'RE ***MARRIED!***

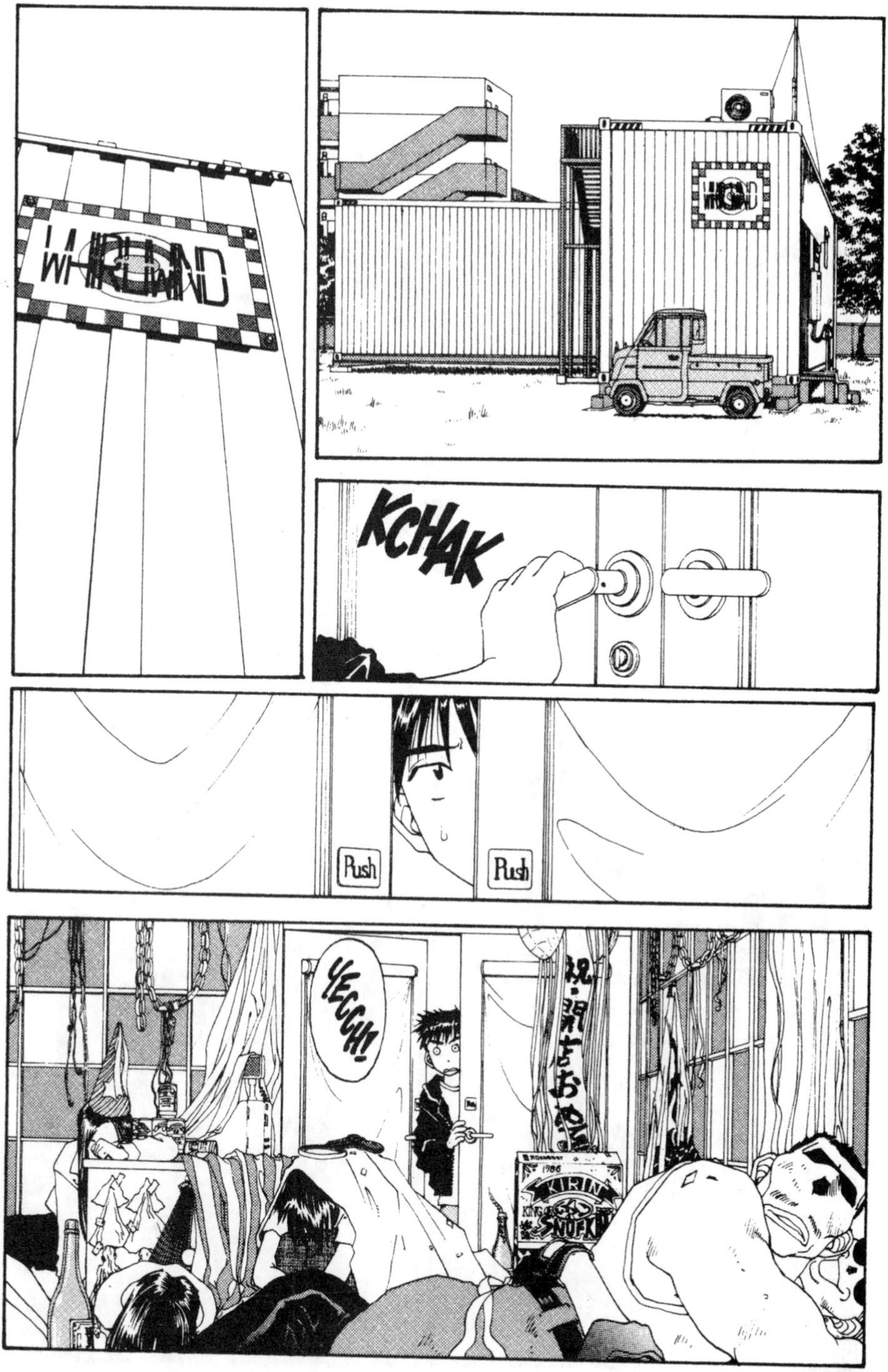
WHIRLWIND
KCHAK
Push
Push
YECCH!
KIRIN

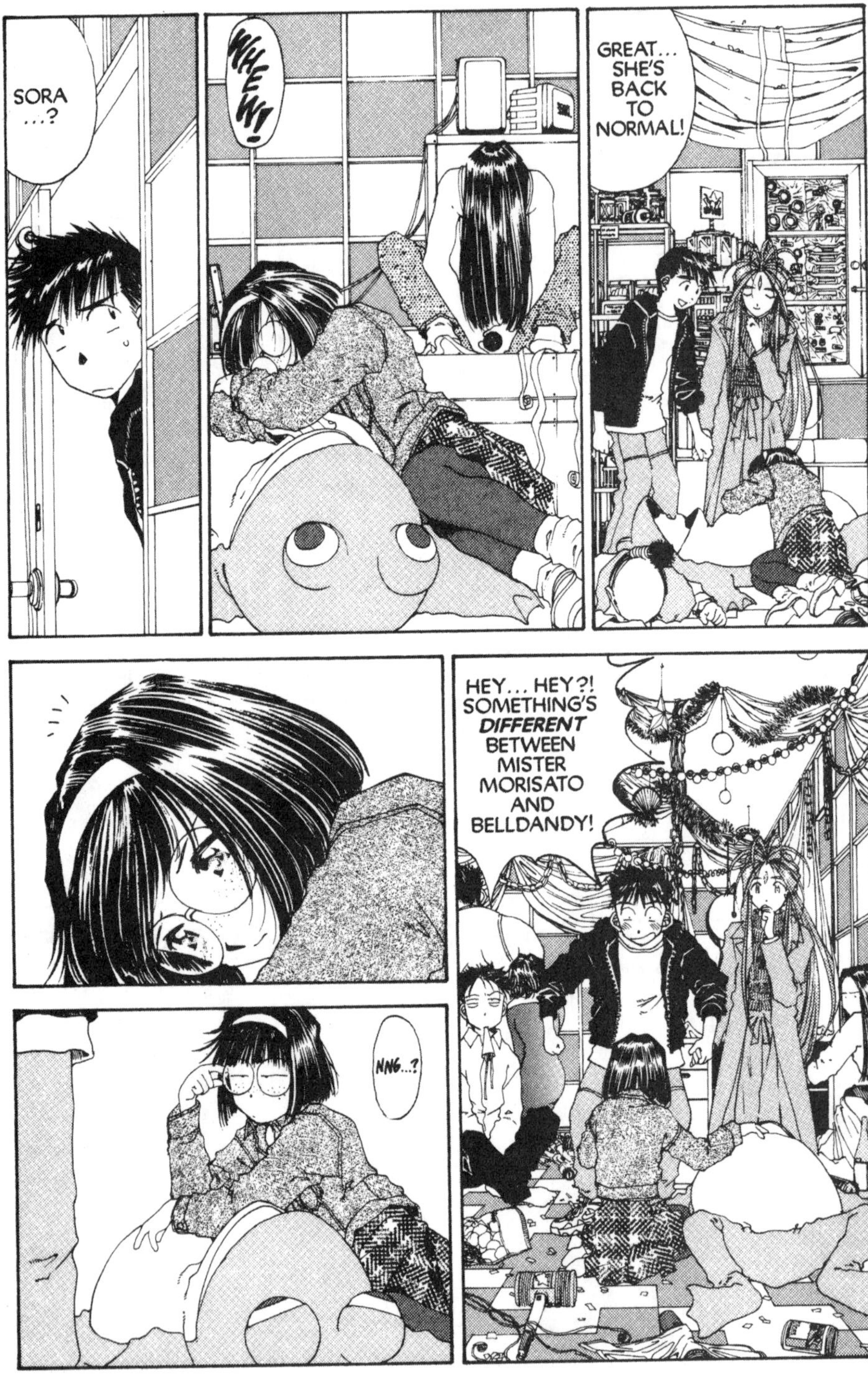
SORA ...?
WHEW!
GREAT... SHE'S BACK TO NORMAL!
HEY... HEY?! SOMETHING'S *DIFFERENT* BETWEEN MISTER MORISATO AND BELLDANDY!
NNG...?

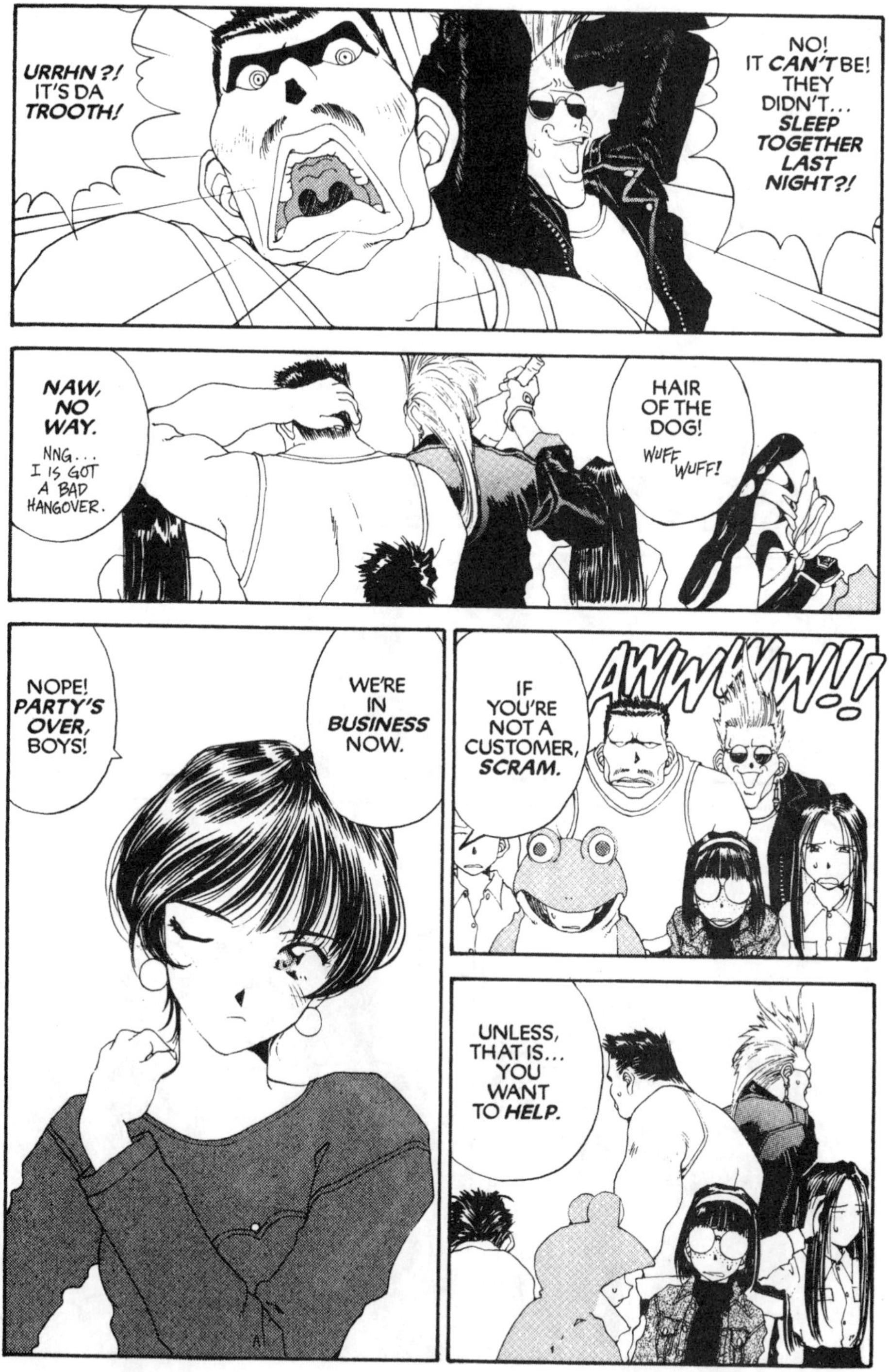
URRHN?! IT'S DA TROOTH!
NO! IT CAN'T BE! THEY DIDN'T... SLEEP TOGETHER LAST NIGHT?!
NAW, NO WAY.
NNG... I IS GOT A BAD HANGOVER.
HAIR OF THE DOG!
WUFF WUFF!
NOPE! PARTY'S OVER, BOYS!
WE'RE IN BUSINESS NOW.
IF YOU'RE NOT A CUSTOMER, SCRAM.
AWWWW!!
UNLESS, THAT IS... YOU WANT TO HELP.

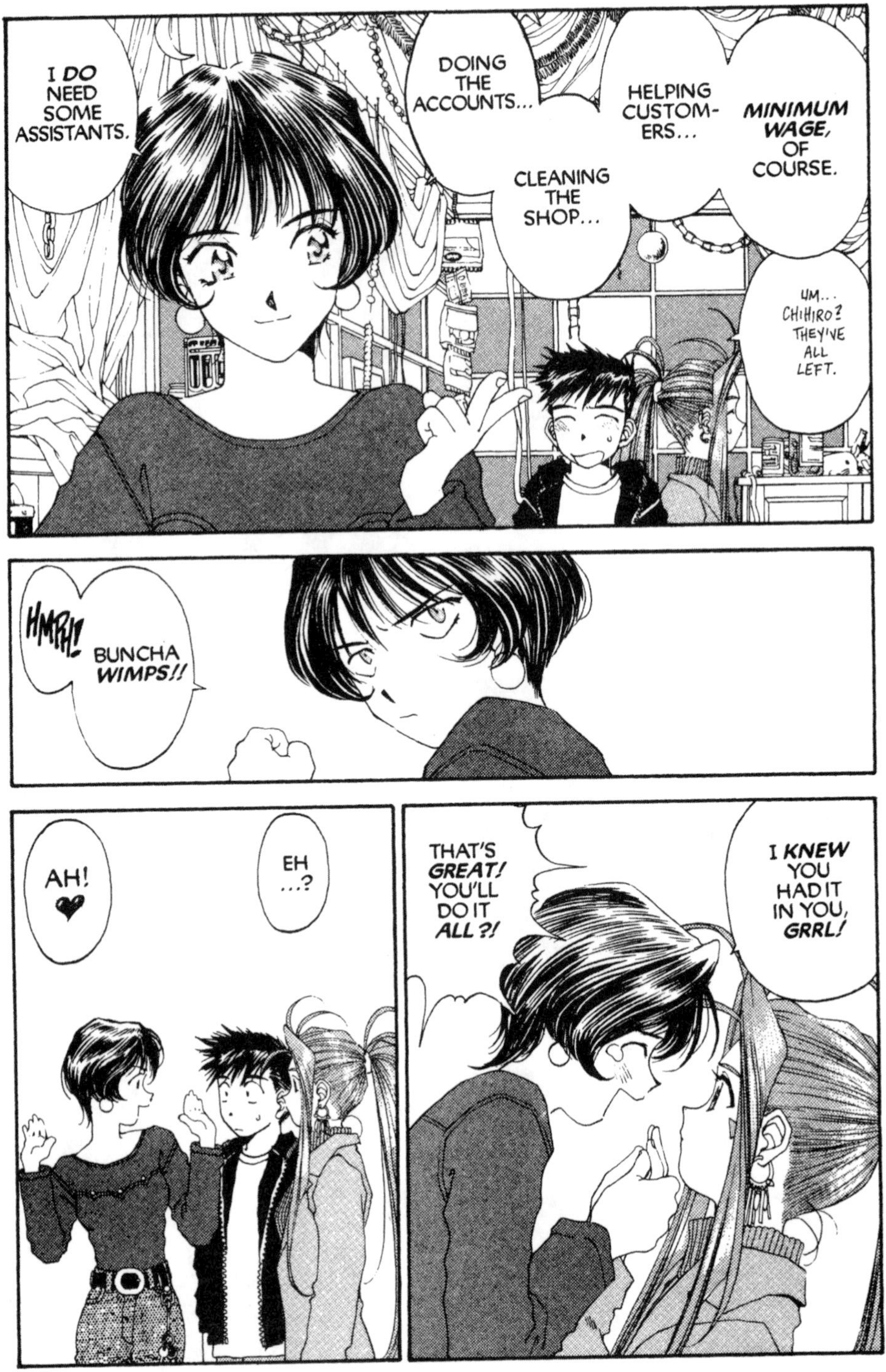
I *DO* NEED SOME ASSISTANTS.
DOING THE ACCOUNTS...
CLEANING THE SHOP...
HELPING CUSTOM-ERS...
MINIMUM WAGE, OF COURSE.
UM... CHIHIRO? THEY'VE ALL LEFT.
HMPH! BUNCHA *WIMPS!!*
AH! ♥
EH ...?
THAT'S *GREAT!* YOU'LL DO IT *ALL?!*
I *KNEW* YOU HAD IT IN YOU, *GRRL!*

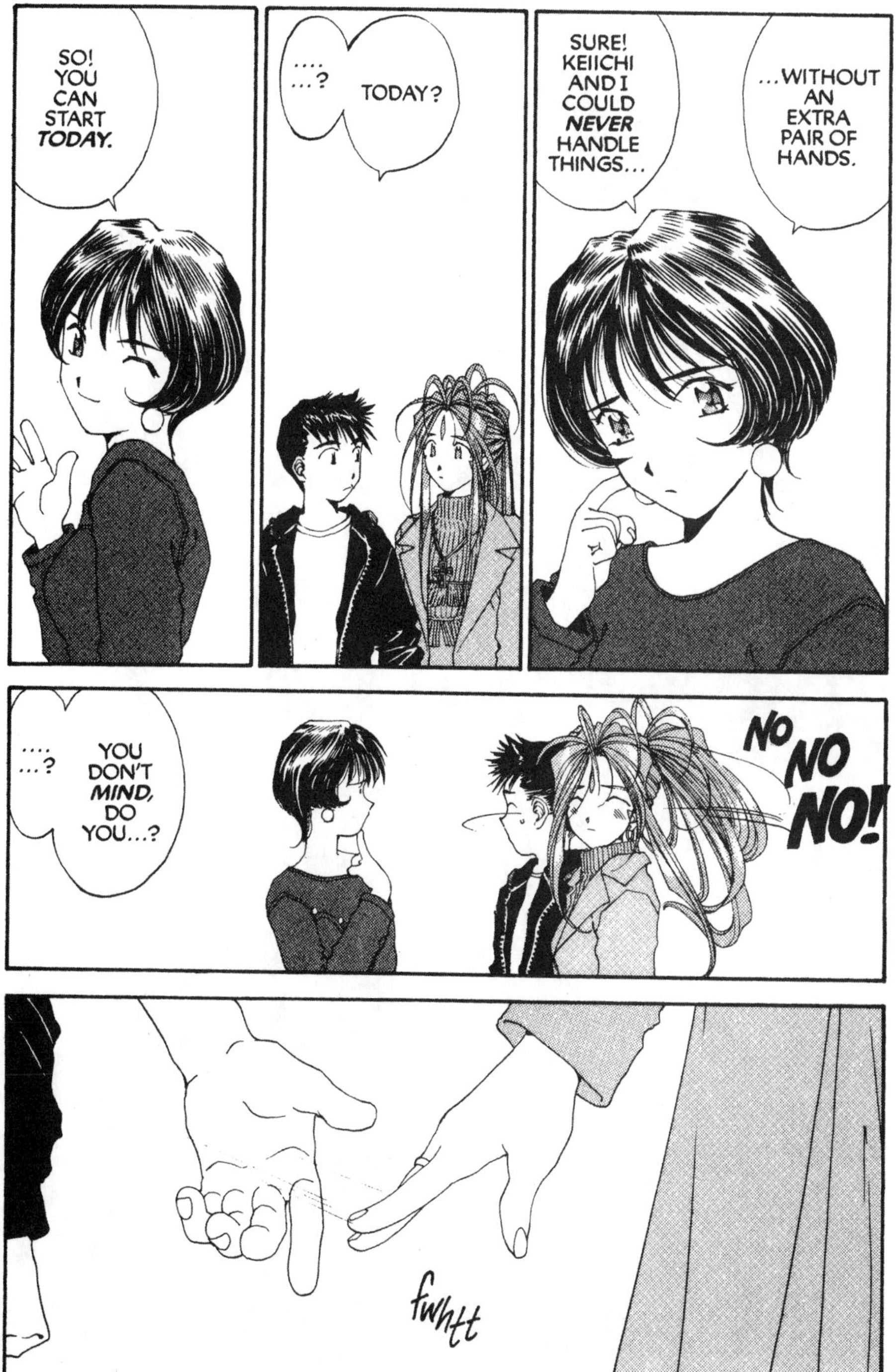
SO! YOU CAN START TODAY.
....
...?
TODAY?
SURE! KEIICHI AND I COULD NEVER HANDLE THINGS...
...WITHOUT AN EXTRA PAIR OF HANDS.
....
...?
YOU DON'T MIND, DO YOU...?
NO NO NO!
fwhtt

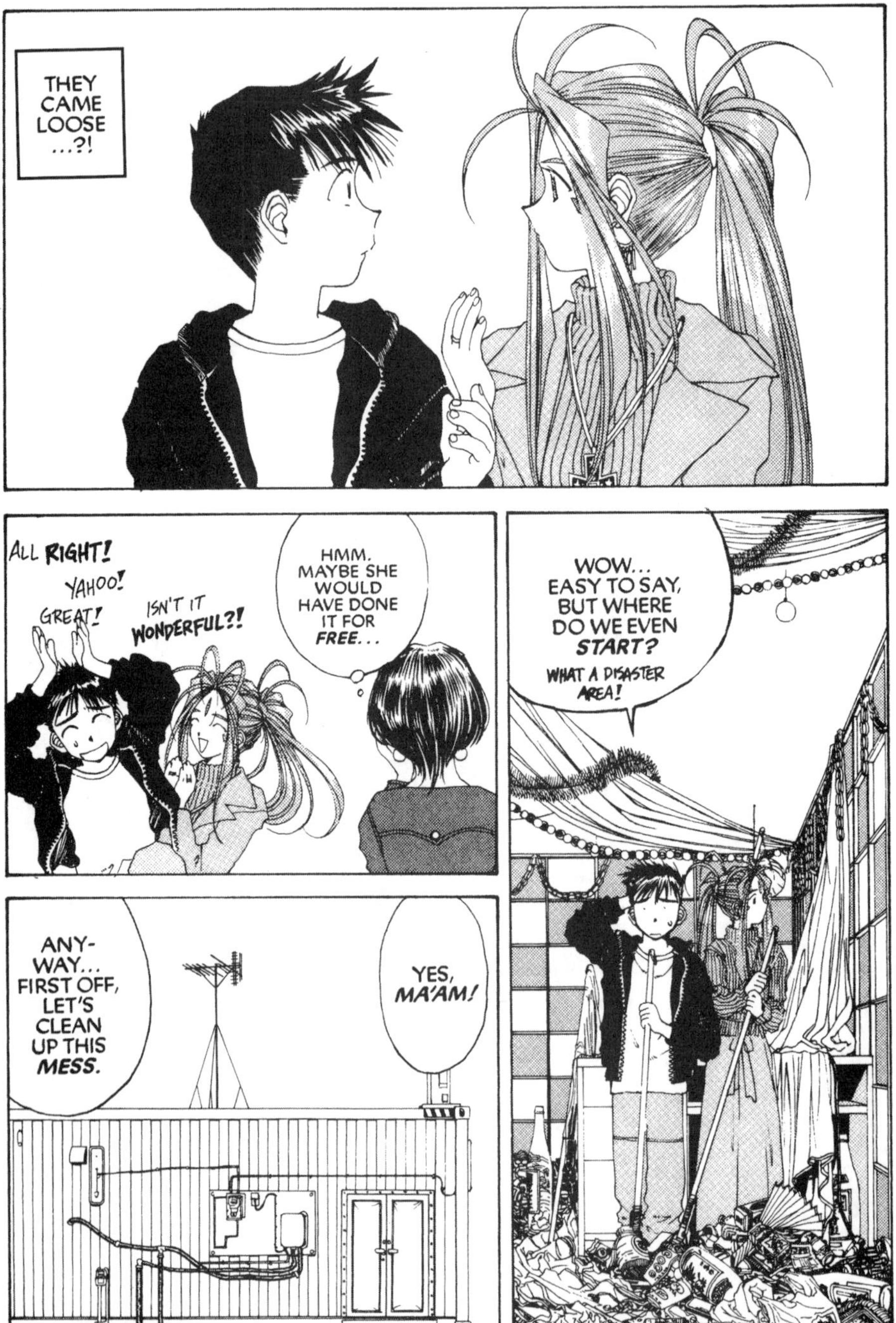
THEY CAME LOOSE ...?!
ALL RIGHT!
YAHOO!
GREAT!
ISN'T IT WONDERFUL?!
HMM. MAYBE SHE WOULD HAVE DONE IT FOR FREE...
ANY-WAY... FIRST OFF, LET'S CLEAN UP THIS MESS.
YES, MA'AM!
WOW... EASY TO SAY, BUT WHERE DO WE EVEN START?
WHAT A DISASTER AREA!

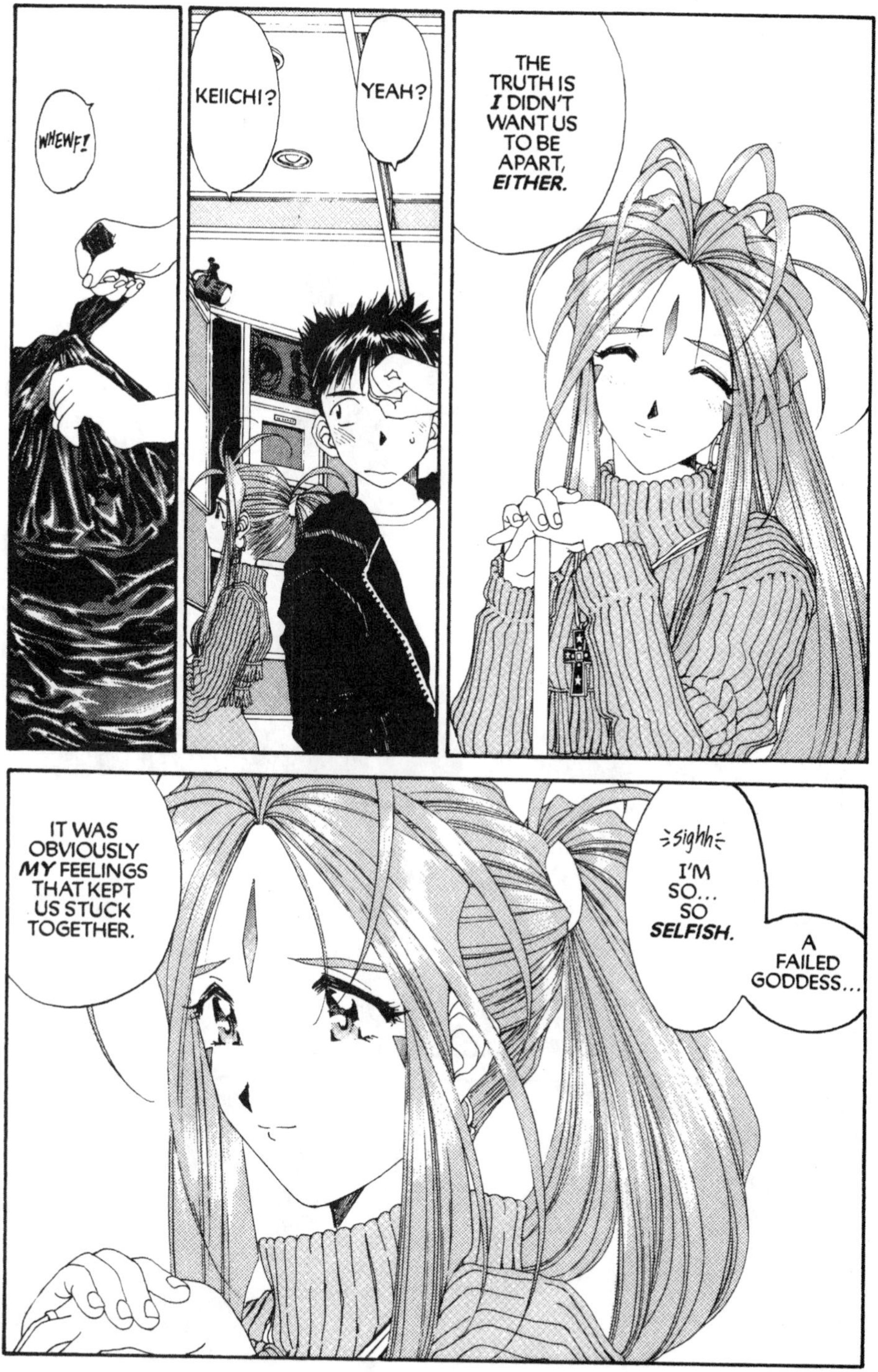
WHEWF!
KEIICHI?
YEAH?
THE TRUTH IS I DIDN'T WANT US TO BE APART, EITHER.
IT WAS OBVIOUSLY MY FEELINGS THAT KEPT US STUCK TOGETHER.
sighh
I'M SO... SO SELFISH.
A FAILED GODDESS...

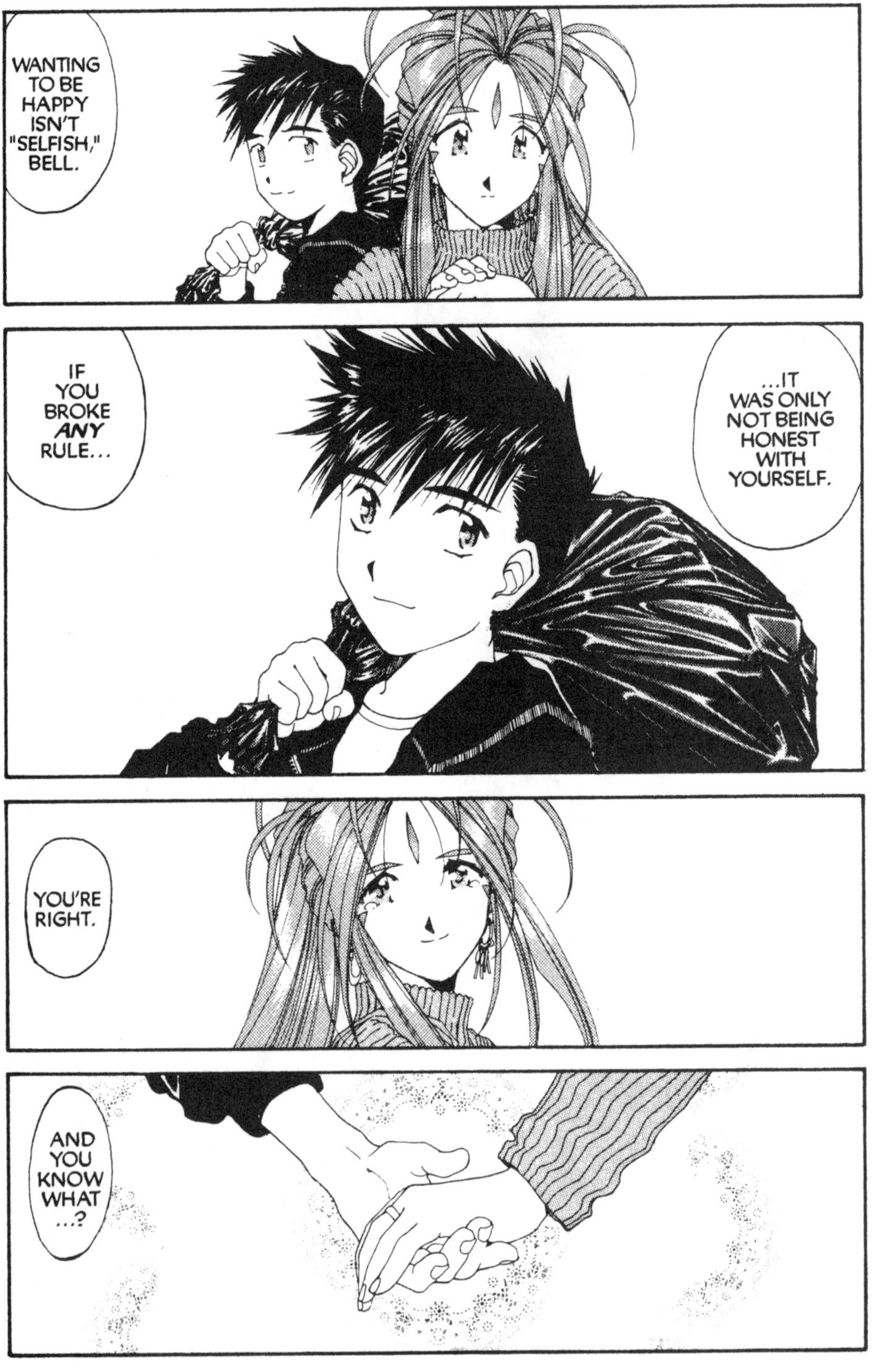
WANTING TO BE HAPPY ISN'T "SELFISH," BELL.
IF YOU BROKE ANY RULE...
...IT WAS ONLY NOT BEING HONEST WITH YOURSELF.
YOU'RE RIGHT.
AND YOU KNOW WHAT ...?

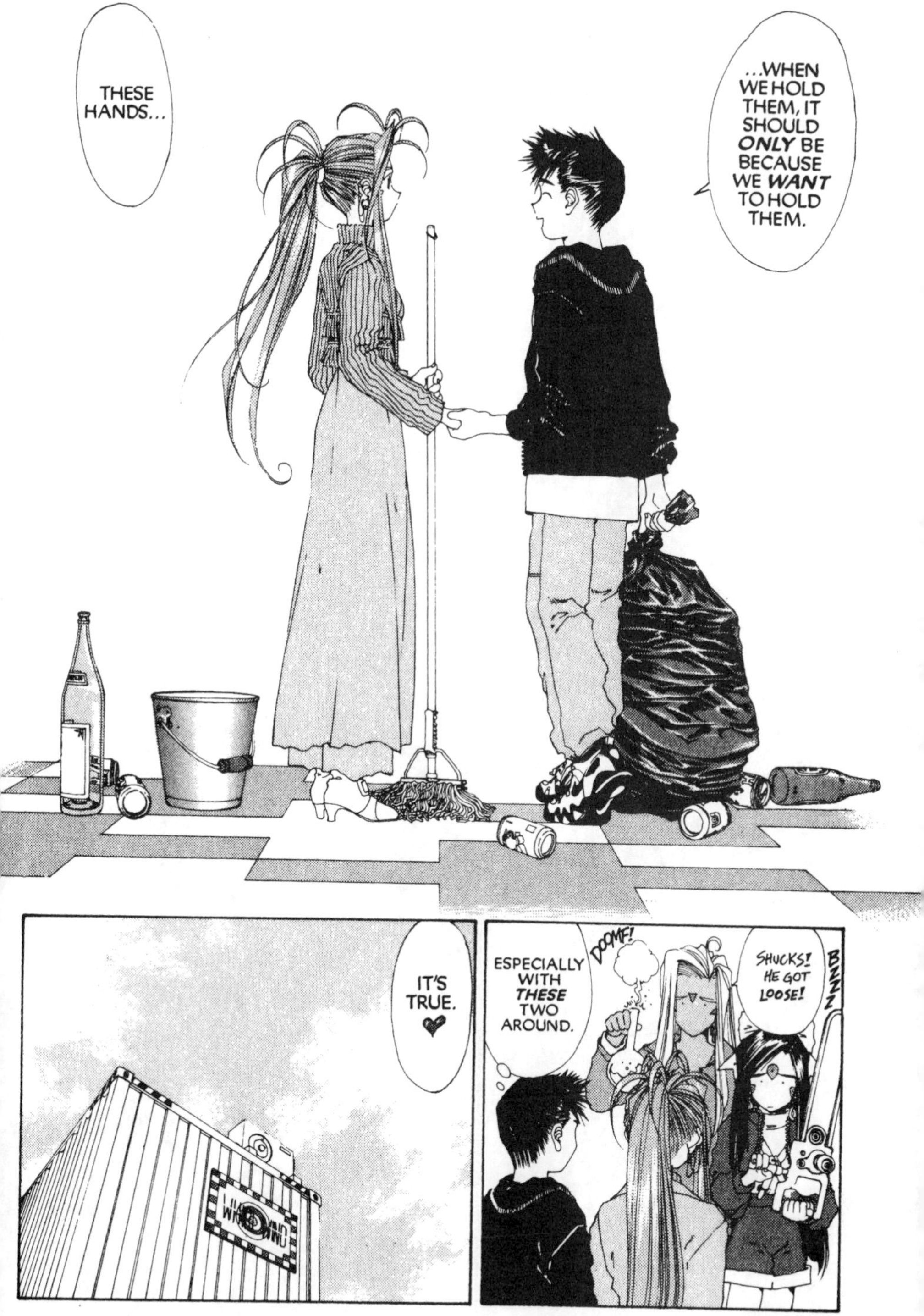
THESE HANDS...
...WHEN WE HOLD THEM, IT SHOULD ***ONLY*** BE BECAUSE WE ***WANT*** TO HOLD THEM.
IT'S TRUE. ♥
ESPECIALLY WITH ***THESE*** TWO AROUND.
DOOMF!
SHUCKS! HE GOT LOOSE!
BZZZ

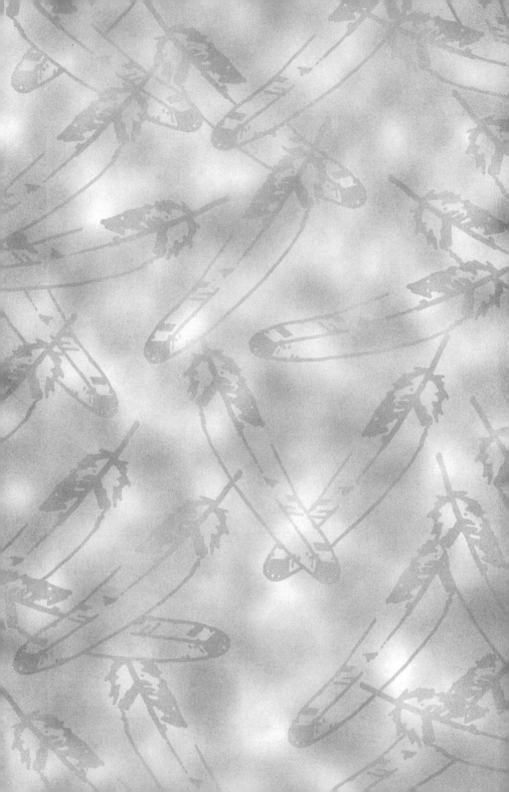

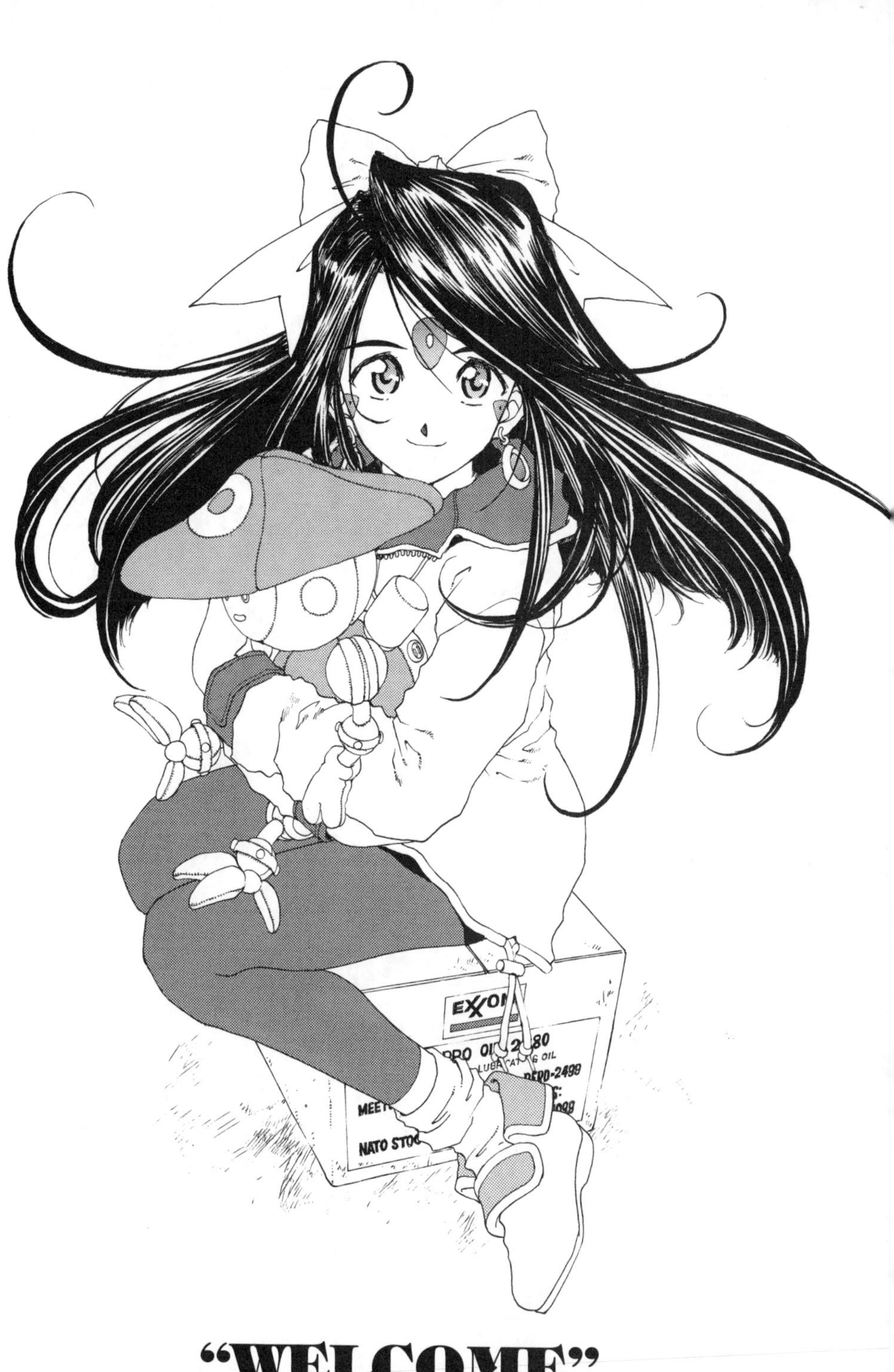

"WELCOME"

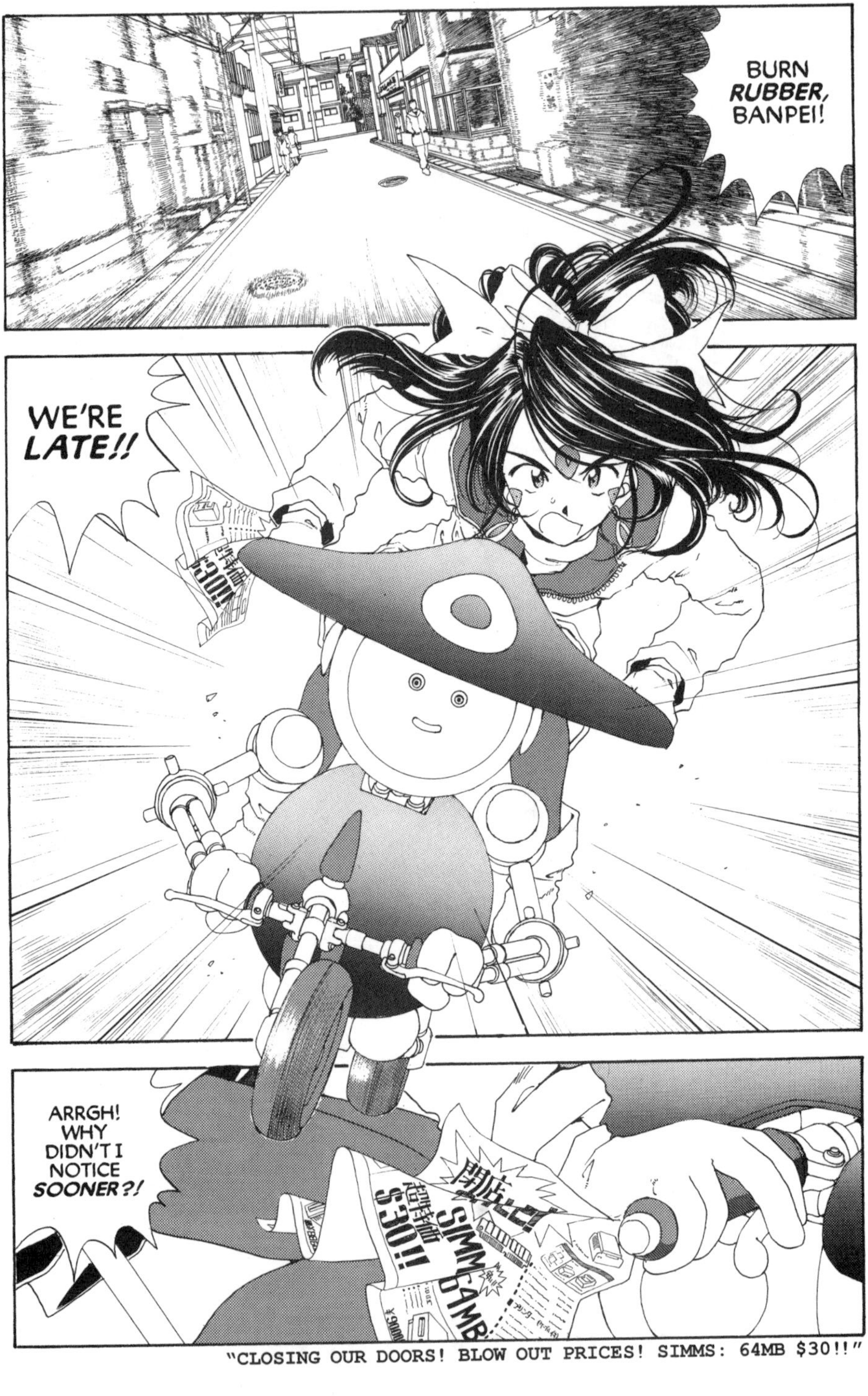
BURN *RUBBER*, BANPEI!
WE'RE *LATE!!*
ARRGH! WHY DIDN'T I NOTICE *SOONER?!*

"CLOSING OUR DOORS! BLOW OUT PRICES! SIMMS: 64MB $30!!"

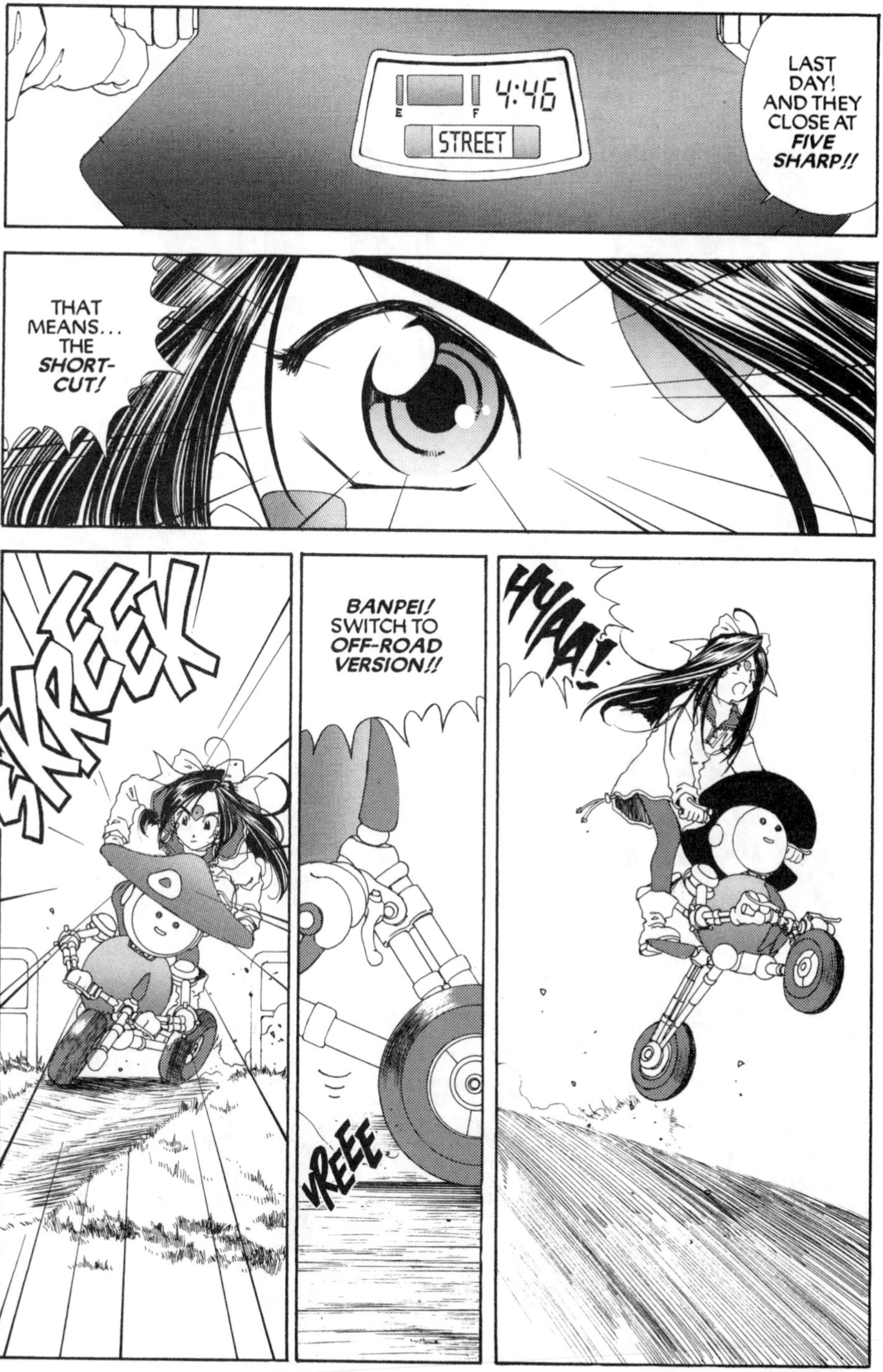
4:46
E
F
STREET
LAST DAY! AND THEY CLOSE AT FIVE SHARP!!
THAT MEANS... THE SHORT-CUT!
SKREEEK
BANPEI! SWITCH TO OFF-ROAD VERSION!!
VREEE
HYAAA!

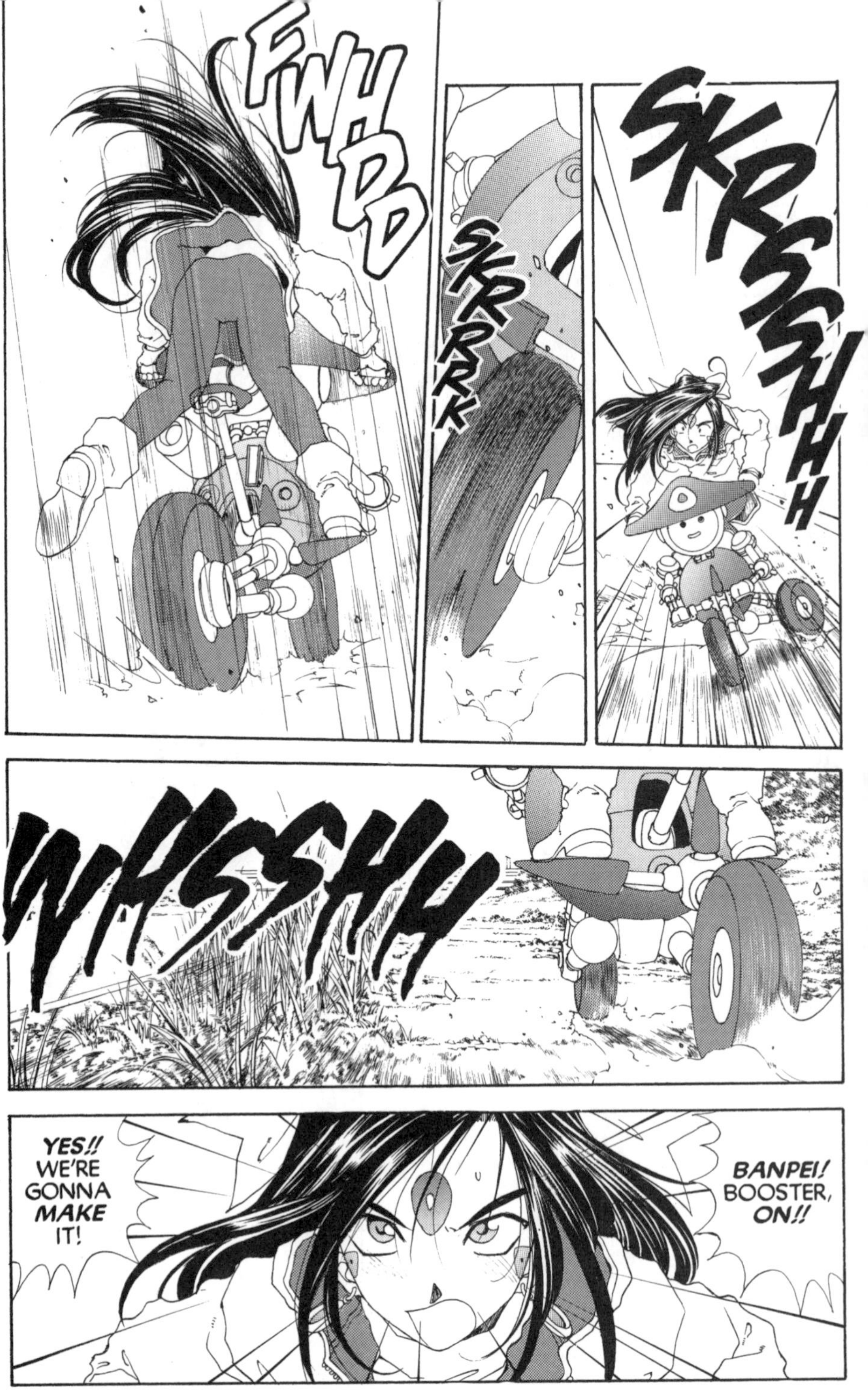
FWHDD
SKRRRK
SKRSSHHH
WHSSHH
YES!! WE'RE GONNA MAKE IT!
BANPEI! BOOSTER, ON!!

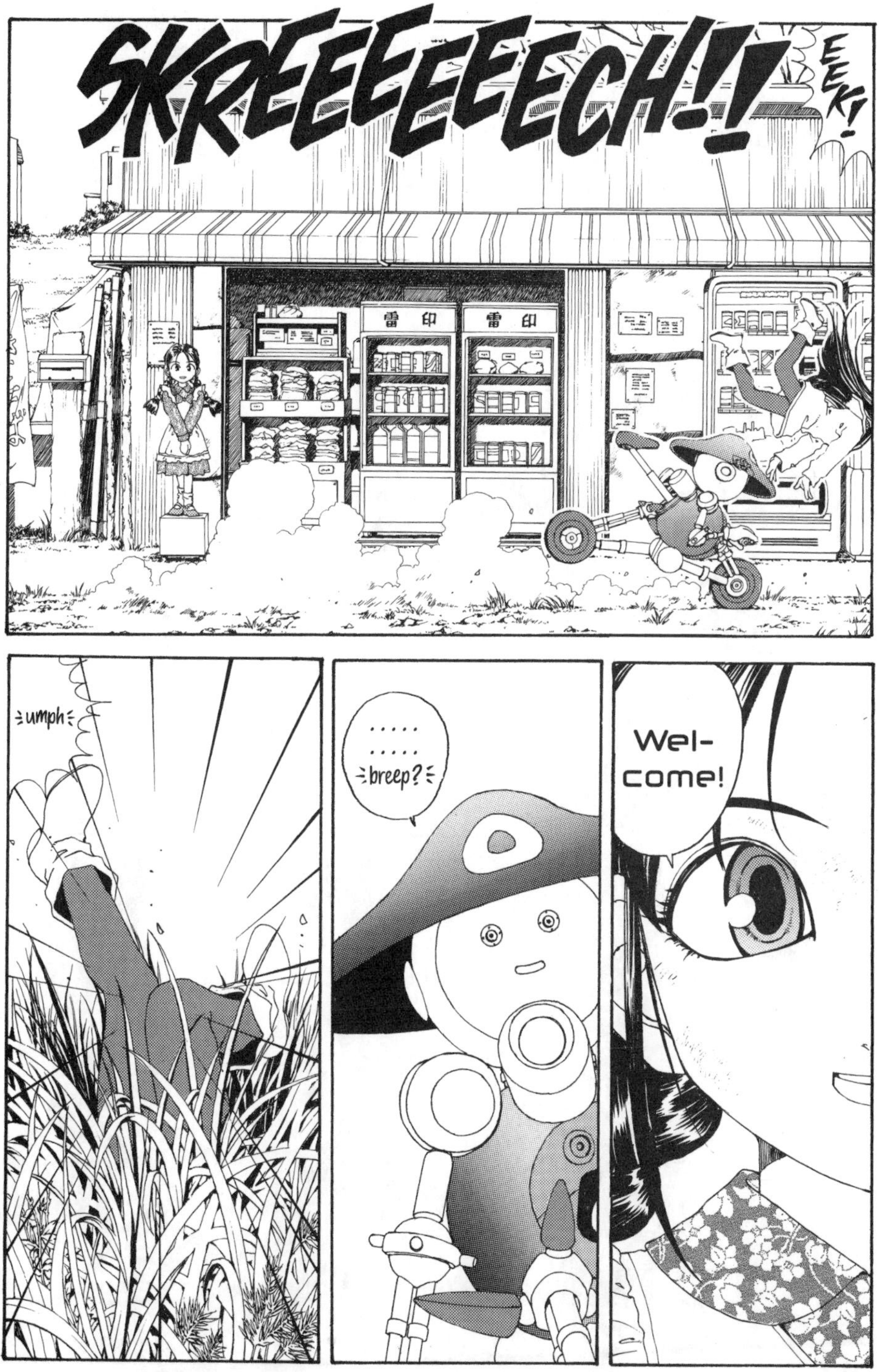
SKREEEEEEECH!!
EEEK!
雷印
雷印
umph
......
......
breep?
Wel-
come!

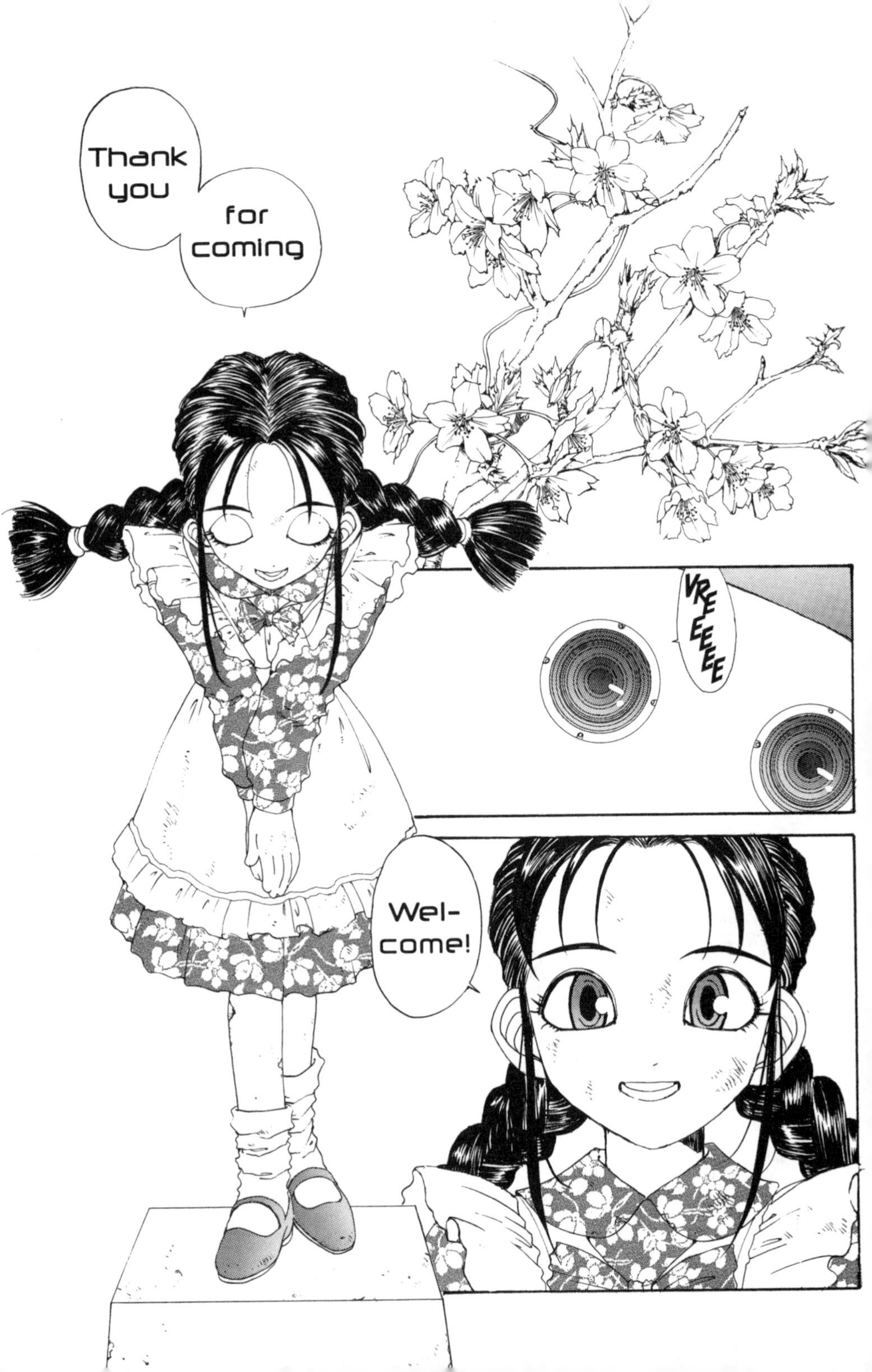
Thank you for coming
VREEEEE
Wel-come!

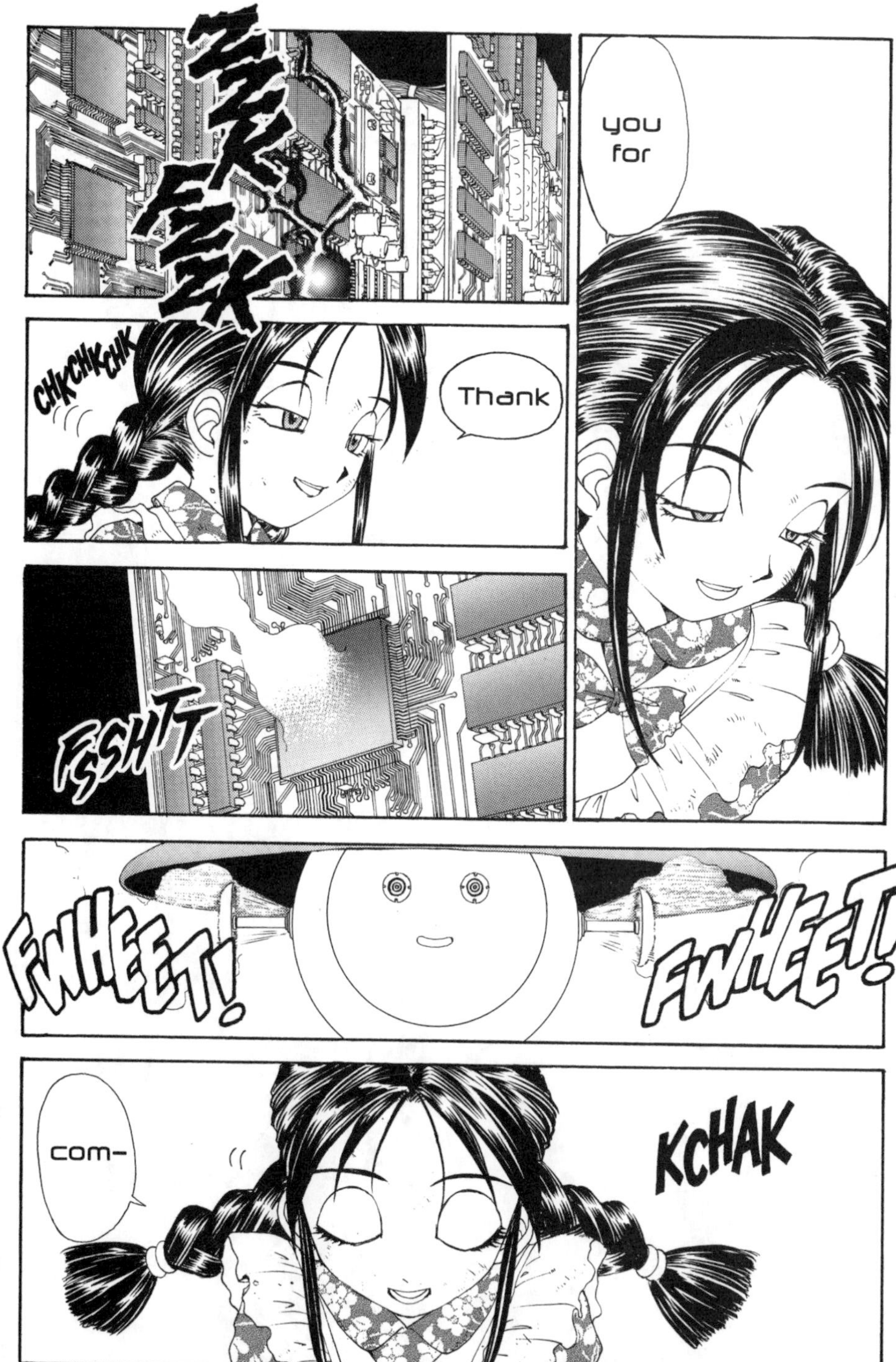
CHKCHKCHK
Thank
FSSHTT
you for
FWHEET!
FWHEET!
com-
KCHAK

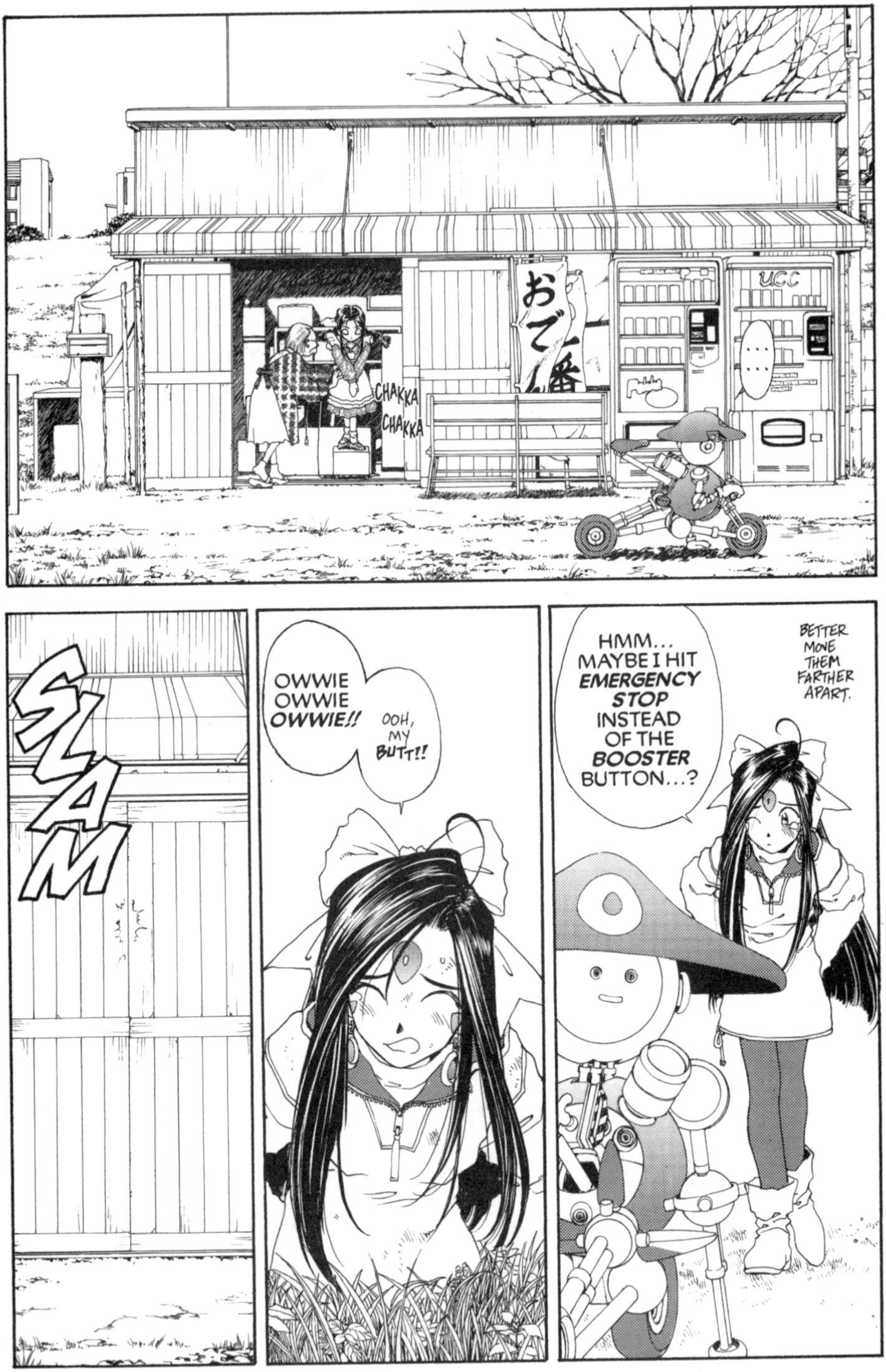
CHAKKA
CHAKKA
UCC
. . .
SLAM
OWWIE OWWIE OWWIE!!
OOH, MY BUTT!!
HMM... MAYBE I HIT EMERGENCY STOP INSTEAD OF THE BOOSTER BUTTON...?
BETTER MOVE THEM FARTHER APART.

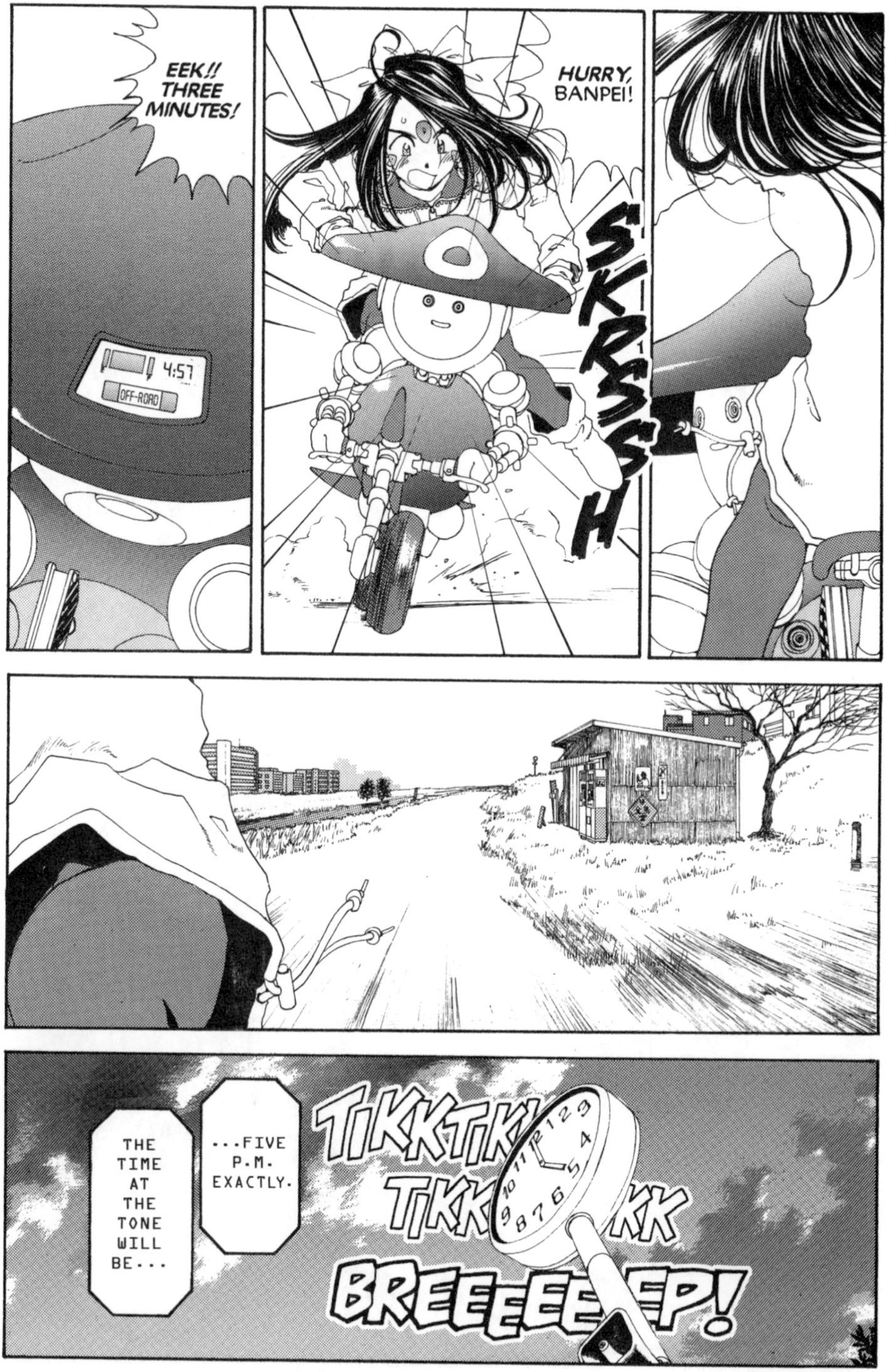
EEK!! THREE MINUTES!
4:57
OFF-ROAD
HURRY, BANPEI!
SKRSSSH
THE TIME AT THE TONE WILL BE...
...FIVE P.M. EXACTLY.
TIKKTIKK TIKKTIKK
BREEEEEEEP!

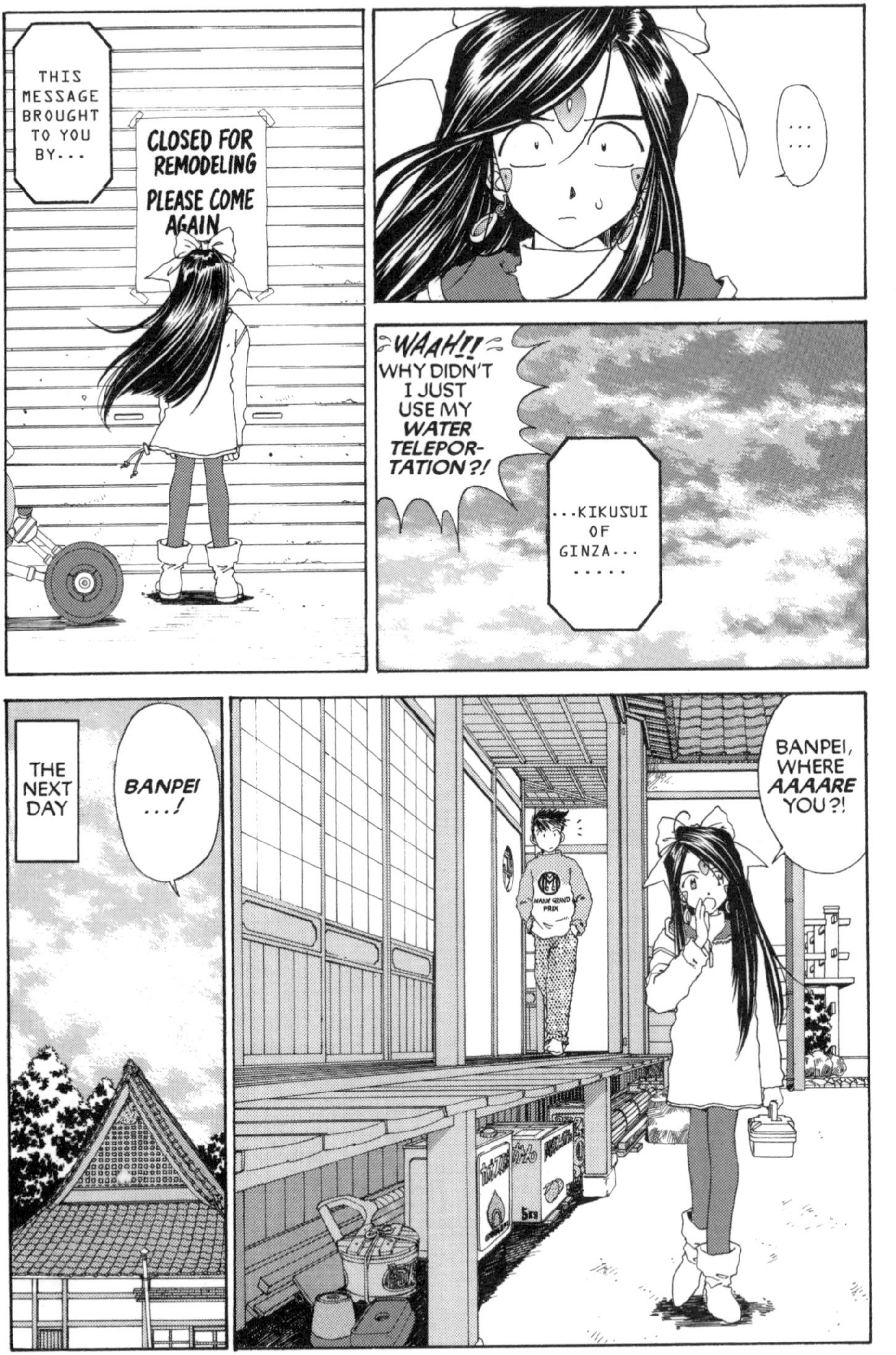
THIS MESSAGE BROUGHT TO YOU BY...
CLOSED FOR REMODELING
PLEASE COME AGAIN
... ...
WAAH!! WHY DIDN'T I JUST USE MY WATER TELEPORTATION?!
...KIKUSUI OF GINZA... .....
THE NEXT DAY
BANPEI ...!
MANX GRAND PRIX
BANPEI, WHERE AAAARE YOU?!

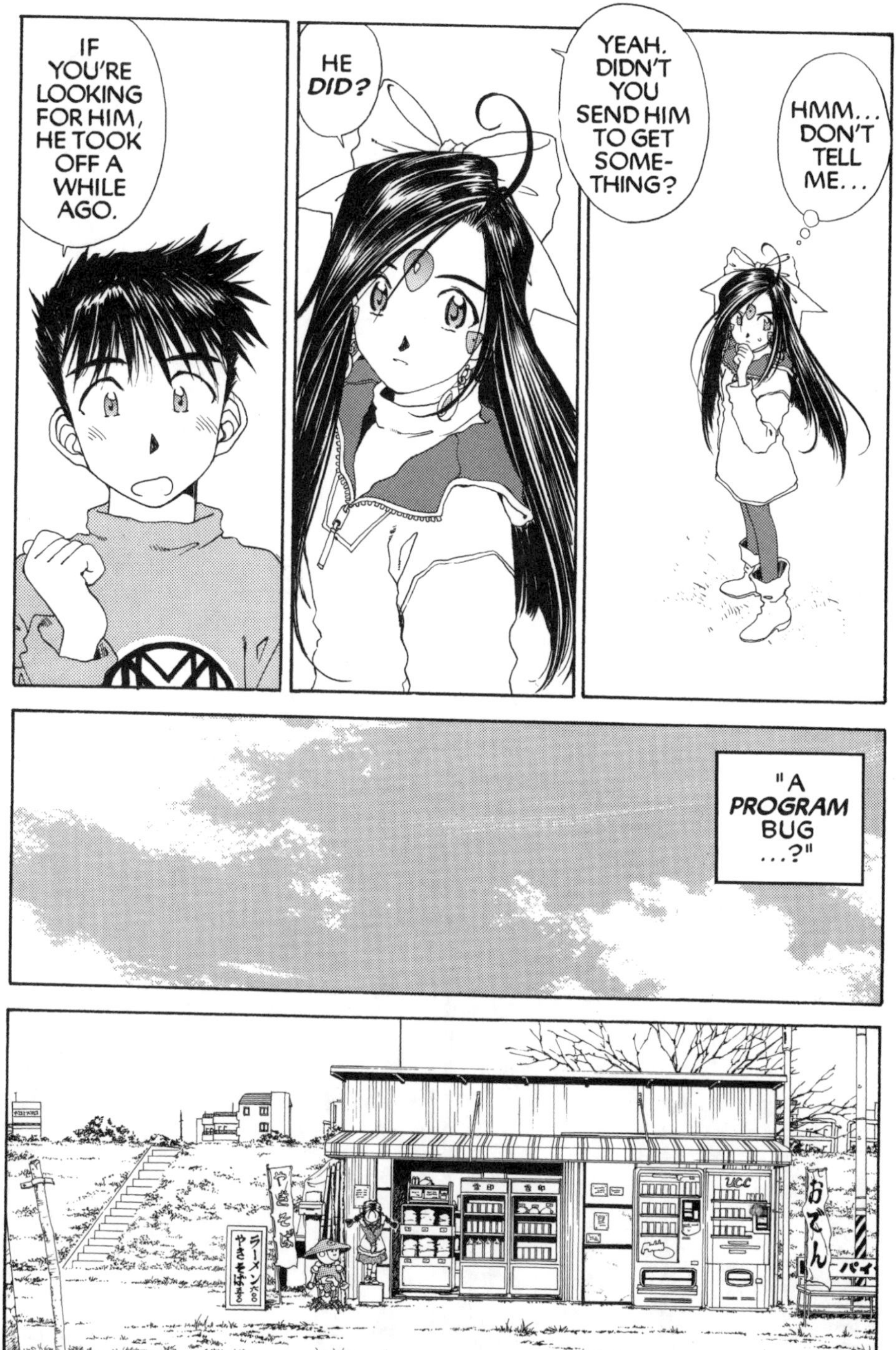
IF YOU'RE LOOKING FOR HIM, HE TOOK OFF A WHILE AGO.
HE *DID?*
YEAH. DIDN'T YOU SEND HIM TO GET SOME-THING?
HMM... DON'T TELL ME...
"A *PROGRAM* BUG ...?"
ラーメン
やきそば
やきそば
UCC
おでん

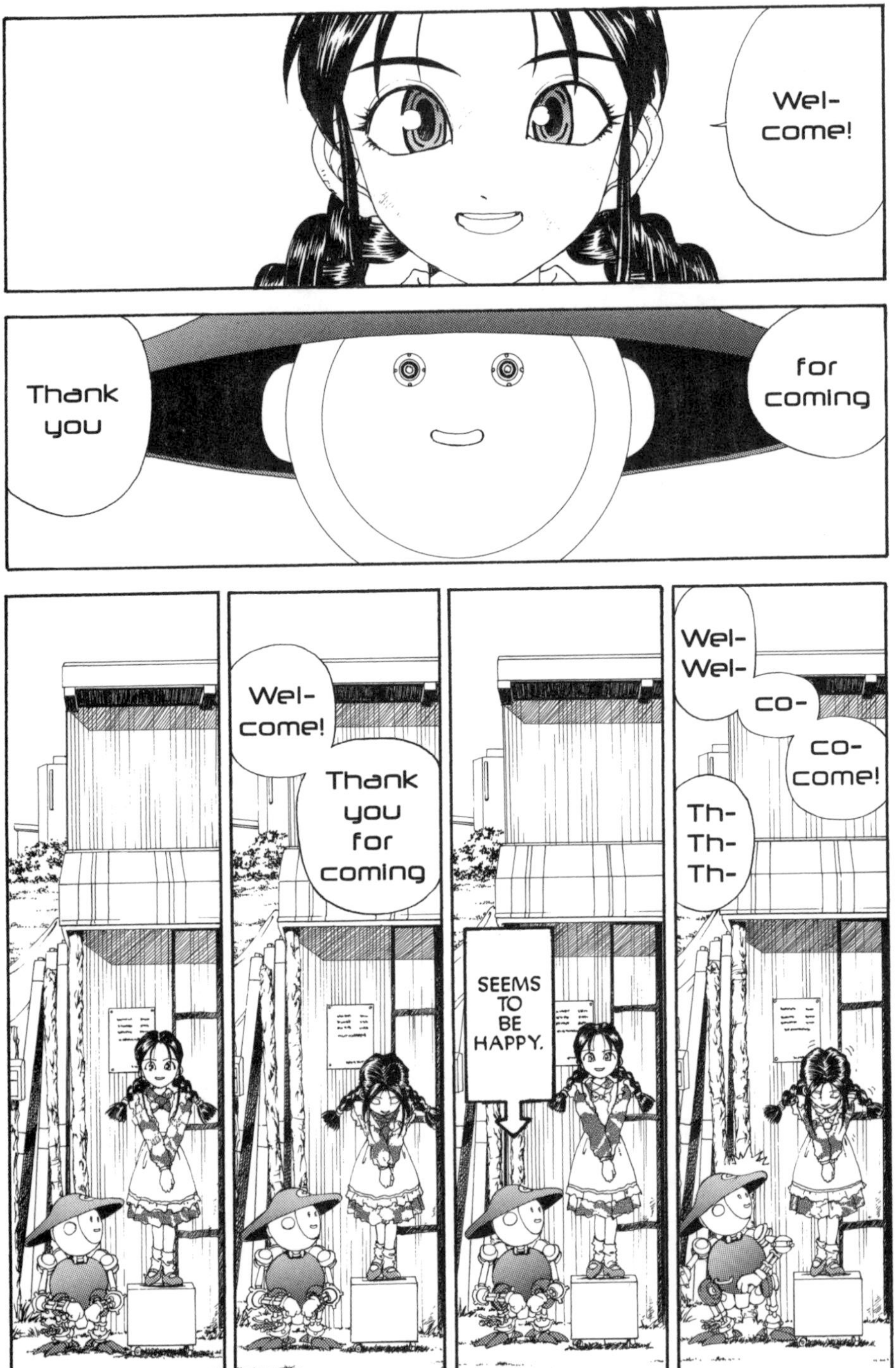
Wel-
come!
Thank you
for coming
Wel-
come!
Thank you for coming
SEEMS TO BE HAPPY.
Wel-
Wel-
co-
co-
come!
Th-
Th-
Th-

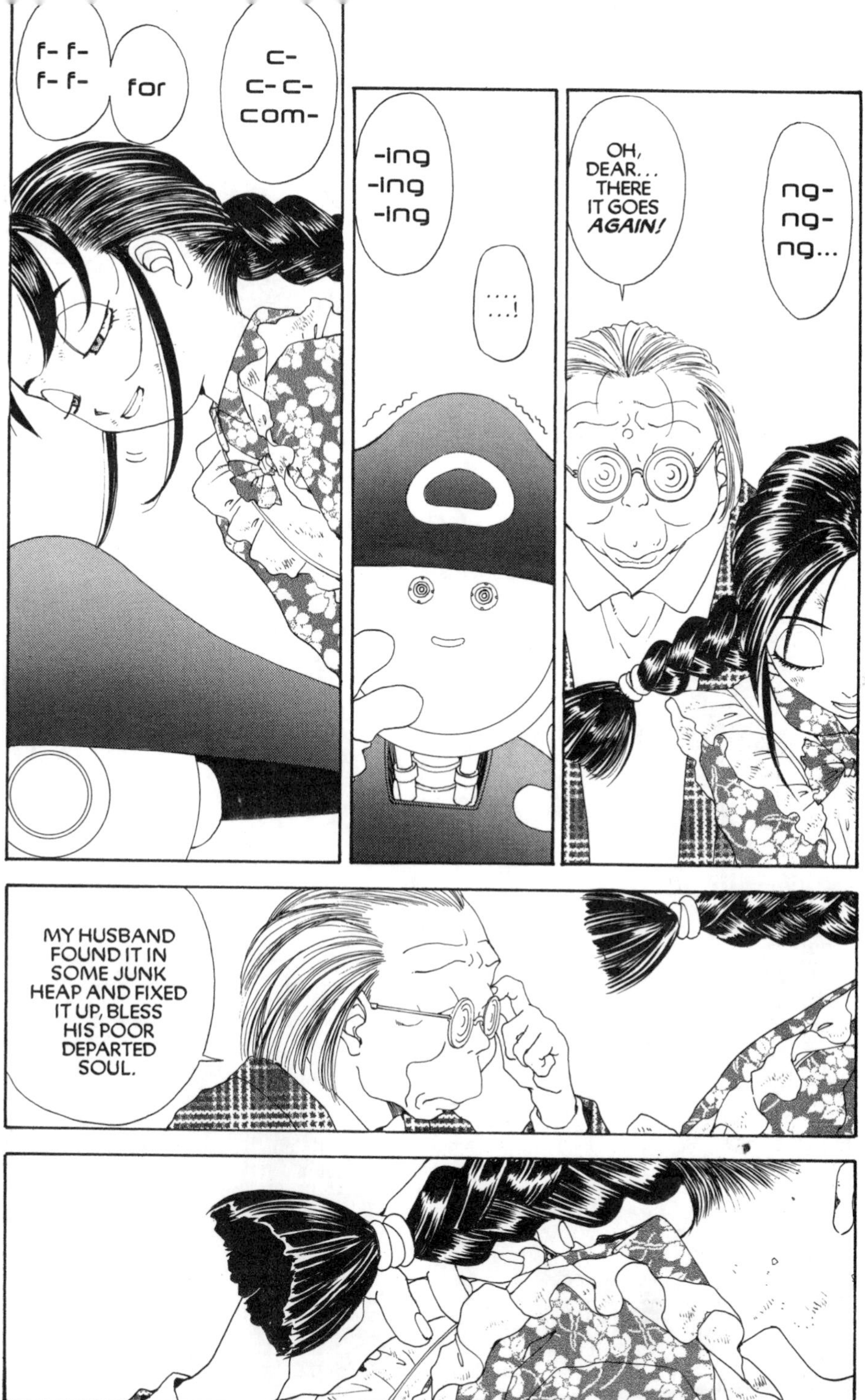
f- f- f- f-
for
c- c- c- com-
-ing -ing -ing
...; ...!
OH, DEAR... THERE IT GOES *AGAIN!*
ng- ng- ng...
MY HUSBAND FOUND IT IN SOME JUNK HEAP AND FIXED IT UP, BLESS HIS POOR DEPARTED SOUL.

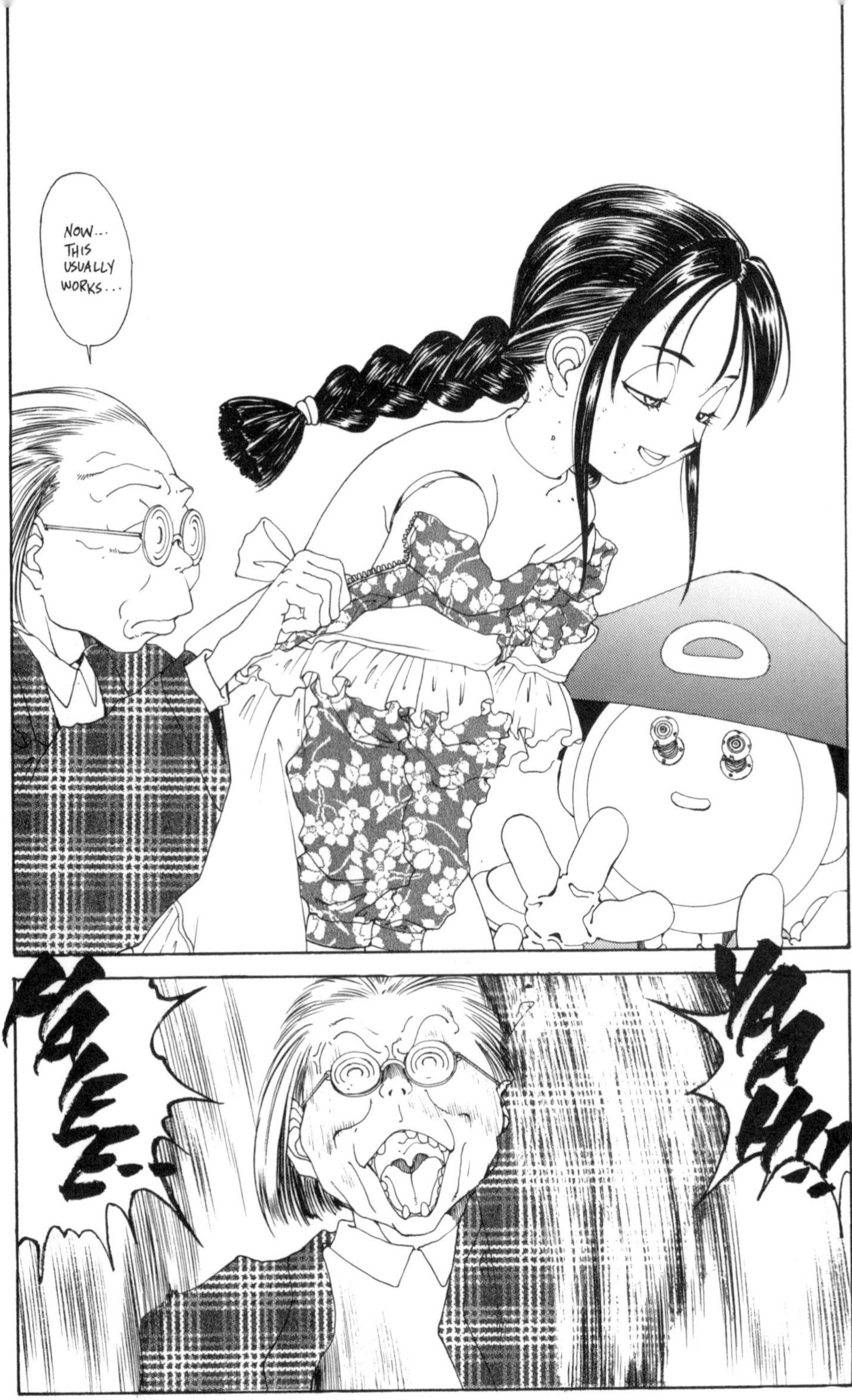
NOW... THIS USUALLY WORKS...

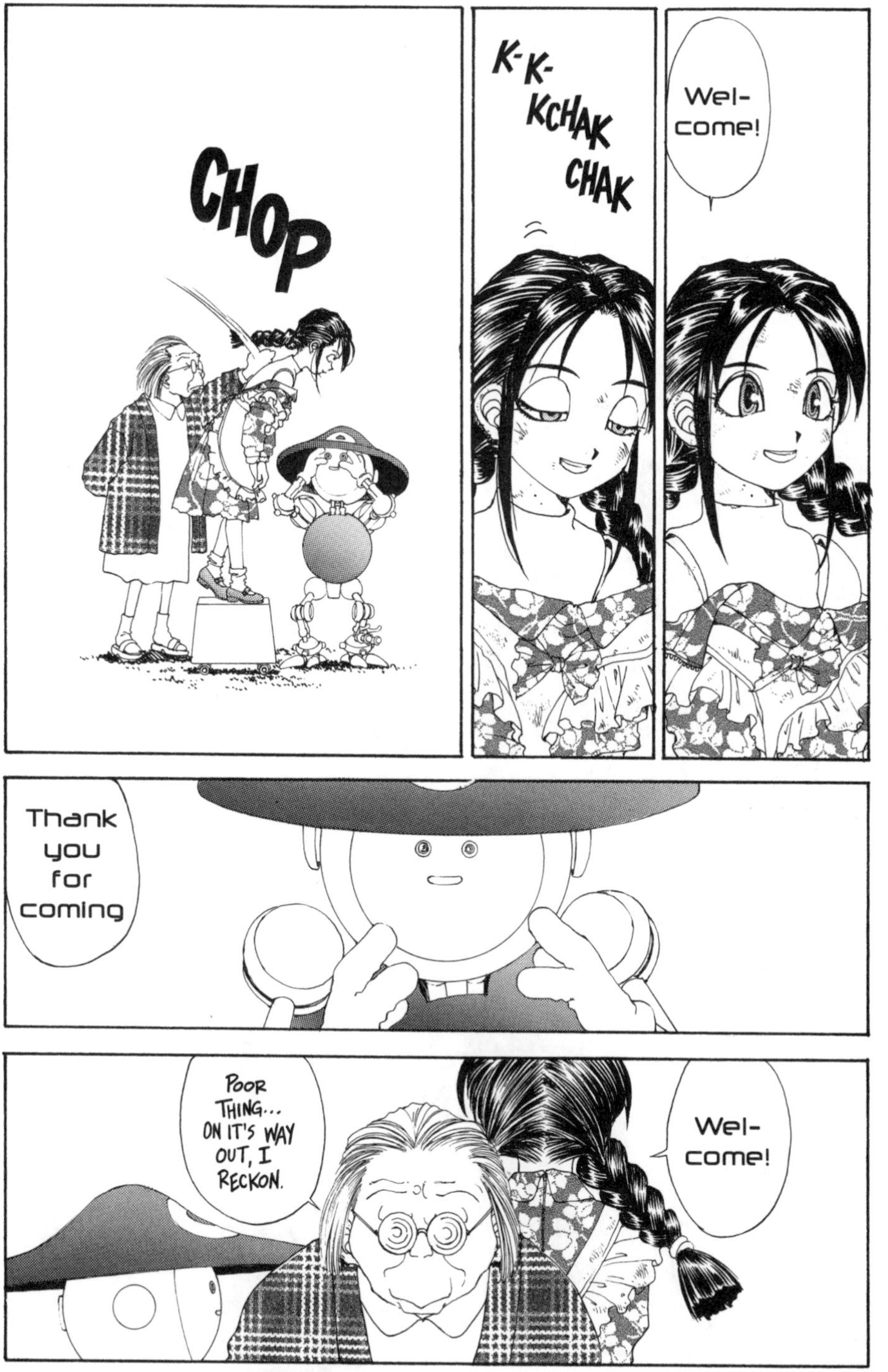
CHOP
K-K-KCHAK CHAK
Wel-come!
Thank you for coming
POOR THING... ON IT'S WAY OUT, I RECKON.
Wel-come!

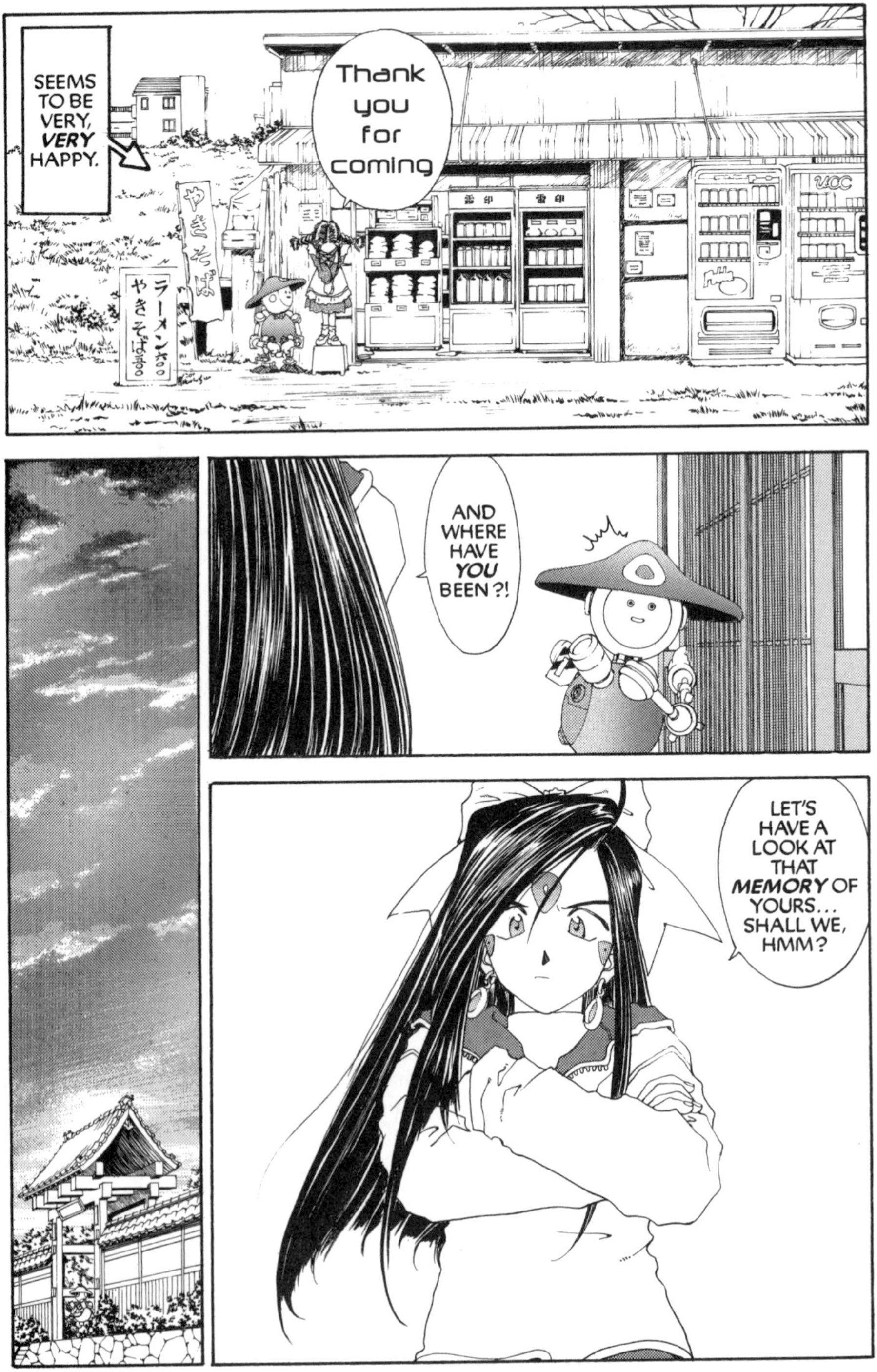
SEEMS TO BE VERY, ***VERY*** HAPPY.
やきそば
Thank you for coming
雪印
雪印
UCC
AND WHERE HAVE ***YOU*** BEEN?!
LET'S HAVE A LOOK AT THAT ***MEMORY*** OF YOURS... SHALL WE, HMM?

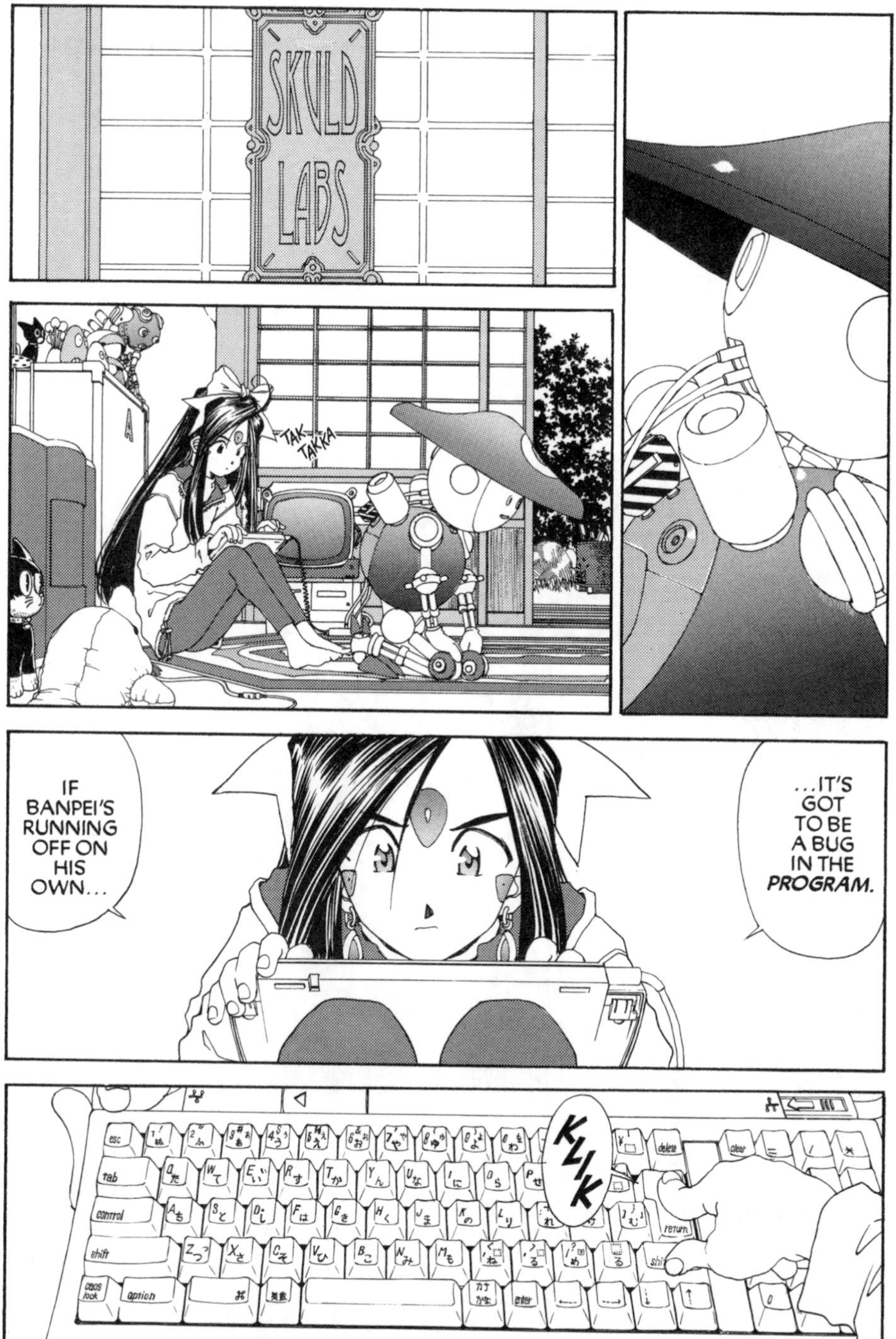
SKULD LABS
TAK TAKKA
IF BANPEI'S RUNNING OFF ON HIS OWN...
...IT'S GOT TO BE A BUG IN THE ***PROGRAM.***
KLIK

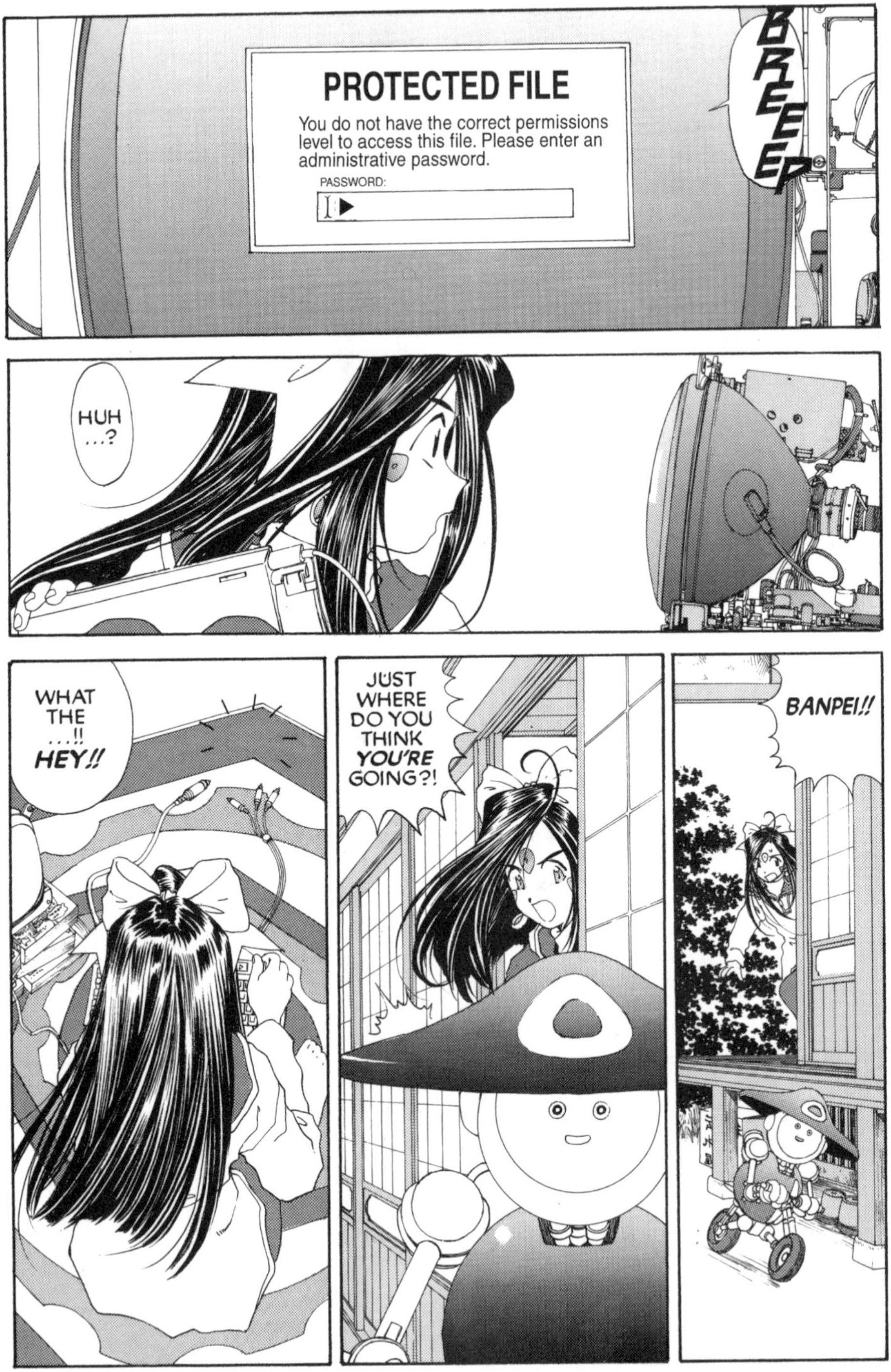
PROTECTED FILE
You do not have the correct permissions level to access this file. Please enter an administrative password.
PASSWORD:
BREEEP
HUH ...?
WHAT THE ...!! HEY!!
JUST WHERE DO YOU THINK YOU'RE GOING?!
BANPEI!!

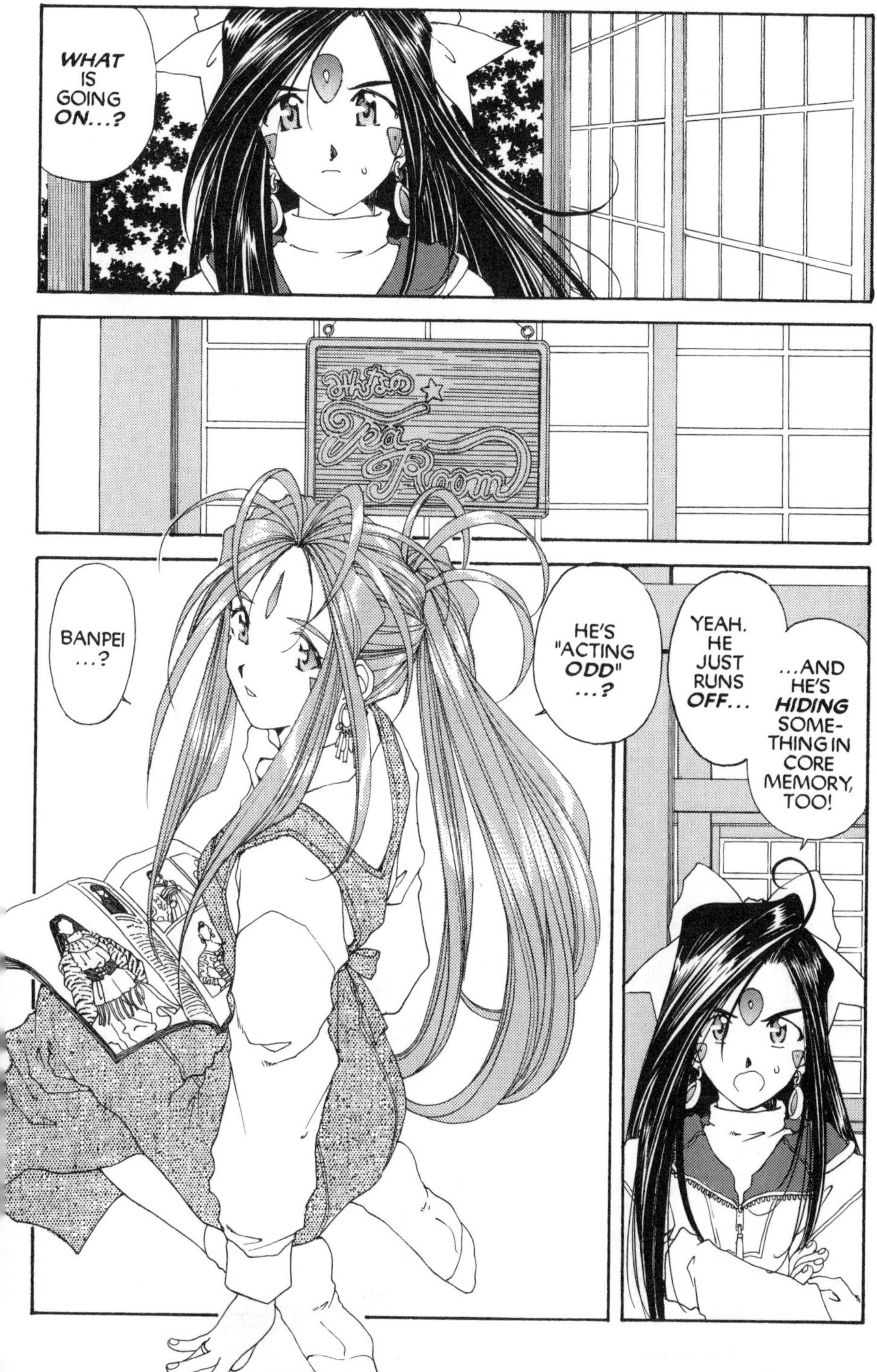
WHAT IS GOING ON...?
BANPEI ...?
HE'S "ACTING ODD" ...?
YEAH. HE JUST RUNS OFF...
...AND HE'S HIDING SOMETHING IN CORE MEMORY, TOO!

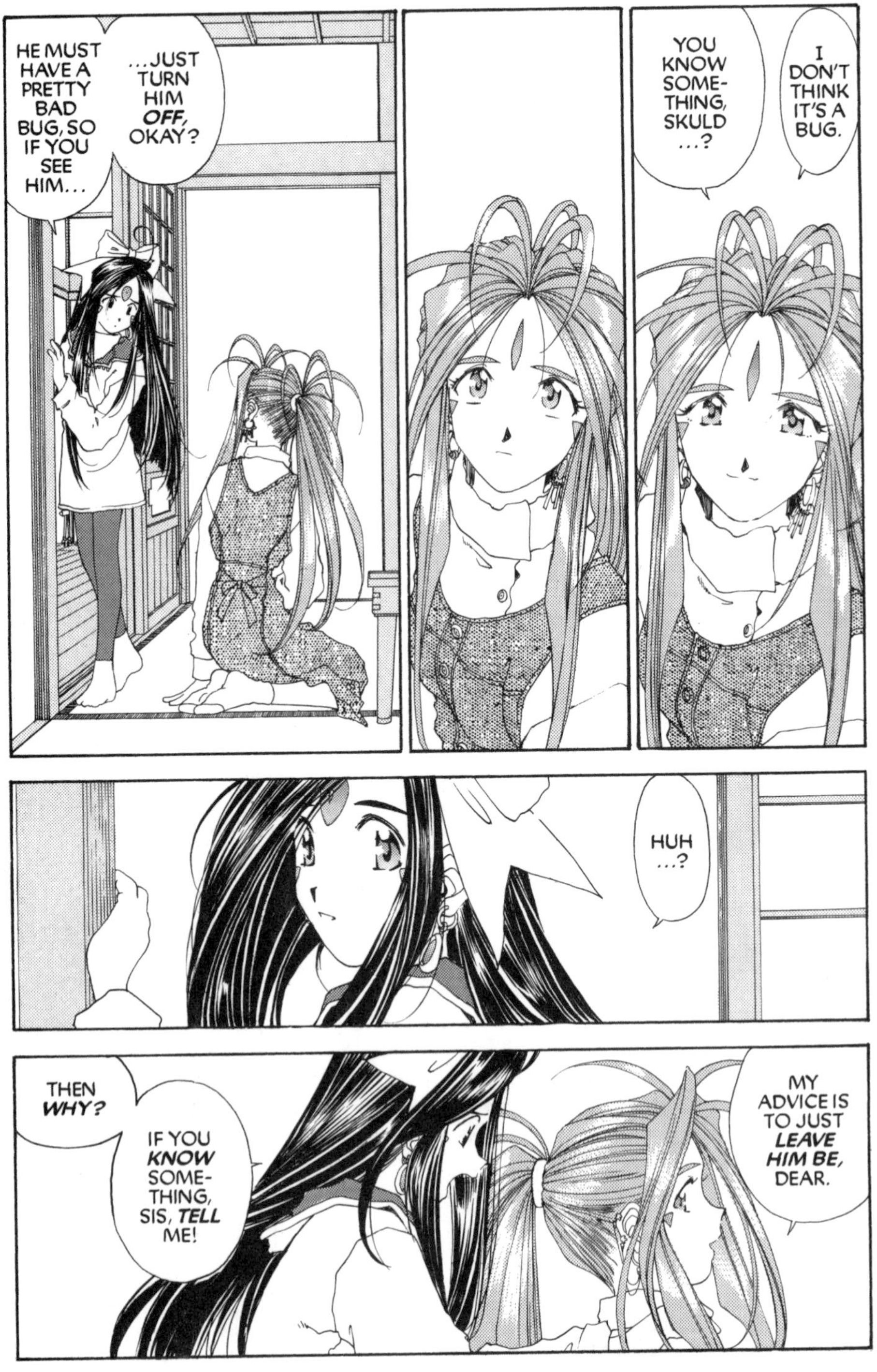
HE MUST HAVE A PRETTY BAD BUG, SO IF YOU SEE HIM...
...JUST TURN HIM OFF, OKAY?
YOU KNOW SOMETHING, SKULD ...?
I DON'T THINK IT'S A BUG.
HUH ...?
THEN WHY?
IF YOU KNOW SOMETHING, SIS, TELL ME!
MY ADVICE IS TO JUST LEAVE HIM BE, DEAR.

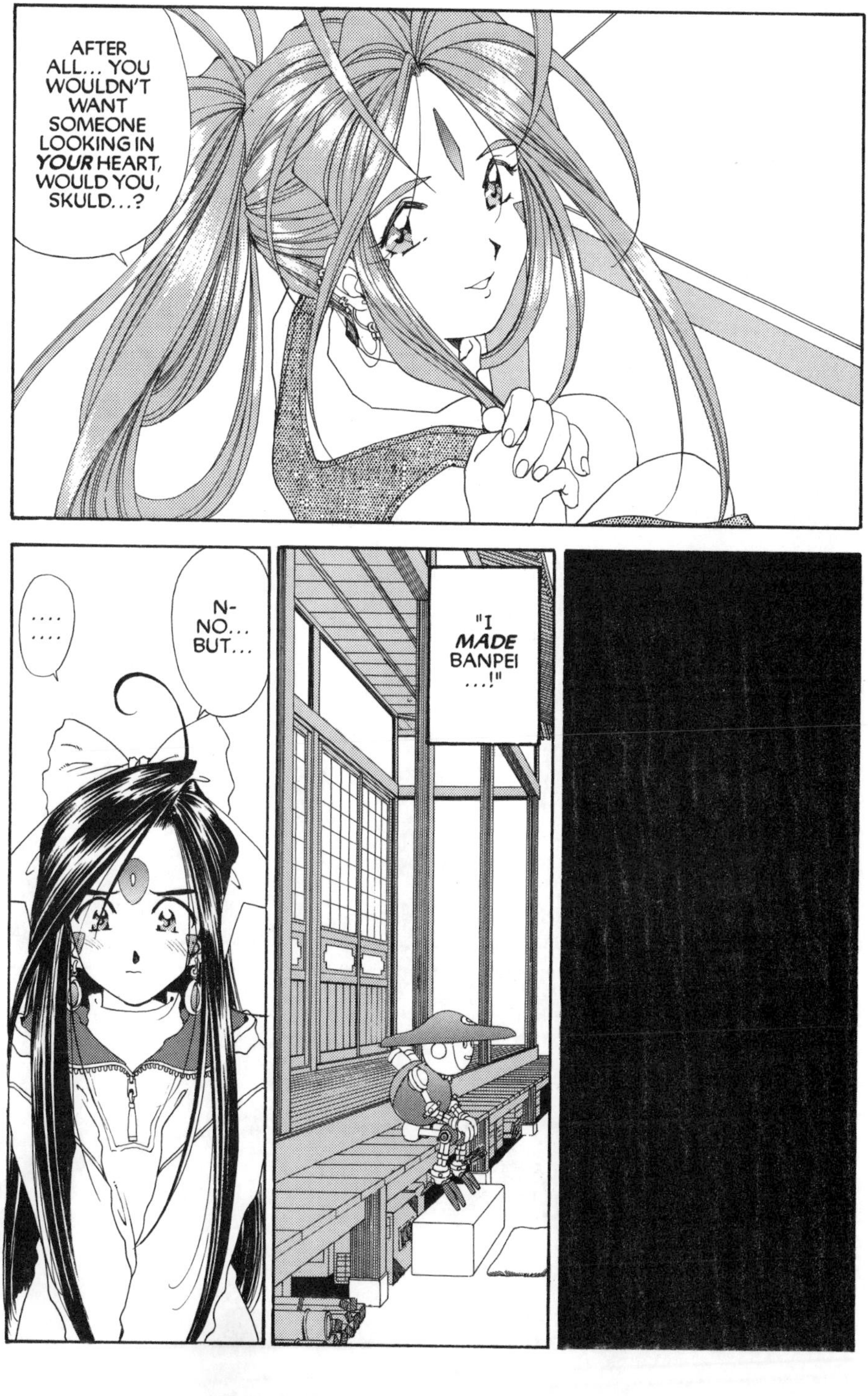
AFTER ALL... YOU WOULDN'T WANT SOMEONE LOOKING IN *YOUR* HEART, WOULD YOU, SKULD...?
....
N-NO... BUT...
"I *MADE* BANPEI ...!"

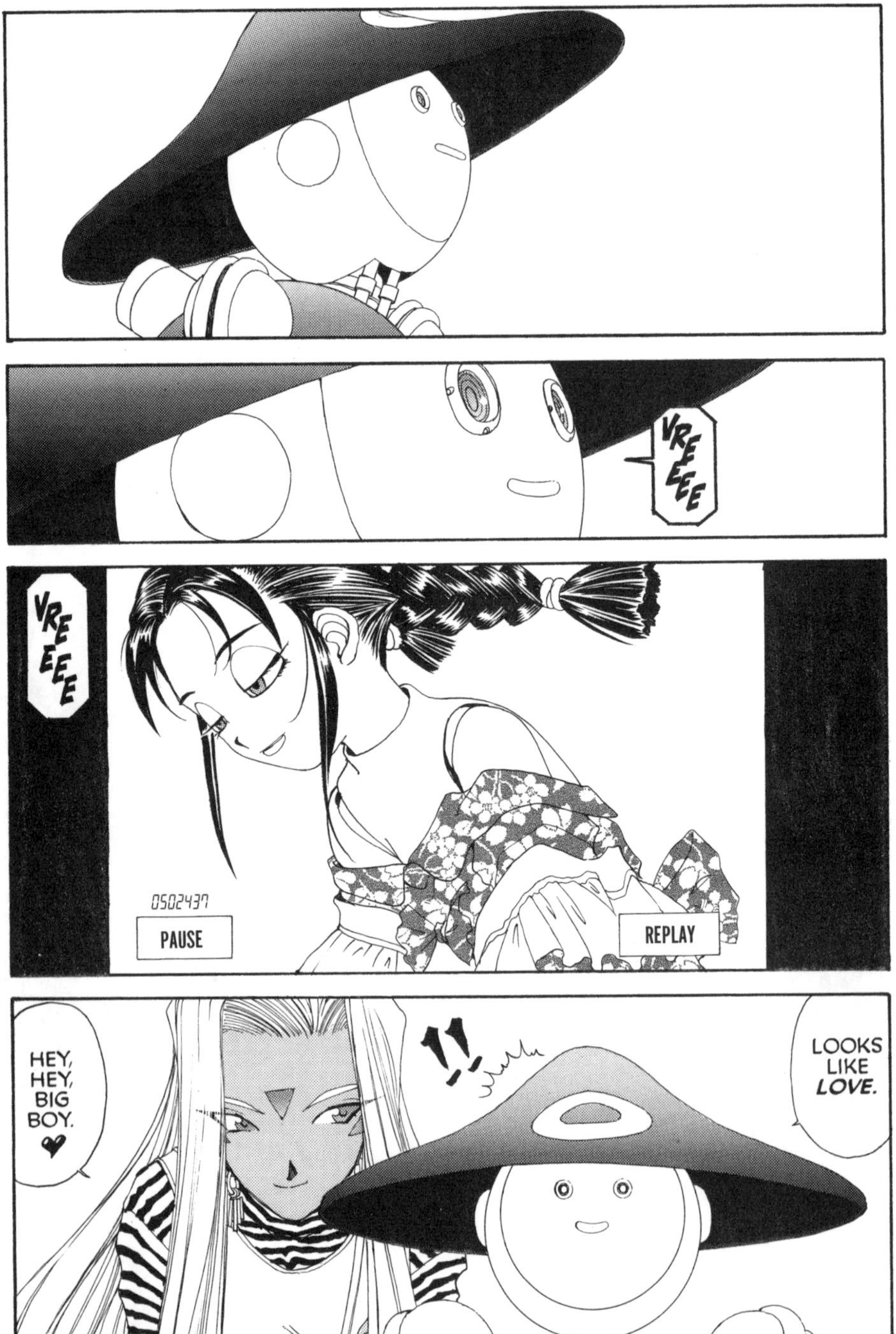
VREEEE
VREEEE
0502437
PAUSE
REPLAY
HEY, HEY, BIG BOY. ❤
!!
LOOKS LIKE LOVE.

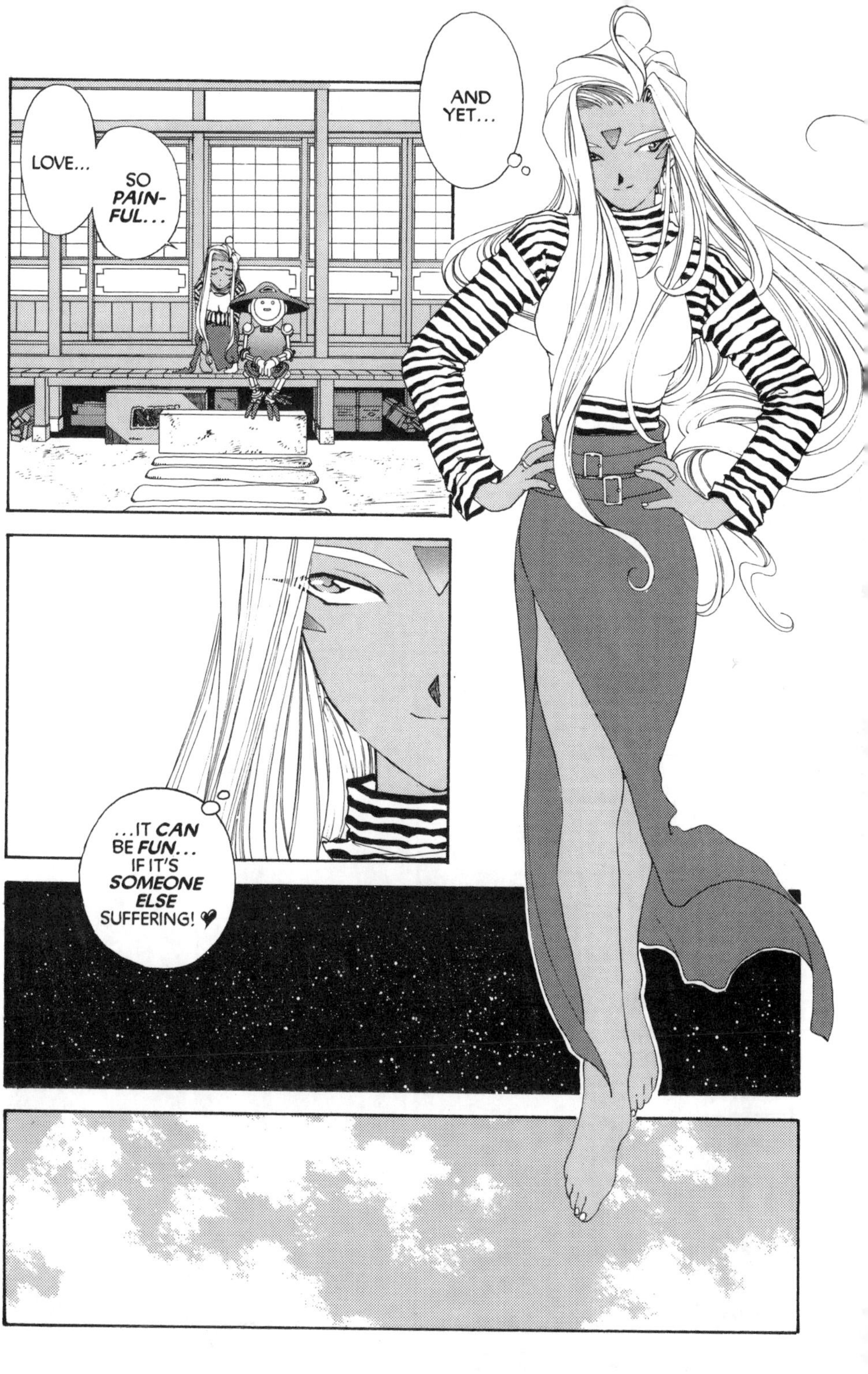
LOVE...
SO PAINFUL...
AND YET...
...IT CAN BE FUN... IF IT'S SOMEONE ELSE SUFFERING! ♥

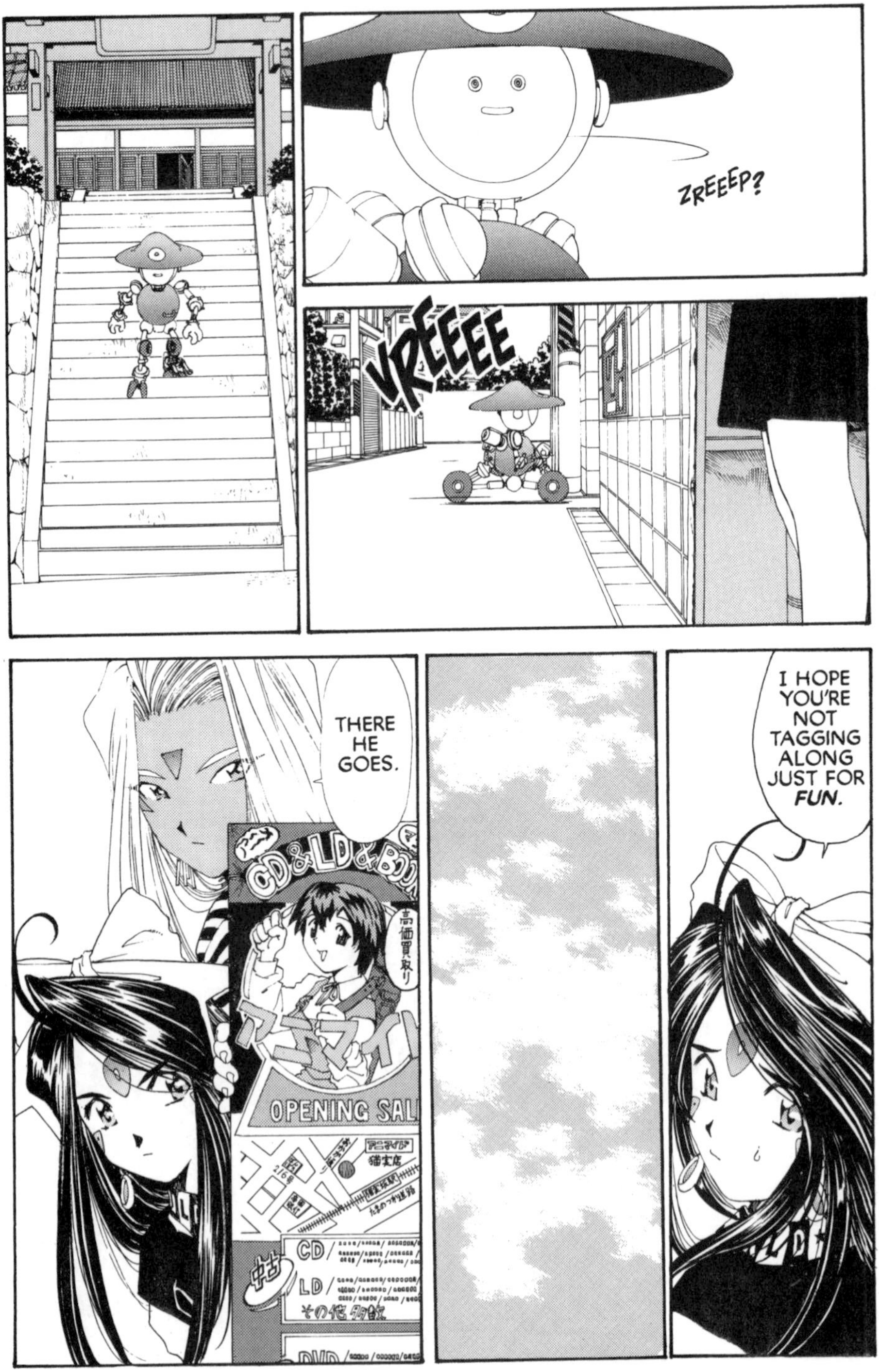
ZREEEP?
VREEEE
THERE HE GOES.
高価買取り
CD/
LD/
I HOPE YOU'RE NOT TAGGING ALONG JUST FOR *FUN*.

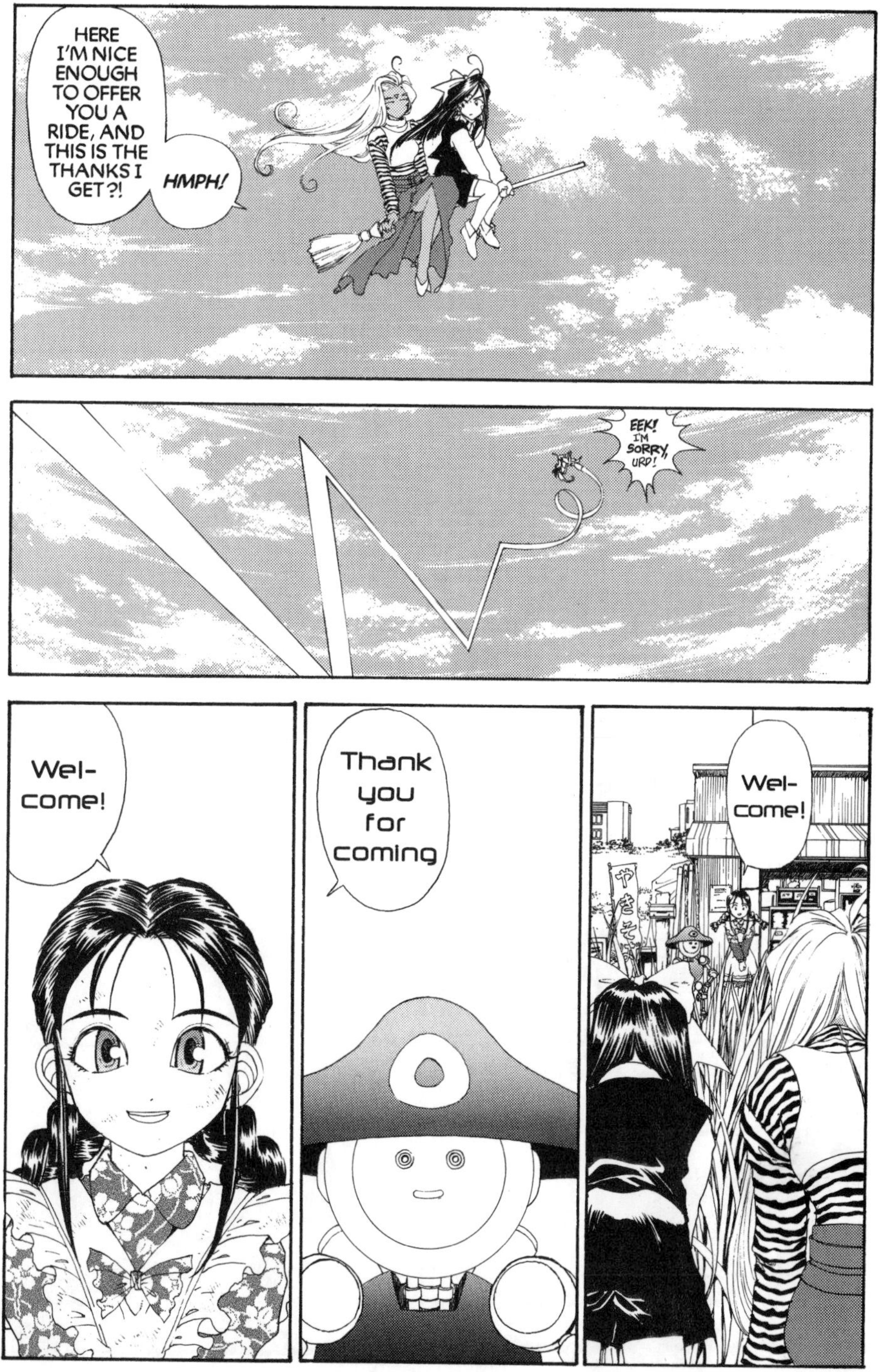
HERE I'M NICE ENOUGH TO OFFER YOU A RIDE, AND THIS IS THE THANKS I GET?!
HMPH!
EEK! I'M SORRY, URD!
Wel-come!
Thank you for coming
Wel-come!

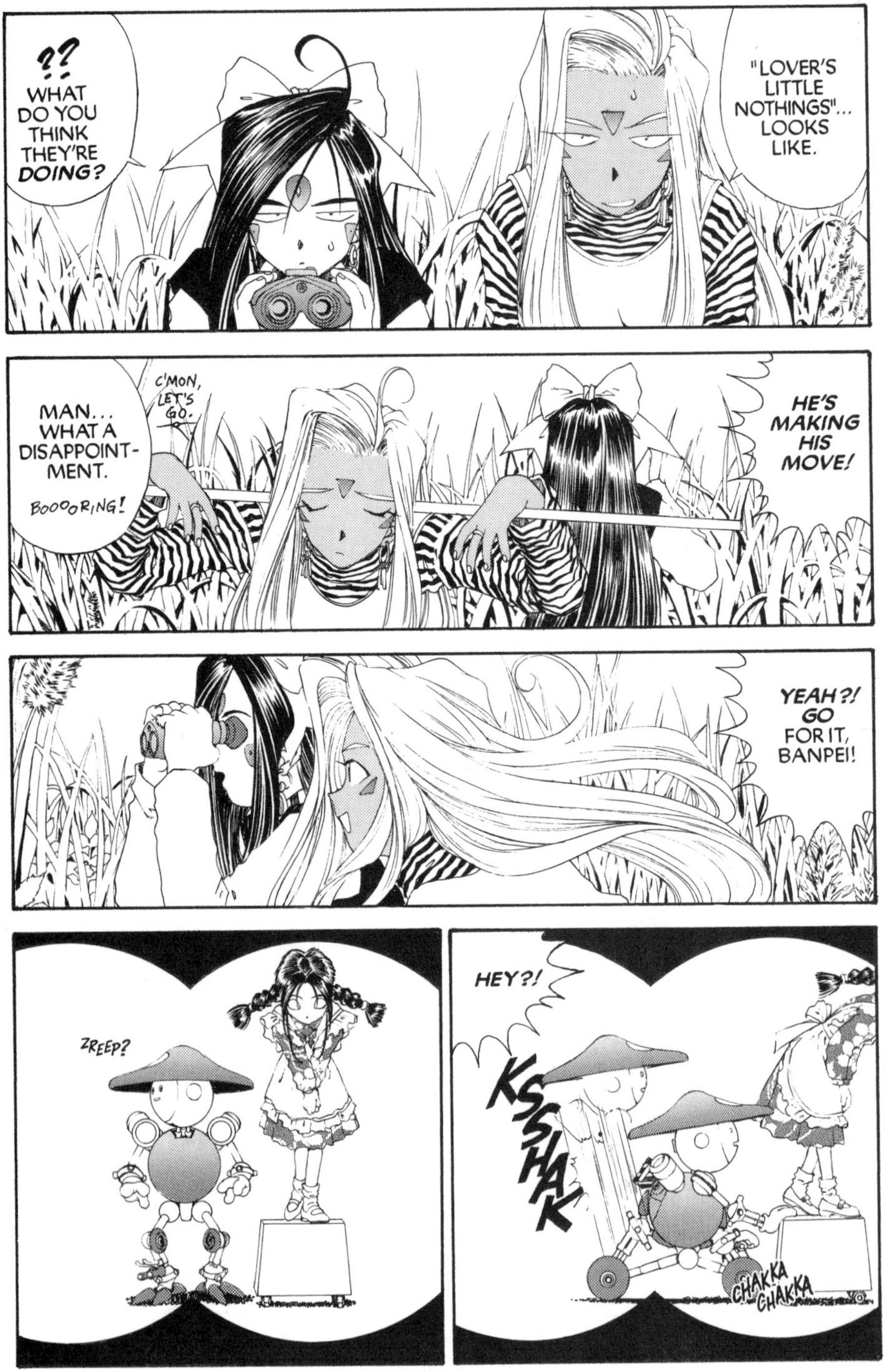
??
WHAT DO YOU THINK THEY'RE DOING?
"LOVER'S LITTLE NOTHINGS"... LOOKS LIKE.
MAN... WHAT A DISAPPOINTMENT.
BOOOORING!
C'MON, LET'S GO.
HE'S MAKING HIS MOVE!
YEAH?! GO FOR IT, BANPEI!
ZREEP?
HEY?!
KSSHAK
CHAKKA CHAKKA

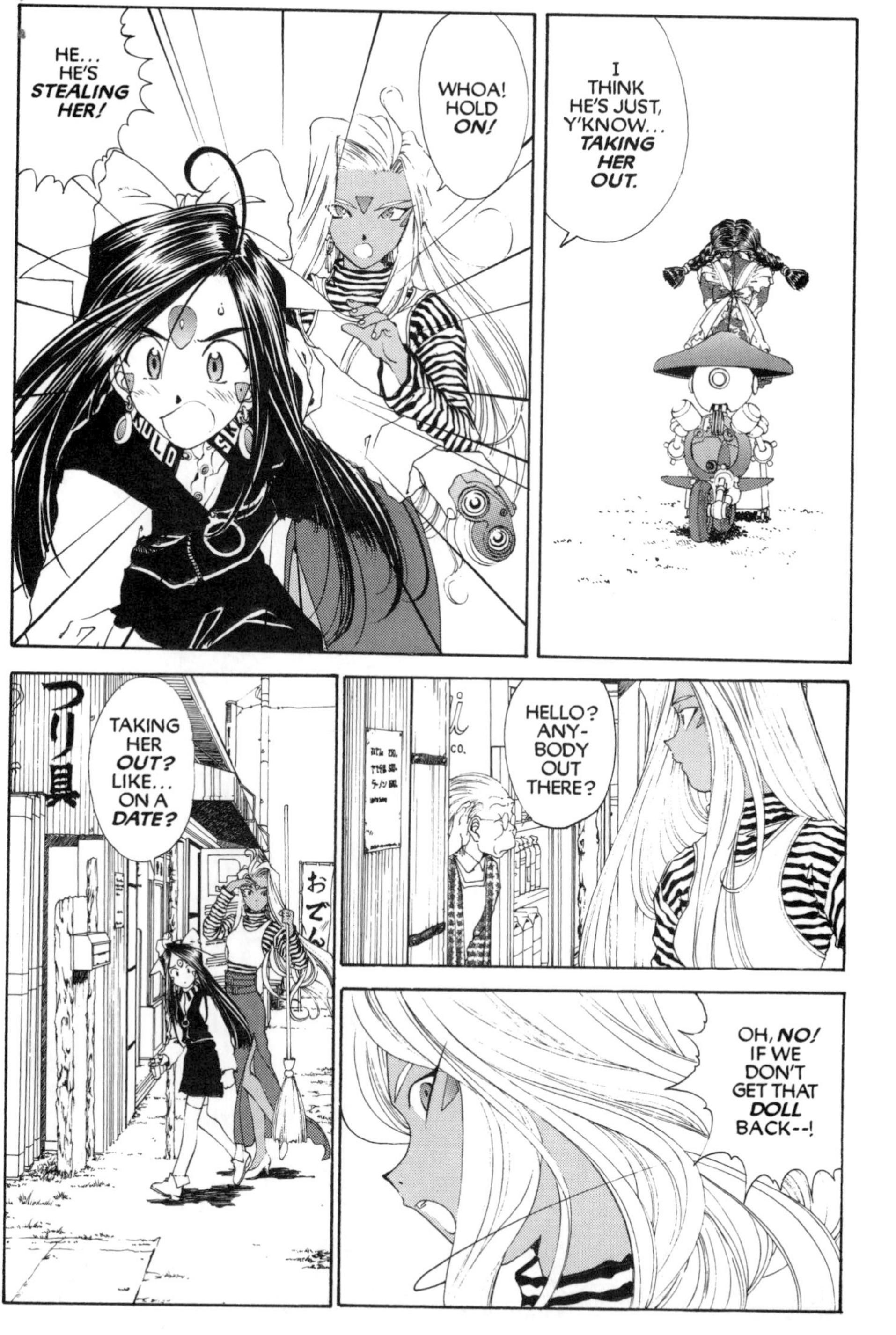
HE... HE'S *STEALING HER!*
WHOA! HOLD *ON!*
I THINK HE'S JUST, Y'KNOW... *TAKING HER OUT.*
つり具
TAKING HER *OUT?* LIKE... ON A *DATE?*
おでん
HELLO? ANY-BODY OUT THERE?
OH, *NO!* IF WE DON'T GET THAT *DOLL* BACK--!

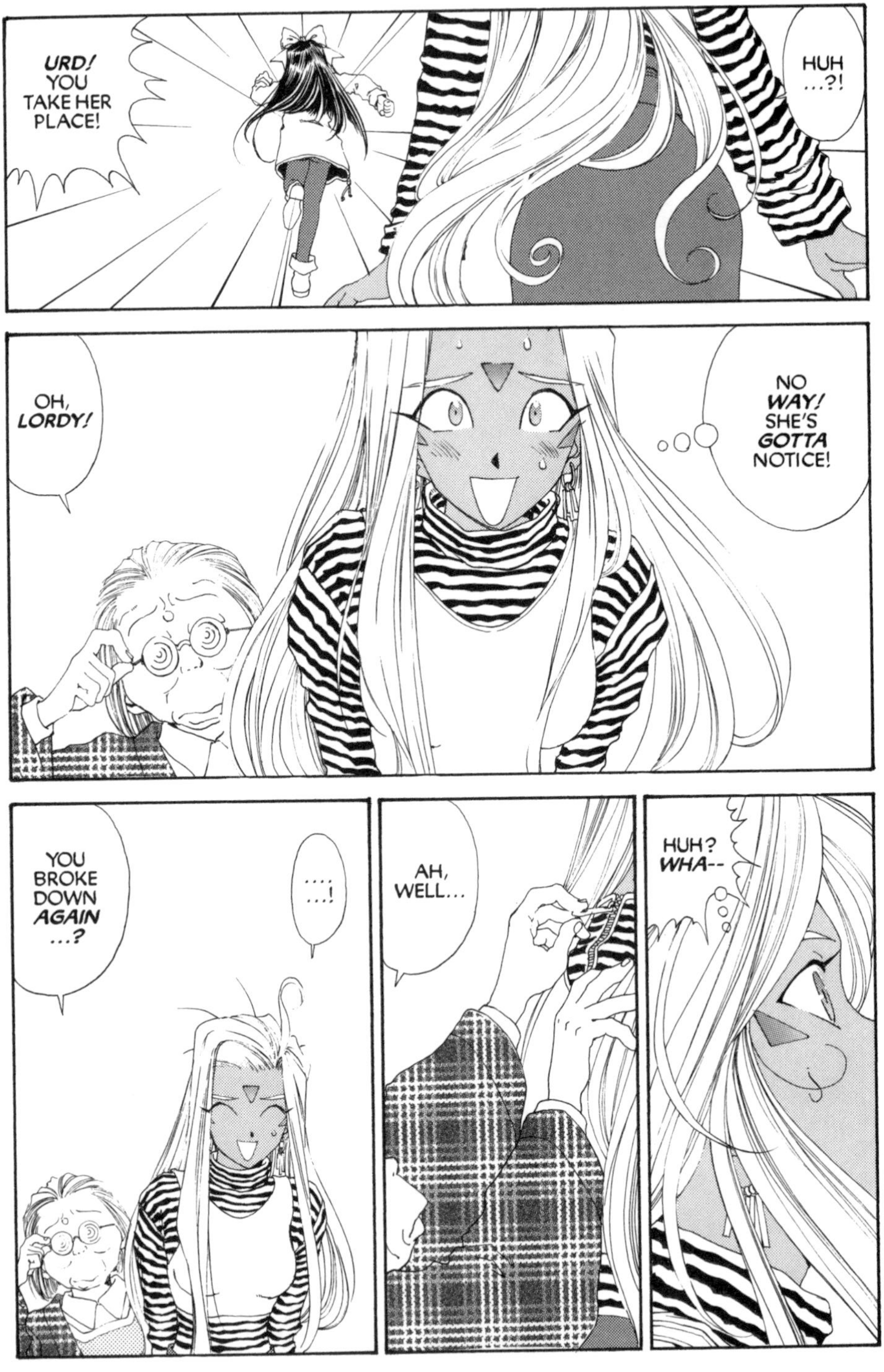
URD! YOU TAKE HER PLACE!
HUH...?!
OH, LORDY!
NO WAY! SHE'S GOTTA NOTICE!
YOU BROKE DOWN AGAIN...?
...., ...!
AH, WELL...
HUH? WHA--

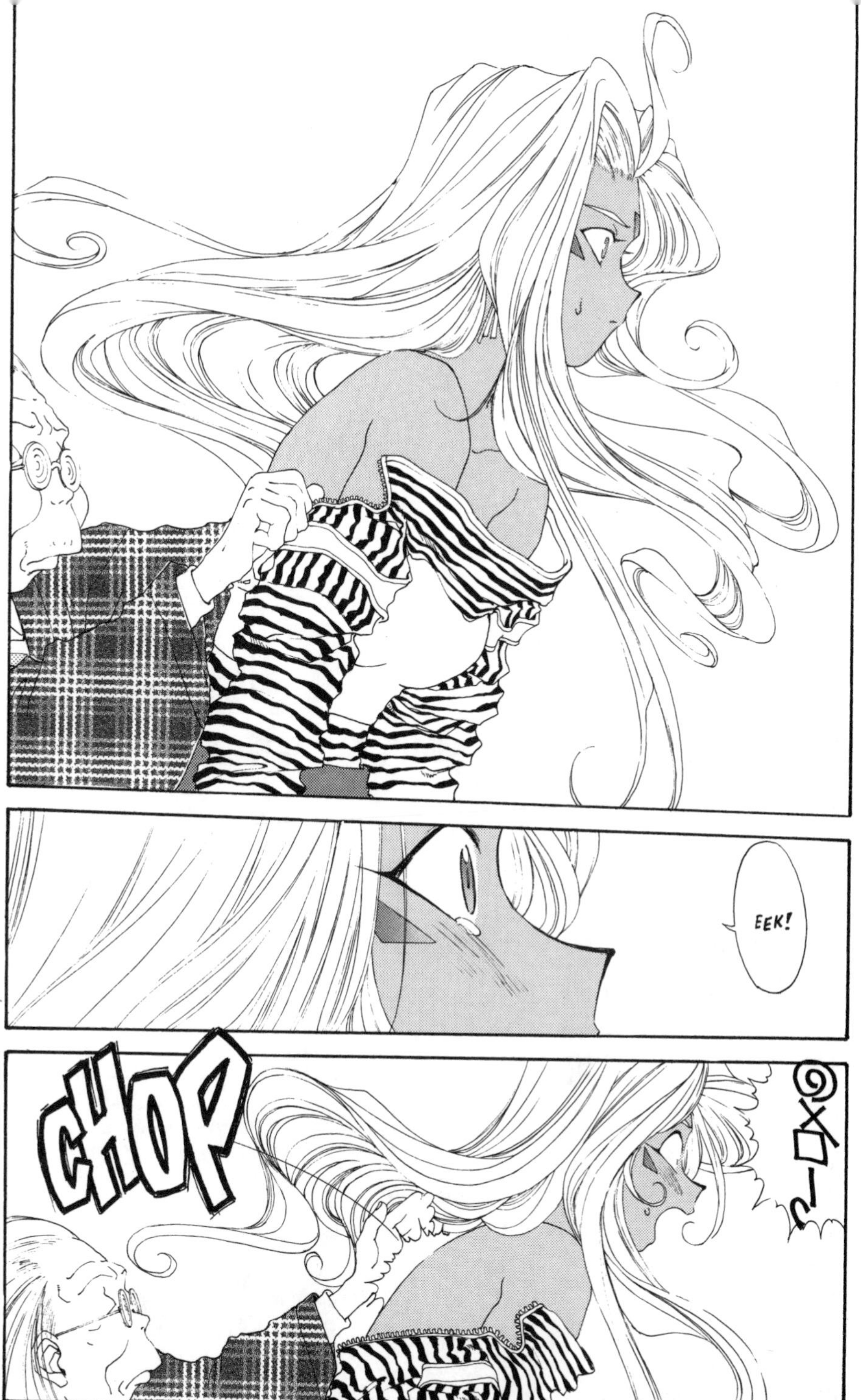
EEK!
CHOP

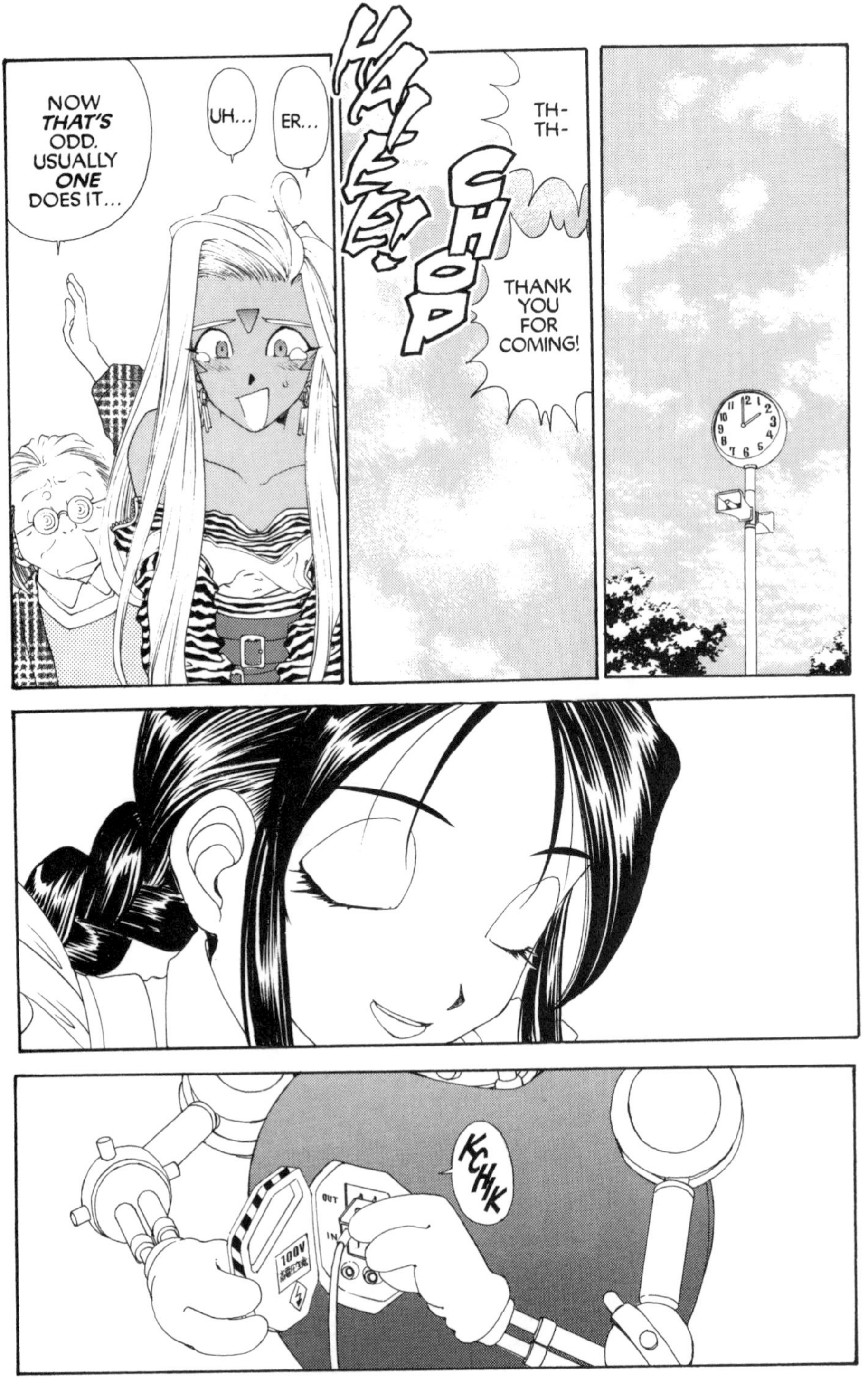
NOW THAT'S ODD. USUALLY ONE DOES IT...
UH...
ER...
HA! HEE!
TH- TH-
CHOP
THANK YOU FOR COMING!
KCHIK

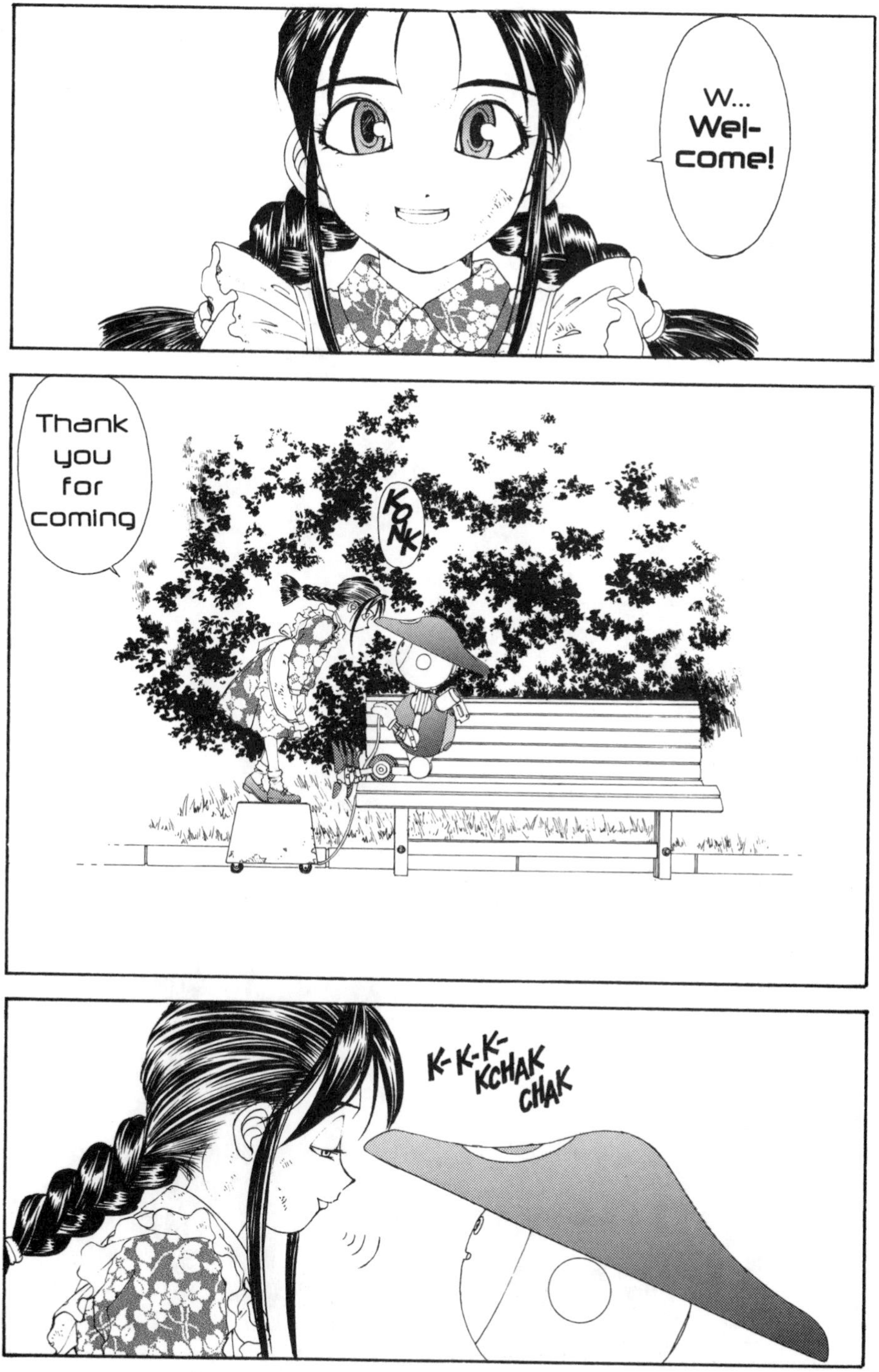
W... Wel-come!
Thank you for coming
KONK
K-K-K-KCHAK CHAK

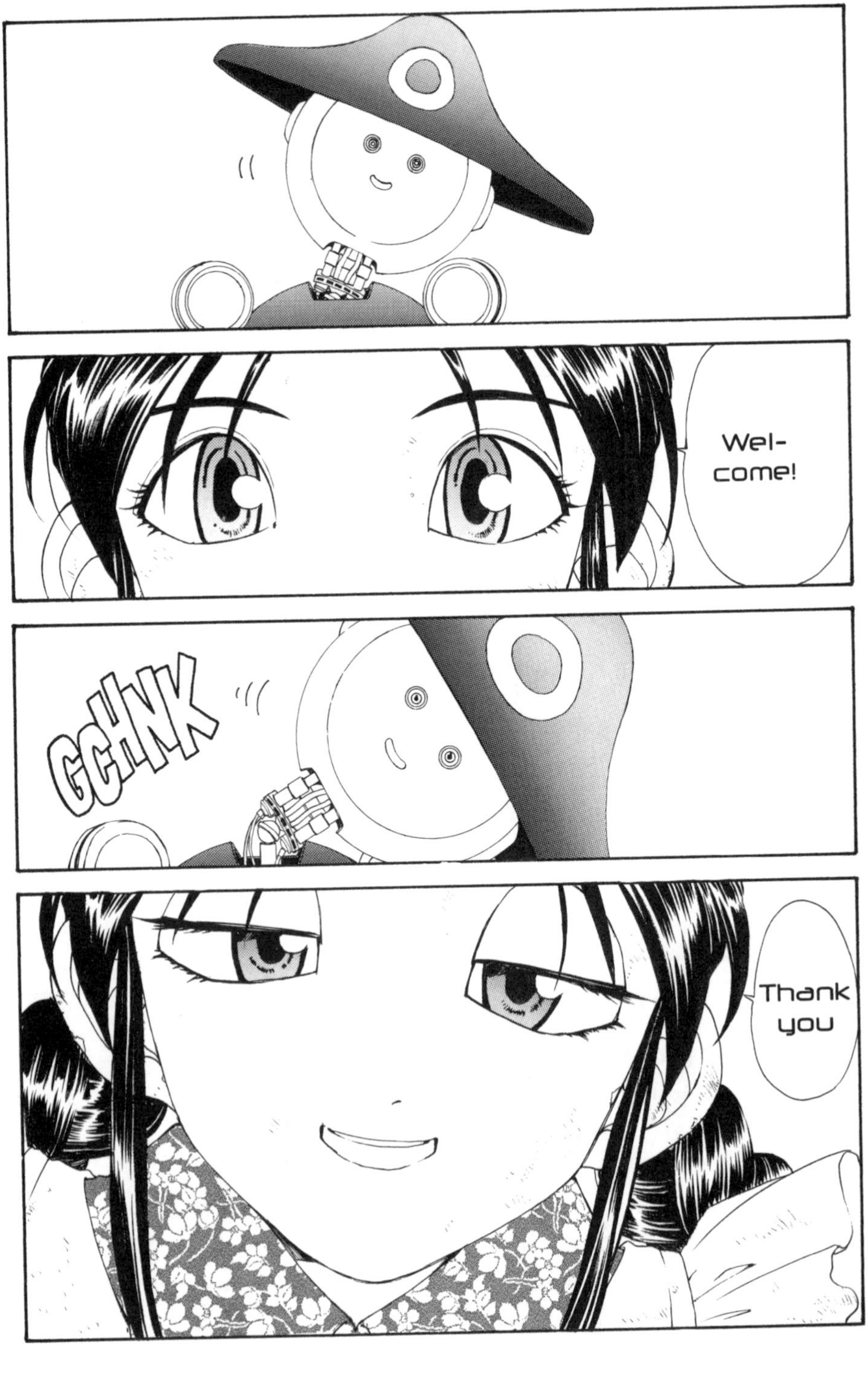
Wel-
come!
GCHNK
Thank
you

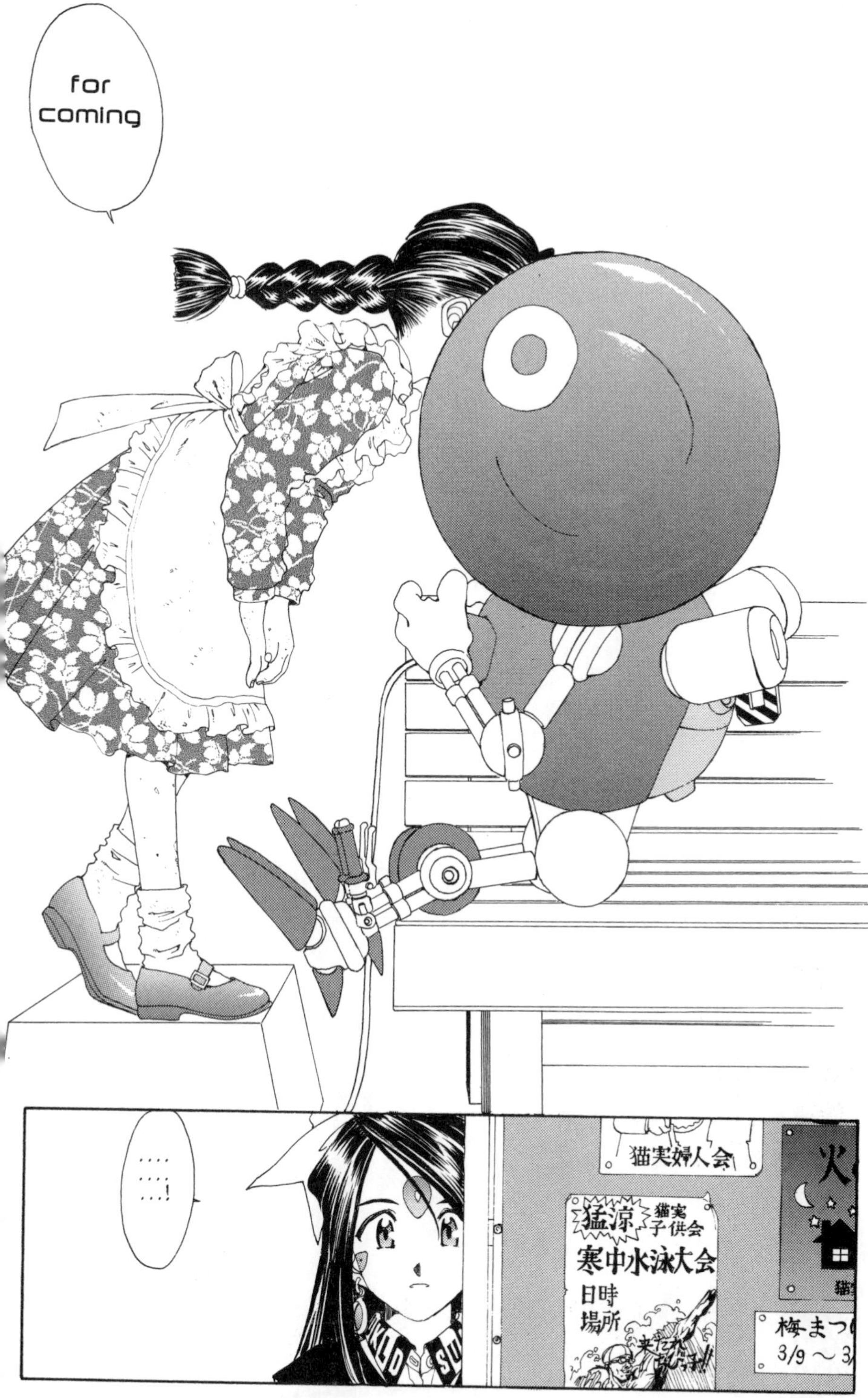
for coming
....
....
...!
猫実婦人会
猛涼
猫実子供会
寒中水泳大会
日時
場所

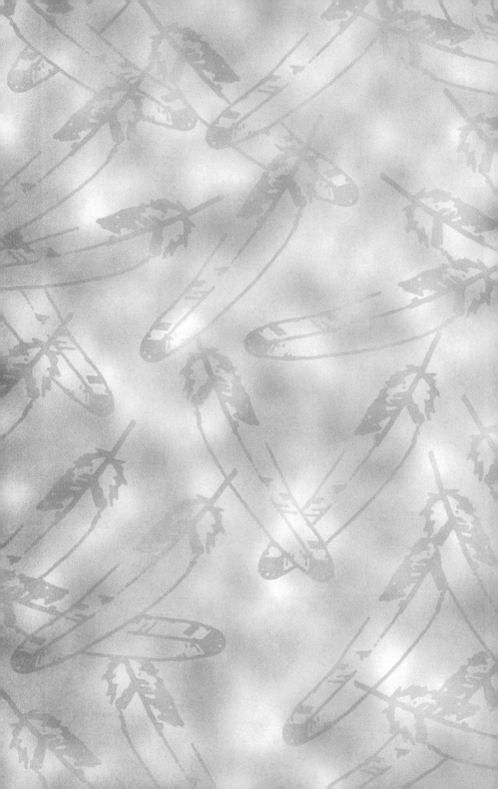

THE SORROWS OF BANPEI

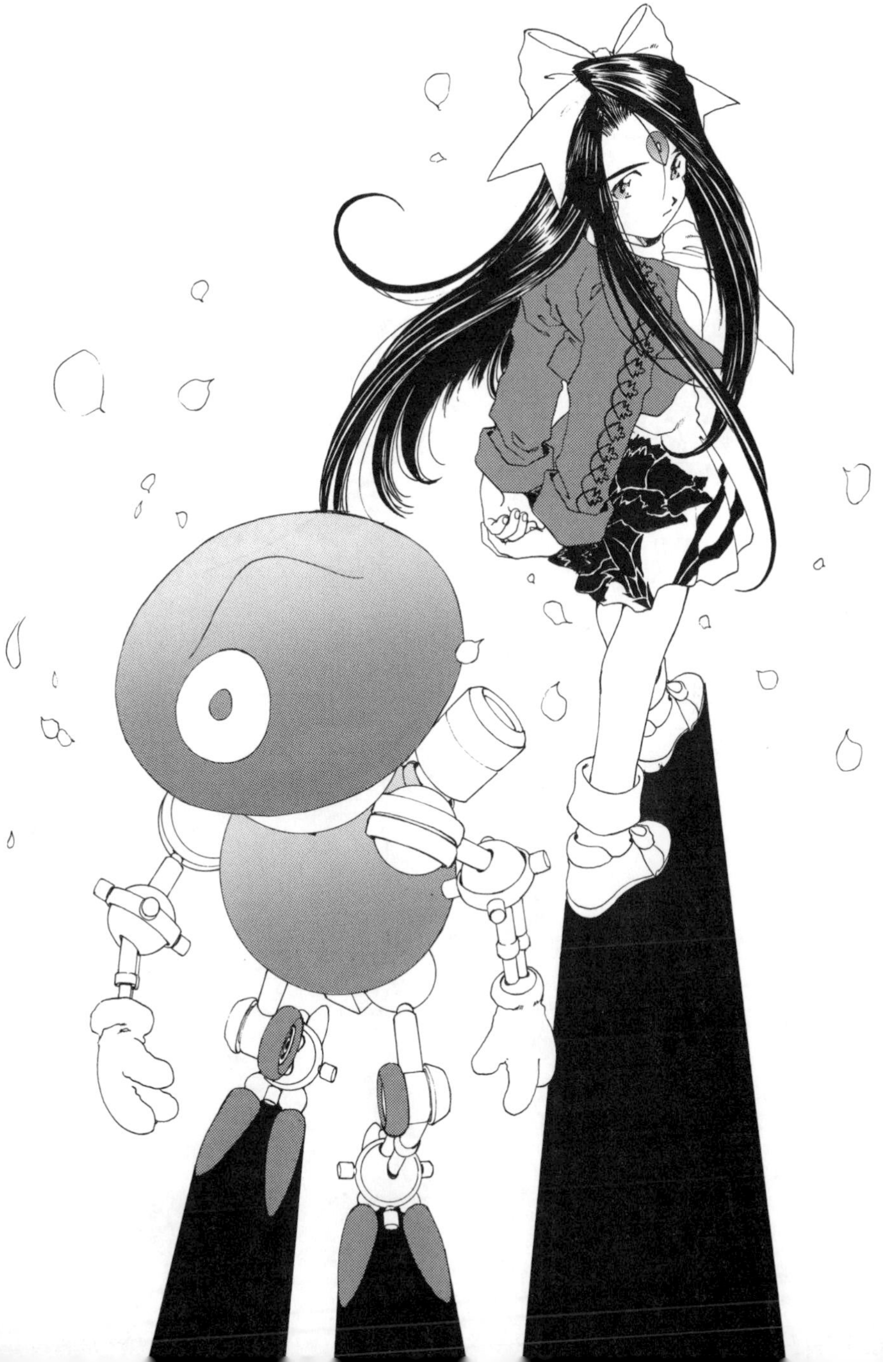

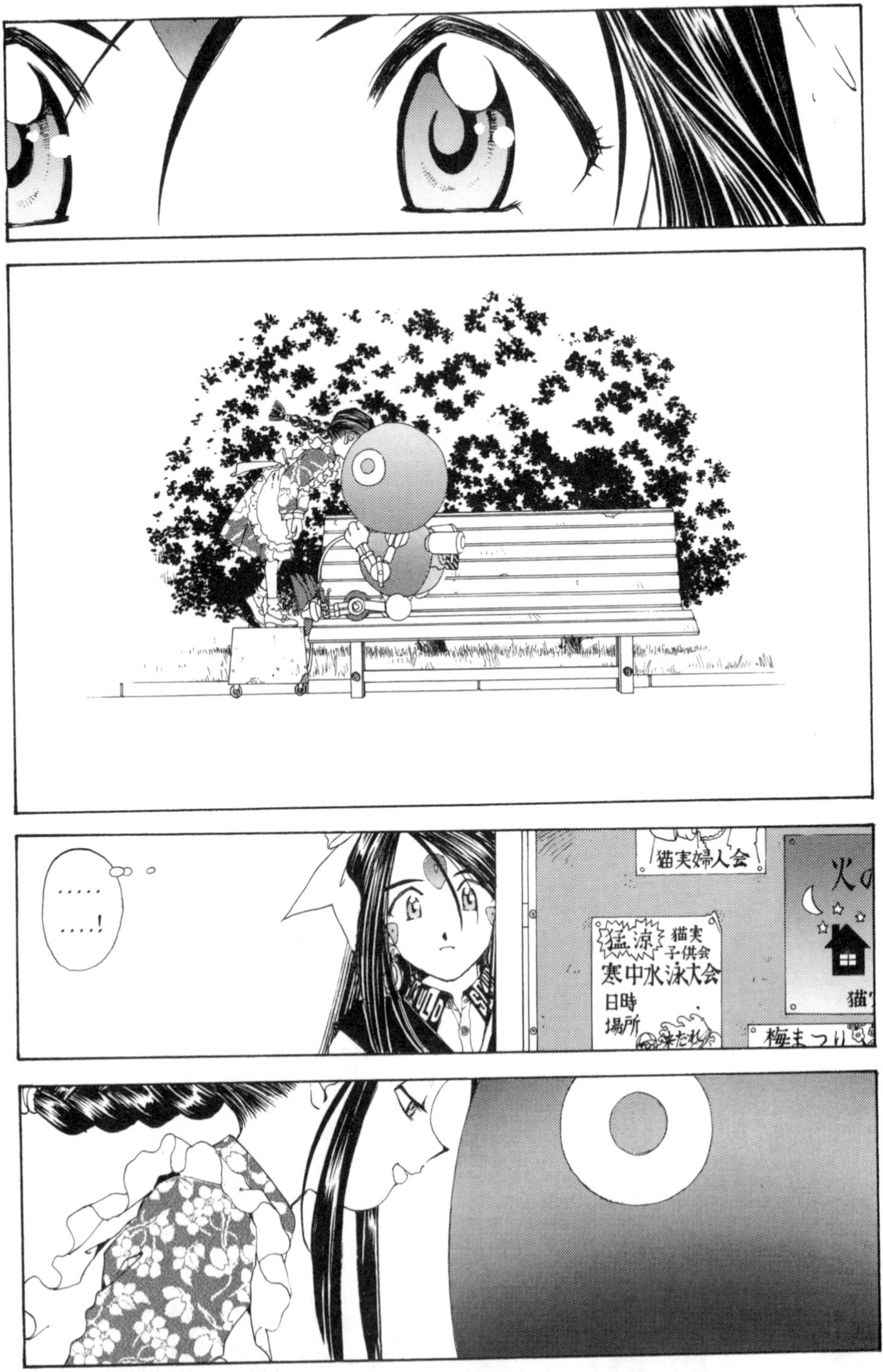
.....
.....!
猫実婦人会
猛涼
猫実
子供会
寒中水泳大会
日時
場所
梅まつり

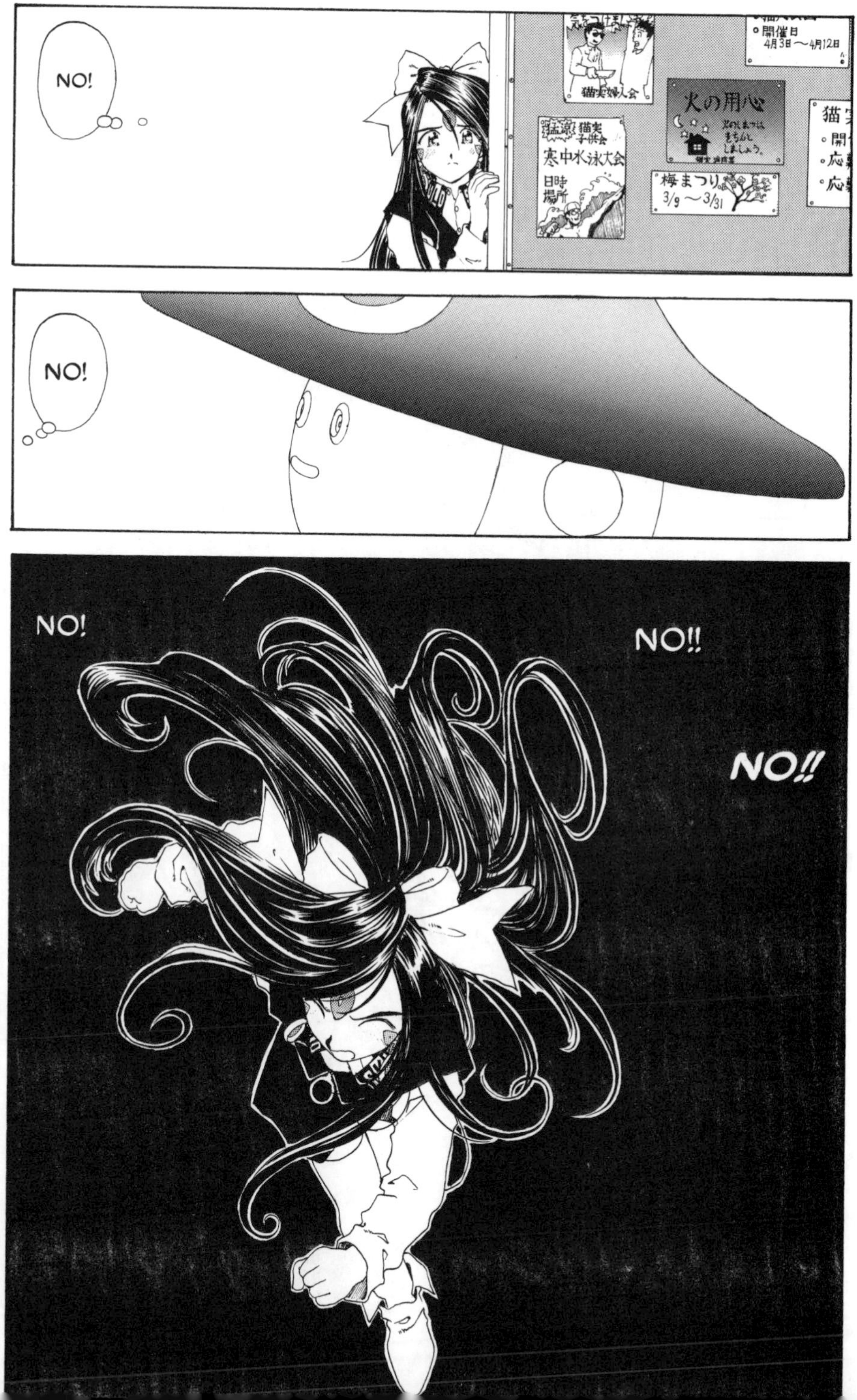
NO!
開催日
4月3日～4月12日
猫実婦人会
火の用心
猫実
子供会
寒中水泳大会
日時
場所
梅まつり
3/9～3/31
NO!
NO!
NO!!
NO!!

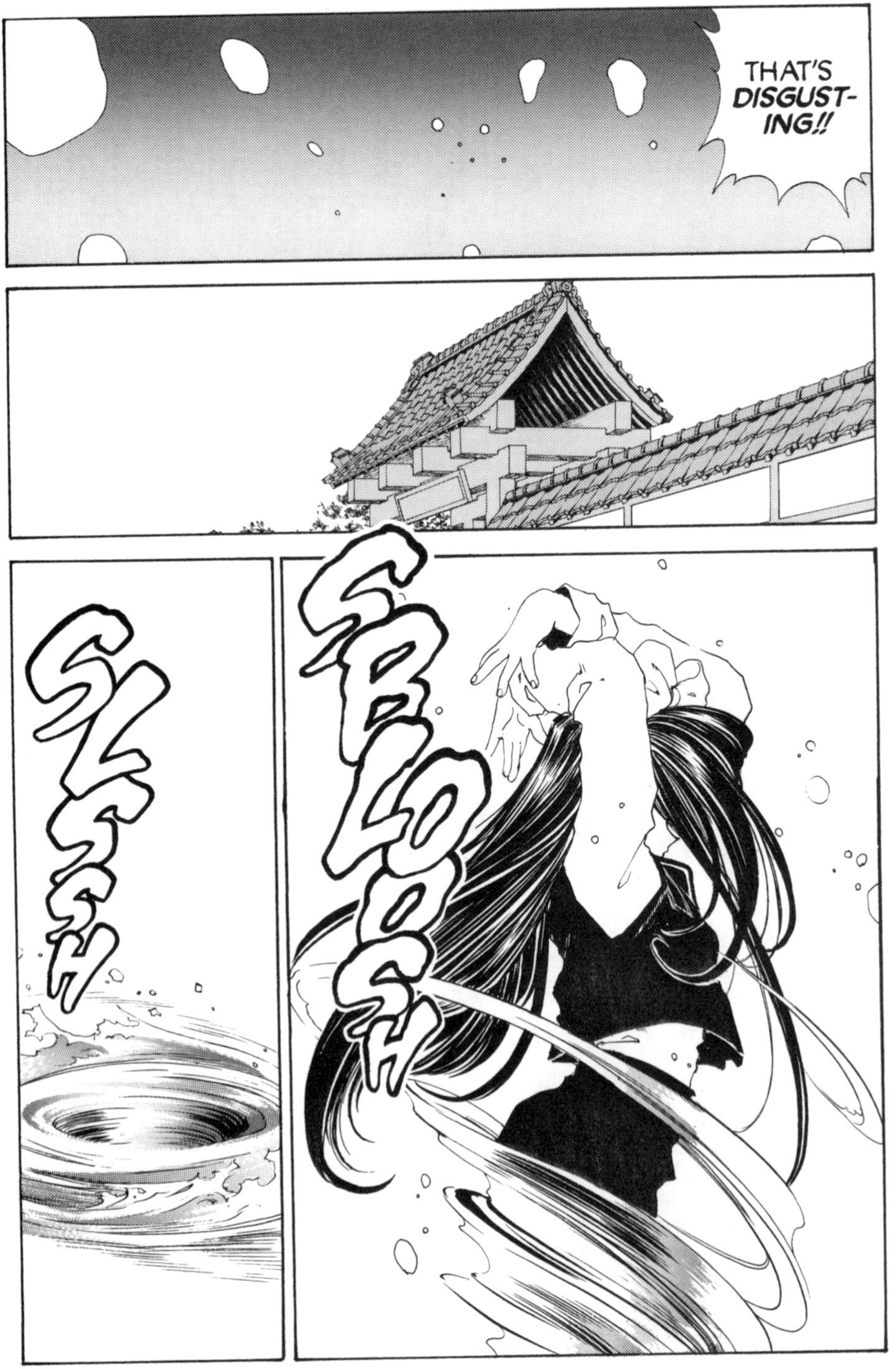
THAT'S DISGUST-ING!!
SLSSSH
SPLOOSH

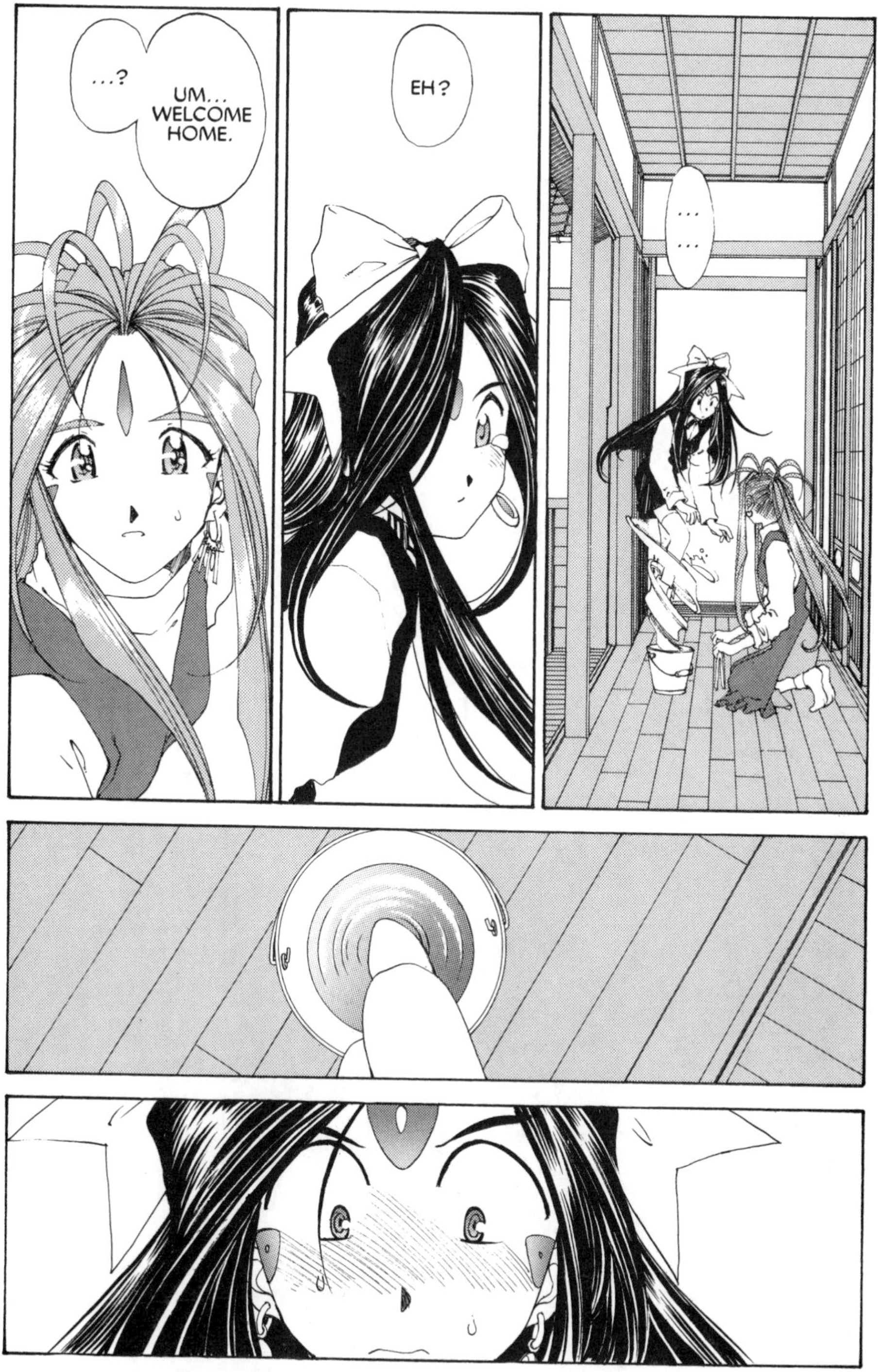
...?
UM... WELCOME HOME.
EH?
......

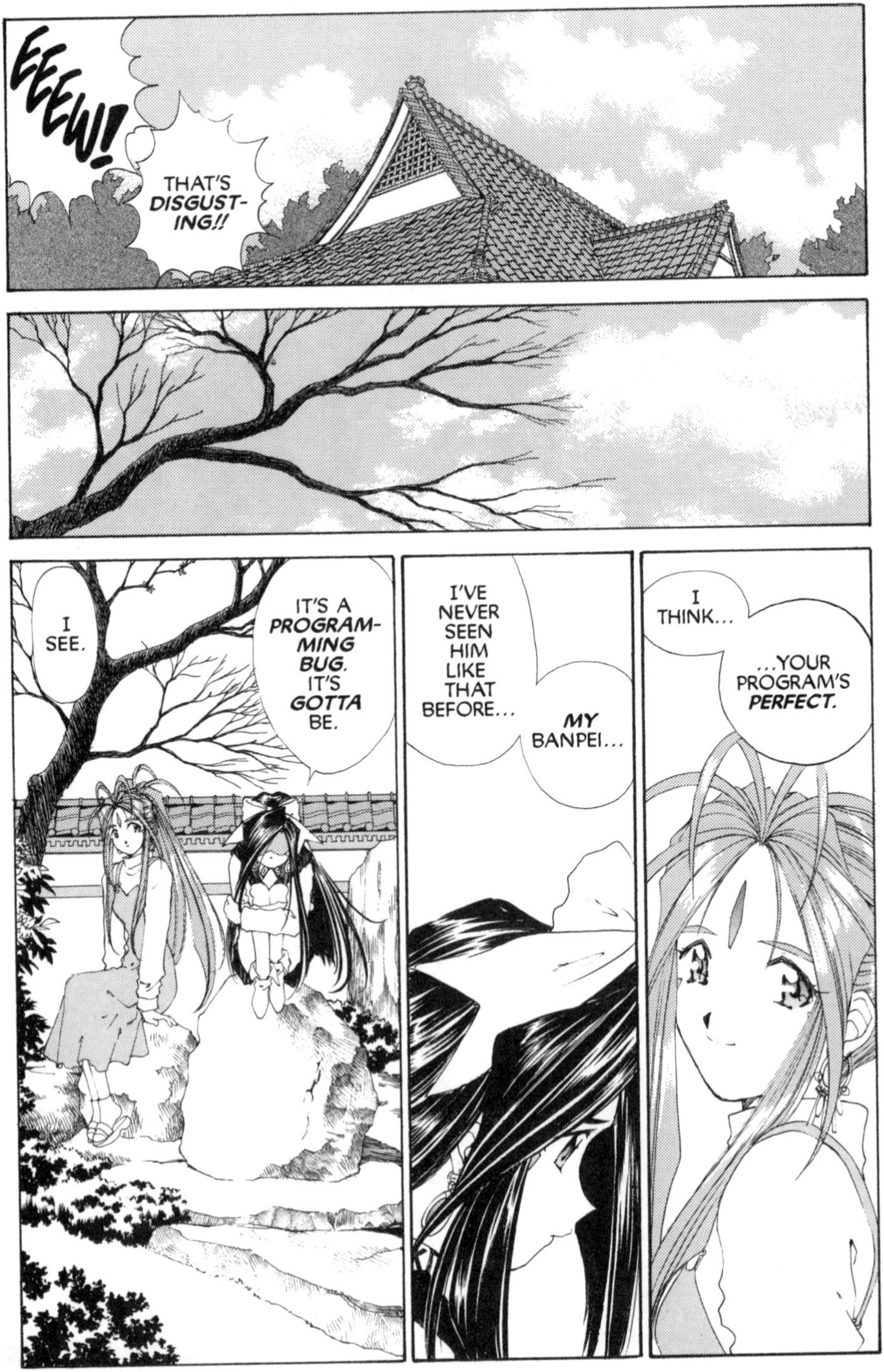
EEEW!
THAT'S DISGUSTING!!
I SEE.
IT'S A PROGRAMMING BUG. IT'S GOTTA BE.
I'VE NEVER SEEN HIM LIKE THAT BEFORE...
MY BANPEI...
I THINK...
...YOUR PROGRAM'S PERFECT.

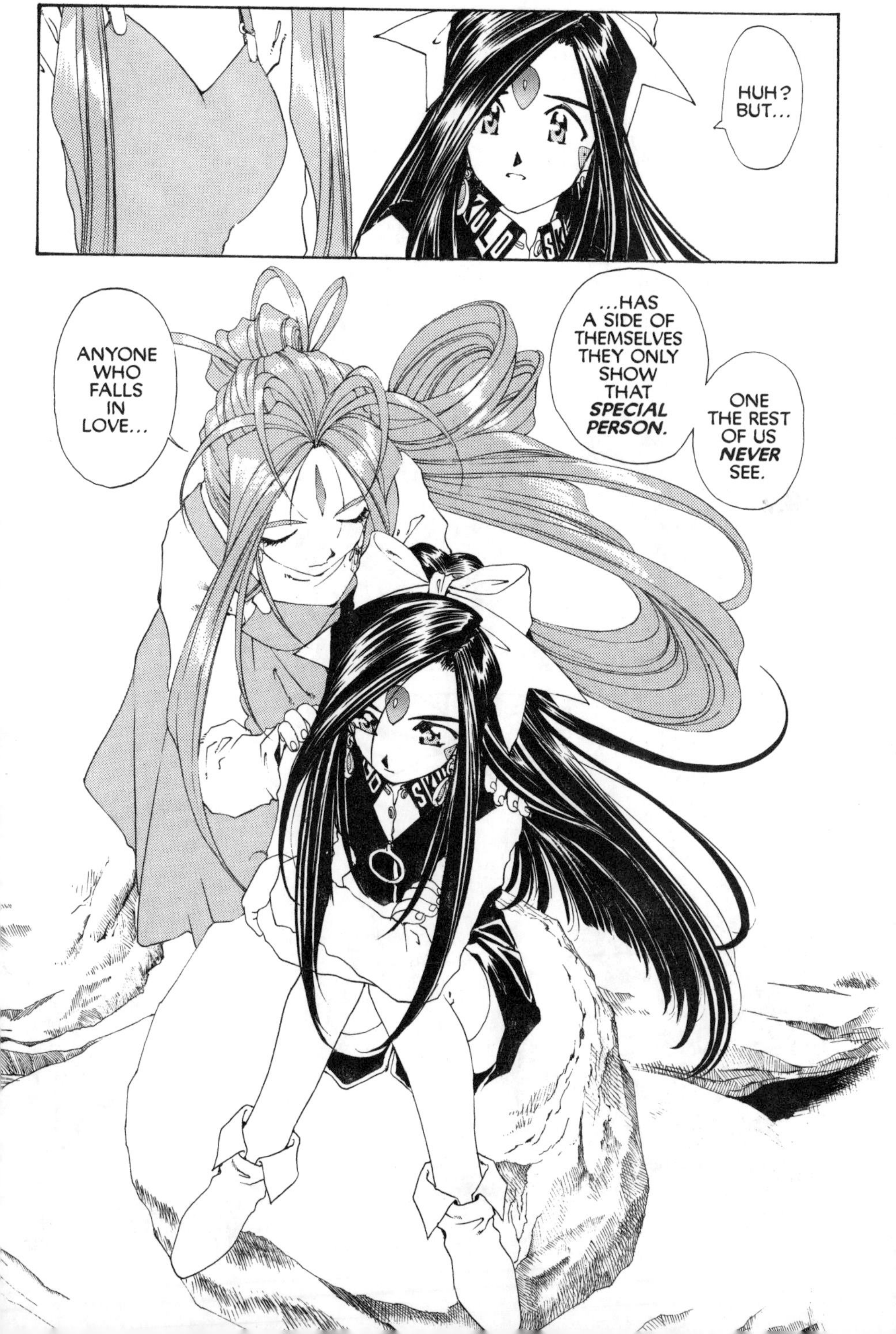
HUH? BUT...
ANYONE WHO FALLS IN LOVE...
...HAS A SIDE OF THEMSELVES THEY ONLY SHOW THAT **SPECIAL PERSON.**
ONE THE REST OF US **NEVER** SEE.

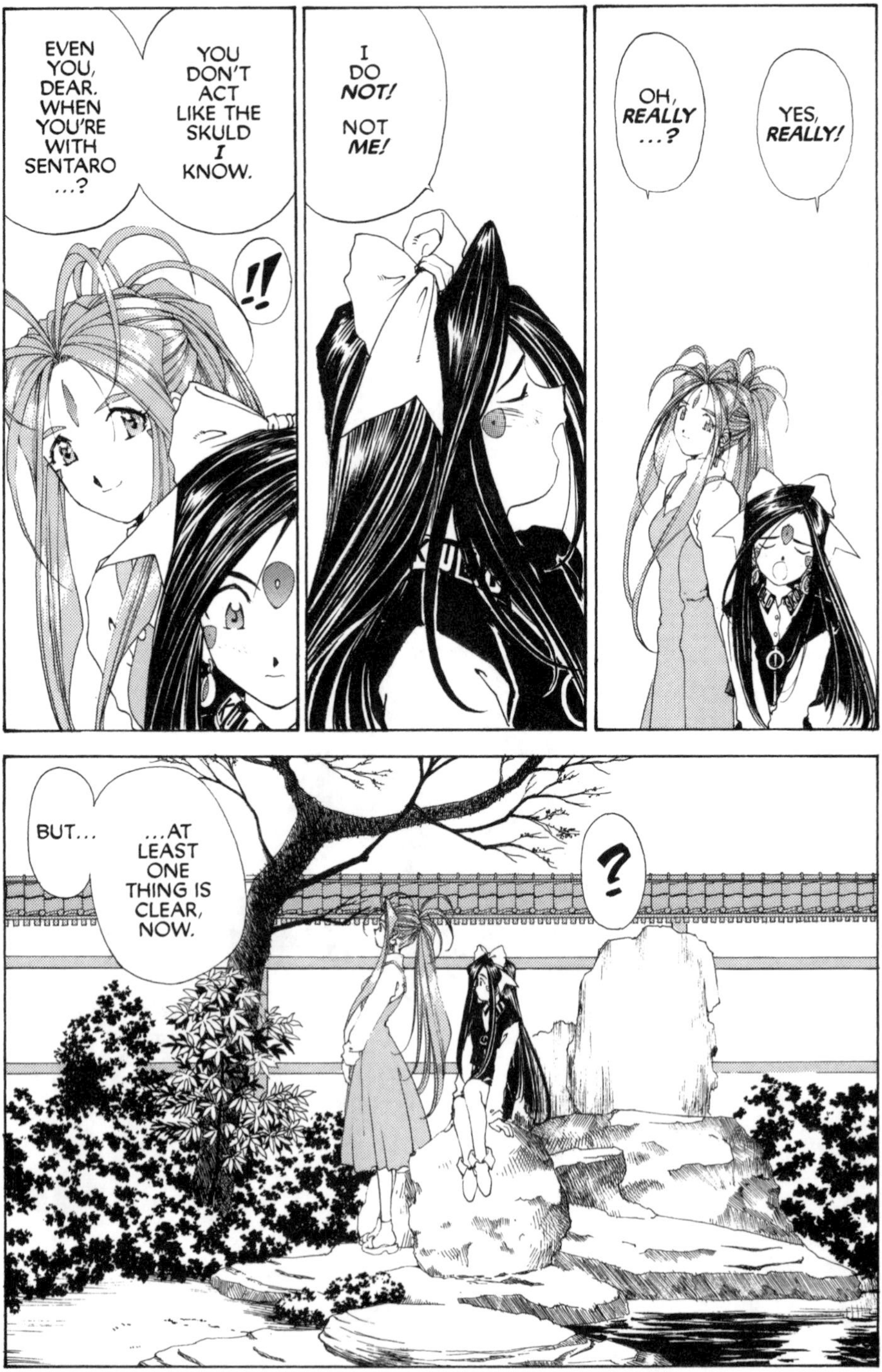
EVEN YOU, DEAR. WHEN YOU'RE WITH SENTARO ...?
YOU DON'T ACT LIKE THE SKULD *I* KNOW.
!!
I DO *NOT!*
NOT *ME!*
OH, *REALLY* ...?
YES, *REALLY!*
BUT...
...AT LEAST ONE THING IS CLEAR, NOW.
?

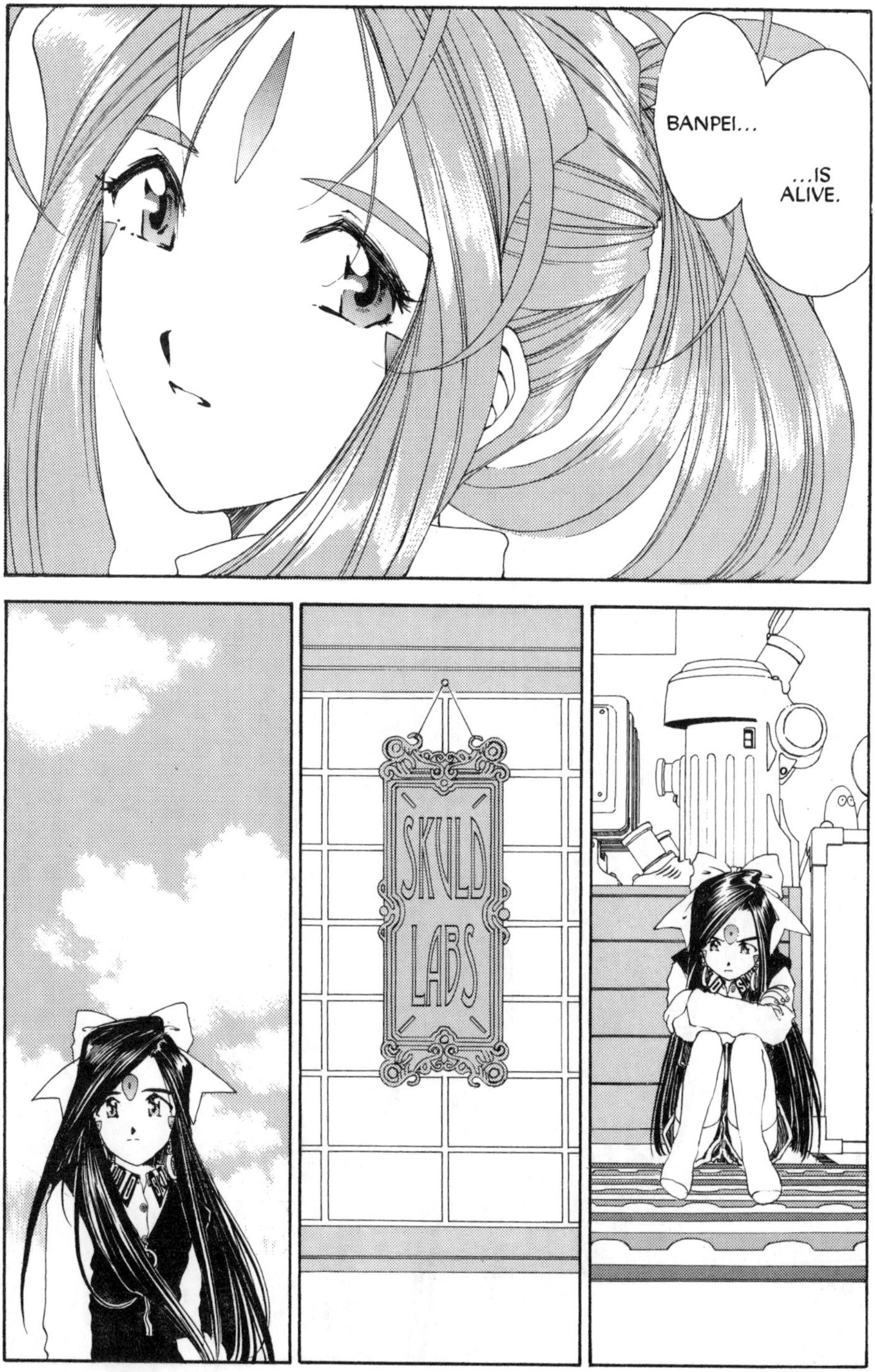
BANPEI...
...IS ALIVE.
SKULD LABS

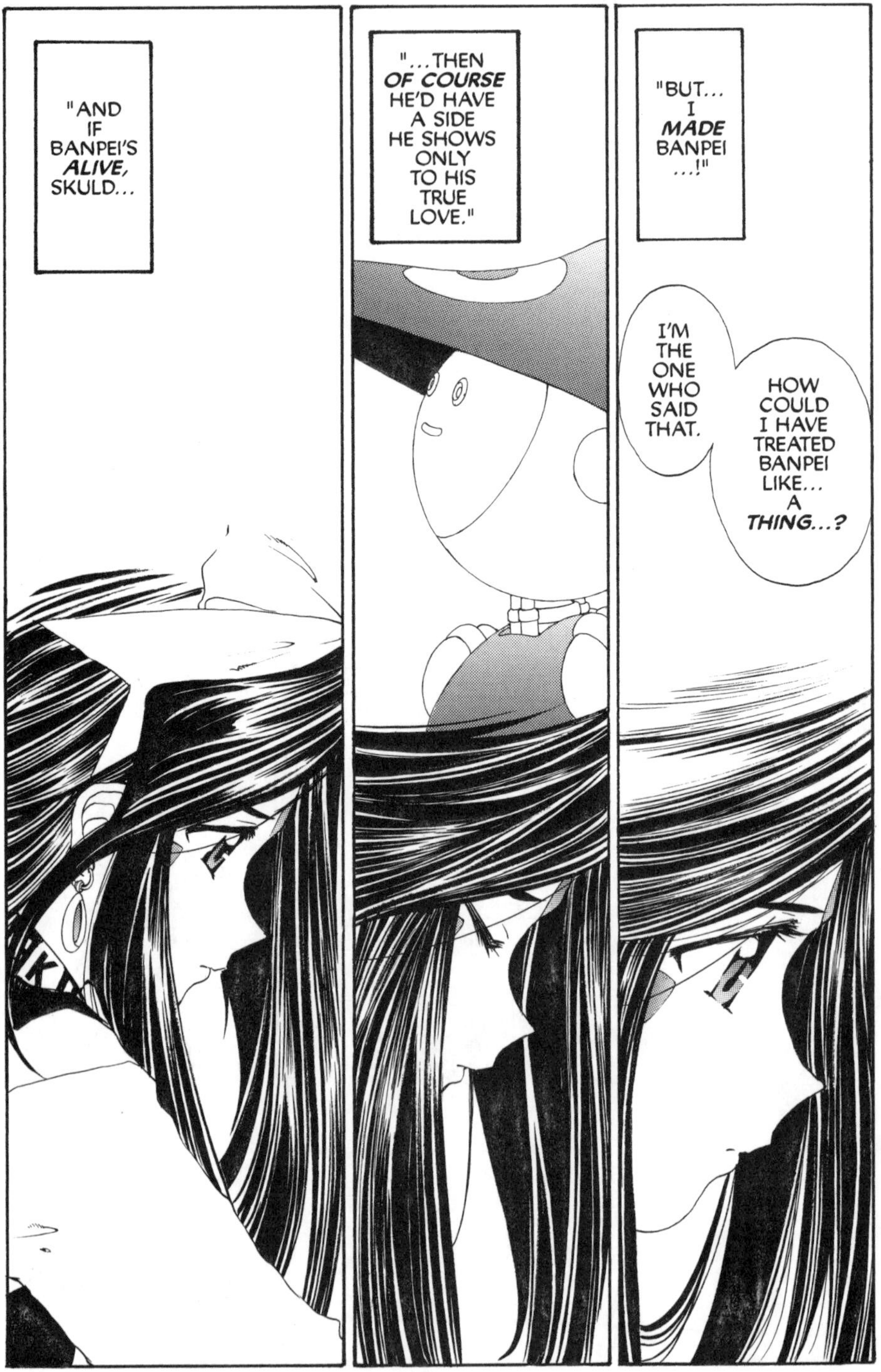
"AND IF BANPEI'S ALIVE, SKULD...
"...THEN OF COURSE HE'D HAVE A SIDE HE SHOWS ONLY TO HIS TRUE LOVE."
"BUT... I MADE BANPEI ...!"
I'M THE ONE WHO SAID THAT.
HOW COULD I HAVE TREATED BANPEI LIKE... A THING...?

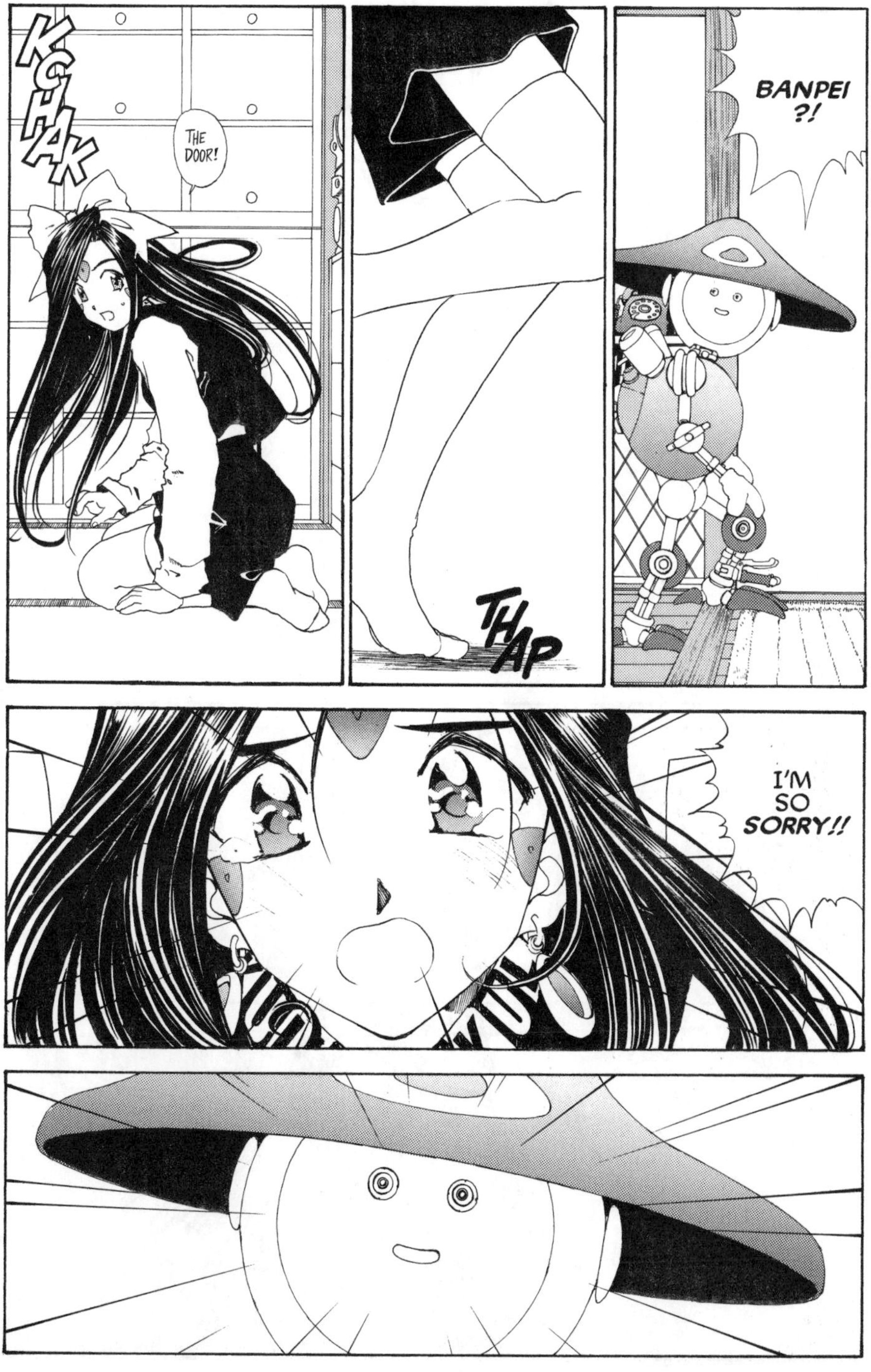
KCHAK
THE DOOR!
THAP
BANPEI ?!
I'M SO SORRY!!

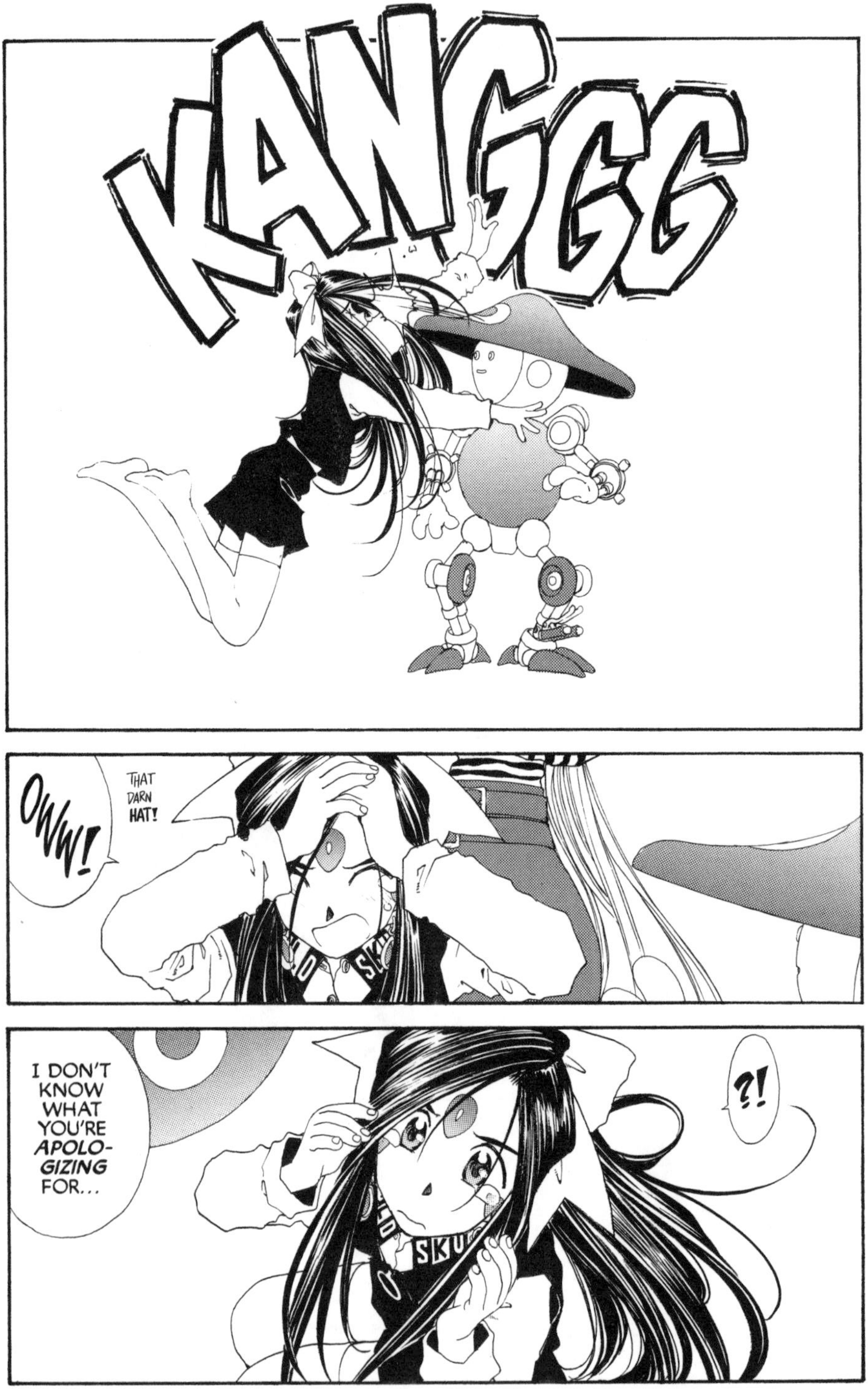

KANGG
OWW!
THAT DARN HAT!
I DON'T KNOW WHAT YOU'RE *APOLOGIZING* FOR...
?!

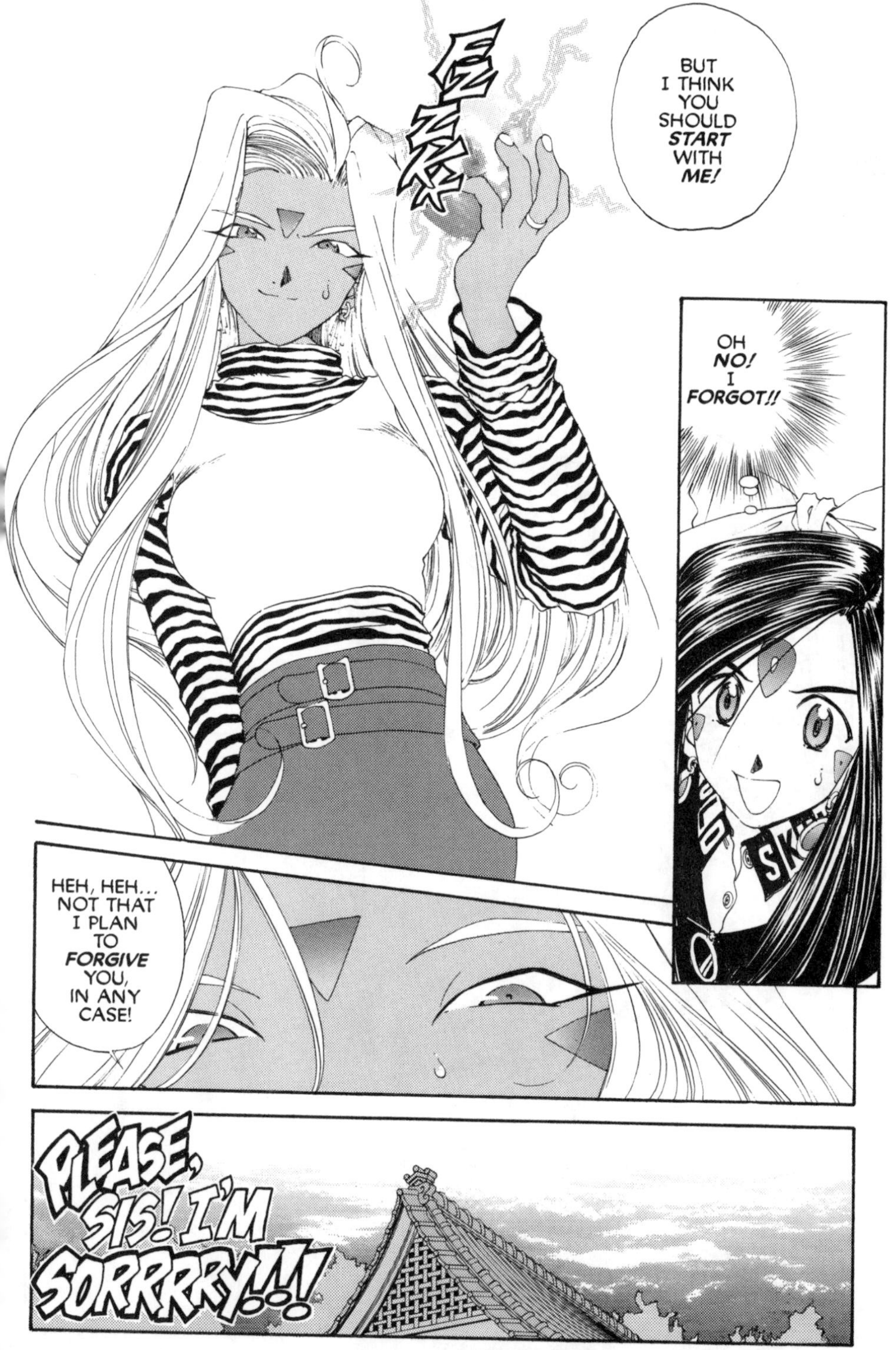
BUT I THINK YOU SHOULD START WITH ME!
OH NO! I FORGOT!!
HEH, HEH... NOT THAT I PLAN TO FORGIVE YOU, IN ANY CASE!
PLEASE, SIS! I'M SORRRRY!!!

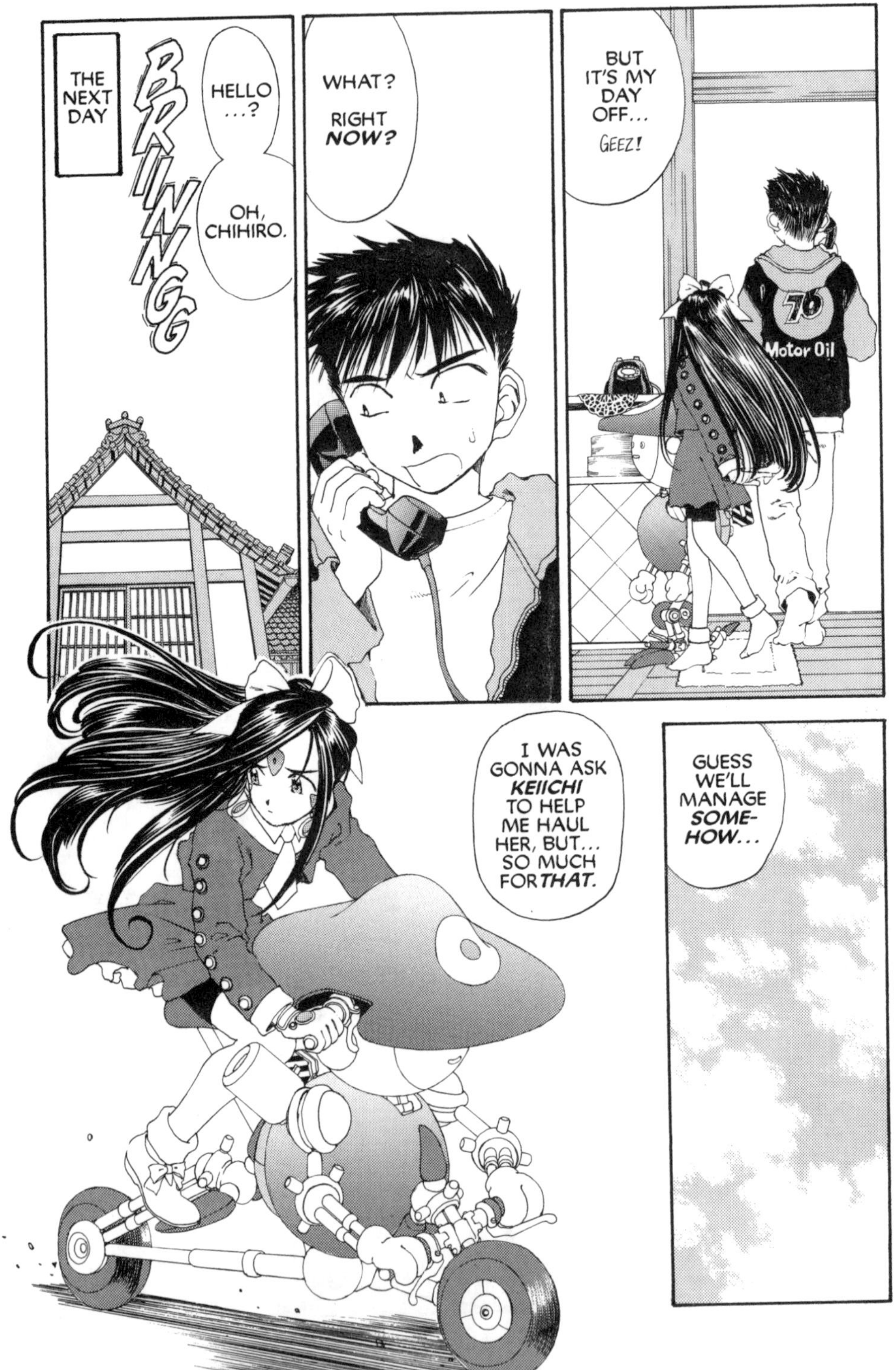
THE NEXT DAY
BRIINNGG
HELLO ...?
OH, CHIHIRO.
WHAT? RIGHT NOW?
BUT IT'S MY DAY OFF... GEEZ!
76 Motor Oil
I WAS GONNA ASK KEIICHI TO HELP ME HAUL HER, BUT... SO MUCH FOR THAT.
GUESS WE'LL MANAGE SOME-HOW...

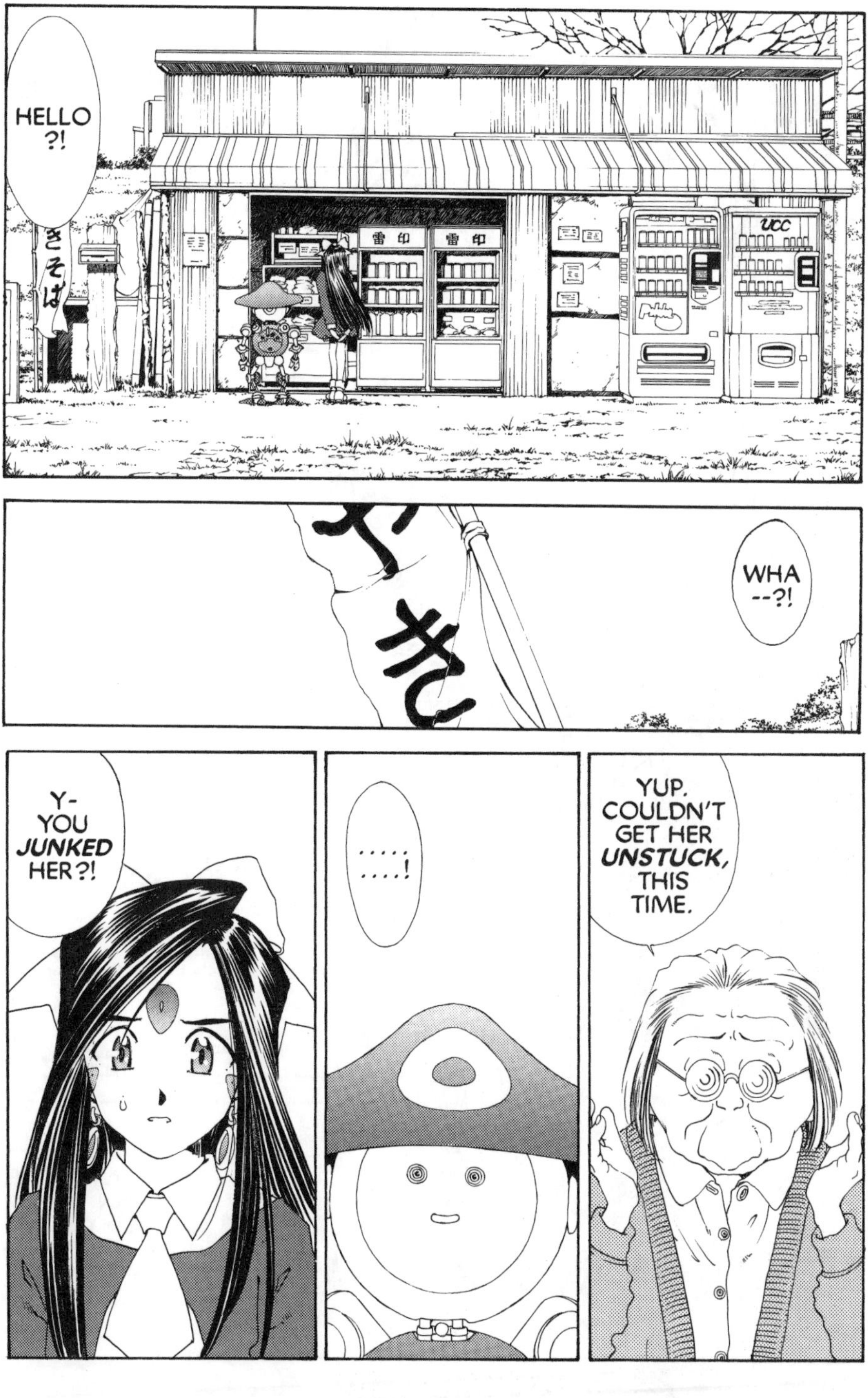
HELLO ?!
きそば
雷印
雷印
UCC
WHA --?!
Y- YOU JUNKED HER?!
....., ...!
YUP. COULDN'T GET HER UNSTUCK, THIS TIME.

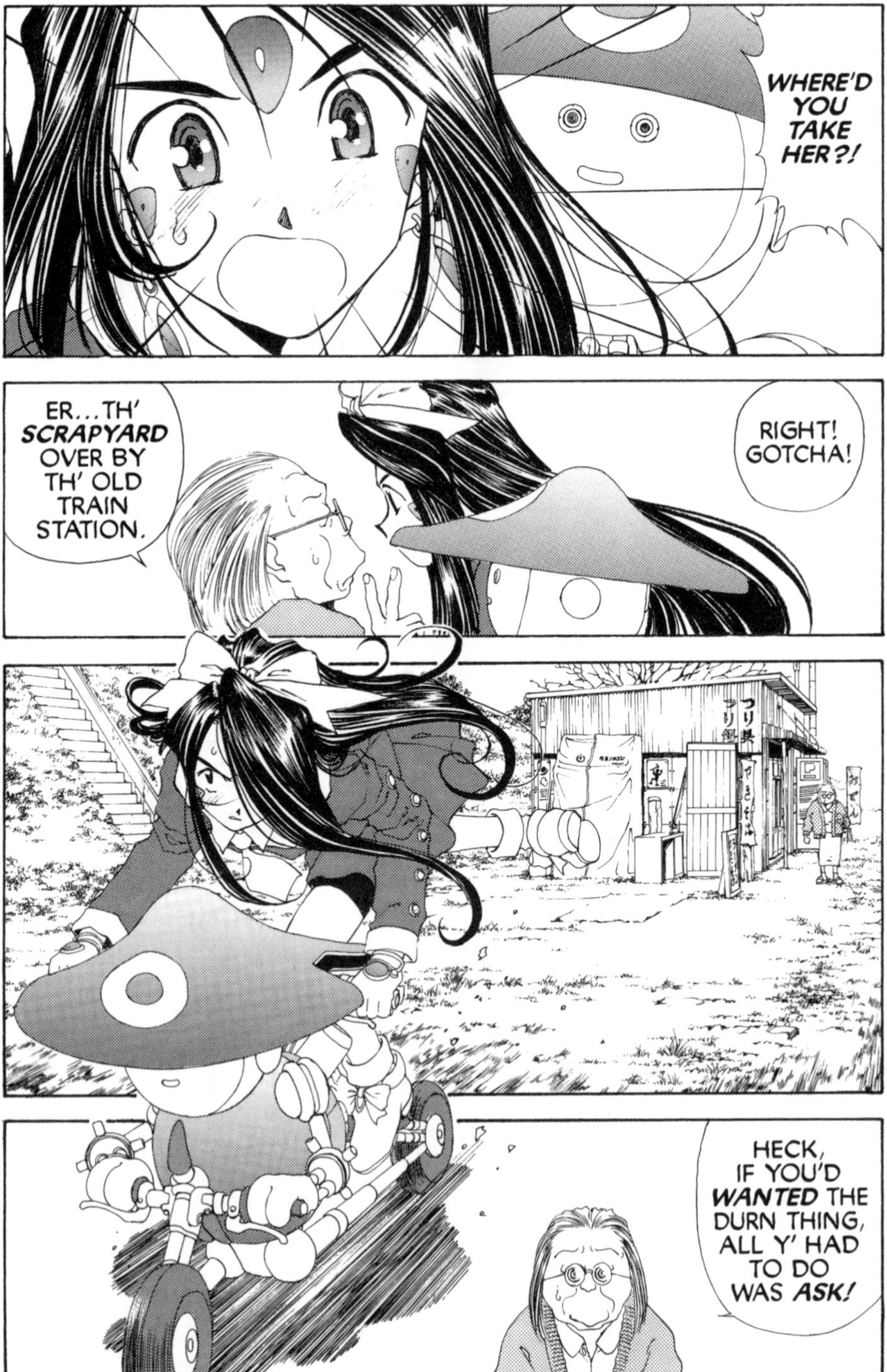
WHERE'D YOU TAKE HER?!
ER...TH' SCRAPYARD OVER BY TH' OLD TRAIN STATION.
RIGHT! GOTCHA!
HECK, IF YOU'D WANTED THE DURN THING, ALL Y' HAD TO DO WAS ASK!

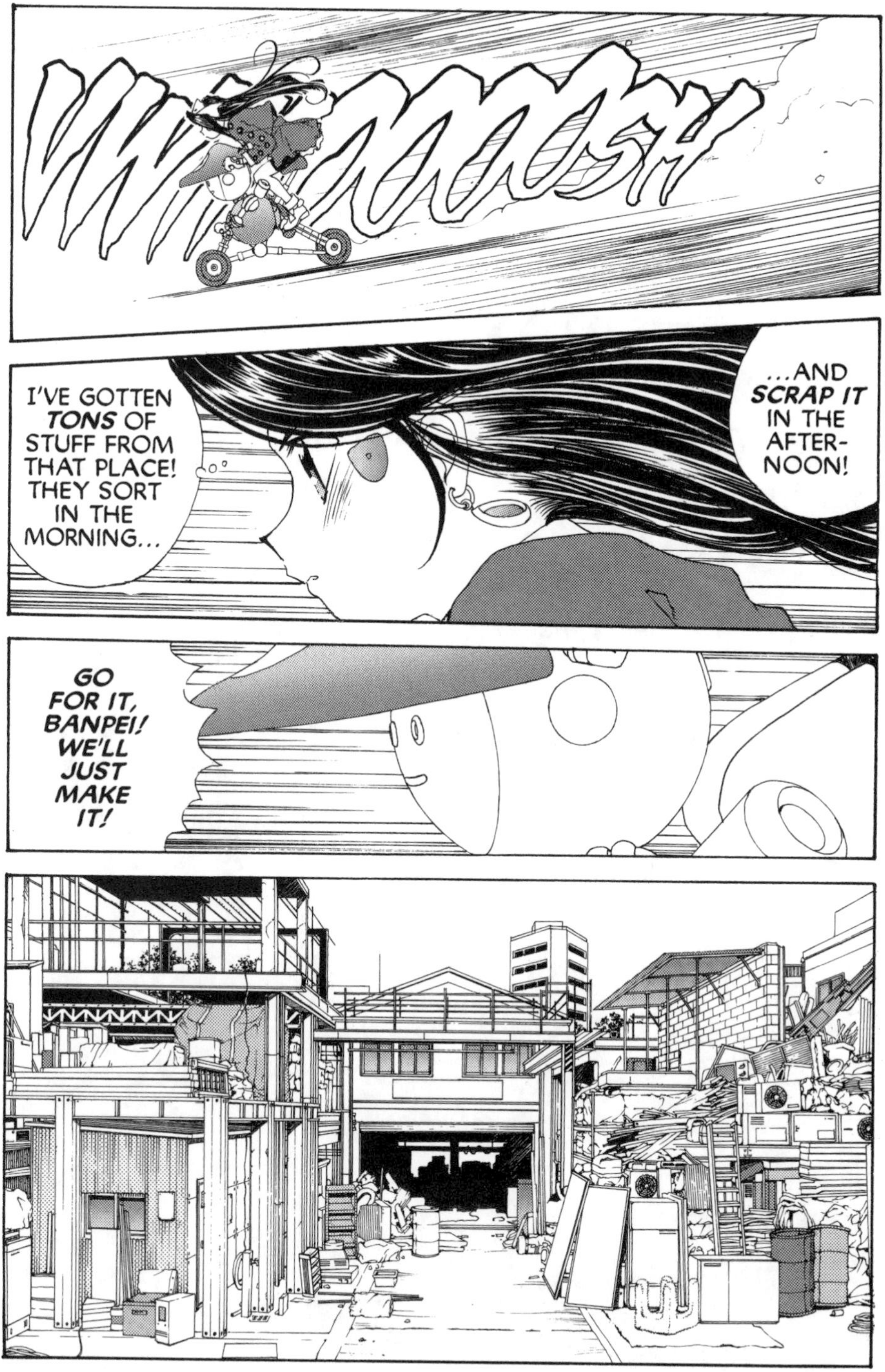
WHOOOOSH
I'VE GOTTEN *TONS* OF STUFF FROM THAT PLACE! THEY SORT IN THE MORNING...
...AND *SCRAP IT* IN THE AFTER-NOON!
GO FOR IT, BANPEI! WE'LL JUST MAKE IT!

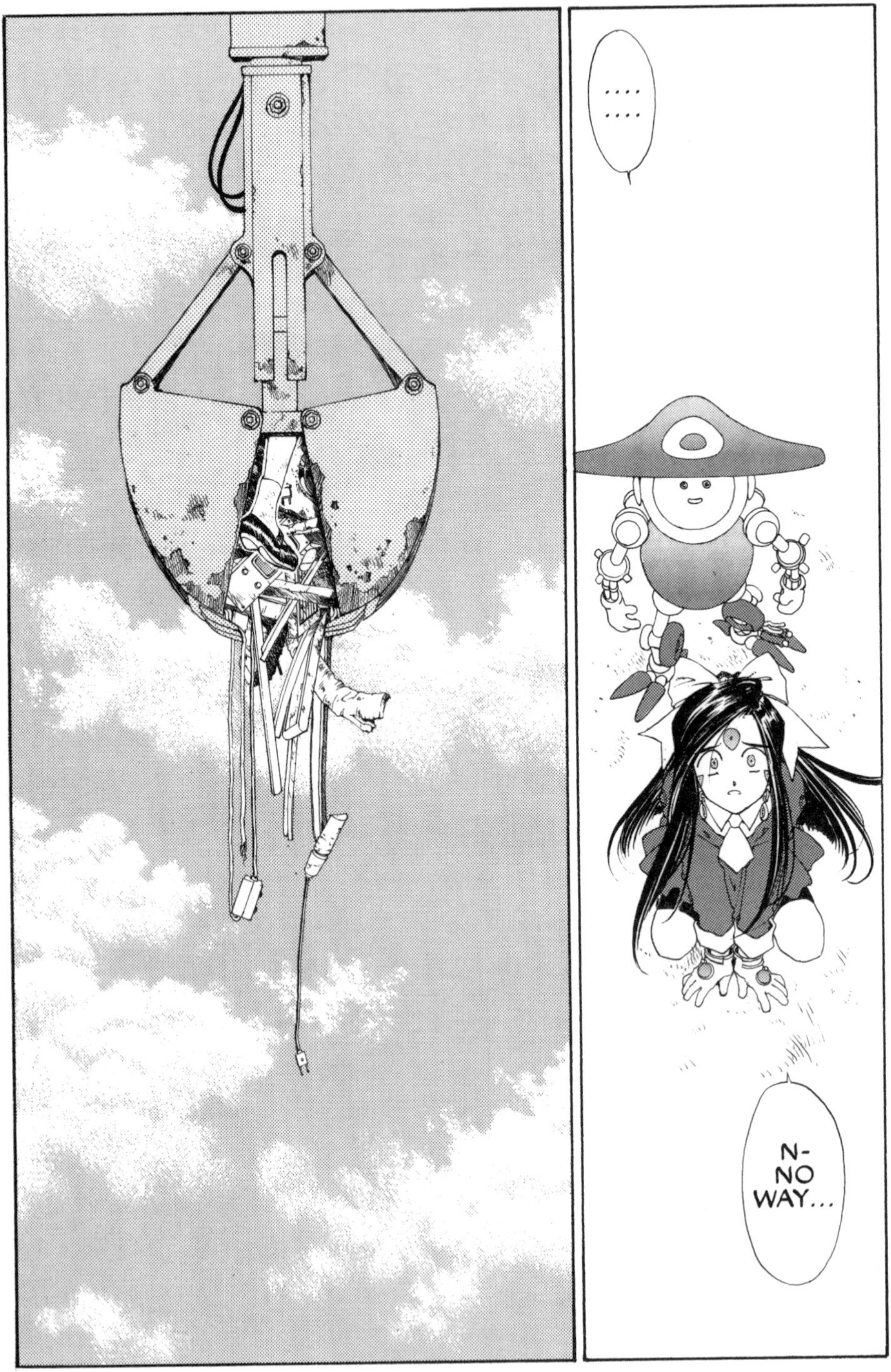
....
....
N-NO WAY...

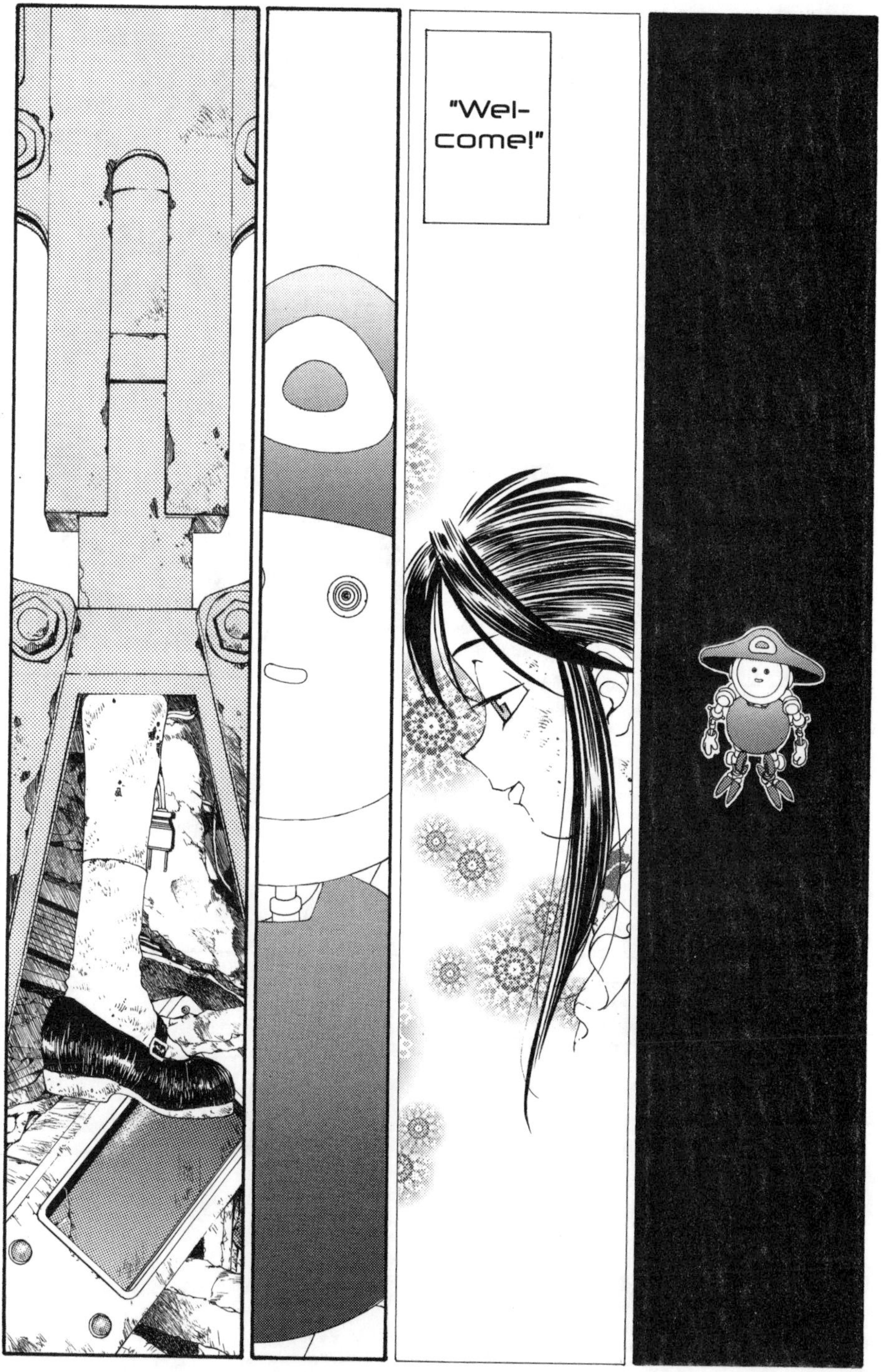
"Wel-
come!"

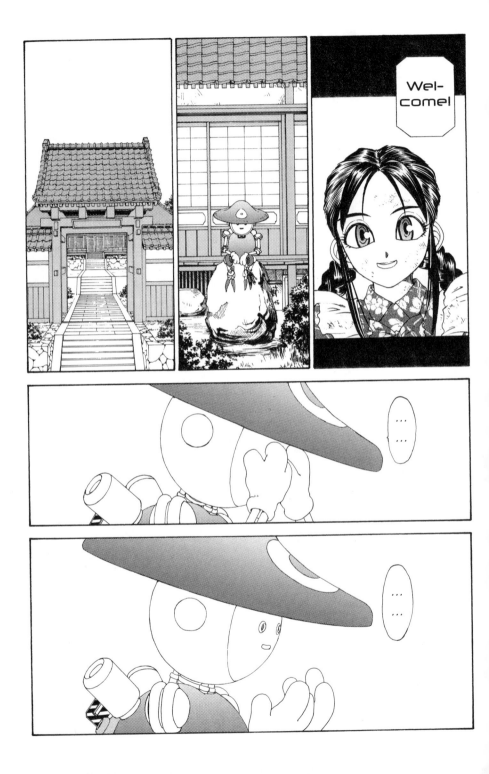

Wel-
come!

...
...

...
...

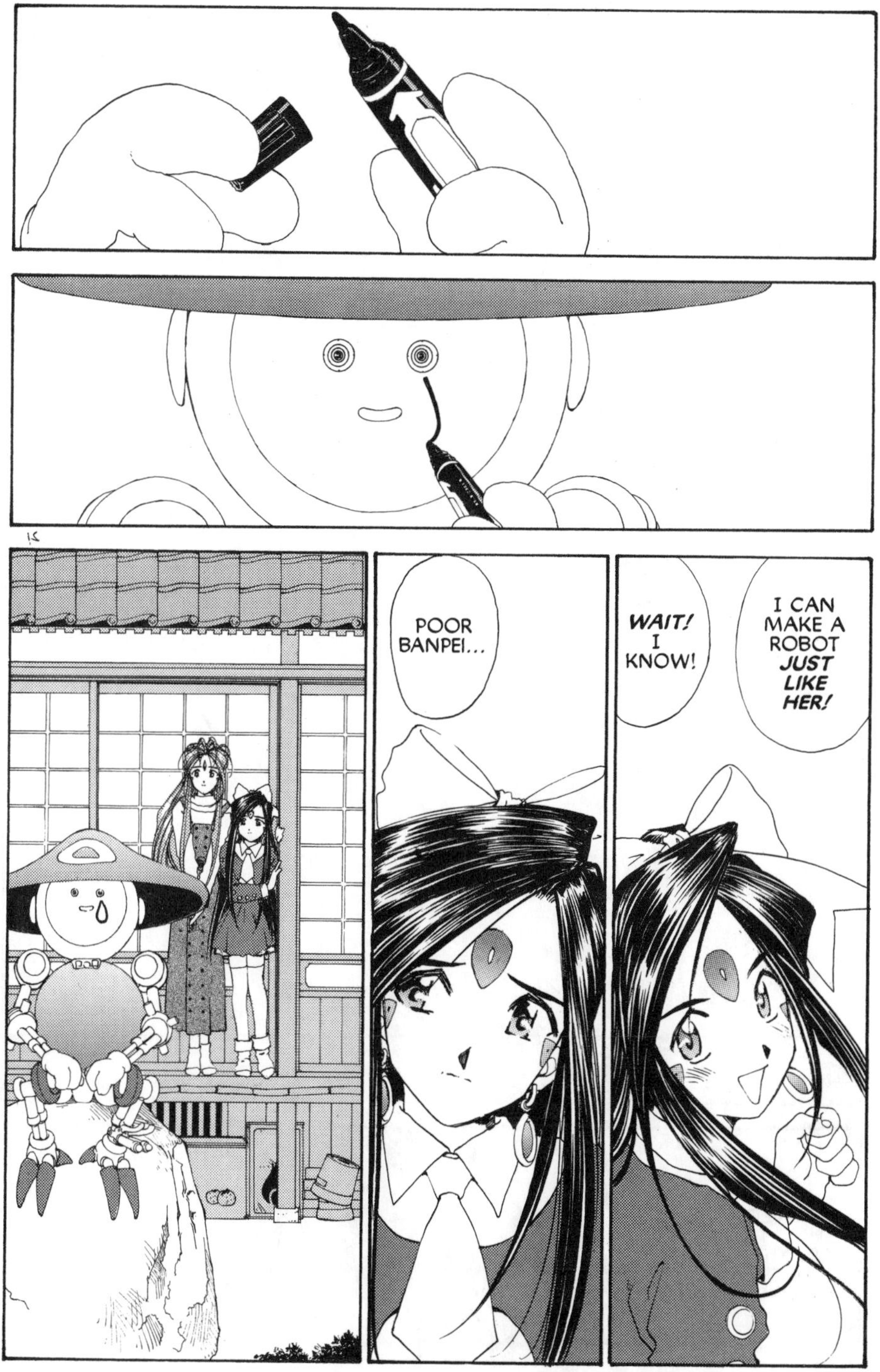
POOR BANPEI...
WAIT! I KNOW!
I CAN MAKE A ROBOT JUST LIKE HER!

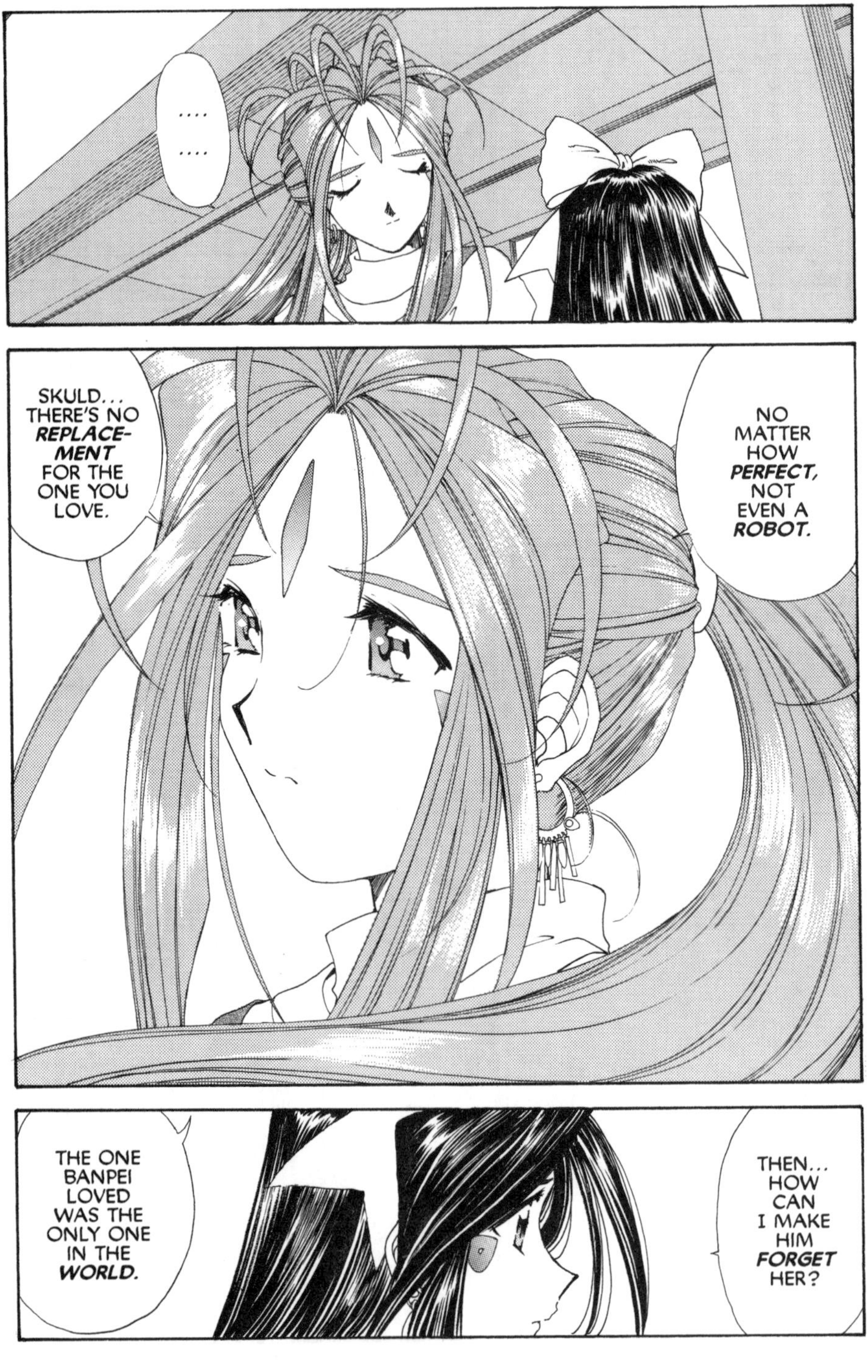
....
....
SKULD... THERE'S NO *REPLACEMENT* FOR THE ONE YOU LOVE.
NO MATTER HOW *PERFECT,* NOT EVEN A *ROBOT.*
THE ONE BANPEI LOVED WAS THE ONLY ONE IN THE *WORLD.*
THEN... HOW CAN I MAKE HIM *FORGET* HER?

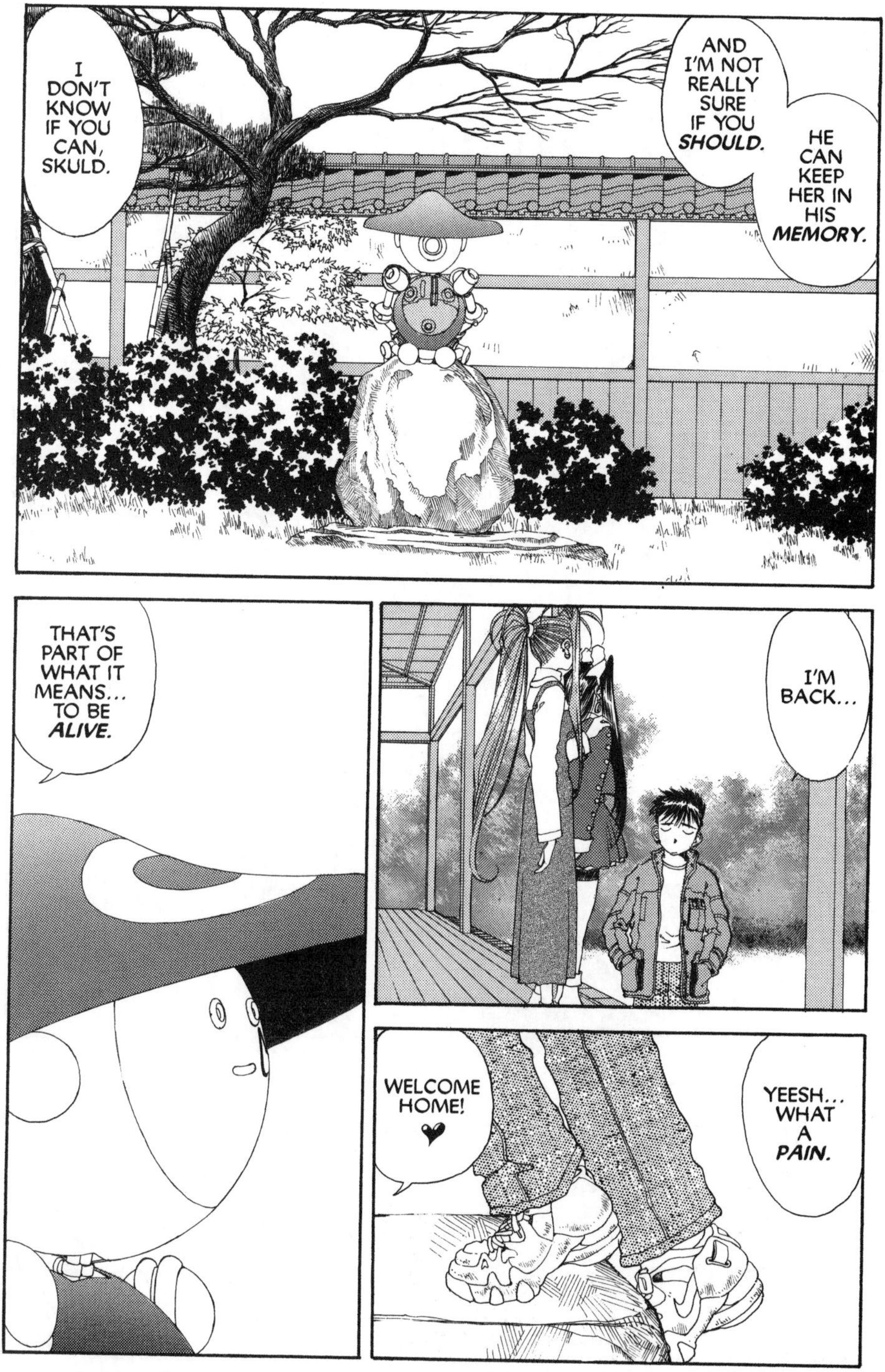
I DON'T KNOW IF YOU CAN, SKULD.
AND I'M NOT REALLY SURE IF YOU *SHOULD.*
HE CAN KEEP HER IN HIS *MEMORY.*
THAT'S PART OF WHAT IT MEANS... TO BE *ALIVE.*
I'M BACK...
WELCOME HOME! ♥
YEESH... WHAT A *PAIN.*

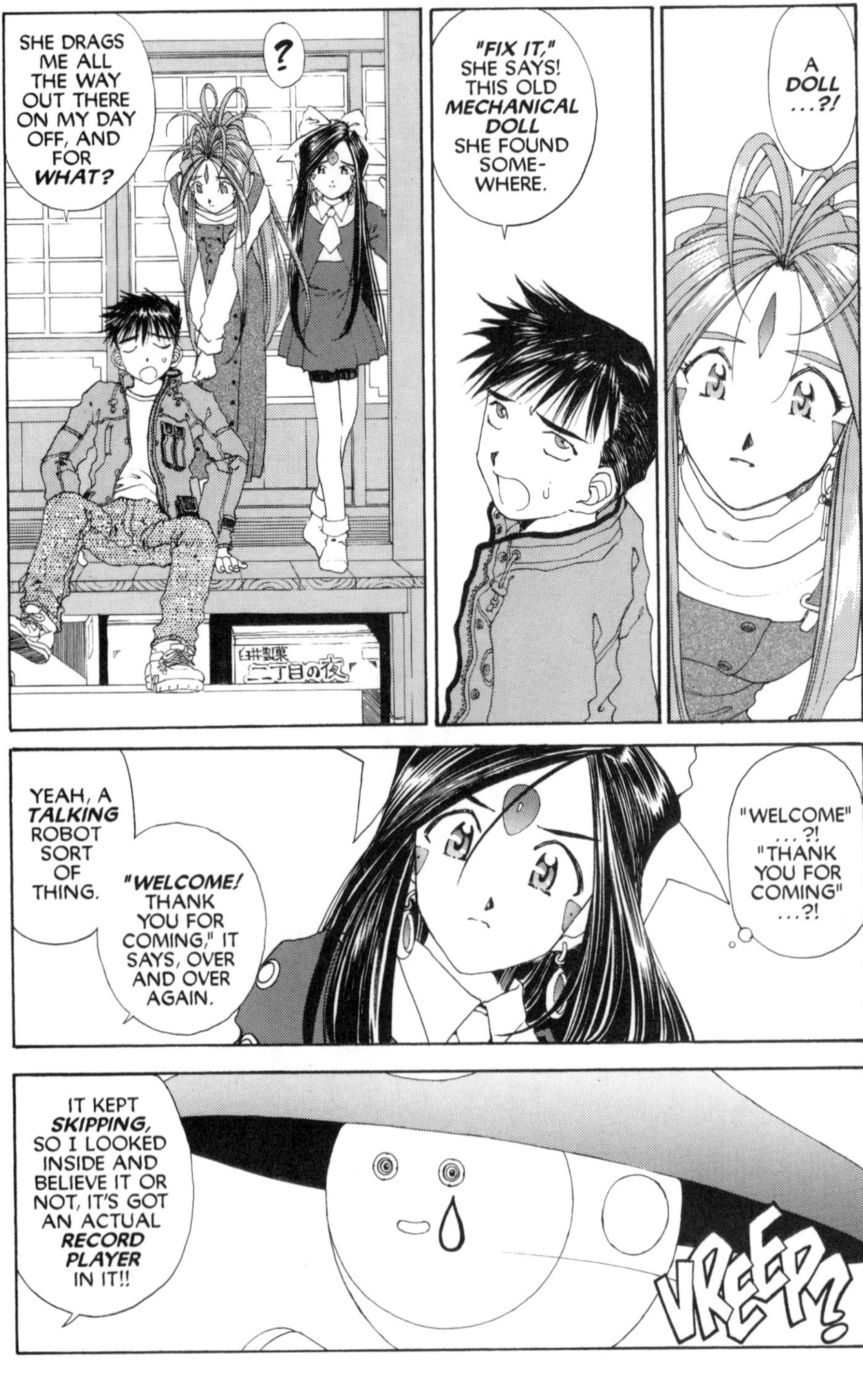
SHE DRAGS ME ALL THE WAY OUT THERE ON MY DAY OFF, AND FOR *WHAT?*
?
白井製菓
二丁目の夜
"FIX IT," SHE SAYS! THIS OLD *MECHANICAL DOLL* SHE FOUND SOME-WHERE.
A *DOLL* ...?!
YEAH, A *TALKING* ROBOT SORT OF THING.
"WELCOME! THANK YOU FOR COMING," IT SAYS, OVER AND OVER AGAIN.
"WELCOME" ...?! "THANK YOU FOR COMING" ...?!
IT KEPT *SKIPPING,* SO I LOOKED INSIDE AND BELIEVE IT OR NOT, IT'S GOT AN ACTUAL *RECORD PLAYER* IN IT!!
VREEP!

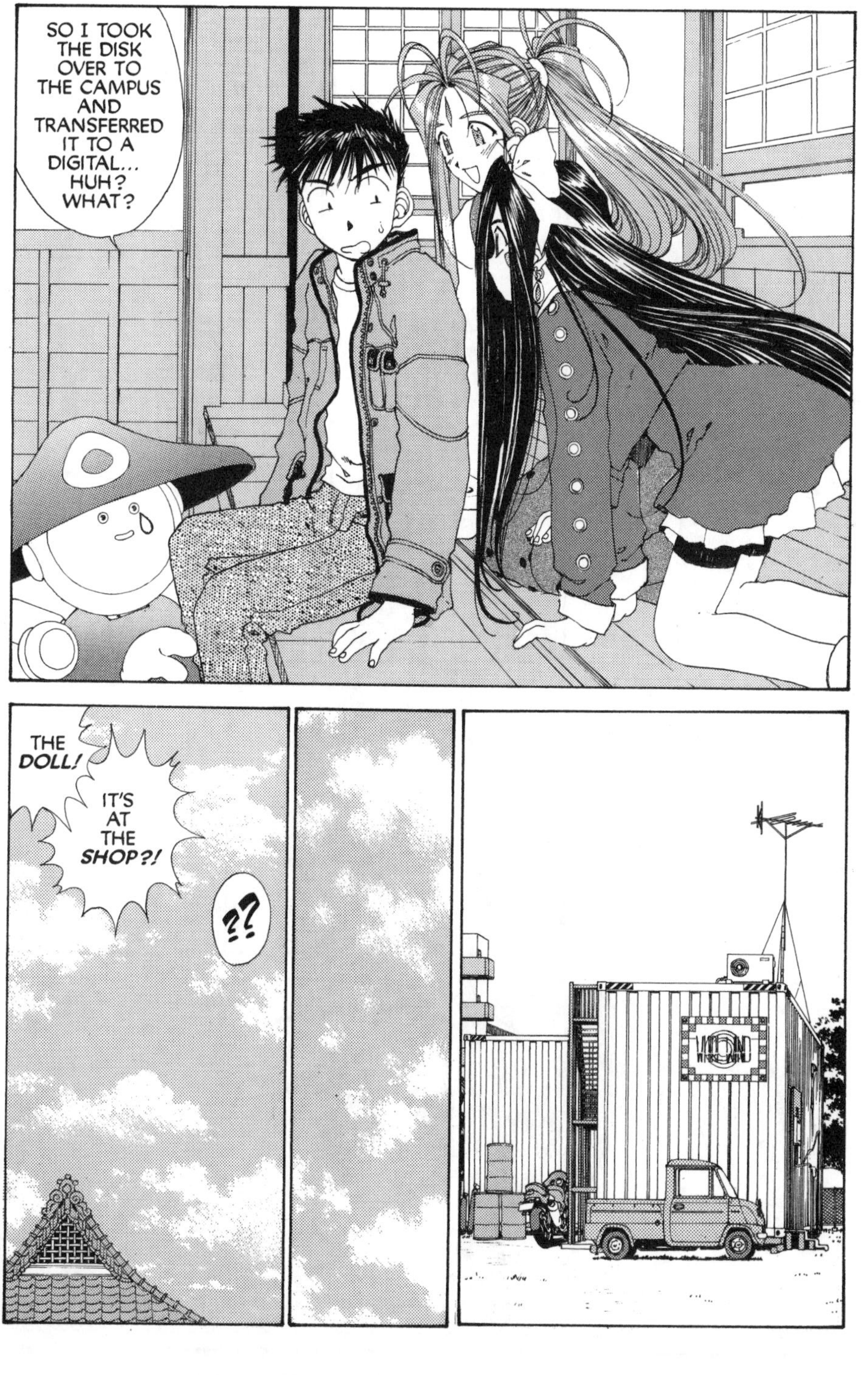
SO I TOOK THE DISK OVER TO THE CAMPUS AND TRANSFERRED IT TO A DIGITAL... HUH? WHAT?
THE *DOLL!*
IT'S AT THE *SHOP?!*
??

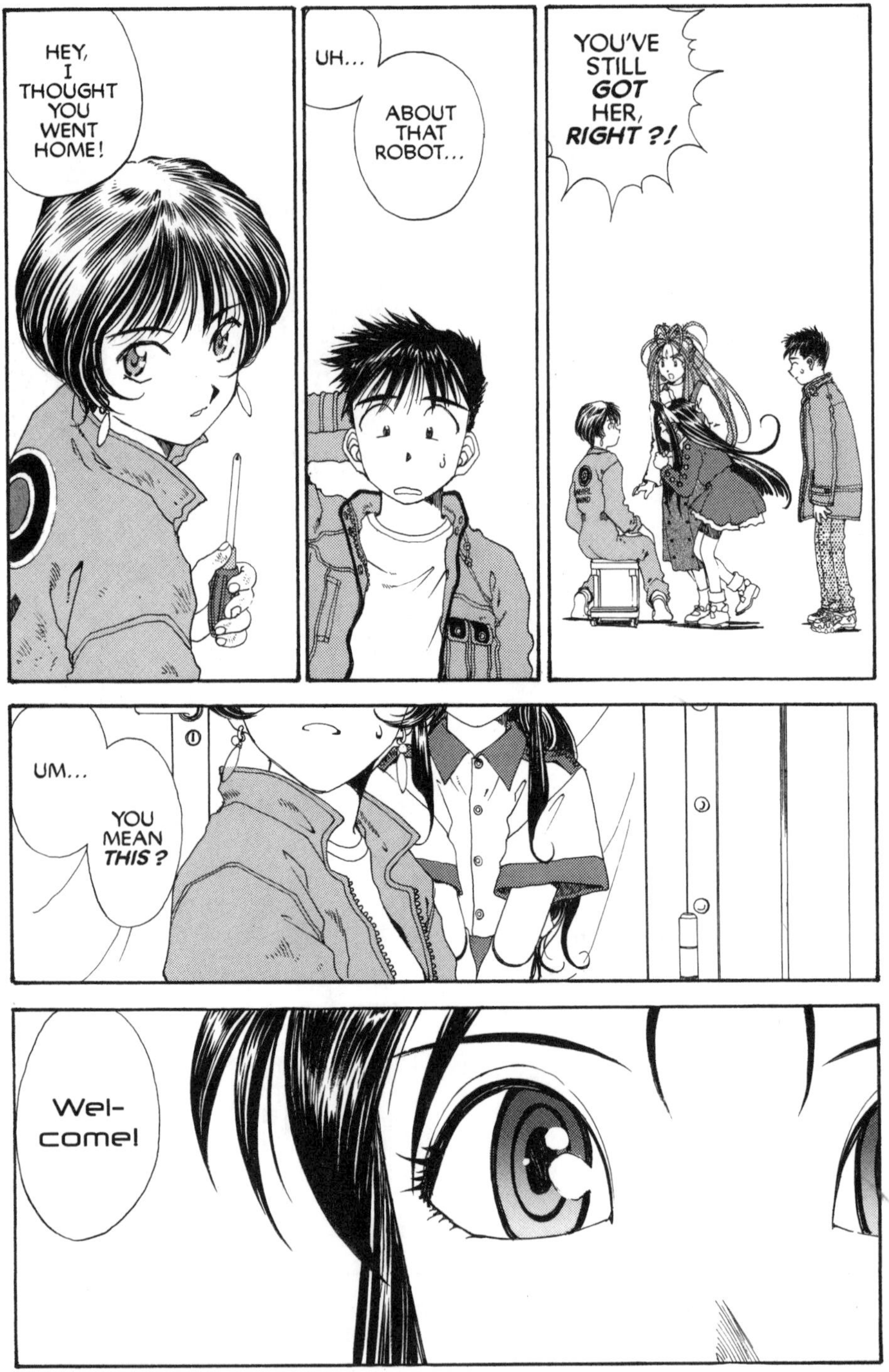
HEY, I THOUGHT YOU WENT HOME!
UH...
ABOUT THAT ROBOT...
YOU'VE STILL **GOT** HER, **RIGHT ?!**
UM...
YOU MEAN **THIS ?**
Wel-come!

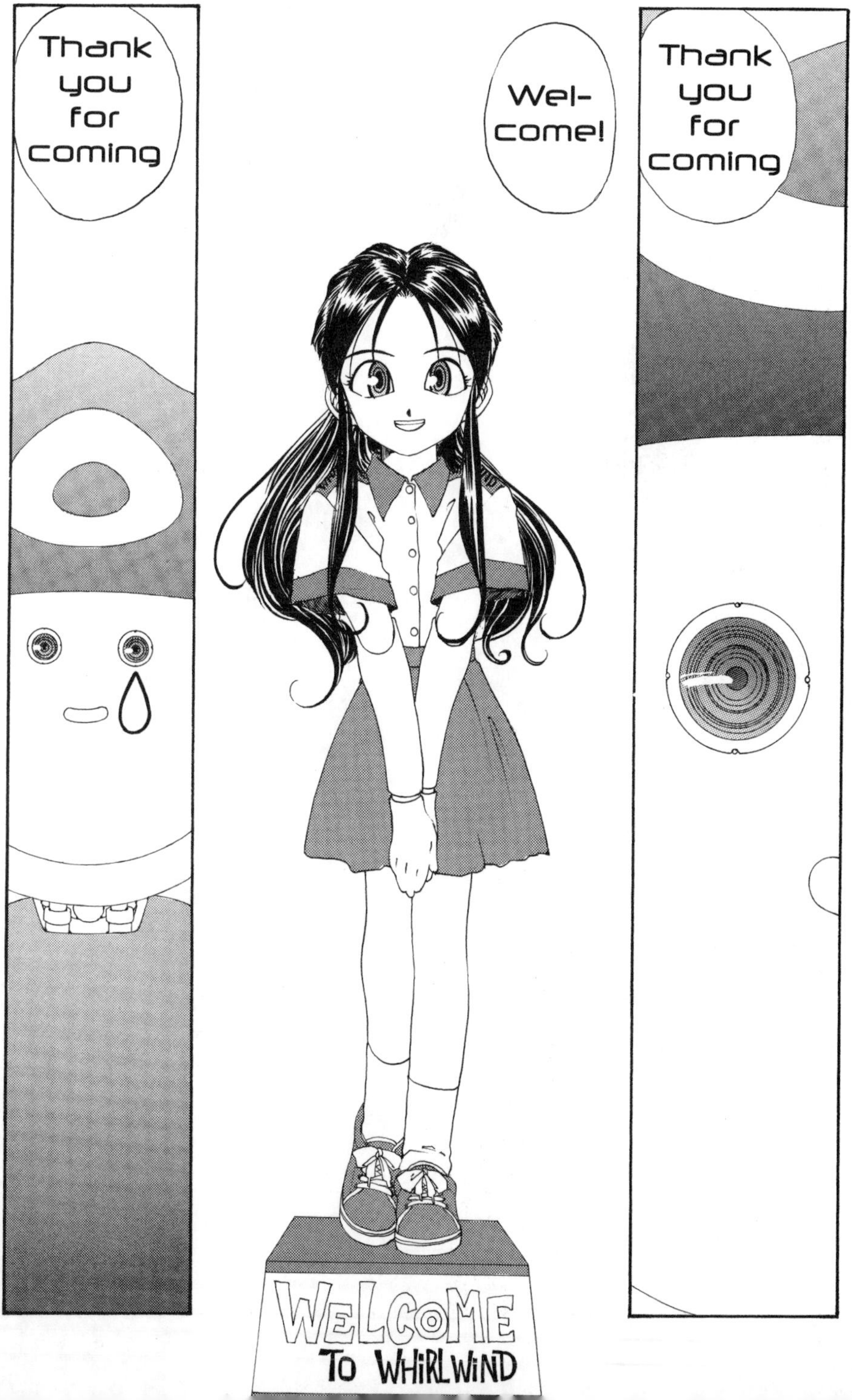
Thank you for coming
Wel- come!
Thank you for coming
WELCOME TO WHIRLWIND

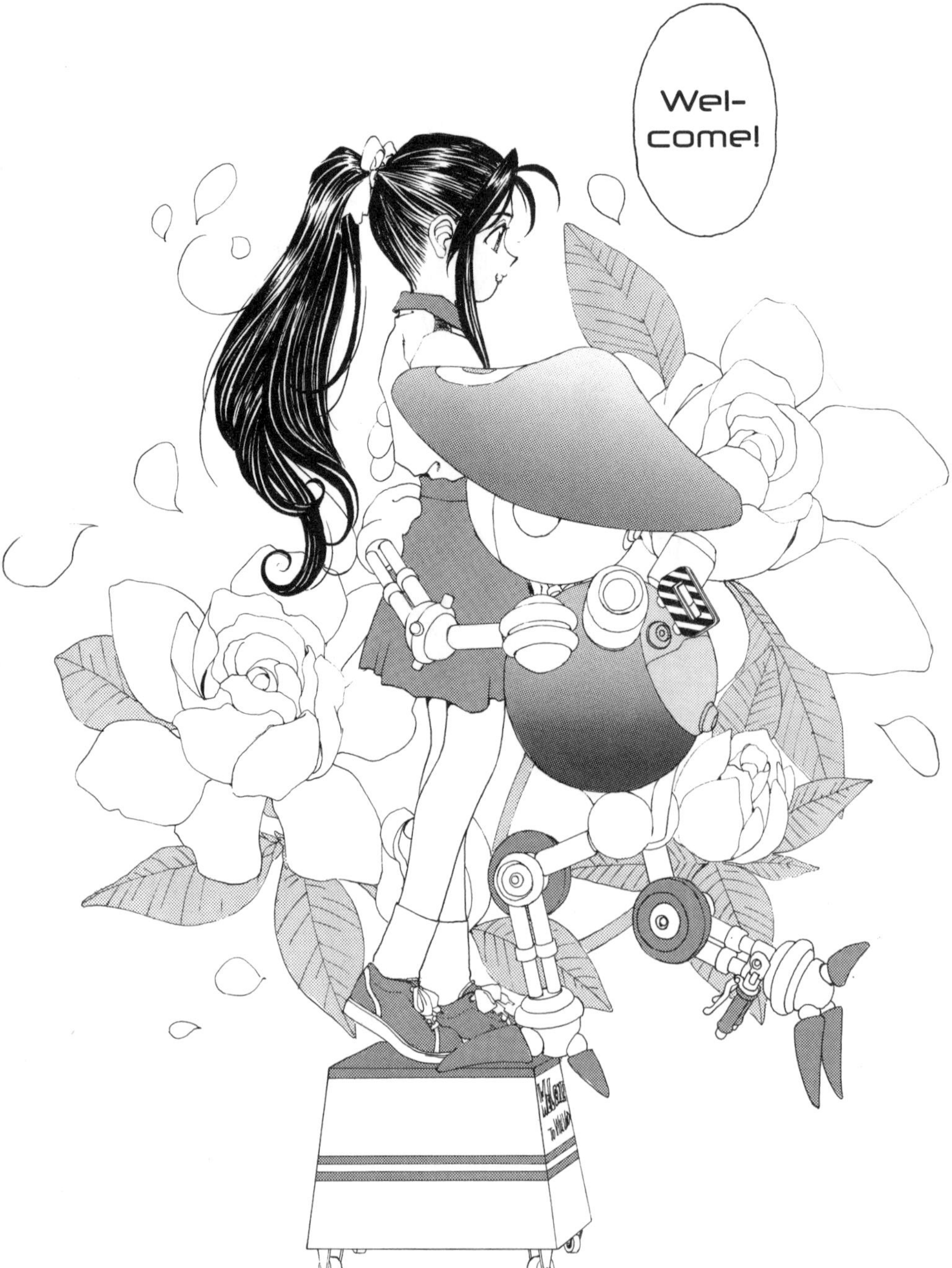
Wel-
come!

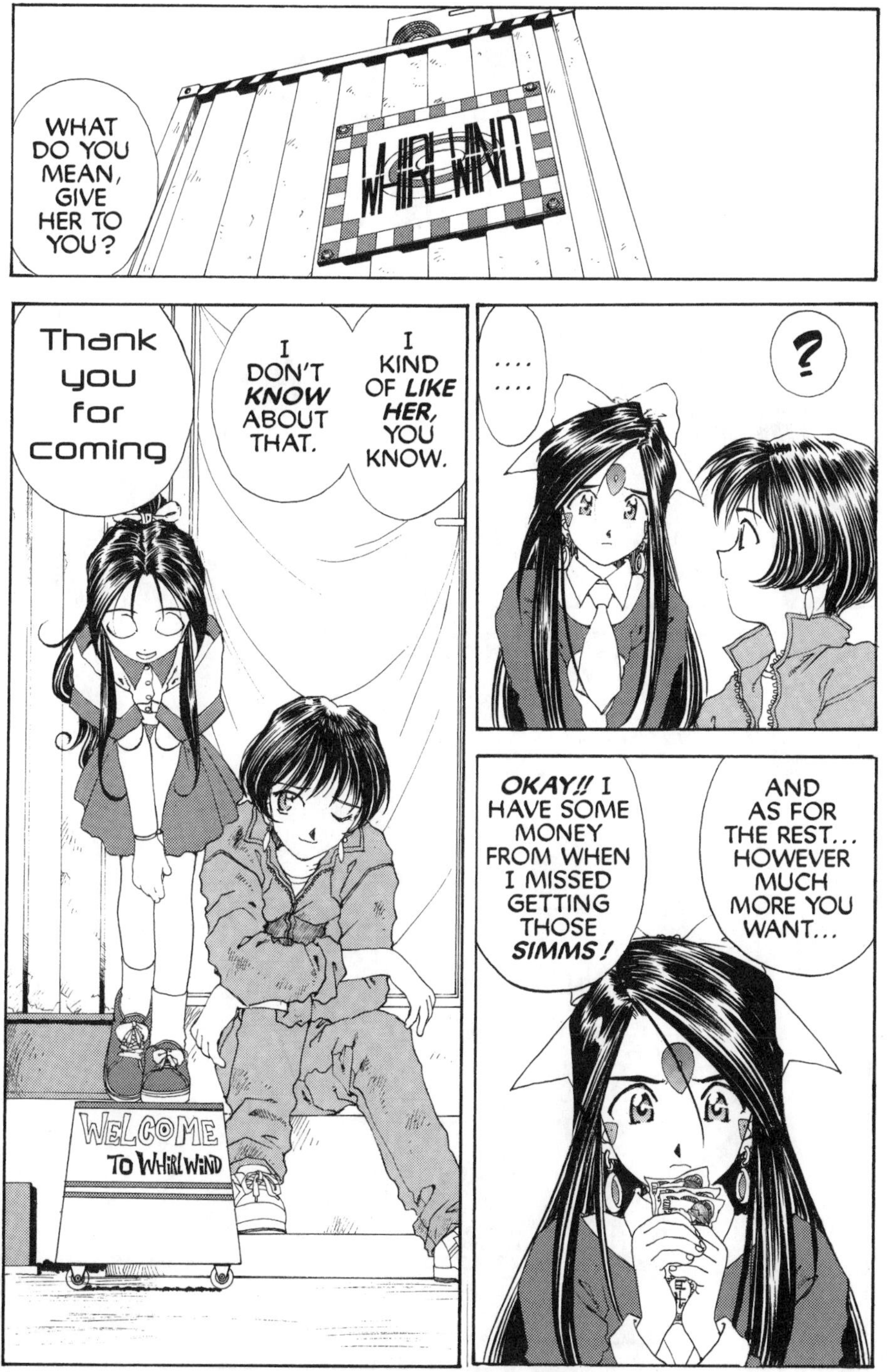
WHAT DO YOU MEAN, GIVE HER TO YOU?
WHIRLWIND
Thank you for coming
I DON'T KNOW ABOUT THAT.
I KIND OF LIKE HER, YOU KNOW.
WELCOME TO WHIRLWIND
....
?
OKAY!! I HAVE SOME MONEY FROM WHEN I MISSED GETTING THOSE SIMMS!
AND AS FOR THE REST... HOWEVER MUCH MORE YOU WANT...

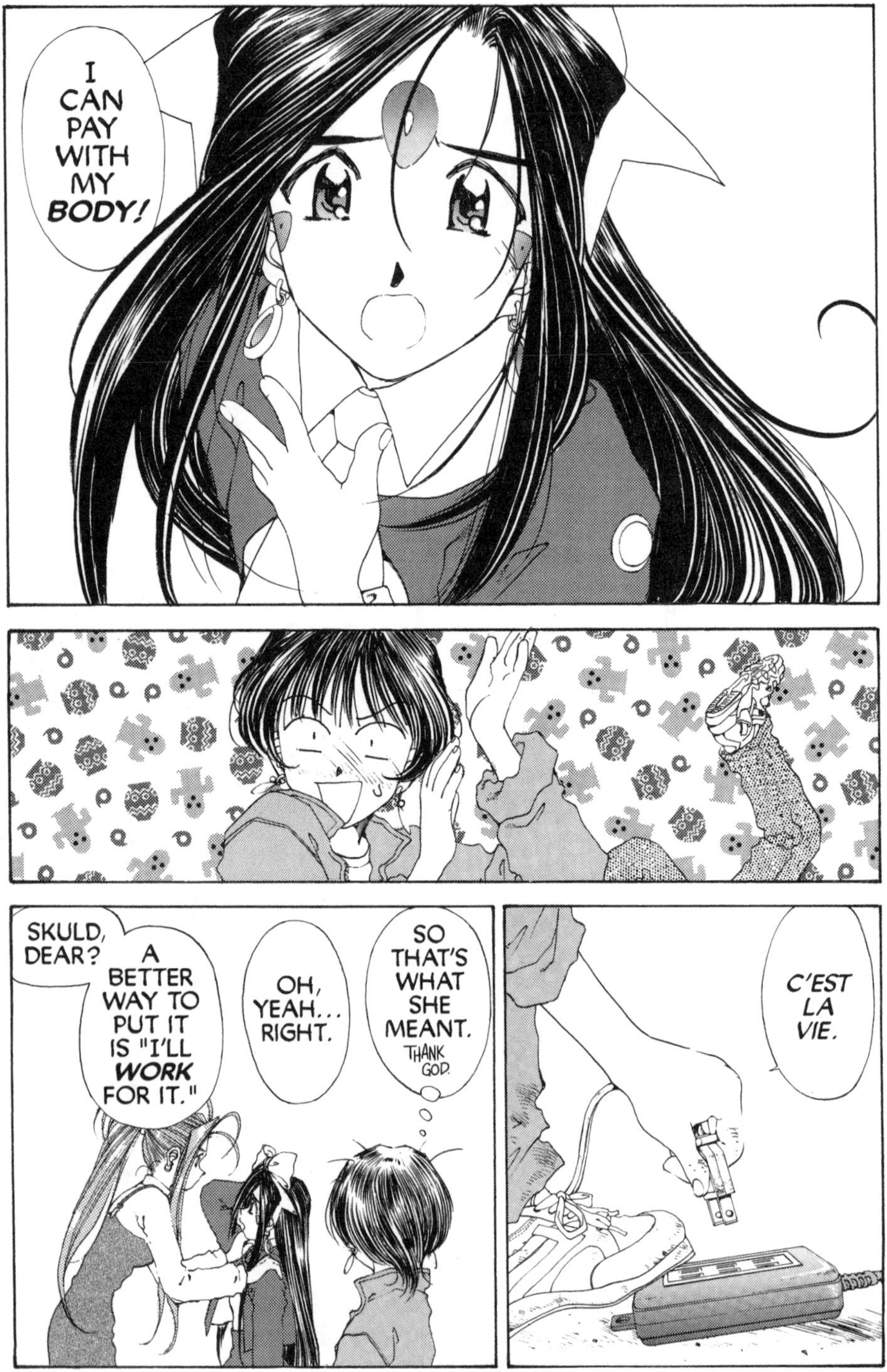
I CAN PAY WITH MY BODY!
SKULD, DEAR?
A BETTER WAY TO PUT IT IS "I'LL WORK FOR IT."
OH, YEAH... RIGHT.
SO THAT'S WHAT SHE MEANT.
THANK GOD.
C'EST LA VIE.

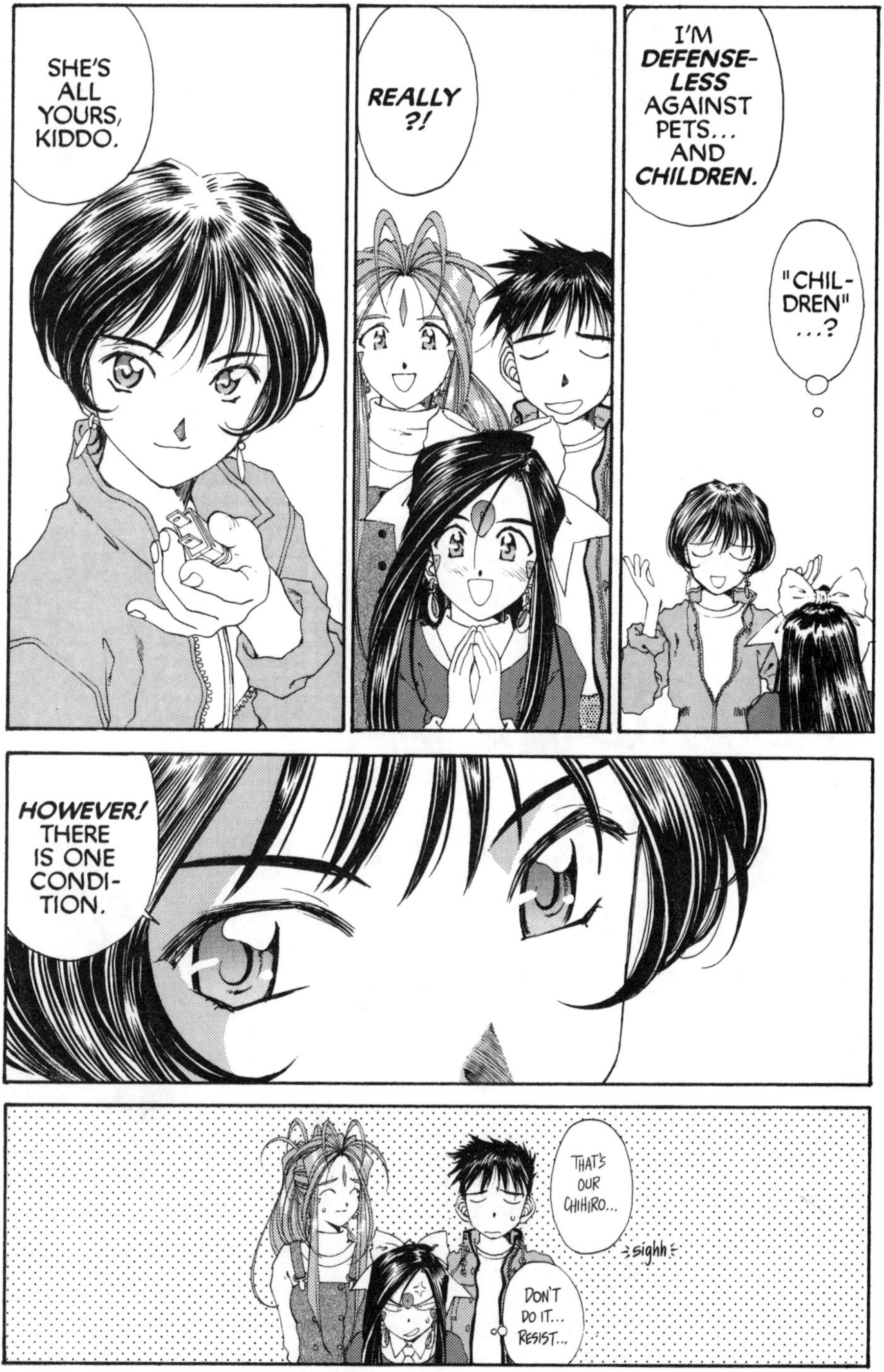
SHE'S ALL YOURS, KIDDO.
REALLY ?!
I'M DEFENSE-LESS AGAINST PETS... AND CHILDREN.
"CHIL-DREN" ...?
HOWEVER! THERE IS ONE CONDI-TION.
THAT'S OUR CHIHIRO...
sighh
DON'T DO IT... RESIST...

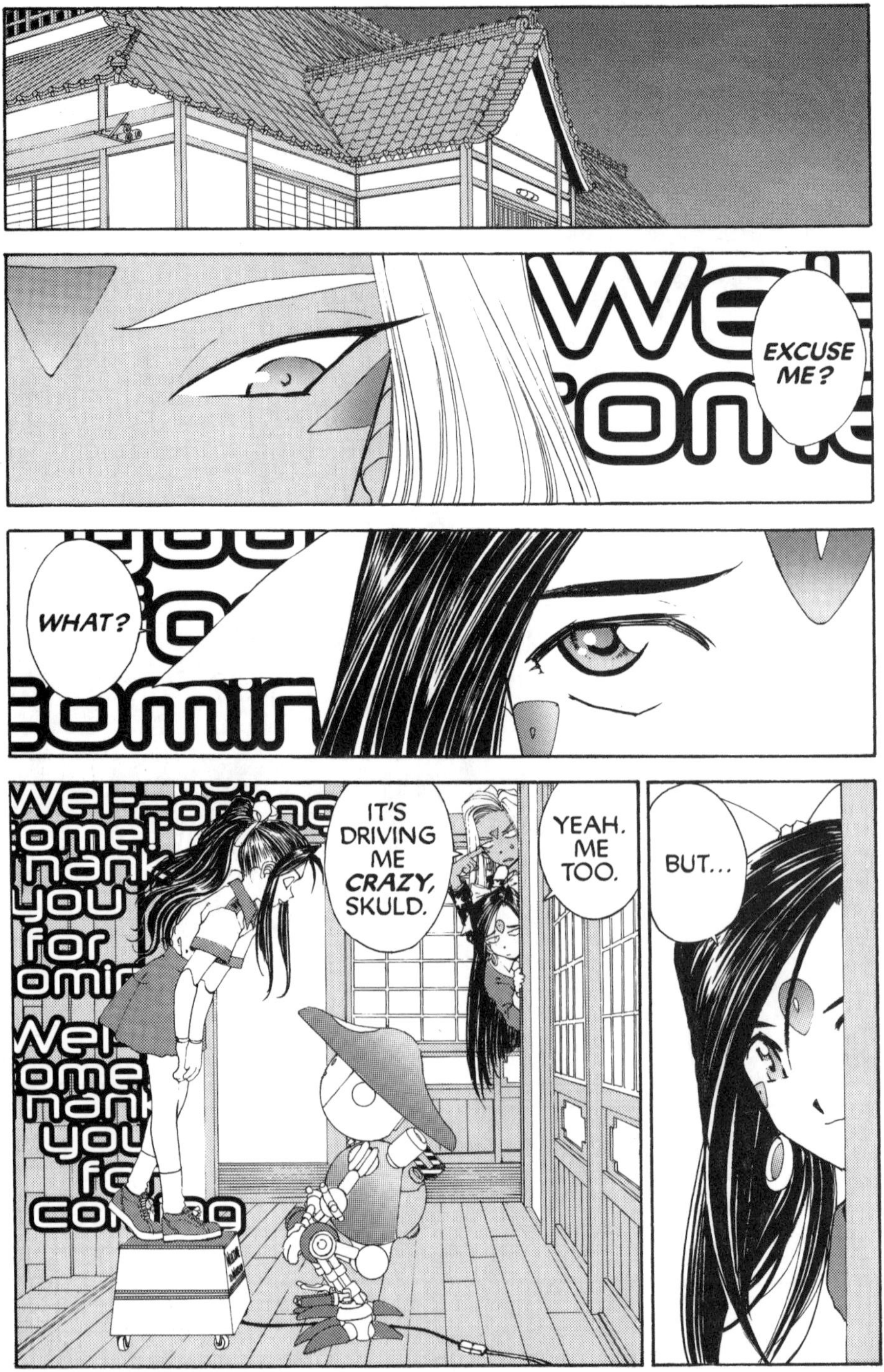

EXCUSE ME?
WHAT?
IT'S DRIVING ME CRAZY, SKULD.
YEAH. ME TOO.
BUT...

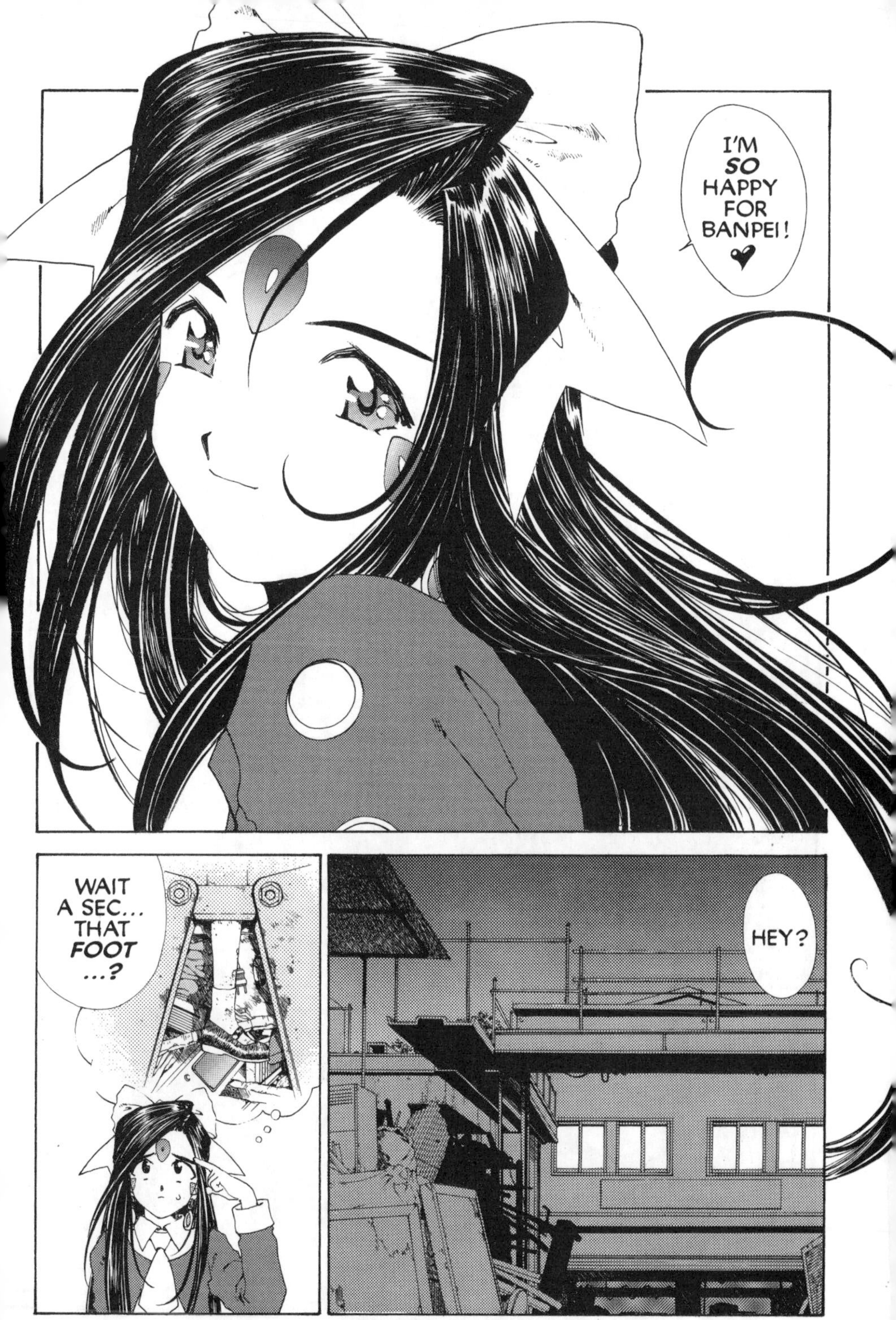
I'M *SO* HAPPY FOR BANPEI! ♥
WAIT A SEC... THAT *FOOT* ...?
HEY?

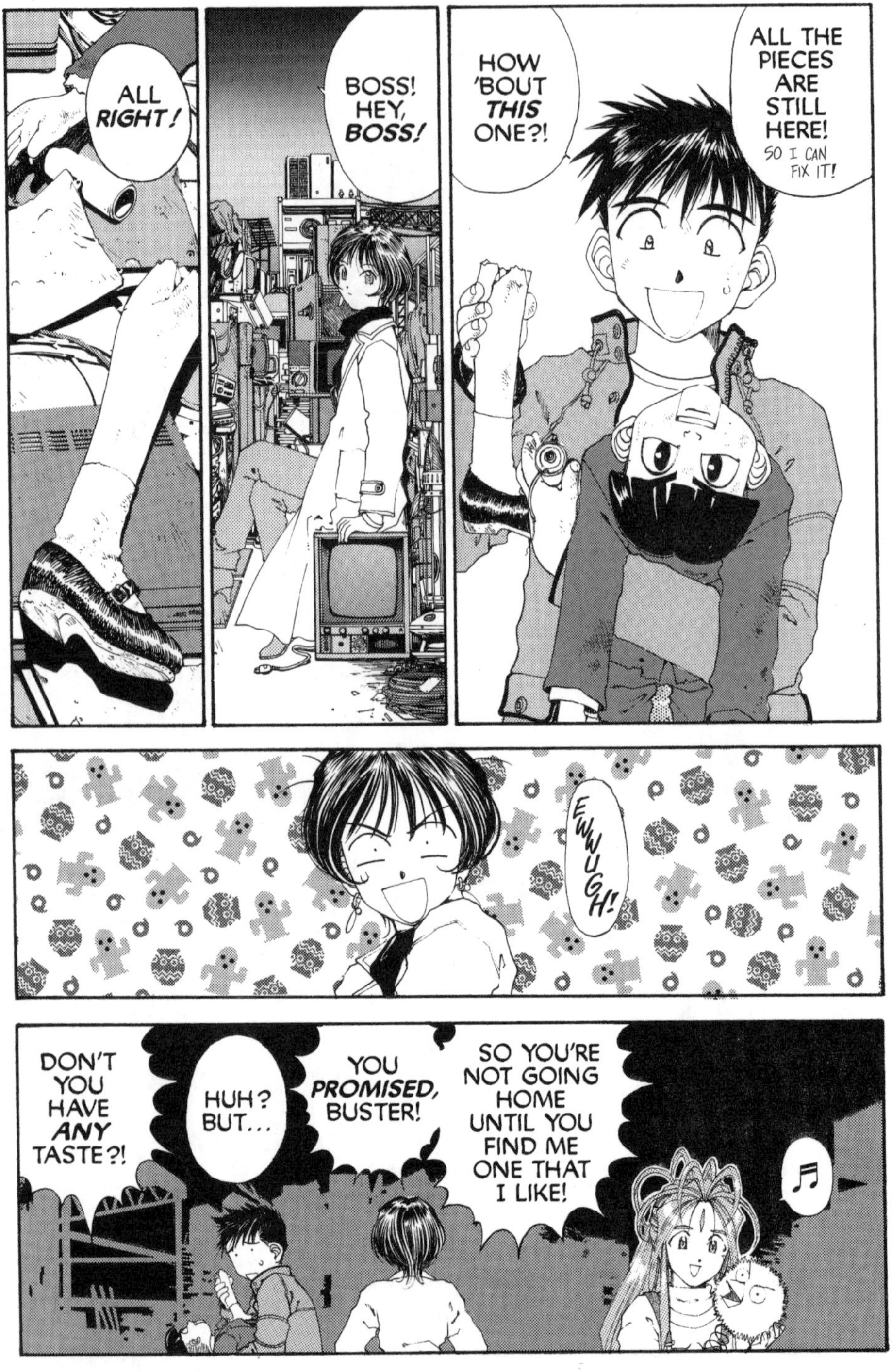
ALL RIGHT!
BOSS! HEY, BOSS!
HOW 'BOUT THIS ONE?!
ALL THE PIECES ARE STILL HERE! SO I CAN FIX IT!
EWWUGH!
DON'T YOU HAVE ANY TASTE?!
HUH? BUT...
YOU PROMISED, BUSTER!
SO YOU'RE NOT GOING HOME UNTIL YOU FIND ME ONE THAT I LIKE!

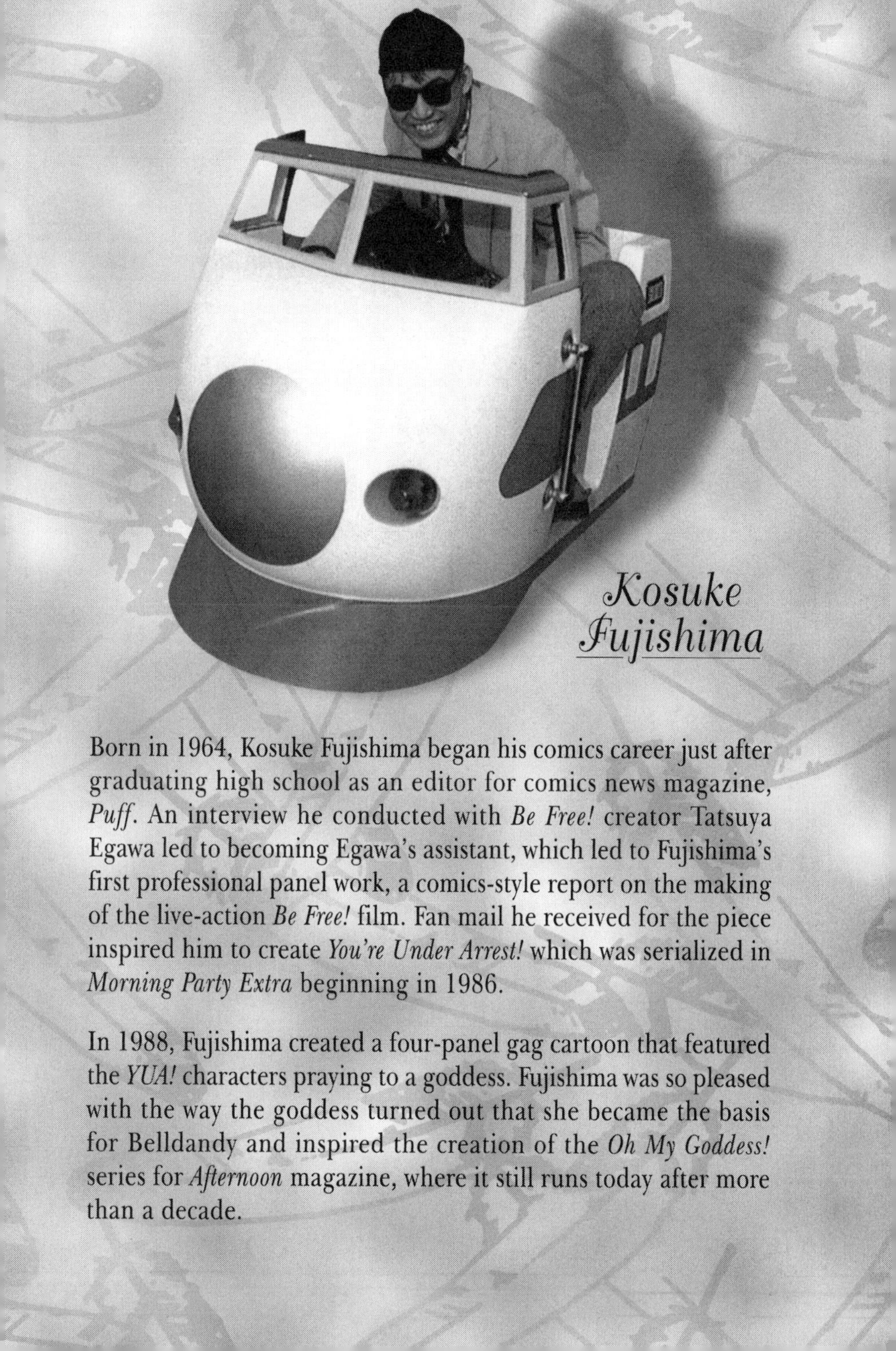

Kosuke Fujishima

Born in 1964, Kosuke Fujishima began his comics career just after graduating high school as an editor for comics news magazine, *Puff*. An interview he conducted with *Be Free!* creator Tatsuya Egawa led to becoming Egawa's assistant, which led to Fujishima's first professional panel work, a comics-style report on the making of the live-action *Be Free!* film. Fan mail he received for the piece inspired him to create *You're Under Arrest!* which was serialized in *Morning Party Extra* beginning in 1986.

In 1988, Fujishima created a four-panel gag cartoon that featured the *YUA!* characters praying to a goddess. Fujishima was so pleased with the way the goddess turned out that she became the basis for Belldandy and inspired the creation of the *Oh My Goddess!* series for *Afternoon* magazine, where it still runs today after more than a decade.